Lecture Notes in Computer Science 1080
Edited by G. Goos, J. Hartmanis and J. van Leeuwen

Advisory Board: W. Brauer D. Gries J. Stoer

Springer-Verlag Berlin Heidelberg GmbH

Panos Constantopoulos
John Mylopoulos Yannis Vassiliou (Eds.)

Advanced Information Systems Engineering

8th International Conference, CAiSE '96
Heraklion, Crete, Greece, May 20-24, 1996
Proceedings

Volume Editors

Panos Constantopoulos
Foundations for Research and Technology - Hellas
Institute of Computer Science
P.O. Box 1385, GR-711 10 Heraklion, Crete, Greece

Yannis Vassiliou
National Technical University of Athens, Department of Computer Science
and: Foundations for Research and Technology - Hellas
P.O. Box 1385, GR-711 10 Heraklion, Crete, Greece

John Mylopoulos
University of Toronto, Department of Computer Science
Toronto, Canada M5S 1A4

Cataloging-in-Publication data applied for

Die Deutsche Bibliothek - CIP-Einheitsaufnahme

Advanced information systems engineering : 8th international conference ; proceedings / CAiSE '96, Heraklion, Crete, Greece, May 20 - 24, 1996. Panos Constantopoulos ... (ed.). - Berlin ; Heidelberg ; New York ; Barcelona ; Budapest ; Hong Kong ; London ; Milan ; Paris ; Santa Clara ; Singapore ; Tokyo : Springer, 1996
(Lecture notes in computer science ; Vol. 1080)

NE: Constantopoulos, Panos [Hrsg.]; CAiSE <8, 1996, Hērakleion>; GT

CR Subject Classification (1991): H.2, D.2, H.5.2-3, H.1, K.6.3-4, H.3.3

DOI 10.1007/978-3-540-68451-0

MyCopy version of the original edition 1996

Typesetting: Camera-ready by author
SPIN 10513013 06/3142 – 5 4 3 2 1 0 Printed on acid-free paper
www.springer.com/mycopy

Preface

The Foundation for Research and Technology - Hellas (FORTH) is proud to host the 8th Conference on Advanced Information Systems Engineering (CAiSE). Initially a Nordic conference, CAiSE quickly evolved into a truly European one. After staying in the North for seven years (Sweden, Norway, United Kingdom, France, The Netherlands, Finland) CAiSE now moves to the southeastern border of Europe, in the capital of the Greek island of Crete, Heraklion.

CAiSE*96 continues the tradition of previous conferences in the series in bringing together people from academia and industry in a lively meeting. The major theme of this year's CAiSE is ''Software Engineering Challenges in Modern Information Systems''. An indicative list of such information systems includes open client/server-based, interoperable, global IS in the Internet, and re-architectured legacy systems. The call for papers also included the traditional CAiSE topics and was given a wide international distribution.

One hundred papers were received from 29 countries and were reviewed by an international programme committee consisting of 45 well reputed researchers in the information systems engineering community. There were 3 reviews for each paper and 30 papers of high academic quality were selected to be presented and discussed at the conference. The papers assembled in this volume represent authors from 16 countries and cover a wide spectrum of topics in the major theme of the conference. The main CAiSE scientific programme is completed by two invited speeches and two panels on important and interesting topics.

Before the main conference, continuing the very successful practice of the recent CAiSE conferences, three workshops were organized on the topics: Requirements Engineering in a Changing World, Next Generation CASE Tools, and Evaluation of Modeling Tools in Systems Analysis and Design, as well as the 3rd Doctoral Consortium on Advanced Information Systems Engineering.

CAiSE*96 and these proceedings would not have been possible without the contribution of many individuals and institutions. We take the opportunity to thank the authors, the programme committee members, the additional referees, the local organizers, the participants, the publisher, and the sponsors.

March 1996

Panos Constantopoulos
John Mylopoulos
Yannis Vassiliou

CAiSE'96 Conference Organization

General Conference Chair

John Mylopoulos
University of Toronto, Canada

Programme Chair

Yannis Vassiliou
National Technical University of Athens and
Foundation for Research and Technology - Hellas, Greece

Organizing Chair

Panos Constantopoulos
University of Crete and
Foundation for Research and Technology - Hellas, Greece

Programme Committee

Rudolf Andersen, Norway
Francois Bodart, Belgium
Leonardo Botacci, United Kingdom
Sjaak Brinkkemper, The Netherlands
Janis Bubenko, Sweden
Panos Constantopoulos, Greece
Valeria De Antonellis, Italy
Eric Dubois, Belgium
Richard Due, Canada
Panagiotis Georgiades, Greece
Andreas Geppert, Switzerland
Georges Grosz, France
Jean-Luc Hainaut, Belgium
Igor Hawryszklewycs, Australia
Matthias Jarke, Germany
Keith Jeffery, United Kingdom
Juhani Iivari, Finland
Hannu Kangassalo, Finland
Eva Lindecrona, Sweden
Frederick Lochovsky, Hong Kong
Pericles Loucopoulos, United Kingdom
Kalle Lyytinen, Finland
Robert Meersman, The Netherlands
Nikolay Mehandjiev, United Kingdom
Ron Norman, United States
Antoni Olive, Spain
Barbara Pernici, Italy
Peter Peters, Germany
Klaus Pohl, Germany
Naveen Prakash, India
Colette Rolland, France
Matti Rossi, Finland
Timos Sellis, Greece
Anne-Helga Seltveit, Norway
Amilcar Sernadas, Portugal
Arne Solvberg, Norway
Stefano Spaccapietra, Switzerland
Bernhard Thalheim, Germany
Babis Theodoulidis, United Kingdom
Juha Pekka Tolvanen, Finland
Yair Wand, Canada
Benkt Wangler, Sweden
Roel Wieringa, The Netherlands
Gerard Wijers, The Netherlands
Roberto Zicari, Germany

Additional Referees

A. Ait-Braham
A. Behm
G. Brataas
F. Buddrus
H. Burg
C. Caleiro
B. A. Farschian
D. Gouscos
P. Gouveia
T. R. Henriksen
B. Karakostas
M. Kradolfer
G. Laskaridis
J. Kaipala
S. Kelly
P. Kerola
L. Krzanik
S.-E. Lautemann
M. Leppdnen
S. Ligoudistianos
H. Liu
D. Martakos
P. Marttiin
I. Petrounias
P. Resende
H. Ronneberg
M. R. Sancho
C. Schommer
C. Sernadas
A. Sotiropoulou
D. Stamoulis
M. Stefanakis
I. Tervonen
D. Tombros
T. Urpi
B. van der Vos
C. Vassilakis
M. Vazirgiannis
V. Vescoukis
S. Visala

Table of Contents

Formal Methods in System Development

Novel Architectures and Information Bases

Workflow Management and Distributed Information Systems

Information Modeling and Methodologies

Object-Oriented Database Design

Semantic Links and Abstractions

MetaEdit+
A Fully Configurable Multi-User and Multi-Tool CASE and CAME Environment

Steven Kelly, Kalle Lyytinen
Matti Rossi
Department of Computer Science and Information Systems
University of Jyväskylä
PL 35
FIN-40351 Jyväskylä
Finland
email: stevek@hyeena.jyu.fi
fax: +358 41 603011

Abstract: Computer Aided Software Engineering (CASE) environments have spread at a lower pace than expected. One reason for this is the immaturity of existing environments in supporting development in-the-large and by-many and their inability to address the varying needs of the software developers. In this paper we report on the development of a next generation CASE environment called MetaEdit+. The environment seeks to overcome all the above deficiencies, but in particular pays attention to catering for the varying needs of the software developers. MetaEdit+ is a multi-method, multi-tool platform for both CASE and Computer Aided Method Engineering (CAME). As a CASE tool it establishes a versatile and powerful multi-tool environment which enables flexible creation, maintenance, manipulation, retrieval and representation of design information among multiple developers. As a CAME environment it offers an easy-to-use yet powerful environment for method specification, integration, management and re-use. The paper explains the motivation for developing MetaEdit+, its design goals and philosophy and discusses the functionality of the CAME tools.

Keywords: CASE, CAME, method, software engineering environments, repository, metamodeling, conceptual modeling, object oriented modeling, tool interoperability, tool integration

1. Introduction

CASE (Computer Aided Systems Engineering) environments have been one of the major technological innovations in systems development during the last decade. Many have claimed that CASE technology will solve the information systems (IS) development problems (Cha86, McC89) that have plagued the community for so long. These include, among others, mediocre productivity (e.g. unrealistic time schedules and cost overruns), and insufficient quality (e.g. low product validity and lack of verifiability) (Bro75, Cha86, Ost87). CASE technologies are expected to provide task related support for software developers in analyzing, designing and implementing a set of information systems (IS) or their components according to a *method.* A method can be defined as a language (vocabulary and grammatical composition rules) which can be used to represent features of the information system to a number of actors (including technical actors such as specific abstract machines like a Smalltalk machine) and a set of rules which define by whom, when, and how such representations are derived and/or used.

The origins of CASE date back to the mid 70's when such well-known software tools as PSL/PSA (Tei77) and SREM (Alf77) were launched. Despite this early start, the breakthrough of these technologies has only occurred during the 90's. One reason for this is the declining cost of computing technologies and its increasing functionality — especially graphical user interfaces. Another is the increased need for disciplining the art of software development and maintenance through standardized process and product models. Finally there is a continuing need to improve the quality and productivity of software production through investments in capital intensive technologies.

In spite of these developments the rate of adopting CASE has been laggard, and the success of adoptions doubtful (Wij90, Aae91). One reason for this is software organizations' lack of the necessary maturity to adopt highly sophisticated technologies such as CASE. Another is the cost of adopting, using and maintaining the technological infrastructure and associated know-how. The third reason is the inadequate technological sophistication of CASE. Most tools in use are stand alone tools that support creation and maintenance of graphical models and can generate code to limited problem domains. Accordingly technologies have not matured for software development in the large and by many. The major deficiencies are thus: insufficient support in integrating methods, inadequate support for alternative representation paradigms, lack of mechanisms to cater for multiple users, rigid method and process support, and focus on task automation (Hen90).

In this paper we report on the development and use experiences of a prototype next generation CASE tool, MetaEdit+. The environment seeks to overcome all the above deficiencies, but pays particular attention to the requirements concerning flexibility, method integration and representational richness. In line with this MetaEdit+ is a multi-method, multi-user, multi-tool platform for both computer aided software engineering (CASE) and computer aided method engineering (CAME). As a CASE tool it establishes a versatile environment for flexible creation, maintenance, manipulation, retrieval and representation of design objects (information) structured and created according to a method. As a CAME tool it provides a flexible and easy-to-use environment for method specification, management, integration and re-use. This paper will explain the motivations for developing MetaEdit+, its design goals and philosophy, its design architecture, its current tool set, and its future development.

2. Related Research

Weaknesses in current CASE tool support can be divided into the following aspects:

1. lack of mechanisms for integrating sets of methods while maintaining consistency between various models (Kel95, Mar95, Kel94a)

2. lack of support for multiple users to create, modify and delete sets of partly overlapping model instances,

3. inadequate catering for multiple representational requirements ranging from fully diagrammatic to fully textual or matrix representations. These are dictated by different method families (Mar95),

4. failure to provide consistent mapping mechanisms between different representational paradigms (Kel95, Mar95),

5. lack of flexibility and evolvability in method support ranging from syntactic variation in methods to crafting totally new method components (Lyy89), and

6. insufficient catering for different information-related needs of a diverse set of stakeholders (Mar95).

2.1 Lack of Method Integration Mechanisms

Several mechanisms are available for method integration or interaction. At the most rudimentary level these deal with mechanisms that enable translations from one representation format to another. Attempts to develop such CASE "EDI" solutions abound, e.g. CDIF (CDI91). Their weakness is that they do not support any inter-model consistency checking, semantic validation and tool interoperability. Accordingly, they can only be used in static model transfer from one environment to another. A more advanced approach has been to develop generic and universal method specification schemata. This "super-schema" would provide a common and universal semantic model onto which all methods used in the environments could be mapped. This can be done directly as in the A/D Cycle information model (Mer90), or through method reference models (Hey92) where the mapping takes place through a reference model. An early solution of this kind was the mapping of system development methods into generic modeling constructs of PSL/PSA (Tei77). The limitation of this approach is its closed nature of method integration which cannot tolerate any flexibility in the mappings. Moreover, it cannot cater for future evolution in the method arena. Finally, it can only support a limited number of method integration solutions which deal solely with object sharing and associated consistency checks.

2.2 Insufficient Multi-User Support

A large body of literature exists on concurrency control and alternative strategies to deal with multiple user operations in software engineering repositories (for a review see Bro91). A number of strategies have emerged recently for achieving varying levels of optimistic concurrency control (Kat84). Despite these advances it is still not known which granularity levels are appropriate for effective concurrency, what are suitable transaction notions, and how much locking and what types of locks are needed. Moreover, it is not clear how much transaction management should be left to users' awareness of others' operations. In this respect, most commercial CASE environments provide solutions that are too crude or inefficient, while advanced mechanisms suggested by researchers can be computationally too demanding (e.g. use of work spaces and merge strategies) or cannot be adapted to the existing CASE architectures. Moreover, a big unsettled issue is how well semantics-driven and dedicated locking strategies operate in such environments and whether we should cater for differences between conceptual and representational objects, or between the different tools that operate on the design data (Kel94a).

2.3 Insufficient Support for Multiple Representation Paradigms

Whilst today's methods contain various representation paradigms — graphical diagrams, matrices, tables, etc. — most existing CASE tools operate on only one: graphical diagrams. If other representation forms are needed they are generated by some user triggered operations such as generating a report. Because of this, CASE tools do not offer the *representation independence* that could make them fully adaptable to differing representation demands. Thus most CASE tools offer only limited syntactic and graphical modifiability in supported methods. Another weakness is the lack of hypertext support for semi-structured and non-structured linking of design objects in different representation formats or model parts. Either the available functionality provides hypertext features *as* the CASE environment (Cyb92), or the support functionality is limited to some model areas (Poh94) or to user interface and user support (Oin93).

2.4 Lack of Method Modifiability and Evolution

The importance of CAME in CASE has been noticed in several studies (Kum92, Che88, Bri90, Wij91, Hey93, Ste93). To this end CASE shells — metaCASE tools, or fully customizable CASE environments — have been developed. Such environments are expected to overcome the inflexibility of method support. According to Bubenko (Bub88) "a CASE shell includes mechanisms to define a CASE tool for an arbitrary technique or a chain of techniques". Yet, metaCASE technology has not yet matured sufficiently to provide adequate method modifiability though the number of CASE products leveraging method modification facilities is increasing. Commercial products offering such features include *Customizer*™ (Ind87), *VSF* (Poc91), *MetaEdit*™ (Smo91a) and *Paradigm+* (Pro94). Research versions of CASE shells include *RAMATIC* (Ber89), *ConceptBase* (Hah91) and *MetaView* (Sor88). Integration of CASE shells and their CASE environments comes in various kinds. A CASE shell can be a separate tool that produces a methodology specification which the CASE environment uses (e.g. *Customizer*), or it can be an integral part of the CASE environment (e.g. *RAMATIC*). *MetaEdit* ™ was one of the first that offered CAME and CASE functionality within the same tool. In MetaEdit methods are specified graphically (Smo91b) and these specifications are converted into a textual form, before compiling and loading the complete method specification into a CASE environment. All these have been steps in the right direction. However, environments that can offer powerful and easy to use modification facilities, method component libraries, method re-use and run-time adaptability are still largely non-existent.

2.5 Lack of Information Retrieval and Computational Facilities

One problem in current CASE tools is their limited information retrieval and reporting capability. Some general and computationally powerful solutions exist in environments that apply a logic programming paradigm (such as ConceptBASE (Hah91)). Though sufficient in their expressive power and generality the use of such query functions is limited by their computational complexity and insufficient user-friendliness. This is due to the lack of data base schema representations and user friendly query formulation. Another problem is that all existing query systems center around retrieving and representing textual information while most of the design information is input and viewed in a graphical format. Finally, few environments provide a means to browse through the repository via hypertext links or various browsing mechanisms.

2.6 Summary

The record of CASE research in each area demonstrates that most concerns have been addressed during the last decade and considerable progress has been made in rendering CASE environments useful. Yet, what seems to be lacking is a comprehensive approach that seeks to tackle most, if not all of, these weaknesses *simultaneously.* Though this may require some compromises and difficult trade-offs in achieving all these goals (like improving multi-user facilities and method flexibility) our contention is that the real impact of future CASE — in the large and by many — will depend on our capability to offer more comprehensive solutions that address most of these concerns within the same environment. Unless such environments emerge the adoption of CASE will in all likelihood continue to be a frustrating experience.

3. The MetaEdit+ Environment

As a meta-CASE environment MetaEdit+ seeks to address most of the above concerns (2.1–2.5) in a comprehensive manner by offering an environment which is:

- **multi-user**, i.e. several users can operate concurrently on the repository (2.2),
- **multi-tool**, i.e. each user can operate several tools simultaneously where each tool provides a different view to the same object (2.3, 2.5),
- **multi-method**, i.e. the environment offers several mechanisms for method integration and consistency checking (2.1),
- **multi-form**, i.e. the environment provides several representation formats for the same design object (2.3), and
- **multi-level**, i.e. the environment is a true metaCASE environment in that both an IS and its design methods can be engineered within the same environment (2.4).

The environment seeks to improve the usability (by multiple users, forms, methods and tools), flexibility (by offering a multi-tool, multi-method approach), and open nature of CASE (i.e. by enabling evolution and plugging of new tools through well defined service protocols). The design goal of the environment has been to base its architecture in principles of *conceptual modeling, layered data base architectures*, and *object orientation.* In this respect, the approach differs to some extent from other metaCASE approaches which focus more on the representation of methods as first order logical theories (Hah91), or on the graphical behavior of design objects (Ber89). From the viewpoint of conceptual modeling the design of a method specification is akin to the development of a conceptual schema for a software repository, and the design of a software tool resembles a design of an external view to a conceptual schema (ANS75). Hence, the method specification language is at the same time the conceptual modeling language for the repository schema, or forms the meta-metamodel level in the IRDS standard (ISO89). The adoption of full object orientation enables flexible organization and re-use of software components in the environment and a high level of interoperability between tools. This is achieved through both data integration (via shared conceptual schemata) and control integration (via object organization) thus making the environment fairly open.

Our motivation in using conceptual modeling and object orientation in the design of MetaEdit+ has suggested three principles for the design: *data independence, representation independence,* and *level independence. Data independence* is defined in a similar way as in traditional data base theory i.e. tools operate on design information without "knowledge" of its physical organization, or logical access structure. *Representation independence* forms a continuum with data independence and it allows conceptual design objects to exist independently of their alternative representations as text, matrix or graphical representations. This principle allows flexible addition of new tools, each one only responsible for its own paradigmatically different view on the same underlying data. *Level independence* means that the environment follows a symmetrical approach in its treatment of data and metadata. Accordingly, the specifications of methods and their behaviors can be managed and manipulated in a similar way to any other object in the environment (therefore the name metaCASE). Moreover, the specifications can be concurrently operated through the same or somewhat specialized tools in the environment.

3.1 General Architecture

The functional architecture of MetaEdit+ is illustrated in Fig. 1. The heart of the environment is the MetaEngine, which handles all operations on the underlying conceptual data through a well-defined service protocol (Smo93a). In other words, the MetaEngine embodies the implementation of the underlying conceptual data model and its operation signature. Accordingly, software tools request services of the MetaEngine in accessing and manipulating repository data. Thereby they avoid the need to duplicate the manipulation code. This design choice allows flexible integration of new tools, each only responsible for its own paradigmatically different view (including operations) on the same underlying repository data. A tool, as the term is used within the MetaEdit+ environment, is a window type with its associated functionality, through which a user can view and possibly alter a design objects in a particular way.

The architecture has similarities with that of the ECMA-PCTE (ECM91) — e.g. common services, separation of components at different levels of integration — but differs from it, most noticeably in the enforcement of no direct communication between components at the same level, or over a common bus between components separated by more than one level: tools communicate only via the MetaEngine.

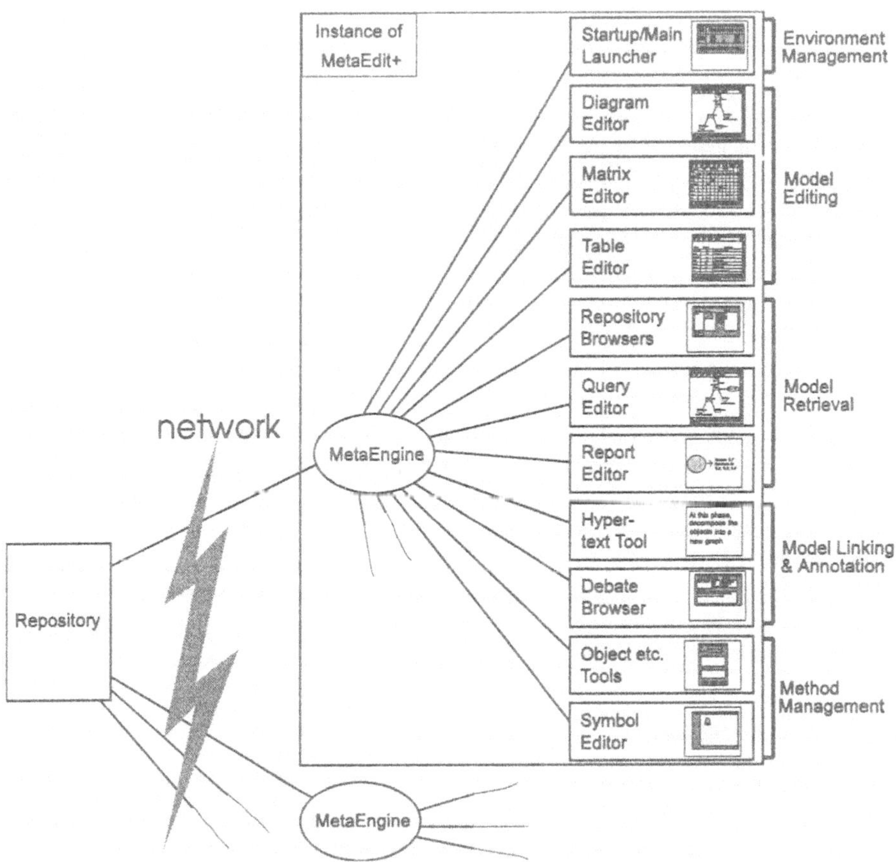

Fig. 1: MetaEdit+ Architecture

MetaEdit+ can run either as a single-user workstation environment, or simultaneously on many workstation clients connected by a network to a server. Each client has a running instance of MetaEdit+, including all its tools and the MetaEngine. The MetaEngine takes care of all issues involved in communicating with the server. Tools communicate with each other only through the MetaEngine, and thereby through the shared data in the repository. Thus the major integration mechanism applied is data integration.

The server forms the software repository holding all the data contained in models, and also in the metamodel(s), in addition to user and locking information. In particular the MetaEdit+ repository includes: *object specification base* containing all the method specifications represented as GOPRR concepts; *symbol specification base* containing all symbols needed to represent Objects, Relationships and Roles; *tool related information base* containing all information needed to represent conceptual objects in different tools (such as spatial coordinates, or size), *user information base* containing all information related to various users such as their passwords, access rights, or current locks held; r*eport specification base* containing all report and other output specifications.

MetaEdit+ applies pessimistic concurrency control in dealing with user and multi-tool interactions with the repository. We have found locks useful despite some of their disadvantages such as stricter user control, interference with users' work, and poorer overall performance. The gains are greater as locks prevent conflicts from occurring between different copies of the repository data, help users to be warned about possible interference, and prevent gaining access to design objects already used in another's transaction. All these are of utmost importance in software repositories. Transactions are understood as long transactions. Their length is defined by a user triggered *commit* operation (automatically requested by the end of the session). The burden of deciding what to lock and when is removed from user's responsibilities and decided by the system. Another feature of the locking strategy is that MetaEdit+ follows more than one level of granularity in locking repository objects. It distinguishes locking granularities between metamodels, graphs, conceptual objects, and representation data. It can thus achieve the following desired features in locking: locks are acquired only when needed, they are well-placed, and are not too small to overburden the system. During their work users can gain information about locked objects and are thus aware of who has locks on which design objects. Accordingly, they can coordinate their actions through negotiating about how locks are freed and transferred. Although no formal testing has been carried out as yet, initial experiences suggest that with this strategy lock conflicts are surprisingly rare in normal CASE work.

3.2 Tool Architecture

In the design of the environment we have classified tools into five distinct families according to their purpose and underlying common functionality. From the viewpoint of conceptual data in the repository each family portrays similar demands in terms of manipulation, locking and retrieval of conceptual design objects, though the different representational paradigms underlying the tools may pose additional demands on retrieval and locking. This has to be dealt with individually in each tool. Each tool family contains one or more tools (Fig. 1). The five tool families are the following:

1. **Environment management tools**: these tools are used to manage features of the environment, its main components and to launch it.
2. **Model editing tools**: these tools are used to create, modify and delete model instances or their parts. In addition, these tools can be used to view the model

instances from different representational viewpoints, and/or to derive new information from existing design information.

3. **Model retrieval tools**: these tools are used for retrieving design objects and their instances from the repository for reuse and review. These tools can operate on both models and metamodels.
4. **Model linking and annotation tools**: these tools are used for linking design objects for traceability and memorization, annotating model instances, finding specific "locations" in the design space, or maintaining conversations about design issues.
5. **Method management tools**: these tools are for method specification, management and retrieval.

4. Conceptual Data Model

Because all method specifications in MetaEdit+ are interpreted as high level conceptual models of method (or methodology) the kernel of the MetaEdit+ functionality and architecture is determined by the underlying conceptual data model called GOPRR. MetaEdit+ uses the GOPRR conceptual data model as a universal and generic meta-metamodel i.e. as a sole language to specify methods. Very little if any method "knowledge" is buried into the code in tools. In addition, GOPRR is primarily intended to model observed, interpreted and recorded development reality *as seen through the methods* (including the world of thought and abstract ideas). In this respect it differs from the ontological IS models (see e.g. Wan93), which attempt to model what actually *is*, rather than just what is perceived and recorded.

4.1 The OPRR Model

Basically, GOPRR (Smo93b) forms an evolutionary extension of the OPRR model which has been successfully used in specifying methods for MetaEdit (Wel92, Smo91b). Whereas the original ER model (Che76) provided only sketchy concepts of attribute: features the object can possess; and of role: the part an object plays in a relationship; the OPRR model has defined these notions in full.

The basic OPRR modeling constructs are:

- Objects, which consist of independent and identifiable design objects. These typically appear as shapes in diagrams, and can have properties such as names. Examples of objects are an Entity in an Entity Relationship Diagram or a Process in a Data Flow Diagram.
- Properties are attributes of objects and can only be accessed as parts of objects or relationships. Properties typically appear as textual labels in diagrams, and they can contain single data entries such as a name, text field or number. An example of a property is the number of a Process in a Data Flow Diagram (Gan79).

- Relationships are associations between objects, and can also have properties. Relationships typically appear as lines between shapes in diagrams, or verbs in texts. An example of a relationship is a Data Flow in a Data Flow Diagram.
- Roles define the ways in which objects participate in specific relationships. In diagrams roles typically appear as the end points of Relationships (e.g. an arrowhead). Roles too can have properties. An example of a role is the specification by directed arrow which end of a data flow relationship is 'to' and which 'from' part of the flow.

In addition OPRR provides constructs for defining cardinality constraints for relationships (i.e. as properties of relationship meta-objects), and means to determine properties which uniquely identify each object instance. The OPRR model is founded on fixed mapping rules between modeling constructs and their graphical behaviors (Ros92).

OPRR is further designed to be applicable to both the instance (model) and the type (metamodel) levels. Thus an instance object, say a Process '3.1' in a Data Flow Diagram model, has an object type of 'Process' on the metamodel level, while a flow relationship instance 'order info' on the model level is an instance of a relationship type 'Data Flow' on the metamodel level.

4.2 Extensions in the GOPRR Model

GOPRR extends OPRR as a conceptual meta-metamodel in several ways. First, unlike OPRR the GOPRR model allows multiple representations of the same underlying conceptual object (e.g. graphical, matrix, text), and even different graphical representations of the same object in the same representation paradigm. This is achieved by making available mechanisms that can override the default representation. In this sense GOPRR forms a true conceptual "kernel" on which varied representations of data, including not only graphical diagrams but also hypertext, text and matrices, can be built. This allows GOPRR to support a wide range of methodologies including matrix, table or text oriented ones, and gives users the ability to see and manipulate design information in a variety of representations.

Second, the conceptual modeling constructs offered by OPRR have been extended in the GOPRR in several ways which yields a powerful but yet ease-to-use modeling language. These new Graph, object orientation, method integration and rule constructs are described below.

Concept of Graph

The GOPRR model adds the concept of Graph into the modeling constructs. A graph denotes an aggregate concept which contains a certain set of objects and their relationships (with specific roles). Graphs typically appear as windows on whole diagrams which contain objects and their bindings of roles and relationships; a graph also has its own properties. An example of a graph is a whole Data Flow Diagram (as a whole or just one level of it). In use, the Graph concept is fundamentally a generalized decomposition graph: it can be included in a parent graph, attached to an object, role or relationship therein. For instance, in Data Flow Diagrams a top level graph may contain a Process ‘3’, which has a decomposition graph called ‘Decomposition of 3’, containing Processes ‘3.1’, 3.2’ etc. Relationships from ‘1’ and ‘2’ to ‘3’ in the top level graph are actually interface relationships, as we can specify that in the lower-level graph they link to e.g. ‘3.2’ and ‘3.1’ respectively. The interface to the object, and hence to the elements in its decomposition graph, can be shown in the child graph to any degree between ‘not at all’ and ‘show copies of external objects’. The interface is maintained distinct from the elements of the decomposition graph itself, allowing reuse of the decomposition graph in different parent graphs. The interface ‘specification’ remains the same in all decompositions, but the elements attached to the interface at the higher level can be different in different parent graphs, thus allowing reuse of the graph as a white or black box.

The design of Graph is such that many “representational” graphs can be made for one “conceptual” graph. For instance, a matrix and diagram representation can be made of the same conceptual Data Flow Diagram. In this situation changes in conceptual graphs are propagated between different tools and their “representational” graphs according to their usefulness to the user. Currently, objects added in one graph are immediately available to other graphs, but not automatically added. Changes to properties are made instantly (on transaction commit, if different users are working on different graphs), and additions to or changes of relationships or roles are made instantly in the relationship-oriented Matrix Editor, but buffered in the Diagram Editor, so the user can control their layout when they are added.

The addition of the concept of Graph allows GOPRR to represent multiple methods, and multiple models, whilst still maintaining the contents of each as a coherent distinguishable whole. In this way graph enables modeling and representation of recursive structures such as decompositions, or complex objects as often found in development methods. The graph notion has also been specialized into a modeling unit called *Project,* which can contain other Graphs, and sub-projects. A Project type thus helps manage the allowed linkages between methods used in a particular project.

It is noteworthy that all concepts included in GOPRR are designed for reuse: both types and instances of object, relationship, role, property and graph can be reused within other graph or project types (or instances).

Object Orientation

Another extension, in line with object orientation is the inclusion of *generalization* and *specialization* constructs into the GOPRR language. This extension helps to organize complex method libraries, enhances reuse, and together with the graph notion enables to model in economical way most method components.

In line with object orientation objects a third extension is *polymorphism* of modeling constructs: objects, relationships, roles and properties are polymorphic in the sense that an object seen in one method as an object can be seen in another method as a relationship, or a property. This enables method component re-use and provides a powerful and flexible method integration mechanism. In this way the method specifications can include specifications of a set of interconnections between different IS models.

Method Integration

In addition to decomposition and polymorphism, GOPRR also adds other powerful method integration constructs. Objects, relationships and roles can be reused in many different graphs: a change to the object via one graph is also visible in the other graphs. Similarly, properties can be shared between several objects, with changes affecting all objects referring to that property. These two constructs allow different degrees of saying that two objects in different places are 'the same': an important factor in representing the same 'real world' fact in two different methods. Explosion works similarly to decomposition, but with freer semantics. For instance, each object may have only one decomposition, wherever it occurs, but can have multiple explosion links for every graph in which it takes part.

Integrity Checking Rules

Finally GOPRR provides enhanced rules for checking the model integrity. It is possible to attach rules to properties, in addition to the normal type restrictions. For example, in modeling Data Flow Diagrams, a rule has been added to the property 'DFD Number' which constrains the contents of the string property to be a dot separated sequence of numbers, disallowing combinations like 'Fred', '2.', '3..2.1', '.'. It is also possible to add constraints on the collection of properties for a given object, role, relationship, graph or project type. For example, a rule could be added to specify that a 'start date' must come before an 'end date' in an activity modeling diagram. These rules, too, are inherited by descendant types, but may be overridden.

4.3 Example

Although the improvements in GOPRR are best seen with complicated methods, for ease of understanding we take a simple Data Flow Diagram metamodel as our example. One way to model Data Flow Diagrams with GOPRR is to note the similarities between the various object types (i.e. processes, externals and stores), and how they may be connected. For instance, instances of all three object types must have a name and a description, and they can connect via a Flow relationship with a Process. These similarities motivate the creation of a generalized 'DFDObject' type, which is specialized into 'Process', 'External' and 'Store' types. DFDObject itself is marked so that it can never be instantiated: it is purely an abstract type.

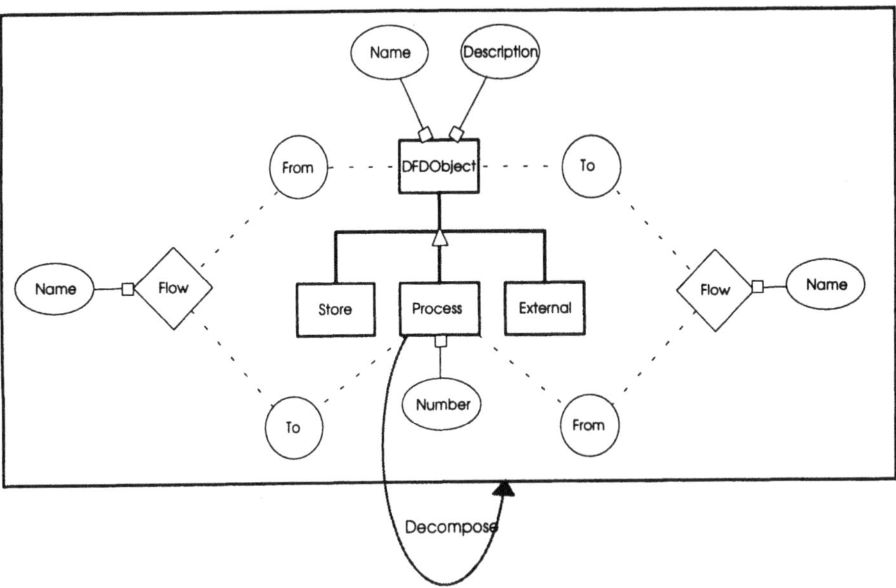

Fig. 2: A GOPRR metamodel of Data Flow Diagrams

This inheritance hierarchy can be seen in the center of Fig. 2, where the rectangles are object types, diamonds are relationship types, circles role types, and ovals property types. DFDObject thus has two properties, Name and Description, and Process inherits these two and adds a third, Number. Objects can be connected by a Flow relationship, with the proviso that one of the objects must always be a Process: on the left, the Process is in the To role, and on the right, in the From role.

The whole figure within the rectangle represents the Graph type of Data Flow Diagrams. The fact that a Process can decompose to a lower-level Data Flow Diagram is represented by the curved gray 'Decompose' relationship between Process and the DFD graph type's rectangle.

5. Method Management Tools

5.1 Motivation and Purpose of the Method Management Tools

In MetaEdit+ the method management tool family has been developed to ease the creation and testing of methods, their management and evaluation support. The primary goal of the tool family is to allow flexibility in method creation and management and ease method construction. Therefore the environment supports alternative ways of method engineering: 1) creation from scratch, where all the parts of the method being defined contain new types, 2) component oriented, where methods are constructed through using prefabricated parts, and 3) reuse oriented, where method engineering seeks to achieve maximal generality of the repository types, and then by specializing these components derive new methods.

5.2 Design Principles of Method Management Tool Family

The development of the MetaEdit+ method management tool family has been influenced by earlier method engineering frameworks (Har93, Hey93, Ros95b, Wel92). These frameworks have sought to consider those aspects that are necessary in a completely functional method engineering environment. Functionally such an environment consists of the following parts:

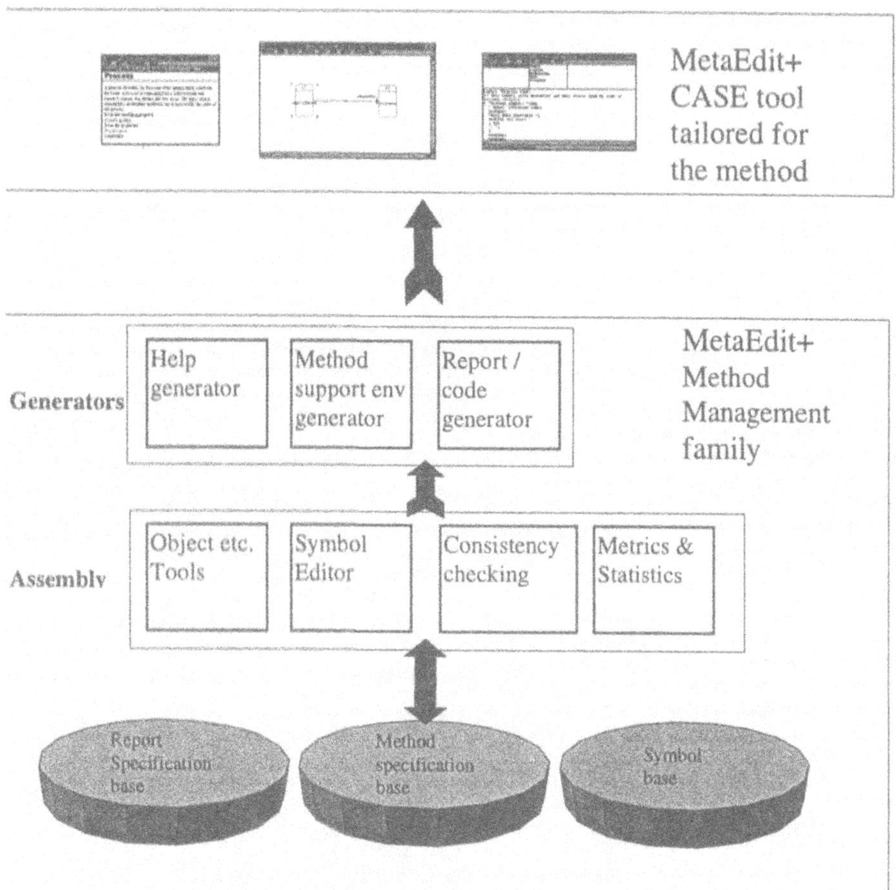

Fig. 3: Method Management Tools in MetaEdit+

Below each subsystem component will be discussed in more detail.

The Method Assembly System

This system part consists of several specialized editors and model retrieval and analysis tools that are needed in method assembly. These tools together allow one to specify a method's objects and relationships and their representations, so that they can be immediately tested within the environment. The most important components are the *metamodel editors* (including object, relationship, role, property and graph editors) by which every method's components and their connections are specified. Due to their different semantics and graphical behaviors Objects, Properties, Relationships and Roles all have their own specification tools. This helps to define their specialized semantics separately, but in particular allows re-use of existing object, relationship and role specifications. These concepts are then collected into complete method specifications using the Graph tool. This also allows the re-use of existing graph "patterns". Each tool also has a dialog definition subsystem, which allows custom definition of dialogs associated with each object type.

The *Symbol Editor* helps specify symbols that are used to distinguish each object type from other object types. Symbols are defined by a specialized drawing tool and are thereafter connected to the appropriate metamodel type. The Symbol Editor also improves re-use as new symbols can be derived by combining or modifying existing symbol patterns and templates retrieved from the repository. The *Consistency checking system* in MetaEdit+ incorporates several rules that ensure the syntactical completeness and consistency of the resulting method specification. Completeness checking covers checking for missing values and missing links between different method components. Consistency checks verify the internal integrity of the method specification by analyzing that the method specification does not include contradictory specifications. The *Metric & statistics system* of the environment offers a number of reports developed using the report generator tool, that analyze the method specification (Ros94, Ros95a). The metrics reports provide a set of computed values, which can be used to review and analyze the properties of the specifications. Examples of metrics are the number of Object, Relationship and Property types in the method (Tei80), and the average number of Properties or Relationships per Object type.

Environment Generation System

This subsystem features several generators that help to deliver a usable and user-friendly CASE tool by using the information contained in the method specifications. The *Method support environment generation system* compiles the method's object specifications into parts of the metamodel repository as soon as they have been defined. As noted above such specifications define the structure of MetaEdit+'s repository data and the symbols to represent and forms to view the object instances. The *Method help generation system* generates an on-line help component associated with each method. This help can then be accessed through a model editing tool interface from the repository. The generation is based on the defined properties of the metamodel types such as a definition what is an External and how it is used in different situations. *Report and transformation generation system* is used for delivering various reports and conducting checking on the models. These reports can be defined using the generic report generator discussed above.

Parts not available in the current MetaEdit+ method management tool family but recognized in the earlier frameworks are: a selection assistant for selecting the right method or its parts for a specific project (Kum92, Har94), and process description and support (Wij91). These needs are not currently addressed in MetaEdit+, but there are ongoing activities in the project that aim at adding these features.

5.3 An Example of a Method Specification

Here we show how to develop part of the Data Flow Diagram metamodel. The example depicts how the defined components of the DFD are connected together to form the actual method. The tools used to manipulate the GOPRR concepts in the concept specification database are form-based.

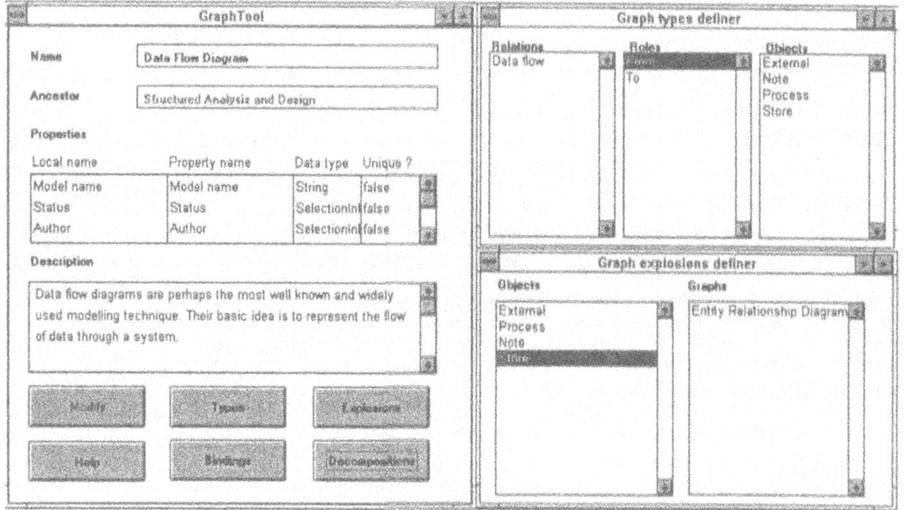

Fig. 4: A Graph Tool

Fig. 4 shows the resulting graph specification of the DFD method. The Graph Tool allows the user to add, remove and edit components of the method (the components, i.e. Objects, Relationships and Roles, are modified with similar tools) and to add and delete method connections. The window on the left shows the definition of the DFD, its properties (i.e. model name and documentation) and related documentation text for method help. The window in the upper right corner of the figure shows the components of the method. The window in the lower right corner shows the possible explosion connections between objects in the DFD and other Graph types: Processes can be exploded into lower level DFD's.

6. Discussion and Conclusions

The limited functionality and rigidity of the current information systems development environments continues to pose a considerable challenge to both academia and practice. In this paper our goal has been to demonstrate how the prototype metaCASE environment called MetaEdit+ deals with these concerns. Overall, we have sought to develop MetaEdit+ as a platform for trying out different tools and tool construction principles, and also to try out the use of object oriented architecture in designing and implementing a metaCASE tool. This is well reflected in its current implementation. MetaEdit+ has been implemented using VisualWorks Smalltalk environment using the ArtBase object repository system and NEDT graphical programming environment, with ENVY as code management system. By doing this, we have been able to re-use about 70% of all code needed to implement the current functionality.

Our goal in developing MetaEdit+ environment has been to develop an environment which:

- Supports high level specification of methods with a powerful yet easy to use method specification language
- Has an open architecture which separates the conceptual specification of the repository and the view (or representation) adopted in different tools and thus conveys a high-level object-oriented API for the tool-repository interactions
- Offers mechanisms for concurrent access of repository data through different tools and users
- Features a comprehensive and well-organized tool set for diverse and complex information handling tasks with some new functionality such as matrices, hypertext tools and the query tool
- Includes flexible, and varying mechanisms for tool integration and both vertical and horizontal method integration support
- Provides symmetrical treatment of IS models and metamodels, and thus enables re-use, metamodel management and utilization within the same environment
- Provides novel support for alternative representational paradigms including matrices, and tables.

We believe that with these features MetaEdit+ addresses many flaws found in current CASE tools. First, through its novel method integration mechanisms it provides innovative ways to organize methods and method families into methodologies, and also to organize methodologies with alternative levels of connectedness and inter-method integrity constraints. Second, through its concurrency management mechanisms MetaEdit+ is able to cater for varying needs and demands for concurrency management for different repository objects. Third, through its open architecture and tool interoperability MetaEdit+ can support the highly diverse representational paradigms and information processing needs which are demanded from software engineering environments. Fourth, through its meta-metamodel MetaEdit+ provides flexibility and evolvability in the method specification and use which is unmatched by any other existing metaCASE tool. Fifth, through the availability of a varied yet uniform (in terms of user accessibility and user interface) tool set the MetaEdit+ environment is able to cater for diverse needs of different system development stakeholders. In this sense MetaEdit+ achieves the design goals of better usability, improved flexibility and a open architecture.

Despite these advances MetaEdit+ is not currently a fully complete environment, suitable for all types of development tasks. First, it does not address the need for multiple distributed repositories which is typical for large scale software development. Second, its concurrency management strategies can be too demanding for large scale software repositories. Third, it does not provide flexible integration mechanisms with other tools (such as electronic publishing or CSCW tools).

Future work in MetaEdit+ will take several directions. First, we want to expand the flexibility and evolvability to cater not only for method representation specifications, but also process and actor models for ISD (Mar94). Second, we will finish the ongoing implementation of the concurrency management system and expand it with the possibility to try out alternative concurrency management strategies which may be applicable in different environments. The third direction is to increase the capabilities to describe integrity constraints within and between method specifications.

On the tool and MetaEngine level the following expansions are currently underway. The applicability of the concept of reusable graphs with 'interface ports', analogous to principles encountered in chip design, will be examined on the model and metamodel levels. The three constructs to represent different levels of 'two things being the same' in a model (multiple representations of the same concept, property sharing, hypertext links) will be examined in the light of current practice in methods. The possibilities of polymorphism based on bindings and metatypes will be examined further in particular as a solution to the problems of metatype polymorphism in existing methods (e.g. objectified associations in NIAM (Nij89), which can be viewed as both objects and relationships). Similarly, the possibilities of the matrix paradigm will be investigated.

To conclude, MetaEdit+ forms a bold attempt to build a versatile platform for implementing flexible design information systems that will form the necessary organizational memory and design resource for knowledge intensive systems and software engineering required in the next millennium. If any improvement has been made in realizing this vision we have achieved our goals.

Acknowledgments. This research was in part funded by the Ministry of Education, University of Jyväskylä, and the Academy of Finland, as the MetaPHOR project (Lyy94). We are also grateful to our colleagues in the MetaPHOR project who have been involved in designing and implementing some parts of the system.

Bibliography

Aae91 Aaen, Ivan, Carsten Sørensen, "*A CASE of Great Expectations,*" Scandinavian Journal of Information Systems 3(**1**) (1991) pp.3–23.

Alf77 Alford, M., "*A Requirements Engineering Methodology for Real Time Processing Requirements,*" IEEE Transactions on Software Engineering 3(**1**) (1977) pp.60–69.

ANS75 ANSI, "*Study Group on Data Base Management Systems: Interim Report 75-02-08,*" ACM SIGMOD Newsletter 7(**2**) (1975).

Ber89 Bergsten, Per, Janis Bubenko jr., Roland Dahl, Mats Gustafsson and Lars-Åke Johansson, "*RAMATIC - A CASE Shell for Implementation of Specific CASE Tools,*" Tempora T6.1 Report, first draft, SISU, Gothenburg (1989).

Bri90 Brinkkemper, Sjaak, "*Formalisation of Information Systems Modelling,*" Ph.D. Thesis, Univ. of Nijmegen, Thesis Publishers, Amsterdam (1990).

Bro75 Brooks, F., "*The Mythical Man Month: Essays on Software Engineering,*" Addison-Wesley, Reading, Mass, USA (1975).

Bro91 Brown, Alan W., "*Object-oriented Databases: their applications to software engineering,*" McGraw-Hill, Maidenhead UK (1991).

Bub88 Bubenko, J. A., "*Selecting a Strategy for Computer-Aided Software Engineering (CASE),*" Report 59, SYSLAB, University of Stockholm, Sweden (1988).

CDI91 CDIF, "*CASE Data Interchange Format Interim Standards vol. 1-3,*" Electronic Industries Association Engineering Department (1991).

Cha86 Charette, R., "*Software Engineering Environments, Concepts and Technology,*" McGraw-Hill, New York, USA (1986).

Che76 Chen, P. P., "*The Entity-Relationship Model: Toward a Unified View of Data,*" ACM Transactions on Database Systems 1(**1**) (1976) pp.9–36.

Che88 Chen, Minder, "*The Integration of Organization and Information Systems Modeling: A Metasystem Approach to the Generation of Group Decision Support Systems and Compute-aided Software Engineering,*" PhD Thesis, University of Arizona, Tuscon, USA (1988).

Cyb92 Cybulski, Jacob L., Karl Reed, "*A Hypertext-Based Software Engineering Environment,*" IEEE Software (March 1992) pp.62–68.

ECM91 ECMA, "*Reference Model for Frameworks of Software Engineering Environments,*" Technical Report ECMA TR/55, 2nd Edition (1991).

Gan79 Gane, C., T. Sarson, "*Structured Systems Analysis: Tools and Techniques,*" Prentice Hall, Englewood Cliffs, NJ (1979).

Hah91 Hahn, U., M. Jarke and T. Rose, "*Teamwork Support in a Knowledge-Based Information Systems Environment,*" IEEE Transactions on Software Engineering 17(**5**) (1991) pp.467–481.

Har93 Harmsen, F., S. Brinkkemper, "Computer Aided Method Engineering based on existing Meta-CASE technology," pp. 125-140 in *Proceedings of the Fourth Workshop on The Next Generation of CASE Tools*, Sjaak Brinkkemper, Frank Harmsen (Ed.)No. 93-32, Univ. of Twente, Enschede, the Netherlands (1993).

Har94 Harmsen, Frank, Sjaak Brinkkemper and Han Oei, "Situational Method Engineering for Information System Project Approaches," pp. 169–194 in *Methods and Associated Tools for the Information Systems Life Cycle (A-55)*, A. A. Verrijn-Stuart and T. W. Olle (Ed.), Elsevier Science B.V. (North-Holland) (1994).

Hen90 Henderson, J., J. Cooprider, "*Dimensions of IS Planning and Design Aids: a functional model of CASE technology,*" Information Systems Research 1(**3**) (1990) pp.227–254.

Hey92 Heym, M., H. Österle, "A Reference Model of Information Systems Development," pp. 215–240 in *The Impact of Computer Supported Technologies on Information Systems Development*, K. E. Kendall, K. Lyytinen, J. L. DeGross (Ed.), North-Holland, Amsterdam (1992).

Hey93 Heym, M., H. Österle, "*Computer-aided methodology engineering,*" Information & Software Technology 35(**6/7**) (1993) pp.345–354.

Ind87 Index Technology Corporation, "*Excelerator Reference Guide,*" Index Technology Corporation, Cambridge, USA (1987).

ISO89 ISO, "*Information processing systems: Information Resource Dictionary System (IRDS) Framework,*" Draft International Standard ISO/IEC DIS 10027 (1989).

Kat84 Katz, Randy H., "Transaction Management in the Design Environment," in *New Applications of Databases*, Georges Garderin and E Ge (Ed.), Academic Press, London UK (1984).

Kel94a Kelly, Steven, Veli-Pekka Tahvanainen, "Support for Incremental Method Engineering and MetaCASE," in *Proceedings of the 5th Workshop on the Next Generation of CASE Tools*, B. Theodoulidis (Ed.) Memoranda Informatica 94-25, Universiteit Twente, Enschede, the Netherlands (1994).

Kel94b Kelly, S., "*A Matrix Editor for a MetaCASE Environment,*" Information and Software Technology 36(**6**) (1994) pp.361–371.

Kel95 Kelly, Steven, Kari Smolander, "*Evolution and Issues in MetaCASE,*" Information and Software Technology (to appear) (1995).

Kum92 Kumar, Kuldeep, Richard J. Welke, "Methodology Engineering: A Proposal for Situation Specific Methodology Construction," pp. 257–269 in *Challenges and Strategies for Research in Systems Development*, Kottermann W. W. and Senn J. A. (Ed.), John Wiley & Sons, Washington (1992).

Liu95 Liu, H., "A Visual Interface for Querying a CASE Repository," in *Proc. of the Eleventh IEEE Symposium on Visual Languages (VL'95)*, Darmstadt Germany (1995).

Lyy89 Lyytinen, Kalle, Kari Smolander and Veli-Pekka Tahvanainen, "Modelling CASE Environments in Systems Development," in *Proceedings of the first Nordic Conference on Advanced Systems*, SISU, Stockholm (1989).

Lyy94 Lyytinen, K., P. Kerola, J. Kaipala, S. Kelly, J. Lehto, H. Liu, P. Marttiin, H. Oinas-Kukkonen, J. Pirhonen, M. Rossi, K. Smolander, V.-P. Tahvanainen and J.-P. Tolvanen, "*MetaPHOR: Final report,*" University of Jyväskylä, Finland (1994).

Mar94 Marttiin, P., "Towards Flexible Process Support with a CASE shell," pp. 14–27 in *Advanced Information Systems Engineering, Proceedings of the Third International Conference CAiSE'94, Utrecht, The Netherlands, June 1994*, G. Wijers, S. Brinkkemper and T. Wasserman (Ed.), Springer-Verlag, Berlin (1994).

Mar95 Marttiin, Pentti, Kalle Lyytinen, Matti Rossi, Veli-Pekka Tahvanainen and Juha-Pekka Tolvanen, "*Modeling requirements for future CASE: issues and implementation considerations,*" Information Resources Management Journal 8(**1**) (1995) pp.15–25.

McC89 McClure, C., "*CASE is Software Automation,*" Prentice Hall, Englewood Cliffs, NJ (1989).

Mer90 Mercurio, V. F., B. F. Meyers, A. M. Nisbet and G. Radin, "*AD/Cycle strategy and architecture,*" IBM Systems Journal 29(**2**) (1990) pp.170-188.

Nij89 Nijssen, G. M., T. A. Halpin, "*Conceptual Schema and Relational Database Design: A fact oriented approach,*" Prentice-Hall, Englewood Cliffs, NJ (1989).

Oin93 Oinas-Kukkonen, H., "*Hypertext Functionality in CASE Environments: Preliminary Findings,*" Conference on Computers and Hypermedia in Engineering Education, Vaasa, Finland (May 24–26 1993).

Ost87 Osterweil, L. J., "Software processes are software too," pp. 180–188 in *Proceedings of the 9th International Conference on Software Engineering* (1987).

Poc91 Pocock, John N., "VSF and its Relationship to Open Systems and Standard Repositories," pp. 53-68 in *Software Development Environments and CASE Technology*, A. Endres, H. Weber (Ed.), No. 509, Springer-Verlag, Berlin (1991).

Poh94 Pohl, K., R. Dömges and M. Jarke, "PRO-ART: PROcess based Approach to Requirements Traceability," in *Poster Outlines: 6th Conference on Advanced Information Systems Engineering, Utrecht, Netherlands, June 1994* (1994).

Pro94 ProtoSoft Inc., "*Paradigm Plus/ Cadre Edition Reference Manual,*" ProtoSoft Inc. (1994).

Ros92 Rossi, M., M. Gustafsson, K. Smolander, L.-Å. Johansson and K. Lyytinen, "Metamodeling editor as a front end tool for a case-shell," pp. 547–567 in *Advanced Information Systems Engineering*, P. Loucopoulos (Ed.), Springer Verlag, Berlin, Germany (1992).

Ros94 Rossi, M., J.-P. Tolvanen, *"Metamodeling approach to method comparison: A survey of a set of ISD methods,"* Working Paper, University of Jyväskylä, Jyväskylä (1994).

Ros95a Rossi, M., S. Brinkkemper, "Metrics in Method Engineering," pp. 200-216 in *Advanced Information Systems Engineering, Proceedings of the 7th International Conference CAiSE'95*, J. Iivari, K. Lyytinen and M. Rossi (Ed.)No. 932, Springer-Verlag, Berlin (1995).

Ros95b Rossi, M., *"The MetaEdit CAME environment,"* Proceedings of the MetaCase 95, University of Sunderland press, Sunderland (1995).

Smo91a Smolander, Kari, Kalle Lyytinen, Veli-Pekka Tahvanainen and Pentti Marttiin, "MetaEdit — A Flexible Graphical Environment for Methodology Modelling," in *Advanced Information Systems Engineering, Proceedings of the Third International Conference CAiSE'91, Trondheim, Norway, May 1991*, R. Andersen, J. A. Bubenko jr. and A. Solvberg (Ed.), Springer-Verlag, Berlin (1991).

Smo91b Smolander, Kari, "OPRR: A Model for Modelling Systems Development Methods," in *Next Generation CASE Tools*, K. Lyytinen and V.-P. Tahvanainen (Ed.), IOS Press, Amsterdam, the Netherlands (1991).

Smo93a Smolander, Kari, *"MetaEdit+ Protocols and standard operations for processing GOPRR information structures: the Application Programmer's Interface,"* Internal Technical Document, MetaPHOR project, Univ. of Jyväskylä, Jyväskylä, Finland (1993).

Smo93b Smolander, Kari, *"GOPRR: a proposal for a meta level model,"* University of Jyväskylä, Finland (1993).

Sor88 Sorenson, Paul G., Jean-Paul Tremblay and Andrew J. McAllister, *"The Metaview System for Many Specification Environments,"* IEEE SOFTWARE (March 1988) pp.30–38.

Ste93 Stegwee, Robert A., Ria M. C. van Waes, "Flexible CASE tools for Information Systems Planning," pp. 248–292 in *Computer-Aided Software Engineering — Issues and Trends for the 1990s and Beyond*, T. Bergin (Ed.), Idea Group Publishing (1993).

Tei77 Teichroew, Daniel, Ernest A. Hershey_III, *"PSL/PSA: A Computer-Aided Technique for Structured Documentation and Analysis of Information Processing Systems,"* IEEE Transactions on Software Engineering (1977).

Tei80 Teichroew, Daniel, Petar Macasovic, III Ernest A. Hershey and Yuzo Yamamoto, "Application of the entity-relationship approach to information processing systems modeling," pp. 15–38 in *Entity-Relationship Approach to Systems Analysis and Design*, P. P. Chen (Ed.), North-Holland (1980).

Wan93 Wand, Yair, Ron Weber, *"On the ontological expressiveness of systems analysis and design grammars,"* Journal of Information Systems (1993).

Wel92 Welke, R. J., "The CASE Repository: More than another database application," in *Challenges and Strategies for Research in Systems Development*, William W. Cotterman and James A. Senn (Eds.) (Ed.), Wiley, Chichester UK (1992).

Wij90 Wijers, G. M., H. E. van Dort, *"Experiences with the use of CASE-tools in the Netherlands,"* Advanced Information Systems Engineering (1990) pp.5–20.

Wij91 Wijers, G. M., *"Modelling Support in Information Systems Development,"* Ph.D. Thesis, Delft University of Technology, Thesis Publishers, Amsterdam (1991).

MENTOR : A Computer Aided Requirements Engineering Environment

S. Si-Said, C. Rolland, G. Grosz
University Paris-1 Sorbonne, CRI, 17, rue de Tolbiac, 75013 Paris, FRANCE
EMAIL : {sisaid, rolland, grosz}@masi.ibp.fr

Abstract : In this paper, we present the Computer Aided Requirements Engineering (CARE) environment named MENTOR. This environment offers various viewers, editors and tools and can be customised by a method engineer to any existing requirements engineering methodology. The core component of the environment is the "Guidance Engine". It executes - or enacts- in a flexible manner any process model -that we call way-of-working. A way-of-working is defined as an instance of a process meta-model. We illustrate, through a comprehensive example, how MENTOR provides support and guidance based on the execution of process models to both application engineers (who construct system specifications) and to method engineers (who construct ways-of-working) in a flexible and efficient way.

1. INTRODUCTION

Requirements Engineering (RE) refers to that part of the system development life-cycle in which application engineers investigate the needs and requirements of the users community and abstract from those requirements the formal specification of the system to be built. Therefore, RE is a very intellectual and creative activity. As we see it, guidance plays a crucial role in the RE process [Rolland94, Rolland95]. Providing guidance for this activity is far more knowledge intensive than for any other system development activity. The required support is based, for example, on suggestions on how to proceed in a certain situation, and on providing alternatives to solve the problem raised by this situation. It is clearly beyond the simple automated control of sequences of activities provided by most methods in practice and, also, by process software engineering environments. Application engineers need to be guided and advised, locally to handle the particular situation they are faced to, and globally, to monitor the flow of decisions they have to make.
Process representations must take into account the guidance requirement. This requirement is not fulfilled by existing process representation formalisms. The Information Systems Engineering (ISE) community has been involved with prescriptive methods as a means for process representation. Methods most often use large-grained life cycle descriptions and provide guidance at a high level of granularity (i.e. it mostly consists of a step-wise organisation of the system development life-cycle). They do not contain the know-how needed to make the application engineer efficient in practice. These process descriptions are informal. This eases their use but makes difficult their control. Conversely, new software process modelling notations emerging from the Software Engineering (SE) community are formal enough to allow correctness checking of process representations but allow only process programs [Tominaga94] restricted to enforcement of constraints [Finkelstein94] and are thus, limited in their use [Curtis92].
CASE tools supporting current ISE methods and SE centred software environments are unable to provide today the kind of heuristics and experience based guidance required in the early phases of system development. Current CASE tools are essentially passive, they help in capturing, storing and documenting IS products but do not support application engineers in their creative development activities

[Martiin93]. Most process centred software environments [Belkhatir94, Bandinelli93, Lonchamp93, Kaiser88] are used to describe the activity of tools and to allow automatic invocation of tools [Tominaga94]. They are essentially enforcing the process performance that conforms to some perceptive software process definition [Dowson93]. They guide the usage of tools but are similar to CASE tools in that they do not support the engineer in the performance of his intellectual activities.
We claim that providing guidance to application engineers relies on :
- an accurate definition of the RE processes described at different levels of granularity,
- a tool environment allowing the definition of such processes and their execution in a flexible manner.
In this paper, we present the Computer Aided Requirements Engineering (CARE) environment MENTOR [Grosz94, Si-Said95] which complies with these requirements. It offers means :
- to define process models as instances of a situation and decision based process meta-model [Rolland94, Rolland95]. Such process models combine within a single representation both a global description of activities and a fine grain description of the different steps to be performed. The underlying process theory has been developed in the NATURE[1] project.
- to dynamically execute process models. Execution is seen as model interpretation to allow flexibility and non-determinism in human-machine interaction. Flexibility and non-determinism are mandatory because RE cannot be fully automated in a pre-defined sequence of actions.
The current prototype of the environment is implemented on top of the O2 O.O.D.B.M.S. [O2] and comprises about 150 O2 classes, 600 methods and 13400 O2c lines of code.
The O2 D.B.M.S. has been chosen because we needed a flexible object oriented data model allowing to store and manipulate classes as instances of others classes and therefore to implement the process meta-model based on a specialisation of generic concepts provided by O2, process models as instances of the process-meta model. and enacted process models as instances of process models.

The paper is structured as follows. The next section presents the general architecture of the MENTOR environment. The different tools together with the repository of this CARE environment are also described. Section 3 is the core of the paper. Through a scenario, we present both, the concepts underlying our approach and the manner in which guidance is provided. Conclusions are drawn and future work is identified in section 4.

2. THE MENTOR ENVIRONMENT

2.1 PROCESS TERMINOLOGY

Before introducing the architecture of the MENTOR environment, we shall clarify the terminology used in the rest of the paper.
Process : we follow the definition proposed by [Feiler93] : *a process is defined as "a set of partially ordered steps intended to reach a goal"*. A *process step* is "*an atomic*

---

[1] NATURE (BRA N° 5363) is an ESPRIT project funded by the European Commission from 10/92 to 10/95. NATURE reports are available via anonymous ftp on ftp.informatik.rwth-aachen.de in /pub/NATURE

action of a process that has no externally visible sub-structure. The process step is the basic process abstraction".

Product : the output of a process is a product, it can be a requirements specification or a conceptual schema. A process keeps track of how the product has been constructed in a descriptive manner. If the product comprises an entity type "User" with the attribute "name", the process comprises elements stating that "User" has been identified first and then, the attribute "name" has been identified and attached to the entity type.

A process and its related product are application dependant.

Process model : A process model is a description of processes at the type level. Most often a process model is used for a prescriptive purpose i. e. to prescribe "how things must/should/could be done" in contrast to the process itself which is really what happens. A process model is more or less a rough anticipation of what the process will look like. What it will be in detail is, however, determined during actual system development. Following [Seligmann89], we refer to process models as ways-of-working.

Product model : In any RE process model, the structure of the product plays an important role. The product model defines the concepts used for building the product and their relationships. For instance, the product model of ER [Chen76] specifies that an ER diagram comprises a set of entities and relationships, an entity-type has a key and a set of attributes, a relationship may have attributes, entities and relationship are related through the concept of role, cardinalities are associated to a role, etc..

A process model and its related product model are methodology dependent.

Process meta-model : a process meta-model provides a set of generic concepts to represent process models. This ensures the genericity of the process representations constructed from the meta-model and, when combined with the product meta-model (see below), makes for methodology independence. The process meta-model implemented in MENTOR is described in [Rolland 95 and Grosz96].

Product meta-model : it is a set of generic concepts to represent product models. The product meta-model implemented in MENTOR is described in [Schmitt93 and Plihon96].

A process meta-model and its related product meta-model are methodology independent.

2.2 GENERAL ARCHITECTURE

In this section, we introduce the architecture of the CARE environment along with the functionalities of the different components that will be used in the scenario described in section 3.

Figure 1 illustrates the different components of the Computer Aided Requirements Engineering (CARE) environment MENTOR. It intends to provide guidance to both method engineers and application engineers. Method engineers are in charge of defining ways-of-working whereas application engineers are in charge of defining systems specifications. Despite the fact that MENTOR is guidance-centred, the environment includes tool such as editors and viewers allowing the method and application engineers to work freely, without the support of the guidance facility. In this respect, MENTOR offers similar functionality -i.e. product and process models definition and construction - as existing Meta CASE tools (e.g. MetaEdit [Smolander91], RAMATIC [Bergsten89], etc.)

As shown in figure 1, the environment is organised in four main components :

- the repository to store both ways-of-working and product models as shown in figure 2.
- the method engineer environment for guiding method engineers.
- the application engineer environment for guiding application engineers.
- the guidance mechanism composed of the guidance engine as the kernel for the whole CARE environment, and the session manager to co-ordinate access to all tools.

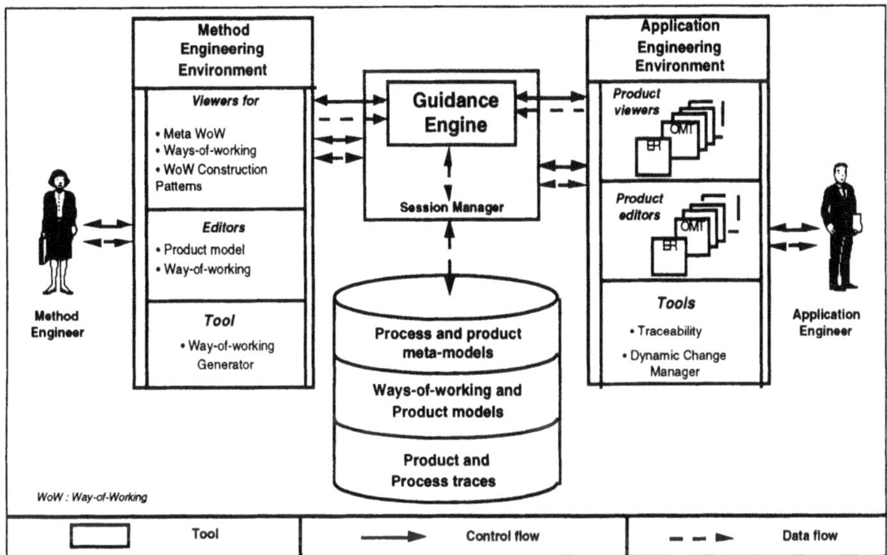

Fig. 1. MENTOR : general architecture

In the rest of this section, we consider each of these components in detail

2.2.1 The repository

The repository uses the O2 O.O.D.B.M.S. to store and manage data.

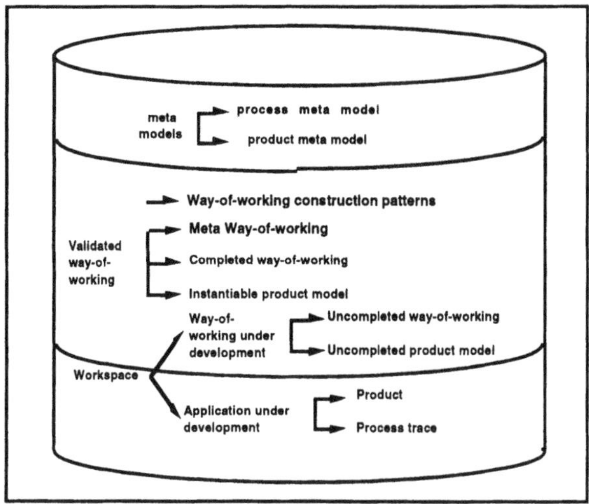

Fig. 2. Structure of the repository

As shown in figure 2, it is structured in three levels :

- the meta level corresponding to the implementation as O2 classes of both process and product meta models.
- the model level corresponding to ways-of-working and product models related to different methodologies. We distinguish a special way-of-working called the meta way-of-working which aims at guiding the method engineer while defining a way-of-working. It is described as any other way-of-working. This level also comprises the way-of-working construction patterns for rapid ways-of-working generation. These patterns will be exemplified in section 3.
- the work space level, composed of ways-of-working and product under development. When a way-of-working is completed and validated by a method engineer, it is integrated in the model level. An application is composed of a product corresponding to the specification under development and a process trace resulting from the enactment of a validated way-of-working.

These three levels are interrelated. Indeed, the ways-of-working and the product models of the model level are instances of the process and product meta model contained on the meta level. Similarly, specification and process traces of the work space levels are instances of product models and ways-of-working of the model level.

2.2.2 The Method engineering environment

It includes viewers, editors and tools. They are introduced in turn.

Three viewers for visualising the current state of any type of product are available to a method engineer. The *way-of-working viewer* provides facilities for displaying the description of any way-of-working contained in the repository, be it under development or validated. Select and copy facilities are available, which allow the engineer to construct ways-of-working out of existing ones. The *meta way-of-working viewer* is used to display the current state of the process of defining a way-of-working. The *way-of-working construction patterns viewer* offers means to browse through the graphical description of the generic knowledge related to method definition (see [Plihon 96 and Rolland96] for details).

The *way-of-working viewer* offers means for scrutinising the complete repository of ways-of-working and provides facilities for reducing the search space through filters. It eventually uses the way-of-working viewer.

The two editors, namely the *way-of-working editor* and the *product model editor* support the method engineer in the description of both the product model and the way-of-working related to a specific methodology. This is done through graphical notations

The way-*of-working generator* offers a means for accessing the library of generic way-of-working construction patterns and embedding facilities for quickly generating chunks of ways-of-working out of the construction patterns.

2.2.3 The Application engineering environment

The Application engineering environment includes a set of specific graphical *product editors* and *product viewers* to develop specifications. A *traceability* tool and a *process change manager* are also available. They are described in the following.

A *product viewer* allows an application engineer to display the current state of a product in a window whereas a *product editor* provides him means to directly modify the product under development (in the current version of the prototype, tools are

available for ER and static OMT [Rumbaugh91] specifications, these can easily be extended). These tools are developed within the O2 environment. The *traceability tool* offers means for keeping track of product and process traces. The generated trace can be used for documentation purposes but can also be used as the raw material necessary for later improvement of ways--of-working.
The *process change manager* aims at keeping coherent the elements used during the enactment of a way-of-working after modifications of the way-of-working. Assume an application engineer aborts the execution of a way-of-working and asks a method engineer to modify it. When he resumes guidance then the state of the enacted way-of-working is not anymore coherent towards the updated way-of-working. In this case, the *process change manager* is automatically triggered.

2.2.4 The guidance engine

The guidance engine is the set of enactment mechanisms able to guide any process governed by a way-of-working [Si-Said95]. We use the term enactment, as in the software community, to refer to the fact that the process is performed not only by machines but by the symbiosis of human beings and computers [Armenise93]. However whereas software centred environments look at process enactment as *program execution* we take the view of process enactment being *model interpretation*. This provides more flexibility in human-machine interaction and permits non-determinism.

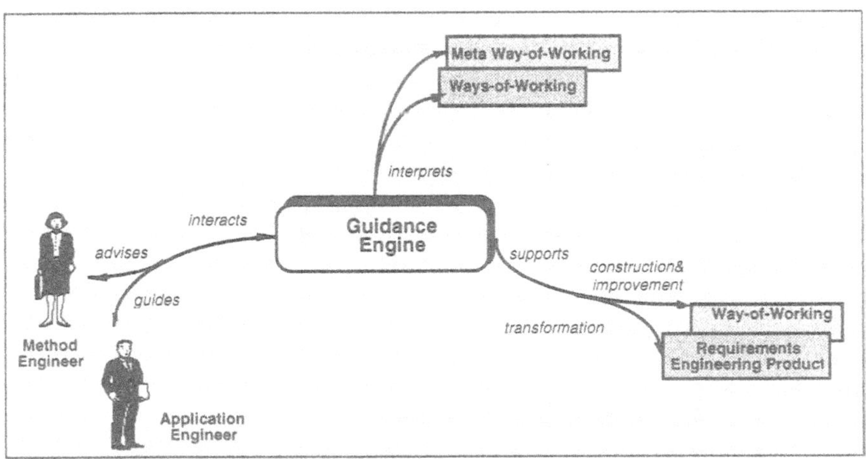

Fig. 3. The guidance engine

As illustrated in figure 3 the guidance engine interacts with the process agent to whom it provides guidance based on the process knowledge stored in the way-of-working. In so doing, it controls the incremental construction of the product under development. The guidance engine can be viewed as an active object which interacts with three other kinds of objects : the product under development, the process agent and the process model.
The guidance engine is generic in the sense that it can guide the enactment of any process modelled in terms of the process meta-model we propose. For example, the process leading to the construction of a way-of-working (represented in a meta way-of-working) is guided in the same way as the process for constructing a specific

application. Obviously the objects interacting in each case are different. During the process of constructing a specific application, the guidance engine interprets the way-of-working to provide advice to the application engineer (the agent) and to support the construction of the requirements specification. The input is a way-of-working and the output is the RE specification. When the guidance engine guides the construction of a way-of-working it uses the meta-way-of-working as an input and the way-of-working is the output. It interacts with an agent who is, in this case, the method engineer and monitors the construction of a way-of-working.
The various functionalities of the MENTOR environment are illustrated in the next section through a comprehensive example.

3. AN EXAMPLE OF A MENTOR SESSION

The scenario presented in this section aims at illustrating how the MENTOR environment provides guidance to both method engineers and application engineers. The scenario comprises two parts. The first one illustrates how a method engineer can retrieve and customise a way-of-working stored in the MENTOR repository. Thus, this part emphasises the support provided to a method engineer for constructing a way-of-working. The second part shows how an application engineer can be guided during an application engineering. It looks at the support provided by a way-of-working and its enactment by the guidance engine. The presentation is based on simple examples extracted from the construction of the E/R schema describing a lending system in a library.

3.1. ILLUSTRATING THE METHOD ENVIRONMENT

• **Selecting the right environment**

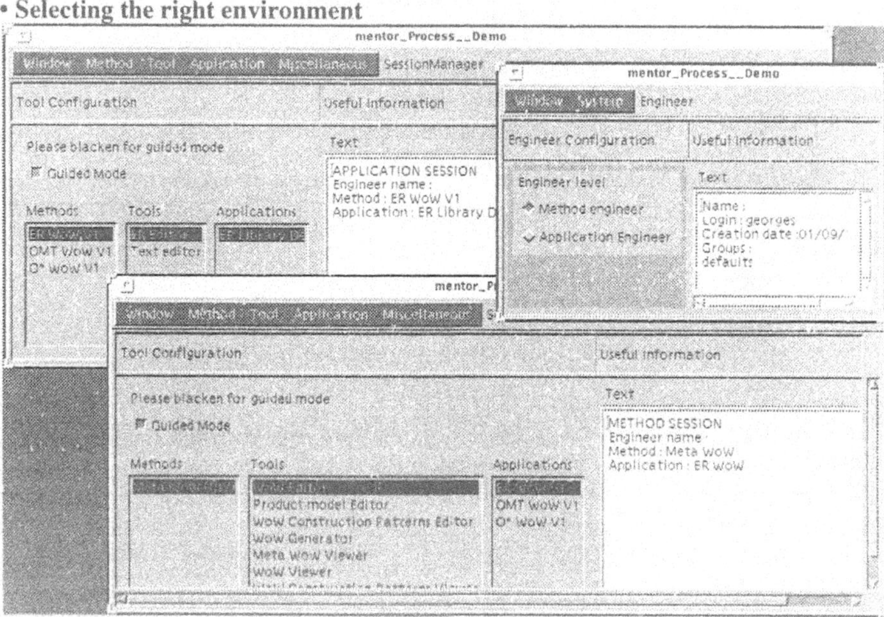

Fig. 4. The session manager windows

The first contact with MENTOR is made through the *session manager window* to select the working mode, i.e. guided mode or free mode (see figure 4).We will see later on that the engineer is able to switch at any moment from one mode to the other. Selecting a mode activates the suitable set of tools and opens the corresponding window as depicted in figure 4.

• Retrieving and editing a way-of-working

Using the application engineering window, the user can browse through the list of ways-of-working stored in the repository, the associated editors and existing applications (columns "Methods", Tools" and "Applications" in figure 4). The current version includes the description of several E/R ways-of-working, an OMT [Rumbaugh91] and an O* [Brunet91] ways-of-working. A temporal version of OMT developed within the TOOBIS [TOOBIS95] project as well as a scenario-based OMT ways-of-working are under development. When needed, the user can edit a way-of-working using the *way-of-working editor*. This is exemplified in figure 5 with an E/R way-of-working.

As shown in figure 5, we view a way-of-working as *a forest of process trees*. Each tree represents an independent piece of process knowledge related to a specific goal. For example, Tree 1 describes one way to fulfil the intention of constructing an ER schema, Tree 2 describes how to refine a relationship-type whereas Tree 3 and 4 are related to schema validation.

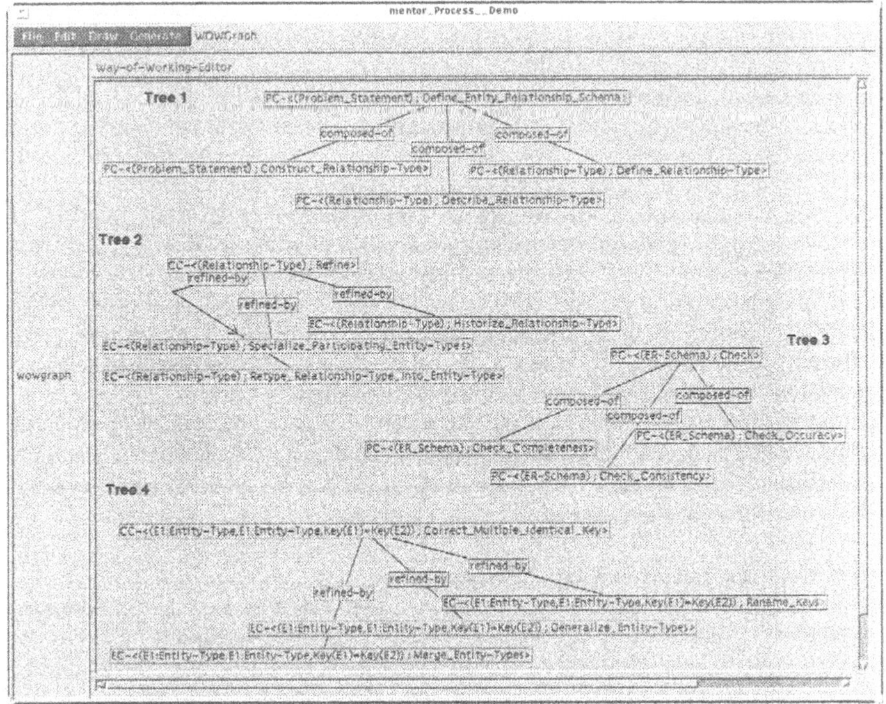

Fig. 5. A partial ER way-of-working

The description of a tree is based on the contextual paradigm defined as part of the NATURE process theory [Rolland94, Rolland 95]. The key concept of this theory is the one of a *context*, the basic block used to model processes. A context is a meaningful association of a *situation* and a *decision*. A situation is a part of the product it makes sense to make decision on and a decision is the expression of the intention the engineer has in mind, it is a goal. For example in figure 5, the context <(Relationship-Type); *Historize_Relationship-type*> of Tree 2 describes the fact that an application engineer can make the decision of historizing a relationship-type.
Tree 2 expresses the fact that there are several alternative ways for refining a relationship-type : one can historize or retype the relationship-type or specialise the participating entity-types. When the decision of a context can be fulfilled in different ways, it is called a *choice context.* Alternatives of a choice context are also contexts, they are related to the choice context through links labelled "refined-by". To support the application engineer in the selection of the most appropriate alternative, *choice criteria* have been associated with each alternative. A choice criteria expresses heuristic knowledge.
In Tree 2, we assume that historizing, retyping a relationship-type, or specialising the participating entity-types are process steps which do not necessitate any decision to be made. Following the process theory, such process steps are represented by *executable contexts.* Executable contexts are the leaves of trees. They cannot be decomposed any further and implement the decision through a deterministic action.
There exists a third type of context for describing a way-of-working, namely *plan contexts.* They help in expressing the fact that in order to fulfil a decision, an application engineer has to follow a plan composed of a set of sub decisions to be made on sub situations. Similarly to the alternatives of a choice contexts, the components of a plan context are also contexts of any of the three possible types (plan, choice and executable). The components are related to the plan context through links labelled "composed-of". For example in Tree 1 of figure 5, the definition of an ER schema is described as a plan context composed of three component contexts : <(Problem_Statement); *Construct_Relationship-Type*> for the identification of a relationship-type and the identification of its structure, <(Relationship-Type); *Define_Relationship-Type*> for the definition of the elements of the structure (i.e. participating entity-types) and <(Relationship-Type); *Describe_Relationship-Type*> for the description of its properties, constraints. A *precedence graph* is associated with each plan context. It defines either the possible ordered transitions between component contexts or their possible parallel enactment.
Let us assume that the method engineer in charge of the development of the lending system wants to provide application engineers with E/R guidance and to that end he selects the way-of-working depicted in figure 5. The way-of-working editor becomes active (blacken zone in figure 4).

• **Customising an existing way-of-working**

However, the method engineer is not satisfied with this existing way-of-working and would like to complete it by adding guidance for the description of Entity-types (which in not included in Trees 1,2,3 and 4 at the moment). In order to do so, he has to activate the Method Engineering Window. Within this environment he can be supported in two ways : using the *meta-way-of-working* and the *way-of-working construction patterns*. The *meta-way-of-working* aims at guiding a method engineer in the construction from scratch (i.e. from a set of method requirements) of a new way-of-working (see [Rolland96] for more details). The meta-way-of-working is modelled as any way-of-working - i.e. as a forest of process trees - and therefore can be enacted under the control of the guidance engine. The *way-of-working construction patterns* are generic and reusable ways-of-working fragments which are modelled as process trees with parameters. They can be used with the Way-of-Working generator. Figure 6 gives one example of such a construction pattern - which is applicable to the description of any concept (denoted C) - and its use for the generation of a process tree dealing with the description of the concept of Entity-Type. The construction pattern uses a classification of concepts into constructional concepts and definitional concepts. The former participate to the structure of the product whereas the latter are used for the definition of the constructional concepts. In the E/R approach, an entity-type is a constructional concept while a domain is a definitional concept. Definitional concepts are further subtyped into *property* (denoted *Prop*), *constraint* (denoted *Const*) and *Cd-concepts* (denoted *Cd*) which are concepts to define other concepts. The valuation of an attribute is a property, the key of an entity-type is a constraint and the attribute is considered as a Cd-concept participating in the construction of an entity-type.

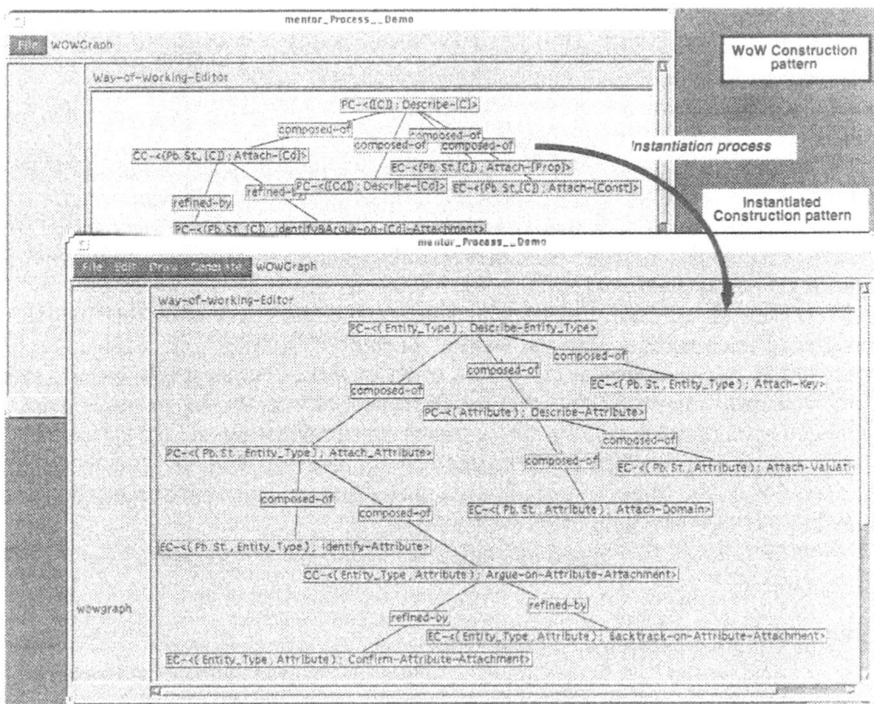

Fig. 6. Instantiating the *Describe Construction Pattern* with the concept of Entity-type

The *Describe_Pattern* illustrated in figure 6 is a plan context which predefines the way any concept C is described. It consists in attaching its properties, its constraints and its Cd-concepts which, in turn, are described by recursively applying the same pattern. Based on this pattern and on the types of concepts of the product in the method under construction, the way-*of-working generator* generates automatically one *Describe* Tree for each of the concepts of the way-of-working product. This is exemplified in figure 6 for the entity-type concept. An entity-type does not have any properties, has one constraint - the key constraint - and is a constructional concept whose definition is based on the attribute concept. Therefore, the description of an entity-type is a plan context composed of three component contexts for the attachment of attributes <(Pb_St, Entity-Type); *Attach_attribute*>, the description of each attribute <(Attribute); *Describe_Attribute*>and the attachment of the key <(Pb_St., Entity-Type); *Attach_Key*>. The context <(Pb_St, Entity-Type); *Attach_attribute*>, for the attachment of the attribute, is its itself a plan context which suggests that the attachment of the attribute shall be argued. The <(Attribute); *Describe_Attribute*> context takes into account that the concept of attribute is a Cd-concept which has one property, the valuation property and the concept of Domain as a Cd-concept participating to its definition.

The library of way-of-working construction patterns currently includes patterns for the Construction of a structure of concepts, its Definition based on the Description of concepts, its Checking and Refinement.

Let us now move to the illustration of the Application Environment based on the assumption that the application engineer who specifies the lending system will be guided by the E/R way-of-working we just described.

3.2. ILLUSTRATING THE APPLICATION ENGINEERING ENVIRONMENT

The core of the application engineering environment is the guidance engine which guides the RE process based on the enactment of a way-of-working. The guidance engine offers two types of guidance :

strategic guidance to help the application engineer in controlling the flow of situations and decisions he has to handle; i.e. to control the flow of contexts.

tactical guidance to provide guidance to the application engineer based on a process tree which matches the situation and intention in hand; i.e. to monitor the enactment of a context.

In the latter, the guidance engine guides the application engineer by interpreting the process rules captured at the type level in a context description, i.e. within a process tree. It acts in a manner similar to that of an inference engine of an expert system which executes rules matching with the current set of facts. In the former, it helps the application engineer in (a) selecting a strategy for progressing and (b) by retrieving a process tree to be used in the next steps of the process. Strategic guidance allows progression in the forest of trees in a non predefined manner introducing thus more flexibility in the enactment of ways-of-working.

We illustrate these two aspects of guidance within the library scenario in the next paragraph.

• Requesting for guidance "a posteriori"

Let us consider the following situation : while the method engineer was working on the customisation of the E/R way-of-working retrieved from the library, the application engineer started working in a free mode and designed the library E/R schema depicted in figure 7. He captured problem-statements given by the users community using the window dedicated to natural language statements capture (figure 7). He considered some and still has to work on the rest. The pending problem statements are shown in figure 7.

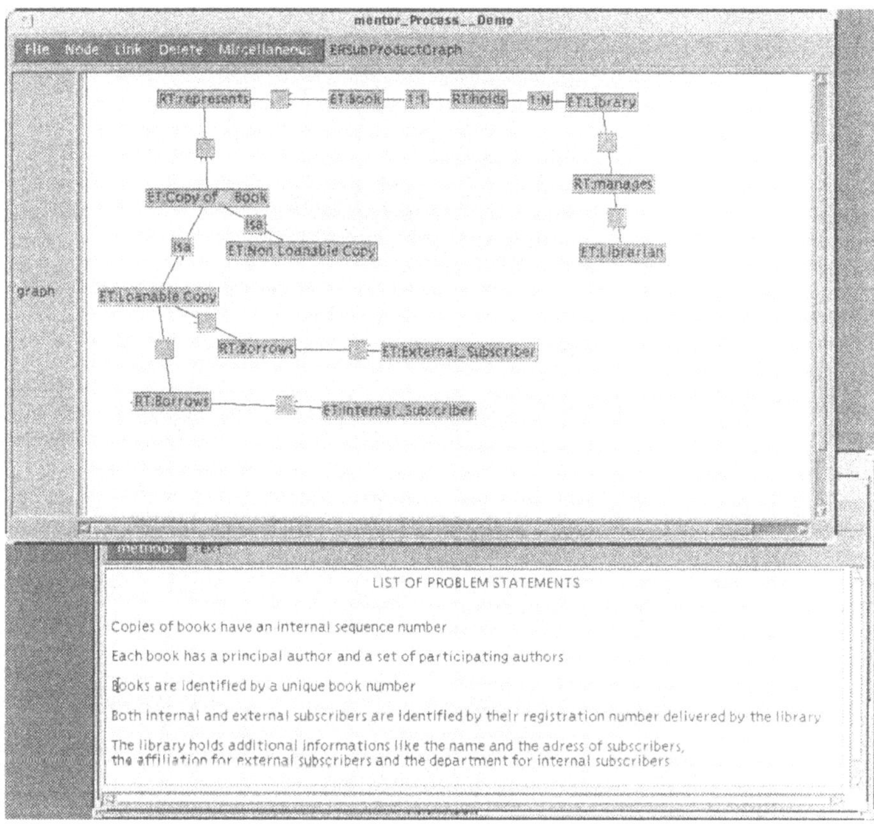

Fig. 7. The current status of the E/R schema

The need of the application engineer at this stage is to be guided "a posteriori". The guidance engine offers three strategies (figure 8), namely the *intention driven strategy, the situation driven strategy and the context match strategy*. They aim at retrieving a set of candidate contexts for which the guidance engine is able to provide guidance corresponding to respectively, the *intention* the application engineer would like to fulfil, the *situation* to be handled, and the contexts which match the contexts *of process trees*. Finding contexts which can guide for further *description* is an example of the first type, selecting contexts whose *situations* are entity-types for further guidance is an example of the second strategy and retrieving *all contexts for which guidance* can be provided by the whole way-of-working is an example of the third strategy.

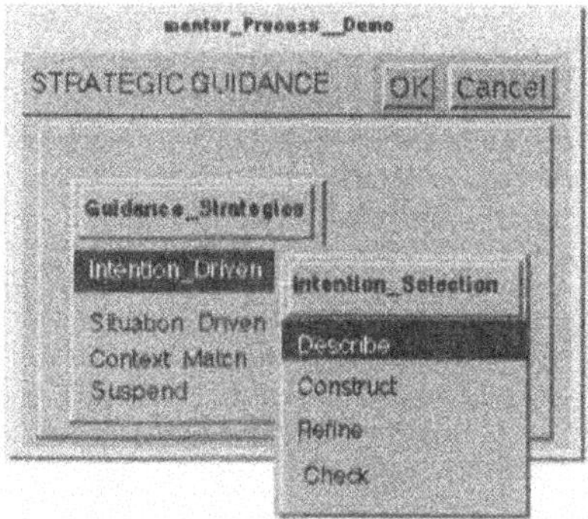

Fig. 8. The different strategies offered to the application engineer

In figure 8, the application engineer has chosen an *intention driven strategy* and selected the *Describe* intention. In response to this selection MENTOR calculates the list of candidate contexts. This is done by matching the situations of the trees' top level contexts having the selected intention with the elements of the specification under development. The result is shown in figure 9. The description of the entity-types belonging to these contexts will be guided by the tree shown in figure 6. Let us examine in more detail the guided enactment of the first of these contexts, namely <(ET[1] :Copy_of_Book);*Describe-Entity-Type(Copy_of_Book)*>.

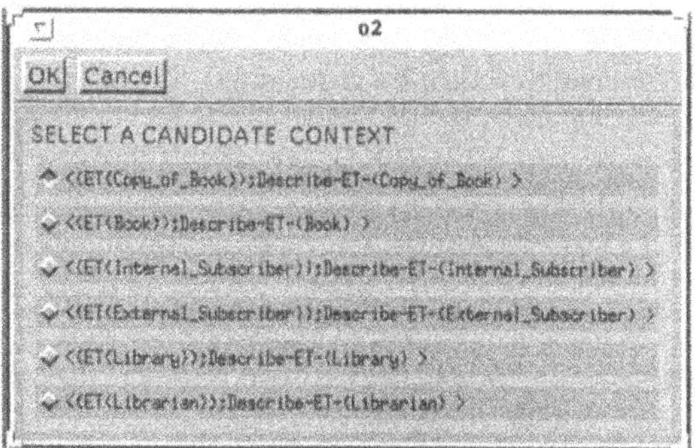

Fig. 9. The list of candidate contexts

• Enacting a process tree

The guidance engine monitors the enactment of a process tree as shown in figure 10. We use a spiral analogy to represent the incremental nature of the RE process where tactical and strategic guidance are alternatively performed. The input of each turn is a context selected in quadrant 1 according to the strategy selected in the previous turn. Quadrant 2 supports the decomposition and refinement of the input context until an executable context is reached and executed in quadrant 3. This is tactical guidance. Based on the presentation of possible strategies and computed candidate contexts, a strategy is selected in quadrant 4. The two lower quadrants implement tactical guidance whereas the two upper quadrants correspond to strategic guidance. Both pairs of quadrants include a selection phase and an execution phase.

---

[1] ET stands for Entity-Type and RT for Relationship-Type

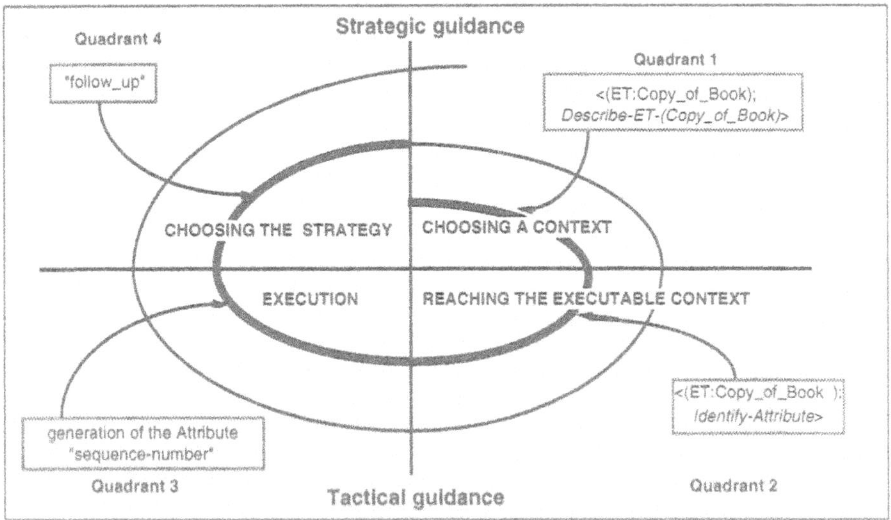

Fig. 10. The spiral view of a way-of-working execution

In quadrant 1,the context <(ET:Copy_of_Book);*Describe-ET(Copy_of_Book)*> is selected.

In quadrant 2, following the hierarchy of figure 6 from the root to the leaves, the guidance engine advises the engineer step by step. In the current example, the description of an entity-type starts by the attachment of its attributes. This is a plan context. The guidance engine computes the set of executable contexts and proposes the first one to the agent. Quadrant 2 ends with the selection of the executable context <(ET:Copy_of_Book); *Identify-Attribute*>.

Quadrant 3 is concerned with the implementation of the executable context resulting from the refinement and decomposition performed in quadrant 2. The guidance engine automatically executes the corresponding action on the product. Guidance at this point is process automation. This corresponds in the example at hand to the creation of the attribute "Sequence-Number" in the E/R schema.

As illustrated by this example, the product under construction is systematically modified at the end of quadrant 3 A step in the process has been performed and a strategy for proceeding further must be selected. This occurs in quadrant 4. There exists a strategy called *"the follow-up" strategy* which is implicitly applied by the guidance engine when it monitors the execution of a plan context. According to this strategy, the guidance engine starts a new step automatically by selecting the context corresponding to the next component context of the plan. In the example on hand, this corresponds to the selection of the context <(Attribute (sequence-Number)); *Describe-Attribute-(*sequence-Number*)*>.

At any moment the application engineer can display the process window which shows the progress in the performance of the plan (see figure 11). He is also authorised to suspend the process enactment (we will see an example later on) and to move to a free mode i.e. without guidance.

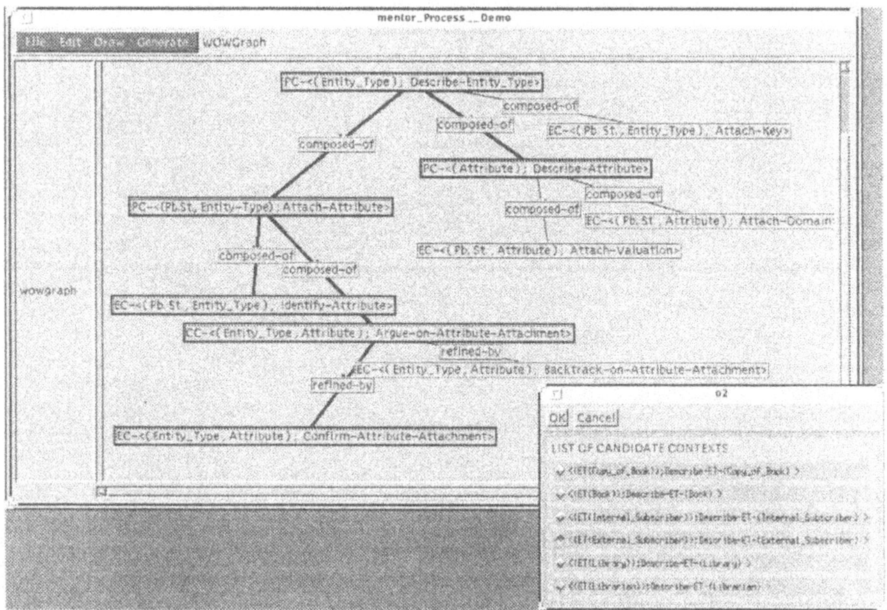

Fig. 11. Displaying process execution

The iterative enactment of the Describe process tree to each of the candidate contexts presented in figure 9 leads to a more complete E/R schema as shown in figure 12.

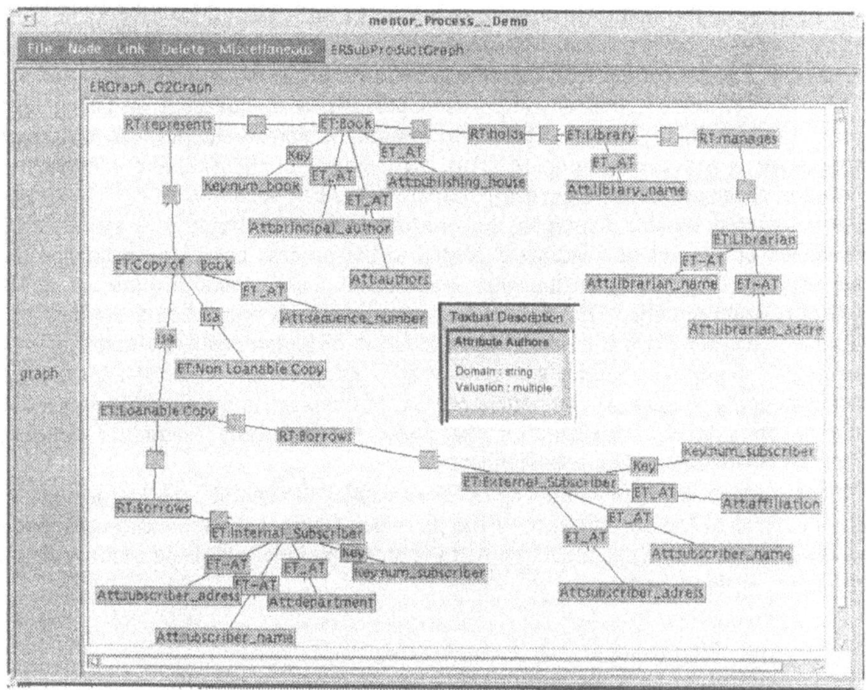

Fig. 12. The current ER specification

At the end of the last step, since the follow-up strategy is not applicable anymore, the application engineer is asked to select one of the proposed strategies to proceed further in the process. Let us assume he selects the *intention driven strategy* with the *Check* intention (figure 13).

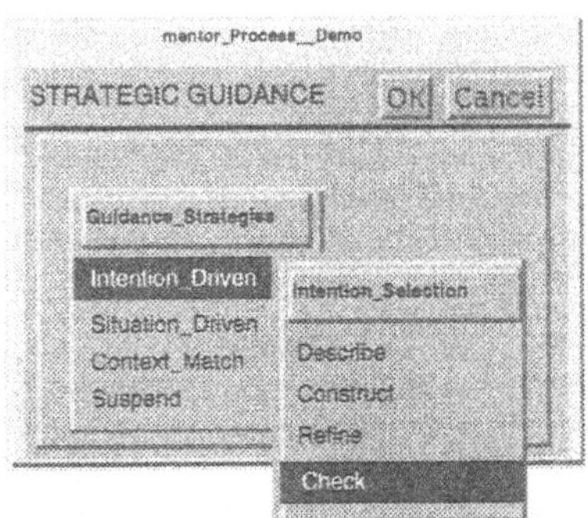

Fig. 13. The list of proposed strategies

• Guiding the E/R schema checking

The guidance engine selects the trees of the way-of-working matching the *Check* intention (Trees 3 and 4 in figure 5) and then identifies the set of candidate contexts in the product under construction matching the context types of these trees. In figure 14, we limit ourselves to the candidate contexts matching Tree 4.

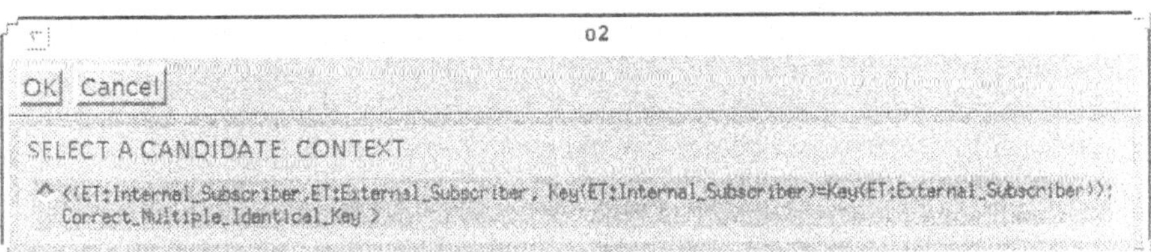

Fig. 14. List of candidate contexts matching the Check intention

The Check tree (Tree 3 in figure 5) detects inconsistent, incomplete and inaccurate situations and proposes ways to solve the detected problems. In the example outlined figure 14, the check permits the detection of two entity-types with the same key, the external subscriber and the internal subscriber. Tree 4 proposes three alternative ways of correcting the situation : merging the entity-types, generalising them, or renaming at least one of the keys. Each alternative is supported by and objected to by a set of arguments. During the enactment process the three alternatives are proposed to the application engineer (quadrant 2) together with the attached arguments. The selection of one of the alternatives by the engineer, say, the generalisation of the two entity-types "External-Subscriber" and "Internal-Subscriber", leads to the execution of a composite action (quadrant 3) which changes the current E/R schema as shown in figure 15. This action asks the engineer to name the generic entity-type, creates the IS_A hierarchy and attaches the attributes common to the specialised entity-types to the generic one. The execution of this action results in the E/R schema depicted in the partial screen dump shown in figure 15.

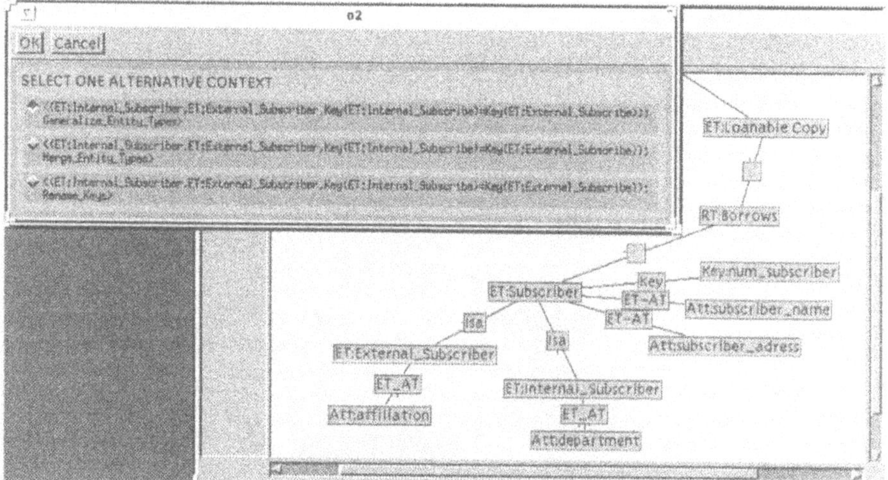

Fig. 15. Correction of the Library specification

Now, the guidance engine again proposes to the application engineer to select a strategy to proceed further. Let us suppose that the engineer wanted to work on the *Borrows* relationship. This means that he selects a *situation driven strategy* and the *Borrows* situation.

• **Improving a selected situation**

Then, the guidance engine computes all contexts having a relationship-type as situation part. Based on the way-of-working presented in figure 5, the guidance engine proposes the candidate context <(RT: Borrows)); *Refine*>. to the application engineer. This context is a choice context and the engineer is requested to select one of the following alternatives :

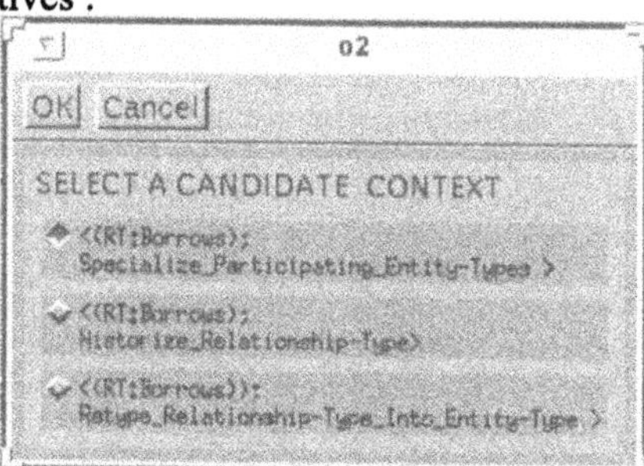

Fig. 16. Selecting an alternative

However, none of these alternatives corresponds to the intention the engineer has in mind, which is to differentiate regular loans - corresponding to loans that respect all the conditions (loan duration, number of loaned books, etc.) with problematic loans - loans in which some of these conditions are violated. A possible action is first to suspend the process (the tool environment keeps track of this suspension in order to be able to resume it), second to change dynamically the way-of-working for including a fourth alternative in tree 3 presented in figure 5 and third to resume to process with the updated way-of-working. This corresponds to a dynamic improvement of a way-of-working in use. This improvement is performed on the fly. Let us examine this option in more detail.

• Changing the way-of-working on the fly

The engineer selects the *way-of-working editor* through the method engineering window and loads Tree 2 in the working space of the editor. Using the graphical facilities, he adds a new alternative to the choice context <(Relationship-Type), *Refine*> : <(Relationship-Type);*Decompose_Relationship-Type*> as shown in figure 17. This alternative is about decomposing a relationship-type into several ones with distinct semantics. To complete the definition of the new alternative context, a choice criterion based on arguments has to be provided.

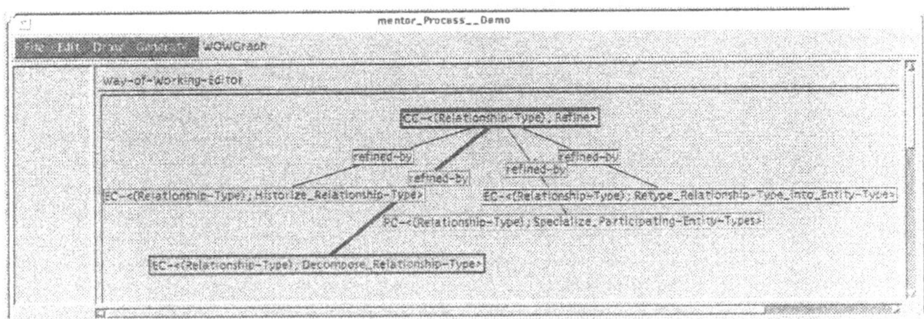

Fig. 17. The modified way-of-working

The application engineer can now resume enactment of the suspended process.

• Resuming a suspended process

This requires the intervention of the *process change manager* which helps in maintaining coherence between the way-of-working and its enacted version. In the case at hand, this leads to the dynamic modification of the window (see figure 17) in order to change the instantiated choice context <(RT:Borrows); *Refine*> according to the change performed on the way-of-working. This results in the addition of the new alternative <(RT: Borrows); *Decompose_Relationship-Type*> to the initial list of alternatives presented in figure 16.

We can assume that the application engineer selects the new alternative in order to decompose the *Borrows* relationship-type into two relationship-types, namely the *regular_loan* relationship-type to manage loans satisfying all the lending rules established by the librarian and the *problematic_loan* relationship-types to manage problematic loans. The selection of this alternative leads to the execution of the composite action which changes the E/R schema as shown in figure 18.

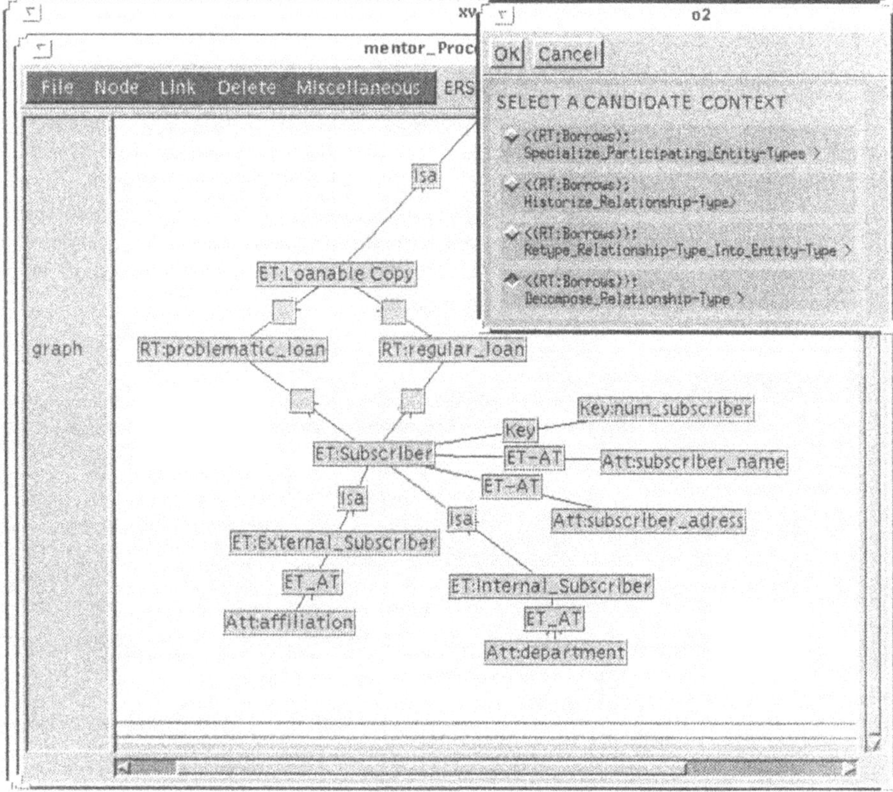

Fig. 18. Managing the way-of-working change

4. CONCLUSION

In this paper, we have presented MENTOR, a Computer Aided Requirements Engineering (CARE) environment which aims at providing flexible and effective guidance to application engineers while constructing system specifications (e.g. ER, OMT, etc.) as well as to method engineers while defining ways-of-working.

Using a scenario, we have illustrated :

- the construction of a way-of-working and its usage by an application engineer
- various types of guidance :
    - tactical guidance based on the execution of process trees, and
    - strategic guidance driven by intention, situation, and context matching
- the manner in which ways-of-working can be dynamically changed on the fly, executed and customised based on a set of generic way-of-working construction patterns

The tool we propose can be related to at least three different classes of software environments :

- (1) *CASE environments*. Traditionally, these environments have been product-oriented. However, they have a restricted view of a product and are not able, for instance, to treat a way-of-working as a product. In MENTOR, the guidance engine treats all products in the same way. Thus, even the way-of-working is just another product for the meta way-of-working. This allows us to use the same software facilities to support both, the process of developing an application and the process of constructing a way-of-working. CASE environments [Oquendo92] have been strong in offering documentation and validation support but have been deficient in providing guidance. MENTOR has been developed to provide guidance in both the creative and the routine parts of the RE process.

- (2) *Process centred software engineering environments(PCSEE).* In these environments, the idea of supporting the development process rather than using individual tools within a process is an important concept [Finkelstein94]. Most of the PCSEEs are articulated around a model or a language to describe processes and a mechanism to execute them [Fuggetta92, Fernström92, Arbaoui93, Belkhatir94, Lonchamp94]. In MENTOR, plan contexts subsume the activity centred process models of PCSEEs. In addition choice contexts and the strategies for context flow make process enactment more flexible, more interactive and more rationally guided.

- (3) *CAME environments.* These environments support method engineers in adapting and constructing methods [Saeki94, Harmsen94, Smolander91]. As in situated methods [Harmsen94], the meta-way-of-working uses the notion of way-of-working construction patterns which is similar to the notion of process fragments. However, these patterns are defined at a higher level of abstraction and, therefore have more potential to be reused. In [Smolander91] and [Saeki94] CAME environments have been defined to support the improvement and customisation of existing methods and help in the specification of a new method, respectively. In these environments, the underlying assumption is that the way-of-working of method engineers is conceptually so different from that of application engineers that special CAME environments are needed. We have shown that it is possible to treat the meta-way-of-working as any other way-of-working. This brings about a conceptual unification of the application and method engineering environments. As a result, it is possible to use the same software facilities to provide guidance in these two environments.

Future work concerns (1) the improvement of the first version of the MENTOR environment, (2) the application of the process theory to real-world case studies and (3) the extension of the theory to deal with co-operative processes, (4) the development of techniques to support learning from process traces..

5. References

[Arbaoui93] S. Arbaoui, F. Oquendo. " *Software Process Performance Support In Peace* ". 6 th International Conference On Software Engineering and its applications pp 39-54, 1993.

[Armenise93] : P. Armenise, S. Bandinelli, C. Ghezzi, A. Morzenti : "*A survey and assessment of software process representation formalisms*", Int. Journal of Software Engineering and Knowledge Engineering, Vol. 3, No. 3, 1993.

[Bandinelli93] : S. Bandinelli, A. Fugetta, S. Grigoli : "*Process Modelling in the large with SLANG*", Proc. of the 2nd Int. IEEE Conf. on Software Process, Berlin, Germany, pp 75-93, 1993.

[Belkhatir94] N. Belkhatir, W. L. Melo, "*Supporting Software Development Processes in Adele2*", Computer Journal, vol 37, N°7, pp 621-628, 1994.

[Bergsten89] : P. Bergsten, J.A. Bubenko, R. Dahl, M. Gustafsson L.A. Johasson : "*RAMATIC - a CASE Shell for Implementation of Specific CASE Tools*", Tech. report SISU, Stockholm, Sweden, 1889.

[Brunet91] : J. Brunet: "*Modelling the World with Semantic Objects*", Proceedings of the IFIP Conference, Quebec, Canada, October 1991.
[Chen76] : P. P. S. Chen : "*The Entity-Relationship Model : Towards an unified view of data*", ACM Transactions on Database Systems, Vol 1, N°1, March 1976.
[Curtis92] B. Curtis, M. Kellner, J. Over : "*Process Modeling*", Communications of ACM, vol 35 n°9, pp 75-90, September 1992
[Dowson93] M. Dowson : "*Software Process Themes and Issues*", Proc. of the 2nd Int. IEEE Conf. on Software Process, Berlin, Germany , pp 28-40, 1993.
[Feiler93] : P. H. Feiler, W. S. Humphrey : "*Software Process Development and Enactment : Concepts and Definitions*", Proc. of the 2nd Int. IEEE Conf. on Software Process, Berlin, Germany, 1993.
[Fernström92] : C. Fernström, " *Tools And Environments To Improve The Software Process*". Information And Software Technology Vol. 34 N° 10, pp 659-674, 1992.
[Finkelstein94] : A. Finkelstein, J. Kramer, B. Nuseibeh (eds) : "*Software Process Modelling and Technology*", John Wiley (pub), 1994.
[Fuggetta92] : A. Fuggetta, Bandinelli, C. Ghezzi, S. Grigolli. "*Process Enactment In SPADE*", Proceedings of the 2nd European Workshop on Software Process technology, Throndeim, Norway, 1992.
[Grosz94] : G. Grosz : "*MENTOR : a Step Forward in Guidance for Information System Development*", Proceedings of the fifth Workshop on the Next Generation of CASE Tools, Utrecht, The Netherlands, June 1994.
[Grosz96] : G. Grosz, C. Rolland, S. Schwer, C. Souveyet, V. Plihon, S. Si-Said, C. Ben Achour, C. Gnaho : "*Modelling and Engineering the Requirements Engineering Process : An Overview of the NATURE Approach*", submitted paper, 1996.
[Harmsen94] : Harmsen A.F., Brinkkemper J.N., Oei J.L.H.; "*Situational Method Engineering for information Systems Project Approaches*", Int. IFIP WG8.1 Conference in CRIS series : "Methods and associated Tools for the Information Systems Life Cycle" (A-55), North Holland (Pub.), 1994.
[Kaiser88] : G. E. Kaiser, N. S. Barghouti, P. H. Feiler, R. W. Schwanke : "*Database Support for Knowledge-Based Engineering Environments*", IEEE Expert, 3(2), pp18-32, 1988.
[Lonchamp93] : J. Lonchamp : "*A structured Conceptual and Terminological Framework for Software Process Engineering*", Proc. IEEE Int Conference on Software Process, 1993.
[Lonchamp94] : J. Lonchamp. " *A Collaborative Process-Centered Environment Kernel*". Proc. of The 6th International Conference CAISE'94. Springer-Verlag 28-41, 1994.
[Martiin93] : P. Martiin, M. Rossi, V-P. Tahvainen, K. Lyytinen : "*A comparative review of CASE shells - a preliminary framework and research outcomes*", published in Information and Management, 25, pp11-31, 1993
[O293] "*The O2 User Manual December*", 1993.
[Oquendo92] : F. Oquendo, J-D Zucker, P. Griffiths. " *A Meta Case Environment For Process-Centered CASE Environments* ", 1992.
[Plihon96] : V. Plihon : "*Un Environnement pour l'Ingénierie des Méthodes*", PhD thesis, University of Paris 1, January 1996.
[Rolland94] : C. Rolland, N. Prakash : "*Guiding the Requirements Engineering Process*", in the Proceedings of the IEEE Asia-Pacific Software Engineering Conference (APSEC), 1994.

[Rolland95] : Rolland C., Souveyet C., Moreno M. : "*An Approach for Defining Ways-Of-Working*", Information Systems Jounral, 1995.
[Rolland96] : C. Rolland, V. Plihon : "*Using Generic Method Chunks to Generate Process Models Fragments*", to be published in the Proc of the Third International Conference on Requirement Engineering (ICRE'96) Conference, 1996.
[Rumbaugh91] : J. Rumbaugh, M. Blaha, W. Premerlani, F. Eddy, W. Loresen : "*Object-oriented modeling and design*", Prentice Hall international, 1991.
[Saeki94] : Saeki M. and Wenyin K., PCTE based Tool for Supporting Collaborative Specification Development, Proc. Int. Conf PCTE'94, San Francisco 1994.
[Schmitt93] : : Schmitt J. R. : "*Product Modeling in Requirements Engineering Process Modeling*", IFIP TC8 Int. Conf. on "The Information Systems Development Process", North Holland (Pub.), 1993.
[Seligmann89] : Seligmann P. S., Wijers G. M., Sol H. G., "*Analyzing the structure of I. S. methodologies, an alternative approach*", in Proc. of the 1st Dutch Conference on Information Systems, Amersfoort, The Netherlands, 1989.
[Si-Said95] : Si-Said S. Ben Achour C. : "*A Tool for Guiding the Requirements Engineering Process*", in Proceedings of the 6th Workshop on the Next Generation of CASE Tools, Jyvaskyla, Finland, pp 23-42,1995.
[Smolander91] : K. Smolander, K. Lyytinen, V.P. Tahavanainen, P. Martiin : "*MetaEdit : A Flexible Graphical Environment for Methodology Modelling*", Proc. of CAiSE91, LNCS N° 498, pp168-193, Tomdheim, Norway, 1991.
[Smolander91] : Smolander K., Lyytinen K., Tahvanainen V.-P., Marttiin P., "*Meta-Edit - A flexible graphical environment for methodology modelling*", Advanced Information Systems Engineering, (Eds. Andersen R., Bubenko J. and Solvberg A.), LNCS#498, Springer-Verlag, 1991, pp. 168-193.
[Tominaga94] : K. Tominaga, T. Tokuda : "*Constraint-Centered Descriptions for Automated Tool Invocation*", IEEE Asia-Pacific Software Engineering Conference (APSEC), pp92-101, 1994
[TOOBIS95] : "*The TOOBIS project (Temporal Object-Oriented Data Base within Information System"*), technical annex , ESPRIT project N°20671, Framework4, 1995.

A Logic-Based Framework for Reasoning Support in Software Evolution

Vassilios C. Vescoukis, Nikolaos Papaspyrou and Emmanuel Skordalakis

{bxb, nickie, skordala}@softlab.ntua.gr

National Technical University of Athens
Electrical & Computer Engineering Department
Computer Science Division, Software Engineering Laboratory

Abstract. Software development has been acknowledged as a complicated problem-solving activity done in a complex, multi-dimensional space. People actively involved in software development need support in understanding and documenting not only the description of the software developed, but also the problem domain and the reasons behind decisions taken during evolution. Development methods do not provide such support, and researchers begin to explore the recording of reasoning in specific phases of software evolution. Several data models have been presented, aiming to support developers by maintaining a repository of deliberation elements of decisions taken during development; these models are usually supported by a special CASE tool that can be classified as a Software decision management system. Using experience gained in the development of large-scale applications in an industrial environment, and experimenting with prototype software design decision management systems, we introduce PROFILE, a conceptual logic-based meta-model that integrates software evolution process modelling with deliberation representation and decision factors. PROFILE enhances existing models by providing support throughout the whole software evolution, by capturing assumptions as real-world reasoning elements, and by maintaining a Knowledge Base of decision-making factors. A prototype Software Evolution Decision Support System based on an instance of PROFILE is also presented in this paper.

Keywords: meta-models, decision-based software development, logic-based models, knowledge-based software engineering, conceptual modelling, reasoning, software evolution support.

1. Introduction

For the past 30 years there has been an intensive effort to improve the software development process by resolving what has been called *software crisis*. Software development methods have been introduced to help produce "good" software, focusing on *how* this should be done. As they where introduced, new development methods appeared to be very promising, but soon enthusiasm was replaced by realism, and yet today, there is no doubt that *the crisis is still here*.

Documentation is the only means stakeholders have for understanding a software system. It must, therefore, be as complete, understandable and easy-to-communicate, as possible. Practice has shown that *everything* changes in the time allocated to a software development effort: requirements are never the same as they were when the development begun, assumptions and constraints change, too. It is the real world that changes, which has an effect in software and these changes must be reflected in software documentation.

We can consider *documentation* as the result of a problem-solving activity defined by a software development method. It is an answer to a "*what needs to be done...*" or "*how should something be done...*" question. Experience shows that this kind of documentation is not equally well understood by all stakeholders involved in software development. *Users* familiar to the problem domain, *might* understand some "what-type" answers, provided that they are properly expressed. *Software engineers* are supposed to understand everything, but this claim cannot be supported in a "court of realism". *Managers* do not need, nor do they want to understand such documentation. Finally, *marketeers* usually derive their own version of documentation which is not necessarily exact or up-to-date.

For the past few years, research has focused on reasoning in software development. During software development several artifacts are produced; before the production of each artifact a deliberation takes place (Figure 1). Several conceptual models have been introduced to capture elements of this deliberation either in the software requirements specification phase, or in the software design phase. A new dimension in software documentation has been introduced. Researchers try to enhance documentation by giving answers to "*why-type*" questions, which is believed that will make documentation more useful, conceivable and easy-to-communicate. So far, focus is on two discrete phases in software development: requirements engineering and design. New data models and tools have been developed to support those involved in these phases of development, capture and exploit reasoning in their work. However, little has been published about experience in using such tools and on practical results of the proposed approaches.

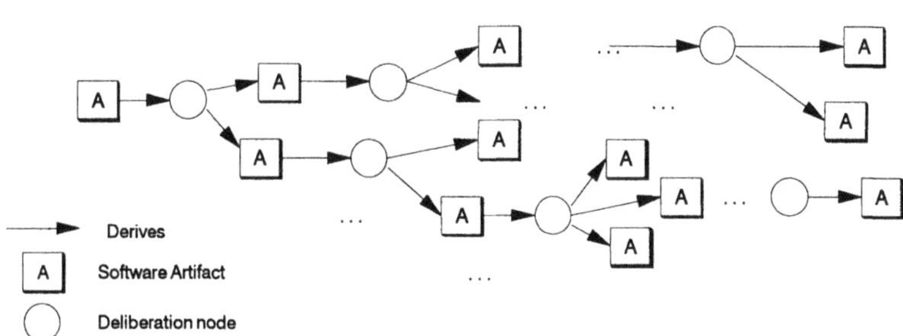

Figure 1. A software evolution graph.

Our central thesis is that a wider perspective is needed in representing reasoning in software development. Supporting only the phases of design and requirements specification, can provide limited help. Reasoning needs to be supported through the whole software life cycle, in a flexible and customizable way (in the sequence, the terms *software evolution* and *software life cycle* will be considered equivalent). Assumptions should be recorded at a global level so that their role can be thoroughly understood. A Knowledge Base containing knowledge about problem-solving practice in software evolution should also be maintained. PROFILE, introduced in this paper, is a logic-based conceptual meta-model aiming to provide a framework for reasoning support in software evolution. It enhances existing models by providing support for the whole software life cycle, by handling assumptions as global reasoning elements, and by maintaining a Knowledge Base for software evolution.

This paper is organized as follows: in section 2, we briefly present our experience with existing deliberation representation models in capturing software design rationale, and give a detailed description of a new logic-based conceptual meta-model. A prototype system implementing an instance of this meta-model is presented in section 3. In section 4 we discuss the related work and in section 5 we make some concluding remarks and present directions for our future work.

2. A new logic-based approach

2.1. Experience

We have been experimenting with software deliberation representation in the phase of design, using qualitative prototypes of existing data models [Potts88], [Lee90], [Lee91], [Conklin88], [Vesc95]. Our experimentation has been done on the design of three software applications: a small-sized *text formatter* developed for illustrative purposes, a medium-scale *document manager*, and a large-scale *technical construction cost estimation* application. We came out with a few useful observations:

- The representation of software design deliberation is a relatively new topic in software engineering. It is not obvious *what* is useful to be captured and *how* to exploit such information.
- A limitation of the models we used, is that the notion of *Design Artifact* is not well-defined [Potts88] [Lee91]. It is not clear neither what exactly an *Artifact* is, nor what its difference from an *Alternative* is.
- Not all alternatives are compatible to each other: selection of another alternative at a later time, may not be possible because of incompatibility with alternatives selected up to then.
- The notion of "design policy" does not exist in any model we have considered.
- *Assumptions* taken into consideration during design were not represented as such, although they are the bridge between the real world and a software system and their representation in a conceptual model should clearly reflect this fact [Lehman91].

2.2. A hierarchy of reasoning in software evolution

From our experimentation, it has been made clear that there are two levels of hierarchy of practical reasoning in software evolution (Figure 2). The lower one is the *application-specific* level and contains reasoning information which is unique to the software application during the life cycle of which reasoning is supported. Such information includes the deliberation elements during evolution problem-solving and is captured using the *Deliberation Representation Data Model.* The higher level is called *global* and contains reasoning information which is global to a software development organization, or at least, to a specific problem-domain in which many software applications can be developed.

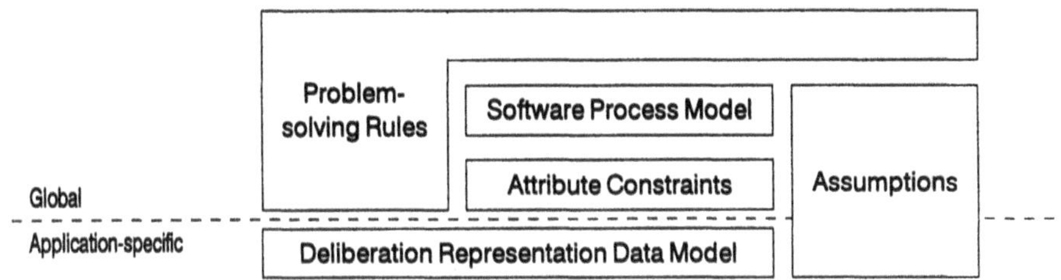

Figure 2. Levels of reasoning in software evolution.

The global level contains the following elements:

The software process model followed, which represents the phases in software evolution, an analysis of each phase in a hierarchy of tasks, and the software artifacts produced in each task. If the definition of the software process model is done at a highly-detailed level, the internal structure of the software artifacts, is also represented.

The constraints that are applied on the evaluation of software artifacts using any measurable attributes, and

A rule base containing knowledge about the implementation of the process model and the practice followed by the developer during evolution problem solving.

Assumptions represent conditions or the real world and in particular of the software development environment or the problem domain, which are true for a period of time and can be used as reasoning elements in deliberation recording. Usually, the scope of an *assumption* is wider than a single evolution problem; however, an *assumption* could also be used as a reasoning element at the application-specific level as shown in Figure 2. With respect to this classification, current approaches provide reasoning support at the application-specific level [Potts88][Lee90][Arango93], and only partially embody the notion of assumption [Ramesh92] as a reasoning element.

2.3. Requirements from a data model

Based on the discussion so far, we present several requirements from a model that will be used to capture deliberations in software evolution.

Software life cycle representation. Software life is divided in discrete phases in which several actions take place. A software evolution model is a set of software engineering activities, methods and practices, needed to produce, enhance, repair, and maintain software [Humphrey89]. Such a model defines what actions should be performed and in what sequence. As these actions take place, software *Artifacts* are produced. Software evolution models do not define the same types of artifacts, or consider similar types of artifacts in an equivalent way. Reference to the software evolution model is necessary for a fine definition of *Artifact*. Hence, the software life cycle followed, should be a part of the model. Apart from a better definition of *Artifact*, this could be useful in classifying decisions, and in understanding the impact and the importance of decisions according to the evolution phase they have been made in.

Development practice representation. Developers use software metrics to define quality measures for the software applications they produce, and require software artifacts to comply to certain norms or constraints when evaluated using these measures. This is a global software development organization's policy that can justify decisions in a proper context, independently of the specific software application in the development of which these decisions have been made. Another case of policy is that of specifying steps that should be taken in solving specific problems. Such requirements can be considered as *decision factors*, because they provide guidance on what piece of information should be considered significant in a problem-solving activity in software evolution. *Decision factors* can therefore be (a) constraints on evaluation, if metrics are well-defined, (b) logic rules, in the case of problem-solving steps, or (c) free-text containing general guidelines, if neither can be formulated. All three types of *decision factors* can be expressed as rules using predicate logic.

User-defined deliberation representation model. In a deliberation, it is not clear what the most useful information to keep is. The different semantic orientation of the models introduced so far, suggests that this information is not the same in all phases of software evolution. The argument that it can be different even among developers, has a standing basis, too. It is therefore required that any deliberation representation schema, not necessarily the same throughout the whole evolution, should become a part of the model under discussion.

Representation of assumptions in a proper context. Assumptions play an important role in software development [Lehman91]. In e-type applications [Lehman80], they can be considered as a bridge between the real world and software. Attaching assumptions in any software engineering artifact, provides a basis for better reasoning in software evolution by capturing important deliberation information in an appropriate context.

2.4. Description of PROFILE

Figure 3 shows the main elements of a conceptual meta-model developed to satisfy the requirements presented in section 2.3, called PROFILE (**PRO**cess modelling and decision **F**actors **I**n software de**L**iberation and **E**volution). This is an abstract view of PROFILE; as will be described later, many elements need to be replaced with a specific data model, in order to have a real implementable model instance. We call this process "model instantiation".

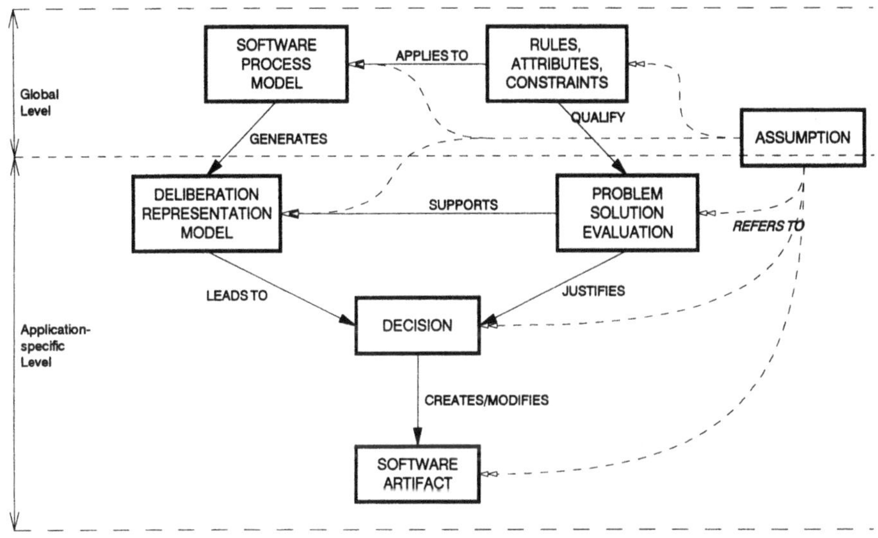

Figure 3. An abstract view of PROFILE.

The first element to define is the software evolution model. This requires representation of phases and their sequence in software evolution. Such a definition can be made in any of three levels of detail as described in [Humphrey89]. In the most detailed level (called the *Atomic* level) a complete definition of all *Artifact* types including their internal structure, is possible.

The next step is the representation of policies followed by developers during software evolution. *Quality measures* is a set of software metrics, formal or not, used by a developer. They usually have a description, a measurement scale, and an applicability scope in terms of *Artifacts* and *Evolution Phases.* A *Decision Factor* is either a constraint upon *Artifacts* evaluation, a sequence of actions taken in problem-solving, or a generic guideline expressed using natural language.

A deliberation representation model for capturing rationale at the *application-specific* reasoning level is the next element of the model to define. It can be the same throughout the whole evolution, or it can be different according to evolution phases. In the latter case, we have a three-dimensional model with reference to the software evolution model used. This implies a higher overhead in software evolution and should be carefully balanced with expressiveness and exploitation of collected information.

Using *Quality Measures* defined previously, alternative solutions to software evolution problems are qualified by assigning values to attributes of *Artifacts*. This is a key in justifying decisions in software evolution. It is well known that software metrics have failed to provide objective measures of software characteristics, except maybe for program code, but metrics is all we have. Defining *Viewpoints* for supporting multiple qualifications made under different assumptions or by different persons, is a realistic solution to this.

The notion of *Assumption* in PROFILE is rather universal than part of the deliberation representation model. *Assumptions* can be attached to any entity of the model to represent a condition that is true within a time frame. Implementations are responsible for handling the temporal dimension of assumption validity, and determine what happens when an *Assumption* is no longer true.

A *Decision* is a trigger for the creation or modification of software Artifacts. Removal of *Artifacts* is a special case of modification. A fine definition of *Decision* depends upon the deliberation representation model that will be used, and can only be done in an instantiation of PROFILE. A *Decision Signature* is a key notion in PROFILE and is defined as a set containing references to the context in which a *Decision* was made. We thus have: $DSig = \{ DPh, DF^*, Q^*, A^*, J, S^* \}$ where DPh = design phase, DF = applicable decision Factors, Q = solutions qualification, A = standing assumptions, J = justification as recorded in the deliberation representation model, S is the scope of the decision in terms of *Artifacts*, and (*) denotes a set instead of a single element. *DPh*, and *J* are pointers to the corresponding entities of the software evolution and deliberation representation models, respectively. A *Decision* is valid as long as all the elements of its *Signature* are valid. Decision Signatures can be used in submitting queries to the model to extract information about software evolution rationale and will be further discussed in section 2.5.

2.5. Instantiation, implementation and use

In this section we present the actions that need to be taken in order to specify an implementable instance of PROFILE, we address some implementation issues and discuss a few aspects of using such an implementation in a real software development environment. From now on, such an implementation will be called a Software Evolution Decision Support System (SE-DSS). We believe that the data model of a SE-DSS highly depends upon the user characteristics; hence, a SE-DSS cannot be regarded as “one more CASE tool”. The use of a SE-DSS implies a measurable overhead, however its necessity cannot be considered well understood by development teams: things could easily end up in a documentation-mess. A developer should proceed in small steps, evaluating experience and using as much feedback as possible from those who actually do the “dirty job” in software development.

At first, the software development organization should specify its requirements from the use of this new dimension of software documentation. The next thing to do, is to conduct some kind of organization-wide research in order to collect some useful characteristics and knowledge that will be embodied in the SE-DSS. These characteristics are: the software life cycle model, the quality measures, the decision factors, and those elements of deliberation in software evolution that will be recorded. Determining the first two, is the easy part of this work. Determining the decision factors is more or less equivalent to creating a special knowledge base by acquiring experts' knowledge on software evolution, which is not an easy thing to do. The initial set of decision factors will contain constraints about metrics and maybe a few guidelines expressed in natural language; as experience is gained, this set will contain fruitful knowledge on software development. It is apparent that a SE-DSS can be best implemented in an environment suitable for knowledge representation. Such a "standard" environment is Prolog, in which we have chosen to implement a prototype presented in section 3; frame-based environments such as ConceptBase [Jarke91] can also be used. In the following discussion we consider Prolog as the implementation environment.

The main functions of a SE-DSS are the maintenance of software evolution history and the relevant information extraction, the maintenance and handling of trigger events whenever certain conditions become true, the maintenance of the knowledge base, and the support of decisions by consulting the knowledge base and examining similar situations of the past. The evolution of a SE-DSS is shown in Figure 4.

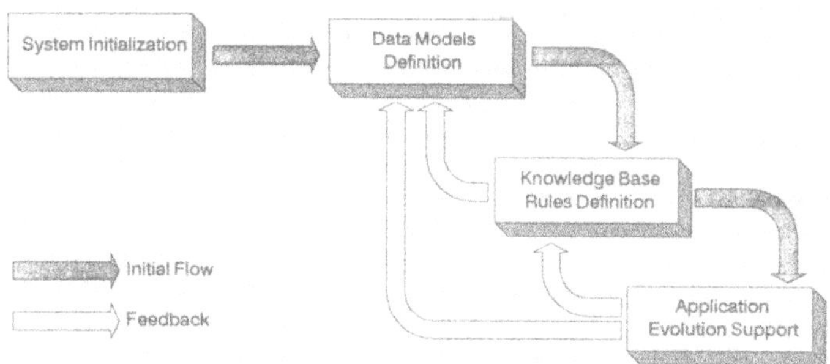

Figure 4. Evolution of a SE-DSS using a PROFILE instance.

3. A prototype SE-DSS system

3.1. Architecture

Figure 5 shows an instance of PROFILE which embodies a deliberation representation model based on DRL [Lee91]. DRL was initially oriented to software design, however, in the context of PROFILE, we think it is generic enough to represent deliberations throughout the whole life cycle.

A prototype SE-DSS system based on this model, called Ictinus*, has been implemented and we have been experimenting with it in the development of several applications. Ictinus's architecture is shown in Figure 6. It is based on the Windows environment where a RDBMS and a Prolog system host a relational database and a rule base respectively. A set of interconnected data models for the representation of the software process model, of the software artifacts and of the deliberation at the application-level, implement the data model shown in Figure 5. A set of Prolog queries implement most of ICTINUS's functions. The main user interface elements are a set of forms for data entry and a graphical browser for browsing through an evolution graph. A front-end user interface provides a working environment to users.

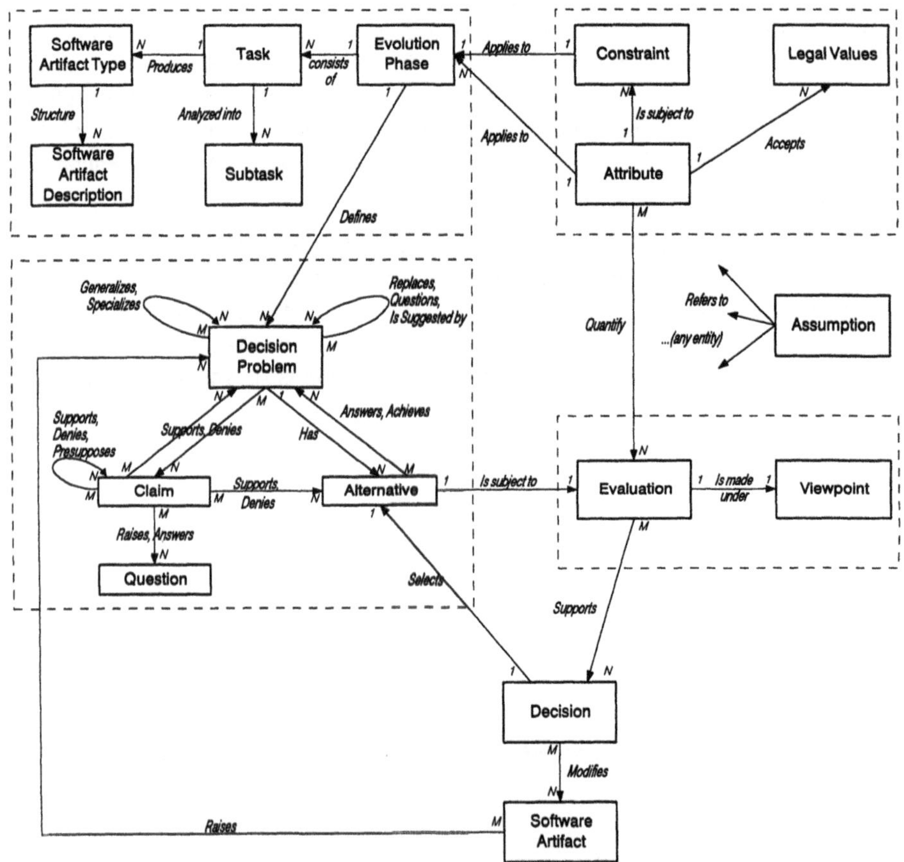

Figure 5. An instance of PROFILE implemented in the Ictinus system.

* *Named after one of the architect designers of Acropolis in Athens.*

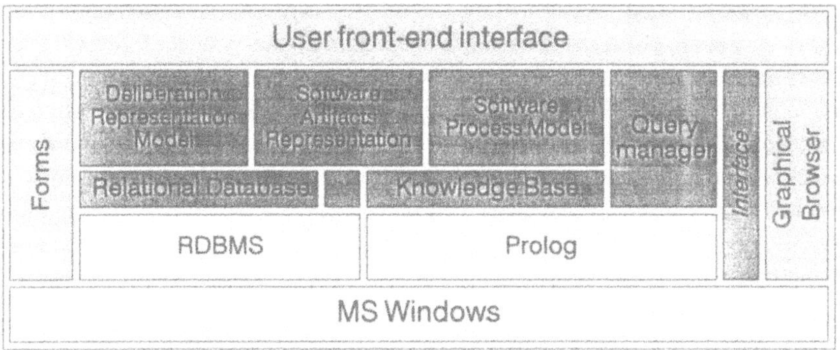

Figure 6. The architecture of the ICTINUS system.

3.2. Services

In the following paragraphs we briefly discuss the main services provided by Ictinus.

Software Process Model management. The user can describe the steps taken in software development at any required level of detail, as a basis for reasoning support during evolution. If this description is done at a high level of detail, the internal structure of software artifacts is also represented and managed. The current implementation of ICTINUS embodies the Waterfall life cycle model at the *Atomic* level of detail, which is the highest with reference to [Humphrey89].

Software Deliberation Representation model management. Several elements of the deliberation representation model (e.g. Viewpoints, Evaluation formulas) reflect the user's policy on evaluation of alternative solution to evolution problems, and therefore are user-defined.

Assumption management. The true state of an assumption is subject to change which results in a set of chain-effects to the decisions in the justification of which this assumption is used. This situation is automatically managed by ICTINUS.

Evolution history recording and playback. Recording of the evolution history is done using either the form-based interface, or the graphical editor. Playback is done using a customizable graphical browser that supports layers of information and can zoom into specific entities to display the required detail. The user decides which classes of entities and what details will be displayed at any time. Walking through the history graph is done using semantic guidance through Prolog queries - not by scrolling a graphical display.

Deliberation management at the application-specific level. Using the deliberation representation data model as a basis, the evolution problems, the alternative solutions and a set of arguments and mathematical evaluations of the alternatives, are stored and managed. Evaluation of alternatives can be made using multiple Viewpoints.

What-if analysis using Assumptions. Modifying current assumptions can affect the validity of decisions taken and change the status of the system. In many cases the system becomes unstable, since some issues cannot be resolved in the new context, and a new problem-solving activity has to take place. Such situations are common during maintenance, where changes in the real world can affect the validity of assumptions and make the system out-of-date, and can be explored using this feature. If some artifacts are modified during this procedure, references to the assumption that initiated the problem are automatically generated and attached to the deliberation information of these artifacts.

What-if analysis using Viewpoints. A similar situation occurs when considering different evaluations of artifacts' quality measures. Depending on the set of decision factors applied, some issues cannot be resolved, which initiates a new problem-solving activity. This is a common situation when doing scenario analysis. Ictinus provides support in such cases by generating alternative evolution graphs that correspond to Viewpoints and by marking unresolved issues. The original evolution graph is modified only when a scenario is accepted and the necessary references to the new viewpoint are automatically generated.

Synthesis library maintenance. A synthesis is a reusable collection of artifacts that share the same qualitative attributes and assumptions in the same functional domain. It can be a set of assumptions, of requirements, of design artifacts, of program elements, or of any type of entities that exist in the software life cycle. A synthesis is *viable* when all attributes and assumptions of its members are valid. Ictinus provides support for maintaining synthesis libraries, for verifying synthesis viability and for performing what-if analysis of the viability of a synthesis in a similar way as in the previous cases.

Decision support is provided through the notion of decision signature. A deliberation takes place in a certain context that is determined by the problem domain, the life cycle phase, the valid assumptions and the applicable decision factors. These elements, except for the problem domain, are part of the *Decision Signature* as defined in section 2.4. We can therefore formulate a query to the knowledge base and extract information about "what has been decided in similar situations". The result of this query can be a long list that can be somehow shortened by running successive refinement queries. The real information obtained from this procedure depends on two factors: The first one is the use of *Assumptions*. Proper use of *Assumptions* can help in effectively characterizing situations and similarities between situations. The second one is the *Decision Factors* rule base. Every time a decision is taken, the user should consider if adding a new rule to the KB is possible. The system's behaviour in decision support is expected to improve as the KB accumulates knowledge about software development practice in the user's organization.

Two other services provided by Ictinus are **event triggering** and **model statistics.** Event triggering is the ability to automatically trigger an event when a condition is met. This is useful whenever a decision becomes invalid for some reason and no other solution exists. The user is notified of the situation and can take the necessary actions.

Finally, using the model statistics feature, the user can determine which elements of the KB are most used. These elements should correspond to policies and situations of the real world, which is an indication that Ictinus is well-tuned to the software development organization.

3.3. Intended use

Figure 7 shows the use of ICTINUS in a software development environment. Chief software engineers are responsible for the initialization of the system by defining the global characteristics of the software development organization, and an initial set of rules and constraints. Software development teams use the system for application-specific deliberation recording and support and provide chief software engineers with feedback regarding the development process itself, and the domain experts with feedback concerning the application domain. Chief software engineers and domain experts are responsible for formulating software practice knowledge and domain knowledge respectively, and updating ICTINUS's knowledge base.

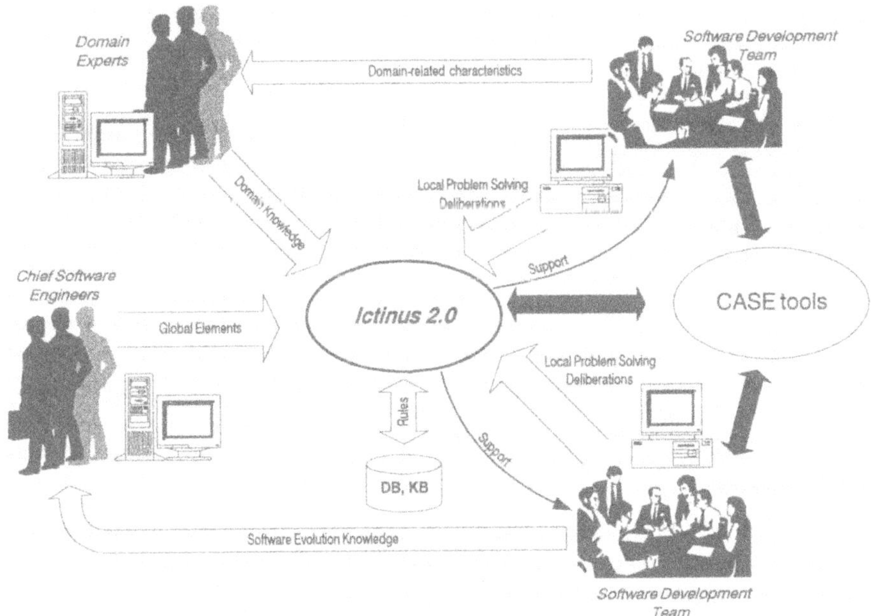

Figure 7. Use of Ictinus in a software development organization.

4. Related work

Potts & Bruns have presented a first approach in capturing deliberations in software design [Potts88]. The data model they proposed is a simple and easy-to-use one. A *justification* is a free-text description of the reasons why a decision has been made. Their model cannot capture several arguments on the same issue and relations among them. The software development organization's practice (software evolution model) is not represented, and neither is the problem-solving policy using metrics, constraints and rules. Furthermore, their model is not supported by an integrated tool but instead one has to switch between a hypertext editor and a Prolog environment.

SYBIL is a decision management system [Lee90] implementing DRL (Decision Representation Language) that supports *goals, alternatives, claims* and relations among them, in software design deliberation. DRL provides better support for representing argumentation than P&B, and has some common qualitative semantic elements with the IBIS model (DRL's *decision problem* vs. IBIS's *issue*, *alternative* vs. *position*, *claim* vs. *argument*). However, IBIS and its implementations such as gIBIS [Conklin88] and IBE [Lease90] can be considered as generic systems for capturing deliberations in engineering disciplines and do not support explicit representation of goals, or the results of deliberations. Neither of these models supports knowledge acquisition and reuse, or domain characteristics representation. Approaches for domain-oriented design support have been presented by Fisher *et al.* [Fischer92] and Arango *et al.* [Arango93], [Arango93b] however, they are not integrated with deliberation representation schemes, which, we believe, should be done in the future.

REMAP [Ramesh92] is a conceptual model used to capture deliberations during requirements analysis that *relates process knowledge to the objects that are created during the requirements engineering process*. It embodies the IBIS model for capturing argumentation and is supported by a system based on the Telos [Mylop90] language implemented using the ConceptBase [Jarke91] environment. REMAP is useful in *capturing deliberations and knowledge when transforming requirements into design* and enhances previous approaches by adding explicit representation of *decisions*, *constraints* and *assumptions*, and by introducing *process knowledge components*. REMAP does not support all phases of software evolution and the necessity for the *development of a generic model for capturing and representing process knowledge across various phases of systems development* is clearly pointed out by the authors.

The development of such a generic model is the main objective of our approach. The representation of the software process model at a highly detailed level (step hierarchy, products and product internal structure), the maintenance of a software evolution KB, and the ability to use a variable deliberation recording model, are the principal REMAP enhancements that PROFILE suggests. As a consequence, we handle *constraints* and *assumptions* in a different way. *Constraints* are regarded as special cases of *decision factors*, which are rule-based representations of evolution knowledge and are applicable to *evolution phases* instead of to *decisions* and *design objects*. *Assumptions* can be assigned to any entity instead of to *arguments* only, which allows a better understanding of their role in software development. In addition, we provide a set of mechanisms for decision support in software evolution.

Several other models for representing deliberations have been presented [Fischer92] [Dong91] [Siddiqi90] [Rose91] [Toulmin84], but they are either less complete than REMAP, or have a different orientation such as group coordination or domain semantics capturing. Relevant studies also include [Rich92], [Oivo90],

5. Discussion

Reasoning is a new dimension in software documentation. Its necessity is not well understood by developers, and existing data models and tools that support reasoning, seem to be immature and not integrated with other tools used in software development. Although there is much discussion of this topic, a common terminology has not yet been agreed. Furthermore, little has been published about experience and so far, there is not any commercially available CASE tool that supports any of the models that have been presented.

We believe that further research is needed in integrating deliberation representation models with existing methods and tools. A unified approach in using AI techniques in Software Engineering is also useful, especially in determining qualitative similarities among problem-solving contexts. These tasks cannot be accomplished unless enough experience from real software development environments has been gained.

We are currently conducting experiments on the topic of measuring the overhead as well as the long-term gain for developers when capturing deliberations. Such an investigation could provide a basis for a classification of existing deliberation representation models according to a *cost-benefit* ratio. We are also preparing a new series of experiments in commercial software development organizations to support both evaluation of the data model and measurements collection. Experience that will be gained is expected to be valuable for this research.

Bibliography

[Arango93] Arango, Guillermo, and Eric Schoen, and Robert Pettengill, ***A Process for Consolidating and Reusing Design Knowledge***, Proceedings of the 15th International Conference on Software Engineering, IEEE Computer Society Press, pp. 231-242, 1993.

[Arango93b] Arango, G., and E. Shoen, R.Pettengill, and J.Hoskins, ***The Graft-Host Method for Design Evolution***, Proceedings of the 15th International Conference on Software Engineering, IEEE Computer Society Press, 1993.

[Conklin88] Conclin, j., and M.L.Begeman, ***gIBIS: A Hypertext Tool for Exploratory Policy Discussion***, Vol 6, No 4, pp. 303-331, 1988.

[Devanbu91] Devanbu, P., and R. Brachman, P. Selfridge, and B. Ballard, ***LaSSIE: A Knowledge-Based Software Information System***, Communications of the ACM, Vol 34, No 5, pp. 3549, May 1991.

[Dong91] Dong, Jinghuan, and Chris Wild, and Kurt Maly, ***A Software Development and Evolution Model Based on Decision-making***, Proceedings of the 3rd International Conference on Software Engineering and Knowledge Engineering, Knowledge Systems Inst., Skokie, IL, USA, pp. 9-14, 1991.

[Fischer92] Fischer, Gerhard, and A. Girgensohn, K. Nakakoji, and David Redmiles, ***Supporting Software Designers with Integrated Domain-Oriented Design Environments***, IEEE Transactions on Software Engineering, Vol 18, No 6, pp. 511-522, June 1992.

[Jarke91] Jarke, M., ***Conceptbase 3.0 user manual***, Univ. Passau, Passau, Germany, Tech. Rep. MIP-9107, March 1991.

[Lease90] Lease, M., and M. Lively, and J. Leggett, ***Using an Issue-based hypertext system to capture the software life-cycle process***, Hypermedia, vol. 2, no. 1, 1990.

[Lee90] Lee, Jintae, ***SIBYL: A Qualitative Decision Management System***, Artificial Intelligence at MIT: Expanding Frontiers, Winston and Shellard, editors, MIT Press, Cambridge, MA, Vol 1, Ch. 5, 1990.

[Lee91] Lee, Jintae, ***Extending the Potts and Bruns Model for Recording Design Rationale***, Proceedings of the 13th International Conference on Software Engineering, IEEE Computer Society Press, pp. 114-125, 1991.

[Lehman80] Lehman, M.M., ***Program life cycles and laws of software evolution***, Proceedings IEEE special issue on Software Engineering, pp.1060-1076, September 1980,

[Lehman91] Lehman, M.M., ***Software Engineering, the software process and their support***, IEE Software Engineering Journal, special issue on Software Environments and Factories, 6(5), pp. 243-258, September 1991

[Mylop90] Mylopoulos, J., and A. Borgida, and M. Jarke, and M. Koubarakis, ***Telos: Representing knowledge about information systems***, ACM Trans. Inform. Syst., vol 8, pp. 325-362, October 1990.

[Oivo90] Oivo, Markku, ***Knowledge-Based Support for Embedded Computer Software Analysis and Design***, Technical Research Centre of Finland, ISBN 951-38-3763-7, September 1990.

[Potts88] Potts, Collin, and Glenn Bruns, ***Recording the Reasons for Design Decisions***, Proceedings of the 10th International

Conference on Software Engineering, IEEE Computer Society Press, pp. 418-427, 1988.

[Ramesh92] Ramesh, B., and V. Dhar, ***Supporting Systems Development by Capturing Deliberations During Requirements Engineering***, IEEE Transactions on Software Engineering, Vol 18, No 6, pp. 498-510, June 1992.

[Rose91] Rose, T., and M. Jarke, and M. Gocek, and M. Maltzahn, and H. Nissen, ***A decision based configuration process environment, Software Eng. J.***, vol. 6 no.5, pp. 332-346, 1991.

[Rich92] Rich, Charles, and Yishai A. Feldman, ***Seven Layers of Knowledge Representation and Reasoning in Support of Software Development***, IEEE Transactions on Software Engineering, Vol 18, No 6, pp. 451-469, June 1992.

[Siddiqi90] Siddiqi, J.I., and J.H.Sumiga, and B. Khazaei, ***Use of a Blackboard Framework to Model Software Design***, Empirical Foundations of Information and Software Science V, Edited by P.Zunde and D.Hocking, Plenum press, NY, pp. 99-107, 1990.

[Toulmin84] Toulmin, S., and R. Rieke, and A. Janik, ***An introduction to reasoning***, 2nd edition, NY Macmillan, 1984

[Vesc95] V.C.Vescoukis, ***Software Design Decisions***, proceedings of CAiSE 95 W3, Jyvaskyla, Finland, June 1995.

[Humphrey89] Humphrcy, S. Watt, ***Managing the Software Process***, SEI, Addison-Wesley 1989, ISBN 0-201-18095-2.

TALE — A Temporal Active Language and Execution Model

Avigdor Gal*, Opher Etzion**[1] and Arie Segev***[2]

[1] Department of Information Systems Engineering,
Faculty of Industrial Engineering and Management,
Technion-Israel Institute of Technology,
Haifa, 32000,
Israel

[2] Haas School of Business, University of California and
Information & Computing Sciences Division,
Lawrence Berkeley Laboratory Berkeley,
CA 94720, USA

Abstract. Complex applications in domains such as decision support systems and real time systems require a functionality that is achieved by combining the active and temporal database technologies. In this paper we present TALE, a Temporal Active Language and Execution model. TALE is a temporal active database programming language, combined with an execution model that enables a correct and efficient processing of operations. As such, TALE is a step in accommodating software engineering challenges in modern information systems. TALE primitives are presented using examples and an EBNF. The run-time control mechanism of the model is introduced and TALE properties, namely active and temporal capabilities, and reflective programming capabilities are discussed.

Keywords: Active databases, Temporal databases, Information modeling, Database programming languages

* The work was conducted while the author was in the Technion. He is currently at the Department of Computer Science, University of Toronto, Toronto, Ontario, M5S 3H5 CANADA.

** The work of this author was supported by the fund for the promotion of research at the Technion.

*** The work of this author was supported by the Applied Mathematical Sciences Research Program of the Office of Energy Research, U.S. Department of Energy under Contract DE-AC03-76SF00098.

1 Introduction

Complex applications in domains such as decision support and real time systems require the processing of temporal data and the execution of programs as a response to events. For example, in decision support applications the validity of current decisions may be dependent upon data that was valid in the past. Consequently, these decisions should be re-evaluated whenever there are retroactive changes of data. A temporal active database [9] provides the required support for those applications by combining the functionality of both temporal databases [16] and active databases [3]. A temporal active database supports time stamped data, and contains a mechanism to activate operations in response to detected events. This combination of the temporal and the active capabilities enables the execution of direct updates, derived updates and retrieval operations that refer to past, present and future time points.

In this paper we introduce TALE, a Temporal Active Language and Execution model. TALE is an extension of the model presented in [9], [19], in which rules that affect past or future valid times were briefly discussed. The model consists of a high level language[3] that enable the use of *events, conditions* and *actions* relating to past, present and future time points. An execution model translates the definition language into a *dependency graph,* an executable data structure that directs the correct and efficient execution of transactions.

The main contribution of this paper is the execution model that provides a wide range of temporal and active inter-relationships. The need for such a model was recognized during the 1993 ARPA/NSF Workshop on an infrastructure for temporal databases. However, only limited discussions of the temporal and active inter-relationships exist in both research areas. Several works (e.g. [3] and [14]) in the active database research area discuss the use of temporal events in active databases. Since these works do not utilize temporal data models, temporal conditions and temporal actions are disabled. Temporal models (e.g. [17], [22], [23] and [20]) discuss the propagation of the temporal effect on a reactive activation of programs, while TALE enables the use of reflective programming [7] as well. Temporal query languages (e.g. [21]) enable the manipulation of time attributes as part of the language, and the use of defaults in defining time bounded values. However, none of the existing temporal query languages offers the wide range of possible inter-relationships between a valid time of a deriving value and a valid time of a derived value that is supported in TALE. Dependency graphs are used in several active data models (e.g. [1] and [7]). In [1], the dependency graph is generated for analysis purposes only, using a given set of ECA rules. TALE and PARDES [7] use the dependency graph as an executable data structure, with a well defined translation mechanism from the user definition of operation clauses to the graph. Both [1] and [7] lack the capability of handling temporal conditions and temporal actions.

As a concrete motivating case study, we present a simple example of a traffic law enforcement system, that imposes a fine as a penalty for speeding offenses.

[3] The support of the language for constraints was discussed in [13].

If a fine is not paid within 30 days of the traffic violation, the fine is doubled. If a fine is not paid within 60 days of the traffic violation, a court order to summon the driver is requested. In addition to the fines, a demerit point system is used. A driver that violates the speed limit in a residential area receives 2 demerit points that are valid for a period of two years. A driver that violates the speed limit in roads other than residential roads receives 3 demerit points that are valid for a period of three years. A driver that acquires 6 demerit points or more must pass a traffic school course; otherwise, the driver's driving license is revoked until the driver passes the course, at which point the driver gets a new driving license.

Basic concepts of the underlying data model are defined in Section 2. Section 3 presents the language primitives, and the execution model of TALE is given in Section 4. Section 5 presents the properties of TALE, including the temporal and active capabilities of the model. The EBNF definition of the language's grammar is presented in Appendix A.

2 The temporal database

The underlying temporal data model is a bi-temporal database [16] with a valid time (t_v) which designates the time points at which the value is considered to be true in the modeled reality, and a transaction time (t_x) which designates the time when a value becomes current in the database. In this paper, we focus on the manipulation and use of valid times, while assuming an automatic assignment of a transaction time to each new value. We use a generic data model, in which an *object* is generically defined as an instance of a class or a tuple in a relation, and a *property* is defined as an attribute in the object-oriented model and a column in the relational model. The term *class* is used to define either a class in the object-oriented model, or a relation in the relational model.

Figure 1 presents a partial schema definition that consists of the name and the properties of three classes: *Driver, Traffic-Citation* and *Speed-Violations* of the traffic law enforcement system. *Driver* includes seven properties that are relevant to each driver. *Traffic-Violations* is a set property where each member of the set (called *Violation*) is a reference to an object in the *Traffic-Citation* class. *Points* is the number of demerit points associated with the driver, and *Traffic-Course-Deadline* is the deadline for participating in a traffic course before the driver's license is revoked. *Driving-License?* is a boolean property (with a domain of "true" and "false" values) that represents the status of the driver's driving license, and *Civil-Service-Employee?* is a boolean property that identifies the driver as a civil service employee. It is worth noting that although Figure 1 consists of a compound property (*Traffic-Violations*), it can be easily translated into a relational data model, as well as into an object-oriented data model.

Points, Traffic-Course-Deadline and *Driving-License* are derived properties. Derived properties, characterized using *(derived)* in Figure 1, are those properties whose value is derived from the values of other properties. The exact definition of their derivation formula is given in Section 3.

Class = *Driver*
Properties = *Driving-License-Number*
Name
Traffic-Violations: set of
Violation (reference to Traffic-Citation)
Points (derived)
Traffic-Course-Deadline (derived)
Driving-License? (derived)
Civil-Service-Employee?

Class = *Traffic-Citation*
Properties = *Citation#*
Driving-License-Number
Date
Violation (reference to Speed-Violations)
Violating-Speed
Fine-Due (derived)
Paid?
Court-Order-Request (derived)
Violation-Points (derived)

Class = *Speed-Violations*
Properties = *Violation-Code*
Road-type
Speed-Limit
Road-Points
Maximal-Fine

Fig. 1. Schema definition of the traffic law enforcement system

Traffic-Citation contains nine properties that are relevant to a single traffic violation: *Citation#*—an identifier of the specific traffic violation, *Driving-License-Number*—the violating driver's driving license, *Date*—the date of the violation, *Violation-Code*—a reference to an object in the *Speed-Violations* class, *Violating-Speed*—the violating speed, *Fine-Due*—the amount of the due fine, *Paid?*—a boolean property that record whether a fine is paid or not, *Court-Order-Request*—the date when a court order should be requested, and *Violation-Points*—the number of demerit points due for the violation.

Speed-Violations stores the general details of violations in different types of roads. It consists of five properties: *Violation-Code*—the code of the violation type, *Road-Type*—the type of the road, *Speed-Limit*—the legitimate speed limit, *Road-Points*—the number of demerit points that a driver obtains as a result of being caught violating the speed limit of the specified road, and *Maximal-Fine*—the maximal possible fine limit.

A *variable* is an instance of a property that is associated with a specific

Points=

2,	*Dec* 1 1994,	[*Dec* 1 1994, *Dec* 1 1996)
5,	*Nov* 12 1995,	[*Nov* 12 1995, *Dec* 1 1996)
3,	*Nov* 12 1995,	[*Dec* 1 1996, *Nov* 12 1998)
	t_x	t_y

Fig. 2. Values of John Doe's *Points*

object. A variable in a temporal database consists of a set of values, such that each value has its own time stamp. For example, Figure 2 illustrates the changes to the variable *Points* of the driver John Doe. The variable *Points* of John Doe has overlapping values ("2" and "5") during [Nov 12 1995, Dec 1 1996), since during that time interval the variable consists of demerit points that relate to two different violations. A selection criterion that chooses the value(s) that is (are) valid in an interval for which a variable has overlapping values can be based on several preference relations. As a default, we assume that a value val_j is preferred to a value val_i iff $t_x(val_j) > t_x(val_i)$.[4] It is worth noting that in this figure, and in the rest of the paper, a single day granularity is assumed.

An *event* is an instantaneous occurrence that can be detected by the database's event detector. It can be the result of a user-initiated signal operation (e.g. the conclusion of a trial), a sensor's output (e.g. the date of requesting a court order as signaled by the system clock), or an update operation (e.g. a change in a *Speed-Limit*). A thorough discussion of events' classification and detection techniques can be found in [2] and [5].

A *user update* operation in a temporal active database updates a single object in a given temporal element. For example, an object can be *inserted* to the database or *deleted* from it. Object's variables are modified as part of an update operation using a *modify* operation, or as part of an *insert* operation.

3 TALE — the language primitives

An *operation* is an executable entity that is activated as a result of an event detection, either conditionally or unconditionally. The set of operations in a temporal active database are partitioned according to their level of interaction with the database variables. *User update* operations are operations that update the database but do not retrieve it. *Apply* operations are operations that possibly retrieve the database but do not update it. There are two types of operations that can retrieve and update the database, namely the *enforce* operation and the *derive* operation. In this section we present the language primitives of TALE

[4] In the temporal model as presented in [10], the t_x is replaced with a *decision time*, a time type that captures the time of the real-world event(s) that lead to the transactions that affect the temporal database.

using examples. The EBNF definition of the language's grammar is given in Appendix A.

TALE language primitives define *operation clauses*, a behavioral description of operations. Operation clauses are defined in a declarative fashion, with the possible use of auxiliary programs, when the execution logic of a desired operation is too complex to be easily represented in a declarative form, or when the database uses existing programs (e.g. *legacy systems*).

Temporal relationships are specified through the use of *participants*, a valid time bound properties of the form ⟨property-name, t_v⟩. A property name followed by a t_v defines the values that are retrieved by the operation, or the bounded effect of the operation on the generation of new values.

An operation clause is composed of four components: an *expression* that defines the execution logic of the operation, a *when* clause that denotes a precondition for activation, a *triggered-by* clause that consists of events that trigger the operation, and a *signals* clause that consists of events that are signaled by the operation. If the *triggered-by* statement is omitted, an implicit triggering is assumed, such that any change to a variable that is part of the operation clause activates the operation. For example, consider the following example:

Driving-License?:= *Renew-License(Driving-License-Number, Name)*
when not(*Driving-License?*)
triggered-by Pass-Traffic-Course

The expression consists of an auxiliary program *Renew-License* that updates an instance of the property *Driving-License?*. The operation is triggered whenever the event *Pass-Driving-Course* occurs, and is activated if the value of *Driving-License?* is false. If the *triggered-by* clause is omitted in this example, then any change of an instance of *Driving-License-Number, Name* or *Driving-License?* triggers the operation. Hence, the following two examples carry the same semantics:

(a) *Driving-License?*:= *Renew-License(Driving-License-Number, Name)*
when not(*Driving-License?*)

(b) *Driving-License?*:= *Renew-License(Driving-License-Number, Name)*
when not(*Driving-License?*)
triggered-by Driving-License-Number, Name, Driving-License?

Several operation clauses can be joined to a single *compound operation*, using the form, as follows.

exp_1 *when* $cond_1$
[*triggered-by* $ev_{11}, \ldots, ev_{1i}$]
[*signals* $ev_{21}, \ldots, ev_{2j}$];
$\ldots$;
exp_i *when* $cond_i$ | *otherwise*
[*triggered-by* $ev_{31}, \ldots, ev_{3m}$]
[*signals* $ev_{41}, \ldots, ev_{4n}$]

The operation clauses are assumed to have a total order priority according to their location in the compound operation. Thus, $cond_2$ is interpreted as $cond_2 \wedge \neg cond_1$. The *otherwise* element is interpreted as $\neg cond_{i-1} \wedge \neg cond_{i-2} \wedge \ldots \wedge \neg cond_1$. The following sections consist of the description of the different types of operations, namely enforce, derive and apply.

3.1 Enforce

An enforce operation evaluates the truth value of a boolean expression on the database state. The primitives that are used by the enforce operation consist of auxiliary programs, participants, constants, binary predicates (e.g. $=$, $>$) and logical connectors (e.g. $\wedge$, $\vee$, $\neg$). For example, the operation clause *Fine-Due* ≤ 500 limits a fine to be less than $500. Although it is equivalent to the first order logic formula $\forall x \in$ *Traffic-Citation* : *Fine-Due*$(x) \leq 500$, the former representation is much easier to write and comprehend [11].

A constraint violation results in invoking a *stabilizer* [8], an alternative operation activated in the wake of a constraint violation to restore the database's consistency. The trivial, and most conservative stabilizer is *abort*, according to which a transaction that violates the constraint fails. An alternative mechanism for the example given above is the *repair transaction* which changes the input transaction's value to be exactly $500.

When the participants of an operation clause are not of the same class, a *matching* process, similar to a join operator in relational algebra, is used to identify the objects that are involved in the operation. In this paper we use an implicit matching, based on [6].

3.2 Derive

A derive operation preserves a data dependency by deriving the values of variables. For example, *Fine-Due* := 15 * (*Violating-Speed* − *Speed-Limit*) defines an operation that derives the fine that is due for a given violation.

While an enforce operation clause (usually) defines merely a dependency that should be preserved, a derive operation also infers update operations required to restore the dependency. The right hand side of a derive operation clause contains a formula for maintaining the correct values of the elements in the left hand side. The derivation expression has the following general form.

$$\text{derivative} := \text{assignment [valid-in } \tau]$$

The derivation expression includes the *valid-in* argument which denotes the valid time of the derived values. As a unique property of TALE, it is possible to specify an explicitly defined valid time for a derived value that is not necessarily related to the valid times of the deriving values. If the valid time is not specified, then it is derived from the temporal characteristics of the deriving values, using default derivation rules. For example, consider the derive operation clause $x := 5 * b$, and suppose that x and b are properties of the same class. If the value of $\alpha.b$ changes during [Sep 1 93, Sep 3 93), then the new value of $\alpha.x$ would be valid during [Sep 1 93, Sep 3 93) as well. However, in $x := 5 * \langle b, t\rangle$ *valid-in* t+6, if $\alpha.b$ changes during [Sep 1 93, Sep 3 93), then the new value of $\alpha.x$ would be valid during [Sep 7 93, Sep 9 93). In the latter example, t is an argument bound to the valid time of b.

A special case of the derive operation is when the database is updated by an auxiliary program. In this case the derivative may not be unique and is written as a sequence $\langle derivative_1, \tau_1\rangle, \ldots, \langle derivative_n, \tau_n\rangle$.

3.3 Apply

An *apply* operation calls an auxiliary program that is applied by the database, but does not affect it. For example, an existing software for planning traffic school's class schedules uses the knowledge that exists in the traffic law enforcement system, yet it does not affect it. Hence, the following apply operation clause is available in the system.

apply Plan-Schedule (Driving-License-Number, Name, Driving-Course-Deadline)
triggered-by Traffic-Course-Deadline

The properties that the auxiliary program requires for its operation appear in the parenthesis. It is worth noting that operations that do not interact with the database can also be specified using the apply operation clause. Such an operation takes the following form.

apply auxiliary-program *triggered-by* $ev_1, \ldots, ev_n$

3.4 An example

Figure 3 presents an exemplary set of operation clauses for the case study. (o_1) computes the fine that is the result of a single traffic violation as a function of the violating speed and the valid time of the violation. According to (o_1), the fine is 15 times the difference between the legal speed and the actual speed during the first month, and is doubled during the second month. The fine balance is reduced to 0 when the fine is paid. The approach taken in (o_1) updates the database proactively, as if the temporal event has already occurred. This approach can assist in answering queries of the form: according to the knowledge that is available today, what would be the fine that is due in 80 days from today? This approach is especially helpful in decision support systems, where decisions that affect the future are based on assumptions that are known today. An alternative approach is to update the database only when the event has actually occurred, using an event *Double-Fine* that signals whenever now=t+31 for some instance. According to this approach, operation (o_1) would be:

(o_1) *Fine-Due* := 15 * ($\langle$*Violating-Speed*, t$\rangle$ – *Speed-Limit*) *valid-in* [t,t+31)
30 * ($\langle$*Violating-Speed*, t$\rangle$ – *Speed-Limit*) *valid-in* [t+31, t+61)
triggered-by Double-Fine
0 valid-in [now, ∞) when *Paid?*

(o_1) *Fine-Due* :=
*15 * (⟨Violating-Speed, t⟩ − Speed-Limit) valid-in [t,t+31)*
*30 * (⟨Violating-Speed, t⟩ − Speed-Limit) valid-in [t+31, t+61)*
0 valid-in [now, ∞) when Paid?
(o_2) *Fine-Due* ≤ *Maximal-Fine*
stabilizer=(Fine-Due:=Maximal-Fine)
(o_3) *Court-Order-Request* :=
null when Paid?
t_s(Violating-Speed)+61 otherwise
(o_4) *Violation-Points* :=
0 valid-in [now, ∞)
when Violation-Points ≠0
triggered-by Pass-Traffic-Course
Road-Points valid-in [t, t+2years)
when Road-type=residential
Road-Points valid-in [t, t+3years)
otherwise
(o_5) *Points* := *sum(Violation-Points)*
(o_6) *Traffic-Course-Deadline* :=
null when Points < 6
t_s(Points)+30 when not(Civil-Service-Employee?)
t_s(Points)+60 otherwise
(o_7) *Driving-License?* :=
Renew-License(Driving-License-Number, Name)
when not(Driving-License?)
triggered-by Pass-Traffic-Course
false valid-in [now, ∞)
when now=Traffic-Course-Deadline
triggered-by Nullify-Driving-License,
Traffic-Course-Deadline
(o_8) *Apply Plan-Schedule (Driver.Driving-License-Number, Name,*
Traffic-Course-Deadline)
triggered-by Traffic-Course-Deadline

Fig. 3. Operations of the traffic law enforcement system

(o_2) limits the maximal fine to be paid. In case of a violation, the *Fine-Due* variable receives the maximal possible fine, using a repair transaction stabilizer. (o_3) computes the date for a court order to be requested. This date is nullified if the payment of the fine was confirmed. The *Violation-Points* are computed in (o_4). If the driver passes a traffic school course, then all of the driver's previous points are erased. Otherwise, the number of the points and their validity is defined according to the type of road on which the violation occurred. The driver's total points are calculated in (o_5) as the sum of points of all violations. Due to the bounded temporal effect of operations, the sum of points accumulates with respect to their validity, as presented in Figure 2.

(o_6) computes the traffic course deadline. A driver that gained 6 demerit points or more should participate in a traffic course. t_s represents "the starting time point of a valid time." If a driver has less than 6 points, then the *Driving-Course-Deadline* receives a "null" value. If a driver has more then 6 points (total order priority assumption) and the driver is not a civil service employee, then the traffic school deadline is set to one month after the first time the driver has passed the 6 points limit. If a driver has more then 6 points and the driver is a civil service employee (total order priority assumption), then the traffic school deadline is set to two months after the first time the driver has passed the 6 points limit. (o_7) computes the validity of the driving license, using the auxiliary program *Renew-License*. (o_8) applies the *Plan-Schedule* program, triggered by changes to *Traffic-Course-Deadline* variables.

4 From definitions to executable entities

In this section we present the basic manipulation of operation clauses to generate executable entities (Section 4.1), and a temporal dependency graph (Section 4.2), which monitors the execution process of a temporal active database (Section 4.3).

4.1 The relationships of operations with database elements

Operations are generated from a given set of operation clauses (o_1)-(o_n). Compound operation clauses are decomposed to basic operation clauses, and the relationships among database elements are determined. We define the relationships of an operation o with database elements by using the following four sets.

UPDATE-SET(o): a set of pairs $\langle p, t_v \rangle$, where p is a property that can be updated as a result of the activation of o and t_v is a temporal element during which p is updated.

TRIGGER-SET(o): a set of pairs $\langle p, t_v \rangle$, where p is a property, an operation, or an event that can activate o, and t_v restricts the temporal range in which o is triggered. For example, if p is a property, then a modification of p during t_v triggers o.

REQUEST-SET(o): a set of pairs $\langle p, t_v \rangle$, where p is a property that can be retrieved as a result of the activation of o. By definition, if p is in the request set of o, than p cannot trigger an operation; thus, TRIGGER-SET(o) $\cap$ REQUEST-SET(o) $= \emptyset$.

SIGNAL-SET(o): a set of events that are signaled as a result of the activation of o. For example, in a warehouse inventory system, the activation of an operation for supplying a product may result in signaling a *Low-Inventory* event. A central order system is signaled by this event and issue, as a result, an order for the product. Since events are the means of notifying the external world on occurrences within the application, we assume that events are not further related with other operations. Therefore, there are no implicit relationships among operations due to *signals* clauses.

These sets are directly inferred from the linguistic constructs, and no additional information is required. For example, $x := \langle a, t_{v2}\rangle + \langle b, t_{v3}\rangle$ *valid-in* t_{v1} is a derive operation that infers the following relationships sets:

- UPDATE-SET(o)=$\{\langle x, t_{v1}\rangle\}$.
- TRIGGER-SET(o)=$\{\langle a, t_{v2}\rangle, \langle b, t_{v3}\rangle\}$, due to the implicit triggering property.
- REQUEST-SET(o)=SIGNAL-SET(o)=$\emptyset$.

These relationships are interpreted as follows. Assume that x, a and b are properties of the same class. If the value of $\alpha.a$ is modified in t_{v2}, then the value of $\alpha.b$ in t_{v3} is retrieved, and the value of $\alpha.x$ in t_{v1} is derived and updated.

According to the sets definitions, an operation clause with an explicit *triggered-by* clause imply that the REQUEST-SET consists of all the participants that do not trigger the operation. For example, in $x := \langle a, t_{v2}\rangle + \langle b, t_{v3}\rangle$ *valid-in* t_{v1} *triggered-by* a, TRIGGER-SET(o)=$\{\langle a, t_{v2}\rangle\}$, and REQUEST-SET($o$)=$\{\langle b, t_{v3}\rangle\}$ ($\{\langle a, t_{v2}\rangle, \langle b, t_{v3}\rangle\}$−TRIGGER-SET($o$)).

Table 1 presents the relationship sets of the operations of the case study. The SIGNAL-SET in this example equals $\emptyset$ for each operation; thus, it is eliminated from Table 1. Each operation has a two-digit number, the first of which defines the original operation-clause.

Paid? is included in the TRIGGER-SET of operation (o'_{32}), although it does not appear explicitly in the second clause of operation (o_3) (Figure 3). This is a result of the negation of the condition of the first operation. The same applies for operations (o'_{42}),(o'_{43}) (*Violation-Points*), and (o'_{62}),(o'_{63}) (*Points*). The properties that participate in the matching process are added to the TRIGGER-SET of operations (o'_{11}), (o'_{12}), (o'_{21}), (o''_{21}), (o'_{42}), (o'_{43}), and (o'_{51}). Operation (o'_{21}) appears in the TRIGGER-SET of the stabilizer (o''_{21}), since the stabilizer is (conditionally) activated by the operation.

4.2 The temporal dependency graph

The control of a transaction at runtime is based on a *temporal dependency graph*, an executable data structure that monitors the activation of operations to achieve consistency in a minimal number of update operations and using maximal parallelism [10]. The temporal dependency graph extends previous works in active databases [15], [7], [1] to include the temporal functionality. It consists of all the relationships among properties, events and operations in a database. The temporal dependency graph is generated from a given database structure, a given set of operation clauses, and a given set of events. The operation clauses are translated into operations, and the relationship sets are defined for each operation (Section 4.1).

The temporal dependency graph TDG = (V, E) is a directed graph. The set of nodes V designate the application's elements, properties, events and operations. The set of edges E denote relationships through which the application elements interact. There are three types of edges, *data edges*, *trigger edges*, and *request*

Operation number	Update-Set	Trigger-Set	Request-Set
(o'_{11})	{⟨Fine-Due, [t, t+31)⟩}	{⟨Violating-Speed, t⟩, Speed-Limit, Speed-Violations.Violation-Code, Traffic-Citation.Violation-Code}	∅
(o'_{12})	{⟨Fine-Due, [t+31, t+61)⟩}	{⟨Violating-Speed, t⟩, Speed-Limit Speed-Violations.Violation-Code, Traffic-Citation.Violation-Code}	∅
(o'_{13})	{⟨Fine-Due, [now, ∞)⟩}	{Paid?}	∅
(o'_{21})	∅	{Fine-Due, Maximal-Fine, Speed-Violations.Violation-Code, Traffic-Citation.Violation-Code}	∅
(o''_{21})	{Fine-Due}	(o'_{21})	{Maximal-Fine, Speed-Violations.Violation-Code, Traffic-Citation.Violation-Code}
(o'_{31})	{Court-Order-Request}	{Paid?}	∅
(o'_{32})	{Court-Order-Request}	{ Violating-Speed, Paid?}	∅
(o'_{41})	{⟨Violation-Points, [now, ∞)⟩}	{Pass-Traffic-Course}	{Violation-Points}
(o'_{42})	{⟨Violation-Points, [t, t+2year)⟩}	{Road-Points, Violation-Points, Speed-Violations.Violation-Code, Traffic-Citation.Violation-Code, Road-Type}	∅
(o'_{43})	{⟨Violation-Points, [t, t+3year)⟩}	{Road-Points, Violation-Points, Speed-Violations.Violation-Code, Traffic-Citation.Violation-Code, Road-Type}	∅
(o'_{51})	{Points}	{Violation-Points, Driver.Driving-License-Number Traffic-Citation.Driving-License-Number}	∅
(o'_{61})	{Traffic-Course-Deadline}	{Points}	∅
(o'_{62})	{Traffic-Course-Deadline}	{Points, Civil-Service-Employee?}	∅
(o'_{63})	{Traffic-Course-Deadline}	{Points, Civil-Service-Employee?}	∅
(o'_{71})	{Driving-License?}	{ Pass-Traffic-Course}	{Driving-License?, Name, Driving-License-Number}
(o'_{72})	{Nullify-Driving-License,	{Traffic-Course-Deadline} Traffic-Course-Deadline}	{Driving-License?}
(o'_{81})	∅	{Traffic-Course-Deadline}	{Driver.Driving-License-Number, Name}

Table 1. The relationship sets of the case study

edges. Data edges connect properties in the relationship sets with operations, and enable the transfer of data values from variables to operations, and vice versa. A valid time temporal element can be associated with a data edge, to designate the edge's temporal range of effect. A temporal element τ that is associated with a data edge (p, o) restricts the retrieval of any variable $\alpha.p$ to τ. A temporal element τ that is associated with a data edge (o, p) restricts the update of any variable $\alpha.p$ to τ. This association enables reasoning about the temporal relationships in the database, which cannot be done in other dependency graph based models. However, the temporal dependency graph can be reduced to a dependency graph in the non temporal case by omitting the time restrictions of data edges.

Trigger edges connect events with operations and constraints with their associated stabilizers. A trigger edge between two operations o_i and o_j, that do not origin from the same operation is generated if exists a property that is in the UPDATE-SET(o_i) and in the TRIGGER-SET(o_j), with a possible temporal overlapping. For example, *Points* is in the update set of operations (o_{51}), and in the trigger set of operation (o_{61}), (o_{62}), and (o_{63}) (Table 1). A trigger edge is generated between operation (o_{51}), and each of the operations (o_{61}), (o_{62}) and (o_{63}), since there are no temporal limitations associated with these edges. In similar, a request edge between two operations o_i and o_j that do not origin from the same operation is generated if exists a property that is in the UPDATE-SET(o_i) and in the REQUEST-SET(o_j), with a possible temporal overlapping.

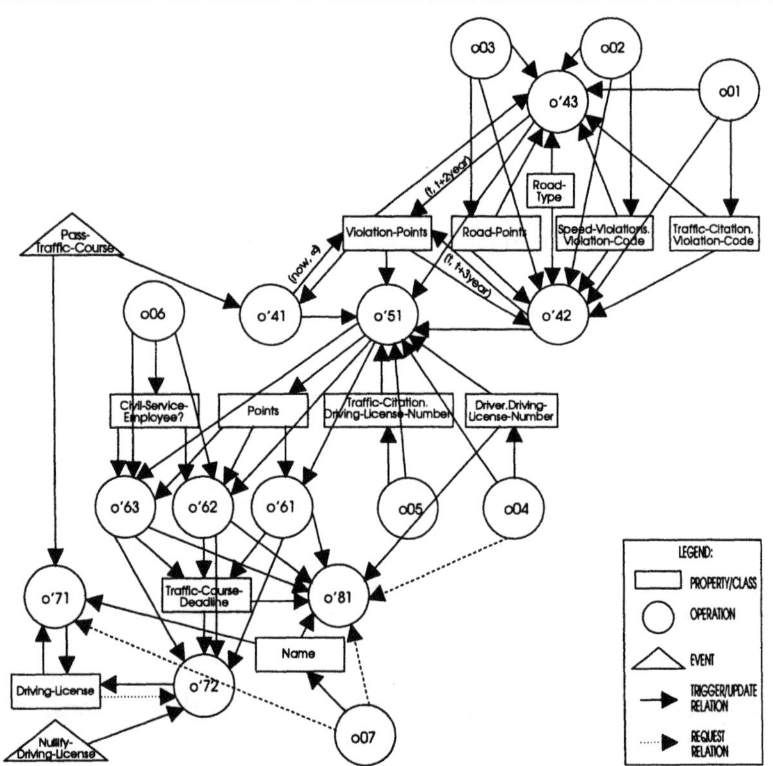

Fig. 4. A partial temporal dependency graph of the traffic law enforcement system

Figure 4 presents a partial example of the temporal dependency graph, with operation clauses (o4)-(o8) of Figure 3. Temporal elements are associated with data edges and represent the effect of operations in a given temporal element. Trigger edges between operations represent the triggering of an operation as a result of the activation of one of its predecessors. request edges are designated by dotted edges. Operations o_{01}-o_{07} are user update operations, designating the update of a single variable. For example, o_{03} updates the *Road-Points* variable.

The time complexity of generating the temporal dependency graph is computed in [10]. Its worse case is bounded by $O(|V|^3)$, the time complexity of generating the trigger and request edges that are not explicitly given by the relationships sets. The number of nodes and edges reflects the number of schema-elements and the relationships among them, and not the number of objects represented in the database. Thus, the space complexity of the graph, which is bounded by $O(|V| + |E|)$ is much smaller than the size of the data stored in the database. It is worth noting that the generation of the graph is a pre-processing phase, carried out only whenever there is a change in the database structure, either changes to static schema definitions or changes in operation clauses.

4.3 The execution process

The execution process uses the temporal dependency graph as an executable data structure that monitors the activation of operations. The execution process consists of three main modules, namely *initialization, triggering*, and *activation*, as follows.

Initialization: Each transaction contains a sequence of signal events and operations that are initiated by the user. Each update operation is decomposed into primitive operations $u_1, \ldots, u_n$, where each primitive operation is designated to update a single variable or object. A *transaction subgraph* is constructed, consisting of all the operations that should be activated as a result of the activation of the primitive operations. An operation o is activated as a result of an update operation u_i iff there exists a path in the temporal dependency graph from u_i to o. For example, Figure 5 is a transaction subgraph of a transaction that was initiated as a result of signaling a *Pass-Traffic-Course* event.

Triggering: An operation is triggered once its predecessors in the transaction subgraph have terminated. A triggered operation consults the transaction subgraph to assess its status. If there are no more incoming edges to be triggered, then the operation is activated; otherwise, the operation waits.

Activation: The activation of an operation entails the retrieval of values, the call for auxiliary programs, and the calculation of formulae to decide upon new values to be inserted to the database. Upon completion of these phases, the database is updated, and any outgoing edges are triggered.

For example, On January 29, 1995, a traffic school course has concluded, and a transaction is issued, updating the database, to confirm that ten drivers has passed. This is done by signaling a *Pass-Traffic-Course* event. The transaction is as follows.

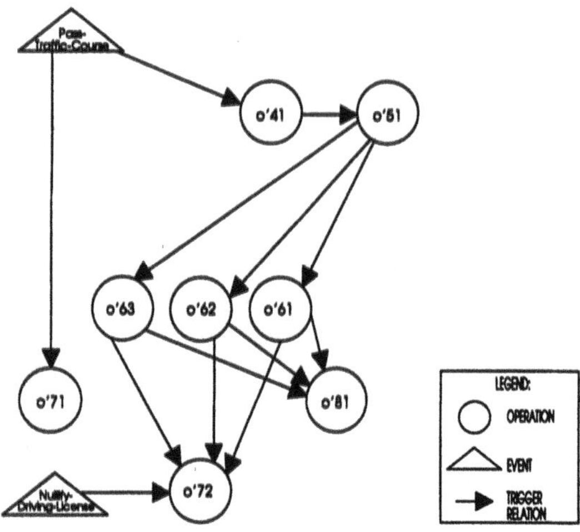

Fig. 5. A transaction subgraph

Begin transaction
Signal Pass-Traffic-Course for
Driver.Driving-License-Number=12345678,
...,
Driver.Driving-License-Number=34467978,
End transaction

The transaction is transformed into primitive operations. Figure 5 represents a transaction subgraph of the given transaction. For each driver, (o'_{41}) retrieves the valid value of *Violation-Points* of each traffic violation the driver committed. If it is not 0, then a new value of the *Violation-Points*, with the value 0 and validity [Jan 29 1995, ∞) is generated. The edge $\langle(o'_{41}),(o'_{51})\rangle$ is triggered, and for each driver, (o'_{51}) derives *Points* to be 0 in the interval [Jan 29 1995, ∞). The edges $\langle(o'_{51}),(o'_{61})\rangle$, $\langle(o'_{51}),(o'_{62})\rangle$, $\langle(o'_{51}),(o'_{63})\rangle$ are then triggered. Of the three operations, (o'_{61}), (o'_{62}), and (o'_{63}), (o'_{61}) is the only one that generates new values, since the precondition of processing (o'_{62}) and (o'_{63}), requiring the number of demerit points to be more than 6, is not valid. For each driver, (o'_{61}) derives *Traffic-Course-Deadline* to be "null" in the interval [Jan 29 1995, ∞). The edges $\langle(o'_{61}),(o'_{72})\rangle$ and $\langle(o'_{61}),(o'_{81})\rangle$ are then triggered. (o'_{71}) renews the driving-license of each of the drivers whose driving-license was revoked. As a result, a new value of the *Driving-License?* property, with the value "True" and a validity of [Jan 29 1995, ∞), is generated for each driver. (o'_{72}) does not result in any new value, since *Traffic-Course-Deadline* is nullified for each driver. (o'_{81}) is triggered with the names of the drivers and a nullified driving course deadline. At this point, there are no outgoing edges to trigger, and the transaction is terminated.

The execution process preserves the database consistency [10]. Therefore, applying a transaction on a database Δ that all of its operation clauses are satisfied, results in a database $\Delta^{'}$ in which all operation clauses are satisfied as well. In addition, to handle the problem of long transactions [4], the update process minimizes the time required for processing a transaction, due to the use of a temporal dependency graph [10].

5 The properties of TALE

This section discusses three of TALE properties, namely active properties (Section 5.1), temporal properties (Section 5.2) and linguistic properties (Section 5.3).

5.1 Active capabilities of TALE

TALE is aimed at defining operations that contain valid times. However, TALE is also a rule language for active databases. As such, every ECA statement[5] has an equivalent operation clause in TALE. Consider the following ECA rule:

Event *ev*
Condition *cond*
Action *prog*

An equivalent operation clause in TALE is written as follows:

- If *prog* is an updating program that updates the elements $\{el_1, \ldots, el_n\}$: $\{el_1, \ldots, el_n\}$:= *prog triggered-by ev when cond.*
- If *prog* is not an updating program: *apply prog triggered-by ev when cond.*

While TALE subsumes ECA rules, the uniqueness of the model over other active database languages, is the combination of the capability of representing time dependent operations (Section 5.2), and reflective capabilities (Section 5.3) besides the standard reactive capabilities of active databases. Some other issues that are not discussed in this paper relate to composite events and coupling modes. The issue of composite events is an issue orthogonal to the temporal capabilities as discussed in this paper. Therefore, any model of composite events definition and manipulation (e.g. [3]) can be adopted by TALE. The default coupling mode used in TALE falls into the *deferred* category. An extension to support other coupling modes is not discussed in this paper. Conflict resolution among different operations are resolved by syntactic restriction as well as by imposing a totally ordered priority.

[5] The term *ECA statement* refers to a *simple ECA rule* [3].

5.2 Temporal capabilities of TALE

TALE enables three temporal effect types on operations.

Derived valid-time temporal projection: An activation of an operation results in the generation of values with bounded temporal validity. For example, consider the operation clause $x := y + 3$, and assume that x and y are properties of the same class. On January 1994, $\alpha.y$ is modified to be 7, valid in [Jan 1 1994, Jan 8 1994). As a result, $\alpha.x$ is modified to be 10, valid in [Jan 1 1994, Jan 8 1994). The valid time is derived as an intersection of the valid times of the participants' instances.

Temporal conditions: An operation consists of a condition expression that can take temporal variables as arguments. For example:

```
x:= y+3        when ⟨z, [t_s − 365, t_e)⟩ >100
    2 * y+8    otherwise
```

$t_v = [t_s, t_e)$, is the valid time of the derived value. The condition is a function of the start time (t_s) and end time (t_e) of that interval. Assume that x, y and z are properties of the same class. On January 1 1994, $\alpha.y$ is modified to be 7, valid during [Jan 1 1994, Jan 8 1994). $\alpha.x$ is modified to be 10, valid during [Jan 1 1994, Jan 8 1994), only if the value of $\alpha.z$ was more than 100 throughout the interval [Jan 1 1993, Jan 8 1994). Otherwise, $\alpha.x$ is modified to be 22, valid during [Jan 1 1994, Jan 8 1994). These conditions are depicted in the temporal dependency graph as temporal elements associated with a triggering edge.

Explicit valid-time temporal projection: An operation can result in the generation of values with bounded temporal validity that is a function of the temporal validity of other values. For example, the operation clause $x := y + 3$ *valid-in* $[t_s, t_e + 4)$ defines an explicit valid time for the derivative. On January 1 1994, $\alpha.y$ is modified to be 7, valid in [Jan 1 1994, Jan 8 1994). As a result, $\alpha.x$ is modified to be 10, valid in [Jan 1 1994, Jan 12 1994). Explicit valid-time temporal projection is depicted in the temporal dependency graph as a temporal element associated with an update edge.

TALE presents new temporal capabilities. To emphasize these capabilities, other common temporal aspects are kept to the minimum. For example, a natural extension of this language, not discussed in this paper, is the support of temporal operators. Ongoing work focuses on an extensive temporal support in the TALE framework.

5.3 Reflective programming capabilities

TALE employs both the reactive programming style of active databases, and a higher level approach of reflective programming, according to which implicit properties of operations define their relationships with the database. As discussed in the previous section, the activation of an operation o depends on the contents of the TRIGGER-SET(o). The contents of this set can be inferred by the operation definition and does not require an explicit definition. For example, consider a derive operation o that uses the operation clause $x := a + b$. The implicit contents of TRIGGER-SET(o) is $\{a, b\}$. Thus, any modification to an instance of either a or b activates o. By definition, when the TRIGGER-SET(o) is inferred, it contains all the participants, thus REQUEST-SET(o)=$\emptyset$.

The TRIGGER-SET(o) and the REQUEST-SET(o) sets are inferred, unless the TRIGGER-SET(o) is defined explicitly. For example, the operation clause $x := a + b$ *triggered-by* a, (which means the event "a is updated"), defines an explicit TRIGGER-SET(o). In these cases, the REQUEST-SET(o) is defined as the set of all participants that are not included in the TRIGGER-SET(o).

6 Conclusion

In this paper we have presented TALE, a Temporal Active Language and Execution model, that encapsulates a wide range of inter-relationships of temporal and active capabilities. TALE language primitives define operation clauses, a behavioral description of executable entities called operations. TALE handles operations that define the relationships among values and time-stamps of variables in a database, in addition to other types of operations. Operation clauses are defined in a declarative fashion, with the possible use of auxiliary programs. Temporal relationships in operation clauses are given through the use of participants, a valid time bound properties of the form ⟨property-name, t_v⟩. Each value in the temporal active database has a bounded temporal validity, that is either given explicitly by the user or derived through the use of operation clauses. TALE extends active databases (that traditionally support temporal events), to support also temporal conditions and temporal actions. Consequently, TALE provides an easy-to-use built-in temporal capabilities in an active database environment. In the degenerate case, when TALE works on a non-temporal active database, TALE would be able to represent ECA rules, as demonstrated in the previous section.

The use of TALE in complex applications facilitates the programming and debugging tasks, and assists in creating a reliable environment for applications that use retroactive and proactive updates. A prototype of a system that is based on TALE is currently under development on the basis of MS-Access 2.0 for Windows, in the Windows 3.11 environment. A temporal database model is mapped to the MS-Access environment using an extension to the Temporal Normal Form (TNF) [18], in which a relation consist of all the variables that share the same time stamp. An ongoing work focuses on the parallel execution model of the update process of a temporal active database, and the use of parallel execution to support schema versioning [12]. An additional work focuses on an extensive temporal support in the TALE framework.

References

1. A. Aiken, J. Widom, and J.M. Hellerstein. Behavior of database production rules: Termination, confluence and observable determinism. In *Proceedings of ACM SIGMOD*, pages 59–68, June 1992.
2. S. Chakravarthy and D. Mishra. An expressive event specification language for active databases. *Data and Knowledge Engineering*, 13(3), Oct. 1994.
3. U.S. Chakravarthy. Rule management and evaluation: An active DBMS perspective. *ACM SIGMOD Record*, 18(3):20–28, Sep 1989.
4. U. Dayal, M. Hsu, and R. Ladin. A transaction model for long-running activities. In *Proceedings of the 17th VLDB*, pages 113–122, Sep 1991.
5. K.R. Dittrich and S. Gatziu. Time issues in active database systems. In R.T. Snodgrass, editor, *Proceedings of the International Workshop on Infrastructure for Temporal Databases*, Arlington, TX, June 1993.
6. O. Etzion. Active interdatabase dependencies. *Information Sciences*, 75:133–163, 1993.
7. O. Etzion. The reflective approach for data-driven rules. *International Journal of Intelligent and Cooperative Information Systems*, 2(4):399–424, December 1993.
8. O. Etzion and B. Dahav. Self-stabilization in databse consistency maintenance. Technical Report ISE-TR-95-1, Technion-Israel Institute of Technology, Feb 1995.
9. O. Etzion, A. Gal, and A. Segev. Temporal active databases. In *Proceedings of the International Workshop on an Infrastructure for Temporal Database*, June 1993.
10. A. Gal. *TALE — A Temporal Active Language and Execution Model.* PhD thesis, Technion—Israel Institute of Technology, Technion City, Haifa, Israel, May 1995. Available through the author's WWW home page, http://www.cs.toronto.edu/~avigal.
11. A. Gal and O. Etzion. Maintaining data driven rules in databases. *IEEE Computer*, 28(1):28–38, Jan 1995.
12. A. Gal and O. Etzion. A parallel execution model for updating temporal databases. to appear in the International Journal of Computer Systems Science and Engineering, 1995.
13. A. Gal, O. Etzion, and A. Segev. A language for the support of constraints in temporal active databases. In *Proc. Workshop on Constraints, Databases and Logic Programming*, pages 42–58, Portland, Oregon, Dec 1995.
14. N. Gehani, H.V. Jagadish, and O. Shmueli. Composite event specification in active databases. In *International Conference on Very Large Databases*, Vancouver, Canada, Aug 1992.
15. S. Hudson and R. King. CACTIS: A database system for specification functionality defined data. In *Proceedings of the IEEE OOBDS Workshop*, pages 26–37, Sep 1986.
16. C.S. Jensen et al. A consensus glossary of temporal database concepts. *ACM SIGMOD Record*, 23(1):52–63, 1994.
17. M.R. Klopprogge and P.C. Lockmann. Modeling information preserving databases; consequences of the concept of time. In *Proceedings of the International Conference of VLDB*, Florance, Italy, 1983.
18. S.B. Navathe and R. Ahmed. A temporal relational model and a query language. *Information Sciences*, 49:147–175, 1989.
19. N. Pissinou. Towards an infrastructure for temporal databases—A workshop report. *ACM SIGMOD Record*, 23(1):35, 1994.

20. N.L. Sarda. HSQL: Historical query language. In *Temporal Databases*, chapter 5, pages 110–140. The Benjamin/Commings Publishing Company, Inc., Redwood City, CA., 1993.
21. R. Snodgrass et al. TSQL2 language specification. *ACM SIGMOD Record*, 23(1):65–86, Mar 1994.
22. S.Y.W. Su and H.M. Chen. A temporal knowledge representation model OSAM*/T and its query language OQL/T. In *Proceedings of the International Conference on VLDB*, 1991.
23. G.T.J. Wuu. SERQL: An ER query language supporting temporal data retrieval. In *The Proceedings of the 10th International Pheonix Conference on Computers and Communications*, Mar 1991.

A Appendix: The EBNF form of the Language's Grammar

The EBNF form of the Language's Grammar is as follows.

Operation-Clause	::= *derive* Derivation-Operation
	| *enforce* Enforce-Operation
	stabilizer= Derivation-Operation
	| *apply* Apply-Operation
Derivation-Operation	::= Derived-Variable *:=* Derivation-Formula
	| Set-Derived-Variable *:=* Set-Derivation-Formula
Derivation-Formula	::= Derivation-Expression
	| Derivation-Clause {; Derivation-Clause }*
	[; Derivation-Expression *otherwise*]
Set-Derivation-Formula	::= Set-Derivation-Expression
	| Set-Derivation-Clause { Set-Derivation-Clause }*
	[Set-Derivation-Expression *otherwise*]
Enforce-Operation	::= Enforce-Expression
	| Enforce-Clause { Enforce-Clause }*
	[Enforce-Expression *otherwise*]
Apply-Operation	::= Apply-Expression
	| Apply-Clause { Apply-Clause }*
	[Apply-Expression *otherwise*]
Derivation-Clause	::= Derivation-Expression *when* Prerequisite
Set-Derivation-Clause	::= Set-Derivation-Expression *when* Prerequisite
Enforce-Clause	::= Enforce-Expression *when* Prerequisite
Apply-Clause	::= Apply-Expression *when* Prerequisite
Prerequisite	::= Cond-Spec
Derivation-Expression	::= Numeric-Exp Derive-Exp-Prefix
	| Routine-Call-Exp Derive-Exp-Prefix
	| Cond-Spec Derive-Exp-Prefix
Set-Derivation-Expression	::= Numeric-Exp Exp-prefix
	| Routine-Call-Exp Exp-prefix
	| Cond-Spec Exp-prefix
Enforce-Expression	::= Cond-Spec Exp-Prefix
Apply-Expression	::= Routine-call-Exp Exp-Prefix
Derive-Exp-Prefix	::= Exp-Prefix [*valid-in* Temporal-Element]
Exp-Prefix	::= [*triggered-by* Event-list] [*signals* Event-list]
Routine-call-Exp	::= Routine-Name *(* {Param}* *)*
Numeric-Exp	::= Data-Element
	| Numeric-Exp Numeric-Oper Numeric-Exp
	| *(* Numeric-Exp *)*
Derived-Variable	::= Property
Set-Derived-Variable	::= {participant}*
Data-Element	::= Property
	| Participant
	| Sequence-Oper
	| Constant
Sequence-Oper	::= Seq-Func*(* Seq-Spec *)*
Seq-Spec	::= Seq-Def

```
                      |   Mod-Seq
Mod-Seq               ::= Seq-Def Numeric-Oper Numeric-Exp
Cond-Spec             ::= [Sign] Cond-Unit
                          { Connective [Sign] Cond-Unit }*
Cond-Unit             ::= Data-Element Binary-Pred Numeric-Exp
                      |   Seq-Spec
Participant           ::= Data-Element Temporal-Element
Property              ::= Identifier
Routine-Name          ::= Identifier
Seq-Def               ::= Identifier
Binary-Pred           ::= =
                      |   <
                      |   >
                      |   ≤
                      |   ≥
                      |   ≠
Seq-Func              ::= sum
                      |   max
                      |   min
                      |   first
                      |   last
                      |   count
Numeric-Oper          ::= +
                      |   −
                      |   *
                      |   /
                      |   **
Sign                  ::= ¬
Connective            ::= ∧
                      |   ∨
Constant              ::= {x | x is a number }
                      |   {x | x is a string }
                      |   now
Param                 ::= Identifier
Event-list            ::= Event {, Event}*
Event                 ::= Property | Identifier
Temporal-Element      ::= Time-Point
                      |   Time-Interval
                      |   { Temporal-Elements }*
Time-Interval         ::= [ Time-Point, Time-Point )
Identifier            ::= LABEL
Time-Point            ::= {t | t is a time-stamp }
```

DEGAS: Capturing Dynamics in Objects

Johan van den Akker* and Arno Siebes

CWI
P.O.Box 94079, 1090 GB Amsterdam, The Netherlands
e-mail: {vdakker,arno}@cwi.nl

Abstract. In this paper we introduce DEGAS (Dynamic Entities Get Autonomous Status), an active temporal data model based on autonomous objects. The active dimension of DEGAS means that we define the behaviour of objects in terms of production rules. The temporal dimension means that the history of an object is included in the DEGAS data model. Novel features of DEGAS are the encapsulation of the complete behaviour of an object, both potential and actual. Thus, DEGAS combines dynamic and structural specifications in one model. In addition, DEGAS allows easy evolution of object capabilities through a clear distinction between inherent types and capabilities that can be acquired and lost. This addon mechanism makes DEGAS very suitable as a formalism for role modelling. Finally, the rule model in DEGAS is both simple, through the use of finite automata, and general, because it allows different strategies for dealing with constraints and reacting to events in other objects.

1 Introduction

It is widely recognised that information systems (IS) modelling should include both static and dynamic aspects of their universe of discourse. To facilitate effective IS design, integration of these aspects must be supported in all phases of the IS development process. This includes implementation platforms for informations systems, database management systems, that have traditionally focussed on the static side of information systems.

Encapsulation of methods and data in object-oriented databases is a step forward in the integration of the dynamic and static parts of an application. Active databases [21, 11] integrate another dynamic element into databases, viz., production rules. Originally rules were introduced to deal flexibly with constraints in a database. Much wider use, however, has been found for them. In fact, it is possible to encode the entire dynamics of an information system as rules in an active database system.

In DEGAS we unify both approaches in one active, object-oriented data model. To achieve an effective unification we also incorporate elements of a third area,

* This research is supported by SION, the Foundation for Computer Science Research in the Netherlands through Project no. 612-323-424.

temporal databases. The specification of a DEGAS object has a static part, attributes, and a dynamic part, described by methods, production rules, and lifecycles. Thus, DEGAS achieves the encapsulation of the complete dynamic aspect of an information system. This total encapsulation is a means to achieve object autonomy. Systems built of autonomous components are necessary for the development of networked information systems across multiple organisations.

Roadmap First, we introduce the main concepts of the DEGAS model. Next, we show the use of these concepts by modelling an example. Then, we discuss the DEGAS model on a more formal level. After that we look at the broader context, motivating the development of DEGAS. We conclude with issues for future research.

2 Main Concepts

The fundamental notion of the DEGAS model is the object. It has structure and behaviour. The structure of an object is determined by the attributes. The behaviour of an object has three components: methods, lifecycles, and rules. Methods specify *what* an object can do. The lifecycles specify what methods the object is willing to execute in a certain context, by specifying sequencing and preconditions of method execution. A rule states *when* an object will execute a given action as far as can be modelled within the system. In other words, rules specify actual actions to be executed in certain situations, described in terms of events and object states.

Thus, methods and lifecycles specify *potential* behaviour of an object, whereas rules describe *actual* behaviour. Traditionally only potential behaviour is specified, whereas DEGAS objects also contain their actual behaviour as far as that can be pre-determined.

In DEGAS relations are modelled as objects. Thus, we have a place for data and behaviour of a relation. A more abstract motivation of this objectification is that a relation is a kind of contract, a view also found in, for example, NIAM [15].

The class of an object defines the intrinsic capabilities, i.e., attributes, methods, rules and lifecycles. Addons are used to model transient capabilities. That is, addons are used to define capabilities that can be added and deleted from an object dynamically. Addons can be likened to roles and are DEGAS' only mechanism for object specialisation.

3 An Example

Challenging applications to model are those with high dynamics. An application with fast changing data and rapidly evolving relations is the stock market. New data emerges constantly in the form of buying and selling orders, economic news items through newsreels etc. Both new and historical data influence the behaviour of the parties in the market. In order to introduce the concepts of DEGAS, we model this example. Our example is a simplification of the system used in the Netherlands.

Let us briefly describe the example in more detail. Companies are owned by persons. A person can buy shares and sell them again. He can subscribe to a newspaper to get news about the companies he is interested in. The buying and selling of shares goes through a marketmaker. If a person wants to buy or sell, he informs the marketmaker. Periodically, the marketmaker determines the price that balances supply and demand. Buying and selling orders that agree with this price are fulfilled.

We start to model this example with the marketmaker. The marketmaker matches supply and demand for his market. This means that the actions he can execute are to accept buying and selling orders and to try to match these. This is specified by the following DEGAS definition of the marketmaker object's attributes and methods. The methods in this object only contain actions to engages in a relation or to extend the object with an addon.

```
Object Marketmaker
Attributes
   currentPrice : real
Methods
   takeSellOrder = {
      SupplyClass.initiate
   }
   takeBuyOrder = {
      DemandClass.initiate
   }
   makeMarket = {
      SupplyDemandAddon.extend
   }
```

This defines possible actions the object may execute, but we know more about the actions of a marketmaker. Therefore, an object includes a lifecycle description. Lifecycles are specified by guarded basic process algebraic expressions [5] with method names as basic actions. The following operators can be used in lifecycle specification:

Sequence	$A; B$	A followed by B
Choice	$A + B$	A or B
Repetition	A^*	One or more times A
Merge	$A \| B = A; B + B; A$	A and B in parallel

Each basic action can be prefixed by a condition as a guard as follows.

$$[\langle Condition \rangle] \langle Methodname \rangle$$

It can be used to express a precondition of a method, or to restrict access to the method by other objects.

The lifecycle of a marketmaker consists of taking buying and selling orders. If these are both present, he is allowed to match supply and demand.

```
Lifecycles
    ((takeSellOrder* || takeBuyOrder*);makeMarket)*
```

The specification of the actual execution of actions by a DEGAS object is given by rules. The behaviour of a marketmaker is to extend himself, if he has both supply and demand relations. This is specified by the following rule, that completes the definition of the marketmaker object.

```
Rules
    On (takeSellOrder||takeBuyOrder) do makeMarket
EndObject
```

This rule only extends the Marketmaker with the SupplyDemandAddon, that contains a rule that periodically triggers the necessary actions to clear the market.

In our example a person can buy shares. To do this he should place a buying order. If this order can be met by supply in the market, he will actually buy the shares. If it is unsuccessful, a cancellation will be the result. In addition to buying shares, a person can take a subscription to a newspaper in order to obtain information. If he owns shares and also reads a newspaper, he will use the information from the newspaper to influence decisions about his shares. This is specified in the person object as follows:

```
Object Person
Attributes
    name : string
    birthday : time
    birthplace : string
Methods
    tryToBuy(company:string, number:integer, maxPrice:real) = {
        DemandClass.initiate(company,number,maxPrice)
    }
    readPaper(paper:string) = {
        SubscriptionClass.initiate(paper)
    }
    useNews = {
        InformedOwnerAddon.extend
    }
Lifecycles
    (tryToBuy)*
    ((extend-Shareholder||extend-InformedPerson);useNews)*
Rules
    On (extend-Shareholder||extend-InformedPerson) do useNews
EndObject
```

In the person and marketmaker objects the methods define that the object engages in relations. Relations in DEGAS are objects themselves. A relation object can have the same capabilities as an ordinary object. For example, a share is modelled as an ownership relation between a person and a company. In the relation object, the partners in the relation are present as implicit attributes. Other information it contains, is the price of the share when it was bought. The definition of the share relation object shows the use of guard conditions in the lifecycle. The action after a condition can only be executed, if the condition is satisfied. In the Share relation object, guards are used to restrict access to its methods.

```
Object Share
Relation Person, Company
Attributes
   buyPrice : real
   currentPrice : real
   value : real
Methods
   transferOwnership(newOwner:oid,price:real) = {
      Person = newOwner
      buyPrice = price
   }
   payDividend(div:real) = {
      value = value + div
   }
Lifecycles
   ([sender==Person]transferOwnership)*
   ([sender==Company]payDividend)*
EndObject
```

A person object does not have the capability to deal with the share relation built-in. Instead it acquires these when it engages in this relation. This is represented by the shareholder addon. An addon defines a temporary specialisation of an object, which is lost when the relation is terminated. In this example, a person who is also a shareholder gains capabilities to sell the shares again.

```
Addon Shareholder
Extends Person
Attributes
   share : oid
Methods
   tryToSell(company:string, number:integer, minPrice:real) = {
      SupplyClass.initiate(company,number,minPrice)
   }
   Sell(buyer,price) = {
      share.transferOwnership(buyer,price)
      Supply.drop
   }
   cancelSupply = {
```

```
    Supply.drop
  }
Lifecycles
  (tryToSell;(Sell+cancelSupply))*
EndAddon
```

The *SupplyClass.initiate* action in this addon specification also occurred in the specification of the Marketmaker object. A call to an *initiate* method is done by an object to express its wish to engage in a relation. Since the relation object does not exist at this time, *initiate* is a method of the relation class object. In this case a Shareholder object will send an *initiate* call to the Supply class object. In response it will send a *takeBuyOrder* message to the marketmaker to ask, if it is willing to accept the relation. As we can see in the specification of the Marketmaker object, it will respond with an *initiate* call to express its agreement. The Supply class object will then proceed to instantiate the relation.

As we can see above in the specification of the Person object, an addon can also be used to link two relations. In our example, the information a person reads in the paper will influence his decisions as a shareholder. This is achieved by extending the person with a further addon, if he owns shares and reads a newspaper. First, we give the specification of the InformedPerson addon, that extends a person who has a subscription to a newspaper.

```
Addon InformedPerson
Extends Person
Attributes
  subscription : Oid
  transactionPrice : real
Methods
  goodNews(company : string) = {
    transactionPrice = subscription.priceAdvice(company)
  }
  badNews(company : string) = {
    transactionPrice = subscription.priceAdvice(company)
  }
Lifecycles
  ([sender==subscription]goodNews*)
  ([sender==subscription]badNews*)
  (ExtendInformedPerson;DropInformedPerson)*
Rules
  On goodNews(company)(t1);goodNews(company)(t2)
  if t2 - t1 ≤ 7 days
  do tryToBuy(company,transactionPrice)
EndAddon
```

The rule specification in these addon definitions shows the use of time in DEGAS. Historical values of attributes can be referenced by a time parameter. Likewise, we can refer to the timestamp of an event. The following specification gives an example of how the informed owner of shares would deal with bad news. This addon extends a person, if it has both the Shareholder and the InformedPerson addons. Therefore, the *extends* specification gives two original object names. Please note, that this does not introduce a form of multiple inheritance. It simply specifies, what the addon may assume to be present.

Addon InformedOwner
Extends InformedPerson,Shareholder
Attributes
  Key : $\mathcal{P}\langle$ Subscription : Oid, Share : Oid $\rangle$
Lifecycles
  ExtendInformedOwner*
  DropInformedOwner*
Rules
  On badNews(company)(t_1);badNews(company)(t_2)
  if $(t_2 - t_1) \leq 7$ days && transactionPrice(t_2) $\leq$ transactionPrice(t_1)
  do tryToSell(transactionPrice)
  On goodNews(t_1);badNews(t_2)
  if $t_2 - t_1 \leq 7$ days && transactionPrice(t_1) == max(transactionPrice, t_1, t_2)
  do tryToSell(transactionPrice)
  On DropShareHolder **do** DropInformedOwner
  On DropSubscription **do** DropInformedOwner
EndAddon

The diagram in Figure 1 shows the complete model of the stock market example. In this picture, large boxes represent objects and small boxes represent addons. The dashed boxes are relation objects. The outgoing arrows from relation objects indicates the partners in the relation, they do not imply any arity constraint on the relation.

4 Discussion of DEGAS concepts

In this section we discuss the different elements of the DEGAS model in more detail. First, we will look at the different parts of a DEGAS object specification. After that, we will take a closer look at relations and addons. For a full formal description of DEGAS, including its semantics, the reader is referred to [3].

Attributes and Methods Attributes and methods are straightforward in DEGAS. Attributes in an object are typed. From a number of simple types, like integers, reals, strings, and object identifiers, additional types are formed using set and tuple constructors. The type system underlying DEGAS follows Cardelli [7] and Balsters [6]. In DEGAS method definition allows assignment to attributes. In addition, we can map a method over a set. A method can also call other methods.

Lifecycles A method call can be executed on an object, if it follows one of the lifecycles specified. The semantics of lifecycles follows process algebra [5]. If multiple lifecycles are specified, then these are executed in parallel. Suppose we have defined the following set of lifecycles on an object O.

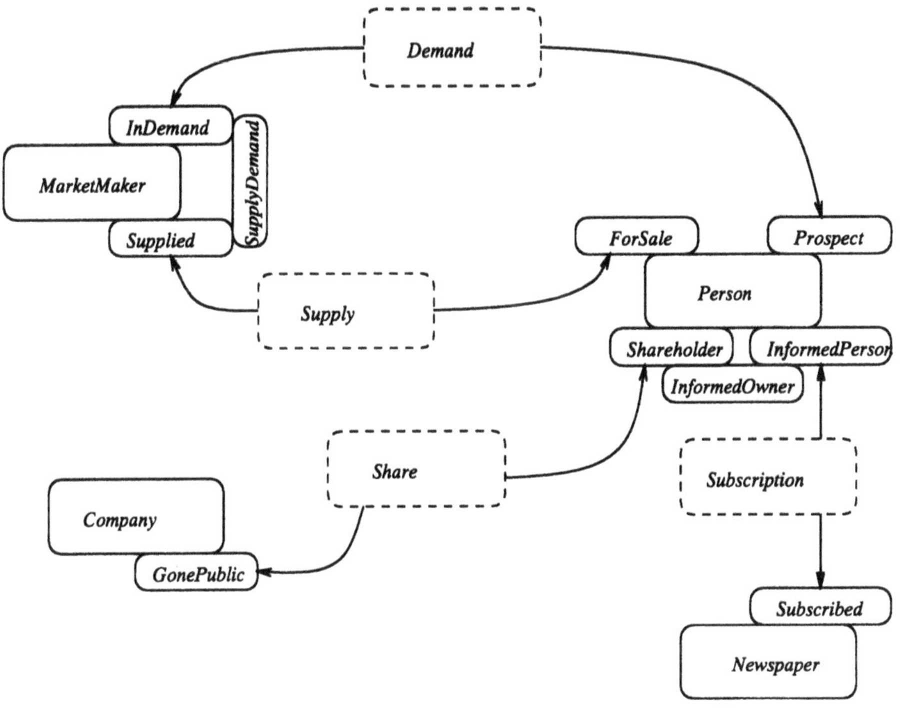

Fig. 1. The DEGAS model for a financial market

Lifecycles
C_1
C_2
$\vdots$
C_n

This means that the execution of methods on O must follow the process

$$C_1 \| C_2 \| \ldots \| C_n$$

This means that the lifecycles specified are executed in parallel. Lifecycles can be checked using finite automata. This follows from the fact that lifecycles are regular expressions. In an object we have a finite automaton associated with every lifecycle. The transitions in this automaton are labelled with method names and conditions. If there is an appropriate transition available, a method call can be executed.

The History of an Object The execution of a method modifies the state of an object. In DEGAS, an object's state is its complete history, which is represented as a sequence of snapshot states. In temporal database research [20], the term snapshot state denotes the state of an object at a point in time when we abstract from the temporal dimension [14]. In DEGAS a snapshot state contains a timepoint, the attributes and their valuation at that time, and the method call that brought the object in the state. As an example, the following is a piece of the history of a share object:

$$\begin{aligned}(13:00:00, &\langle \mathit{currentPrice}: \mathit{real}, \mathit{person}: \mathit{oid}, \mathit{company}: \mathit{oid}, \rangle,\\ &\langle \mathit{currentPrice} = 54.25, \mathit{person} = \mathit{Johan}, \mathit{company} = \mathit{Philips}\rangle,\\ &\mathit{transferOwnership}(\mathit{Johan}, 54.25))\end{aligned}$$

$$\begin{aligned}(13:02:00, &\langle \mathit{currentPrice}: \mathit{real}, \mathit{person}: \mathit{oid}, \mathit{company}: \mathit{oid}\rangle,\\ &\langle \mathit{currentPrice} = 55.25, \mathit{person} = \mathit{Arno}, \mathit{company} = \mathit{Philips}\rangle,\\ &\mathit{transferOwnership}(\mathit{Arno}, 55.25))\end{aligned}$$

The information in the snapshot state is valid from the given time until the time given in the next snapshot state. The last snapshot state gives the information valid at the current time. Type information is included because of the dynamic nature of the capabilities of DEGAS objects, which can be changed through addons.

Historical values of attributes are accessed in DEGAS through the addition of a time parameter. This can be used, for example, in the condition of a rule:

Rules
  On share.newPrice
  if price(T_{now} − 15 min) - price(T_{now}) > 10
  do tryToSell

The history is the central element in the formalisation of DEGAS. Method definitions specify the state transitions possible in DEGAS. The sequence of method calls is restricted by the lifecycles of an object. In addition rule triggering is described in terms of the state history.

Although the natural combination of temporal and active databases has been suggested by different authors [10, 21], there are no active data models that incorporate the history of a database. Work on the temporal specification of rules has been done by Sistla and Wolfson [19]. This approach is based on temporal logic. It focusses only on the condition of the rules, which means that there is no general history mechanism in their approach.

Rules In the specification of rules, DEGAS follows the ECA format, originally introduced by Dayal [9] and now commonly accepted in the active database community. Rules are specified as an Event-Condition-Action (ECA) triple. If the event occurs and the database state satisfies the condition, the action is executed. This is specified in a DEGAS object as:

On ⟨*Event*⟩ **if** ⟨*Condition*⟩ **do** ⟨*Action*⟩

The event specification is a basic process algebraic [5] expression constructed from a set of method calls. The event expression of a rule differs from a lifecycle by the absence of guard conditions. In addition a negation operator can be used in the event specification of a rule.

Negation $A; \neg B$ A not followed by B

A rule condition is a condition on the state of the object. The action is a method call, either local or to a method in another object.

The presence of rules means that there are two possible sources of actions in an object. The first consists of method calls from other objects. The second is the execution of actions from triggered rules. Both are subject to the lifecycles specified on the object. This is reflected in the execution model of an object. Basically, an object first executes a method and then executes triggered rules until no more rules are triggered. This loop is depicted in Figure 2.

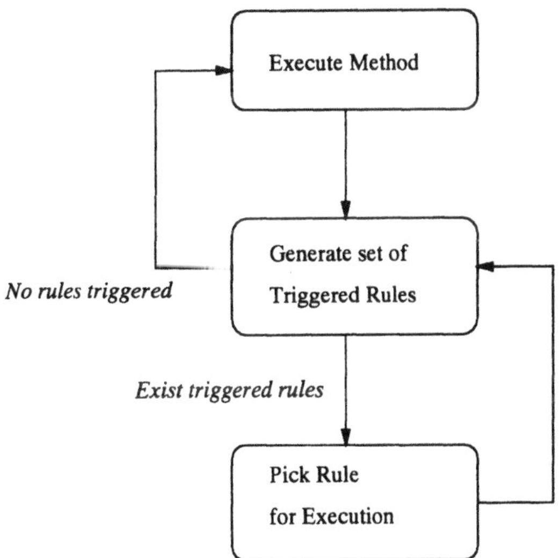

Fig. 2. The execution of an autonomous object

The execution of rules is a two phase process. During a method call, a set of rules that are triggered by that method call is built up. After a method has terminated, one rule is picked at random for execution from the set of triggered rules at random. If the condition of the rule is satisfied at the time it is picked, its action is executed. The rules not picked are dropped. During execution of a rule's action, a new set of triggered rules is constructed.

The rule model ensures both simplicity and generality. The former originates from the fact that all event specifications can be checked using finite automata.

The latter can be found in the different strategies that can be applied to the interaction of lifecycles and rules. If the action of a rule is not allowed by any lifecycle the moment it is triggered, we have two options. Either the action is tried again later, or the action is simply dropped. DEGAS offers both strategies through the negation operator ¬ in event expressions. If we want the action of a rule to be retried, the event includes the negation of the rule's action. For example, the marketmaker might have the rule that he *must* clear the market after he has determined a price:

Rules
  On determinePrice;¬ clearMarket **do** clearMarket

Rules where only an immediate reaction is of interest, are, for example, those rules defining the reactions to news events in the InformedOwner addon in the previous section. In this case, the reaction is only useful if it is executed immediately.

A number of design issues are simplified by the DEGAS rule model. An example is the risk of non-termination, which is already undecidable for very simple rule languages [18]. In DEGAS this risk is taken explicitly by the designer by using the negation operator. Thus, he knows that a certain rule will be triggered again and again until it is executed. This assists in the identification of possibly problematic rule sets.

Other examples of object-based active database systems are HiPAC [9], SAMOS [12] and Chimera [8]. SAMOS and Chimera offer encapsulation of rules, but the object is not the exclusive location of rule definition. HiPAC treats rules as separate objects, thus separating part of the behaviour from the objects. The motivation given for this objectification of rules is that it allows easy run-time manipulation of rules. In DEGAS this kind of manipulation is offered through the addon mechanism.

Relations and Addons Relations in DEGAS are objects themselves. Hence, the discussion of the elements of DEGAS objects above also applies to relation objects.

The initiative for a relation comes from one of the partners. To this end it sends a message to the class object of that relation. Before the relation is established there might be a number of conditions that need to be satisfied. These are checked by the relation class object. If the relation class approves, it instantiates the relation object and instructs the partners to extend themselves with the appropriate addon.

An addon specifies an extension to an object's capabilities. It is a general purpose object specialisation mechanism. Hence, it is not tied to one particular form of specialisation, such as e.g. roles. An addon can be added to an object, if the object has a method to do this. This means that the object knows the name of the addon, but does not know anything about the contents of an addon. Thus, changes in an addon are transparent to the object.

An addon can add attributes, if it does not duplicate names. Usually, the addon will contain the identity of the relation object it is tied to. In case of an $1 - n$ relation, this attribute is a set. The addon is only added the first time an object engages in a relation. When the object engages in more relations of the same type, extension with an addon only means that an element is added to this set.

Methods can only be added. There is no mechanism to modify the behaviour of existing methods, other than specifying a rule on an existing method. Rules are treated the same as methods with regard to specialisation.

In an addon, lifecycles can be added to the set of existing lifecycles. As an example, suppose we have the following lifecycle definition in object O:

Lifecycles
$(A; B)^*$
$(C; D)^*$

Clearly, O follows the process:

$$(A; B)^* \| (C; D)^*$$

If O is extended with addon A with the following lifecycle definition:

Lifecycles
$(K; L)^*$

The specialised object O will follow the process:

$$(A; B)^* \| (C; D)^* \| (K; L)^*$$

The addon mechanism offers a number of advantages over using inheritance to specialise objects. The key to these advantages is the observation that object specialisation is tied to the role of an object. An object is specialised in order to play a role. In an inheritance hierarchy we would need a separate class for each possible combination of object extensions. Clearly, this leads to a combinatorial explosion of the number of classes in the hierarchy [13]. In DEGAS, this observation has lead to the extension of an object with an addon, when it engages in a relation. The addon defines the role the object plays in the relation. It gains methods to deal with the relation. Rules specify what information must be passed to the relation, while lifecycles define the access of the relation to the methods of the object.

A number of other approaches are based on this observation. For example, Aspects by Richardson and Schwarz [16] are also dynamic extensions to objects. There is no link between aspects and relations. Although aspects can have aspects themselves, there is no possibility of interaction between aspects of the same object. This means that interaction between relations of an object, or multiple roles, in the way shown in our example is not possible using aspects. A database programming language offering an extensive role mechanism is Fibonacci [4]. Its object specialisation mechanism is more complex than the DEGAS addon mechanism. For example, it has multiple inheritance between roles. This is caused by the strongly typed functional nature of Fibonacci. In DEGAS multiple inheritance is not needed, since addons need no information about other addons. There is no treatment of rules or time in both Aspects and Fibonacci.

An extensive conceptual study and formalisation of objects with roles can be found in [22]. Here it is observed that there are static classes, dynamic classes and roles. Objects cannot migrate between static classes. Hence, these are equivalent to the classes in DEGAS. Dynamic classes are based on dynamic partitions of a static object class. Objects can migrate between dynamic classes, although this may be subject to lifecycles. Roles are dynamic classes that do not partition an object class. In addition an object can play multiple roles. In DEGAS the latter two are both modelled using addons. Dynamic class migration is specified in the lifecycle of an object. Migration is achieved through the gain and loss of addons. Roles are tied to relations. When engaging in a relation an object will gain the addon that specifies its role in the relation. The main difference is that DEGAS only distinguishes between inherent and transient capabilities of an object.

5 DEGAS in a broader context

In this section we show DEGAS in a broader context than active databases. Not only is the DEGAS notion of object autonomy the natural consequence of the integration of rules in an object database, it also supports currently foreseen developments in computing, networking and integration of information systems. These contribute to the need for systems built of autonomous components. Autonomy in this case implies extreme distribution. A more elaborate motivation for object autonomy can be found in [2].

Developments in Technology Extreme distribution is motivated by a number of developments foreseen in computer systems in the nearby future. These are the emergence of massively parallel computer systems and the coupling of existing computer systems over networks. These have in common that any form of central control will pose a large amount of overhead on the system. In a massively parallel computer centralisation of decisions, for example regarding resource allocation or invocation of active rules, poses overhead on the system. Enough overhead to make it a considerable factor in the performance of such a system.

Similar problems are posed by the possibility of information systems running on networks of mobile computers. A lot of effort has been put into making databases interoperable over a network. Still, it will be very difficult to come up with a scheme that can keep up with the sheer size of such a network and the speed of changes in the network caused by its mobile character. It seems a better idea to build an inherent flexibility into the components, such that they can function with as little global information as possible.

Because of the problems of central control in these environments, control must be distributed to components of the system. In other words, the components are forced to be autonomous.

Integration of Information Systems There is a strong trend to increasing integration of systems in chain information systems or through a public information infrastructure. Such systems merge (parts of) information systems of various owners into one big information system. Examples are integrated information systems for suppliers and customers and the trading system at the stock exchange, as shown in this article. However, nobody wants to give up control over his part of such a system. In addition one organisation may want to integrate its information system with a number of inter-organisation systems. An example of this is a supplier of tyres, who sells these to several car manufacturers, that all have an information system for their own chain of suppliers and resellers.

An inter-organisation information system is made up of parts that are not subject to any form of central control. This means that we need information systems that function without central control of the components. In addition, different parts of an organisation's information system may be exported to different inter-organisation systems. This means that access control can differ at a very fine grain in the system. For each component we want to be able to define who has access to what.

These developments again force components of a system to function without central control. In addition they point at a need to be able to define access control in a system at a very fine grain. Autonomy of components makes this possible.

Autonomy is the Solution All the developments mentioned above foster a need for systems composed of autonomous components. The difficulties with central control of a system can be overcome by distributing control to parts of the system, or by building inherent flexibility into the parts of the system. The result will be autonomy for the components of such a system. We also signalled a development towards the sharing of data with outsiders. Approaching data from multiple sources as one database while the owners retain control, means autonomy for the components. Exporting data to multiple inter-organisation information systems at a time, asks for an inherent flexibility that autonomous components can offer.

DEGAS offers a formal model to support the development of systems of autonomous components. This is achieved by basing the DEGAS model on autonomous objects. We have chosen object as the level of autonomy, because of its obvious advantages in modelling an information system. Object autonomy also has the advantage of generality, because the complexity of the objects may be arbitrary. This means that the model can also be used for autonomous components at a higher abstraction level, as long as its behaviour can be described in DEGAS.

Autonomous objects and Agents In recent years the notion of agents has received considerable attention as a paradigm for software development. Research has focussed either on the specification of agents by logic, see for example [17], or on the implementation of special purpose agents, for example to schedule meetings (see [1]). Since the logics used to specify agents are relatively complex, there is a gap between these two approaches. To bridge this gap we need simple general purpose agents. Autonomous objects are a first step towards this kind of agents.

Another area where agents can be useful, is the design and analysis of information systems. For example, Yu et al [23] propose an agent-oriented framework for the specification of information systems. This framework consists of two parts, one, Albert, to specify agents in an information system and the other, **i***, to understand and redesign the organisational context of the information system. If we want to apply this framework also to the design and implementation phase of information system development, we need a database programming language that supports the modelling notions used in the specification phase. Autonomous objects in DEGAS offer such support through their rule and lifecycle specifications.

6 Conclusion

In this paper we introduced DEGAS, an active temporal data model, using an application with a highly dynamic content, the stock market, as an example. The relation and addon mechanism of DEGAS, where capabilities are only present when they are needed makes DEGAS especially useful for this kind of applications. In addition addons and relations offer a clean mechanism to implement roles.

DEGAS emphasises the integration of the dynamic and static parts of an application. This integration is achieved through the complete encapsulation of an object's behaviour. This contributes to the autonomy of objects, an important factor in the construction of highly distributed information systems.

An important contribution in the field of active databases is the temporal element of DEGAS. The notion that the state of an object is formed by its complete history makes it possible to achieve temporal database functionality in DEGAS. We elaborate on the temporal aspects of DEGAS in a forhtcoming paper.

A prototype implementation is underway. The simplicity of the DEGAS rule model is expected to facilitate a performant system. To complement the data model a query model will be formalised for DEGAS. Basically, a query is the specification of a set of objects. Further research will focus on the integration of temporal and active databases.

References

1. Special issue on intelligent agents. *Communications of the ACM*, 37(7), July 1994.
2. J.F.P. van den Akker and A.P.J.M. Siebes. A data model for autonomous objects. Technical Report CS-R9539, CWI, Centre for Mathematics and Computer Science, Amsterdam, The Netherlands, 1995. Available through WWW (`http://www.cwi.nl/~vdakker/Publications.html`).
3. J.F.P. van den Akker and A.P.J.M. Siebes. DEGAS: A temporal active data model based on object autonomy. Technical Report CS-R9608, CWI, Amsterdam, The Netherlands, 1996. Available through WWW (`http://www.cwi.nl/~vdakker/Publications.html`).
4. A. Albano, R. Bergamini, G. Ghelli, and R. Orsini. An object data model with roles. In Rakesh Agrawal, Sean Baker, and David Bell, editors, *Proc. of the 19th Intl. Conf. on Very Large Data Bases (VLDB)*, Dublin, Ireland, 1993.
5. J.C.M. Baeten and W.P. Weijland. *Process Algebra*. Number 18 in Cambridge Tracts in Theoretical Computer Science. Cambridge University Press, Cambridge, UK, 1990.
6. Herman Balsters and Maarten M. Fokkinga. Subtyping can have a simple semantics. *Theoretical Computer Science*, 87:81-96, 1991.
7. Luca Cardelli. A semantics of multiple inheritance. In G. Kahn, D.B. MacQueen, and G. Plotkin, editors, *Proceedings of the International Symposium on the Semantics of Data Types*, pages 51-68, Berlin, Germany, 1984. Springer.
8. Stefano Ceri and Rainer Manthey. Consolidated specification of Chimera (CM and CL). Technical Report IDEA.DE.2P.006.01, IDEA, ESPRIT Project 6333, 1993. Available by FTP from rodin.inria.fr:/pub/IDEA/DE.2P.006.ps.gz.
9. U. Dayal et al. The HiPAC project: Combining active databases and timing constraints. *SIGMOD Record*, 17(1):51–70, March 1988.
10. Klaus R. Dittrich and Stella Gatziu. Time issues in active database systems. In N. Pissinou, R.T. Snodgrass, and R. Elmasri, editors, *Towards an Infrastructure for Temporal Databases: report of an international ARPA/NSF workshop*, Tucson, AZ, USA, 1994. University of Arizona, Dept of Computer Science, TR 94/01.
11. Klaus R. Dittrich, Stella Gatziu, and Andreas Geppert. The active database management system manifesto: A rulebase of ADBMS features. In T. Sellis, editor, *Rules in Databases: Proc. of the 2nd International Workshop*, pages 3-17, Berlin, Germany, 1995. Springer.
12. Stella Gatziu, Andreas Geppert, and Klaus R. Dittrich. Integrating active concepts into an object-oriented database system. In Paris Kanellakis and Joachim W. Schmidt, editors, *The Third International Workshop on Database Programming Languages: Bulk Types and Persistent Data*, pages 399-415, San Mateo,. CA, USA, August 1991. Morgan Kaufmann.
13. David McAllester and Ramin Zabih. Boolean classes. In M. Meyrowitz, editor, *Proceedings OOPSLA'86*, pages 417-423, 1986.
14. L. Edwin McKenzie Jr. and Richard T. Snodgrass. Evaluation of relational algebras incorporating the time dimension in databases. *ACM Computing Surveys*, 23(4):501-543, December 1991.

15. G.M. Nijssen and T.A. Halpin. *Conceptual schema and relational database design : a fact oriented approach.* Prentice-Hall, New York, USA, third edition, 1990.
16. Joel Richardson and Peter Schwarz. Aspects: Extending objects to support multiple, independent roles. In *Proceedings of the ACM SIGMOD International Conference on the Management of Data*, pages 298-307, 1991.
17. Yoav Shoham. Agent-oriented programming. *Artificial Intelligence*, 60:51-92, 1993.
18. A.P.J.M. Siebes, J.F.P. van den Akker, and M.H. van der Voort. (un)decidability results for trigger design theories. Technical Report CS-R9556, CWI, Amsterdam, The Netherlands, 1995. Available through WWW (`http://www.cwi.nl/~vdakker/Publications.html`).
19. A. Prasad Sistla and Ouri Wolfson. Temporal conditions and integrity constraints in active databases. In *Proc. of the 1995 SIGMOD International Conference on the Management of Data*, pages 269-280, San Jose, CA, USA, 1995.
20. A.U. Tansel, J. Clifford, S. Gadia, S. Jajodia, A. Segev, and R. Snodgrass. *Temporal Databases: Theory, Design, and Implementation.* Benjamin/Cummings, Redwood City, CA, USA, 1993.
21. Jennifer Widom and Stefano Ceri. *Active Database Systems: Triggers and Rules for Advanced Database Processing.* Morgan Kaufmann, San Francisco, CA, USA, 1995.
22. Roel Wieringa, Wiebren de Jonge, and Paul Spruit. Using dynamic classes and role classes to model object migration. *Theory and Practice of Object Systems*, 1(1):61-83, 1995.
23. Eric Yu, Philippe Du Bois, Eric Dubois, and John Mylopoulos. From organization models to system requirements: A "cooperating agents" approach. In *Proc. of the Third International Conference on Cooperative Information Systems (CoopIS'95)*, Wien, Austria, May 1995.

From Rules To Rule Patterns

G. Kappel, S. Rausch-Schott, W. Retschitzegger, M. Sakkinen[1]

Institute of Computer Science, Department of Information Systems
University of Linz, AUSTRIA
email: {gerti, stefan, werner, markku}@ifs.uni-linz.ac.at

Abstract. Rule-based systems are a commonly accepted solution for smoothly capturing the context-dependent and time-dependent organizational knowledge of large enterprises, also known as business policies. At the same time, however, the design of rule-based applications is one of the most pressing open research problems. This is largely because of the expressive power and flexibility of existing rule-based models together with a lack of design guidelines on how to apply these models. Learning from analogous problems in object-oriented system development and borrowing their solution metaphor we introduce *rule patterns* as generic rule-based solutions for specifying business policies. The advantage of rule patterns is their predefined, reusable, and dynamically customizable nature allowing the designer to reuse existing experience for building new rule-based applications. The paper introduces the general notion of rule patterns and illustrates the approach by sample rule patterns for specifying interaction policies in workflow applications.

Keywords and Phrases. rule patterns, specification of business policies, workflow management

1 Introduction

Non-standard applications have to cope with frequently changing requirements which are, to a large extent, due to changes in the business environment [Louc91]. Those aspects of the business environment which are subject to frequent changes are often referred to as business policies. Business policies typically capture context-dependent and time-dependent organizational knowledge. They may be based on ethics, law, culture and organizational commitments by either prescribing a certain action or by constraining the set of possible actions [Herb95, Odel94, Schr95]. To cope with changing business policies, it should be possible to easily adapt the application implementing the respective policies. The introduction of the object-oriented paradigm has been one step in this direction. Object-oriented languages and development environments help to intuitively model the universe of discourse and to adapt to changing requirements [Fugi92, Tsic89]. However, a mechanism for explicitly specifying business policies in a natural and straightforward way is still missing. In most object-oriented systems business policies are implemented by some methods or parts thereof, and thus business

1 On leave from the Department of Computer Science and Information Systems, University of Jyväskylä (Finland), until July 1996.

knowledge is mixed with code realizing the basic functionality with a low modification probability. Within this respect there exist some suggestions for distinguishing methods containing policy, i.e., the "making of context-dependent decisions", from methods containing implementation, i.e., the "execution of fully specified algorithms" [Rumb91]. It has been shown, however, that a more intuitive way to describe business policies is in terms of rules, not least since domain specialists usually do so in expressing their system requirements [Petr94].

Approaches for integrating rules with object-oriented concepts have been widely accepted as a powerful means for explicitly modeling business policies [Odel94, Rubi94, Tsal91]. These approaches are also known as rule-based models, or more accurately as *active object-oriented models* whose most prominent basic mechanism is the Event/ Condition/Action rule (ECA rule)[2]. Such a rule monitors the situation represented by an event and a condition and executes the corresponding action when the event occurs and the condition holds true [Diaz91, Ditt95]. ECA rules allow for an explicit, localized, and transparent specification of business policies. With ECA rules, on the one hand, reusability of methods and thus of classes is enhanced since they no longer contain application-specific policies. On the other hand, reusability of a business policy itself is enhanced, since it is encapsulated within rules.

Unfortunately, designers are overtaxed with the power of the provided concepts, especially with the amount of possibilities for implementing a certain business policy. Thus, they would need some guidelines for defining rules realizing specific business policies. Learning from analogous design problems in object-oriented system development and borrowing their solution metaphor, we introduce rule patterns in analogy to design patterns [Coad95, Copl95, Gamm94, Pree95]. Rule patterns provide templates for an easy specification of business policies. They both categorize rules according to different types of business policies, and at the same time provide an abstraction mechanism for specifying rules in an application-independent manner. If we try to draw a rough analogy between rules and rule patterns, respectively, and standard object-oriented constructs, we can say that an ECA rule corresponds to a single method. However, there is no widely adopted concept or construct for combining several rules that would correspond to an ordinary class, even less to a parameterized (generic) class. Patterns in object-oriented programming represent a still higher level of abstraction and granularity. In the current paper, we will present only quite simple rule patterns corresponding to generic methods or procedures.

To illustrate the potential of rule patterns we fall back upon workflow applications as one prominent application area. In these applications, rules are used for specifying different kinds of business policies such as the order of processed activities, agent selection and interaction, and worklist management [Bußl94, Casa95, Eder95, Kapp95ab, Rein93]. We pick up interaction policies which, in addition to workflow applications, have been recognized to be crucial concerning the interaction between objects within object-oriented modeling as well as concurrent object-oriented programming languages.

2 Note that there are approaches which integrate the ECA paradigm into non-object-oriented environments like extended relational database systems.

The remainder of this paper is organized as follows: Section 2 introduces the general notion of rule patterns. Section 3 illustrates the approach by describing sample rule patterns for interaction policies in workflow applications. A comparison to related work follows in Section 4. Section 5 concludes with a discussion of the approach and ongoing research. Due to space limitations the paper can only discuss some rule patterns within a small fraction of a real world example. A more complete list of interaction rule patterns together with their application to a fully-fledged running example is available as a technical report [Kapp95c].

2 Rule Patterns for Specifying Business Policies

There exists a broad range of business policies which can be realized by using rules. Business policies encountered in workflow applications, such as those mentioned above, are a small fraction thereof. For a discussion of different classifications of business policies the interested reader is referred to [Gert93, Herb95, Kapp95c, Odel94]. The motivation of introducing rule patterns as abstraction of rules is at least threefold. Firstly, and as already mentioned, there exist no design guidelines for applying rules in application development. Secondly, the amount of business rules found in simple case studies reported in literature is beyond several hundreds [Knol94]. Clearly, one needs some kind of structure and/or classification in order to manage such an amount of rules. And thirdly, we have found out that rules realizing business policies can be abstracted in that they are no more restricted to a specific application domain but rather can be easily applied to other domains with little adaptation effort. Consequently, when looking at a rule realizing a specific policy, one can find components which are applicable for a number of application domains as well as components specific to a single application domain. Let us consider the following two policies. A business policy in a warehouse could be that every time the stock-keeper takes out goods, the number of goods in stock has to be checked and, if fallen below a given limit, new goods have to be ordered. A similar business policy in a bank could be that every time a customer withdraws a certain amount from his/her account, the balance is checked and if overdrawn, the bank charges are increased. It can be seen that there are a lot of similarities between these two policies. Consequently, it is possible to factor out common components valid for both application domains. An abstract formulation of these two policies could be: As soon as a certain value is changed and this value falls below a certain limit some reaction has to be undertaken.

To avoid that the application designer has to consider such fixed, i.e., common components of a rule realizing some business policy again and again for each application domain and to support the adaptation of such a rule to other application domains, rule patterns are introduced. *Rule patterns* are descriptions of rules, predefining certain event/condition/action-pairs. They are an *abstract means* to capture a certain kind of business policy in a generic and thus application-independent manner. Some rule patterns realize business policies by abstracting from a single rule only. At a higher level of abstraction, however, rule patterns are a *composition* of several rules working together to realize some specific kind of business policy. *Parameterization* makes rule patterns even more general and versatile than they could be otherwise. Parameterized rule patterns consist of components independent from particular applications, i.e., *predefined components*, as well as components specific to particular applications, i.e., *parameterized components*. The kinds of parameters as well as the degree of parameterization, i.e., the relation between parameterized components and predefined components, vary according to the different kinds of policies.

Figure 1 illustrates the process of working with rules and rule patterns. In the long run, for each kind of business policy rule patterns are provided within a pattern library. Within our research prototype, this library is organized as a set of dictionaries wherein the patterns are all stored as first-class objects. At this time, of course, we are far from claiming that our set of rule patterns is complete. Consequently, this pattern library must be extensible by both defining new patterns and specializing existing ones (① in Figure 1). At the same time, existing patterns or parts of them can be easily reused. In order to use rule patterns within an application, they have to be customized by the application designer. This is done by binding the parameters of a selected pattern on the basis of the application semantics. The system guides the application designer during the process of parameter binding by providing on-line help for each required parameter and by restricting the binding alternatives to those that do not contradict the specification of the underlying pattern (cf. the application of a rule pattern shown in Figure 4). Once a rule has been fully and correctly specified, it can be automatically generated and stored in the rule base attached to the corresponding application (② in Figure 1).

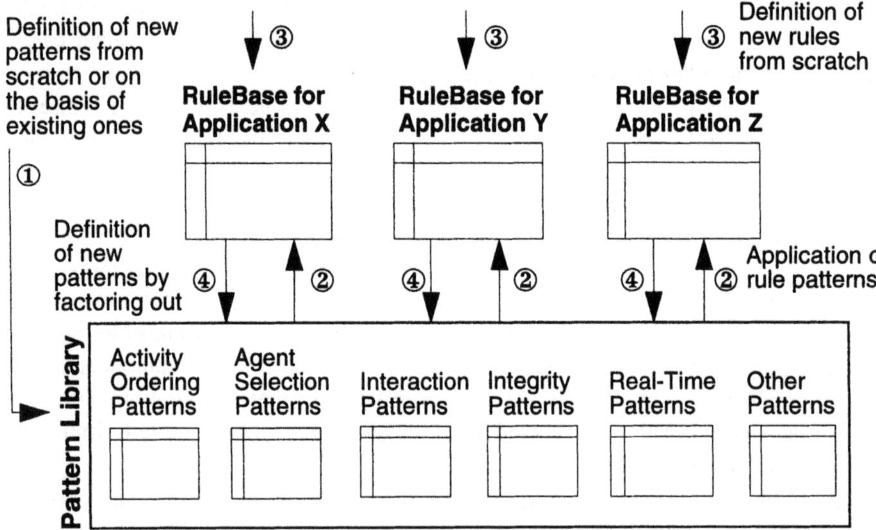

Fig. 1. Working with Rules and Rule Patterns

Furthermore, it is still possible to specify rules without using a pattern and to store them directly within the appropriate rule base (③ in Figure 1). This is normally done for rules without reusability in mind. If sometimes later an application designer recognizes that a specific design situation recurs and thus is worth to be specified by a corresponding rule pattern, existing rules can be used for this abstraction process (④ in Figure 1).

3 Rule Patterns by Example: Interaction Rule Patterns

In the following, we want to illustrate our approach by sample rule patterns specifying different policies concerning interactions between a sender object and a receiver object. These rule patterns are called *interaction rule patterns*. Interaction rule patterns represent interaction structure abstractions similar to the already well known data structure abstractions (e.g., classification, association, aggregation, and generalization/ specialization) and to control structure abstractions (e.g., sequence, condition, and iteration). They enhance sequential message passing in two different ways. Firstly, in contrast to sequential message passing based on a single thread of control where any receiver object has to accept messages implicitly, i.e., unconditionally, interaction rule patterns model interactions in a concurrent object-oriented environment based on multiple threads of control. Thus, any receiver object accepts messages explicitly, i.e., depending on its actual state. Secondly, interaction rule patterns support different kinds of interaction policies such as synchronous, asynchronous and future synchronous [Nier93, Yone87]. In the following, two interaction rule patterns are described by means of an example situated in the area of active object-oriented workflow systems [Kapp95ab], where it is crucial to flexibly model the synchronization between concurrently executing tasks within activities. In a first step, each interaction policy is described by means of an application-specific rule. The syntax and semantics of these rules are based upon our underlying research vehicle TriGS (Triggersystem for GemStone) [Kapp94a] and will be described, if necessary, on the fly. In a second step, the corresponding generic rule pattern is factored out. Note that the reader should not get too much diverted with details of TriGS. The approach is intended to be applicable much more generally than just for TriGS. For a complete description of the example as well as of eight currently existing interaction rule patterns we refer to [Kapp95c].

3.1 Synchronous Interaction Policy

Problem. The first interaction policy we want to realize is synchronous interaction. Synchronous interaction means that the sender of a message blocks until the receiver has finished the requested method execution. The receiver on its part is not able to execute the requested method until it is in the right state for satisfying the request. That is, a received message is explicitly accepted on the basis of the receiver object's actual state. A state is specified in the sense of a state transition diagram [Rumb91, Hare88]. For sake of simplicity, we assume that every object has an implicit multi-valued instance variable `state` holding its actual state(s).

Example. Our running example is a typical workflow application realizing a computerized reservation management system for a nationwide consortium of motels connected via a wide area network. Each motel manages rooms grouped into different categories. In order to be able to check the availability of rooms for a certain reservation request, a motel has to retrieve a list of rooms from a `category` object corresponding to the desired room category stored within the reservation object (`resObj`). For this task, the `motel` object interacts with the `category` object by sending the message `getRooms` within the context of the method `tryRes` synchronously, i.e., blocking until the result is available.

This situation is shown in Figure 2. The notation of the interaction diagram in Figure 2a is based partly on the notation for event-trace diagrams of OMT [Rumb91], and on the interaction diagram notation of OSA [Embl92]. Sender object, i.e. the `motel`, and receiver object, i.e., the `category`, are denoted by vertical bars. Time progresses from top to bottom of the lines. Solid lines designate active threads of control and dashed lines designate inactive, i.e., blocked threads of control. Arrows denote interactions between objects. Furthermore one sequence of states of the receiver object as it might occur during a certain interaction is shown. These states are all part of the state transition diagram in Figure 2b. Note that we assume multiple threads of control in the sense that either the receiver object has its own thread of control, or another thread of control executes methods of the passive receiver object. Multiple threads are necessary since, if the receiver object is currently not in the right state for satisfying a certain request, it must be possible to execute one or more other methods in parallel, assuring that the receiver object eventually reaches the correct state. In Figure 2a, for example, `getRooms` has to wait until the `category` object has been transformed from the state `Updating` into the right prestate `Idle`, necessary for performing `getRooms`.

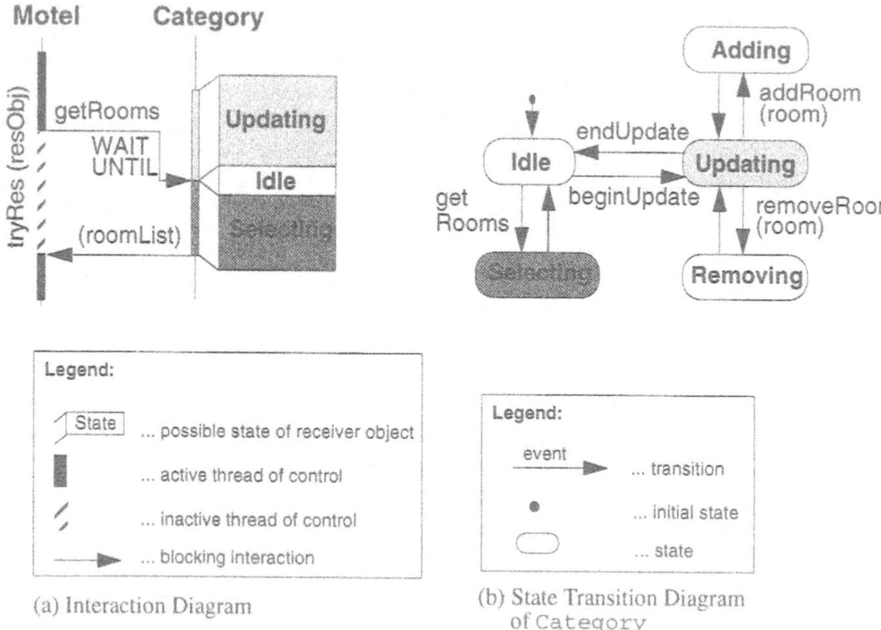

(a) Interaction Diagram

(b) State Transition Diagram of `Category`

Fig. 2. Synchronous Interaction Between `Motel` and `Category`

Figure 2b shows the state transition diagram based on OMT notation [Rumb91] for class `Category`. According to it, an object of class `Category` remains in state `Idle` until receiving one of the requests `getRooms` or `beginUpdate`. In the first case, the object changes its state to `Selecting` and automatically returns to the state `Idle` upon finishing the execution of the corresponding method. In the second case, the object changes its state to `Updating`. Within this state, a `category` object accepts the messages `addRoom`, `removeRoom` and `endUpdate`. Upon receiving the messages `addRoom` and removeRoom, respectively, the object changes its state; it automatically returns to the state Updating upon finishing execution of the corresponding methods. When receiving the message endUpdate it returns to the state Idle.

Concrete Solution by using Rules. The rule blocker_getRooms depicted in Figure 3 has to be specified in order to realize the synchronous interaction between a motel object and a category object. Note, we use a simplified notation borrowed from our underlying active object-oriented model TriGS. Rules in TriGS extend the ECA paradigm to ECEA, therewith allowing a more flexible definition of rule execution points [Kapp94b]. The *condition event selector* (*Esel*$_C$) of the rule blocker_getRooms defines all events which are able to trigger the rule. The rule blocker_getRooms is triggered each time any object of class Motel sends the message getRooms to any object of class Category from within the method tryRes. The keyword PRE denotes that the rule is triggered *before* the requested method getRooms, further on called *triggering method*, is executed. Moreover the triggering method getRooms is blocked at least until the condition is evaluated. The *condition* part of the rule checks whether the receiver receiver is not in the appropriate prestate Idle for executing the requested message getRooms. If the condition is false, the action part is not considered at all and the triggering method getRooms proceeds immediately. If it is true, getRooms is further blocked until the correct state is reached (keyword WAIT UNTIL).

DEFINE RULE blocker_getRooms **AS**	Rule Name
ON PRE(Motel,tryRes:aResObj,Category,getRooms) **DO**	Condition Event Selector (Esel$_C$)
IF not (receiver.state includes: "Idle") **THEN**	Condition
WAIT UNTIL ON POST (receiver, getRooms) **OR** **POST** (receiver, endUpdate)	Action Event Selector (Esel$_A$)
EXECUTE NIL.	Action

Fig. 3. Synchronous Interaction Rule

The *action event selector* (*Esel*$_A$) of the rule blocker_getRooms is responsible for monitoring the transitions leading to the correct state Idle. Therefore the Esel$_A$ is specified as a *composite event selector* whose components are two simple messages connected by disjunction. Each of these messages, when sent to the actual receiver, leads to the state Idle (cf. also Fig. 2b). After one of these messages has finished execution (keyword POST), the *action* is executed. Since the action is defined as NIL, the triggering method getRooms is allowed to proceed immediately.

One benefit of this approach is the fact that the motel object does not have to check periodically for the right state of the category object (polling) since reaching the appropriate state is signalled by the category object itself. However, even more important is the fact that already implemented sequential message passing can be enriched with this additional synchronization semantics without any modifications of the existing implementation.

Generic Solution by using Rule Patterns: The Blocker. Although the realization of a interaction policy by using rules provides some important advantages, there still exists one major drawback. Since the policy of synchronous interaction is not only used for the message getRooms but also for other parts within our reservation example and for other application domains, too, those components of the rule remaining the same for any synchronous interaction would have to be specified again and again. What we want to do is to relieve the application designer from this task. For this purpose, the application-dependent rule for synchronous interaction depicted in Figure 3 is abstracted to a generic rule pattern for synchronous interaction, called *Blocker*.

DEFINE RULE PATTERN blocker_<name> **AS**	Rule Pattern Name
ON PRE (<sender>,<senderMethod>, <receiver>,<message0>) **DO**	Condition Event Selector ($Esel_C$)
IF not (receiver.state includes: <prestate>) { **AND** not (receiver.state includes: <prestate>) }* **THEN**	Condition
WAIT UNTIL ON (**POST** (receiver, <message>) ['[' receiver.state includes: <prestate> ']']) { **OR** (**POST** (receiver, <message>) ['[' receiver.state includes: <prestate> ']']) }*	Action Event Selector ($Esel_A$)
EXECUTE NIL.	Action

Fig. 4. Synchronous Interaction (Blocker) Rule Pattern

This abstraction process is done by factoring out the recurring components of the rule and by explicitly specifying the formal parameters which have to be bound when applying the pattern. The structure of the Blocker rule pattern is depicted in Figure 4. The first parameter of each rule pattern is used for generating the specific name of each rule being deduced from the pattern at hand (<name>). The $Esel_C$ of the Blocker rule pattern consists of four different parameters denoted by angle brackets. Note that for all parameters specified within angle brackets actual parameters have to be provided. Any unbracketed occurrence of a parameter name is bound to the nearest preceding bracketed (defining) occurrence. For the parameters <sender> and <receiver>, classes as well as objects may be specified. In case of classes being specified, the corresponding rule is triggered whenever <message0> is sent from/to any instance of the <sender>/ <receiver> class[3]. If the same rule shall be applied for several classes and/or methods, wildcards may be used instead of specifying actual parameters. For example, if it is immaterial from which method <message0> is sent, <senderMethod> is not specified and the rule is triggered whenever the specified <sender> sends <message0> to <receiver>. The *condition* of the rule pattern consists of a conjunction of one or more actual state checks (cf. the EBNF meta symbols "{...}*"). It checks whether the set of actual states of the receiver (receiver.state) includes one of the prestates of the transition denoted by the incoming message. If one of the prestates is already reached, the action part is not considered at all and the triggering method

3 Note that class methods can be specified by the keyword CLASSMETHOD within the parameters <senderMethod> and <message0>. In that case the rule is triggered whenever the <message0> is sent from/to the respective class.

(<message0>) can be executed. If the receiver is in none of these prestates, the sender blocks (keyword `WAIT UNTIL`).

The $Esel_A$ specifies that the action should be executed after one of the methods corresponding to a transition leading to one of the prestates has been executed. In case that one distinct message is used as event in different transitions, the resulting state set has to be checked within a *guard* (enclosed in square brackets). A guard specifies a boolean expression further restricting the set of events able to trigger the condition or action, respectively. The action of the rule pattern is defined as `NIL` indicating the fact that the Blocker pattern is just used for blocking the triggering method until the receiver is able to accept the sent message.

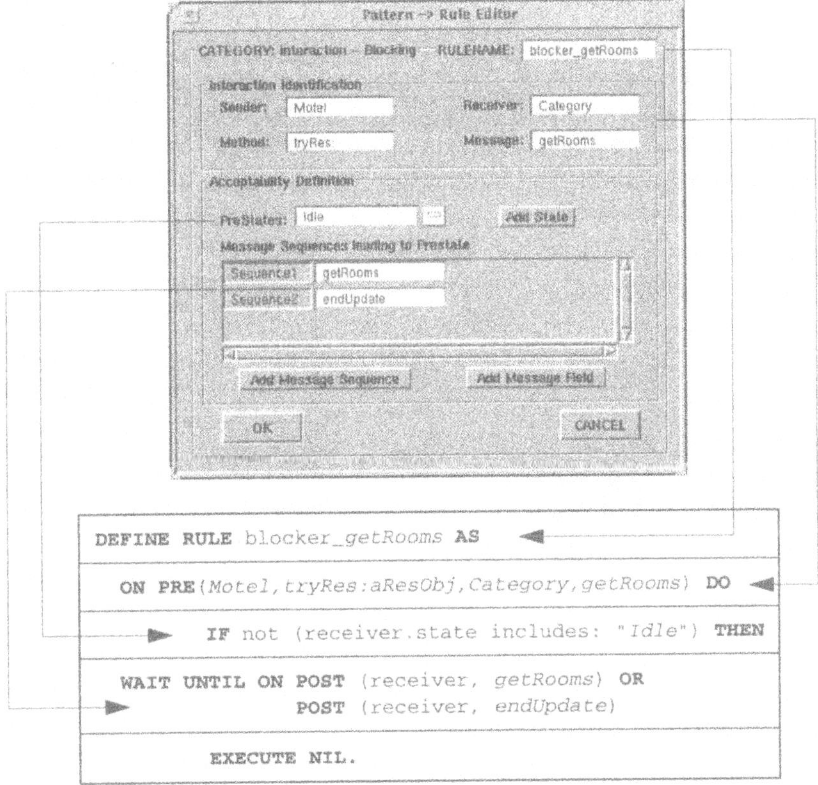

Fig. 5. Application of a Blocker Rule Pattern

Due to its generic nature, at a first glance the proposed rule pattern looks admittedly much more complicated than the application-dependent rule described above. But once a rule pattern is defined it can be easily applied just by defining its parameters using a corresponding form. On the basis of this parameter binding, the system automatically generates a rule. Anyway, the application designer is not concerned with the complexity of the rule pattern. Figure 5 illustrates the approach of generating the business rule realizing synchronous interaction as described in Figure 3 out of the Blocker rule pattern. Note that actual parameters are shown in italic. The remaining components are generic and are, thus, together with formal parameters the basic ingredients for the rule pattern.

3.2 Asynchronous Interaction Policy

Problem. The second interaction policy we want to realize on the basis of rules is asynchronous interaction. Asynchronous interaction considerably increases concurrency since the sender just initiates the interaction. This is useful for all those cases where the sender does not need any result of the task it delegated. From the sender's point of view neither a check for the receiver's actual state is necessary, nor does the sender have to wait for the receiver to finish method execution. Of course, the receiver may not satisfy the request before having entered the appropriate prestate.

Example. Continuing with our running example, reservation transactions can be concurrently submitted to the consortium from any node within the network. The consortium is responsible for delegating such requests to the appropriate motels. Consequently, the `consortium` object asynchronously propagates the message `tryRes` from within the method `newRes` to all motels satisfying the user's request stored within `resObj`, quits its current thread of control and gets ready for further requests. Figure 6 illustrates this scenario. Within the interaction diagram in Figure 6a asynchronous interaction is denoted by a flash line with two arrows, indicating the fact that interaction is done with one or more motels.

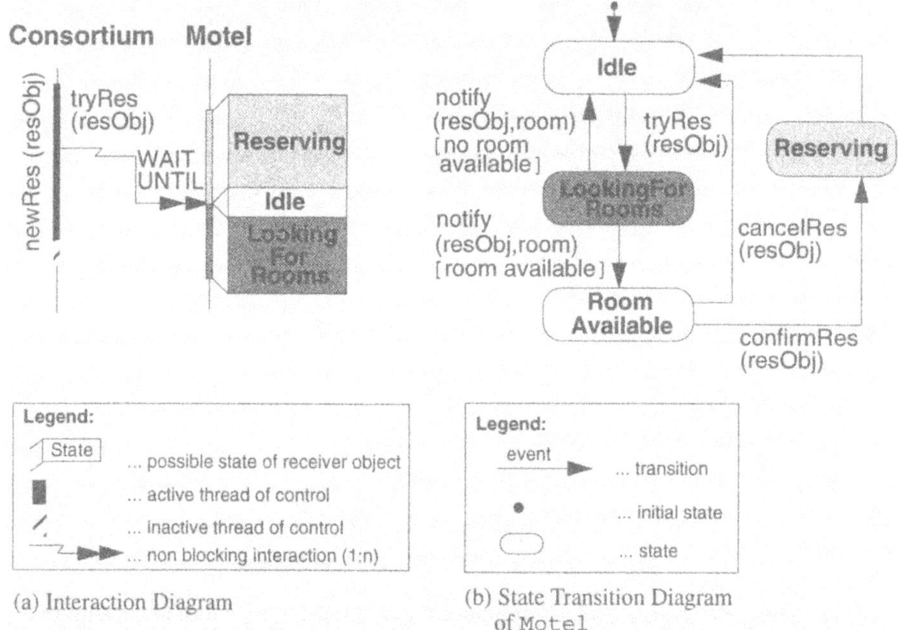

(a) Interaction Diagram

(b) State Transition Diagram of `Motel`

Fig. 6. Asynchronous Interaction Between `Consortium` and `Motel`

Figure 6b shows the state transition diagram for class `Motel`. According to it, a `motel` object remains in state `Idle` until it receives the message `tryRes`, which changes the state to `LookingForRooms`. Within that state the motel selects appropriate rooms (cf. synchronous interaction `getRooms` in Section 3.1) and asks whether one of them is available. If not, the motel returns to state `Idle`. If yes, the first available room notifies the motel and, thus, changes the motel's state to `RoomAvailable`. Finally, the `consortium` object is asked to confirm or cancel the reservation, and the motel reserves the room within state *`Reserving`* or immediately returns to state *`Idle`*, accordingly.

Concrete Solution by using Rules. This asynchronous interaction policy is realized by a rule depicted in Figure 7. The $Esel_C$ specifies an event which is signalled every time a *`consortium`* object sends the message *`tryRes`* to a *`motel`* object from within *`newRes`* (cf. also Figure 6). The condition is set to *`TRUE`* since asynchronous interaction requires that the sender has to proceed execution immediately after initiating a request, independent of the receiver's state.

DEFINE RULE async_tryRes **AS**	Rule Name
ON PRE(Consortium, newRes, Motel, tryRes:resObj) **DO**	Condition Event Selector ($Esel_C$)
IF TRUE **THEN**	Condition
ON (**POST** (receiver, notify: from:) **OR** **POST** (receiver, cancelRes:) **OR** **POST** (receiver, confirmRes:)) **OR** ((**POST** (Motel, CLASSMETHOD new) **OR** **POST** (receiver, notify: from:) **OR** **POST** (receiver, cancelRes:) **OR** **POST** (receiver, confirmRes:)); **PRE**(sender, newRes:, receiver, tryRes:)) [left.left.retVal = right.receiver]	Action Event Selector ($Esel_A$)
EXECUTE INSTEAD ASYNC receiver tryRes: resObj.	Action

Fig. 7. Asynchronous Interaction Rule

However, the interaction should be accepted by the `motel` object only if it is in state `Idle`. Thus, the composite event selector $Esel_A$ specifying the acceptability consists of two main components: The first component resembles the $Esel_A$ of synchronous interaction rules. It is responsible for recognizing transitions to the state `Idle`, if the motel is not already in this state. In our example, these transitions are represented by three simple messages which are connected by `OR` operators. The second component is responsible for recognizing the case that the `motel` object is already in the appropriate state `Idle` upon request of `tryRes`. The `motel` object is in state `Idle` either if the object has just been created (classmethod `new`) or if one of the messages which are part of the first component of the $Esel_A$ has been sent. After this, the action has to wait on the request of the triggering method `tryRes`. This is denoted by the sequence operator "`;`". In case that the `motel` object has just been created, a guard ensures that the receiver (`right.receiver`) of the request is identical to that object (`left.left.retVal`). Note that a composite event selector is stored as a tree and its components can be recursively accessed by the keywords `left` and `right`. The *action* of the rule starts the execution of `tryRes` within an asynchronous thread of control (keywords `INSTEAD ASYNC`).

Generic Solution by using Rule Patterns: The Asynchronizer. In analogy to the Blocker rule pattern, the Asynchronizer rule pattern depicted in Figure 8 can be derived from the application-dependent rule shown in Figure 7, accordingly:

DEFINE RULE PATTERN async_<name> **AS**	Rule Pattern Name
ON PRE (<sender>,<senderMethod>, <receiver>,<message0>) **DO**	Condition Event Selector ($Esel_C$)
IF TRUE **THEN**	Condition
ON ((**POST** (receiver, <message>) ['['receiver.state includes: <prestate>']']) { **OR** (**POST** (receiver, <message>) ['['receiver.state includes: <prestate>']']) }*) **OR** (((**POST** (receiver, <message>) ['['receiver.state includes: <prestate> ']']) { **OR** (**POST** (receiver, <message>) ['['receiver.state includes: <prestate> ']']) }*); (sender, senderMethod, receiver, message0))	Action Event Selector ($Esel_A$)
EXECUTE INSTEAD ASYNC receiver message0.	Action

Fig. 8. Asynchronous Interaction Rule Pattern

4 Related Work

There exist different approaches both from the database area and the programming language area related to parameterized rules on the one hand, and to flexible interaction specification on the other hand.

Casati et.al. [Casa95] use rules in the area of workflow management systems. Similarly to [Kapp95ab] rules provide the control and data flow between processing steps, thereby serving as an implementation mechanism for workflow enactment. In addition, *rule templates* are used to define the general structure of rules whose actual code depends on each specific workflow definition. Rule templates are quite similar to rule patterns. They are translated into rules at the time of their application, i.e., when a workflow definition is compiled. Unlike rule patterns where generic components are represented by parameters, the generic components of rule templates are represented by macros. The intention behind rule patterns was to specify business policies and therefore to be independent of a specific application domain. In contrast, the discussion of rule templates is restricted to the domain of workflow management systems.

The *AMOS* active database management system [Risc92, Sköl95] supports *parameterized rules* where the parameter might be either some value or a type. This resembles simple rule patterns consisting of a single rule. However, rule patterns in general go a step further in that they may be composed out of several parameterized rules.

The *composition filter* approach [Aksi93] is an extension to a conventional object-oriented model and offers composable techniques for specifying different aspects of the behavior of objects such as inheritance and delegation, multiple views and roles, synchronization and real-time constraints. New aspects of an object's behavior can be added by introducing new filter types. The behavior of an object can be enhanced through the manipulation of incoming and outgoing messages by using input and output filters. A filter is, similarly to a rule, a first-class object that determines via a *condition* whether a particular message identified by a *matching part* is either accepted or rejected and what *action* is to be performed in either case. At the conceptual level, composition filters are similar to our approach because they also aim to be adaptable to "constraints and requirements imposed by different application domains" what we call business policies. At the implementation level to the contrary, composition filters are somewhat different. Unlike rules, composition filters are specified statically within a class's definition as instances of a certain filter type. Furthermore, TriGS rules can not only be triggered by message passing events but also by time events and, above all, by composite events. Rule Patterns are comparable to filter types. However, filter types define only the actions which have to be taken when a filter of this type is applied. The situation *when* the action has to be executed has to be specified again and again when applying the filter type to a certain application class. Rule patterns predefine not only the action but also the situation which should trigger the rule independently of a concrete application, thus allowing automatic generation of rules out of the corresponding rule patterns.

The following approaches in object-oriented systems also have intentions similar to our rule patterns, or can possibly be applied for similar purposes. However, coming from the programming and not from the database community they do not consider database aspects such as persistence and transactions. The first two of them have also been presented strictly for sequential programs, but the ideas might be easily adaptable to concurrent systems.

The main purpose of the *Law-governed* approach [Mins87, Mins91] is the expression and enforcement of global regularities within an object-oriented system. It is based on rules, which are typically used to intercept message sends (thus corresponding to ON PRE condition event selectors in TriGS). The collection of all rules belonging to a system is called the Law of the system; rules can pertain to both static and dynamic aspects of the system, and even specify how the Law itself may be changed. The rules are specified in a variant of Prolog, so they can be very powerful. On the other hand, their evaluation can be very expensive (in general, there is no guarantee that the evaluation of a rule will even terminate), so they would be unsuitable for active databases. As a consequence of the global view, message sends can be intercepted only if *every* message sent to every object is passed through the law; in TriGS and similar systems events are caused only by *interesting* message sends. Instead of the parameterization of our rule patterns, the law-governed approach has the conventional unification of logical variables. The Law is always a "flat" collection of rules; there is no structuring facility analogous to composite rule patterns.

The *Contract* [Helm90, Holl92][4] is a construct for explicitly specifying (complex) interactions among groups of objects. A contract is thus analogous to a *composite* rule pattern: both express patterns of behavior that cannot be specified by a method interface or by a single rule. In the development of object-oriented software, contracts are intended to be defined mostly *before* classes; the Demeter system can automatically generate methods for a class from the contracts in which it participates [Lieb96]. This aspect is rather opposite to rules and rule patterns, which are largely intended to specify dynamically changing behavior. Contracts do not allow the behavior of a method to be

4 This is a specific technical meaning different from the well-known idea of "programming by contract" [Meye88].

changed, for instance. However, for the purpose of enforcing certain interactions to occur in a certain sequence, contracts and rule patterns seem to be equally useful.

Transverse activities [Kris93] are a new approach similar to Contracts. Being based on BETA [Lehr93], this work does take concurrency into account. (Any object can be genuinely active in the sense of having its own thread of control, while objects in most active databases could more precisely be called *reactive*.) The continuation of this research may yield results that are useful also for rule patterns.

5 Outlook

The basic idea of rule patterns can be applied to underlying systems that are very different from TriGS. TriGS is a prototype built with small resources, and has some rough edges, in part because the underlying system could not be modified. Good rule patterns can hide a lot of those rough edges. However, most object-oriented database systems are less dynamic and less reflexive than GemStone; in particular, classes in them are not objects themselves. In such a system, it would be sensible to treat rule patterns as static entities, instead of objects. Actually it is not necessary even for *rules* to be first-class objects.

There are some systems, e.g., ODE [Geha92] and Sentinel [Anwa93], in which rules are always declared within class definitions. In the majority of active object-oriented systems as well as in TriGS, rules do not belong to classes but are defined and stored separately from them. This is really the natural choice for rule patterns, which can have a more global purpose than single rules, and where classes can appear as formal parameters. However, when one has patterns, or modules, or other constructs larger than a single class for building the static structure of an object-oriented system, it seems far more promising that also rules and rule patterns could be incorporated in them. We will investigate this issue in the further course of our work.

Finally, let us consider rules and rule patterns within the software life-cycle. At the stage of *analysis*, domain specialists state their requirements more naturally by means of IF ... THEN constructs, i.e., by means of rules. Within *design*, for rules stated during requirements analysis appropriate rule patterns are identified. These rule patterns provide a specification of how the rules found during analysis can be transformed to the design of the system by means of active object-oriented technology. The *implementation* phase comprehends parameter binding on the basis of the rules found during analysis followed by an automatic generation of the corresponding "implementation rules". Since the concept of rules and rule patterns is used within each phase of the software life-cycle traceability of frequently changing requirements for the whole software life-cycle is facilitated.

Future work will include the development of additional rule patterns for business policies other than interaction policies introduced in this paper, and the further implementation of a design environment for active object-oriented applications based on rule patterns. In the long run, designers of active object-oriented applications should not be concerned with decisions on how a recurring design problem is realized by using objects and rules. They should rather be able to compose their applications out of a framework of predefined parameterized rule patterns.

References

[Aksi93] M. Aksit, K. Wakita, J. Bosch, L. Bergmans, A. Yonezawa, *Abstracting Object Interactions Using Composition Filters,* Proc. of the ECOOP'93 Workshop on Object Based Distributed Programming, R. Guerraoui, O. Nierstrasz, M. Riveill (eds.), Springer LNCS 791, Kaiserslautern, July 1993

[Anwa93] E. Anwar, L. Maugis, S. Chakravarthy, *A New Perspective on Rule Support for Object-Oriented Databases*, Proc. of the ACM-SIGMOD Int. Conf. on Management of Data, SIGMOD Record, 22 (2), pp. 99-108, June 1993

[Bußl94] C. Bußler, S. Jablonski, *Implementing Agent Coordination for Workflow Management Systems Using Active Database Systems*, Proc. of the IEEE Fourth Int. Workshop on Research Issues in Data Engineering (RIDE), Houston, 1994

[Casa95] F. Casati, S. Ceri, B. Pernici, G. Pozzi, *Conceptual Modeling of Workflows*, Internal Report no. 95.018, Dipartimento di Elettronica e Informazione, Politecnico di Milano, Milan, Italy, 1995

[Coad95] P. Coad, D. North, M. Mayfield, *Object Models - Strategies, Patterns & Applications*, Yourdon Press Computing Series, Prentice Hall, 1995

[Copl95] J.O. Coplien, D.C. Schmidt (eds.), *Pattern Languages of Program Design*, Addison-Wesley, 1995

[Diaz91] O. Diaz, N. Paton, P. Gray, *Rule Management in Object Oriented Databases: A Uniform Approach,* Proc. of the 17th Int. Conf. on VLDB, Barcelona, pp. 317-326, 1991

[Ditt95] K.R. Dittrich, S. Gatziu, A. Geppert, *The Active Database Management System Manifesto: A Rulebase of ADBMS Features*, Proc. of the 2nd Workshop on Rules in Databases (RIDS), T. Sellis (ed.), Springer LNCS, Athens, Greece, Sept. 1995

[Eder95] J. Eder, H. Groiss, *Ein Workflow-Managementsystem auf der Basis aktiver Datenbanken (A Workflow Management System Based on Active Databases)*, Geschäftsprozeßmodellierung und Workflow-Management, G. Vossen, J. Becker (eds.), International Thomson Publishing, Bonn, 1995 (in German)

[Embl92] D.W. Embley, B.D. Kurtz, S.N. Woodfield, *Object-Oriented System Analysis - A Model-Driven Approach,* Yourdon Press, 1992

[Fugi92] M. Fugini, O. Nierstrasz, B. Pernici, *Application Development through Reuse: The ITHACA Tools Environment*, ACM SIGOIS Bulletin, 13 (2), pp. 38-47, August 1992

[Gamm94] E. Gamma, R. Helm, R. Johnson, J. Vlissides, *Design Patterns - Elements of Reusable Object-Oriented Software*, Addison-Wesley Professional Computing Series, 1994

[Geha92] N.H. Gehani, H.V. Jagadish, O.Shmueli, *Composite Event Specification in Active Database Systems,* Proc. of the 18th Int. Conference on VLDB, August 1992

[Gert93] M. Gertz, U.W. Lipeck, *Deriving Integrity Maintaining Triggers from Transition Graphs*, Proc. of the 9th Int. Conf. on Data Engineering (DE'93), IEEE Computer Society Press, Vienna, 1993

[Hare88] D. Harel, *On Visual Formalisms*, Communications of the ACM, 31 (5), May 1988

[Helm90] R. Helm, I.M. Holland, D. Gangopadhyay, *Contracts: Specifying Behavioral Compositions in Object-Oriented Systems*, Proc. of the conjoint OOPSLA/ECOOP Conf., ACM Press, pp. 169-180, Ottawa, Canada, 1990

[Herb95] H. Herbst, *A Meta-Model for Business Rules in Systems Analysis*, Proc. of the 7th Int. Conf. on Advanced Information Systems Engineering (CAiSE'95), J. Iivari, K. Lyytinen, M. Rossi (eds.), Springer LNCS 932, Jyväskylä, Finland, June 1995

[Holl92] I.M. Holland, *Specifying reusable components using Contracts*, Proc. of ECOOP92, O. Lehrmann Madsen (ed.), Springer LNCS 615, Utrecht, 1992

[Kapp94a] G. Kappel, S. Rausch-Schott, W. Retschitzegger, S. Vieweg, *TriGS - Making a Passive Object-Oriented Database System Active*, Journal of Object-Oriented Programming (JOOP), 7(4), July-August, 1994

[Kapp94b] G. Kappel, S. Rausch-Schott, W. Retschitzegger, *Beyond Coupling Modes - Implementing Active Concepts on Top of a Commercial ooDBMS,* Int. Symposium on Object-Oriented Methodologies and Systems (ISOOMS), Springer LNCS 858, 1994

[Kapp95a] G. Kappel, B. Pröll, S. Rausch-Schott, W. Retschitzegger, *$TriGS_{flow}$ - Active Object-Oriented Workflow Management*, Proc. of the 27th Hawaiian Int. Conf. on System Sciences (HICSS'95), 1995

[Kapp95b] G. Kappel, P. Lang, S. Rausch-Schott, W. Retschitzegger, *Workflow Management based on Objects, Rules and Roles*, IEEE Bulletin of the Technical Committee on Data Engineering, 18 (1), March, 1995

[Kapp95c] G. Kappel, S. Rausch-Schott, W. Retschitzegger, *Rule Patterns for Designing Active Object-Oriented Database Applications,* Technical Report, Dept. of Information Systems, University of Linz, June 1995 (also available at http://www.ifs.uni-linz.ac.at/ifs/publications.html)

[Knol94] G. Knolmayer, H. Herbst, M. Schlesinger, *Enforcing Business Rules by the Application of Trigger Concepts*, Proc. Priority Programme Informatics Research, Information Conference Module 1, Swiss National Science Foundation, Bern, 1994

[Kris93] B. B. Kristensen, *Transverse Activities: Abstractions in Object-Oriented Programming*, Object Technologies for Advanced Software, S. Nishio, A. Yonezawa (eds.), Springer LNCS 742, 1993

[Lehr93] O.Lehrmann Madsen, B. Moeller-Pedersen, K.Nygaard, *Object-Oriented Programming in the BETA Programming Language*, Addison-Wesley, 1993

[Lieb96] K. Lieberherr, *Adaptive Object-Oriented Software: The Demeter Method with Propagation Patterns*, PWS Publishing Company, 1996 (to be published)

[Louc91] P. Loucopoulos, C. Theodoulidis, D. Pantazis, *Business Rules Modelling: Conceptual Modelling and Object-Oriented Specifications*, IFIP WG8.1 Working Conf. on the Object-Oriented Approach in Information Systems, F. Van Assche, B. Moulin, C. Rolland (eds.), North-Holland, Quebec City, Canada, October 28-31, 1991

[Meye88] Bertrand Meyer, *Object-oriented Software Construction*, Prentice Hall, 1988

[Mins87] N. H. Minsky, D. Rozenshtein, *A Law-Based Approach to Object-Oriented Programming*, Proc. of the OOPSLA '87 Conf. (Orlando, Florida, 1987), N. Meyrowitz (ed.), ACM SIGPLAN Notices, 22 (12), pp. 482-493, December 1987

[Mins91] N. H. Minsky, *Law-Governed Systems*, The IEE Software Engineering Journal, September 1991

[Nier93] O. Nierstrasz, *Composing Active Objects*, Research Directions in Concurrent Object-Oriented Programming, G. Agha, P. Wegner, A. Yonezawa (eds.), MIT Press, 1993

[Odel94] J.J. Odell, *Specifying requirements using rules*, Journal of Object-Oriented Programming (JOOP), 6 (2), 1994

[Petr94] I. Petrounias, P. Loucopoulos, *A Rule-Based Approach for the Design and Implementation of Information Systems*, Proc. of the 4th Int. Conf. on Extending Database Technology (EDBT'94), M. Jarke, J. Bubenko, K. Jeffery (eds.), Springer LNCS 779, UK, March 1994

[Pree95] W. Pree, *Design Patterns for Object-Oriented Software Development*, Addison-Wesley, 1995

[Rein93] B. Reinwald, *Workflow Management in Verteilten Systemen (Workflow Management in Distributed Systems)*, Teubner, Stuttgart-Leipzig, 1993 (in german)

[Risc92] T. Risch, M. Sköld, *Active Rules based on Object Oriented Queries*, IEEE Bulletin of the Technical Committee on Data Engineering, Vol. 15, No. 1-4, Dec. 1992

[Rumb91] J. Rumbaugh, M. Blaha, W. Premerlani, F. Eddy, W. Lorensen, *Object-Oriented Modeling and Design*, Prentice Hall, 1991

[Rubi94] K.S. Rubin, P. McClaughry, D. Pellegrini, *Modeling rules using Object Behavior Analysis and Design*, Object Magazine, June 1994

[Schr95] M. Schrefl, G. Kappel, *Modelling Object Behavior: To use methods or rules or both?* Workshop "Semantics in Databases", Prague, 1995

[Sköl95] M. Sköld, E. Falkenroth, T. Risch, *Rule Contexts in Active Databases - A Mechanism for Dynamic Rule Grouping*, Proc. of the Rules in Database Systems Conference (RIDS'95), Athens, Greece, 1995

[Tsal91] A. Tsalgatidou, P. Loucopoulos, *An Object-Oriented Rule-Based Approach to the Dynamic Modelling of Information Systems*, Proc. of the Int. Working Conf. on Dynamic Modelling of Information Systems, H.G. Sol, K.M. Van Hee (eds.), pp. 165-188, North-Holland, 1991

[Tsic89] D. Tsichritzis, *Object-Oriented Development for Open Systems*, Proc. of Information Processing 89 - IFIP World Computer Congress, G.X. Ritter (ed.), North-Holland, 1989

[Urba92] S.D. Urban, A.P. Karadimce, R.B. Nannapaneni, *The Implementation and Evaluation of Integrity Maintenance Rules in an Object-Oriented Database*, Proc. of the 8th Int. Conf. on Data Engineering (DE'92), 1992

[Yone87] A. Yonezawa, E. Shibayama, T. Takada, Y. Honda, *Modelling and Programming in an Object-Oriented Concurrent Language ABCL/1*, in: Object-Oriented Concurrent Programming, A. Yonezawa, M. Tokoro (eds.), MIT Press, 1987

Tool-Based Re-Engineering of a Legacy MIS: An Experience Report

Thomas Kudrass, Marco Lehmbach[1], Alejandro Buchmann
Technical University Darmstadt, Dept. of Computer Science, Database Research Group
Frankfurter Str. 69 A, D-64293 Darmstadt, Germany
{kudrass | buchmann}@dvs1.informatik.th-darmstadt.de

Abstract. In the process of restructuring its computing facilities, Rhône-Poulenc Rorer is eliminating its mainframes. As a consequence, existing legacy systems must be migrated. We present an experience report on the use of CASE tools for re-engineering a legacy MIS and illustrate the process of current state analysis and generation of a re-engineered target system. Based on the experience gained in evaluating representative CASE tools for their suitability in the data re-engineering process and the actual use of the ISEE tool we present a list of needed features missing from today's tools.

1. Introduction

The case study presented in this paper was inspired by the decision of Rhône-Poulenc Rorer to give up its mainframe systems by mid 1997. This implies that existing mainframe systems have to be substituted or migrated. Subject of this study is a custom-made Management Information System for in-house controlling data (CMIS) based on an IBM SQL/DS system running on a mainframe.

Because of a lack of documentation and in-house know-how concerning the legacy MIS it has to be analysed and documented before being replaced. In addition, the documentation is supposed to act as an online help system for the MIS administrator. The documentation should further include an analysis of the system's interfaces in order to maintain these more efficiently.

As a result of multiple modifications over time the data structure of the MIS is messy and the data is partially inconsistent. Therefore, it makes no sense to substitute the MIS by a system with the same data structure. Instead, a target model is to be developed.

The capabilities of the MIS exceed the functionality of a data warehouse because it comprises also operational functions that are logically a part of various operational subsystems (see section 2). The aim is to extract these functions in order to assign them to the subsystems to reduce the MIS to a data warehouse system. In this paper, we address three issues: (a) the procedure of analysing and documenting an existing legacy infor-

---

1. current address: Rhone-Pôulenc Rorer, Nattermannallee 1, D-50792 Cologne

mation system, (b) deriving a target model in an I-CASE-Tool and (c) describing the specification of an ideal documentation and analysis tool.

This paper is organized as follows. Section 2 describes the environment of the case study. Section 3 contains a short introduction into the I-CASE methodology in general and into the I-CASE tool ISEE in detail. We discuss the procedure of documenting the system's current state and deriving the target model of the data structure in section 4. That leads to the catalogue of requirements concerning an ideal business process analysis and data documentation tool. Finally, section 6 concludes with some remarks about the availability of the discussed features.

2. A Case Study: The Controlling Managament Information System

The pharmaceutical branch of Rhône-Poulenc (France) consolidated with Rorer (USA) in 1990. This consolidation constituted Rhône-Poulenc Rorer Inc., a company with 22,500 employees in more than 140 countries. The former German company A. Nattermann & Cie. GmbH in Cologne acts as the headquarter of Rhône-Poulenc Rorer Germany. More than 1,400 employees in production, marketing, administration and sales work with the German subsidiary of Rhône-Poulenc Rorer Inc. in Cologne and achieved revenues of $ 400 million in 1992. Rhône-Poulenc Rorer Germany is one of the top German pharmaceutical companies and it is the biggest company in terms of revenue in production and sale of over-the-counter drugs.

This study [Lehm95] analyses the mainframe SQL- based Controlling Management Information System (CMIS), which was developed by the information system department (now disbanded) of A. Nattermann & Cie GmbH in 1989. CMIS handles and provides in-house controlling data such as costs, revenues, budgets, etc.

CMIS integrates the order, production and accounting systems in a broad sense. Most of the master data originates from the production system, e.g. the *selling unit*. A selling unit contains all relevant information about the sold products. In order to guarantee a minimum of tolerable inconsistency between the material master data in the production system and the selling unit in the CMIS, a daily batch job is executed which updates the selling unit. The accounting system delivers the actual amount of money that was paid by the customers, and the order system passes information about the amount of products sold to the CMIS. This happens daily, too.

The CMIS is divided into several subsystems like master data administration, reporting, budgeting, key customer management, accounting, investment controlling and advertisement expenditures controlling: Within the budgeting module the expected expenditures for the upcoming year applied to each cost center are planned and transferred to the accounting and to the production system in order to control the budgets. Hence, the CMIS contains also subsystems providing calculation functions that need additional manual input. The subsystems investment controlling and advertisement expenditures

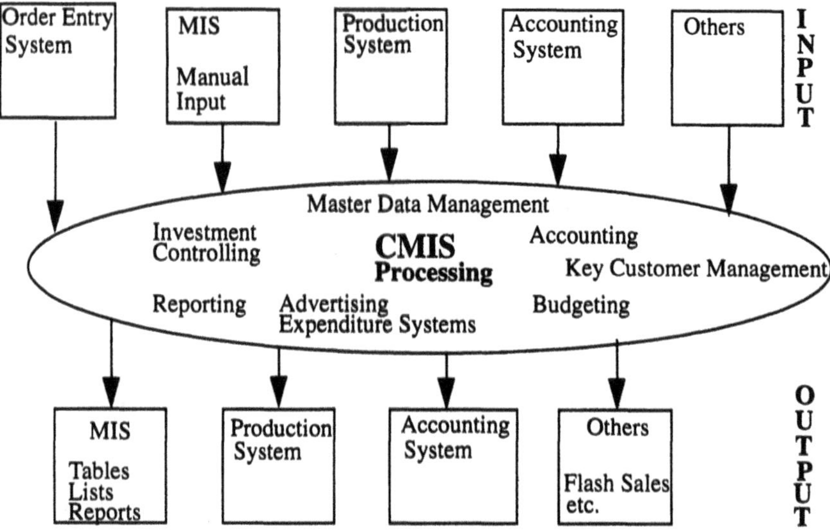

Figure 1: System Environment of the Controlling MIS

collect data about planned investments and advertisements. These data are partially used by the accounting system. The key task of the accounting module within the CMIS is reporting on the sales. The reporting module consists of a collection of standard reports and a query management tool. The standard reports present the development of costs, turnover etc. The reporting functionality could migrate into a future data warehouse system substituting the existing CMIS.

Some key facts about the CMIS are: The size of the data is roughly 1.6 Gigabyte. This quantity is distributed among 250 tables (entity types), characterized by 2000 different attributes. Some of the tables contain more than 700,000 records (e.g. monthly inventory), some only one or two. The SQL system catalogue contains information about 120 different primary keys. Some of these keys occur very often, e.g. the primary key of the selling unit, occurs in 60 tables as a foreign key. There are also tables specified by up to 100 attributes like the master employee data table with a record length of around 2000 bytes.

Figure 2 contains part of the CMIS data structure that will be used as an example throughout the whole paper. Rhône-Poulenc Rorer used to be divided into divisions and subdivisions. After a reorganization of the company the differentiation of subdivisions was eliminated. Due to legal requirements some data (e.g. in the bookkeeping department) have to be available five years which implies the existence of historical data. Therefore, the former one-to-many relationship between division and subdivision was replaced by a one-to-one relationship. A division has several cost centers, e.g. one for human resources, another one for marketing, etc. Every employee belongs to exactly one cost center. A brand has many possible forms of administering (e.g. liquid form or pills). Since pills can be sold in packages of ten, twenty or more units and different laws

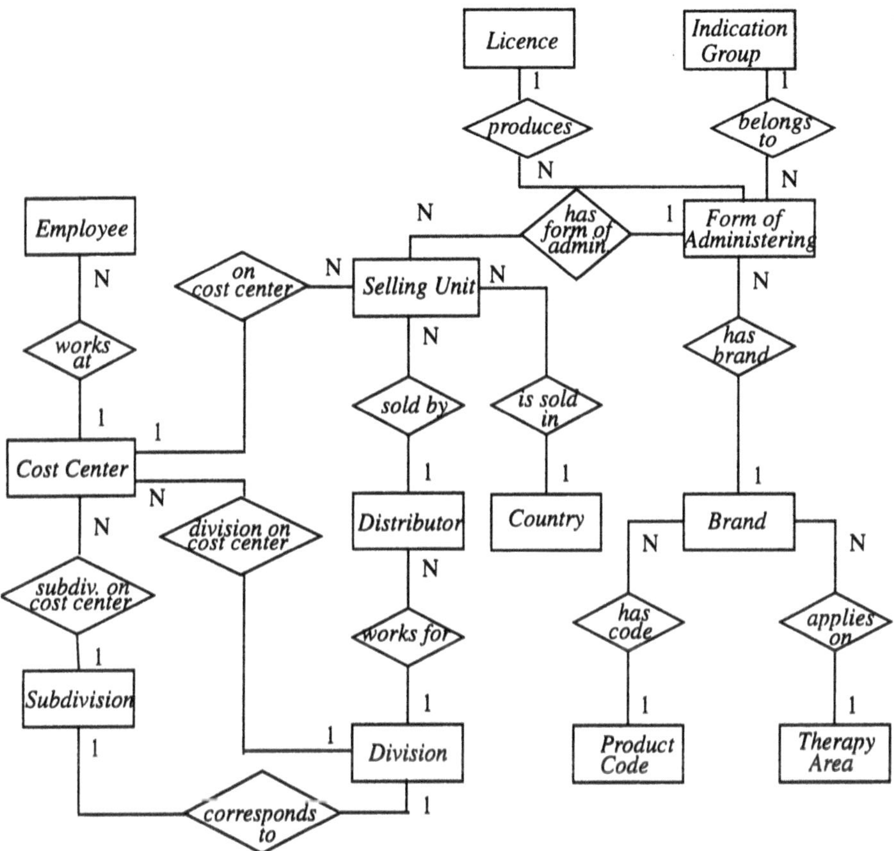

Figure 2: A Part of the CMIS Data Structure

and languages require different packages for each country, various packages, so-called selling units, have to be produced. They are sold by company owned distributors.

3. The Usage of the I-CASE Methodology

3.1 Selecting a Tool

Within the second phase of the software life cycle [Royc70, Somm92], the software and system design, the developer is supported in several tasks by different development tools. We chose three tools which are representative for three different modelling approaches. These approaches are the Structured Design Methodology by Constantine/ Yourdon [CoYo79], the Integrated Computer Aided Manufacturing (ICAM or IDEF) notation of ER diagrams [Chen76] and the ARIS approach (Architecture of Integrated Information Systems) [Sche92]. Because of the widespread use of the IDEF modelling and the Structured Design Method, there are many tools available that are based on them. As representative tools we chose the system design tool ERWin/BPWin from Logic Works [ERwi95] and the I-CASE tool ISEE, version 3.2., from Westmount B.V.

[UMIS93]. The ARIS approach is often referenced with respect to business process re-engineering, especially in the context of SAP/R3. The corresponding product is the ARIS Toolset, our third choice.

Main prerequisites for the application of a tool are:

1. the possibility to document separately single applications in subsystems based on a common enterprise-wide data repository
2. openness and interfaces to other development tools
3. graphical support of data flow diagram (DFD) and ERD techniques
4. access to the data repository
5. a reverse engineering of the data structures

Due to space restrictions we sketch only briefly ERwin/BPwin and ARIS, ISEE is described in more detail in section 3.3.

The DB design tool ERwin by Logic Works represents every application system by a single ER diagram which implies the creation of separate data repositories for each system. Thus, it is impossible to manage several systems and their interfaces (e.g. interdependent data, batch jobs) centrally in one repository. The ARIS Toolset 3.0 comprises a process modelling component as an essential part which supports the detailed registration of all business processes and participating objects. By means of reference models comparison analyses with limited expressiveness can be executed. Within the data view such comparison analyses - like a reverse engineering of the existing data structure - are not supported. There is no possibility to create SQL scripts from the given entity relationship diagrams (forward engineering) in a straightforward manner. Due to the strong coupling of the ARIS Toolset to the SAP software there are few interfaces to other database design and CASE tools.

Table 1 shows that ISEE was the most appropriate tool among the candidates in meeting the above requirements. That led to the decision to apply ISEE for analysis and documentation of all existing application systems at Rhône-Poulenc Rorer.

Tool	Subsystens/ Common Repository	Openness and Interfaces	DFDs and ERDs	Access to Data Repository	Re-Engineering of Data Structures
ERwin & BPwin	-	√	√	(√)	√
ARIS Toolset	√	(√)	(√)	(√)	-
I-CASE ISEE	√	√	√	(√)	(√)

–	not available
√	available
(√)	partially available

Table 1: Evaluation of CASE Tools according to the Selection Criteria

Regardless of the positive evaluation of ISEE it can be stated that its focus is more on the Lower CASE than on the Upper CASE because it is not mandatory to pass through the phases of the Upper CASE during software development. They serve primarily the development preparation and the documentation of the procedure. Hence, online-queries are only limited and analyses of current and target states are impossible. Furthermore the reverse engineering only deduces table structures without relationship types. Because ISEE is a so-called multi-user tool enabling the definition of subsystems within a project it makes possible an appropriate mapping and separation of different application systems of the corporation using one data repository.

In section 5 it is shown that no approach or tool meets the additional requirements we extracted from our experience in the given CMIS environment.

3.2 The I-CASE Methodology

The process of software and system design is commonly divided into subprocesses which is reflected in the structure of the CASE tools. The terms Upper CASE and Lower CASE arrange CASE products in groups depending on their focus. Upper CASE products serve the corporate planning, the description of the corporation and its plans. Lower CASE supports among other things the non-graphic generation of specifications as a first step in the straightforward mapping of data modeling (e.g. data definitions, triggers, stored procedures) to programs. Integrated CASE tools (I-CASE) comprise both the Upper and the Lower CASE using a common repository. The repository, or data dictionary, acts as documentation and information base for all structured and standardized data which are being created or accessed during system development. The repository gives the CASE components access to the necessary information, keeps this data consistent and non-redundant and, hence, guarantees a seamless integration of these components.

3.3 The I-CASE tool ISEE / Westmount

3.3.1 General structure

ISEE from Westmount is based on the Structured Design methodology by Constantine/ Yourdon [CoYo79] supporting I-CASE. ISEE divides the development process into four phases, the analysis, architecture, design and programming phase (see figure 3). The analysis and architecture phases represent the Upper CASE, the design and programming phases the Lower CASE. All phases are passed through gradually, beginning the next phase after the end of the previous one.

ISEE distinguishes three modelling viewpoints: processes, data structures and user interfaces. For each combination of phase and view several modelling techniques are available to the developer.

Within the data view the developer can use the entity-relationship modelling technique in all phases. The process modelling is supported by ISEE only in Upper CASE by a

Data Flow Diagram (DFD) editor in the analysis phase and by a System Architecture Diagram (SAD) editor in the architecture phase. A SAD enhances the data flow modelling by taking required hardware and software components in the system development into account.

Besides the editors, ISEE incorporates a report generator, which gives the developer access to information in the repository and several checking mechanisms, so-called check routines, for the consistency maintenance of the whole system which is to be analysed.

The subsequent discussion is restricted to the two Upper CASE phases because the Lower Case plays a minor role in the analysis and documentation process. Due to the restriction to Upper CASE the consideration is reduced to the DFD and ERD techniques.

			VIEWS		
			Process	Data	User Interface
Upper CASE	PHASES	Analyst	DFD	ERD DSD	
		Architect	SAD	ERD DSD	FSD
Lower CASE		Designer	SCD	ERD	FSD
		Programmer	ERD PRG	ERD PRG	PRG
REPOSITORY					

Techniques & Diagrams

DFD: Data Flow Diagram
DSD: Data Structure Diagram
ERD: Entity Relationship Diagram
PRG: Program Editor
SAD: System Architecture Diagram
SCD: Structure Chart Diagram

Figure 3: Main Components of the I-CASE tool ISEE

3.3.2 Top-Down Design in I-CASE - Analysis Phase

The design begins with the DFD, which captures data flows between processes and / or data stores from the process view. DFDs allow to form arbitrary hierarchies of complex processes counting each hierarchy level by a current number beginning with level 0 at the topmost layer. While modelling the data view the data stores are analysed and a more detailed specification of the data stores through ERDs is developed. Graphically speaking, each ERD is attached to a data store. Each data flow can be specified in more detail by DSDs. The references originating from these attachments establish relation-

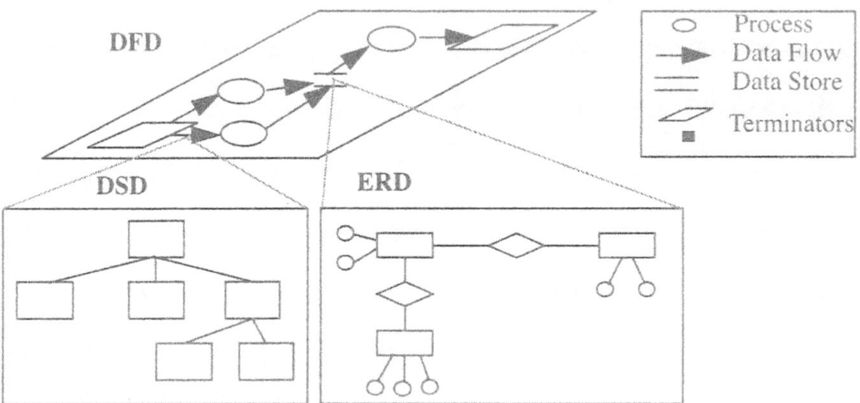

Figure 4: Interdependencies between DFDs, DSDs and ERDs [Prui93]

ships between different diagrams. Those references are managed centrally in the data repository (maintained in a project database in ISEE), which leads to a network of diagrams representing the system to be modelled. This network is built at the bottom layer. ISEE permits forming a hierarchy by creating a project database for each project and decomposing a project into several subsystems.

In the first phase, the analysis phase, a project database is created and the necessary subsystems are defined by a level 1-DFD. The division of subsystems can be done according to the underlying requirements dependent on organizational aspects, applications or tasks. Those classification possibilities of subsystems are valid for all subsequent phases, too. Following this stage the current state of the existing systems is understood by decomposing each level-0-subsystem (their totality is equivalent to the level-1-DFD) of the project. When obtaining a predetermined degree of accuracy the data structure is documented by ERDs.

Only after finishing the current state analysis the derivation of a target model takes place in the second phase, the architecture phase. This phase is characterized by a modification of existing data structures due to revealed anomalies and disadvantages. See section 4.2 for a detailed description of the procedure with an example taken from the CMIS.

4. The Case Study

4.1 Documenting the Current State at Rhône-Poulenc Rorer

This section deals with an actual analysis and documentation procedure using the I-CASE tool ISEE of the existing CMIS at Rhône-Poulenc Rorer. The repository database used in the case study was based on the Ingres database system running on a Unix machine. The procedure of documenting the existing system consists of the following four steps: (1) set up the ISEE project, (2) import the existing datastructure, (3) design the DFDs and (4) design the ERDs.

(1) Set up the ISEE project

First of all we have to define a project database, e.g. the project "Analyse all of the company's systems". Therefore, we name our project "rpr_cologne.pdb". Afterwards we design the level-1-DFD by decomposing the process 0 = "rpr_cologne" into the company's organizational departments like controlling, research, production etc. As a result of this decomposition the subsystems are defined.

(2) Import the existing data structure

In the next step we have to prepare the existing data structure for the ISEE re-engineering option. The data structure has to be in the same format as the project database. Therefore, we import the data structure from the mainframe to the Unix based Ingres database by converting the SQL system *create table* scripts into flat files. After creating the CMIS data structure in an Ingres database, we execute the option *Generate from Database*, which is provided in the analysis phase of ISEE. As a result ISEE creates one ERD for each table containing the table as an entity with its attributes. In addition to that a so-called Top ERD is designed, where all tables without any attributes are included. Since the tables have technical names, we have to extend those names by adding self-explaining aliases, e.g. entity "T11607" is changed to "T11607@division", to facilitate the understanding. Unfortunately, relationships can not be extracted automatically, they have to be deduced manually using foreign keys.

(3) Design the DFDs

Because the CMIS is mainly used and maintained by the controlling department, we will handle all the collected information about the CMIS in the subsystem "Controlling" (figure 5). In doing so we relate an application system to one department. But there is a possible conflict in the separation of organizational units. Problems may arise from their assignment to application systems because two DFDs cannot correspond with one superior DFD at the same time.

The level-1-DFD of the project occurs within the corresponding subsystems as level-0-DFDs with one process representing the subsystem. Since the CMIS ist not a stand-alone-system we create a process "Interfaces", which handles the data transfers between the CMIS and other systems. The CMIS collects most of its data by using batch jobs. These batch jobs are documented in the level-2-DFD "Interfaces". If the desired level of detail is reached one can stop decomposing processes.

(4) Design the ERDs

When the design of the DFDs is completed the process modelling is finished. In the next step we switch to the data view. The task is now to focus on the data stores in the DFDs by creating ERDs for each relevant store. While designing a new ERD of a DFD's data store it is strongly suggested to use the top ERD as a reference copy and modify it as necessary in order to maintain a consistent data repository.

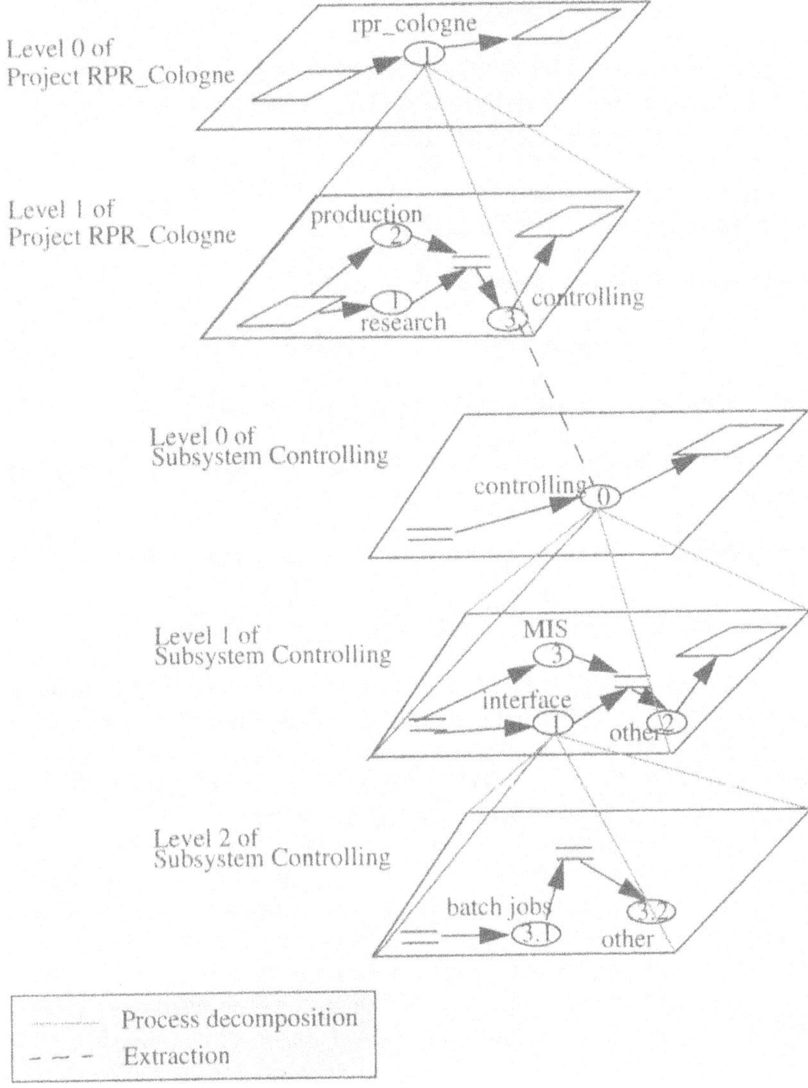

Figure 5: An example of top-down design at Rhône-Poulenc Rorer

4.2 Procedure of Deriving the Target Data Structure in ISEE

As discussed in section 3.5. the ISEE analyst phase is used for documenting the current state of processes and data structures and the ISEE architect phase for modelling the target data structure. Since the project does not include the task of re-engineering the business processes we are not going to modify the DFDs from the analysis phase. This leaves only two steps for deriving the target data structure from the current state: (1) initialize the ISEE architect phase and (2) modify the current data structure.

(1) Initialize the ISEE architect phase

Because we use the same DFDs and therefore the same level-1 DFD, which is the basis for the process of creating the subsystems, we have to create the same subsystems in the architecture phase as there are in the analysis phase.

Afterwards we execute the option "*Import from previous Phase(Analyst)* ", which creates a one-to-one copy of all ERDs and DFDs.

(2) Modify the current data structure

The need to modify the existing ERDs has various reasons. We give three examples:

a) Additional relations in order to enhance query performance

b) Specialization of entities due to encoded semantic information and wrong level of abstraction

c) Decomposition in order to avoid redundancies and to save disk space

a) Additional relations in order to enhance query performance

Most of the daily, weekly and monthly reports are based on queries where relationships between brand and e.g. distributor, country or other entity types are built related directly to selling unit. These queries always use the same two joins to create the relationship between selling unit and brand. In order to enhance the querie's performance an additional persistent table *Selling Unit-Brand* is to be modelled in the target state (figure 6). The update frequency is very low in the given example because the affected data are master data, which means a number of about 5 updates per year (as a result of the introduction of a new brand). There are around 20 weekly and 40 monthly reports using the combination of selling unit, form of administering and brand. In the given example redundant base tables or materialized views are possible solutions. The decision of what approach to use depends on the availability of materialized views in the target system and can only be made after the commitment to a new platform.

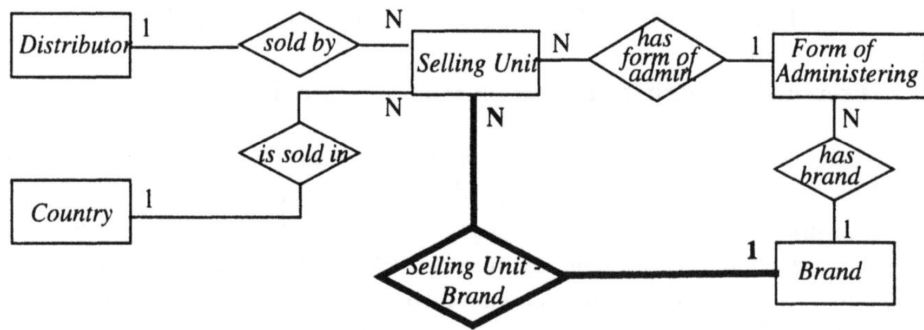

Figure 6: Additional relations (Example)

b) Specialization of entities due to encoded semantic information and wrong level of abstraction

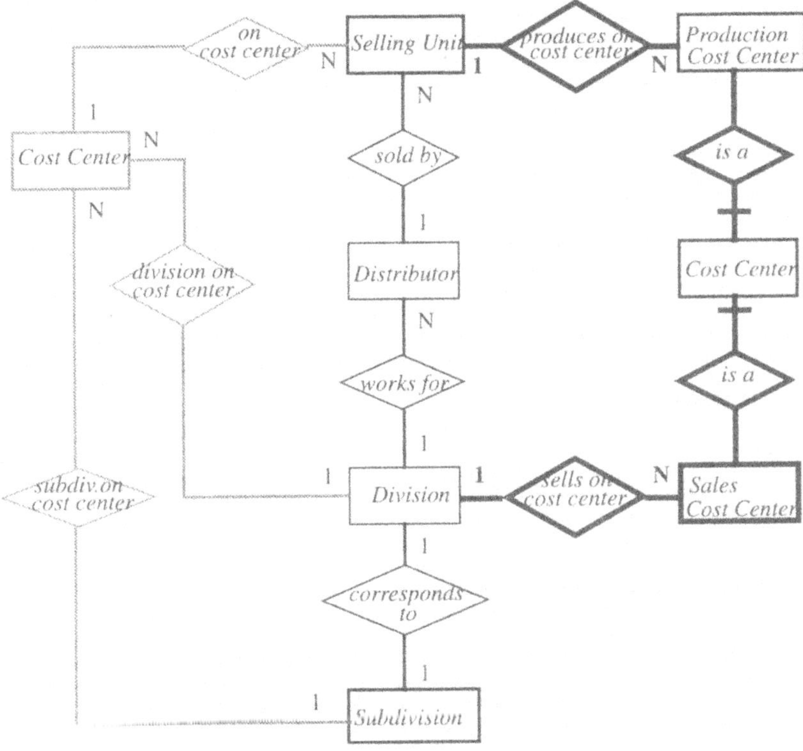

Figure 7: Specialization (Example)

Right now the MIS manages all cost centers in one entity type *cost center* where *cost center id* is the primary key with a domain ranging from 1000 to 9999. The primary key contains encoded semantic information. Cost center numbers 1000 to 1999 are reserved for production cost centers, 2000 to 2999 are reserved for sales activities. In order to integrate that kind of information in the target model a decomposition of the entity cost center has to take place. In our example we broke the *cost center* down into *production* and *sales cost center* and related them to their corresponding entities (figure 7, bold face). The entity *cost center* in the target model results from the disjoint generalization of the two specialized cost centers. Because *division* and *subdivision* have a one-to-one relationship, a relationship between *subdivision* and *sales cost center* is not necessary.

c) Decomposition in order to avoid redundancies and to save diskspace

The MIS manages information about the employees. The main table representing that information is named *employee master data*. This table is characterized by 174 attributes with a record length of 1976 byte. The table keeps the following information about the employees: personal data, children, education, position and status (job description), wages, savings agreements, pension data, health insurance, social insurance, information about handicaps, etc.

The table structure to be redesigned is characterized by all the teething troubles of the early data processing period causing many problems now. For example, there are 10 columns to store a variable number of children to capture the "worst case" of 10 children.

It is obvious that a lot of disk space is wasted, because information about handicaps exists only for handicapped employees, information about pension data, health insurance, social insurance is only relevant for regular employees and not for temporary workers. Since all former employees receive a company pension the actual table contains more than 3000 records, where only 1400 people are working with the company right now. In order to enhance the performance of application modules reading this table and in order to save disk space it is necessary to split up the table into its logical units, as itemized above.

5. A Requirements Catalogue for Analysis and Documentation Tools

5.1 Features Facilitating the Modelling

In this section we describe features that are desirable and identify tools supporting these features. However, at present no tool supports the combination of all features.

5.1.1 Powerful Database Re-Engineering

We focus on the case of re-engineering relational databases. Given a relational schema, the database re-engineering process aims at the creation of a conceptual model like the ER model by extracting the design elements from the existing tables. There are some authors ([BaCN92], [HCTJ93],[ChBS94]) giving a comprehensive overview about algorithms how to reverse engineer a conceptual model from a source relational schema. They presuppose some knowledge about the relational database by analysing not only the relational schema, but also data instances. There are commercially available tools providing a "Reverse Engineering" option (e.g. Bachman/Analyst [Bach88]), but most of them restrict themselves to reading the data structure, e. g. the data dictionary. Typically, the captured information comprises the names of tables and attributes, attribute properties (like type, length) and primary key information. Assuming the ER model is the target, the result of the re-engineering is a collection of ER diagrams each corresponding to one table or a global ER diagramm corresponding to the whole data structure. In both cases relationships between entities are often ignored.

Based on the assumption that the underlying database supports the primary key concept and there is a consistent naming policy, tools should apply search algorithms, as e.g. proposed in [BaCN92], capable of detecting all potential relationships and transform them into the graphic ER representation of the tool. Furthermore, if the tool can process the extension of the database to be re-engineered, the cardinalities of the relationships can be determined by simple rules. But it has to be considered that the usage of such rules may lead to wrong results. The main reasons for it are the evaluation of small data sets that do not cover all cases or the analysis of historical data producing incorrect findings. Considering the relationship in our universe of discourse between *division* and *subdivision*, before January 1 1993 one *division* was related with several *subdivisions*. After a reorganization of the company now there is a one-to-one relationship between both entity types. Because the corresponding table contains also the historical assignments due to book-keeping reasons an algorithm would deduce a one-to-many relationship which is not valid at present time.

In order to use the advantages of an automatic deduction of relationships it is desirable to mark the relationships as confirmed or proposed. The analysis is only finished after the verification of all relationships. Up to now there are no tools available providing this kind of interactive capabilities.

5.1.2 Support of Task Orders in DFDs

There are processes that have to be executed in a fixed order like batch jobs with several subroutines (processes). A technique has to be provided or the DFD methodology has to be enhanced to become capable of taking into account precedence relationships. Some mechanisms like task chain diagrams or event-driven process chains as they are available in the ARIS Toolset are good enhancements.

5.1.3 Support of Complexity and Modularity

Because of the complex system structure it is desirable to have facilities to create subsystems within subsystems. Assuming the ER diagram is the dominant conceptual model it is necessary to support the designer in decomposing ER diagrams in different views and to merge smaller diagrams containing common entities. View integration algorithms as proposed in [DaHw84] and [NaEL86] could be a good basis of tools supporting this functionality. The analysis of existing systems requires a modular approach which conflicts with the top-down approach supported by most tools. Because many CASE tools follow the top-down strategy no links between different subsystems can be drawn. Within the considered project logical links like input/output relations and common used data could not be ignored. A technique for logical links between different subsystems is still missing.

As already stated in section 4.1 there is a conflict of the organizational hierarchy vs. the application system hierarchy.

5.1.4 Detection of Synonyms

It is desirable to register synonyms in the tool. We found in the data structure of the CMIS many synonyms. Synonyms are caused by the integration of different subsystems, e.g. the ident number of the type selling unit identifies the same objects as they are stored in the production system identified by a material number. The hardest problem is to define detection algorithms because they require user-specific knowledge.

5.1.5 Global ERDs and Local ERDs

A global ERD is a part of the whole conceptual model that is frequently used in describing the structure of multiple data stores, for example master data and the product hierarchy. By way of contrast a local ERD is used by only one data store. A change of a global ERD has to be propagated to all ERDs where this global ERD has been used as a component. Figure 8 illustrates the use of a global ERD for the product hierarchy, used in various local ERDs. The global ERDs are marked in bold face.

The definition of global and local ERDs can not be described in a uniform way. Commonly, useful local ERDs are composed of one global ERD and directly adjacent entity types. Global ERDs model typically hierarchical master data or recurrent concepts.

When creating local and global ERDs it has to be considered that global ERDs are not only black boxes, i.e. it must be possible to establish relationships between entities inside and outside the global ERD that can be maintained by the data repository.

After modelling the DFDs and the attached ERDs of one subsystem a subsystem ERD could be generated automatically by merging local ERDs. Thus, local as well as global ERDs are parts of the project ERD. That makes it possible to use search algorithms as the basis of an object browser.

The concept of global and local ERDs serves the simplification of the modelling, the consistence maintenance after changes, a better control of complex ERDs and supports the modular procedure common in the current state analysis. A tool realizing this concept should provide the capability of merging single local ERDs to project or subsystem ERDs which leads to more clarity. Up to now there are no tools available supporting this concept.

5.2 Presentation

5.2.1 Interactive Data Repository Query Facilities

To support the DB administrator in changing the schema towards the target model in the re-engineering process it is necessary to have an "Interactive Data Repository Query Tool". While modelling or changing the data structure questions like "Which entities also contain this attribute ?", "In which relationships / subsystems does this entity occur ?" etc. arise very often. In case of erroneous queries or batch jobs[1] the DB administrator needs information about the participating tables and their relationships

Figure 8.a: DFD "*Get Tables of the product hierarchy*"

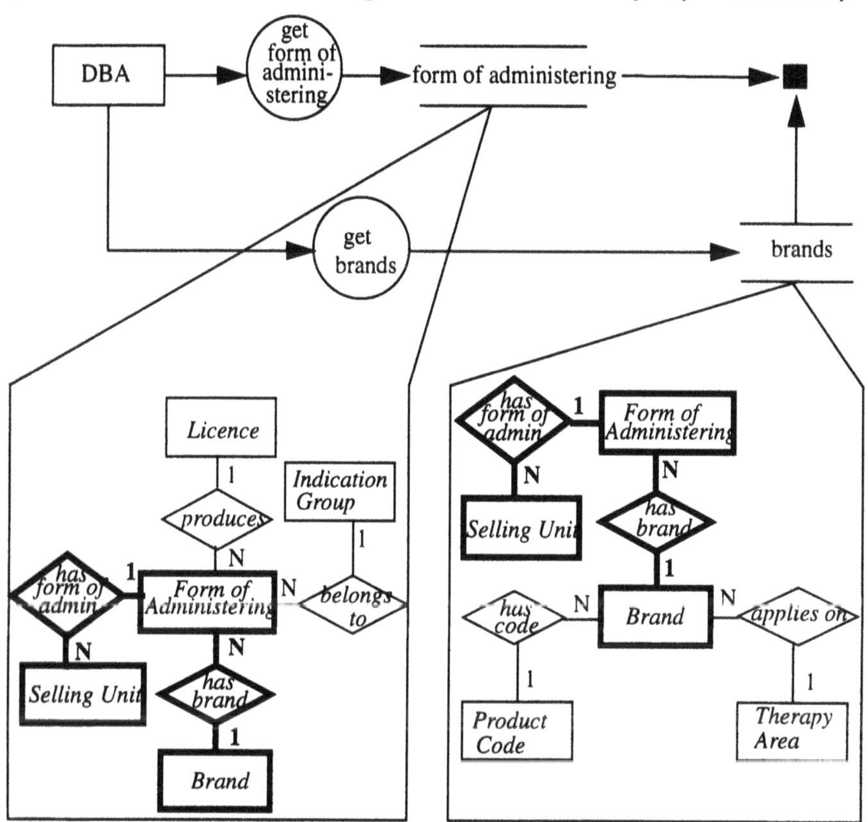

Figure 8.b: Local ERD "*Form of Administering*" **Figure 8.c:** Local ERD "*Brand*"

with other tables and the key attributes to assess the consequences of necessary changes. Furthermore, similar information is required for the integration of new batch jobs. CASE tools often provide only report components that do not allow interactive queries on the data dictionary / repository. Our experience shows that it is desirable to enhance documentation and analysis tools by interactive data repository query facilities as sketched above.

If a tool supports several views, e.g. data or process views, a navigation component should be available to traverse an object within different views in order to find out the connection with other objects. Simultaneous presentation of the various views with cross links among views would improve overall clarity. Unfortunately, none of the tools we analysed offers this feature.

1. Batch jobs handle most of the data transfers between the MIS and the other systems.

5.2.2 Requirements of the ER Model Representation

Complexity notation

We want to sketch some features that make an ER diagram more comprehensible according to our experience.
Many facts require the (min,max) notation to capture structural constraints between the modeled entities going beyond the cardinality definitions. In our model a *selling unit* is the unit of sale of a certain product or a certain brand. A *sample* is a free sample in the form of a selling unit that is, however, marked as sample not for sale. A selling unit is assigned at most n or even no samples. A sample is assigned at least one or n selling units, for example the sample "Biovital 50 ml" is used as sample for the selling unit "Biovital 50 ml" as well as for all other offered sizes.

Figure 9: Complexity Notation (Example)

Some design tools [ERwi95] use alternative notations that render readability difficult instead of the clear (min,max) notation.

Representation of relationships

The representation of relationships as diamonds facilitated the clearness of our models. Other notations like the representation in ERwin using edges to symbolize relationships lead to a tangled net of edges when more than 50 entity types are modelled. The ERwin tool only creates one ER diagram for each application system. In our CMIS case study that implies a diagram containing more than 200 entity types and around 800 edges (relationship types). Hence, subsystems have to be formed which is not supported by ERwin.

5.2.3 Storing Unstructured Information

When analysing data and processes it is desirable to keep information about objects (processes, entities) that can only be modeled as unstructured text. This information comprises general descriptions of objects or specific object information, such as its history or the old structure of a table that was changed. The old structure is a specific object information because it may be important for the understanding of old reports or queries. This information cannot easily be structured and has to be stored in so-called memo fields. The main drawback of memo fields is that they are costly to generate without being accessed later. Many tools provide the feature to store unstructured information with the definition of objects. However, unstructured information is rarely retrieved, because it is not visible. The proposal is to mark objects in the diagram (ERD, DFD) whether they carry unstructured information.

5.3 Treatment / Analysis of Current and Target System States

5.3.1 Support of a Dynamic Transition between Desired State and Current State

The long-term goal of the case study is to develop an enterprise-wide data and process model. Application systems are assigned to different subsystems. From the analysis of the current state a target model is derived which serves as a guideline in the decision making process. It must be decided how single modules, systems or subsystems within the target concept can be realized, either by standard software, by enhancing existing application systems or by proprietary solutions. The aim is to update the enterprise model in the future to document when a desired state has become a current state.

At present, the current state is documented in the first phase, the analysis phase, and the target state in the second phase, the architecture phase. Following the top-down approach the transition from the current to the target state is feasible. Once the target state has been realized, it becomes in fact a current state which has to be documented in the analysis phase. This kind of bottom-up shift is not foreseen in the I-CASE tool ISEE we used and in many others.

5.3.2 Analysis Tool with Respect to Current and Target States

Several tool vendors provide so-called analysis components. For example, the analysis component of the business re-engineering tool ARIS compares reference models with desired models derived from them. The result of the analysis is a comparison of single objects. The differences between original and derived model can comprise object changes, insertions or deletions and are displayed by graphical means.

CASE tools contain similar comparison components. They are based on a version comparison related to objects but are only available within one phase (the comparison result is printed as report).

In our case study the current and the desired state are split up into two phases. That implies a comparison component that works across both phases top-down and bottom-up. At the deduction of the desired state from the current state the object structures are affected. Only few application systems are stand-alone systems, most of them deal with interdependent data objects. Structure changes of these objects require propagation processes that guarantee a continuous communication with dependent systems.

6. Conclusion

Both data warehousing and business process re-engineering require a data re-engineering process which has been described in this paper. To develop the CMIS towards a data warehouse system the existing subsystems have to be analysed and described in a clear manner.

Within the re-engineering process a tool is needed, which supports the phase of documenting the current state of processes and data structures of an information system and provides help in deriving a target model from the generated documentation.

This paper addressed the issues of presentation, modelling and analysis techniques, which will ease the process of restructuring existing information systems and maintaining the system's documentation. Hence, the paper is supposed to encourage (motivate) business tool and I-CASE tool producers to develop a truly integrated and comprehensive process and data documentation and analysis tool that meets all requirements as mentioned above.

As far as we know there is no satisfying tool available. Most of our requirements are realized seperately by different software tools, but no tool combines all of them. The main reasons are:

- CASE tools provide most of the necessary techniques, but they always start from zero and strictly follow the top-down philosophy, which makes it impossible to describe an existing system because the analysis requires a modular procedure.
- The presentation of repository data in CASE tools can be considered as rather poor, because most of the time they only provide a more or less standard report interface.
- Business re-engineering and database design tools rarely support the decomposition of systems into subsystems, and a differentiation between current and target state is not intended. On the other hand they offer the necessary presentation techniques.
- Aspects like decomposition and merging of ERDs must be better supported.

Acknowledgements

We would like to thank Rhone-Poulenc Rorer, Cologne, for their support of the work of Marco Lehmbach while doing his Masters Thesis there.

References

[Bach88] Bachman C.: A CASE for Reverse Engineering, *IEEE Datamation*, July 1988.

[BaCN92] Batini C., Ceri S., Navathe S.B.: Conceptual Database Design: An Entity-Relationship-Approach, The Benjamin/Cummings Publishing Company, Inc., 1992, pp. 328-340.

[Chen76] Chen P.: The Entity Relationship Model - Toward a Unified View of Data, *ACM Trans. on Database Systems*, Vol. 1, No. 1 (March).

[ChBS94] Chiang R.H.L, Barron T.M., Storey V.C.: Reverse engineering of relational databases: Extraction of an EER model from a relational database, *Data & Knowledge Engineering*, Vol. 10, No. 12 (March).

[CoYo79] Constantine, Yourdon: Structured Design, Prentice Hall, Englewood Cliffs, N.J., 1979.

[DaHw84] Dayal U., Hwang H.: View definition and generalization for database integration in a multidatabase system, *IEEE Trans. Software Engineering*, Vol. 10, No. 6 (Nov.).

[ERwi95] Logic Works: Erwin Users Guide, 1995.

[HCTJ93] Hainaut J.-L., Chandelon M., Tonneau C., Joris M.: Schema Transformation Techniques for Database Reverse Engineering. In *Proc. of the 12th Int. Conf. on ER Approach,* 1993.

[UMIS93] Westmount Technology B.V.: ISEE User Manual 3.0, Delft, 1993.

[Lehm95] Lehmbach M.: Development of an enterprise-wide data model by analysis of existing applications, Masters thesis, Tech. Univ. Darmstadt, Dept. of Computer Science, 1995 (in German).

[NaEL86] Navathe S., Elmasri R., Larson J.: Integrating user views in database design, *IEEE Computer*, Vol. 19, No. 1 (Jan.).

[Prui93] Pruijt: Structured Analysis and Design with ISEE, Westmount Technology B.V., Delft, 1993.

[Royc70] Royce, W.: Managing the Development of Large Software Systems: Concepts and Techniques, IEEE Report R-77-320, 1970.

[Sche92] Scheer A.W.: Architecture of Integrated Information Systems, Springer Verlag, 1992 (in German).

[Somm92] Sommerville, I.: Software Engineering, Addison Wesley, Wokingham, 1992.

Developing an Information System using TROLL - an application field study *

M. Krone**, M. Kowsari, P. Hartel, G. Denker, H.-D. Ehrich

Technische Universität Braunschweig, Informatik, Abt. Datenbanken
Postfach 3329, D–38023 Braunschweig, Germany
e–mail: {M.Kowsari|P.Hartel|G.Denker|HD.Ehrich}@tu-bs.de

Abstract. In this paper we present a national project located in the area of computer aided testing and certifying (CATC) of physical devices. The objective of this project is to develop an Information System that supports the various activities of different user groups in a German federal institute of weights and measures. We decided to use formal methods right from the beginning of the project. Our approach is based on the formal object oriented specification language TROLL . Starting point of the development is an abstract model of the organization which will serve later on as a formal basis for implementation. We present parts of this specification and its relations with the underlying formal semantics. The experiences we made so far are rather positive and we expect further effects in the future.
keywords: object oriented specification, case study, information system, information modelling, requirements engineering, formal method

1 Introduction

The development of a large Information System is by far no trivial task. One main problem with it is to ensure "that we get what we want". In the past 25 years many suggestions have been made on how to tackle complex software engineering projects. However, there is no silver bullet yet [Bro87]. There is a small but growing community of people who propose and promote formal methods in Software Engineering [WL93, BH94]. Most times these people come from academia. The acceptance of formal methods in industry is still low. This is mainly due to the fact that formal methods are thought to be complex, hard to handle and not suitable for real world applications [GSW93].

In order to make formal methods attractive for industry they have to fulfill several requirements. They have to be easy to learn and to teach [Har95] [BS93]. In today's organizations we do not find many people who know formal methods [BH94]. This means we have to invest in their education. If this investment is

* Work reported here was partially supported by CEC under ESPRIT-II Basic Research Working Group No. 6112 COMPASS and by CEC under ESPRIT BRA WG 6071 IS-CORE, PTB, OBLOG SOFTWARE S.A. Lisbon.

** Now at Siemens AG, Transportation Systems, Systems Engineering, P.O.Box 3327, D-38023 Braunschweig, email:Maren.Krone@bwg4.erl1.siemens.net too high or people feel that they are not able to master the formalism then there will be a low chance of success. Formal methods have to be supported by tools (e.g. semantic editor, testing, prototyping) [Esp93]. The formalism allows us to build intelligent tools which allows us to speed up development drastically. Graphical representations help to overcome the fear of embarking on formalisms. Methodological guidelines [BS93] are another important issue for the acceptance of formal methods.

We present in this paper the use of formal methods for the development of an Information System in an industrial environment. The project is located in the area of computer aided testing and certifying (CATC) which is conducted by the federal institute of weights and measures of Germany. About 100 employees settled in three labs will use the system. When the project started in the beginning of 1994 no formal methods were applied. At the end of the year it got clear that the chance of success with the chosen approach was rather low [HS94]. At that time we decided to use a formal approach [KH95]. This paper presents the problem domain of our project and gives a brief introduction into the mathematical formalisms underlying our approach. It exemplifies the use of the method by presenting a small part of the development. After almost one year we have already collected several experiences, positive as well as negative ones. Furthermore, we will give some hints, why our first approach without formal methods did not succeeded.

The objective of the project is to develop an Information System that supports the activities of different user groups in the federal institute. Such activities are often called business processes [HJ95]. The complexity of the organization and the system that is supposed to support this organization is rather high. Besides, the system has to integrate already existing applications and re-specified ones. In order to be able to develop such a system we have to get a deep understanding of the organizational structures. This understanding is the prerequisite for deciding which part of the organization shall be computerized and how this system is embedded into the organization.

An abstract model of the organization can help us to achieve the required understanding. This model has to cover all aspects which are relevant with respect to the organizational activities. These aspects define what we call the Universe of Discourse (UoD).

Based on the UoD model we decide what will actually be supported by the Information System. The model defines the functional requirements of the later system. It abstracts from non-functional requirements, like technologies that shall be used for implementation.

A formal adequate method should allow for the modelling of the intended system on a high abstract level. Existing and widely accepted formal languages like Z [Spi89], VDM [Jon89] do not provide the right level of abstraction for modelling. Further on they emphasize on structural aspects and do not allow for an intuitive modelling of complex behavioral aspects. On the other hand there exist numerous formal approaches towards process modelling. Most of them either neglect the static aspects like CSP [Hoa85] or do not come with the concepts needed for Information Systems modelling.

Object orientation is a typical answer towards this problem. The object oriented paradigm recognizes as primary concept the object. An object allows for an intuitive presentation of real world entities and may reflect their behavioral and static properties. Methods like OMT [RBP+91] or "Object-Oriented Software Engineering" [Jac92] are quite popular. However, they miss the required formality. The project we are going to present started with such an informal method and did not achieve the desired results. This resulted in a loss of confidence in such informal approaches.

The solution of this dilemma can be the combination of formalisms and object oriented methods. Some formal specification languages have already object oriented extensions e.g., VDM++ [DK92], MooZ [MC90]. Even with this adaption of object orientation they still cope with a low level of abstraction.

We decided to apply the formal and object-oriented specification language TROLL [JSHS96]. The TROLL approach incorporates many ideas which have been developed over the past 8 years. Much work in the theoretical foundations [SSE87, ESS88, EJDS94, DE95, ES95] and on methodological [SJ92, SJH93, HJ95] issues has been done.

The TROLL approach supports the declarative specification of conceptual models. It integrates concepts for the modelling of dynamic, structural and process aspects. With the TBench [KHHS95] a specification tool for TROLL is available. The TROLL method [JWH+94] combines an intuitive diagrammatic notation with a textual one.

In this paper we introduce the problem domain, the Information System to be developed and our first experiences we made by using a formal approach. In the next section we give an introduction to the application field of the federal institute. Section 3 depicts an overview of the formalisms underlying our method. We introduce in Sect. 4 a small part of the conceptual model, some methodological guidelines and the relationship between the mathematical formalism and the conceptual model. Our first experiences are summed up in Sect. 5. We end the paper in Sect. 6 with future expectations and some conclusions.

2 Description of the problem domain

In this section we provide an introduction to the problem domain of our case study. We want to give some idea about important aspects of our specific application, the requirements of the intended system, and the complexity we have to deal with.

Our case study is located in the area of the Physikalisch-Technische Bundesanstalt[3] (PTB).

The PTB [JB87] is a federal institute for science and technology and the highest technical authority for metrology and physical safety engineering in Germany. Its tasks are research in physics and technology, realization and dissemination

[3] federal institute of weights and measures

of SI units [4], cooperation in national and international technical committees, physical safety engineering serving the protection against explosions etc.

The group 3.5 'explosion protected electrical equipment' is concerned with the testing and certifying of explosion proof electrical equipment. The basis are the European standards EN 50014-50028 [EN 78a, EN 78b]. Such equipment is allowed to be set into hazardous areas because it has been approved and certified due to European harmonized standards. The assessment procedure consists of testing the formal and informal documents, checking the design papers (i.e., technical drawings) and the tests which are carried out according to European standards. There are experimental tests such as explosion tests, flame propagation tests and thermal-electrical investigations. Currently, all steps which are necessary for this are carried out manually by the staff in charge and are worked out individually. About 100 employees settled in three labs of the group 3.5. are now concerned with testing and certifying.

On average 1000 certificates a year are issued. It is important that all informations in connection with a certificate are available and reusable at any time. Because of the huge amount of data a standardized archive and catalogue of all existing certificates of explosion proof equipment is planned which will be integrated in a software package called CATC (Computer Aided Testing and Certifying). The design and modelling of CATC is the long-term aim of the cooperation with the database group of TU Braunschweig started in 1994.

The technical constraints fixed by PTB for CATC are as follows: In order to support rapid communication between staff and operators on the one hand and between staff and the secretaries who are settled in different buildings on the other hand the group 3.5 is operating a local network. The employed client/server system (IBM LAN SERVER 4.0) supports database application programs. The database management system (DB2/2) is based on the relational model.

CATC has to support several different problem domains. As such it has to:

1. support *experimental test* like PRESSTEST JOINTTEST and others. JOINTTEST will serve as the case study of this paper, which will be introduced in detail in Sect. 4.
2. manage *basic administration data* and
3. allow for *design approval.*

Fig. 1 illustrates the hierarchical structure of the intended Information System.

The *administration* management includes the registration of formal information of the manufacturer, the settlement of accounts and legal matters. This information is essential for the following tests in the certification process and has to be permanently available.

The subsystem dealing with *design approval* includes the assessment of design papers for the equipment based on descriptions and its accordance with the European Standards. It provides the relevant clauses of the standards such that

[4] international system of units

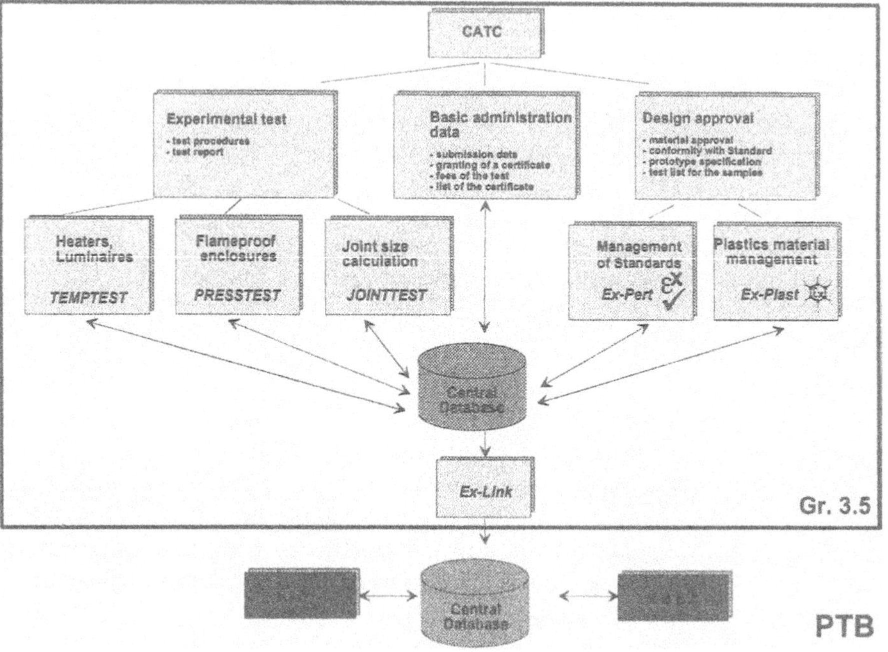

Fig. 1. CATC – Overview

the certification becomes more efficient. Required data can be carried out faster and easier at every desk.

The subsystem for the *experimental tests* performed by operators in the test lab stores all relevant data. The focus is to ensure that for example with flameproof enclosure the parts which potentially can ignite an explosive atmosphere are placed in an enclosure which can withstand the pressure developed during an internal explosion of an explosive mixture and which prevents the transmission of the explosion to the explosive atmosphere surrounding the enclosure. During the explosion every 0.2 second 30 kbyte data are produced. Thus, there is a conflict between hardware, which works in real time, and the multi-tasking operating system (OS/2).

CATC has via LAN access to the central database of the PTB, where common data are stored. There are further programs for administration (RBEZ[5], HASY[6]) which access that database (see Fig. 1, Ex-Link). CATC is not a standalone Information System but it has to be embedded in an existing environment. Besides, we have to deal with existing application programs which have to be re-specified (e.g., JOINTTEST) because they were erroneous. These re-specified parts have to be embedded in the new Information System structure. In addition, there is the link to the multiply accessed PTB wide database.

[5] archive and documentation application

[6] settlement and calculation application

To summarize, we have a safety-critical application area that comprises technical aspects as well as database aspects in a heterogeneous complex environment and that has to consider existing and re-developed applications.

3 A formal model for concurrent object systems

In this section we introduce our basic understanding of systems and objects. We give an introduction to the underlying semantic framework that serves for the formalization of system specifications.

Our intuitive understanding of concurrent object systems can be described as follows: An object system is composed of a number of concurrent objects. These objects are the *nodes* of the system. Every object describes a set of *sequential life cycles* which are sequences of *local actions* of the object. Objects may interact with each other, i.e., an object may call a local action of another object. Such a *global action* forces a synchronization of the participating objects, i.e., all local actions which compose the global action must occur simultaneously.

An object system describes a global web of local life cycles which are glued together at shared communication points. TROLL is a specification language that allows for the modelling of such concurrent object systems. The basic features of the language are:

- A *system specification* is a set of *data type*, *object type*, and *object class* specifications.
- *Parameterized data types* allow for the construction of new date types based on a fixed universe of predefined data types.
- An object type specification consists of a set of *attributes*, *actions* and *constraints*. Attributes describe the state of an object of that type and the actions determine the possible object evolution. Constraints allow for the definition of static and transitional invariants over the object state.
- Object types may be constructed over other object types (*aggregation*). Such types describe complex objects, i.e., objects which are composed of component objects. The specifications of the component objects are embedded into the specification of the aggregation. This allows us to define constraints over the aggregation, i.e., the objects in composition. It also enables the definition of local interactions inside the complex object. In this way we may construct complex local actions of the local actions of the object in composition. Thus, a local action of an aggregated object may consist of different local actions of its components.
- An object type may be the *specialization* of another object type. The specialized type may have additional properties to the inherited ones. Inheritance may be monotone. In this case we talk about save inheritance, i.e., all axioms being valid for an object of the supertype are always satisfied by an object of the subtype.
- Object classes are declared over object types. They describe the potential sets of objects in the system. Interactions between the objects of different classes describe the global synchronization relations.

The case study which will be introduced in Sect. 4 illustrates some of the language features. There we will explain the concepts in more detail.

Semantics is given to TROLL specifications using different techniques: the static structure of an object system is semantically described with algebraic methods, statements over object states are expressed with a logic calculus, the dynamic structure of the system, i.e., the systems evolution, is reflected via a temporal logic which is interpreted in terms of event structures. An exhaustive description of the model theory is given in [ES95]. In the following we intuitively explain these semantic ingredients. Moreover, in Sect. 4 the semantic notions are illustrated by example.

Static structures are needed to describe the state of objects. Such static structures are defined by data signatures and their algebraic interpretation. We assume a *data signature* $\Sigma_D = (S_D, \leq, \Omega_D)$ with a given number of data sorts S_D which are the predefined ones and the constructed sorts, a partial order on data sorts $\leq$, and data operations over these sorts Ω_D, whereby every constructed sort induces a number of operations. For instance, for the data sort `list` there are predefined operations `concat`, `append`, etc. The interpretation of such a signature is a Σ_D*-algebra*. In order to make statements over object states we adapt a logic calculus [Her95, GH91]. This calculus is especially suited in the domain of Information Systems since it provides powerful means to express queries over objects in a declarative way. It goes beyond this paper to explain all the features of this calculus. The interested reader is referred to [Her95, GH91].

In order to specify object systems we have to extend the data signature by sorts and operations which describe objects. For this purpose we introduce so-called *extended data signatures*. This signature extends the data sorts S_D by a special data sort S^i_O of *objects identities* and the data operations by S^a_O, the *object actions*. Thus, data terms are built over an extended data signature $\Sigma = (S, \leq, \Omega)$, $S = S_D \cup S^i_O \cup S^a_O$, $\Omega = \Omega_D \cup \Omega^i_O \cup \Omega^a_O$, which is the basis of data terms as well as identity and action terms, i.e., $i \in T_\Sigma(X)_{id}$ and $\alpha \in T_\Sigma(X)_{ac}$, respectively.

Skipping some technical details which can be found in [ES95] we arrive at a so-called *instance signature* $\Sigma_I = (Id, Ac)$, which consists of a set of identities Id representing all objects of the system, and a set of actions Ac_i for every object $i \in Id$. With the help of the case study which will be presented in the next section we illustrate these notions. Instance signatures will be the basis for constructing models in the framework of event structures. Up to this point we have covered all structural aspects of an object system description.

We introduce a temporal logic to deal with system dynamics. This logic is a first order predicate logic extended by two predicates on actions (*enabling* and *occurrence* of actions) and temporal operators for the future (*tomorrow* and *sometimes in the future*) and for the past (*yesterday* and *sometimes in the past*).

Let $\Sigma = (S, \leq, \Omega)$ be an extended data signature over an S-indexed family of sets of variables $X = \{X_s\}_{s \in S}$ and let $T_\Sigma(X)$ be the set of Σ data terms. The set of formulae L_Σ of the object logic is inductively defined as follows:

- if $t_1, t_2 \in T_\Sigma(X)_s$ then $t_1 =_{ss} t_2 \in L_\Sigma(X)$;
- if $\alpha \in T_\Sigma(X)_{ac}$ then $\rhd\alpha \in L_\Sigma(X)$ (enabled action) and $\odot\alpha \in L_\Sigma(X)$ (occurred action);
- if $\varphi, \psi \in L_\Sigma(X)$ and $x \in X_s$ then $\neg\varphi, \varphi \vee \psi, \exists x\ \varphi \in L_\Sigma(X)$;
- if $\varphi \in L_\Sigma(X)$ and $i \in T_\Sigma(X)_{id}$ then $\mathtt{X}_i\varphi \in L_\Sigma(X)$ (tomorrow), $\mathtt{F}_i\varphi \in L_\Sigma(X)$ (sometimes in the future), $\mathtt{Y}_i\varphi \in L_\Sigma(X)$ (yesterday), and $\mathtt{P}_i\varphi \in L_\Sigma(X)$ (sometimes in the past);

We will give some examples of formulas in Sect. 4 by translating our case study.

Instance signatures together with temporal logic formulas which describe the behavior of objects are interpreted over labelled event structures. Each node of an object system has a labelled sequential event structure as a model, and the object system is modelled by a concurrent labelled event structure built of the sequential event structures by event sharing. Thus, nodes have sequential models whereas concurrency comes into play in the object system.

A sequential event structure is a triple $E = (Ev, \rightarrow^*, \#)$, where Ev is a set of events, $\rightarrow^*$ is a partial order (causality), and $\#$ is a symmetric reflexive order (conflict). Moreover it satisfies three conditions: (1) there exists a unique, minimal element $\epsilon \in Ev$, (2) all configurations $\downarrow e := \{e' \mid e' \rightarrow^* e\}$ are totally ordered, and (3) $e\#e' \Leftrightarrow \neg(e \rightarrow^* e' \vee e' \rightarrow^* e)$ for all $e, e' \in Ev$.

Thus, a sequential event structure is a rooted tree where every branching point indicates conflict. Since conflict is a derived concept we denote sequential event structures by $E = (Ev, \rightarrow)$, where $\rightarrow^*$ is the reflexive transitive closure of the irreflexive step relation $\rightarrow$.

These sequential event structures are put together via event sharing to form concurrent event structures which are models of the system. In the system model concurrency arises and conflict remains to be local, i.e., $e\#f$ for $e, f \in Ev$ iff there is an object i and locally conflicting events $e', f' \in Ev_i : e'\#f'$ such that $e' \rightarrow^* e$ and $f' \rightarrow^* f$. Events are concurrent, $e\ co\ e'$, iff $\neg(e \rightarrow^* e' \vee e' \rightarrow^* e \vee e\#e')$.

Models of object systems are labelled event structures $\bar{E} = (E, \mu)$ which are built for locally sequential event structures E_i: $\bar{E} = \bigcup_{i \in Id}(E_i, \mu_i)$. The labelling function μ maps each event to a global action, i.e., set of local actions: $\mu : Ev \rightarrow \mathcal{P}_f^+(Ac)$, $\mu = \bigcup_{i \in Id} \mu_i$, $\mu_i : Ev_i \rightarrow Ac_i$.

In Sect. 4 we will come back to this. First we specify our case study and afterwards we will depict part of the model.

4 The case study

In Sect. 2 we described our problem domain. For illustrating the use of TROLL in the design of Information Systems, we focus on one part of the CATC system, namely JOINTTEST.

In the following we will describe in detail the relevant aspects. First we briefly explain some *technical notions* which are necessary for the specification. Then we will introduce the specific requirements of JOINTTEST especially the *process of* JOINTTEST. We exclude details of complex obligatory calculations, because it would go beyond the scope of this paper. Afterwards, we present the *modelling of the Universe of Discourse with* TROLL. The textual object oriented specification language TROLL comes along with the graphical notation OMTROLL. After a brief introduction to the development methodology of TROLL we partially present the design of the JOINTTEST. The specification of JOINTTEST which corresponds to the real world is much more complex than the restricted version we present in this paper. We restrict ourselves because of space limitations. Instead of explaining the whole complexity we rather give an intuitive specification of JOINTTEST explaining most of the concepts of TROLL and illustrating their use in requirements analysis and design specification.

The last part *semantics* will forge the link back to Sect. 3 by presenting parts of the semantics of the case study.

Technical Notions
The *flame proof-joint*, *joint* for short, is the place where corresponding surfaces of two parts of an enclosure come together and prevent the transmission of an internal explosion to the explosive atmosphere surrounding the enclosure [HO71].

In Fig. 2 we illustrate a test surrounding for flame proof joint tests. The main components to measure and estimate joints according to the standard given are the *width* and the *gap of a joint*. The width of a joint is the shortest distance from the inside to the outside of an enclosure. The gap of a joint is the distance between the corresponding surfaces when the electrical apparatus has been assembled. The prototype tests on flame proof is comprised of tests on the ability of the enclosure to withstand pressure and of tests on the non-transmission of an internal ignition. Therefore the enclosure is placed in a test chamber called autoclave and some explosive mixture is introduced into the enclosure.

The European Standard specifies the design of flame proof joints in detail. During the testing procedure it is important to compare the standards values of the widths and gaps of the joints with the applicants value resulting from the explosion tests.

Process of JOINTTEST
There are two groups: staff and operators who can manipulate joints. The applicant, i.e., the one who wants some device to be certified by PTB, sends the table of flame path joints (see Fig. 3). There are three different kinds of values:

- Columns 2-4 give the data according to EN 50018.
- Columns 5-8 include data according to construction drawings.
- The last three columns of the table are values resulting from tests.

The staff compares the data according to EN50018 with construction drawing and decides, whether the values are satisfactory. The operators verify the values provided by the applicant and report their results to the staff. The staff is responsible for the assessment of the values measured by the operator.

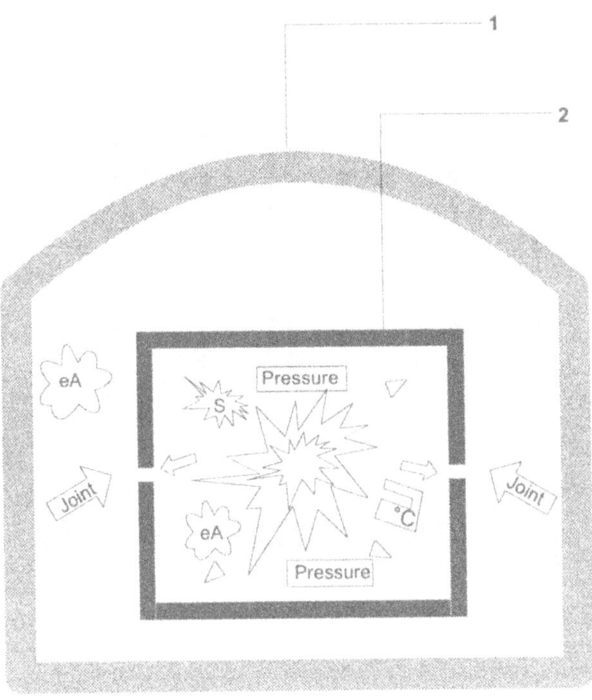

Fig. 2. Flame proof joint test, 1: autoclave , 2: enclosure, eA : explosion atmosphere, s: spark, $^{\circ}C$: surrounding temperature

Modelling the Universe of Discourse with TROLL
In Sect. 1 we mentioned the problems arising with developing huge Information Systems in complex organizational structures. Our method to overcome these problems is to specify the Universe of Discourse of the problem domain rather than the application program itself. The object oriented paradigm is well suited for this. Anyhow, one major problem in UoD modelling is the identification of the relevant objects. The process of finding them is a rather creative one and we believe that there do not exist prefixed rules for it. However, if an entity has been identified to be relevant, we can follow some methodological guidelines to build a model of it.

In order to elaborate a UoD model, the TROLL method integrates a number of diagrams which allow for a pictorial presentation of static and dynamic aspects of the model. These diagrams are easy to understand and therefore well suited for discussing the essential aspects of the system with the client. Thus, we use TROLL in the requirements analysis to fix the functional requirements. Due to the formalism the usual misunderstandings between the developer and the client in what the system really shall do can be diminished. Even in the case when the client does not yet know, what he wants, the formalism helps him and the

	Data acc. to EN 50 018 - 1977/ VDE 0171			all to construction drawing						test sample		
Joint	Minimum length of joint	Distance l (for bores within flamepath)	Maximum width of joint i_K (flat, combined, cyclindric, bearinggap and actuationsgap)	Width of joint L (c+d)	Distance l (a+b)	Size of diameter with ISO-symbol for internal and outside measurement	Dimensions (acc. to DIN 7160, DIN 7161)	Constructional width of gap = difference of diameter between bore and cyclindric bore: min.	max. $= i_c$	Length of joint L	Distance l	Width of testing gap i_E
K1	12.5		0.15	140	-	7.5+00.5 / 7.45-0.05		0.05	0.15	15.42	7.57 / 7.333	0.225
K2	12.5		0.15	141	-	7.5+00.5 / 7.45-0.05		0.051	0.148	15.43	7.57 / 7.333	0.227

Fig. 3. Table of flame path joints

developer in understanding the general setting of the problem domain.

The diagrams also model different aspects like communication, object composition and hierarchies etc. of the system. The textual representation in TROLL syntax is the result of the design specification stage. There is a smooth boundary between these two life cycles and therefore we prefere the database terminology of conceptual design (fixing the functional requirements, UoD) and logical design (textual representation of the model in TROLL syntax). Together they form an evolutional software engineering process consisting of iterations of analysis and design stages.

The following enumeration gives a short overview about the different diagrams textual notation respectively and their usage:

1. The *Community Diagram* (see Fig. 4) defines the static structure of the system. It consists of all object types, their composition and inheritance hierarchies, specialization and aggregation of object types and is the first raw design of the system. As such, it provides a simple and intuitive means to illustrate the structure of the system. The notation is quite similar to OMT and was adapted to TROLL [JWH+94].
2. The next step is to define an *Object Declaration Diagram* (see Fig. 5) for each object type of the community diagram in order to declare its actions and attributes. The attributes are declared by their signature, i.e., name plus optional parameters, and optional classifications (e.g. derived, history, optional, constant). The actions are declared by an identifier and a list of parameters.

3. With the *Object Behavior Diagram* (see Fig. 6) one can define explicitly the lifecycle of an object. The nodes represent the states of an object. The edges represent state transitions and are labelled with the action that causes the state transition. Additionally, constraints can be attached to the state transitions. The diagram is pretty much like state charts of Harel [Har88].
4. Then the *Object Communication Diagram* (see Fig. 7) depicts the communication between object types. A set of interactions may be declared for each action and constraints for each occurrence of an action. These diagrams can be compared to Fusion diagrams [CAB+94].
5. Finally the *Data Type Diagram* represents user defined data types over standard data types.
6. The result of the design is always a textual description in the TROLL syntax. It can now be written down and comprises the details represented in the figures. This is only a frame of the system specification which has to be refined by defining additional constraints, updates, ...

Please keep in mind, that there are usually several iterations of the following described process.

We start our specification of the UoD of JOINTTEST with the Object Community Diagram of JointNode which is depicted in Fig. 4. In this part of CATC we deal with the six object types: `JointNode`, `JointTable`, `Joint`, `ExpJointPart`, `ConstJointPart` and `JointPart`.

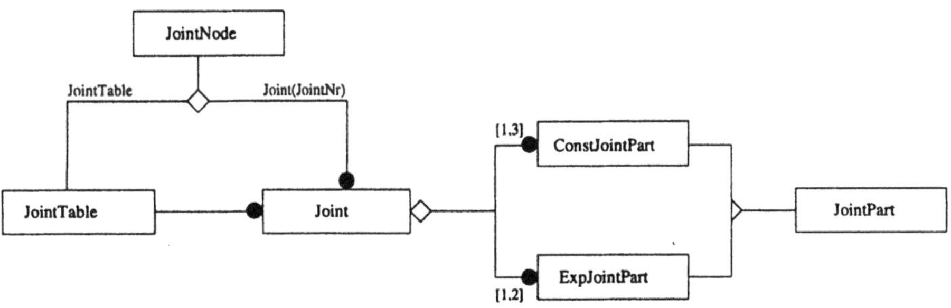

Fig. 4. Object Community Diagram of `JointNode`[7]

`JointNode` is the object type that depicts the special part of CATC concerning joint tests. In this universe we have joints and joint tables. We simplified the specification because of space limitation to one joint table and several joints. 1-n relationships between objects are shown as lines with filled circles at the object type which might occur more than ones. The diamond stands for aggregation of object types and the triangle is the diagrammatic notion for specialization. Thus `JointNode` is an aggregation of one `JoinTable` and one or more `Joints`. Joints

[7] Do not confuse the word table with relational database table.

can be constructed of several parts, a constructive part (**ConstJointPart**) and an experimental part (**ExpJointPart**). The constructive part is concerned with comparing data according to the standard with data according to the construction drawing (see Sect. 4, Process of JOINTTEST). The experimental part deals with the results of test measurement. Up to five parts can belong to one joint which form one row in the table of flame path joints (see Fig. 3). There may be one to three constructive parts and one to two experimental parts. The object type **JointPart** depicts a specialization, which consists of those attributes and actions, the constructive and experimental parts have in common.

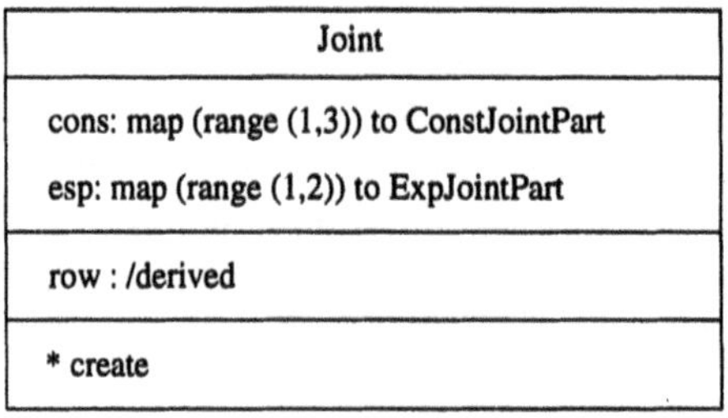

Joint
cons: map (range (1,3)) to ConstJointPart esp: map (range (1,2)) to ExpJointPart
row : /derived
* create

Fig. 5. Object Declaration Diagram of **Joint**

Now we can refine each component of the JointNode and represent it by Object Declaration Diagrams. The diagram for the object joint is represented in Fig. 5.

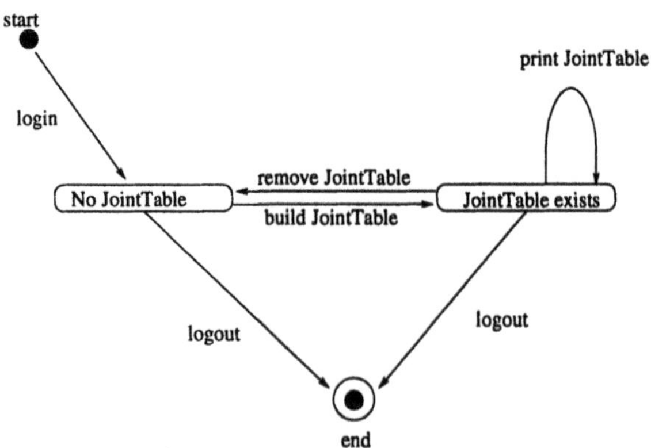

Fig. 6. Object Behavior Diagram of the staff

The behavior of the staff is illustrated in Fig. 6. A staff object is born by login and by it she is in the "NoJointTable" state. This is the beginning of the lifecycle of the object. A staff object may logout immediately after login and by this she will leave the system. Therefore, logout is the *death* action of a staff object and terminates a life cycle. After a login a staff object may build a joint table. By this action the life cycle state changes to the "JointTable exists" state. Now she can work with the joint table, e.g., print it or do other things not specified here. From this life cycle state a staff object may logout or remove the joint table. The latter action will change back to the life cycle state where no joint table exists.

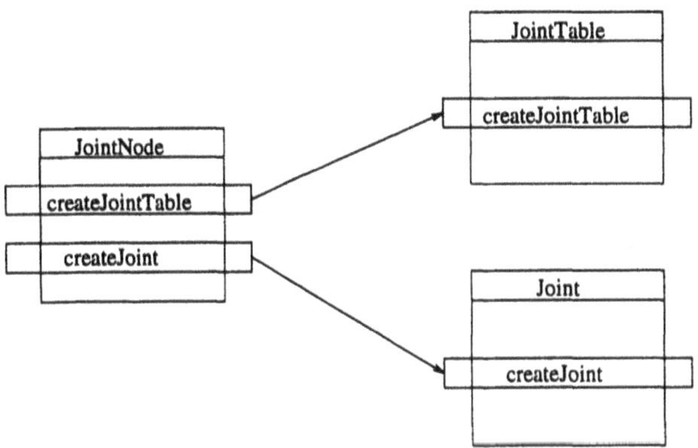

Fig. 7. Object Communication Diagram between `JointNode`, `JointTable` and `Joint`

The communication between object type JointNode and object types JointTable and Joint is depicted in Fig. 7. The action createJoint of object type JointNode corresponds directly to a createJoint action of the object type Joint. The action createJointTable of object type JointNode corresponds to a createJointTable action of object type JointTable. Here the simplification we made is easy to see: in the real world specification of JOINTTEST usually the relations between actions are more complex.

Now we can start with the last step of our specification procedure by collecting all developed details of the figures and constructing TROLL frames which can be enhanced by further details.

```
object type JointNode
uses JointTable, Joint, ...
components
    Joint(nr:int) : Joint
    JointTable : JointTable
attributes JNr: int initial 1
actions
   new  birth
   createJoint  calls Joint(JNr).create
                updates JNr:=JNr+1
   createJointTable calls JointTable.create
end
```

We start with object type `JointNode`. There are two components: A joint node has several joints which are identified by a number (`Joint(nr:int)`) and a joint table (`JointTable`) as components. Moreover, an attribute `JNr` is specified to save the current joint number. The initial value of the attribute is `1`. Thus, after a JointNode has been born by `new`, `JNr` has value `1`. There are two actions specified, one for creating joints another one for creating a joint table. The former one takes the current joint number `JNr`, calls synchronously the *birth* action in `Joint` and assigns the new joint to the name `Joint(JNr)`. These *birth* actions are specified in the corresponding object types, i.e., `JointTable` and `Joint`, respectively.

```
object type JointTable
uses Joint
attributes Joints : listOf Joint
actions
   create birth;
   insertJoint(j:Joint) = updates Joints:= append(Joints,j)
end
```

The object type `JointTable` has a list of joints as attributes. These are object-valued attributes. In contrast to components, object-valued attributes do not belong to `JointTable`, instead they are readable from `JointTable`. In this sense object-valued attributes are links to other objects such that their attributes can be read and used for some computations. `JointTable` has a list of joints as attributes. Besides the *birth* action there is one action specified to append new joints to this list, i.e., to append further links. `insertJoint` is the action which takes a joint as parameter and appends this joint to the list `Joints`.

Before we specify `Joint` we introduce the object types `ConstJointPart` and `ExpJointPart`, as well as the generalization of both `JointPart`. Object type `JointPart` comprises all attributes which are also part of the specializations. Every joint has a `gap`, a `width`, and further attributes named `a`, `b`, etc. See the table of flame path joints in Fig. 3 where these attributes appear.

```
object type JointPart
uses real ...
attributes
    gap, width, a, b ... : real
actions
     ...
end
```

The object types `ConstJointPart` and `ExpJointPart` are specializations of `JointPart` which have further attributes. The inheritance relation is monotone. That means, that we carry over all axioms of the supertype into the subtype. The behavior of the subtype is in full compliance with that of the supertype. For our case study, we specialize `JointPart` to `ConstJointPart` which has a derived attribute:

```
object type ConstJointPart
inherits JointPart  monotone
attributes
   l : real derived (a+b);
actions
     ...
end
```

Now we come to object type Joint:

```
object type Joint
uses ConstJointPart, ExpJointPart, ...
components
    cons : map (range (1,3)) to ConstJointPart
    exp  : map (range (1,2)) to ExpJointPart
attributes
    row : listOf(record(a: real,..., l: real))
          derived
           concat(toList(select jp.a, jp.b, jp.width, jp.gap, jp.l
                            from jp in range(cons)),
                  toList(select jp.a, jp.b, jp.width, jp.gap, 0.0
                            from jp in range(exp)))
actions
   create birth
end
```

An object of type Joint has up to five components. Three components are constructive joint parts and another two are experimental joint parts. The former ones are those which will be derived from the construction drawings, whereas the latter are fixed by explosion test done by the operators in the labs. There is an attribute called `row` for joints. This attribute corresponds to one row of the table of flame path joints in Fig. 3. The sort of this attribute is quite complex. This is due to the fact that in `row` the information of all components are collected. We specified a `select` statement to extract this information and exploited this way the logic calculus which provides concepts for querying object states. We explain this by starting from the innermost select clauses: The select clause returns a bag of records. Each record incorporates five real numbers representing `width`, `gap`, etc. of one joint. We query the constructive joints as well as the experimental joints. We get all joints by the implicitly defined operation `range` for maps. `Range` gives the set of all elements of the co-domain of a map. Here, `range(cons)` delivers all constructive joint parts. We select the values of the attributes and transform the bag to a list. To be able to concatenate experimental and constructive joint part list, we introduced 0.0 as l value of ExpJointPart. The result of this concatenation is one `row`.

Up to now we only specified object types. Thus, we still have no instances of the object types. Those will be generated by specifying object classes. For space limitations we simplify our sets of instances such that we have one object of type `staff` and one object of type `JointNode`. The TROLL specification of `staff` corresponds to the behavior diagram in Fig. 6.

```
object type staff
actions
    login birth
    newJoint
    buildJointTable
end

object class Manager:staff
      interactions
         Manager.newJoint calls JN.createJoint
         Manager.buildJointTable calls JN.createJointTable
end
object class JN:JointNode    end
```

We showed a part of the specification of the UoD of `JointNode`. We abstracted from a lot of details because of space limitations. Though we illustrated the use of TROLL for specifying Information Systems of industrial size, especially, we explained the adequacy of its concepts. Besides the expressive power one of the main advantages of our approach is the well-defined semantics.

Semantics
We will define the semantics of our case study in terms of the notions given in Sect. 3. According to Sect. 3 we will reflect the statical part of the system through an extended data signature. Each object type in the diagram establishes an object sort $b \in S_O$. For instance, we have as object sorts `JointNode, JointTable, Joint, ConstJointPart, ...` $\subseteq S_O$. In Sect. 3 we pointed out that each object sort gives rise to two data sorts, i.e., object identities S^i_O and object actions S^a_O. The former are fixed by the *object class* definitions. Thus, `Manager`$\in$ `Manager`^{i} and `JN`$\in$ `JointNode`^{i}. Each object will constitute a node in the system and each node will be interpreted by a sequential event structure. We will later come back to this. Object actions are given by the specification, i.e., we have `createJoint, createJointTable` $\in$ `JointNode`^{a}.

Passing some technical details which can be found in [ES95] we arrive at an *instance signature* $\Sigma_I = (Id, Ac)$ with

$$\begin{aligned} Id &= \{\texttt{Manager}, \texttt{JN}\} \\ Ac_{\texttt{Manager}} &= \{\texttt{newJoint}, \texttt{buildJointTable}\} \\ Ac_{\texttt{JN}} &= \{\texttt{new}, \texttt{createJoint}, \texttt{createJointTable}, \\ &\qquad \texttt{Joint(1).create}, \texttt{Joint(2).create}, \ldots, \\ &\qquad \texttt{JointTable.create}, \texttt{JointTable.insertJoint(Joint(1))}, \ldots\}. \end{aligned}$$

So far we only reflected the statical part of the specification. TROLL features like *calls*, *updates* determine the behavior of objects of the corresponding type.

To cover the behavior formally we use temporal logic. For illustration purposes we translate parts of `JointNode` into temporal formulas. A *birth* action can only take place at the beginning of an object life cycle. After it has occurred it cannot be executed for the rest of the object life. Thus, we receive for every object `O` of type `JointNode`, $\mathtt{O} \in \mathtt{JointNode}^i$, $\mathtt{x} \in \mathtt{int}$ the following formula

$$\mathtt{O} : \odot\mathtt{new} \Rightarrow \mathtt{F}_{\mathtt{O}} \neg \rhd \mathtt{new}.$$

The formula asserts that whenever the *birth* action has occurred, in the future it will never be enabled.

All other actions are enabled after the execution of the *birth* actions. The following formula reflects this:

$$\mathtt{O} : \odot\mathtt{new} \Rightarrow \rhd\mathtt{createJoint} \wedge \rhd\mathtt{createJointTable}.$$

The *updates* part of the specification intuitively expresses, that after the occurrence of a `createJoint` action attribute `JNr` is increased by one. Therefore, whenever it was possible to read a value `n` for the attribute in a previous state, and when action `createJoint` happened in the current state, it must be possible to read the value `n+1` for the attribute. The reading of attributes is expressed via an action `r`.

$$\mathtt{O} : \mathtt{Y}_{\mathtt{O}} \rhd \mathtt{JNr.r(x)} \wedge \odot\mathtt{createJoint} \Rightarrow \rhd\mathtt{JNr.r(x+1)}$$

The local interaction between components of `JointNode` is translated into the following formula:

$$\mathtt{O} : \odot\mathtt{createJoint} \Rightarrow \odot\mathtt{Joint(x).create} \wedge \mathtt{JNr.r(x)}.$$

That means, whenever a joint is created with a specific number synchronously the *birth* action has to take place in the corresponding component.

The global interaction between `Manager` and `JointNode` corresponds to:

$$\mathtt{Manager} : \odot\mathtt{newJoint} \Rightarrow \odot\mathtt{JN.createJoint}.$$

We only illustrated the translation of some TROLL concepts to temporal logic formulas.

Now we are able to explain the interpretation structures. Models for single objects are sequential event structures. In Fig. 8 we depicted parts of the models of `Manager` and `JN`. Events are framed and labelled with the actions which occur. Lines between events denote causality.

Each branch of a sequential event structure is a possible run of the corresponding object. For `JN` the following life cycles are depicted. After the creation of `JN` either a new joint is created or a joint table is created. In the former case two actions take place concurrently. This corresponds to the interaction rule specified for `createJoint` in `JointNode`. Analogously, the `createJointTable` takes place together with the *birth* action in the corresponding component. After the creation of the joint table, joints may inserted. Similarly, after the creation of a joint further actions may take place.

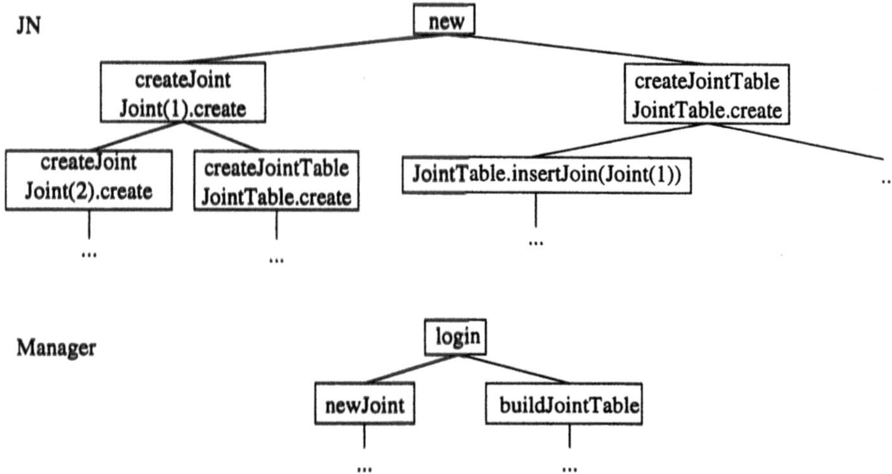

Fig. 8. Sequential event structures of nodes

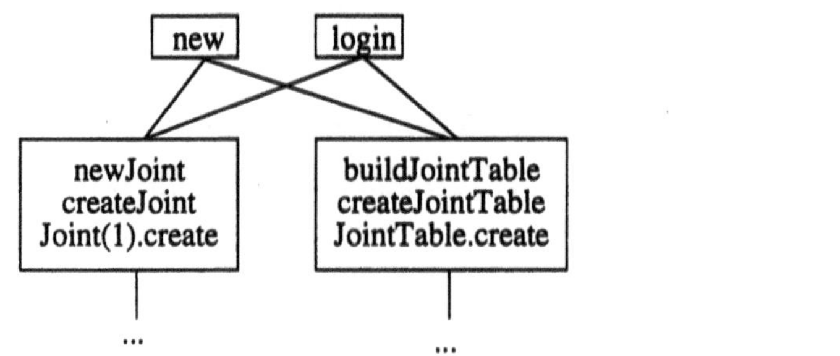

Fig. 9. Concurrent event structure

For `Manager` we specified the beginnings of two life cycles. After the object has been created, a manager may build a new joint table or a new joint.

In sequential event structures events are either causally related or in conflict. There is no concurrency in sequential models. Concurrency comes into play when these sequential event structures are put together to form a concurrent event structure via shared events. For instance, in Fig. 9 we illustrate how this is done. After the concurrent creation of both objects `JN` and `Manager` either the manager may create a new joint and by this calls the `createJoint` action of `JN`, which again calls `Joint(1).create`. Thus, three actions take place concurrently, one of the object `manager` and another two of the compound object `JN`. Analogously, the right branch in Fig. 9 represents the life cycle, where after the concurrent creation of both objects a joint table is built. To summarize, in Fig. 9 the creation events are concurrent, whereas the other two events are in conflict and therefore, denote different possible runs.

5 Experiences

The project we described in this paper is in its initial state. We are still in the phase of modelling the Universe of Discourse of CATC. However, we made already several positive experiences.

The first attempts of managing the project with a popular object oriented analysis and design method [HS94] failed. The team that is developing the system is composed of students and full-time employees. Students did not just have to cope with implementation tasks, they were also involved in the modeling of the system. Since they typically stay for 6 months in the project we had a high personal fluctuation. Students that left the team took a lot of knowledge that was supposed to be documented in their models with them. This was the information supposed to be giving the semantics of the models. Due to the informality there was no common understanding of many models and a lot of things had to be discussed over and over again whenever new people entered the project. This was one of the major reasons for us to restart the project following a formal approach. It turned out to be much less critical when members leave the project. The documentation they leave is less ambiguous.

The current team developing the system is now composed of 11 students and three full-time employees. All team members have similar backgrounds (computer science, mathematics) and therefore use the same terminology. One employee is settled in the federal board and fortunal has a background of computer science and of the problem domain. The two other employees are settled in the university with special interests in formal methods and mathematics. But none of the students had knowledge about TROLL , so we trained them in a special TROLL seminar taking place every two weeks at the very beginning. Both employees at the university are TROLL specialists and one of them is the designer of additional TROLL concepts. He spent a lot of time on answering to specific questions, the students had.

An advantage often mentioned in relation with formal method is the possibility to verify correctness. The verification issue is not of central importance in our project.

The project is located in an federal institute but many developers are students. These students have to communicate with staff member respectively operators. The gap between students and federal board employees in their understanding of technical and administrational processes is evident. Therefore it was important to improve the communication skills. Here especially the support by diagrammatic notations had proven valuable and was confirmed by all project members. The diagrams are based on concepts well known in computer science e.g., entity/relationship diagrams (community diagram), finite automata (behavior diagram) or programming languages (textual representation of TROLL). Indeed, both the diagrams and the TROLL text were intuitive for students as well as for federal board employees. Furthermore the fact that they had to develop with TROLL and thus were compelled to formalize their ideas, brought out a lot of misunderstanding in early stages. Here we had to handle the usual problem, that the federal board employees had some ideas about what the needed in general but not in all details. We had long term discussions about the overall model and this lead in our opinion to a quite good understanding of the general setting of the PTB world.

The specification phase is an iterative process since the discovered misunderstandings came up gradually. Here more tool support is necessary. Re-specifying is an important part of the work and re-doing already developed parts over and over is disappointing enough. Tool support turned out to be one key factor in order to avoid frustration when having to change a model again.

Roughly spoken the specification is twofold: First we dealt with more general aspects by developing the diagrams and secondly we attacked more fine grain problems with the textual notation. This involves two different views of the world, a global and a detailed one. The advantage is that we achieve first a rather stable global view before we consider details. Changes to the finer grained specification documents did not affect the global view.

Most probably the project will move from a pure national one to an international one. This turned out just recently. If this happens, we hope to have a high degree of reuse. Since most business facts and rules are formalized we expect that we can easily adapt our models to this new dimension of the problem domain. This potential future may prove the strategical advantage of our choice of a formal approach.

The specification phase which we have already left behind, has much clarified our minds and helped us to understand what should be implemented. We are still working on the implementation at the moment. About 40000 of C++ code whith 100 object classes resulting from 5000 lines of TROLL have been written so far. That makes a factor of 1:8.

For the next steps we expect little problems with the how and we are almost sure that "we get what we want", due to the fact, that we solved the question of "what to do" in the specification phase. Of course we will have to deal with minor programming errors in the currently coding phase. But these are not the typical problems that result in a failure of the project.

As soon as the first user interface windows are compiled, we can test and verify the functionality of the system and thus compare wether our assumptions meet reality.

6 Conclusions and Outlook

In this paper we presented a field-study where we applied the formal specification language TROLL to the modelling of an Information System of a rather reasonable size.

In the previous sections we introduced the industrial context of our application domain, picked one small part out of it and illustrated the specification of it. We said less about the implementation issues and the integration of existing and re-specified applications since the project is still in its initial state. We are sure that the next stages will bring up much more details and worthy information with respect to these subjects.

Furthermore we think about an automatic generation of application programs or frames from specifications. First steps in that directions have already been made, e.g., an approach to generate a relational database model from TROLL specifications [Dan95] has been developed.

Tool support is crucial for the success of big projects. We do not yet have the support we wished to have. The project lead to a vast list of requirements for adequate tool support. Most important are tools that allow for a fast change of specification documents while ensuring the consistency of the whole project. For presentation and discussion of the models we need documentation support. These documents have to show different views of the models. An example for a specification environment is the OBLOG workbench [Esp93]. Besides providing comfortable support for the modelling of systems based on a mathematical formalism, it facilitates the generation of end applications which serve for model validation. Unfortunately, our system platform made it impossible for us to use this environment.

The reification from specification to implementation is one objective we want to reach in the near future. The first theoretical results have been developed [DE95]. We hope that future developments will provide us with a basis for a practical reification method that allows for error free implementations of specifications.

References

[BH94] J.P Bowen and M.G. Hinchey. Seven More Myths of Formal Methods: Dispelling Industrial Prejudices. In M. Naftalin, T. Denvir, and M. Bertrani, editors, *FME'94: Industrial Benefit of Formal Methods*, pages 105–117. LNCS 873, Springer, Berlin, 1994.

[Bro87] F.P. Brooks. No Silver Bullet – Essence and Accidents of Software Engineering. *IEEE Computer*, 20(4):10–19, Apr. 1987.

[BS93] J. Bowen and V. Stavridou. The Industrial Take-up of Formal Methods in Safety-Critical and Other Areas: A Perspective. In *[WL93]*, pages 183–195, 1993.

[CAB+94] D. Coleman, P. Arnold, S. Bodoff, S. Dollin, H. Gilchrist, F. Hayes, and P. Jeremes. *Object-oriented Development - The Fusion Method.* Prentice-Hall, 1994.

[Dan95] C. Danker. Transformation of TROLLobject specifications into schema of relational databases. Diploma Thesis at Techn. Univ. Braunschweig, 1995.

[DE95] G. Denker and H.-D. Ehrich. Action Reification In Object Oriented Specification. In R. J. Wieringa and R. B. Feenstra, editors, *Information Systems - Correctness and Reusability, Selected Papers from the IS-CORE Workshop*, pages 103–118. World Scientific, 1995.

[DK92] E.H. Dürr and J.v. Katwijk. VDM++, A formal specification language for object-oriented design. In *Proceedings of TOOLS7 (Technology of object-oriented languages and systems).* Prentice-Hall, 1992.

[EJDS94] H.-D. Ehrich, R. Jungclaus, G. Denker, and A. Sernadas. Object-Oriented Design of Information Systems: Theoretical Foundations. In J. Paredaens and L. Tenenbaum, editors, *Advances in Database Systems, Implementations and Applications*, pages 201–218. Springer Verlag, Wien, CISM Courses and Lectures no. 347, 1994.

[EN 78a] *VDE: EN 50014 Elektrische Betriebsmittel für explosionsgefährdete Bereiche - Allgemeine Bestimmung.* VDE-Verlag, 1978.

[EN 78b] *VDE: EN 50018 Elektrische Betriebsmittel für explosionsgefährdete Bereiche - druckfeste Kapselung 'd'.* VDE-Verlag, 1978.

[ES95] H.-D. Ehrich and A. Sernadas. Local Specification of Distributed Families of Sequential Objects. In E. Astesiano, G. Reggio, and A. Tarlecki, editors, *Recent Trends in Data Types Specification, Proc. 10th Workshop on Specification of Abstract Data Types joint with the 5th COMPASS Workshop, S.Margherita, Italy, May/June 1994, Selected papers*, pages 219–235. Springer, Berlin, LNCS 906, 1995.

[Esp93] Espirito Santo Data Informatica, Lisbon. *OBLOG CASE V1.0 - The User's Guide*, 1993.

[ESS88] H.-D. Ehrich, A. Sernadas, and C. Sernadas. Abstract Object Types for Databases. In K. R. Dittrich, editor, *Advances in Object-Oriented Database Systems*, pages 144–149, Bad Münster am Stein, 1988. LNCS 334, Springer, Berlin, 1988.

[GH91] M. Gogolla and U. Hohenstein. Towards a Semantic View of an Extended Entity-Relationship Model. *ACM Transactions on Database Systems*, 16(3):369–416, 1991.

[GSW93] T. Günther, K.-D Schewe, and I. Wetzel. On the Derivation of Executable Database Programs from Formal Specifications. In *[WL93]*, pages 351–366, 1993.

[Har88] D. Harel. On visual formalisms. *Communications of the ACM*, 31(5):514–530, 1988.

[Har95] T. Hartmann. *Entwurf einer Sprache für die verhaltensorientierte konzeptionelle Modellierung von Informationssystemen.* Reihe DISBD. infix-Verlag, Sankt Augustin, 1995. *To appear.*

[Her95] R. Herzig. *Zur Spezifikation von Objektgesellschaften mit TROLL light.* Fortschritt-Berichte Reihe 10, Nr. 336. VDI-Verlag, Düsseldorf, 1995.

[HJ95] P. Hartel and R. Jungclaus. Modeling Business Processes over Objects. *Int. Journal of Intelligent and Cooperative Information Systems*, 1995. *To appear.*

[HO71] W. Wettisch H. Olenik, H. Rentzsch. *Handbuch für den Explosionsschutz.* W.Girardet, Zürich, 1971.

[Hoa85] C. A. R. Hoare. *Communicating Sequential Processes.* Prentice-Hall, Englewood Cliffs, NJ, 1985.

[HS94] T. Hohnsbein and H. Schafiee. *Reengineering des Programms DRUCKMESS in der PTB.* Doppelstudienarbeit an der Universität Braunschweig, Abt.Datenbanken, 1994.

[Jac92] I. Jacobson. *Object-Oriented Software Engineering.* Addison-Wesley, Reading, MA, 1992.

[JB87] H. Rechenberg J. Bortfeld, W. Hanser. *100 Jahre Physikalisch-Technische Reichsanstalt/Bundesanstalt 1887-1987.* VCH Verlagsgesllschaft, München, 1987.

[Jon89] C.B. Jones. *Systematic Software Development using VDM.* Prentice-Hall, Englewood Cliffs, NJ, 1989.

[JSHS96] R. Jungclaus, G. Saake, T. Hartmann, and C. Sernadas. TROLL - A Language for Object-Oriented Specification of Information Systems. *ACM Transactions on Information Systems*, 1996. *To appear.*

[JWH+94] R. Jungclaus, R.J. Wieringa, P. Hartel, G. Saake, and T. Hartmann. Combining TROLL with the Object Modeling Technique. In B. Wolfinger, editor, *Innovationen bei Rechen- und Kommunikationssystemen. GI-Fachgespräch FG 1: Integration von semi-formalen und formalen Methoden für die Spezifikation von Software*, pages 35–42. Springer, Informatik aktuell, 1994.

[KH95] M. Kowsari and P. Hartel. Ein Fallbeispiel zur Evaluation einer Objektorientierten Methodik. In C. Eckert, H.J. Klein, and T. Polle, editors, *7. Workshop Grundlagen von Datenbanken*, pages 88–93. Universität Hildesheim Institut für Informatik, Juni 1995.

[KHHS95] J. Kusch, P. Hartel, T Hartmann, and G. Saake. Gaining a Uniform View of Different Integration Aspects in a Prototyping Environment. In *Proc. 6th Int. Conf. on Database and Expert Systems Applications (DEXA'95)*, pages 38–47. Springer Verlag, Berlin, LNCS 978, 1995.

[MC90] S.L. Meira and A.L.C. Cavalcanti. Modular Object-Oriented Z Specifications. In *Z User workshop, Oxford*. Springer-Verlag, 1990.

[RBP+91] J. Rumbaugh, M. Blaha, W. Premerlani, F. Eddy, and W. Lorensen. *Object-Oriented Modeling and Design*. Prentice-Hall, Englewood Cliffs, NJ, 1991.

[SJ92] G. Saake and R. Jungclaus. Specification of Database Applications in the TROLL-Language. In D. Harper and M. Norrie, editors, *Proc. Int. Workshop Specification of Database Systems, Glasgow, July 1991*, pages 228–245. Springer, London, 1992.

[SJH93] G. Saake, R. Jungclaus, and T. Hartmann. Application Modelling in Heterogeneous Environments using an Object Specification Language. *Int. Journal of Intelligent and Cooperative Information Systems*, 2(4):425–449, 1993.

[Spi89] J.M. Spivey. *The Z notation - a reference manual*. Prentice-Hall, Englewood Cliffs, NJ, 1989.

[SSE87] A. Sernadas, C. Sernadas, and H.-D. Ehrich. Object-Oriented Specification of Databases: An Algebraic Approach. In P.M. Stoecker and W. Kent, editors, *Proc. 13th Int. Conf. on Very Large Databases VLDB'87*, pages 107–116. VLDB Endowment Press, Saratoga (CA), 1987.

[WL93] J.C.P Woodcock and P.G. Larsen, editors. *FME'93: Industrial-Strength Formal Methods*. LNCS 670, Springer, Berlin, 1993.

Active Relationships for Controlling the Propagation of Information and Activities in Databases

Friedrich Kemper, Wolfgang Wilkes, Gunter Schlageter

University of Hagen, Department of Computer Science,
Feithstr. 140, D-58084 Hagen
Germany

Abstract

In many complex applications (design, manufacturing, workflow management, etc.) information about activities on specific objects affect related objects and result in subsequent activities on distant objects. The way in which objects are influenced is dependent on the operational semantics of the relationship. To capture these semantics, we introduce the concept of "active relationships" which contain a description of the activity propagation as an integral part of the relationship type definition. Active relationships allow to separate the specification of local activities and their global consequences and to solve typical problems concerning consistency control, configuration management, resource activation, etc. The paper discusses the features of active relationships and their integration into an object-oriented environment by means of several application examples. In addition, it describes an implementation of active relationships based on an object-oriented database and the use of this implementation for coupling two subsystems to an integrated system.

1 Introduction

Many application areas, as e.g. design, manufacturing, workflow management, etc., are characterised by their complex object structures: The objects are highly interrelated by different types of relationships with other objects. The relationships are more than simple object pointers, they often bear very specific semantics. Unfortunately, in normal object-oriented systems only semantic-less references can be used to model relationships. As a result, the semantics of relationships has to be coded either into object methods or even into the application programs.

This problem has been recognised by several authors, and various models have been proposed to overcome the problem [BaKi85], [FoTa90, [NgRi91]. But most of these models only introduce pre-defined relationship types which cover some situations.

This research was supported by the ESPRIT project 7364, "JESSI-COMMON-FRAME".

They do not provide a mechanism which enables the user to define new relationship types with application specific semantics.
In this paper we focus on the operational semantics of relationships, namely the propagation of activities and information. In several applications, objects are influenced by related objects: As a consequence of an event on an object, activities are invoked on related objects. The way in which activities are propagated is not a property of a single object, but it is a property of the relationship between the objects.

Several applications can be modelled more easily using this view of objects and their relationships:

- *Configuration management*: Design objects are organised by many different relationships: They are composed of other design objects (composition hierarchy), they exist in several versions, and they are represented in different, interrelated representations (e.g. schematic and netlist representation of an electronic circuit). The combination of these relationships require complex activity propagations. Some examples: (1) If a component of a composite design object becomes invalid, the composite design object itself has to become invalid. (2) The creation of a version of a component can enforce the automatic creation of a new version of the composite design object. (3) The update of a schematic representation can result in an automatic re-extraction of the corresponding netlist representation.

- *Coupling of subsystems*: If subsystems are to be coupled, relationships have to be defined between objects in the different subsystems. Activities in one subsystem are propagated via these relationships and cause subsequent activities in the other subsystem.

- *Distributed Systems*: If the objects are located at different nodes within a distributed system, the co-operation of distant objects is determined by the semantics of the relationships which connect them.

From these examples, we can draw several requirements:

⇒ It is important to distinguish between the local activities on single objects and their consequences for other objects. The specification of the propagation of activities determines the way in which different objects interact. Thus, the specification of the activity propagation is part of the description of overall processes and should not be mixed with the specification of local operations.

⇒ The interaction of objects often needs to be adapted to the needs of a specific environment. Even within a single configuration management system, different departments like to add their specific interaction rules to the general enterprise-wide rules. For instance, whereas in general a composite object is set to invalid after one of its components has become invalid, within a design department it might be sensible to invoke a search routine which automatically looks for a similar (valid) component.

⇒ Relationships tend to bear similar semantics. For instance, a *version relationship* may exist between various object types. To avoid replications of similar relationship definitions we need the ability to define generic relationships which can be materialised to concrete relationship types between specified object types.

To fulfil these requirements, this paper introduces the mechanism of *active relationships* (1) to provide relationships as explicit concepts for the modeller, and (2) to specify the propagation of information and the possible invocation of follow-up actions on related objects as an inherent part of the operational semantics of relationships. *Relationship categories* allow the definition of generic relationships, and *rule environments* support a controlled adaptation of the defined activity propagation for specific users and user groups.

The remainder of this paper is organised as follows: In the following section, the technical description of the concept of active relationships is presented. Section 3 describes the implementation of the active relationships in the context of a CAD-Framework's database and the use of active relationships for the integration of different subsystems. Related approaches are discussed in section 4.

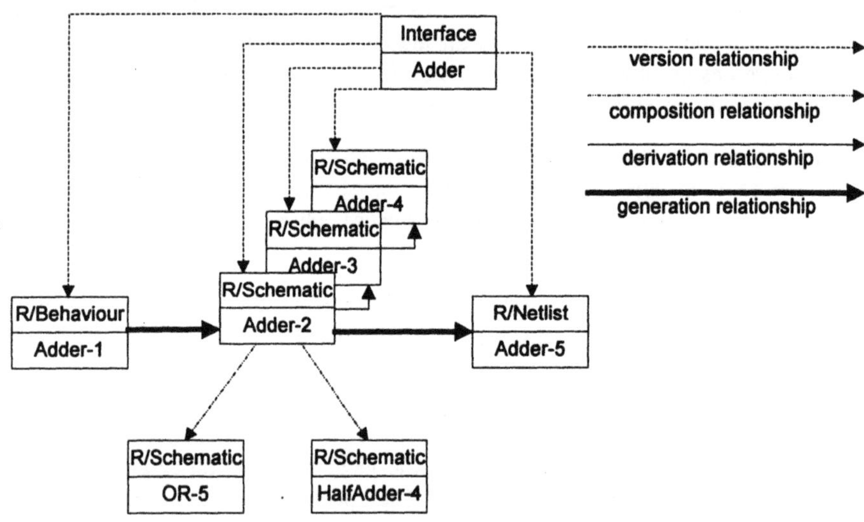

Figure 1: Typical relationships of a CAD application

2 Active Relationships

2.1 Example

We start the description of active relationships with an example from the area of VLSI design which will be used throughout this section. During the design of an Adder several representations are created which are connected to each other by various relationships (figure 1). The consistency of a single object in this structure is determined to a high degree by the objects to which it is related. For example, the schematic representation Adder-2 can only be as valid as its components are, i.e. if a component is invalidated, the same is true for the composite object. Similarly, Adder-2 is dependent on the behavioural representation Adder-1 from which it was generated (e.g. manually by a designer), and the netlist representation Adder-5 is dependent on the schematic representation in the same way. Revisions derived from Adder-2 are influenced by changes of Adder-2 as well. Moreover, if the interface specifications in the interface object Adder change, all representations which are versions of Adder are influenced since then they are based on an outdated specification. Thus, a lot of operations which take place on different objects may affect the consistency of the object Adder-2, and in the same way, operations on Adder-2 may affect other objects.

Figure 2 shows the schema level of our example, i.e. the involved object types and their relationship types.

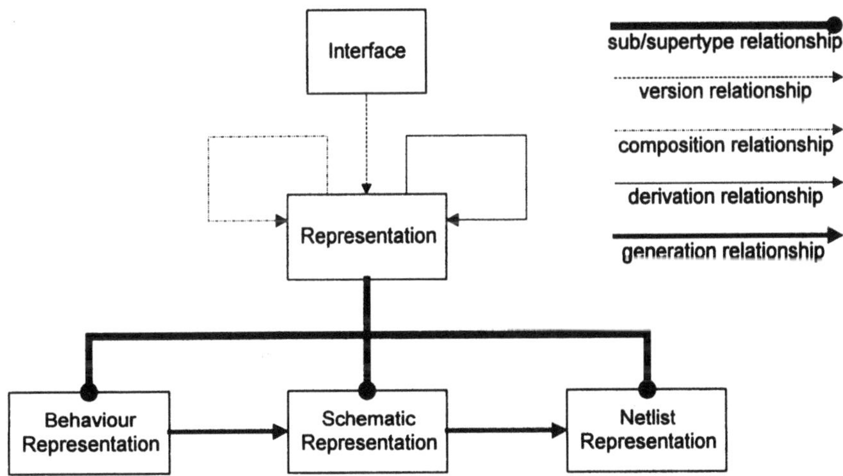

Figure 2: Object types and relationships of the CAD application example

2.2 Object Types

The basis for our model is a basic object-oriented data model: An object type defines the attributes which represent properties of the objects of this type, and it defines a set of methods to manipulate these properties. For each attribute, automatically two methods are created:

<attribute_name> to read the attribute
SET_<attribute_name> to modify the attribute

If an attribute is set-valued, it can be manipulated by three pre-defined methods:

<attribute_name> -- to read the attribute values (this method returns an iterator to run through all elements of the set)
add_to_<attribute_name> -- to add a value to the set
delete_from_<attribute_name> -- to delete a value from the set

Example 1 shows the definitions of the object type *SchematicRep* and its supertype *Representation* (only the explicitly defined methods are shown). The syntax is C++ oriented.

Example 1:

a)

```
OBJTYPE Representation;
// Attributes
  string status;
  string owner;
  date   creation_date;
// Methods
  int validate();
    {...};
  int invalidate();
    {...};
  ...
END OBJTYPE;
```

b)

```
OBJTYPE SchematicRep
        IS_A Representation;
// Attributes
   schematic  contents;
   ...
// Methods
   schematic edit_contents()
     {...};
   netlist extract_netlist()
     {...};
   SchematicRep derive_version()
     {...};
   ...
END OBJTYPE;
```

Of course, the *contents* attribute defined for *SchematicRep* objects is a complex structure consisting of several parts (ports, nets, instances, graphical elements, etc.), but within the context of this paper it is sufficient to treat those parts as a whole.

2.3 Relationship Types

Relationships between object types are defined explicitly by a relationship construct. In the definition of the relationship type, each of the involved object types gets a specific role name ('[ ]' denote optional parts, '|' separates alternative terms):

```
RELTYPE <relationship name> [<category assignment>];
  <role name> : <object type> [(<cardinality constraint>)]
                [<rename clause>];
  <role name> : <object type> [(<cardinality constraint>)]
                [<rename clause>];
  [RULES: <rule section>]
END RELTYPE;
```

Figure 3: Definition of relationship types

In general, it is also possible to have n-ary relationships with n>2. But since active relationships are usually binary, transferring an activity from one side to the other one, we only deal with binary relationships in this paper. The *rule* clause, the *category assignment* clause, and the *rename* clause are discussed in the subsequent sections.
The following example shows the definition of the relationship type *derivation* which is recursively defined on the object type *Representation.* The relationship type defines a 1:n relationship: Each representation may be derived from at most one predecessor.

Example 2:

```
RELTYPE derivation;
   successor     : Representation (n);
   predecessor   : Representation (0..1);
END RELTYPE;
```

As a result of this relationship definition, the object type *Representation* "inherits" some additional methods to manipulate the relationships in which it participates. Due to playing the role *predecessor* in the *derivation* relationship, *Representation* is extended by the following operations:

successors:	returns an iterator to run through the set of successors
add_successor:	to relate the *Representation* object with a new successor
delete_successor:	to disconnect the *Representation* object and a given successor

The following methods are added to *Representation* because it plays the role *successor* in the *derivation* relationship:

predecessor:	returns the predecessor of the *Representation* object
connect_predecessor:	to connect the *Representation* object with a predecessor
disconnect_predecessor:	to disconnect the *Representation* object from its predecessor

As the example shows, the object type "inherits" set oriented methods if it plays a role which can be connected to more than one object of the other role (as the predecessor role), and it gets methods which work on single objects otherwise (as the successor role). It does not matter from which side a relationship was built (from the *successor* via the operation *connect_predecessor* or from the *predecessor* via the *add_successor* operation), it is always visible form both sides.

The inherited methods are directly applicable, for instance to implement the methods of the object. An example: The method *derive_version* copies an object of type *SchematicRep* and relates original and copy by means of the *derivation* relationship. This is performed by using the "inherited" method *add_successor* :

Example 3:

```
SchematicRep derive_version ()
{  SchematicRep  NewSchem;
   NewSchem = copy ();    // local method of each object
   add_successor (NewSchem);
   return (NewSchem); }
```

2.4 Relationship Rules

The operational semantics of a relationship defines how it propagates changes from one side of the relationship to the other one(s). This propagation behaviour is defined by means of *relationship rules*, a special kind of ECA rules known from the area of active databases [Daya88], [Buch94]. A relationship rule is defined locally to a relationship. Consequently, it can only recognise events and use methods of those objects which are related by this relationship. Figure 4 shows the structure of a relationship rule definition.

```
<rule-name> [priority]:
   AFTER|BEFORE <event> AT <role name>
   [WITH <condition>]
   DO <action>
   [MODE   immediately|deferred|detached-dependent|
           detached-independent]
```

Figure 4: Definition of a relationship rule

A relationship rule fires whenever the given event is raised. If the given condition is evaluated to true, the specified action is executed. The *mode* part of the rule definition corresponds to the coupling modes commonly used in active databases [Daya88], [Buch94]. It determines whether the rule is executed in (respectively at the end of) the transaction which raised the event ("immediately"/"deferred") or whether the firing of the rule creates a new transaction ("detached"). If this new transaction is "dependent" to the running transaction, it may not start before the termination of the running transaction. The default mode is "immediately".

Example 4 shows a relationship rule associated to the *composition* relationship. It causes a composite object to become invalid as soon as one of its components is invalidated. The rule is triggered by an invalidation of the *status* attribute of the component object and invalidates the composite object as well.

Example 4:

```
RELTYPE composition;
   composite   :  Representation (m);
   component  :  Representation (n);
RULES:
   status_propagation:
      AFTER   invalidate() AT component
      WITH    composite.status() != "invalid"
      DO      composite.invalidate()
      MODE    immediately;
END RELTYPE;
```

Another example enriches the copy function which was already used in the implementation of the method *derive-version*. In general, a copy can be performed in three different ways (see [Rumb88]:

1. Copy only the local attributes.
2. Copy relationships as well (i.e. relate the copy to those objects which are related to the original).
3. Copy also those objects which are related to the original (deep copy).

If we consider our example (figure 1 and 2), then it is clear, that our copy has to perform for some relationships like alternative 2, for others like alternative 1: Whereas a copy of a *Representation* object R should have the same components as R and should also be related to the same *Interface* object as R, it cannot be connected to other objects by means of the *derivation* relationship in the same way as R. Example 5 describes the effect of a copy operation for the components by a relationship rule.

Example 5:

```
RELTYPE composition;
   ...
   RULES:
   status_propagation:
      ....;

   copy_propagation:
      AFTER   copy AT composite
      DO      component.add_composite (event_par.returnvalue)
      MODE    deferred;
END RELTYPE;
```

The rule causes each component to be automatically connected to the new copy of its composite object. This copy can be accessed via the parameter *event_par.returnvalue* (see below). In the following, the single parts of a relationship rule definition will be discussed in more detail.

Events

Two classes of events are of interest:

- *database events*: events which can be used to observe the manipulation of data, i.e. creation, deletion, or update of an object.
- *method events*: events which indicate the invocation or termination of a method.

In both cases we can distinguish pre- and post-events, i.e. the event may be raised before the update or the execution of a method or after the update or the method execution (indicated by keywords BEFORE or AFTER).

A method event allows to access the actual parameters of the method which raised the event. In case of a post-event, also the return value of the method is provided. The access to parameters and return values is done by *event_par.<parameter-name>* and *event_par.returnvalue* respectively.

Conditions and Actions

Conditions control the execution of the rule action. They can be expressed as arbitrary boolean expressions. Only if the condition evaluates to true, the action part is executed. The action part contains a block of statements of the underlying programming language (in which the object methods are defined).

As an example for a relationship rule with a complex action part consider the specific kind of change propagation which has been introduced in [Katz90] (see figure 5): A derivation of a new version of one of the components of a composite object (a) leads to an automatic creation of a new version of the composite object (b). This mechanism works recursively until the root object of the component hierarchy is reached or the scope of the propagation is limited by means of a flag in one of the composite objects.

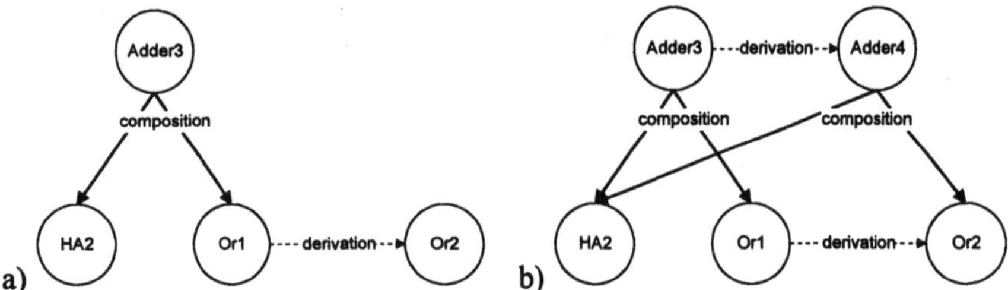

Figure 5: Change propagation according to [Katz90]

This behaviour can be modelled by associating the following relationship rule to the *composition* relationship:

Example 6:

```
RELTYPE composition;
   ...
   RULES:
   change_propagation:
      AFTER   derive_version() AT component
      WITH    composite.propagation_flag == TRUE
      DO    { Representation  new_composite;
              new_composite = composite.derive_version();
              new_composite.delete_component(component);
              new_composite.add_component
                                   (event_par.returnvalue);
            };
END RELTYPE;
```

Synchronisation and Termination

As know from the field of active databases, triggering of activities may cause several problems [Etz93]. One problem is the synchronisation of actions triggered by the same event. A single event may raise more than one relationship rule and may thus lead to the execution of several actions. Those actions can be executed in parallel without any problems if the actions are independent from each other (i.e. if they access different data). But, if dependencies exist between the triggered actions, then appropriate priority numbers which control their execution order must be assigned to the respective rules (see *priority* field in figure 3).

A common problem of all approaches which uses ECA rules is non-termination. In the area of relational databases several models have been developed which allow the detection of (potential) cycles [AWH92], [BCW93], [VoSi93]. Some additional problems arise in the area of object-oriented systems (among other things due to the encapsulation of methods). [Buch94] sketches two possible solution of this problem. In our current implementation we use a simple time-out mechanism.

2.5 Relationship Categories

Usually a lot of different relationship types exist in a specific application, but several of them bear a similar semantics. This has been illustrated in figures 1 and 2, where the same kind of relationship has been used to relate the object types *SchematicRep* and *BehaviourRep* as well as *NetlistRep* and *SchematicRep.*

To support the reuse of relationship definitions we introduce *relationship categories.* A relationship category builds a template for the definition of actual relationship types (see also [KrWi95]). A relationship type which is bound to a specific category inherits the roles and rule specifications of its category. The object types of the inherited roles may be specialised to subtypes. In the following example, generation is a relationship category where both roles are of type *Representation.* This category describes common properties of the relationships between *BehaviourRep* and *SchematicRep* and between *SchematicRep* and *NetlistRep* respectively.

Example 7:

```
RELTYPE CATEGORY generation;
   source : Representation;
   generated : Representation;
   RULES:
   status_propagation:
      AFTER   invalidate() AT source
      WITH    generated.status() != "invalid"
      DO      generated.invalidate()
      MODE deferred;
END RELTYPE CATEGORY;

RELTYPE beh-schem OF CATEGORY generation;
   behav : behaviourRep (1) RENAMES source;
   schem : schematicRep (N) RENAMES generated;
END RELTYPE;
```

Example 7 (continued):

```
RELTYPE schem-netl OF CATEGORY generation;
   schem : schematicRep (1) RENAMES source;
   nl : netlistRep (1)  RENAMES generated;
   ...
   RULES:
   create-netlist-on-demand:
      BEFORE  simulate() AT nl
      WITH    nl.status() == "invalid"
      DO      { nl.contents = schem.extract_netlist;
                nl.validate() }
      MODE    immediately;
END RELTYPE;
```

In this example, the category *generation* defines the rule *status_propagation* which is inherited by both relationship types of this category. In the relationship *schem-netl* an additional rule has been defined to extract the actual netlist structure if a netlist simulator is invoked. The rename clause allows to redefine role names which have been inherited from the category.

2.6 Rule Environments

The activity propagation defined by active relationships determine to a great deal the way how users can work with the system. But often, even within the same project, different designers will have a different understanding of the desired system behaviour. Some of them would prefer an automatic (re-) creation of objects whenever possible. Others – more experienced ones – would prefer to use only status propagation and notification services. To support a flexible usage of relationship rules, we provide the concept of *rule environments* to adapt the system behaviour to the needs of (groups of) designers. Rule environments are extensions of the ETM environments defined in [Kotz89].

A rule environment can be seen as a kind of database view. It contains all object and relationship types defined within the database schema and a (possibly empty) set of relationship rules. Each database access happens via a rule environment and only those rules are active which have been attached to the environment. A rule environment is defined by

```
DEFINE ENVIRONMENT <env_name> [SUB-ENV OF <superenv-name>]
```

and rules are attached to it by

```
ATTACH <rule_name> TO <env_name> [IRREVOCABLE].
```

Rule environments may be created as *sub-environments* of other environments (its *super-environments*). Each environment has at most one super-environment but any number of sub-environments. This results in a hierarchic structure of rule environments, and a single environment inherits the relationship rule attachments of all its predecessors. In addition, further rules can be attached to it.

Our concept supports two different modes of attachment inheritance which depend on the chosen form of the attach-operation.

- *Default inheritance*: If the respective rule has been attached to the environment without using the IRREVOCABLE option, then the rule can be detached in one of the sub-environments. A rule of this kind represents a system behaviour which is recommended but not enforced.
- *Strict inheritance*: A relationship rule which has been attached as IRREVOCABLE must stay active in all sub-environments and cannot be detached there. This allows to enforce a common behaviour within a rule environment and to make it also obligatory for each sub-environment. This feature can be used, for instance, to enforce company or group specific policies.

The combination of these two modes allows to define a common system behaviour which is recommended for all users of the system but can be adapted – within the given limitations – to specific needs of groups of users or even to individual needs of single users. This allows to apply the semantics of relationships in a very flexible way.

3 Implementation and Sample Application

The research presented within this paper has been performed in the context of the ESPRIT project JESSI-Common-Frame [JCF92], a collaborative project of many partners, among them Siemens, Siemens Nixdorf Information Systems, Philips and ICL. The result of the project was a CAD framework for the area of micro electronics called JESSI-Common-Framework (JCF) which is now commercially available under the name SIFRAME. JCF provides - based on an object-oriented database - mechanisms for data and design management, tool integration, tool communication, etc.

Our implementation of active relationships is based on JCF's underlying active object-oriented database system OMS [FFH+91]. This database provides a simple side effect management which monitors the execution of basic database operations (create_object, delete_object, modify_attribute, create_relationship, ...). OMS supports only event/action rules, i.e. the evaluation of conditions is not supported. Actions can be described by arbitrary user-defined methods.

We have implemented an additional layer on top of the OMS database which allows the management of active relationships [KeWi95], [Emam96]. This layer uses the existing OMS event handling component to detect relevant modifications of data. Each event defined within a relationship rule is mapped onto a corresponding OMS event. If the modification of an object has been recognised, the active relationship layer checks whether a relationship is sensitive to this event. If this is the case the given condition is evaluated by the active relationship layer. Conditions are described by expressions in the Lisp-like language Scheme. If the condition evaluates to true, the corresponding action is executed.

The system provides much flexibility: Relationship rules may be defined or deleted at runtime, and they may be temporary deactivated. It is also possible to define specific rule environments for different projects.

The implementation of the mechanism of active relationships has actually been used to support the integration of a subsystem into the existing design management component of JCF. In general, the problem of integrating two subsystems can be sketched as follows (see figure 7):

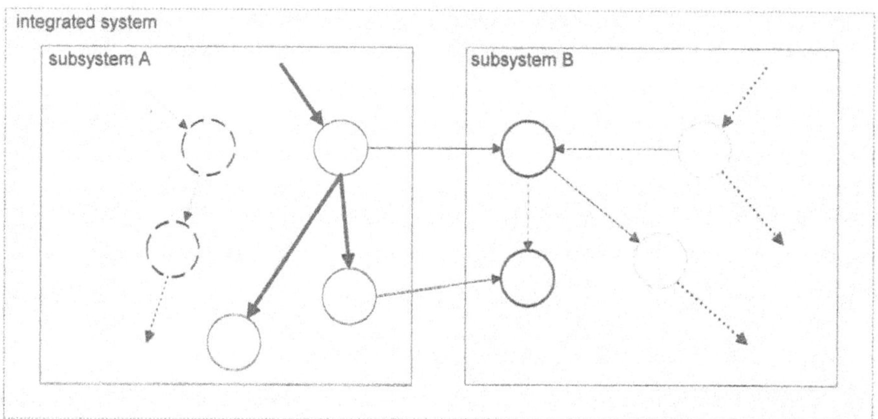

Figure 7: Two subsystems which are related to each other via several relationships

Both subsystems provide inherent functionality which is implemented based on their local object and relationship types and the corresponding methods. To combine the subsystem, some relationships have to be established between objects in different subsystems. Via these relationships, operations in one system influence the objects of the other system. These dependencies can be described and maintained by means of active relationships.

Our extension of the design management component improves the version management of composite design objects. For this purpose we add a so called "configuration tree" to the JCF component hierarchy. Details about the functionality of the configuration tree can be found in [WiKe94]. To integrate our configuration tree to the design management component, we defined relationships between elements of the component hierarchy and the configuration tree. Since it is not possible to change the code of the JCF design management system, we used active relationships to monitor the behaviour of the objects of the design management component, and in case of relevant events, the necessary actions were initiated on related objects in our configuration tree. More details about this coupling can be found in [KWS95], [KeWi95] and [Emam96].

4 Related Approaches

All ER-based models support the concept of relationships as an explicit modelling mechanism. An advanced example of this type of model is presented in [AGO91], where relationships are modelled as n-ary associations. Properties of associations are specified as constraints (like referential, surjectivity, or constancy constraints). By using various declarations it is possible to maintain the referential constraints and even more complex pre- and postconditions for insert and delete operations.

In [Rumb87] and [Rumb88] an approach is presented which is based on an object-oriented language. Rumbaugh introduces n-ary relationships which allow to specify the propagation of operations across relationships via so called *propagation attributes* which are attached to the relationship types. This mechanism supports only the propagation of the triggering operation but not the invocation of different actions.

More possibilities are provided by the software configuration management system Adele [EsCa94] and the SORAC database management system [DPW93]. Normally, frameworks and configuration management systems contain hard-wired strategies for the resolution of consistency conflicts across relationships (e.g. [Katz90], [JCF92], [Wolf94]). But Adele and SORAC allow to more explicitly express the semantics of a relationship. Actions on objects can be associated to events (changes of related objects), and their execution is controlled by boolean conditions.

However, both systems do not provide any means to describe a common behaviour of several relationships. Moreover, all rules are defined as global rules which are operative for the whole system. Adaptations to the special needs of single users are not supported. A major difference of our approach to the SORAC system and to the other approaches is the way how relationships are embedded into an underlying object-oriented system and how objects present themselves to applications. As opposed to the SORAC system which provides specific object structures to capture the relationships which have to be known by the application, in our model the application can use the usual methods for dealing with relationships (like navigation, creation of a new relation or deletion of a relation). The operational semantics of the active relationship is treated as a side effect of operations on the involved objects. Thus, existing applications are not affected by the definition of the activity propagation, they can treat active relationships in the usual object-oriented way. With respect to this aspect, our approach is very similar to ADAM [Diaz95].

5 Conclusion

In this paper, active relationships have been introduced as a mechanism to specify the propagation of activities across relationships. The key features of active relationships are the following:

- Relationship types are represented as explicit constructs for the designer of the system. For the applications, the existence of relationships is visible by specific methods which are inherited by the involved object types.
- The operational semantics of a relationship type, i.e. the way in which activities are propagated across the relationships, is described in relationship rules as part of the relationship type definition.

- Relationship rules can be seen as local ECA rules in the scope of a relationship type, i.e. only the methods defined for the related object types may be used in specifying the condition and the action part of the rule.
- Relationship categories form templates from which actual relationship type definitions can be derived which inherit the specification of the category.
- Rule environments allow the flexible application of relationship rules in different circumstances.

There are several application fields where active relationships can be of help, including

- consistency control in complex relationship structures
- workflow management: description of the activity flow, invoking of automatable activities, notification of people with a specific role about pending activities, etc.
- coupling of subsystems

The concept of active relationships has been implemented on top of an object-oriented database system with active elements. This prototype has been successfully used for the extension of a design management system by coupling an additional module with the existing system via active relationships.

References

[AGO91] A. Albano, G. Ghelli, R. Orsini: *A Relationship Mechanism for a Strongly Typed Object-Oriented Database Programming Language*, Proc. 17th Int. Conf. on Very Large Data Bases (VLDB), Barcelona, Spain, September 1991

[AWH92] A. Aiken, J. Widom, J.M. Hellerstein: *Behaviour of Database Production Rules: Termination, Confluence, and Observable Determinism*, Proc. ACM SIGMOD Int. Conf. on Management of Data, San Diego, USA, June 1992

[BaKi85] D.S. Batory, W. Kim: *Modeling Concepts for VLSI CAD Objects*, ACM Transactions on Database Systems, Vol.10, No.3, September 1985

[BCW93] E. Baralis, S. Ceri, J. Widom: *Better Termination Analysis for Active Databases*, in N.W. Paton, M.H. Williams (Eds.): Rules in Database Systems,Workshops in Computing, Springer, September 1993

[Buch94] A.P. Buchmann: *Active Object Systems*, in A. Dogac. M.T. Özsu, A. Biliris, T. Sellis (Eds.):Advances in Object-Oriented Database Systems, Springer Verlag, 1994

[Daya88] U. Dayal: *Active Database Management Systems*, Proc. 3rd Int. Conf. on Data and Knowledge Bases, Jerusalem, Israel, Juni 1988

[Diaz95] O. Díaz: *The operational semantics of user-defined relationships in object oriented database systems*. Data & Knowledge Engineering, No. 16, 1995

[DPW93] M. Doherty, J. Peckham, V.F. Wolfe: *Implementing Relationships and Constraints in an Object-Oriented Database Using a Monitor Construct*, in N.W. Paton, M.H. Williams (Eds.): Rules in Database Systems,Workshops in Computing, Springer, September 1993

[Emam96] T. Emami: *Integration of Active Relationships into a CAD Framework to realize a flexible Consistency Control*, Diploma thesis, University of Dortmund / University of Hagen, February 1996 (in German)

[EsCa94] J. Estublier, R. Casallas: *The Adele Configuration Manager*, in W.F. Tichy (Ed.): Configuration Management, Trends in Software, Wiley 1994

[Etzi93] O. Etzion: *PARDES - A Data-Driven Oriented Active Database Model*, Sigmod Record, Vol. 22, No. 1, March 1993

[FFH+91] W. Fox, J. Friedrich, R. Hopp, T. Kathöfer, A. Meckenstock, D. Nolte, K. Pielstiecker, G. Reitmeyer, R. Rupprecht, M.Schrew: *The Architecture of the Object Management System within the Cadlab Framework*, in F.J. Rammig, R. Waxman (Ed.): Proc. 2nd Int. IFIP Workshop on Electronic Design Automation Frameworks, North-Holland, 1991

[FoTa90] S. Foo, Y. Takefuji: Databases and Cell Selection Algorithms for VLSI Cell Libaries, IEEE Computer, Vol. 23, No. 2, 1990

[JCF92] B. Steinmüller: *The JESSI-COMMON-FRAME Project - A Project Overview*, in M. Newman, T. Rhyne (Eds): Electronic Design Automation Frameworks, North-Holland, 1992

[Katz90] R.H. Katz: *Toward a Unified Framework for Version Modeling in Engineering Databases*, ACM Computing Surveys, Vol. 22, No.4, December 1990

[KeWi95] F. Kemper, W. Wilkes: *Integration of Active Relationships into JCF*, Esprit Project 7364, Document-No. JCF/FU-Hagen/015-01/28-Apr-95

[Kotz89] A.M. Kotz: *Triggermechanisms in Database Systems*, Informatik-Fachberichte 201, Springer, 1989 (in German)

[KrWi95] T. Kretzberg, W. Wilkes: *EXPRESS+ and SDAI+: Specification and Automatic Derivation of Higher Level Programming Interfaces*. Proc. 5th Int. EXPRESS User Group Conference, Grenoble, October 1995

[KWS95] F. Kemper, W. Wilkes, G. Schlageter: *Active Relationships: A Means for Controlled Propagation of Information and Activities in Databases*, Informatik Berichte 188, University of Hagen, Germany, June 1995

[NgRi91] G.T. Nguyen, D. Rieu: *Representing Design Objects*, Artificial Inteligence in Design, Oxford, Butterworth/Heinemann, 1991

[Rumb87] J. Rumbaugh: *Relations as Semantic Constructs in an Object-Oriented Language*, OOPSLA '87, Special Issue of SIGPLAN Notices, Vol. 22 , No. 12, December 1987

[Rumb88] J. Rumbaugh: *Controlling Propagation of Operations using Attributes on Relations*, OOPSLA '88, SIGPLAN Notices, Vol. 23, No. 11, November 1988

[VoSi93] L. von der Voort, A. Siebes: *Termination and Confluence of Rule Execution*, 2nd Int. Conf. on Information and Knowledge Management, November 1993

[WiKe94] W. Wilkes, F. Kemper: *Application of Indirect Components for Version Management in Design Databases*, International Conference on Data and Knowledge Systems for Manufacturing and Engineering, Hong Kong, May 1994

[Wolf94] P. van der Wolf: *CAD FRAMEWORKS: Principles and Architecture*, Kluwer Academic Publisher, 1994

Multi-Data Models Translations In Interoperable Information Systems

Christophe Nicolle, Djamal Benslimane, Kokou Yetongnon

Laboratoire LIESIB
Facultés de Sciences Mirande
Université de Bourgogne
21000 Dijon, FRANCE
Email : {cnicolle, benslima, kokou}@satie.u-bourgogne.fr

Abstract. Interoperation of heterogeneous and autonomous information systems has traditionally been hampered by semantic differences in their data models. In this paper, we address the problem by defining a methodology called TIME, which is based on an extensible meta model. Its key features are : a set of meta-types which can be used to represent the syntax and the semantics of data modeling concepts, a knowledge base of transformation rules that map a meta-type into other meta-types, and an inference engine which uses the transformation rules to translate schema from source to target models. The extensibility of the meta-model is achieved by organizing the meta-types into a generalization hierarchy that record similarities among modeling concepts. The hierarchy of meta-types allows the reuse of transformation rules during automatic generation of data model translators.

1 Introduction

To facilitate information exchanges between different databases, several systems that highlight the evolution of information sharing have been developed in the course of these last years. This evolution goes from a simple exchange of message (cooperative system) to a total unification of a set of databases as a unique database (federated and distributed system). These systems requires the definition of concepts to allow the interoperation of heterogeneous computers and local databases systems. The heterogeneity can take on several aspects such operating systems, semantics and internal physical organization models. In this article, we are interested only in heterogeneity semantic problems that result from differences in the structure, data manipulation languages and content of database information. These problems complicate the interoperation between the different information systems.

A classic solution is to integrate the local schemas into a global schema. Usually, the global schema is expressed in a common data model, in which the user expresses his queries [12]. The integration of a large number of data schema is nevertheless an expensive and intensive task [11]. An alternative is to place translation tools between the different data models within a federation. Thus, users of the federation access information from their local data model [14, 15].

The responsibility of translating from concepts of one model into another model is left to the user or to the administrator of the local system. But, this solution rapidly becomes too complex to implement when the number of heterogeneous databases wishing to communicate becomes large. This method is not therefore well adapted to a heterogeneous databases federation [8, 9].

Our objective is to define an environment that provides a tool to help solve the problem of translation in a heterogeneous database federation. In order to do so, we propose a methodology of data models translation based on an extensible meta-model called TIME (Traducteur Intelligent avec Métamodèle Extensible). TIME is composed of a minimum set of modelisation concepts which can be specialized to represent different data models. The main advantages of this methodology is that it enables the reuse of translation rules between different models.

The remainder of the article is organized as follows. In section 2, we present a discussion of different approaches of data model translation. Section 3 presents our meta-model (its structure, its meta-types and associated translation rules). In section 4, we describe translation rules that are associated with the meta-model, and we define the notion of meta-type correspondence. Section 5 discusses examples of specifications of the relational and object oriented data models. An example of scheme translation is presented in section 6. And finally, section 7 provides a conclusion to the article and a discussion of our future themes of research.

2 Discussion

Data model translations has been the subject of intensive research recently. The different solutions can be classified into 3 main approaches.

The first approach deals with one to one translations betweem two specific data models. This type of solution can be used for the migration of a database from a semantically poor model to a richer model or for conceptual design of database by first representing the system in a rich data model and translating the conceptual representation into a target model [3, 4]. This type of translation, where each concept of a source model finds its equivalent in the target model insures a great reliability of conversion. Nevertheless it is not well adapted for the interoperability of heterogeneous systems, where a considerable number of translators may be required (for N different models it is necessary N*(N - 1) translators). The addition of a new database with a new model necessitates the creation of as many translators as there are different models in the system.

The second approach, which is based on the utilization of a global model, is generally used in distributed systems. It allows for a one to many type of translation that is used to integrate the various databases into one system. The objective is to provide an interface between a user and the group of databases. The advantage of this solution is the reduction of the number of translators required. To add a database with a new data model and langage, it suffices to create its equivalent in the global model. Users queries are posed on the global schema and mapped into queries on the local schemas.

To facilitate the integration of databases some solutions use a meta-model [1, 2, 10]. A meta-model is well suited for resolving semantic heterogeneity among data models. However, this solution requires users to express their queries with higher order logical predicates. An alternative is to map the meta-model back in the local user model. Thus allowing users to express queries in their native model.

The third approach is based on the utilization of a canonical or pivot model that allow the translation of N data models into M data models. This type of translation is very difficult to implement and generally corresponds to the specification of N+M one to one translations between the pivot model and the other models.

The above approaches have pointed out the need to reduce the number of translators requires to allow interoperability of information systems. Tools that are based on the reuse of pre-defined concepts and translations can be used to facilitate the generation of one to one data model translators [7, 13]. The semi-automatic or automatic generation of one to one translators thus facilitates the translation in both federated and distributed systems. To acheive this goal, we propose a data translation methodology called TIME (Traducteur Intelligent avec Méta-modèle Extensible) that uses an extensible meta-model, a knowledge base and an inference engine. The data model contains a reduced set of meta-types that are linked by generalization/specialization relationships. We use the specialization link as a mechanism for extending the meta-model by specializing existing meta-types to define new meta-types. As in object oriented models, an inheritance link between two meta-types allows the reuse of both structural properties and meta-type constraints. The inference engine uses a knowledge base containing a set of transformation rules to translate schema from source models to target models. The translation rules are expressed in first order logical predicate. The advantage of this methodology is to simplify the translation process by reusing translation paths between different models.

3 Structure of TIME Meta-model

TIME defines two main components : a set of meta-types, and a knowledge base containing a set of basic transformation rules (Figure 1). The meta-types are used to capture the semantics of different categories of modeling concepts. There are two sorts of meta-types. Meta-object types represent concepts which can be used to model real entities while meta-link types denote data model concepts which characterize relationships among entities. To achieve extensibility, the meta-types of the meta-model are organized in a specialization (generalization) hierarchy. Thus, a new meta-type can be defined by specializing an existing meta-type. Initially, the meta-type hierarchy contains 5 basic meta-types: META, MComplex-Object, MSimple-Object, MN-Link and MBinary-link (figure 1). The knowledge base (KB) initially contains a set of basic transformation rules that can be used to transform an instance of a basic meta-type into an other basic meta-type and a set of facts describing meta-types correspondence. These rules are expressed in a first order logical predicates that are utilized by the inference engine.

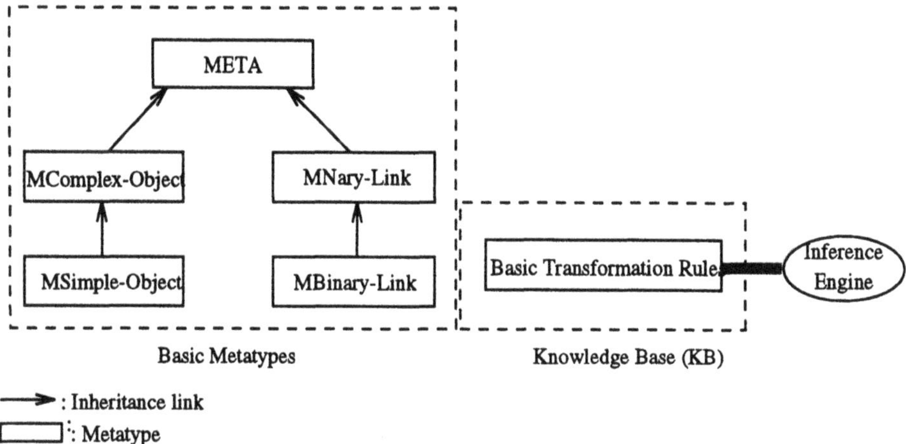

Fig. 1. Structure of the metamodel

A meta-type M is defined by a tuple M = (A_M,C_M,P_M), where A_M is a set of syntactic elements that describe the structure of M. C_M is a set of user defined constraints that are used to restrict the meta data constraints associated with the super meta-type of which M is a specialization. PM is a set operations or methods. It is used to model methods of the object oriented (or any similar) model. P_M is empty for data models (e.g. relational model) which do not allow the encapsulation of data and operations into a type. We give below an informal definition of the meta-types. A formal BNF [1] definition is given in appendix.

3.1 Definition of Meta-type META

The highest meta-type in the specialization (generalization) hierarchy is a generic meta-type, META, with an empty structure. Its purpose is to define meta-data constraints and operations that can be shared by all meta-types. It is defined by META=([ ], C_{Meta}, [ ]). C_{Meta} comprises a set of data modeling constraints. For example, C_{Meta} contains an ID function that uniquely identifies the instances of meta-types.

3.2 Definition of Meta-type MComplex-Object (CO)

Meta-type CO represents modeling concepts that are used to describe complex structure entities such as : OBJECT in object oriented model, ENTITY TYPE

[1] Backus Normal Form

in the Entity-Relationship model and RECORD in the Codasyl data model. Meta-type MComplex-Object is specified by CO = (A_{CO}, C_{CO}, P_{CO}), where A_{CO} is defined using the usual tuple and set constructions on meta-object types. The component C_{CO} and P_{CO} are not redefined at this level, but are inherited from the super meta-type META. An example showing an instance PERSON of meta-type MComplex-Object is given by:

PERSON =(A_{PERSON} := [Name : String ,
Address : [Street : String, Town : String],
Childs : [FirstName : String, BirthDate : String] (0,20),
Age : integer],
C_{PERSON} := [ ],
P_{PERSON} := [ ])

3.3 Definition of MSimple-Object (SO)

Meta-type SO, which is a specialization of meta-type CO, represents modeling constructs with flat structure. It is defined by SO = (A_{SO}, C_{SO}, P_{SO}) where the attribute structure A_{SO} inherits the tuple structure A_{CO} of meta-type CO, but restricts the type of its components to primitive domains. The components C_{SO} and P_{SO} are inherited from the meta-type MComplex-Object.

3.4 Definition of MNary-Link (NL)

Meta-type NL models types that represents connections between real world entities. Links can carried attributes. It is defined by NL = (A_{NL}, C_{NL}, P_{NL}). The component C_{NL} and P_{NL} are not redefined at this level, but are inherited from the super meta-type META. An example showing an instance OWN of an MNary-Link is given by :

OWN = (A_{OWN} := [PERSON : (1,n) , CAR : (1,1), DATE : (1,n)],
C_{OWN} := [ ],
P_{OWN} := [ ])

3.5 Definition of MBinary-link (BL)

Meta-type BL categorizes binary connections involving real world object types. It is a special case of NL and it is defined by BL = (A_{BL}, C_{BL}, P_{BL}).

4 Translation of meta-types

To allow the translation of schema with the meta-model, we define two types of transformation rules. The first, basic transformation rule allow the transformation between instances of two basic meta-types directly linked in the inheritance lattice. The second, non-basic transformation rules allow the transformation between one or more instances of non-basic meta-types (4.2).

4.1 Notion of correspondence

To allow the specification of a new meta-type in the meta-model we define the notion of meta-type correspodences to detect which existing meta-types we link with the new one. A good definition of these correspondences allows for a better definition of transformation rules between these meta-types and avoid semantic losses. In function of these correspondences, the system defined the type of the inheritance link between the meta-types (specialization link, may-be a link).

We define three meta-types correspondences : strong correspondence, simple correspondence and weak correspondence. the correspondence between meta-types M_1 and M_2 can be different from the one between meta-types M_2 and M_1.

Strong Correspondence : M_1 and M_2 are in strong correspondence relationship, that is to say that an instance of one can be transformed into an instance of the other without semantic loss if and only if :

$$M_1 = M_2$$

In this case M_1 and M_2 are equivalents.

The existing meta-type is used to represent the new one. The system establishes a virtual link between the concept of the model and the existing meta-type.

Simple Correspondence : M_1 is in relationship of simple correspondence with M_2, that is to say that during the transformation of an instance of M_2 in an instance of M_1, programs, constraints or structures can be lost, if and only if:

$$(M_1 \subseteq M_2)$$

In this case, a specialization link is introduced between M_1 and M_2. For example, MSimple-Object is in relationship of simple correspondence with MComplex-Objet (Figure 1) .

Weak Correspondence : M_1 is in relationship of weak correspondence with M_2, that is to say that during the transformation of an instance of M_2 in an instance of M_1, constraints and structures can be lost. In this case, a specialization link is introduced between M_1 and M_2. Moreover, to avoid semantic losses, the system compares others meta-types with M_1 in order to link the new meta-type with another type by a Maybe a link. For example, in figure 3, MRelation is in relationship of weak correspondence with MSimple-Object. This is due to inclusion dependencies. The system links MRelation with MBinary-link to represent these dependencies by links during the transformation process.

If more of one existing meta-types are in weak equivalence with the new meta-type, the system choose the existing meta-type where differences are smaller.

4.2 Basic transformation rules

A transformation rule converts an instance of a basic meta-type to one or more instance(s) of the basic meta-type which are directly connected in the specialization (generalization) hierarchy. Transformation rules are expressed in first order logical predicate of general form $R_b(I_1,M_1,I_2,M_2)$, where I_1 is the source meta-scheme, I_2 is the target meta-scheme, M_1 and M_2 are basic meta-types. This rule produces the target meta-scheme I_2 from I_1 by converting all instances of meta-type M_1 in the source meta-scheme I_1 into one ore more instance(s) of meta-type M_2. There are four transformation rules:

- $R_b(I_1,nl,I_2,bl)$ transforms an n-ary meta-type NL into a set of binary Link. Note that in some cases an n-ary link (NL) can be converted into both a meta object MO and a set of binary links where the participant meta-types of the initial n-ary link are linked to MO by the binary links. This is necessary to preserve the semantic correspondence between I_1 and I_2 when the participant object meta-types have cardinalities of (1,N) or (0,N). This rule is formally described in appendix 8.2.
- $R_b(I_1,bl,I_2,nl)$: this transformation rule noted only nas a trivial case since by definition a binary link is a an Nary-Link.
- $R_b(I_1, so,I_2, co)$ by definition this transformation is trivial since simple objects (SO) are complex objects with flat structures. In some cases, however, it may be necessary to restructure two or more simple objects linked by binary links into a complex object.
- $R_b(I_1,co,I_2,so)$ flattens all complex structures into a set of objects with simple structure, and generates a set of binary link meta-types (BL) to connect the newly created simple objects to the original object.

A formal description of the first transformation rule, $R_b(I_1,nl,I_2,bl)$, is given in appendix.

Figure 2 shows the use of the transformation rule $R_b(I_1,co,I_2,so)$. This rule translate the source meta-scheme I_1 into a target meta-scheme I_2 by replacing the complex-object PERSON with three instances of meta-type MSimple-Object PERSON, CHILDS, ADDRESS linked by two instances of meta-type MBinary-Link \$PERSON-CHILDS\$, \$PERSON-ADDRESS\$.

5 Data models specification

The specification of a data model in TIME is accomplished in two steps :

- Step 1 defines meta-types corresponding to the concepts of the data model by specializing existing meta-types or by adding new meta-types.
- Step 2 defines and associates transformation rules between the meta-type created and their respective super meta-types in the generalization hierarchy. In this step meta-type correspondence is defined, and the knowledge base is completed by adding new rules to the set of transformation rules and new meta-types correspondences to the fact base.

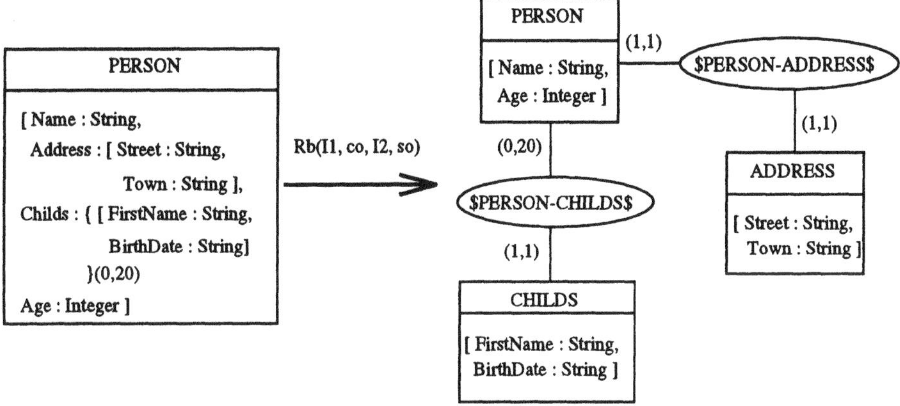

Fig. 2. An example of transformation of MComplex-Object into MSimple-Object and MBinary-Link

In this section we present an example to illustrate the specification of concepts of the relational and object oriented models. The specification of other models in the meta-model TIME is given in [6]. Figure 3 depicts two levels. The top level shows the basic meta-types, basic transformation rules and basic meta-type correspondence. The second level displays the meta-types that correspond to the modeling concepts of the Relational and Object oriented data models, and the transformation rules between these new meta-types, their super-meta-types and the new meta-types correspondences.

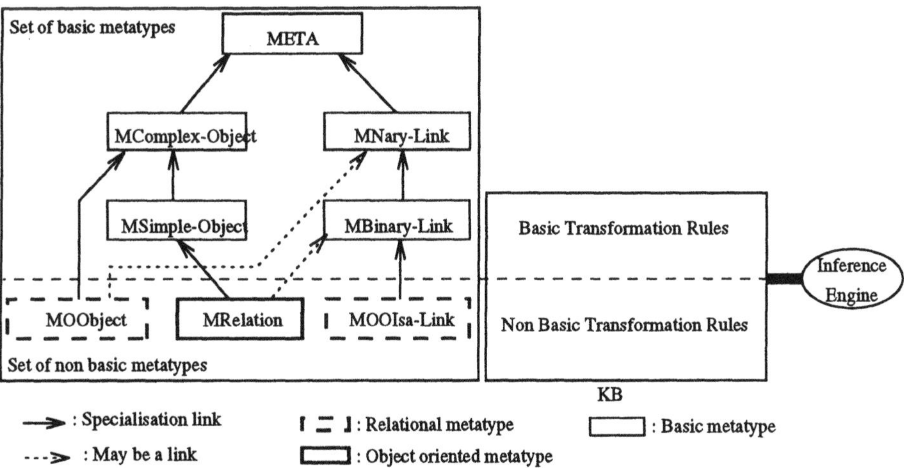

Fig. 3. Specification of two data models

5.1 Specifying the Relational Model in the meta-model TIME

In this section we specify the concepts of the relational model in the meta-model TIME. We follow this with a description of the transformation rules of each concept.

The specification of the relational data model in TIME consists to define a meta-type MRelation (REL) which represents the concept RELATION (relation name, monovalued attributes on simple domains, functional and inclusion dependencies). It is defined by REL=(A_{REL}, C_{REL}, P_{REL}). As shown in figure 3, MRelation specializes the meta-type MSimple-Object. Thus, the structure A_{REL} is identical to the structure of A_{SO}. MRelation, in C_{REL}, refines the ID function defined in META to correspond to the precise definition of the relational primary key; namely, a sub-sequence of attribute labels that uniquely identify the tuples of a relation. P_{REL} is empty.

Two non-basic transformation rules expressed in the first order logical predicate are associated with meta-type MRelation. They are used to convert instances between MSimple-Object and MRelation meta-types. They are informally defined as follows :

- $R_t(I_1$,so,I_2,rel) transforms directly an instance of a meta-type SO into an instance of a meta-type R. To complete the definition of this new instance, the system analyzes links and cardinalities associated with the initial instance of SO to define primary key and foreign key constraints.
- $R_t(I_1$,bl,I_2,rel) transforms an instance of a meta-type BL into attributes defining foreign key constraints on the instance of meta-type REL.
- $R_t(I_1$,rel,I_2,so) transforms an instance of a meta-type REL into an instance of a meta-type SO. The constraint on keys defined in REL is translated into instance of BL to conserve the same semantic during the transformation.

5.2 Specifying the object oriented model in the meta-model TIME

This section presents the specification of the concepts of the object oriented data model, and gives a description of the transformation rules.

Meta-types MOObject (OO) and MOOIsa-Link (OIL) represent the object oriented concepts, object and IS-A link, respectively. As illustrated in figure 3, the meta-type MOObject specializes the meta-type MComplex-Object. It is defined by OO = (A_{OO}, C_{OO}, P_{OO}). The structure A_{OO} is identical to the structure of A_{CO}. Conversely, The meta-type MOObject refines the component P_{CO} to introduce the behavioral aspect of the objects. A detailed and formal description of methods is beyond the scope of this paper. Thus the component P_{OO} is not presented. C_{OO} is empty. The meta-type MOOIsa-link is a binary link. In addition to the constraints inherited from meta-type MBinary-Link, it maintains a subset constraints between the population of the specialized and generalized meta-types which generalizes the concept of inheritance of the object oriented data model. Moreover, MOOIsa-Link specialises the structure of MBinary-Link to represent connection without attribute. The meta-type MOOIsa-Link is defined by OIL = (A_{OIL}, C_{OIL}, [ ]).

- $R_t(I_1$,co,I_2,oo) transforms directly an instance of a meta-type MComplex-Object into an instance of a meta-type MOObject. The composition links are transformed into instance of MNary-Link meta-type.
- $R_t(I_1$,oo,I_2,co) transforms an instance of a meta-type MOObject into an instance of a meta-type MComplex-Object. The transformation of the behavioral aspect is not presented here to simplify our discussion. The composition links are transformed into instance of MNary-Link meta-type.
- $R_t(I_1$,nl,I_2,oo) transforms an instance of a meta-type MNary-Link into reference attribute in the structure of the instance of MOObject meta-type MOObject.
- $R_t(I_1$,bl,I_2,oil) directly transforms an instance of a meta-type MBinary-Link into an instance of a meta-type MOOIsa-Link. The identical attributes in instances O_1 and O_2 in the are absorbed into the sub-type OO_2.
- $R_t(I_1$,oil,I_2,bl) transforms an instance of a meta-type MOOIsa-Link into an instance of a meta-type MBinary-Link. The attributes of the surper type instance are created into the sub-type instance.

6 Translation From Relational to Object Oriented Model

In this section we first describe the principles of the translation process give an example to illustrate the translation between a relational data model and an object oriented data model.

6.1 Principles

Let RS be a relational scheme. Our goal is to use the meta-model TIME to obtain an equivalent scheme in an object oriented data model. This requires three steps:

- **Step 1** : Translate the initial relational scheme into an intermediate meta-scheme I1 that includes instances of meta-type MRelation and key constraints expressions.

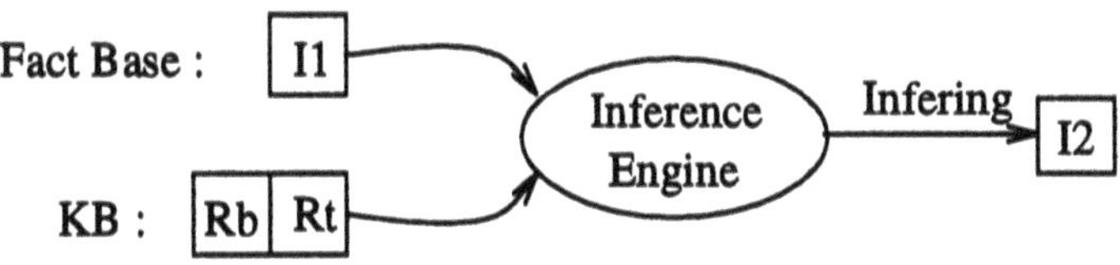

Fig. 4. Transformation of I_1 into I_2

- **Step 2** : Transform I_1 in to I_2 by replacing all instances of meta-type MRelation by instances of meta-types MOObject and MOOIsa-Link.This is done with the inference engine by applying basic and non-basic transformation rules (R_b and R_t) on the instances of meta-scheme (I_1) (cf. Figure 4).
- **Step 3** : Translate the meta-scheme I_2 into a final object oriented scheme.

6.2 Example

Let RS be the following relational scheme :

PERSON (PersonN#, Name)
CHILDREN (PersonN#, BirthDate)
ADDRESS (AddressN#, Number, Street, Town)
LIVE (People, House, Since)
CAR (CarN#, Color, Type, Owner, Date)

and let the constraints which define the foreign keys be given by :

CHILDREN.PersonN# ⊂ PERSON.PersonN#
CAR.Owner ⊂ PERSON.PersonN#
LIVE.People ⊂ PERSON.PersonN#
LIVE.House ⊂ ADDRESS.AddressN#

The first step of the translation process is to create a meta-model instance for each concept in the scheme. In this case, we must create instances of the meta-type MRelation for each relation. The application of the translation rules to the relational scheme example yields the following intermediate meta scheme I_1 that includes instances of meta-type MRelation and key constraints expressions.

I1 = (PERSON = (A_{PERSON}=[PersonN#:String, Name:String],
C_{PERSON}=[PERSON(PersonN#) → PERSON(Name)],
P_{PERSON}=[ ]),

CHILDREN = ($A_{CHILDREN}$=[PersonN#:String, BirthDate:String],
$C_{CHILDREN}$=[CHILDREN(PersonN#) → CHILDREN(BirthDate),
CHILDREN.Person N# ⊂ PERSON.PersonN#],
$P_{CHILDREN}$=[ ]),

ADDR = (A_{ADDR}=[AddrN#:String, Num:String, Street: String, Town:String],
C_{ADDR}= [ADDR(AddrN#) → ADDR(Num,Street,Town)],
P_{ADDR}=[ ]),

CAR = (A_{CAR}=[CarN#:String, Type:String, Owner:String, Date: String],
C_{CAR}=[CAR(CarN#) → CAR(Type), CAR(CarN#,Owner) → CAR(Date),
CAR.Owner ⊂ PERSON.PersonN#],
P_{CAR}=[ ]),

LIVE = (A_{LIVE}=[People:String, House:String, Since:String],
C_{LIVE}=[LIVE(People, House) → LIVE (Since),
LIVE.People ⊂ PERSON.PersonN#,
LIVE.House ⊂ ADDRESS.AddressN#] ,
P_{LIVE}=[ ]))

Next, we map the above instances of relational meta-types MRelation into a scheme containing instances of basic meta-types. The goal is to obtain a meta-scheme that contains object oriented meta-constructs. We achieve this by following the translation paths form MRelation to the meta-type MOOBject and by applying transformation rules among the basic meta-types. We use the foreign key constraints to classify the relations into MSimple-Object or MBinary-Link types. Labels of the form '\$XXX\$' are intermediate instances generated by the translation process. The results of this step are given by following the intermediate meta scheme (I_1).

I1' = (PERSON = (A_{PERSON}=[PersonN#:String, Name:String],
C_{PERSON}=[ ],
P_{PERSON}=[ ]),
CHILDREN = ($A_{CHILDREN}$=[BirthDate:String],
$C_{CHILDREN}$=[ ],
$P_{CHILDREN}$=[ ]),
ADDR = (A_{ADDR}=[AddrN#:String, Num:String, Street: String, Town:String],
C_{ADDR}= [ ],
P_{ADDR}=[ ]),
CAR = (A_{CAR}=[CarN#:String, Type:String, Date:String],
C_{CAR}=[ ],
P_{CAR}=[ ]),
LIVE = (A_{LIVE}=[Since:String],
C_{LIVE}=[ ],
P_{LIVE}=[ ]) ,
\$PEOPLE-LIVE\$ = ($A_{\$PEOPLE-LIVE\$}$ = [PERSON:(1,n), LIVE: (1,1)],
$C_{\$PEOPLE-LIVE\$}$ = [ ],
$P_{\$PEOPLE-LIVE\$}$ = [ ]),
\$HOUSE-LIVE\$ = ($A_{\$HOUSE-LIVE\$}$ = [ADDR:(1,n), LIVE: (1,1)],
$C_{\$HOUSE-LIVE\$}$=[ ],
$P_{\$HOUSE-LIVE\$}$=[ ]),
OWN = (A_{OWN} = [PERSON:(1,n),CAR:(1,1), [Date:String]],
C_{OWN} = [ ],
P_{OWN} = [ ]),
\$PERSON-CHILDREN\$ =
($A_{\$PERSON-CHILDREN\$}$ = [PERSON:(0,1), CHILDREN:(1,1)],
$C_{\$PERSON-CHILDREN\$}$ = [ ],
$P_{\$PERSON-CHILDREN\$}$ = [ ])]

To obtain inheritance link, we transform instances of MBinary-Link (Only instances on the general structure : [Object_1 : (0,1), Object_2 : (1,n)]) into instances of MInheritance Link.

To obtain object types, the simple object meta-types are first changed into complex object meta-types which generalize the object oriented type. This transformation is straightforward. It follows from the generalization link between MSimple-Object and MComplex-Object. Next, we use rules $R_t(I_1$",nl,I_2,co) and $R_t(I_1$",co,I_2,oo) to translate object and relationship meta-types into object oriented meta-type as defined below :

I2 = (PERSON = (A_{PERSON}=[PersonN#:String, Name:String],
C_{PERSON}=[ ],
P_{PERSON}=[ ]),

CHILDREN = ($A_{CHILDREN}$=[BirthDate:String],
$C_{CHILDREN}$=[ ],
$P_{CHILDREN}$=[ ]),

ADDR = (A_{ADDR}=[AddrN#:String, Num:String, Street:String,Town:String],
C_{ADDR}= [ ],
P_{ADDR}=[ ]),

CAR = (A_{CAR}=[CarN#:String, Type:String, Own:PERSON, Date: String],
C_{CAR}=[ ],
P_{CAR}=[ ]),

LIVE = (A_{LIVE}=[Since:String, People:PERSON, House:ADDR],
C_{LIVE}=[ ],
P_{LIVE}=[ ]) ,

$PERSON-CHILDREN$ =
($A_{\$PERSON-CHILDREN\$}$ = [PERSON:(0,1), CHILDREN:(1,1)],
$C_{\$PERSON-CHILDREN\$}$ = [ ],
$P_{\$PERSON-CHILDREN\$}$ = [ ])]

After the step 3 we obtain the following target object oriented scheme :

Class PERSON
Type Tuple (PersonN# : string, Name : String)

Class CHILDREN inherit PERSON
Type Tuple (BirthDate : String)

Class ADDR
Type Tuple (AddrN# : String, Num : String, Street : String, Town : String)

Class CAR
Type Tuple (CarN#:String, Type: String, Own : PERSON, Date : String)

Class LIVE
Type Tuple (Since : String, People : PERSON, House: ADDR)

7 Conclusion

In this paper we have presented a methodology for translating multiple data models. We addressed the problem by defining an extensible meta-model called TIME and used it as a data model translator design tool. The main characteristics of the meta-model are :

- It provides a minimum set of meta-types that capture the semantics of different categories of concepts found in most data models.
- It achieves extensibility by organizing the meta-types in an specialization/generalization hierarchy. Thus, a new meta-type is defined by specializing an existing meta-type.
- It achieves translation by defining a knowledge base composed of a set of transformation rules.

- It allows the reuse of transformation rules and sharing of translation step between multi- models translation.

Our future objectives are first to use the notion of correspondence to place new meta-types in the inheritance lattice of our meta-model. We will work to associate the notion of correspondence with the notion of distance to measure the level of semantic losses during the translation process. Next, we need to extend the above results, and to define a formal methodology and algorithm for heterogeneous query processing. This will allow us to define a query interface for the interoperation or migration of existing systems. Last, to use the meta-types generalization hierarchy, the knowledge base of transformation rules and the reusability property of the model to automatically or semi-automatically generate data model translators.

8 Appendix

8.1 BNF description of the meta-types

This section presents the description for each basic meta-types and for the meta-types MRelation, MOObject and MOOIsa-Link.

MComplex-Object : CO = (A_{CO}, [], []) where A_{CO} is described in BNF by :

Let A a set of labels,
A_{CO} := [structure_CO] | { structure_CO } (m,n) | {structure_CO }
structure_CO := a : T | a : T, structure_CO
where a is an attribute name (a ∈ A),
T := D | A_{CO}
D := String | ... | Integer
m := 0 | n
n := 1 | 2 | ...

MSimple-Object : SO = (A_{SO}, [], []) where A_{SO} is described in BNF by :
A_{SO} := [structure_SO]
structure_SO := a : T | a : T, structure_SO
where a is an attribute name (a ∈ A),
T := D

MNary-Link : NL = (A_{NL}, [], []) where A_{NL} is described in BNF by :
A_{NL} := [structure_NL]
structure_NL := M : (m,n), M : (m,n) | M : (m,n), M : (m,n), A_{CO} |
M : (m,n), structure_NL
where a is an attribute name (a ∈ A),
where the type of M is a CO or SO and M ∈ A

MBinary-Link : BL = (A_{BL}, [], []) where A_{BL} is described in BNF by :
A_{BL} := [structure_BL]
structure_BL := M : (m,n), M : (m,n) | M : (m,n), N : (m,n), A_{CO}

where a is an attribute name ($a \in A$),
where the type of M is a CO or SO and $M \in A$

MRelation : REL = ([], C_{REL}, []), the constraints C_{REL} are defined by three axioms as follows : Let R_1, R_2 be instances of REL, A_i a sub-sequence of attribute labels and F_k the ID function defined in META,

Axiom 1 defines a key is not null is given by :
$\forall R_1 \in REL, \forall A_i \in R_1, \forall F_k \in ID(R_1), R_1.F_k(A_i) \neq NULL$

Axiom 2 defines a primary key, whose attribute(s) define(s) uniquely all non key attribute(s) is given by :
$\forall R_1 \in REL, \forall A_1, A_2 \in R_1, \forall F_k \in ID(R_1)$,
where $R_1.F_k(A_1), R_1(A_1) \rightarrow R_2(A_2)$

Axiom 3 defines a foreign key, who are key attribute(s) of an instance R_1 of REL define(s) uniquely a sub-sequence of non key attribute(s) of an instance R_2 of REL.
$\forall R_1, R_2 \in REL, \forall A_1, A_2 \in R_1, \forall A_2 \in R_2, \forall F_{k1} \in ID(R_1)$
with $R_1.F_{k1}(A_1), \forall F_{k2} \in ID(R_2)$ where $R_2.F_{k2}(A_2), R_1(A_2) \subset R_2(A_2)$.

MOObject : OO = (A_{OO}, [], P_{OO}) where A_{OO} is described in BNF by :
A_{OO} := [structure_OO] | { structure_OO } (m,n) | {structure_OO }
structure_*OO* := a : T | a : T, structure_OO
where a is an attribute name ($a \in A$),
T := D | A_{CO} | t' where the type of t' is a OO and t' $\in$ A
D := String | ... | Integer
m := 0 | n
n := 1 | 2 | ...
The term P_{OO} is not developed in this paper.

MOOIsa-Link : OIL = (A_{OIL}, C_{OIL}, []). The structure A_{BL} and the constraints C_{BL} are refined in the meta-type MOOIsa-Link as follows :
A_{OIL} := [structure_OIL]
structure_OIL := M : (0,1), M : (1,1)
where a is an attribute name ($a \in A$),
where the type of M is a OO and $M \in A$

C_{OIL} is defined as follows,
Let OO_1 and OO_2 instances of the meta-type MOObject,

Axiom 4 : $\forall$, OO_1, OO_2,
OIL = [OO_1 : (0,1), OO_2 : (1,1)] $\Rightarrow$ ($\forall$ e : $OO_1(e) \Rightarrow OO_2(e)$)

This constraint defined that OO_2 is a subtype of OO_1.

8.2 Formal description of $R_b(I_1, nl, I_2, bl)$

$\forall$ $M_{nl} = (A_{nl}, C_{nl}, P_{nl})$ instance of MNary-Link

$r_b(M_{nl}, nl, M_{bl}, bl) \rightarrow M_{bl}$ instance of MBinary-Link,
N_j instances of MBinary-Link (j = 1, 2, ..., m),
M_{oc} instance of MComplex-Object,

- Two objects are linked by the instance of meta-type MNary-Link.
  $\forall$ A_{Mnl} := [M_1 : ($Cmin_1$, $Cmax_1$), M_2 : ($Cmin_2$, $Cmax_2$)] [2]
  $\Rightarrow$ Creation of one instance M_{bl} with the same name of M_{nl} with type of MBinary-Link were

$$A_{Mbl} := [M_1 : (Cmin_1, Cmax_1), M_2 : (Cmin_2, Cmax_2)]$$

- More of two object are linked by the instance of MNary-Link, maximal cardinalities of these object are sup of 1.
  $\forall$ A_{Mnl} := [M_1 : ($Cmin_1$, $Cmax_1$),..., M_n : ($Cmin_2$, $Cmax_2$), [r_i : t_i]], $n > 2$
  $\Rightarrow$ Creation of one instance of M_{oc} where A_{Moc} := [r_i : t_i] [3]
  Creation of a set of instances of MBinary-Link $N_j = (A_j, C_j, P_j)$, linking the new object and each participant object in M_{nl} |

$$A_{Nj} := [M_{oc} : (1,1), M_i : (Cmin_i, Cmax_i)], j = 1, 2, ..., m; i = 1, 2, ..., n$$

- More of two objects are linked by the instance of MNary-Link, at least one object has a maximal cardinalities equal to one [4].
  $\forall$ A_{Mnl} := [M_1 : ($Cmin_1$, $Cmax_1$),..., M_n : ($Cmin_2$, $Cmax_2$)], $n > 2$ and $\exists$ $Cmax_k = 1$, k = 1, 2, ..., n.
  $\Rightarrow$ Creation of a set of instances of MBinary-Link $N_j = (A_j, C_j, P_j)$, j = 1, k, linking objects M_k with others participant objects of M_{nl} |
  $A_{Nj} := [M_k : (Cmin_1, 1), M_i : (Cmin_i, Cmax_i)], k \neq i$

References

1. Paolo Atzeni, Riccardo Torlone : "A Metamodel Approach for the Management of Multiple Models in CASE Tools", Proceedings of the DEXA International Conference in Berlin, Federal Republic of Germany, 1991
2. Thierry Barsalou, Dipayan Gangopadhyay : "M(DM) : An Open Framework for Interoperation of Multimodel Multidatabase Systems",Proceedings of the 8th International Conference of Data Engineering, Tempe, Arizona, pp 218 - 227, Feb 3-7, 1992.

[2] This rule is done if A_{Mnl} has attributes
[3] or A_{Moc} := [ ], if M_{nl} has not attribute
[4] if M_{nl} has attributes, independent of the cardinalities, we apply the last rule.

3. M.Bouzeghoub, G. Gardarin, E. Metais : "Database Design Tools : An Expert System Approach", Proceedings of VLDB 85, Stockholm August 1985.
4. M.Bouzeghoub, E. Metais : "Semantic Modelling of Object Oriented Databases", Proceedings of the 17th International Conference on Very Large Databases (VLDB), Barcelona, pp3-14, September 91.
5. S.A. Demurjian, D.K. Hsiao : "Towards a Better Understanding of Data Models Through the Multilingual Data system", IEEE Trans on Software Engineering, pp 946-958, Vol 14, N7, July 1993
6. Christophe Nicolle, "TIME, un Traducteur Intelligent avec Méta-Modèle Extensible", Technical Report N94/01, November 94, University of Burgundy
7. Christophe Nicolle, Djamal Benslimane, Nadine Cullot, Kokou Yetongnon, "A Metamodel Based Methodology fot Translating Data Models in Interoperable Information System", Procceding of DATASEM, October 8-10, 1995.
8. David K. Hsiao, "Federated Database and Systems : Part I. A Tutorial on their Data Sharing" VLDB journal 1, pp127-179, Dennis Mc Leod Editor, 1992.
9. David K. Hsiao, "Federated Database and Systems : Part II. A Tutorial on their Resource Consolidation" VLDB journal 1, pp285-310, Dennis Mc Leod Editor, 1992.
10. Manfred A. Jeusfeld, Uwe A. Johnen : "An Executable MetaModel for Re-Engineering of Database Schemas", Proceedings in the International Conference on Entity-Relationship Approach, Manchester, December, 1994.
11. Laks V.S. Lakshmanan, Fereidoon Sadri, Iyer N. Subramian. : "On The Logical Foundations Of Schema Integration And Evolution In Heterogeneous Database Systems.", DOOD 93, Phénix, USA, in Computer Sciences 760, Spring Valley, Dec 93.
12. Amit P. Sheth, J.A. Larson : "Federated Database Systems, for Managing Distributed, Heterogeneous, and Autonomous Databases", pp183-235, ACM Computing Surveys, V ol 22, N3, September 90.
13. Stefano Spaccapietra, Martin Andersson, Yann Dupont, Kokou Yetongnon, Christine Parent, Christophe Nicolle, " Integrating Schemas of Heterogeneous Database Systems", in the Second Meeting on the Interconnection of Molecular Biology Databases (MIMBD95), July 20-22, 1995 in Cambridge, United Kingdom.
14. Susan D. Urban : "A Semantic Framework for Heterogeneous Database Environments", First International Workshop on interoperability in Multidatabase Systems, Kyoto, Japan, pp 156-165, April 1991.
15. Susan D. Urban : "Resolving Semantic Heterogeneity Through the Explicit Representation of Data Model Semantics". Sigmod Record, Vol 20, N4, December 1991.

Interoperable Transactions in Business Models – A Structured Approach

H. Weigand, E. Verharen,
Infolab, Tilburg University, Tilburg, The Netherlands
and F. Dignum
Fac. of Maths. & Comp. Sc.,Eindhoven University of Technology,
Eindhoven, The Netherlands

Abstract. Recent database research has given much attention to the specification of "flexible" transactions that can be used in interoperable systems. Starting from a quite different angle, Business Process Modelling has approached the area of communication modelling as well (the Language/Action perspective). The main goal of this paper is to provide some useful structuring mechanisms for interoperable transactions based on the Language/Action perspective. The paper thus tries to build a bridge between two rather separated worlds: the research on interoperable transactions on the one hand, and the research on business process models on the other. Extended deontic logic provides the material for this bridge. To better structure the specification, a distinction is proposed between the transaction level, the task level, and the contract.

Keywords: cooperative information systems, business process models, communication, interoperable transactions, deontic logic

1. Introduction

The field of Information Systems Engineering no longer concerns itself only with the development of 'isolated' Information Systems (IS). With the advent of high-speed local and global network communications, more and more applications, like EDI, Workflow management and collaborative computing, are being developed that access different independent resources inside and outside the organization. Integration of the various resources might not be possible for technical or organizational reasons, hence the growing reliance on *interaction* between systems. Behaviour of such systems, called Information and Communication Systems, or Cooperative Information Systems (CIS), is described by means of interoperable transactions defined as a logical unit of work, involving different autonomous agents. Interoperable systems cooperate by means of message passing; a specification of an interoperable process consists essentially of a set of communicating agents, the possible message types provided by each agent to support its role, and constraints on the synchronisation of messages.

A notorious problem with interoperable transactions, is that isolation cannot be maintained because of the long life-span. This means that certain accomplishments can become invalid later. For example, a flight reservation has been made, but the airline company cancels the flight. In the ConTracts model ([Wächter & Reuter,1992]), exit invariants can be specified that have to be maintained by the system for the duration of the ConTract. If they are violated, specific conflict resolution methods are invoked, such as compensation. In Interactions ([Nodine et al.,1994]), the problem is known as weak conflicts. It is recognised that weak conflicts do not fit well into the block structure of a specification language. They are treated more like exceptions and specified by means of event-condition-action rules. The "action" part is always an abort, that is, backtracking (using compensation) to the point where an alternative can be tried. Backtracking can be a very rude way, as [Nodine et al.,1994] admits, but it seems to be impossible to specify a satisfactory general failure handling mechanism. In general, a weak conflict requires a rescheduling of the task components that preserves as much of the original schedule as possible, optimises costs to be made by compensations etc.

Recent years have shown a growing awareness that linguistic theories are relevant for IS design in general and CIS in particular. The so-called Language/Action approach gives content to a new generation of Business Process Models [Teufel & Teufel,1995]. Examples are DEMO [Dietz,1994] and Action Workflow [Medina-Mora et al.,1992]. Underlying these models, the concepts of *obligation* and *authorization* play an important role. An obligation is the result of a commitment to perform a certain act and authorizations restrain or allow the commitment to and operation of an act (including doing other communicative acts). The logic to reason about obligations and related concepts is called *deontic* logic [Wieringa et al.,1989]. The application of deontic logic to communication modelling was first suggested in [Weigand,1993] and worked out in [Dignum & Weigand,1995].

The "weak conflicts" mentioned above usually originate from a violation of an obligation. For that reason, our approach insists that obligations and authorizations of service providers and receivers are modelled. In this way it is possible to reason over any uncooperative action rather than classify them as a true failure (leading to unnecessary rollback or recovery actions of transactions).

(Extended) deontic logic is a convenient tool for expressing the semantics of interoperable transactions, but does not impose any structure on the specification. Interoperable transaction specifications tend to become rather complicated, because of all possible exceptions that must be envisaged and the absence of one central control agency. This not only causes methodological problems in the design phase, but also reduces evolution and reusability of specifications.

The main goal of the present paper is to provide some useful structuring mechanisms for interoperable transactions based on a Language/Action perspective to communication. Loosely speaking, the paper tries to build a bridge between two hitherto separated worlds: the research on interoperable (extended) transactions on the one hand, and the research an business process models on the other. Extended deontic logic provides the material for this bridge.

In section 2, we start with a business process model proposed by [Goldkuhl,1995] that will be used as leading example in the rest of the paper. To illustrate the feasibility of deontic logic, we use it to formalise the semantics of this model. In section 3, a three-level architecture will be introduced for structuring the specification. A distinction is made between task level and transaction level. Moreover, failure handling is dealt with separately by a contingency plan and a contract, respectively. In section 4, this framework is discussed with a view to reusability and dynamic evolution. We conclude with a brief comparison with related works.

2. Business Process Example

Business process is a central concept in the field of Business Process Reengineering. A business process can be defined as a series of coherent activities (value chain) that creates a result with some value for an external or internal customer. In his paper on communicative action, [Goldkuhl,1995] discusses the well-known framework by Michael Porter, and notes some theoretical weaknesses. As an alternative, he describes a communicative action model of business relations and business processes (figure 1).

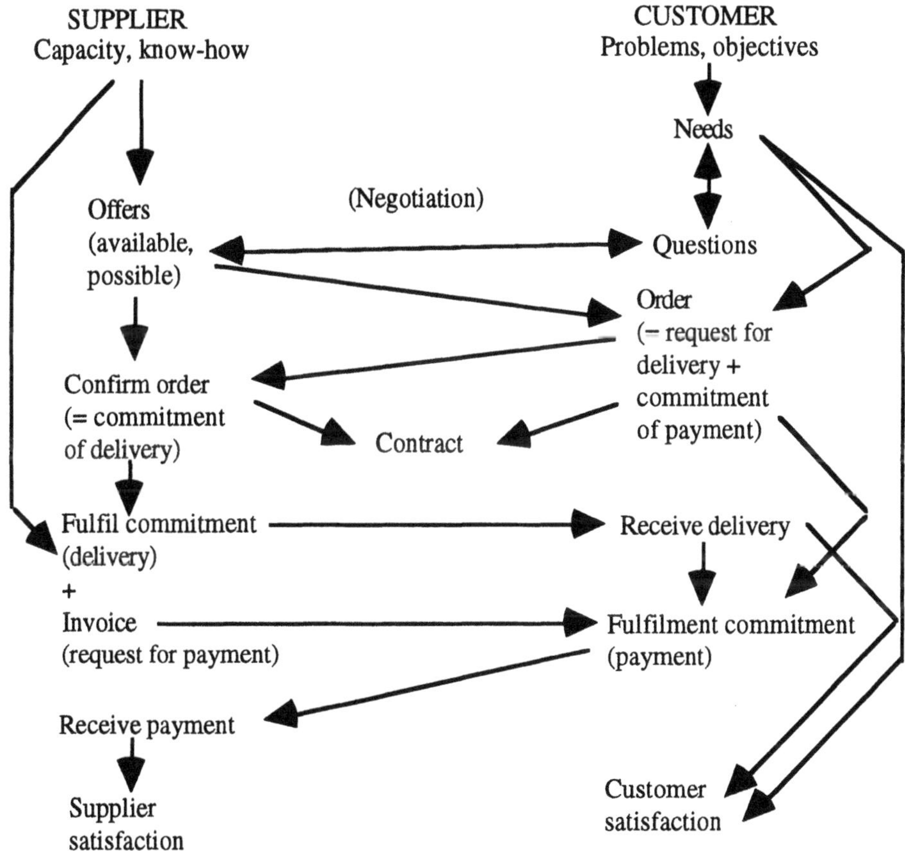

Fig.1. A communicative action model of business relations and business processes (after [Goldkuhl,1995], fig.5)

What distinguishes this model from other BPR models is (a) the focus on interactivity, rather than input-output transformations, and (b), its *generic communicative logic* . For instance, once an order is defined as a mutual obligation (to deliver and to pay, respectively), the fulfilment is a logical consequence, as is the (undesirable) possibility of non-fulfilment (not pictured yet). That the obligation must be mutual can be inferred from the very nature of a business transaction. It is also quite natural that mutual commitments can only be established after a stage of negotiation.

The communicative logic suggests a distinction of four stages in the interchange process between supplier and customer:

1. inquiry and negotiation stage
2. contractual stage
3. fulfilment stage
4. satisfaction stage

It should be noted that no specific messages or actions for the satisfaction stage are given in the model. This is perhaps because satisfaction is often implicit, and only dissatisfaction leads to communicative acts, such as appeals to warrant.

The communicative logic behind the model of Goldkuhl can be made even more precise by formalising the communicative acts (messages) in deontic logic. Deontic logic is an extension of dynamic logic with two operators, `Obl(i,α)` and `Aut(i,α)`, for *obliged* and *authorized*, respectively. Besides `Obl` and `Aut`, we include one more primitive operator in the deontic specification language. This is `Acc`, for accomplishment.

- The semantics of an authorized request to do α is that `Obl(i,α)` holds (as a postcondition) provided that `Aut(i,α)` (as a precondition). In other words, an authorization is a *conditional* obligation.
- `Obl(i,α)` means that i not doing α leads to *violation*. An obligation is weaker than a logical necessity; violation does not lead to inconsistency. Independent rules specify what such a violation implies, e.g. a sanction. These rules are usually expressed in terms of other `Obl` and `Aut` formulas.
- `Acc(α)` means that action α has been executed, and hence the obligation to do α is fulfilled.

The following gives some examples related to Fig.1 now written in Deontic Logic (where `[α]q` means that after action α, q holds, `DIR` (directive) stands for the action `request`):

```
[give-quotation(j,i,g,p)]
  Aut(i,DIR(i,j,deliver(j,i,g,p)))
```

If a company gives a quotation for a certain price (p) the client is authorized to order the product (g) for that price. (This could be a meaning definition for give-quotation).

```
Aut(i,DIR(i,j,deliver(j,i,g,p))) →
    [DIR(i,j,deliver(j,i,g,p))] (Obl(j,deliver(j,i,g,p))
    ∧
    [deliver(j,i,g,p)] Aut(j,DIR(j,i,pay(i,j,p))))
```

If a customer is authorized to order a product for a certain price (i.e. a quotation has been given for that price) then the company is obliged to deliver the product after the customer has ordered it. But after delivery of the product, the company is authorized to order the customer to pay for it.

```
Aut(j,DIR(j,i,pay(i,j,p))) →
  [DIR(j,i,pay(i,j,p))]Obl(i,pay(i,j,p))
```

If an order has been delivered (and authority acquired to request payment) a request for payment induces an obligation for the customer to pay.

Note that the obligation to pay is made conditional: it becomes effective only when the supplier requests for it. This is of course one way of doing it; the obligation can also be instantiated directly when the order is given, and even precede the delivery. These different ways of working can be distinguished in the logic when needed.

Deontic logic can also be used to reason about violations. This part of the specification is not included in Goldkuhl's picture, but will be part of the business contract as well. This holds also for cancellations, which means a retract of an obligation before it has been fulfilled.

Another thing about which the logic can and must be explicit is the expiration of authorizations and obligations. In Deontic Dynamic Logic, this is accounted for by explicit or implicit frame axioms. For example:

```
Obl(i,pay(i,j,p)) →
  [pay(i,j,p)]¬aut(j,DIR(j,i,pay(i,j,p)))
```

After the customer has paid, the company cannot request another payment again.

Goldkuhl emphasises the importance of the satisfaction stage and the *mutual* satisfaction that must be the goal. In the Deontic Logic, two levels of satisfaction can be distinguished. The basic level of satisfaction is reached as soon as the obligations of both partners have been fulfilled, that is, Acc(α) is true for all actions α in the contract. This is in fact the borderline between fulfilment and satisfaction. However, the contract may also describe authorizations for both partners to make claims in the case of dissatisfaction. The second level of satisfaction, and the real end of the interaction, is when these authorizations have expired as well. We will come back to the mutual satisfaction, and Goldkuhl's deviation from the Action Workflow model ([Medina-Mora et al. 1992]) in this respect, in section 4.

The borderlines between the other stages can be expressed in deontic logic as well. The negotiation stage ends with the establishing of certain *authorizations*.. The contractual stage ends with the establishing of certain (usually, mutual) *obligations*, making up the contract. In the case that the authorizations have been negotiated beforehand (cf. section 4), the contractual stage can be entered right away.

More details about the logic can be found in [Weigand et al.,1995] and [Dignum et al.,1995] where it has been extended with temporal deontic constraints, making it possible to describe for instance deadlines and the request to do some action "as soon as possible". Although deontic formulas describe the exchange between the customer and the company exactly and completely, they lack structure. In [Dignum & Weigand, 1995] we have introduced provisionally a language CoLa (Communication Language) with a more readable syntax that structures the (speech) acts into transactions. In the next section, the CoLa framework will be described in more detail, and we will argue for a distinction between task level and transaction level.

3. CoLa Framework

The specification of interoperable transactions needs structure for the sake of complexity reduction and reusability. Besides the notions of messages, transactions and services introduced in our earlier paper ([Dignum & Weigand, 1995]), we distinguish contracts and tasks. We use the general term "agent" for the participants in the interoperable transaction (e.g., the supplier and customer). From an analysis point of view, the agent is a real-world person or company. From a design point of view, the agent can also be a piece of software to which the person or organization has delegated some of his tasks.

Fig. 2 gives a schema in which the CoLa concepts are related. An agent has a certain task that can be split up into subtasks that the agent tries to fulfil. In doing so the agent initiates the necessary transactions. Transactions are seen as a communication process oriented towards a goal, the possible message types provided by each agent and constraints on the synchronisation of messages, together with a specification of what should happen in the case of a failure. In case of an unrecoverable failure the task manager of the agent should be notified so that he can pursue an alternative.

Transactions are part of a contract describing the communication behaviour between two agents concerning some business relation and process. The contract also specifies what should happen in case of violation of one of the obligations or cancellation by one of the agents (by notifying the Contract Manager), possibly leading to other obligations described by another transaction in the contract and triggering the contingency plan, describing what should happen in order to get the subtask fulfilled, managed by the Task Manager.

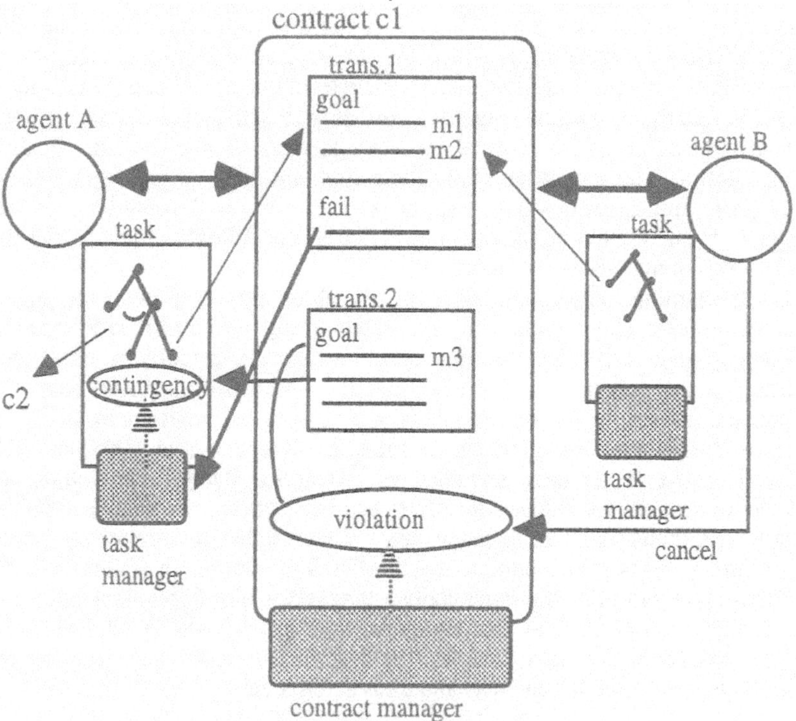

Fig. 2. Tasks, contracts and transactions

3.1. Tasks

A *task* is a meaningful unit of work assigned to an agent. Performing the task often involves communication, that is, using some transactions. However, the task specification and updates thereof do concern the agent in question only, whereas changes in the possible transactions can only be made by consent of the other agent. For that reason, we make a distinction between task and transactions, where the transactions corresponds to the agreements between the two agents and the task draws on this potential for fulfilling an agent's goal.

Tasks can be described in a task language such as TasL [Nodine et al.,1994]. It typically allows the specification of tasks and subtasks, alternatives and temporal constraints. What is crucial in this context, is the way failures are dealt with.

Transactions are prone to many types of failures, including traditional ones like system failures such as system crashes (in the case of interoperable transactions this also includes network failures) and deadlocks caused by concurrent processes. Furthermore a failure occurs when a transaction (as one subtask) is initiated that does not commit (e.g. order product), but also when the transaction does commit first, and the resulting deontic state is violated later (e.g. the company doesn't deliver), or because of cancellation, whereby the other party undoes an achieved effect. These features of transactions directly influence the task specification.

Drawing on previous work in extended transaction models [Elmagarmid,1992], we distinguish the following failure handling methods:

- *fail* - this stops the subtask in a failure state (similar to abort or time out),
- *skip* - this indicates that the subtask is non-vital. The task can be resumed as if the subtask has succeeded,
- *choose* - this prompts for seeking an alternative way to make the subtask run to a successful state (similar to the concept of contingency transaction in DOM [Buchmann et al.,1992]).

A task can be seen as an AND/XOR graph of possible subtasks. The following relations can be defined:

T1 BEFORE T2 (temporal precedence)
Ts = AND(T1,T2, ..) (task/subtask relation)
Ts = XOR (T1, T2, ..) (alternative set)
Ts = XOR (T1, .., skip) (non-vital part)

We can use the temporal logic semantics [Ngu et al,1994] for the precedence relations, while the AND/XOR formula is specified as the Goal of the task. The constraint T1 BEFORE T2 is a paraphrase for the TL expression: ~T2 UNTIL T1.

The execution model is as follows:

- when a task is called, the Task Manager collects the subtasks, puts them into a right order according to the precedence relationships (such an ordering can be stored of course to save computing time). The subtasks are then called one by one. This step continues recursively.
- when a subtask cannot be fulfilled, the next alternative is chosen. If no alternative is available, it means that the subtask fails. It does not mean directly that the parent is aborted, since it is possible that the subtask can still be fulfilled by choosing an alternative in the preceding subtasks. This is tried first (backtracking). Only when no alternative is left, the parent fails.
- the parent also fails when an exit state is reached.
- when an exception occurs , the procedure is basically the same. A next alternative is taken, or, if no alternative is left, backtracking is attempted. To keep the task specification simple, we give the designer the opportunity to specify a contingency plan separately (see below). If no alternatives for backtracking are left, the task fails, but its parent may have alternatives or contingency plans of its own. Every time a task fails, the Task Manager goes up one level in the task hierarchy.

Note that our execution model enforces a "structured approach" in the task specification. We do not allow for arbitrary abort or commit dependencies between subtasks over the boundaries of the parent tasks. This modularity is enforced to keep the specification transparent and maintainable.

A notorious problem with contingencies is that when a subtask is invalidated, later (dependent) subtasks may already have commited, and their result might become obsolete. Whether they have to be retried (and compensated) or not depends on what kinds of results they have produced. We therefore give the designer the opportunity to specify a separate contingency plan. The contingency plan consists basically of a set of *results* (such as supplier list, order-set). Results have an internal object structure, are produced by certain subtasks and can become invalidated by other subtasks. When that occurs, a task can be triggered to repair the damage. This task can make use of the fact that all the essential results obtained so far (and not invalidated) are explicit. For reasons of space, we leave the contingency plan specification for a follow-up paper (Weigand & Ngu, 1995).

We will use the order example to illustrate the task specification (without contingency handling). A task specification consists of a task *name*, a set of *subtasks* (unordered), a set of *temporal constraints*, a *goal* (what makes the task succeed) , and an *exit* (what makes the task fail - abort). Constraints and exit are optional.

```
task order
subtasks
    inquiry
    order-product
    ACCEPT(delivery)
    payment
    cancel-delivery
constraints:
    order-product BEFORE order-delivery;
    inquiry BEFORE order-product;        /*etc
Goal = {delivery}
Exit = {cancel-delivery}
end-task

task inquiry = XOR(get-quotation(abc),
                   get-quotation(xyz))
end-task;
```

- The subtasks are either tasks specified elsewhere or transactions specified in the contract.

- The goal of the task `order` is `delivery`. This goal can only be reached by first an inquiry and a product order.

- In the case of `inquiry` we have used a short-hand notation in which we put the Goal immediately after the task name since there are no constraints.

- The ACCEPT around `delivery` means that this transaction is not initiated by the customer agent himself. Executing the subtask ACCEPT(`delivery`) implies executing that part of the transaction that the customer is supposed to do, in response to the prompt of the supplier.

- A possible contingency part specifies that if the order is cancelled by the other party, the Task Manager has to find an alternative (as if `order-product` had failed).

This will involve finding another supplier. Any contractual matters that need to be resolved (for example, collecting a fine) are not specified here, since they are handled by the Contract Manager (see below). However, dependent subtasks, e.g. reservation for the shipping, if any, are cancelled by the Task Manager in accordance with the contingency plan.

In the example, only two alternative suppliers are taken into account. A better approach would be to first collect a list of possible suppliers. The task specification language should be expressive enough to represent this. At the moment, we are working on a pseudo-Prolog language extension.

Goldkuhl explicitly includes in his model the problems and objectives of the customer and the capacity of the supplier. By embedding the transactions in an agent task, the link to the objectives are now explicit, and relationships with other tasks of the customer company can be described. As far as the supplier is concerned, Goldkuhl makes no reference to objectives, only to capacity. The symmetry between the parties the author argues for is not maintained at this point. In our point of view, the supplier has objectives as well, including producing goods and making money. These can be modelled as supplier tasks. On the other hand, the capacity and know-how do play a role, as constraining factors, but so do they at the customer side, in particular, the financial capacity or liquidity. Therefore we argue for a symmetric treatment of supplier and customer *also* as far as objectives and constraints are concerned. The particular task of the supplier can be modelled as follows:

```
task sell
subtasks
    ACCEPT(get-quotation);
    give-quote;
    ACCEPT(order-product)
    delivery;
    ACCEPT(payment)
constraints:
    give-quote BEFORE ACCEPT(order-product);
    ACCEPT(order-product) BEFORE delivery
Goal = {payment}
end-task
```

3.2. Transactions

Elementary tasks are either executed by the agent as an internal procedure or involve a transaction with another agent. By transactions we mean all *possible* (authorized) messages and message sequences that can be exchanged between the two communicating agents [Dignum et al.,1995]. Real-world events, such as "product delivered" do not play a role directly, but only via messages such as "assert(product delivered)" by means of which a particular agent communicates a certain fact or evaluation. Moreover, since the message interface encapsulates the local database actions of the agent, the latter do not play a role either. Provided that there is agreement on the semantics of the messages exchanged, the specification of these messages is the only concern for the designers of an interoperable transaction. To put it sharply, for an agent sending an "order product" request to a supplier, what counts is that the supplier replies by a positive confirmation, and not what it does in its database. This can and must be sufficient to let the transaction succeed, and, if the supplier might turn out to be unreliable, it is the confirmation message that provides ground for further (for example, legal) action. So we may assume that the speech act "assert(product delivered)" implies the material action of delivery, and we could make an axiom of this, but we refrain from stating it in this paper because the material action is not relevant for the communication model.

Each transaction has a set of agents, the messages, the constraints (in propositional temporal logic), and the goal and exit states. A transaction execution leading to a goal state means that the transaction succeeds, whereas an execution leading to an exit state means that the transaction fails. "States" are identified here by message occurrences. Higher-level transactions are aggregations of subtransactions, and can specify temporal constraints on the subtransactions. The temporal constraints (not included in our previous paper) are temporal logic formulae [Ngu et al,1994].

All messages are specified as an illocution function, such as request, and a propositional content (an action or proposition). This is in accordance with the common practice in the Language/Action perspective. The semantics of the illocutions are specified directly in deontic logic [Weigand et al, 1995]. The advantage of using these illocution functions is that otherwise the illocution is hidden in the message name (e.g. req_quote), so that no generalization is possible over the semantics.

For our example we arrive at the following transactions, among others.

```
transaction quotation
    isa get_authorization(order(Partno, Quantity, Price))
end-transaction
```

```
transaction get_authorization(a:action)
agents:
    c: customer        /* all customers in the network
    s: supplier        /* all suppliers in the network
c can send
  {messages:
    request(authorize(a)) to s
  }
s can send
  {messages:
    authorize(a) to c
    refuse(authorize(a)) to c
  }
constraints
    request(authorize()) BEFORE authorize()
Goal = {authorize(a)};
Exit = {refuse(authorize(a)}
end-transaction;
```

The above states that the transaction quotation is a specialisation of the transaction get_authorization. This transaction is defined as a request to get authorization, followed by an authorization or a refusal. Specialization means inheritance of the message set, the constraints, the Goal and the Exit. All these parts can be extended (not overruled) in the specializaton. The message authorize is predefined and creates an authorization for a certain action. The effect of this sample specification is the same as the give-quotation example in section 2, but here we make use of more generic primitives. Note that the constraint here is so self-evident that it is better built-in in the language as an axiom.

```
transaction order-delivery(O: order)
agents:
    s: supplier
    c: customer
s can send
  {messages:
    assert(delivered(O)) to c
  }
c can send
  {messages:
    accept(delivered(O)) to s
  }
Goal = {accept(delivered(O))}
end-transaction
```

This example shows a typical transaction, in which the two partners express agreement about a situation by means of two messages. In most cases, the accept is essential, since delivery is more than saying the order is delivered, it is also more than just putting the containers in front of the entrance. Only when the customer accepts the goods as such (a speech act), the delivery succeeds.

```
transaction payment(s:supplier,$:amount)
agents:
    c: customer
    b: bank
c can send
  {messages:
    request(transfer_money(s,$)) to b
    request(increase_credit) to b
  }
b can send
  {messages:
    commit(transfer_money(s,$)) to c
    assert(credit(c,$)) to c
    refuse(transfer_money(s,$), "not enough credit") to c
  }
constraints
    refuse(transfer_money(s,$), "not enough credit")
          BEFORE request(increase_credit)
    request(transfer_money()
          BEFORE commit(transfer_money)
Goal = {commit(transfer_money(s,$))}
end-transaction
```

Although the transactions often take the form of a request followed by a commit, or an assert followed by an accept, sometimes intermediary messages are allowed, as with `increase_credit` in the bank payment example, and sometimes the response is superfluous because the request/assert was already authorized. In the method DEMO ([Dietz,1994]), communication is modelled exclusively by means of so-called actogeneous and factogeneous conversations, creating an obligation and a fact respectively. Each of these conversations is required to have at least two messages (request/commit, assert/accept). A limited set of additional messages, to be used in the negotiation, such as refuse, and counter offer, are allowed as well. Although this is not essential for our method, DEMO could be integrated into it as far as the transaction modelling is concerned. DEMO complements this model with an Information Model and an Action model. The Information Model, describing the object structure of the message content, can be easily combined with our transactions as well, but the Action Model is, in our method, divided over the Task specification and the Contract.

3.3. Contracts

Conceptually, in our framework, contracts specify obligations between different parties about services provided to each other. If a particular service is not being fulfilled, it is possible to reason over this violation and take a remedial action without forcing the whole task to abort. In this way, the process is more reactive to failures.

From a technical point of view, a contract is nothing but a protocol binding different parties to their commitments by explicitly specifying the type of services agreed upon, the obligations and the failure recovery methods. From an organizational point of view, a contract between interoperable systems stemming from different organisations also has the purpose of laying down some agreement. By grounding it in other contracts or business law, it may have legal status.

A contract is based on a set of transactions, where a transaction is a set of messages and constraints between them, or, alternatively, an aggregation of reified transaction types. A contract describes the authorized communication behaviour among providers and receivers of services. If the provider does not adhere to the obligation, it is the job of the Contract Manager to impose the violation policies. It would complicate the task specifications and lower the reusability if this communication is included in the task. As stated before the Task Manager should only be responsible in ensuring that a task is brought to its goal, not how violation of commitments are being dealt with.

The reader may have noted that we sometimes use the term "contract" for the specification of the transactions plus the way failures are dealt with, and sometimes for the latter part only, separated from the transactions. This is to avoid inventing yet another term. In the following, the restricted meaning is intended.

A contract is specified as a set of deontic clauses (called 'services' in [Dignum & Weigand, 1995]). The status of an interaction of the two partners can be described in terms of obligations, authorizations and accomplishments. Logically speaking, this is a big deontic logic formula. This formula can be brought into a conjunctive normal form. Each clause in this normal form is a disjunction of literals. The contract describes the deontic clauses and their dynamics, that is, a clause is created by one or more transactions, and is removed by other transactions. So the state of the interaction can be represented by a *set* of clauses, as in a Petri Net, where a state is identified by a set of token placements. Due to lack of space, the formal aspects of the contract will be worked out in another paper ([Weigand& Ngu, 1995]). We restrict ourselves to a few intuitive examples, related to `order-product`:

```
clause S1: Obl(a,deliver)
in
   order product
goal
   delivery              =>    S3
exit
   VIOLATION                   =>    S4
   cancel-order product        =>    S2
   cancel-delivery             =>    S4
modified by
   change-conditions
end {S1}

clause S2: Obl(t,pay($100));
in
   cancel-order product
goal
   fine-payment
end{S2}

clause S3: Acc(a,order)
in
   delivery
end {S3}

clause S4: Obl(a,pay($1000))
in
   cancel-delivery
end{S4}

clause S5: Aut(t,warrant)
in
   delivery
goal
   date(D1)
end{S5}
```

The clause is identified by a number (unique within the contract) and may have a name. Its content is specified as a deontic formula. The "`in`" part sums up the transactions that lead to this state, provided they have been closed successfully. The goal and exit transactions have the effect of moving to another deontic clause. The old clause is no longer valid. The difference between goal and exit is that one involves the fulfilment of the obligation whereas the other involves a violation or cancellation. Violation means the deadline has passed without fulfilment of the obligation (in this example leading to the same state as `cancel-delivery`). Note that in S4 we only record the incoming transactions, and not the fact that violation of S1 also leads to this clause. Finally, the contract also allows the specification of update transactions that do not invalidate the deontic content but only modify certain parameters (e.g. a change of the delivery date).

The contract does not only specify the "success line" of the interaction, but especially the exceptions. In some cases, it is possible to return to the success line. For example, the supplier might have the obligation to offer an alternative product (in `change-conditions`). If this is acceptable, clause S1 remains valid (this can be handled by the Contract Manager). If the supplier does not offer an alternative product, or when it is not acceptable, it is no longer possible to reach the final state, and the interaction fails. Such a failure has to be handled by the Task Manager (see previous section).

Note that this is done only when the contract has no solutions to offer anymore. During the execution of the interaction, other obligations may be instantiated. For example, the obligation to pay a fine or the authorization to warrant. These obligations can be represented explicitly in our framework. However, the further processing of these "side-effects" should not interfere with the task execution. To achieve this independence, we suppose that execution of the interactions takes place in an agent architecture. When the execution of the interaction leads to an obligation of the customer to pay a fine, this obligation is automatically put on the agent's agenda. Since by definition the agent recurrently checks its agenda and executes its tasks, the fine will also be paid in due time. On the other hand, if it is the supplier that has a liability, it is up to the agent to see to it that the payment is actually made.

4. Contracting

Contracts, in the general sense of agreements between commercial partners, can be defined on two levels. In Goldkuhl's model, a contract is the result of the negotiation, and boils down to a commitment to deliver and a commitment to pay. Let us call this an order contract. In the previous section, we have defined a contract as a set of services that specify authorized messages (in transactions) and their deontic effects. We assume that such a contract has been set up by the two partners only once and then frequently used. We call this a procedural contract.

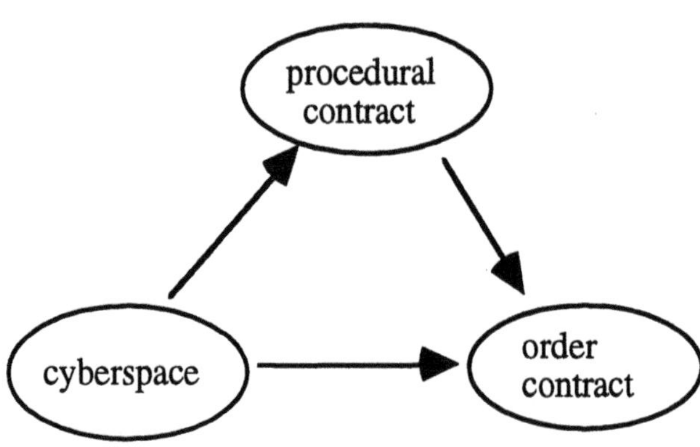

Fig. 3. Contracting in cyberspace

Since "contracts" can be defined on different levels, we should require from any communication modelling approach that it can account for these levels. We want to say a few words about how our approach can do this.

Starting from an empty cyberspace (Fig. 3) in which agents can only communicate, agents must have the possibility to offer services. A service is a publicly accessible interface of the agent, comparable to a method in object-oriented programming. A supplier agent can provide the service of giving an offer. When a customer agent requests for this service, the supplier can refuse or accept. If he accepts, he sends an offer, that is, an authorization for the customer to order a product with the obligation to pay for it. If the customer agent uses this authorization, an order contract in the sense of Goldkuhl has been accomplished. All that is required in this case is a reliable and standardised way of requesting a service, as well as the "umbrella" protection of some international business law that guarantees the legal status of the obligations.

Nowadays it is often considered an economic advantage to have closer business relations with some preferred supplier or customer. In that case, the two parties can make more agreements beforehand, for example about a guaranteed delivery time. Such a contract has to be set up. This can be supported by another service of the agent that offers contracts rather than specific products. If the customer accepts the offer, a mutually agreed contract is accomplished. This can be used then by the customer in the way described in section 3.

The contract can be "symmetric" in the sense of Goldkuhl (section 2), but also establish an asymmetric power relationship, in the same way as an employer can contract a new employee. We then arrive in a situation in which Goldkuhl's critique of Action Workflow - that it is rather one-sided in its customer[initiator] emphasis - is no longer valid. The one-sided Action Workflow loops fit well in an organizational setting with existing power and authorization relationships, whereas the symmetric business process model fits well in the free market context of autonomous negotiating agents. So we feel that both models have their value, depending on the context.

5. Comparison with Related Work

The Interactions model [Nodine et al.,1994] uses "weak constraints" and backtracking when they are violated. Our failure handling uses backtracking as well, but it goes further in two respects. First, we do not abort later (dependent) subtasks immediately, but only when the committed service cannot be maintained (by the Contract Manager). The contract may provide specific alternatives; if these succeed, no abort or backtracking is necessary. Secondly, we have sorted out the complex concept of "compensation" into two more focused notions: compensation of the other party, as specified in the contract, and "compensation", or contingency handling, of the task. For contingency handling, we proposed a separate specification part that monitors the results obtained and invalidated so far. Although exception handling is a complex issue and will remain so, the least we can do is try to manage the complexity. This is the most important but modest goal of the task/contract distinction. We also consider it an advantage that task management can be turned into a local issue, rather than a concern of the (global) multidatabase as in the Interactions model. In this way the global control is kept to a minimum, which makes the specification and implementation much more flexible.

In [Alonso et al, 1996] a comparison is made between the advanced transaction models and workflow models. It is argued that transaction models are too centered around databases, and that (in many respects) workflow models offer a superset of transaction models. This is in accordance with our approach. However, we feel not at ease with the FlowMark workflow model adopted in that paper that (a) still separates activities from data (cf. speech acts) and (b) specifies flow of control in a mechanistic way (cf. contracting, negotiation)

The paper has also aimed at providing a formal way of specifying business process models such as DEMO, Goldkuhl's BPR and Action Workflow. We have shown how these approaches can be put to use. However, it has also become clear that they have different scopes. For example, DEMO offers a rigid methodology, but only on the transaction level. Goldkuhl's BPR is a generic task model that is particularly aimed at free market exchanges, whereas Action Workflow is a generic task model (and perhaps transaction model) that is more oriented towards an organizational context. All models mentioned do not pay much attention yet to failure handling.

Our results are quite compatible with the ideas on electronic contracting developed by Ronald Lee and his colleagues (eg. [Dewitz, 1991]). In this work, attention has been given to the "grounding" of electronic messages in an "umbrella contract" that describes in particular the legal effect of the speech act. Legal rules are formalized in deontic logic and legal procedures are represented by means of Petri Nets. It appears that our use of Petri Nets (contracts) is more restricted: we don't use it for representing temporal constraints, we identify each place node with a deontic clause, and use it in particular for violation handling.

References

[Alonso et al, 1996] G. Alonso, D. Agrawal, A. El Abbadi, M. Kamath, R. Gunthor, C. Mohan, "Advanced Transaction Models in Workflow Contexts", In: Proc. of the 12th Int Conf on Data Engineering, New Orleans, Lousiana, March 1996.

[Buchmann et al.,1992] A. Buchmann, M. Tamer Özsu, M. Hornick, D. Georgakopoulos, F. Manola, "A Transaction Model for Active Distributed Object Systems", in: Database Transaction Models for advanced applications, A. Elmagarmid (ed), Morgan-Kaufman, 1992.

[Dewitz, 1991] S.D. Dewitz, "Contracting on a performative network: using information technology as a legal intermediary", in: Collaborative Work, Social Communications and Information Systems, R.K.Stamper et al (eds), North-Holland, 1991.

[Dietz,1994] J.L.G. Dietz, "Business Modelling for Business Redesign", in: Proc. of 27th Hawaii Int.l. conf. on System Sciences, IEEE Computer Society Press, 1994.

[Dignum & Weigand,1995] F. Dignum and H. Weigand, "Communication and Deontic Logic", in: Information Systems, Correctness and Reusability, Proc. of ISCORE-94 Workshop, R. Wieringa and R. Feenstra (eds.), World Scientific, Singapore, 1995.

[Dignum & Weigand, 1995] F. Dignum and H. Weigand, "Modelling Communication between Cooperative Systems", in: K.Lyytinen, J.Ivari, M.Rossi (eds), "Advanced Information Systems Engineering" (LNCS-932), Springer-Verlag, Berlin, 1995, pp140-153. (Proc. of CAISE-95).

[Dignum et al.,1996] F. Dignum, H. Weigand, E. Verharen, "Meeting the deadline: on the formal specification of temporal deontic constraints", Proc. of ISMIS'96.

[Elmagarmid,1992] A. Elmagarmid (ed.), Database Transaction Models for Advanced Applications, Morgan-Kaufman, 1992.

[Goldkuhl,1995] G. Goldkuhl, "Information as Action and Communication", in: The Infological Equation, Essays in honour of B. Langefors, B. Dahlbom (ed.), Gothenburg Studies in Information Systems, Gothenburg Univ, 1995. (also: Linkoping Univ report LiTH-IDA-R-95-09)

[Medina-Mora et al.,1992] R. Medina-Mora, T. Winograd, R. Flores, F. Flores, "The Action Workflow Approach to Workflow Management Technology", in: Proc. of 4th Conf. on Computer Supported Cooperative Work (CSCW'94), ACM, 1994.

[Ngu et al,1994] A. Ngu, R. Meersman and H. Weigand, "Specification and verification of communication for interoperable transactions", in: Int.l. Journal of Intelligent en Cooperative Information Systems (IJICS) 3 (1), p. 47-56, 1994.

[Nodine et al.,1994] M.H. Nodine, N. Nakos, S.Zdonik, "Specifying Flexible Tasks in a Multidatabase", in: Proc. CoopIS-94, March 1994.

[Teufel & Teufel,1995] S. Teufel and B. Teufel, "Bridging Information Technology and Business - Some Modelling Aspects", in: ACM SIGOIS Bulletin 16 (1), p. 13-17, 1995.

[Wächter & Reuter,1992] H. Wächter and A. Reuter, "The ConTract Model", in: Database Transaction Models for advanced applications, A. Elmagarmid (ed), Morgan-Kaufman, 1992.

[Weigand,1993] H. Weigand, "Deontic aspects of communication", in: Proc. of Deontic Logic in Computer Science (DEON'92), J.-J.Ch. Meyer, R. Wieringa (eds.), Wiley, 1993.

[Weigand et al.,1995] H. Weigand, E. Verharen, and F. Dignum, "Integrated Semantics for Information and Communication Systems", in: Proc of IFIP DS-6 Database Semantics, Stone-Mountain, Georgia, USA, 1995.

[Weigand& Ngu, 1995] H. Weigand, A. Ngu, "Flexible specification of interoperable transactions". Working paper, Tilburg University, 1995.

[Wieringa et al.,1989] R.J. Wieringa, J.-J.Ch.Meyer, and H. Weigand, "Specifying dynamic and deontic integrity constraints", in: Data & Knowledge Engineering (4) 2, pp.157-191, 1989.

On Information Modeling to Support Interoperable Spatial Databases

Nectaria Tryfona
National Center for Geographic Information and Analysis
Boardman Hall, University of Maine, Orono, ME 04469-5711, U.S.A.
nectaria@spatial.maine.edu

and

Jayant Sharma
National Center for Geographic Information and Analysis
Department of Spatial Information Science and Engineering
Boardman Hall, University of Maine, Orono, ME 04469-5711, U.S.A.
jayant@spatial.maine.edu

Abstract. A major research topic in geographic databases is that of interoperability, i.e., the capability of integrating transparently remote data and processes in an open environment. This paper addresses the issue of information modeling for interoperating geographic databases. In particular, it deals with the topic of exchanging semantics at the information systems context. Our proposal is based on the peculiarities of spatial data, namely field- and object-based views of space and spatial relationships, that are critical for the representation of information in an interoperable, yet unified "system". A generic Geographic Data Model that encapsulates these semantics and makes their interchange among remote systems possible and without ambiguities is discussed. We show, with an example, how this model supports interaction among heterogeneous spatial application domains. This research effort is based on (a) the requirements expressed by the OpenGIS community, (b) results from modeling "classical" interoperable applications, and (c) a well-established theory on database modeling of geographic applications.

1 Introduction

Geographic Information Systems (GIS) are decision support tools based on the collection, storage, retrieval and representation of spatial data. An *Interoperable* (or *Interoperating*) *GIS* is one that allows remote systems seamless and transparent access to its functionality and data. It is a distributed yet unified environment, in which all supported models and processes are compatible. The heterogeneous remote systems are autonomous and "logically" connected providing meaningful exchange of data (Goh et. al., 1994). In a multisystem GIS all components conform to generic data and process models, regardless who produced them, how, when and why. The difference between an interoperable and a distributed environment is that, in the former, various applications share and exchange processes and data, while in the latter all processes and data belong to the same application.

Interoperability of GIS is currently a central research and development effort for the geographic data processing community. It is fueled by the growing need for developing applications based on interaction among various hardware and software components located at different sites, owned by different "vendors", and designed for widely differing application domains. It is also observed that current technology is difficult to use when multiple systems are invited to work together, each one independently, forming an integrated environment.

Therefore the range of issues to be dealt in interoperable spatial information systems is quite broad. Starting with designing open architectures that allow access to geographic information on distributed, heterogeneous systems and ranging till the development of data and process models suitable for these open architectures, a requirements analysis for spatial operations, study of the properties of space that contribute to peculiarities in spatial data handling, and specification of complex interdependencies and consistency constraints between geographic data and operations.

Interoperability is not a new concept. It has been around for many years, primarily in the computer science research community, for describing solutions to build systems by combining heterogeneous resources and services (Manola et. al., 1992; Soley, 1992; Elmagarmid and Pu, 1990). Although interoperability of systems is a major research focus for various domains, (see for example, heterogeneous databases (Sheth and Karabaitis, 1993; Sciore et. al., 1994; Sheth and Kalinichenco, 1992; Kashyap and Sheth, 1994), medical information systems (Mannal and Burgara, 1993), and business applications (Chen et. al., 1993)), each one has its own peculiarities that must be addressed. Common to all domains, however, are the issues of cooperation, and capturing and exchanging semantics among multiple databases and applications. There are several approaches to these aspects: Schek and Wolf (1992) describe mechanisms for the cooperation between object database systems and autonomous operation services in a heterogeneous environment. Their architectural framework for interoperability between database management and application-specific computation is based on a kernel model which exists on top a generic data model used by all components. DeLorenzi and Wolf (1993) propose a protocol for Cooperative Spatial Information Managers linking several software components of an open GIS, that is, statistics packages, computational geometric algorithms, record storage managers, spatial storage managers and users' applications. Goh et. al. (1994) address the issue of context interchange in a dynamic environment such as a stock market. Their work tackles more than just schematic and semantic incompatibilities among interoperating systems by providing a mechanisms for expressing and exchanging context. Despite the varied approaches and issues tackled all of the above research efforts assume the existence of a *generic data model* known to all remote systems.

This paper deals with the issue of a generic spatial data model suitable for facilitating interoperability of GIS. In other words, we address the topic of information modeling for interoperable spatial databases. Spatial databases are an indispensable part of GISs and in an interoperating environment their role is to support the exchange of data and operations as well as the semantics of geographic information. This work examines the special semantics of spatial data in an information systems context and describes a geographic model to encapsulate the distinguishing properties of space. The major contribution of this paper is: (a) the study and definition of special issues which arise in spatial databases that any satisfactory model must handle for supporting interoperability among autonomous and heterogeneous applications, and (b) the presentation of a formal model which can serve as the intermediate model understandable by all the remote systems comprising the spatial interoperating environment.

Our current work is based on: (a) the requirements specifically expressed by the Technical Committee of the Open Geodata Interoperability Specification (OGIS, 1995), (b) results from studying interoperability among GISs (Voisard and Schweppe, 1994), (c) research results from modeling "classical" applications in an interoperating environment (Schek and Wolf, 1992; DeLorenzi and Wolf, 1993; Kim, 1995; Goh et.

al., 1994), and (d) modeling issues of spatial databases (Hadzilacos and Tryfona, 1992; Delis et. al., 1994; Tryfona, 1994; Tryfona and Hadzilacos, 1995).

The remainder of the paper is organized as follows: Section 2 gives the conceptual framework of an open environment, presents an overview of levels of an interoperable architecture, and focuses on a specific proposal for interoperable geographic databases. Section 3 describes the semantics of spatial information which must form the basis of a successful model for interoperable databases, while Section 4 presents a generic model for supporting and facilitating interoperability, and proposes its use as the enterprise model for cooperating spatial applications. Section 5 gives an example of the model use and Section 6 concludes with a summary of the results and a discussion of future work.

2 The Conceptual Framework

Specific results from all aforementioned efforts can be used to accomplish an open GIS environment. On the other hand, the complexity of an interoperable GIS leads to the idea of layer decomposition (Voisard and Schweppe, 1994). Each layer corresponds to a different level of abstraction, starting with the application or user level down to the invocation of system services. There are four basic layers: (a) the application layer, which is concerned with application depended user requests, (b) the abstract services layer, which is a uniform view of the overall system (c) the concrete services layer, which has a view of precise operations that can be asked of each system, and (d) the system services layer, which deals with invocation of services to the specialized system (Voisard and Schweppe, 1994) (Figure 1).

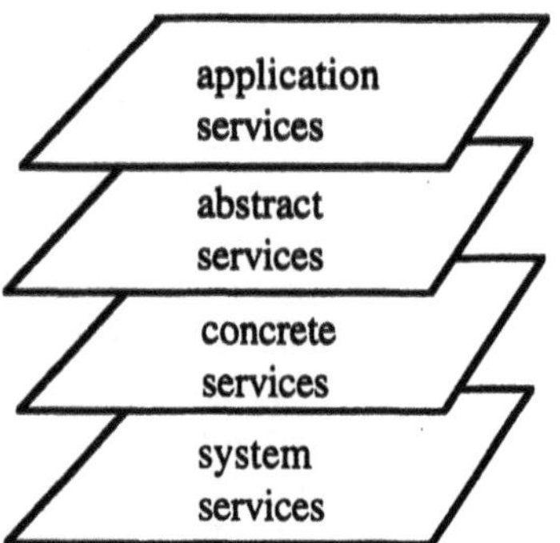

Fig. 1. The layered architecture for an interoperable environment proposed by (Voisard and Schweppe, 1994).

From the perspective of data modeling, the first layer (i.e., application services) deals with *user views*, while the second one (i.e., abstract services) addresses the issue of definitions of *objects*, *properties*, *relationships* and *operations* among them. At these two levels, in an interoperable environment, there is a need to exchange data which correspond to portions of applications and hence databases. Exchanging just computer metaphors, e.g., records, layers and processes among the remote systems, leads to lack of data semantics (Hadzilacos, 1995). Semantics in GISs have a special role since the same information can be represented in different ways and data with similar representations may have totally different meaning (Abel and Kilby, 1994; Pascoe and Penny, 1995), (Hadzilacos, 1995).

We base our proposal on the layered approach of (Voisard and Schweppe, 1994). In particular, we address the issue of exchanging semantics and data by using a Geographic Data Model (GDM). Figure 2 illustrates the rationale of interoperable geographic databases from the database modeling viewpoint. Each remote system provides an interface for the spatial application built on top of a GIS. Each application communicates with the local data by using a local DataBase Management System (DBMS) and with remote data and processes through the GISs. The GISs communicate via GDM by providing a mechanism to translate their particular model to GDM and vice versa.

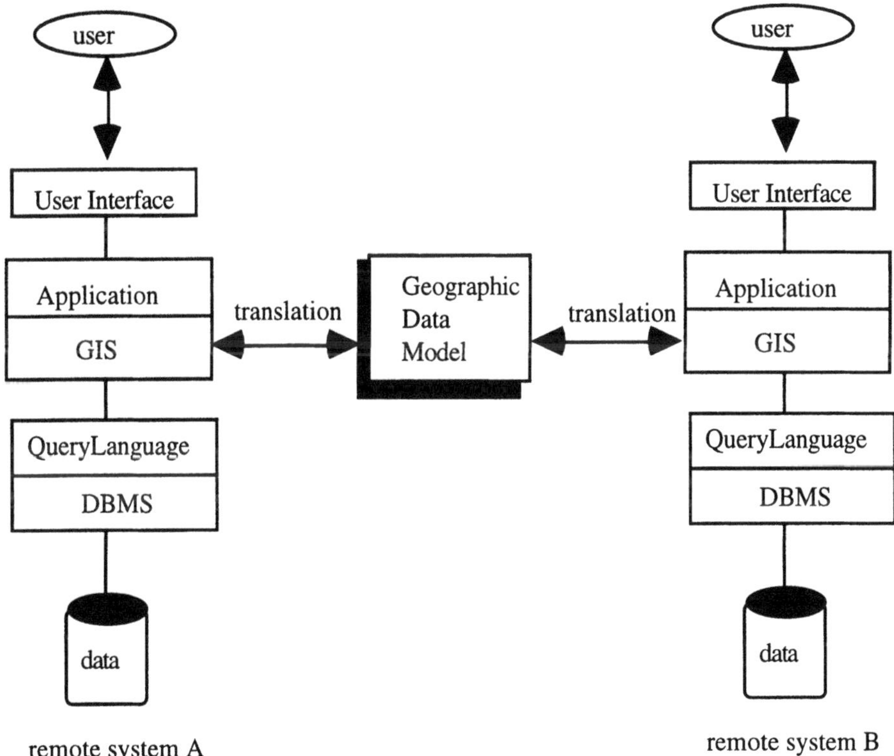

Fig. 2. Interoperating Geographic Databases.

GDM acts as an abstract level communication protocol among the remote systems. It is responsible for representing (a) user views, and (b) objects and operations, formally, without ambiguities, in a way understandable, adaptable and transferable to models that remote systems use. It includes data definition facilities to homogenize different representations of semantically equivalent data in remote systems at different levels of detail. Therefore, GDM corresponds to the application and abstract services layers of Figure 1.

3 Semantics of Spatial Information and Desiderata for Modeling

A clear understanding of the semantics of spatial information will facilitate data modeling for interoperable spatial databases. The *what* and *how* of data semantics, its representation, and exchange is the topic of much discussion. We adapt Sheth's proposal (Sheth, 1995) that:

(a) there is a difference between semantics captured by human beings and computers (we deal with the latter),
(b) in the information systems context, semantics can be viewed as a mapping between an object of the real world and one modeled, represented and/or stored in an information system,
(c) the process of capturing semantics by a computer can be improved by defining the syntax of the data, and
(d) regularities in databases (i.e. constraints) that capture objects' behavior in the real-world are components of the semantics.

We also concern ourselves with the semantics of spatial information as a whole, rather than the semantics of individual spatial entities, since all entities inherit these common properties and behavior (Tryfona and Hadzilacos, 1995).

Based on experience from specific application development (UtilNets, 1994) as well as from general studies (Couclelis, 1992), (Camara et. al., 1992), we came to the result that the modeling framework for the semantics must at least handle:

- the field- and object-based views of geographic space, and
- spatial relationships.

We analyze these concepts and then we show why they are critical for the representation of spatial information in an interoperable environment:

- The domain expert often characterizes geographic objects by using spatial varying properties, such as the soil_type of a land_parcel, or the height of a mountain (Tryfona and Hadzilacos, 1995). In fact these are properties of the space inherited by the geographic object of interest since if one object was replaced by another without changing the spatial location, these properties would remain the same. For example, if two land parcels are combined to form a new one then the soil_type of the combined parcel is that of its predecessors, whereas if the boundaries of a land_parcel change, the soil_type may also change (Tryfona and Hadzilacos, 1995). In general, if several objects occupy the same space then they share the same values for their space-varying properties. Therefore, it would be more accurate to assign these properties to "space" (as fields) and provide a mechanism for objects to "inherit" properties of space at the occupied position (Tryfona and Hadzilacos, 1995). The *orthogonal* object and field views of space are rather deep issues with counterparts in physics and philosophy as atomic and plenum views (Couclelis, 1992). The dichotomy is most likely based on human cognition which "appears to make use of both the object and field views, but at different geographic scales and for different purposes" (Couclelis, 1992). For modeling of geographic applications designers need both field and object views at their disposal. That is, geographic objects can be discrete entities with boundaries separating them (the requirement on handling fuzzy boundaries notwithstanding), however it must also be possible to describe spatial properties, such as ground_elevation and vegetation, without attributing them to specific objects.

- Describing relationships among objects is the key of capturing semantics (Sheth, 1995). A major issue in geographic databases is expressing spatial relationships among geographic entities. Spatial relationships not only express interdependencies among objects but also integrity constraints on a collection of related objects. For example, the spatial relationships A *inside* B and B *inside* C imply the relationship A *inside* C. Any generic model should be able to express spatial integrity constraints, define geographic object classes determined through spatial relationships, and express spatial queries. The definition of a Square, in a cadastral application, as "a land parcel which is not contained in any building block" is an example of using topological integrity constraints. The models should also lead to straightforward solutions for explicitly storing topology in the logical and physical levels -a common practice despite topology being derivable from object positions (Hadzilacos and Tryfona, 1992).

The above concepts and requirements are a consequence of the *nature of the domain -spatial* in this case- rather than individual objects. Therefore a generic model which will make possible the interchange of spatial information in an interoperable environment must encapsulate the special semantics of this domain, as well as permit the standard syntactic and semantic definitions of entities required for an open information system.

4 The Geographic Data Model

This section discusses the Geographic Data Model (GDM) which can serve as the enterprise model of the interoperable environment. GDM captures the semantics of a geographic database, i.e., the concepts described in the previous section. We don't invite others at remote locations to use our model. Each remote system (application) (Figure 2) may use a different model and language. As they express the same aspects, all models are just different syntactic versions of the same underlying spatial concepts encapsulated by GDM; hence, they can be used interchangeably.

The following presentation of GDM is based on Hadzilacos and Tryfona's (1992; 1994) earlier work which uses an object-oriented approach and an unambiguous syntax. We first describe how GDM deals with geographic objects, fields, operations among them, and spatial relationships and integrity constraints. Next we present the mechanism of GDM to accommodate the object-based approach (§4.1), relationships among objects (§4.2), the field-based approach (the concept of layers and operations among them, §4.3) and the interrelationship between the object and field approaches (§5).

4.1 Dealing with Geographic Objects

A *database* is a set of objects which represent part of the real world. Each *object* belongs to an *object class* (or entity set) characterized by a set of *properties* or *attributes*, and a set of *methods* or *operations*. Each attribute is associated with a *domain*, which is an unrestricted set of *values*. Methods are the only means to access the attributes. So each object instance (entity) in a database is represented by a set of values each belonging to the domain of the corresponding attribute of the object class.

In geographic applications spatial objects have a *position* which links the object with *space*. *Position* is a function defined on geographic objects and for each object it returns a part of space (Tryfona and Hadzilacos, 1995). This approach places no restriction on the model of space. For example, 2-dimensional Euclidean space is modeled using an entity set homomorphic to R^2, i.e., the space contains sets of points.

The entity set homomorphic to R^2 corresponds to vector systems, while the one homomorphic to Z^2 corresponds to raster systems.

Objects in geographic databases have another special attribute, namely their *dimension*. Its domain is 0, 1, 2, or *null*, and corresponds to the geometric types *point*, *arc*, and *region*. Objects with a *null* dimension are aspatial (or non-geographic) while non-null dimension objects are called geometric or geographic objects and have a position (Hadzilacos and Tryfona, 1992).

Geometric operations are performed on objects' positions. The primary geometric operations are assumed to be defined together with a domain. Strictly speaking these operations are defined on objects and not on their positions. It simplifies the statement of the definitions, however, and creates no confusion if we describe them as acting on positions (see (Hadzilacos and Tryfona, 1992; Delis et. al., 1994) for the formal treatment, on which the following set of primary geometric operations is based). The set of operations includes: (a) *primary operations* whose range is real, like *distance* and *area*, (b) *primary operations* whose range is a geometric type, like *union*, *difference*, *nodes*, etc., (c) *derived operations* whose range is real, like *perimeter* and *length*, and (d) *derived operations* whose range is a geometric data type, like *intersect*.

The above operations on objects are concerned with the attribute *position* and hence with spatial relationships among the objects. The next section describes the facilities within the GDM for expressing spatial relationships and constraints.

4.2 Dealing with Spatial Relationships

A *relationship* is a condition on a tuple of values of objects' attributes. Relationships which are conditions on the attribute *position* are called *spatial*. In geographic applications *topological relationships* are a critical subset of the various kinds of spatial relationships. An accepted and commonly used definition of topological relationships between two geographic objects is based on point-set topology (Egenhofer and Herring, 1991). Topological relationships between geometric objects are characterized by considering empty and non-empty intersection of their boundaries and interiors and are called *elementary topological relationships*.

In GDM, complex topological relationships, integrity constraints, and queries, are constructed using predicate calculus expressions. A topological sentence is built out of atomic topological formulae with negation, conjunction, disjunction, and universal and existential quantification (Hadzilacos and Tryfona, 1992).

Based on the above, the example of Section 3: "*A square is a land parcel that is not contained in any building block*" is transformed into:

$$\text{CONTAINED\_IN}(lp, bb){:}\, r_6(lp, bb) \vee r_7(lp, bb)$$
$$\text{SQUARE} = \{lp \mid lp \in \text{LANDPARCEL} \wedge \neg\exists bb \in \text{BUILDING\_BLOCK}(\text{CONTAINED\_IN}(lp, bb))\}$$

Thus objects can be interrelated in a geographic database and participate in complex spatial integrity constraints and queries.

4.3 Dealing with Layers (fields)

A fundamental requirement of spatial database design is the ability to model spatial properties, i.e., to *associate parts of space with an attribute*. Spatial applications deal with the two orthogonal generalizations of spatial properties (Hadzilacos and Tryfona, 1994): (a) the association of the whole space with one attribute (the field view), and (b) the associations of sets of attributes with a geometric figure (the object view). The first is modeled with concepts such as *layers*, whereas the second is modeled with concepts oriented towards objects. This section describes how the field view is supported by GDM.

Dealing with spatial varying attributes means dealing with layers. A *layer* is a set of geometric figures (which are representations of geographic objects, consisting of a boundary and an interior) with associated values. Thus, it is natural to define a layer as a function from geometric figures to attributes or as a relation with the geometric figure as the key attribute (Delis et. al., 1994). From the user's point of view layers are often represent derived information. In such cases they are called *virtual* and they are related with the way users need to view data -a concept similar with that of database views. In manipulating layers it is sufficient to be able to modify the geometric figures (i.e. the domain of the function) or the attributes (i.e. the range of the function) and to combine such changes through function composition. There are with four types of operations forming the functional algebra (Delis et. al., 1994):

(a) Operations (COMPUTE ATTRS) on a single layer function, which change its range (by adding, change or delete non-geometric attributes), but leave the same domain, i.e., the same geometric figures. Such operations are used to derive computable attributes.
(b) Operations (COMPUTE SPATIAL) which operate geometrically on the domain of a layer function to produce a layer function with a new set of geometric figures as domain. For example: given a layer with lines and regions (representing rivers and lakes) construct a layer which consists of a buffering zone around the rivers and lakes.
(c) Reclassification (RECLASS), which operates on a single layer and concatenates adjacent figure if their range, i.e., non-geometric attributes, are identical.
(d) Overlay (OVERLAY), which takes two layer functions and produces a new one with the geometric overlay as domain and the combination of the ranges.

Combinations of the four categories, in the mathematical sense of function composition, allow the expression of any operation on layers. Section 5 shows how objects, operations, and relationships are integrated into one model.

5 Combining Objects and Fields - Example of usage

The purpose of an integrated geographic data model in an open GIS environment is expressing the semantics of a geographic database in a way understandable and adaptable by any other model supported by autonomous and remote databases. Any portion of applications running at remote systems must be expressed without ambiguities in an intermediate model, GDM in this case, and vice versa (Figure 2).

GDM provides a formal syntax for describing the five constructs of relations, layers, virtual layers, object classes and constraints as well as the use of the four basic operations among layers. It uses syntactic rules of an Object-Oriented specification described in (Hadzilacos and Tryfona, 1994). Providing a formality for the representation of applications aids capturing semantics and handling important aspects of real-world entities represented in an information systems (Sheth, 1995).

In this section we present a sample usage of the GDM to show how objects (§4.1), layers (§4.3) and spatial relationships (§4.2) can be combined to express portions of geographic information. Objects and layers are combined in an orthogonal way (§3), spatial constraints among objects are translated into spatial relationships, while relations among layers are obtained by using the layer algebra (§4.3).

Consider the following scenario: An application "running" on remote system A "asks" for a portion of the cadastral application located in remote system B using the statements: "*identify sites suitable for a new park. Good candidates must be: within 1.25 Km but no closer that 250m from "motor roads" (accessible but not noisy) and not located in regions designated as "industrial" or "residential"*.

The basic goal -except from transferring the data (maps, records, etc.)- is to distiguish and tranfer objects, relationships among them, space-varying attributes (i.e., fields, layers) and their semantics in an understandable way from one location to the other.

This application requires the creation of a zone at the specified distance from motorways which must be overlaid with sites that are not industrial or residential. The result is a (virtual) layer representing candidate sites for a park. The result is derived from the overlay of two layers: one representing accessible but not noisy sites, and one representing the land use of our area of interest.

The above requirements can be formally stated within GDM as follows:

- DEFINE LAYER 1 LANDUSE
  ATTR (USAGE, STRING)
  GEOMETRIC TYPE REGION
- DEFINE LAYER 2 ROADS
  ATTR (ROAD_TYPE, STRING),
  (WIDTH, REAL)
  GEOMETRIC TYPE ARC
- DEFINE VIRTUAL_LAYER 3 AS COMPUTE SPATIAL
  (2, BUFF_ZONE_≤_1.25KM=BUFFER (1.25, ROAD_TYPE="MOTORWAY"))
- DEFINE VIRTUAL_LAYER 4 AS COMPUTE SPATIAL
  (2, BUFF_ZONE_≥_250M=BUFFER (250, ROAD_TYPE="MOTORWAY"))
- DEFINE VIRTUAL_LAYER 5 AS OVERLAY (3,4)
- DEFINE VIRTUAL_LAYER 6 AS COMPUTE ATTRS
  (5,ZONE =
  $$\left\{\begin{array}{l} true, if\ \mathrm{BUFF\_ZONE} \leq 1.25Km \wedge\ \mathrm{BUFF\_ZONE} \succ 250m = true \\ false, otherwise \end{array}\right\})$$
- DEFINE VIRTUAL_LAYER 7 AS COMPUTE ATTRS
  (1,CANDIDATE_SITES =
  $$\left\{\begin{array}{l} true, if\ \mathrm{USAGE} \neq \text{"Industrial"} \wedge\ \mathrm{USAGE} \neq \text{"Residential"} \\ false, otherwise \end{array}\right\}$$
- DEFINE VIRTUAL_LAYER 8 AS RECLASS OF (7, CANDIDATE_SITES)
- DEFINE VIRTUAL_LAYER 9 AS OVERLAY(6, 8)
- DEFINE VIRTUAL_LAYER 10 AS COMPUTE ATTRS
  $$(9,\mathrm{PARK\_SITES}{=}\left\{\begin{array}{l} true, if\ \mathrm{CANDIDATE\_SITES} = true \wedge\ \mathrm{ZONE} = true \\ false, otherwise \end{array}\right\})$$
- DEFINE OBJECT CLASS PARK_SITE ON LAYER 10

Since remote systems "understand" GDM they can exchange objects, properties, layers, operations on layers and spatial integrity constraints.

6 Conclusions and Future Work

Interoperability among information systems is a major research focus for various domain areas. All approaches used so far assume the existence of a generic data model known to all cooperating remote systems.

In this paper we addressed the issue of information modeling for interoperable geographic database systems. Firstly, we discussed the particular semantics of spatial data whose representation and interchange are critical in an open environment. Next, we described a Geographic Data Model for exchanging spatial data, operations and these semantics among remote systems. GDM provides mechanisms to represent geographic object classes, layers (fields), operations on them, and spatial constraints. It is proposed as the intermediate, enterprise database model understandable by all remote systems comprising the interoperating environment.

Using a generic model as the intermediate step eliminates inconsistencies and redundancies during the phase of exchanging modeled information among systems. Remote systems must therefore (a) understand the domain specific semantics encapsulated by this model, and (b) provide mechanisms for translation from their model to GDM and vice versa. Flexibility and openness are not violated however, since each remote system may use its own model and facilities locally. GDM is used only when communicating with dissimilar systems.

A concept-to-concept mapping and analogies between various spatial data models and our proposed model are critical. Additionally, providing mechanisms for lossless transformation from existing spatial data models to the GDM are required. Prototypes built for different domain areas are also needed in order to understand their special or additional needs.

Acknowledgments

We would like to thank Thanasis Hadzilacos and Max. J. Egenhofer for their fruitful discussions and the Geographic Database Management Group of the Department of Spatial Information Science and Engineering for suggestions on earlier versions of this work.

References

1. Abel, D. J., and Kilby, P. J., 1994, *The Systems Integration Problem*. International Journal of Geographical Information Systems, vol. 8, no. 1, pp. 1-12.

2. Camara, G., Feritas, U.M., Souza, R.C.M., and Casanova, M.A., 1992, *SPRING: Procassemanto de Imagens e Dados Georefenciados*. Proceedings of V Brazilian Symposium on Computer Graphics and Image Processing (SIBGRAPI 92), pp. 233-242.

3. Cohen, D., Larson, G., and Berke, L., 1993, *Role of Interoperability in Business Application Development*. Proceedings of the ACM SIGMOD, 1993.

4. Couclelis, H., 1992, *People Manipulate Objects (but cultivate fields): Beyond the Raster-Vector Debate in GIS.* Lecture Notes in Computer Science, Springer-Verlag (639), Proceedings of the International Conference GIS: From Space to Territory: Theories and Methods of Spatio-Temporal Reasoning in Geographic Space, Pisa, Italy, September 1992.

5. Delis, V., Hadzilacos Th., and Tryfona N., 1994, *An Introduction to Layer Algebra.* Advances in GIS Research, Proceedings of the 6th International Symposium on Spatial Data Handling, Edinburgh, UK, September 1994.

6. DeLorenzi, A., Wolf, A., 1993, *A Protocol for Cooperative Spatial Information Managers*. Proceedings of DBTA Workshop on Interoperability of Database Systems and Database Applications, Fribourg, Switzerland, 1993.

7. Egenhofer, M., and Herring, J., 1991, *Categorizing Binary Topological Relationships Between Regions, Lines and Points in Geographic Databases*. Technical Report, Orono, ME: Department of Surveying Engineering, University of Maine.

8. Elmagarmid A. and Pu, C. (Eds), 1990, *Special Issue on Heterogeneous Databases*, ACM Computing Surveys, 22, 3.

9. Goh, C., H., Madnick, S., and Siegel. M., 1994, *Context Interchange: Overcoming the Challenges of Large Scale Interoperable Database Systems in a Dynamic Environment*. Proceedings of the Third International Conference on Information and Knowledge Management (CIKM), Maryland, 1994.

10. Hadzilacos Th., 1995, Personnal Communication.

11. Hadzilacos Th., and Tryfona N., 1992, *A Model for Expressing Topological Integrity Constraints in Geographic Databases*. Lecture Notes in Computer Science, Springer-Verlag (639), Proceedings of the International Conference GIS: From Space to Territory: Theories and Methods of Spatio-Temporal Reasoning in Geographic Space, Pisa, Italy, September 1992.

12. Hadzilacos Th., and Tryfona N., 1994, *Logical Data Modeling for Geographic Databases*. International Journal of Geographic Information Systems, (9,6).Kim, W., 1995, "Modern Database Systems: The Object-Oriented Model, Interoperability and Beyond", ACM Press.

13. Kashyap, V., and Sheth, A., 1994, *Semantics-based Information Brokering*. Proceedings of the Third International Conference on Information and Knowledge Management (CIKM), Gaithensburg, MD, November, 1994.

14. Mannal, D., and Burgara, K., 1993, *Enhancing Inter-operability and Data Sharing in Medical Informaion Systems*. Proceedings of the ACM SIGMOD, 1993.

15. Manola, F. , Heiler, S., Georgakopoulos, D., Hornick, M., and Brodie, M., 1992, *Distributed Object Management*. International Journal of Intelligent Cooperative Information Systems, 1, 1.

16. Pascoe, R. T. and Penny, J. P., 1995, *Constructing Interfaces between (and within)*. Geographical Information Systems, vol. 9., no. 3, pp. 275-291.

17. Sciore, E., Siegel, M., and Rosenthal, A., 1994, *Using Semantic Values to Facilitate Interoperability Among Heterogeneous Information Systems*. ACM Transactions on Database Systems, vol. 19, no. 2.

18. Schek, H.J., and Wolf, A., 1992, *Cooperation Between Autonomous Operation Services and Object Database Systems in a Heterogeneous Environment*. Proceedings of the IFIP TC2/WG2.6 Conference in semantics of Interoperable DatabaseSystems, Victoria, Australia, November 1992.

19. Sheth, A., 1995, *Data Semantics: what, where and how?*. Technical Report TR-CS-95-003, LSDIS Lab, Dept. of CS, Univ. of GA, September 1995. To appear in "Database Application Semantics," Proceedings of the 6th IFIP Working Conference on Data Semantics (DS-6), R. Meersman and L. Mark (Eds.), Chapman abd Hall, London, UK, 1996.

20. Sheth, A., and Karabaitis, G., 1993, *Multidatabase Interdependencies in Industry*. Proceedings of the ACM SIGMOD, 1993.

21. Sheth and Kalinichenko, 1992, *Information Modeling in Multidatabase Systems: Beyond Data Modeling*. Proceedings of the First International Conference on Information and Knowledge Management (CIKM), Baltimore, MD, November, 1994.

22. Soley, R.M., 1992, *Using Object Technology to Integrate distributed applications*. In *Enterprise Integration Modeling*, Proceedings of the First International Conference, MIT Press, Cambridge, Mass, 446-454.

23. Tryfona N., and Hadzilacos Th., 1995, *Geographic Applications Development: Models and Tools for the Conceptual Level*. Proceedings of the ACMGIS'95 Workshop, Baltimore, MD.

24. Tryfona, N., 1994, *A Structured Database Methodology for Geographic Applications*. Ph.D. Thesis, Dept. of Computer Engineering and Informatics, University of Patras, Greece.

25. Voisard, A., and Schweppe, H., 1994, *A Multilayer Approach to the Open GIS Design Problem*. Proceedings of the ACM GIS' 94 Conference.

26. UtilNets, 1994, Work Program of Brite-Euram Project 7120, GD XII, European Union, Brussels, Belgium.

Guidelines for Formalizing Fusion Object-Oriented Analysis Models

B. W. Bates, J-M. Bruel, R. B. France*, and M. M. Larrondo-Petrie

Department of Computer Science & Engineering
Florida Atlantic University
Boca Raton, FL-33431, USA.
Email: {batesb,bruel,robert,maria}@cse.fau.edu

Abstract. The growing interest in object-oriented analysis and design methods (OOMs) in the software development industry can be attributed to the support they give to some of the more significant software engineering principles, for example, separation of concerns and generality. On the other hand, most OOMs, like their structured analysis and design predecessors, produce models that are not amenable to rigorous semantic analyses. This problem can be attributed to the lack of firm semantic bases for the modeling notations and concepts. In this paper we show how a particular OOM, the *Fusion* analysis method, can be made more formal while preserving its essential qualities. Our approach involves integrating the *Z* formal specification style with the Fusion method. The result is an OOM that produces semantically analyzable Fusion models of behavior at the requirements level.

Keywords: Formal Specification Techniques, Object-Oriented Analysis, Transformations.

1 Introduction

As software developers grapple with the problem of producing high quality software, attention has turned to object-oriented methods (OOMs), mainly because of the support they give to some of the more significant software engineering principles, in particular, separation of concerns, design for change, anticipation of change, and incrementality (e.g., see [4, 18, 21]). As was the case with earlier graphical structured approaches, industry's growing interest in OOMs can also be attributed to the use of simple, visually-appealing concepts and notation. On the other hand, like earlier structured analysis and design (SA/D) approaches (e.g., see [5, 28, 29]), most popular OOMs lack formal semantic bases, making it very difficult to rigorously reason about and with the models they produce. In this sense, most OOMs are *informal* because their applications are likely to produce ambiguous specifications that are not amenable to rigorous semantic analyses.

The lack of semantic bases in most OOMs severely inhibits their use in the specification and analysis of complex information systems. The need to rigorously investigate the behavior of such systems suggests the use of formal specification techniques (FSTs). A FST consists of a formal language (i.e., a language with a precise syntax and semantics), and mechanisms for deriving consequences from specifications expressed in the formal language. FSTs utilize mathematical concepts and notation to precisely define theories and models of application behavior. Precise specifications facilitate effective communication among persons with a stake in the development of the software, while the ability to reason about specified properties allows developers to predict the behavior of implementations during the specification phases of software development.

Other object-oriented and SA/SD methods have been integrated in a formal environment (e.g., see [3, 10, 14, 16, 20]). In this paper we describe some guidelines resulting from our work on formalizing Fusion [4], an OOM developed in industry. We chose Fusion because it incorporates some of the best object-oriented modeling ideas from previous OOMs in a single coherent method. The approach we used can be used to formalize other OOMs as well. We show how Fusion can be integrated with Z [24], a popular and mature FST. We chose Z because of its maturity, expressiveness and the availability of tools (e.g., CADiℤ [25], *f*UZZ [23], and ProofPower [13]). The integrated specification method that we created can be used to develop Fusion analysis models that are amenable to rigorous semantic analysis.

In Section 2 we discuss the benefits of integrating informal specification techniques (ISTs) with FSTs, and give an overview of Z and Fusion. Section 3 provides the rules supporting the translation of Fusion analysis models to Z specifications. Finally, Section 4 gives our conclusions and an overview of our ongoing work in this area.

* This work was partially funded by NSF grant CCR-9410396.

2 Integrating formal and informal specification techniques

The application of OOMs can be made more rigorous by providing formal foundations supporting the semantic analysis of the models. One approach is to interpret the models using underlying formal semantic models. The formal interpretation can be used to reason about and with the models. We describe this approach as *interpretive*. In using this approach one has to make an effort to validate the semantic model. Validation in this sense means ensuring that the semantic model is "consistent" with the intuitive interpretation of the models, that is, that the semantic model does not result in a modeling language that requires the modeler to learn new meanings for old constructs.

Another approach is to use the OOM with a suitable FST. The integration of an OOM and a FST is an instance of a class of specification techniques that we call *integrated formal/informal specification techniques* (FISTs) [6, 7, 8]. The use of FISTs can be beneficial in the following respects:

- *FISTs enable an evolutionary approach to the use of FSTs in industry.* FISTs allow an organization to preserve, and even enhance, its investment in ISTs while taking advantage of FST-related benefits.
- *FSTs and graphical ISTs can complement each other.* The relatively simple and graphical nature of IST specifications often makes them more presentable than the more detailed, often textual, formal specifications. On the other hand, the lack of firm semantic bases for ISTs inhibits their use in rigorous specification and analysis of behavior. FSTs are needed for such activities.

FISTs can be classified as either *supplemental* or *interpretive*, depending on the relative roles of the formal and informal models. In a supplemental FIST the formal and informal concepts supplement each other, that is, the formal and informal specifications developed using the FIST capture complementary aspects of a system's functionality. An example of a supplementary FIST involving the Fusion method [4] and Z [24] is one in which Z is used to express operation specifications, and Fusion models are used to express the static and life-cycle aspects of applications.

In an interpretive FIST, the formal model provides a more precise description of behavior captured by the informal model. In some cases an interpretive FIST can have the same results as the interpretive approach discussed earlier in this section. This happens when there is a formal set of rules that map IST modeling constructs to FST constructs. The existence of formal mappings between the notations is not a necessary part of interpretive FSTs. Formalization of the informal models can be done in a cognitive manner, that is, it can be based on a developer's understanding of the application area and of the intent captured in the informal models. A consequence of this cognitive approach to formalization [6] is that there may not always be a clear connection between parts of the formal model and the informal model, for example, the formal models may have details that are not representable in the informal notation.

The manner in which FSTs and ISTs are integrated in a FIST is usually based on one or more of the following considerations:

- *Preservation of the 'intuitive' interpretation of the informal specification*: The integration should be such that the formal specifications provide interpretations of the informal specifications that are consistent with intuitively-held interpretations of the informal specifications. A FIST that does not support intuitively-held interpretations of its informal specifications may require that the informal specifications be developed in ways that are not consistent with practices associated with the use of the ISTs. In such cases, a specifier learning and using the FIST is not likely to take full advantage of his prior experience with the ISTs.
- *Level of automated support for moving between formal and informal specifications*: Developing formal specifications can be a very arduous task. Well-defined relationships between FST and IST constructs and concepts can provide the basis for mechanical generation of some parts of the formal specification. In the other direction, it is often possible, given a well-defined relationship between formal and informal specification elements, to mechanically generate informal specifications from formal specifications. This transformation is often easier to automate because it usually entails simply choosing what information to hide.
- *Degree of integration*: In some cases it may not be worthwhile to formally interpret all aspects of an informal specification. It may be sufficient to formalize only those parts that can benefit from more rigorous specification and analysis.

In this paper we describe an interpretive FIST that integrates Fusion analysis models [4] with the Z specification style [24]. Transformation rules are defined for some aspects of the formalization, some of which can be mechanized. We made every attempt to preserve the intuitive interpretation of Fusion models in our formalization; empirical investigation is still needed to validate the integration in this sense. In the following subsections we give an overview of Fusion and Z.

2.1 Overview of Fusion

Fusion [4] is an object-oriented software development methodology that combines and extends existing techniques, e.g. Rumbaugh's Objet Model Technique (OMT) [18], Booch's technique [2], Wirfs-Brock's Class Responsibility Collaborator [26] (CRC) technique, and Jacobson's Objectory [12]. Fusion claims to take the best ideas from these methods and incorporate them into a single coherent method that covers software analysis, design, and implementation. In this section we present an overview of the Fusion analysis process and products.

In Fusion's analysis phase the required behavior of the system is described by

- an Object Model that defines the static structure of the information manipulated by the application in terms of classes and the relationships among them; and
- an Interface Model that defines the externally observable behavior of the application. The Interface Model, in turn, consists of two models:

  Operation Model: This model characterizes the effect of application services in terms of the observable state changes they make and the output events they send to the environment.

  Life-Cycle Model: This model characterizes the allowable sequences of service invocations for the application.

A data dictionary is maintained and updated throughout the development process.

The services identified in the interface model are not associated with class operations at the analysis level. In fact, Fusion does not attach operations to classes in this phase; this is done during design.

The notation used in the Object Model is summarized in Fig. 1. There are three different types of associations in Fusion:

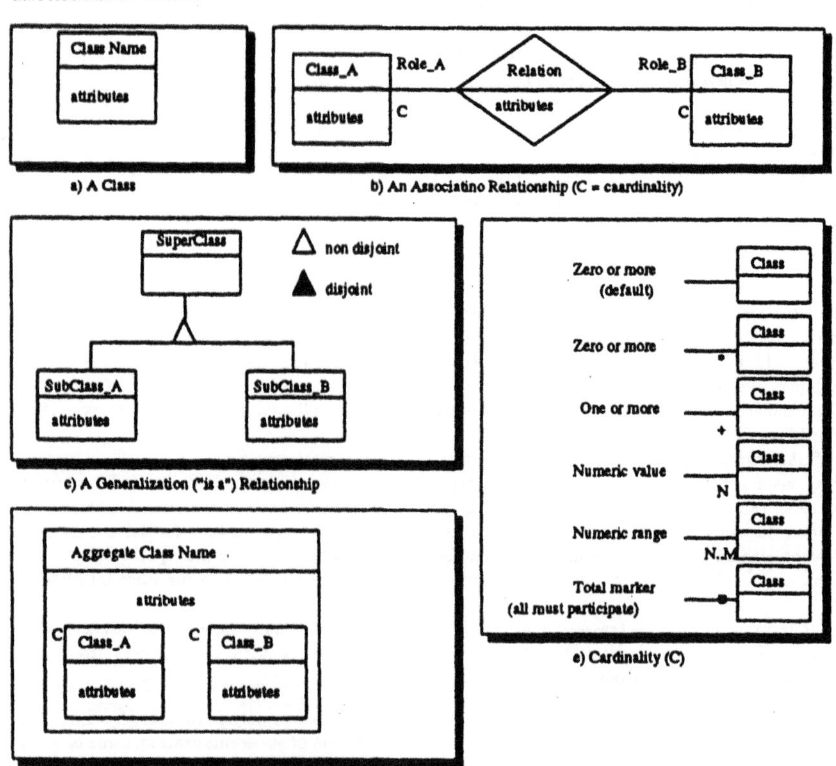

Fig. 1. Summary of Fusion Object Model Notation

Generalization: A triangle symbol Δ symbolizes the "is a" relationship between two classes (see Fig. 1.c). The subclasses may partition the superclass (i.e., can be disjoint), or they may overlap (i.e., can be non disjoint). The disjoint subclasses are joined to their superclass with a filled-in triangle $\blacktriangle$.

Aggregation: The relationship between an aggregate class and its component classes, is shown as classes embedded in the aggregate class (see Fig. 1.d). Cardinality is shown adjacent to each component class. The symbols used for cardinality are given in Fig. 1.e.

Relationship: This represents more general forms of associations between classes. The relationship is assigned a name and can have attributes associated with it (see Fig. 1.b).

A filled-in rectangle or "marker" on a relationship means that all members must participate in the relationship. Relationships can be annotated with assertions (called invariants) that stipulate that certain properties must be maintained, and roles, which indicate the role objects play in the relationships. Invariants can also be associated with individual classes.

The Fusion Operation Model consists of a set of operation schemas. Each schema consists of the following parts:

Description: an informal and concise description of the operation.
Reads: a list of the items that the operation reads.
Changes: a list of the items the operation changes.
Sends: a list of the events the operation sends to other objects in the environment.
Assumes: a condition that describes what is assumed true at the start of the operation.
Result: describes what is true after the operation has completed its execution.

The Life-Cycle Model is expressed in a language that allows one to express relationships such as "event x is followed by event y", "either event x or event y occurs", "event x is optional", "the steps of events x and y are interleaved".

More detailed descriptions of Fusion notation will be given when needed in the remainder of this paper.

2.2 The Z Notation

The Z specification language [11, 24] is a general purpose specification language which was developed by the Programming Research Group at Oxford. It has a strong mathematical basis in predicate logic and set theory. Static aspects of applications are represented by sets and dynamic aspects by operations on sets.

In this section we introduce only the Z notations necessary to understand the specifications given in this paper[2].

The primary structuring construct in Z is the schema. A schema has two parts: a declaration and a predicate part. The declaration part consists of variable declarations of the form $w : Type$, where w is a variable name and $Type$ is a type name. Intuitively, the preceding declaration means that the value of w is a member of the set named by $Type$ (types are sets in Z). The predicate part consists of a predicate that expresses the relationships among the declared variables.

There are two ways of writing schemas, vertically or horizontally:

```
┌─ Schema ──────────────────────
│ Declaration
├──────────
│ Predicate
└───────────────────────────────
```

$Schema \mathrel{\widehat=} [\, Declaration \mid Predicate \,]$

Schemas are used to model both the static and dynamic aspects of a system. A schema that captures the static aspect of a system will be referred to as a state schema, and a schema that captures the dynamic aspect will be referred to as an operation schema. In a state schema the components of a system's state are declared in the declaration section and constraints on the state are given in the predicate part.

[2] The reader is invited to see [24] or the URL: `http://www.comlab.ox.ac.uk/archive/z.html`.

The declaration $w : Schema$, where $Schema$ is a schema name, declares a variable w with components (declared in $Schema$) that satisfy the predicate part of $Schema$.

Let S be a schema defined as:

S
$x : \mathbb{N};\ y : \mathbb{P}\mathbb{N}$
$x \leq \# y$

for the declaration $w : S$

$w.x$ denotes the projection function: $w.x$ is w's x component,
θS is a tuple consisting of (schema variable, value) pairs, where the values are said to be bound to the schema variables (commonly used to equate the before and after state components of an operation),
pred S is the predicate part of a schema.

An operation schema defines the relationship between the state at the start and at the end of an operation's execution. The declaration part of an operation schema declares variables representing the before and after state, inputs, outputs, and any other variables needed to define the relationship. The predicate part of the schema defines the relationship between the before and after states.

The following conventions are used for variable names in operation schemas:

unprimed variable (e.g., w) - value of variable before operation execution;
primed variable (e.g., w') - value of variable after operation execution;
variable ending in '?' - an input to the operation; and
variable ending in '!' - an output from the operation.

$\Delta S == S \wedge S'$ denotes the change of state schema,
$\Xi S == [\Delta S \mid \theta S' = \theta S]$ denotes that the state schema does not change.

3 Fusion to Z translation guidelines

3.1 Object Model

In examining the Fusion Object Model it was noticed that the model has three major classes of constructs: objects (classes), relations, and annotations (invariants). In the following subsections we give rules guiding the translation of instances of these constructs to Z specifications.

Representing objects in Z In Fusion, an object in an Object Model can have zero or more attributes associated with it. The attributes are values, not objects.

Objects that have no attributes associated with them are represented as Z schemas that contain only an object identifier.

Rule 1 (attributeless objects) *Objects that contain no attributes are represented by Z schemas. An object identifier attribute is defined in order to identify the instances of the class.*

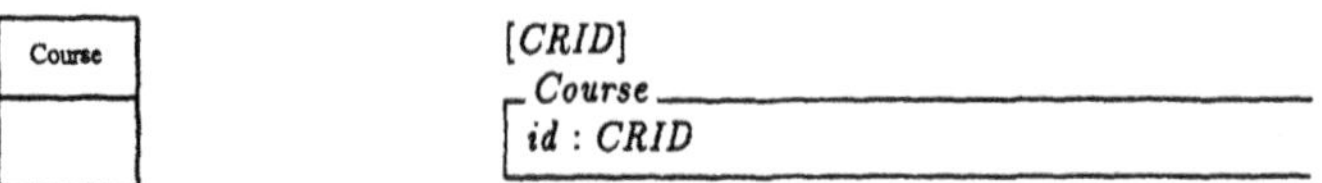

Fig. 2. Formal specification of a class without attributes

Objects with attributes are represented by Z state schemas, in which the attributes are declared as state variables, and any invariant annotations are expressed formally in the predicate part (e.g., see Fig. 3).

Rule 2 *Objects with attributes are made into state schemas. Attributes are declared as state variables, and invariants (if any) are formally expressed in the predicate part. If an attribute is not associated with a type, the capitalized name of the attribute is used as a type name and declared as a basic Z type. Each object instance has a unique identifier that is explicitly defined through an attribute.*

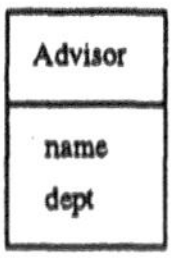

Advisor
name dept

$[ADVID, NAME, DEPT]$

```
┌─ Advisor ─────────────────
│ id : ADVID
│ name : NAME
│ dept : DEPT
└───────────────────────────
```

Fig. 3. Formal specification of a class with attribute

Operations that modify the state of a system may only affect a subset of the variables. In Z one has to specify that state variables that are not affected by operations are left unchanged, for example, if state variable x is unaffected by an operation's execution then the equation $x' = x$ should appear in the predicate part of the operation schema. If an operation affects only a small part of the state consisting of a large number of variables, then numerous equations of the above form need to be written. One can structure state schemas in a way that minimizes the need to write a large number of such equations.

The rule below provides some guidelines for structuring schemas to minimize the impact of this problem. It utilizes schema inclusion to achieve structuring. When a schema A is included in another schema B then B's declaration part includes all the declarations in A, and the predicate part of A is logically 'anded' to the predicate part of B. The rule involves identifying sets of attributes of a class that are unaffected by a group of operations that act on the instances of the class. These attributes are defined in separate schemas which are included in the schema representing the class (e.g., see Fig. 4).

Rule 3 (schema structuring) *Determine sets of attributes that are not changed often by operations and declare them in separate schemas. The schema representing the class is then formed by including these schemas in the declaration part along with any attributes that are not declared in any of the included schemas.*

Rule 4 (instances) *Instances of classes are represented as bindings of values to variables declared in Z schemas representing the classes. The identifier of an instance is the value bound to the identifier variable (id) declared in the Z schema for the instance class (see Fig. 5).*

Representing relationships in Z We created a mathematical toolkit that includes Z definitions of the different types of general binary relationships that can exist between objects in an Object Model. The types are defined by parameterized Z schemas. We utilize graphical symbols in the toolkit to make clear the connection between formalizations and the Fusion representations of relationships. In Fig. 6 we give an example of a toolkit formalization of a Fusion relationship and show how it is used to represent a particular relationship in a model. If the relationship is associated with a cardinality other than 0 and 1, then the cardinality constraint is expressed in the predicate part of the schema (e.g., see Fig. 7).

Rule 5 *Relationships are represented by variables declared in a state schema. The type associated with a relationship variable is obtained from the mathematical toolkit defining standard relationship types (many, 0, 1). If the relationship has a cardinality other than many, 0, and 1 then the cardinality constraint is expressed in the predicate part of the schema.*

Without schema structuring:

STUDENT

$id : STID$
$name : NAME$
$address : ADDRESS$
$ssnum : SS$
$gpa : GPA$
$courseenrolled : \mathbb{P}\, COURSE$
...

AddCourse

$\Delta STUDENT$
$c? : COURSE$

$c? \notin courseenrolled$
$courseenrolled' = courseenrolled \cup \{c?\}$
$id' = id$
$name' = name$
$address' = address$
$ssnum' = ssnum$
...

After schema structuring:

StudentPart

$id : STID$
$name : NAME$
$address : ADDRESS$
$ssnum : SS$

STUDENT

$StudentPart$
$gpa : GPA$
$courseenrolled : \mathbb{P}\, COURSE$
...

AddCourse

$\Delta STUDENT$
$c? : COURSE$

$c? \notin courseenrolled$
$courseenrolled' = courseenrolled \cup \{c?\}$
...
$\theta StudentPart' = \theta StudentPart$

Fig. 4. Illustration of schema structuring

Advisor	
name	dept
Robert	CSE
Maria	CSE

$advisors : \mathbb{P}\, Advisor$
$a1, a2 : Advisor$

$a1.id = 01$
$a1.name = Robert$
$a1.dept = CSE$
$a2.id = 02$
$a2.name = Maria$
$a2.dept = CSE$
$advisors = \{a1, a2\}$

Fig. 5. Particular instances representation

Fig. 8 shows how relationships with attributes are represented in Z.

Rule 6 (attributes) *Relationship attributes are handled by declaring the attributes as basic types (if only one) or schemas. A function that maps the relationship to its attributes is then defined in the relationship schema.*

N-ary relationships are represented in Z as variables of n-tuple types, where the classes (sequences of instances) involved in the tuple are the components of the tuple type. Cardinality constraints are expressed in the predicate part of the relationship schema (e.g., see Fig. 9).

$$
\begin{array}{|l}
[X, Y] \\
\hline
1 \longleftarrow\!\!\!\!\longrightarrow * : \mathbb{P}(X \leftrightarrow Y) \\
\hline
\forall R : X \leftrightarrow Y \bullet \\
\quad R \in 1 \longleftarrow\!\!\!\!\longrightarrow * \Rightarrow R^{-1} \in (Y \rightarrow X) \\
\hline
\end{array}
$$

$$
\begin{array}{|l}
\hline
advisors : \mathbb{P}\, Advisor \\
students : \mathbb{P}\, Student \\
assigned\_to : 1 \longleftarrow\!\!\!\!\longrightarrow * \, [Advisor, Student] \\
\hline
\mathrm{dom}\; assigned\_to \subseteq advisors \\
\mathrm{ran}\; assigned\_to \subseteq students \\
\forall i, j : students \bullet i.id = j.id \Leftrightarrow i = j \\
\forall i, j : advisors \bullet i.id = j.id \Leftrightarrow i = j \\
\hline
\end{array}
$$

Fig. 6. Formal specification of a binary relationship

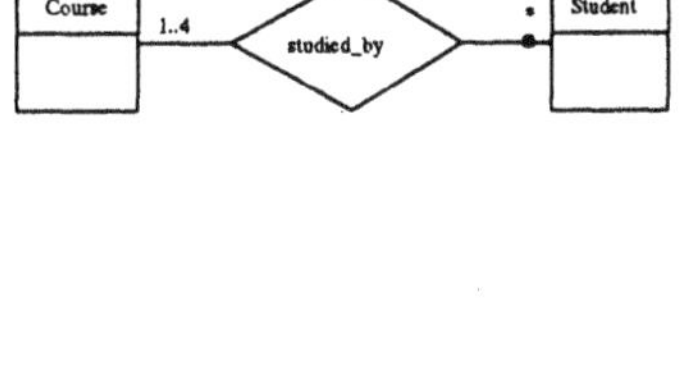

$$
\begin{array}{|l}
\textit{Relationship} \\
\hline
students : \mathbb{P}\, Student \\
courses : \mathbb{P}\, Course \\
studied\_by : Student \leftrightarrow Course \\
\hline
\forall s : \mathrm{dom}\; studied\_by \bullet \\
\quad 1 \leq \#studied\_by(\!|\, \{s\} \,|\!) \leq 4 \\
\mathrm{dom}\; studied\_by \subseteq students \\
\mathrm{ran}\; studied\_by \subseteq courses \\
\forall i, j : students \bullet i.id = j.id \Leftrightarrow i = j \\
\forall i, j : courses \bullet i.id = j.id \Leftrightarrow i = j \\
\hline
\end{array}
$$

Fig. 7. Integration of the cardinality constraints

Rule 7 (n-ary relationship) *Ternary or higher relationships are handled by modeling the relationship as a variable with an n-tuple type, where each class in the relation is a component of the type. Cardinality constraints are expressed in the predicate part of relationship schema.*

Representing aggregation structures An aggregate object is represented in Z by a schema in which the variables representing sets of component parts and relationships among the component parts are declared (e.g., see Fig. 10).

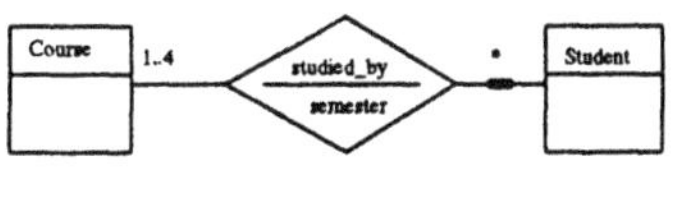

$$
\begin{array}{|l}
\textit{Relationship} \\
\hline
students : \mathbb{P}\, Student \\
courses : \mathbb{P}\, Course \\
studied\_by : Student \leftrightarrow Course \\
semester : (Students \leftrightarrow Course) \rightarrow SEMESTER \\
\hline
\forall s : \mathrm{dom}\; studied\_by \bullet \\
\quad 1 \leq \#studied\_by(\!|\, \{s\} \,|\!) \leq 4 \\
\mathrm{dom}\; studied\_by \subseteq students \\
\mathrm{ran}\; studied\_by \subseteq courses \\
\forall i, j : students \bullet i.id = j.id \Leftrightarrow i = j \\
\forall i, j : courses \bullet i.id = j.id \Leftrightarrow i = j \\
\mathrm{dom}\; semester = studied\_by \\
\hline
\end{array}
$$

Fig. 8. Relationship with attributes

The schema represents a ternary relationship called *takes* involving the classes Student, Room, and Test.

Relationship

takes : $\mathbb{P}(\mathbb{P}\, Student \times \mathbb{P}\, Room \times \mathbb{P}\, Test)$

...

Fig. 9. Formalization of a ternary relationship

Rule 8 *Aggregation is handled by declaring components as sets containing elements of the component schemas types in the aggregate class schema. Relationships among the components are expressed as described by the rules on formalizing Fusion relationships.*

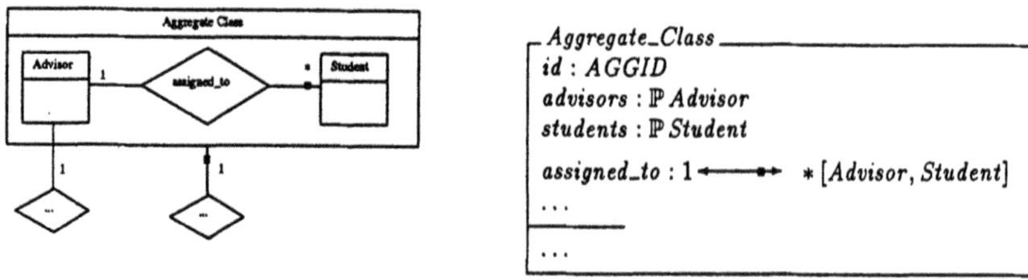

Fig. 10. Formalization of an aggregation

Representing generalization hierarchies A generalization hierarchy is represented in Z by including superclass schemas in subclass schemas. See Fig. 11 for an example.

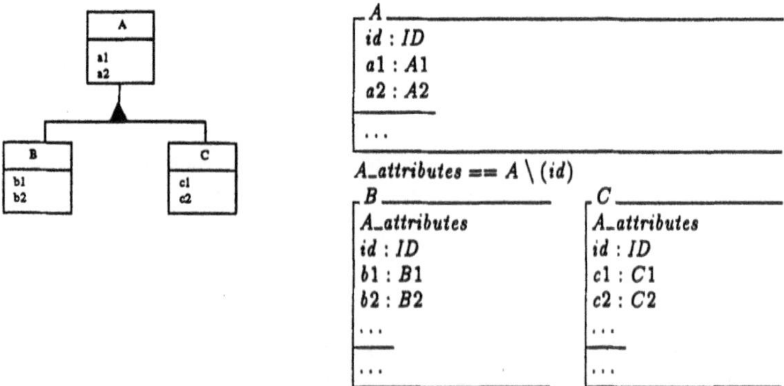

Fig. 11. Generalization hierarchy formalization

Putting it all together Once the parts of the Object Model are defined they are collected in a schema that is a representation of the model. Invariants involving parts that were separately defined are expressed in the predicate part of this schema.

Our rules provide a bottom-up approach to formalizing an Object Model. Some restructuring of the schemas and/or redefinition of the parts may be needed to reduce the complexity of the schemas produced by the rules.

3.2 Formalizing the Interface Model

We formalize only the Operation Model. The Fusion Life-Cycle Model is rigorous and analyzable; reexpression of this model in Z is not necessary.

Representing Operation Models Fusion Operation Models are translated to Z operation schemas in the following manner:

Rule 9 *The following are rules guiding the translation of a Fusion Operation schema to a Z operation schema:*

- *The operation name is used as the schema name.*
- *The informal definition is used to document the Z operation schema.*
- *Variables mentioned in the Reads section are declared as input variables in the Z schema.*
- *If variables are mentioned in the Changes section then the state is declared in the operation schema preceded by the Δ symbol (indicating that the operation causes a change in the state). Equations for variables not changed by the operations (i.e., not mentioned in the Changes section) are generated. For example, if state variable x is not mentioned in the Changes section then the equation $x' = x$ is generated; if no variable in the state schema, S, in which x is declared is mentioned in the Changes section then the equation $\theta S' = \theta S$ is generated.*
- *Variables mentioned in the Sends section are declared as output variables in the Z operation schema.*
- *The condition in the Assumes section, when formalized, is the precondition of the operation.*
- *the formalized content of the Result is given in the predicate part of the operation schema.*

In Fig. 12 the above rule is applied to a Fusion Operation Model.

Operation: *view_WS*
Description: A request to view a worksheet.

Reads: supplied *student* : *stud_id*
Changes: none
Sends: *student* : *worksheet* *advisor* : *worksheet* *sys_adm* : *worksheet* *univ_adm* : *worksheet*
Assumes: *stud_id* is valid and a student can only view their own worksheet.
Result: Displays the student's worksheet.

view_WS
$id? : STID$
$ws! : Worksheet$
$\Xi AdvState$

$\exists\, s : students \bullet$
$s.id = id? \Rightarrow ws! = getsheet(s)$

Fig. 12. Illustration of an operation translation

4 Conclusion

The use of OOMs in the development of complex information systems can be inhibited by their lack of formal semantic bases. In this this paper we discuss how a particular object-oriented analysis method, Fusion, can be integrated with a FST, Z, to produce analyzable object-oriented analysis models. A case study on an application of the Fusion/Z FIST described in this paper can be found in [1].

Our FIST approach can be abstracted as shown in Fig. 13, where the boxes represent models and the ovals represent activities.

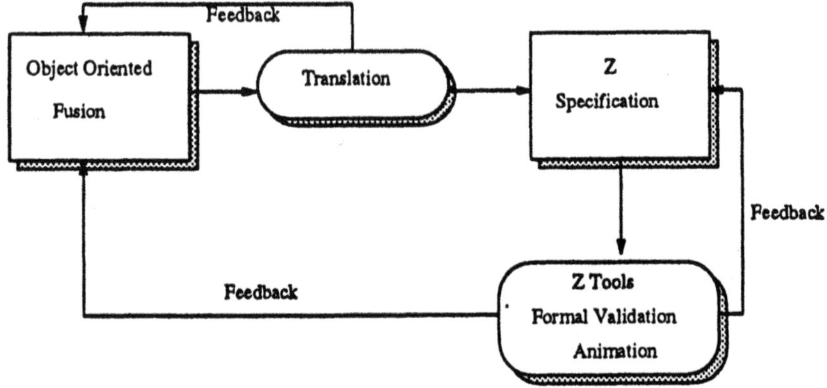

Fig. 13. The integration process

The translation activity is guided by the rules we stated in the previous section. Currently the translation process is manual, but we are working on formalizing the rules in order to identify those that can be mechanized to support partial automation of the translation.

In our experimentations with the Fusion/Z FIST[3], we found that formalizing the Fusion models helped identify problems with the object model, for example, inconsistent use of attribute names, undefined variables, and missing operation arguments. More generally, formalization revealed ambiguities, gaps in our knowledge of the systems being modeled, and inconsistent requirements. The feedback from the translation activity can be used to improve the Fusion models (as indicated by the feedback arrow leaving the translation activity in the figure).

The primary objective of integrating Fusion and Z is to create analyzable Fusion models. The integration allows one to use Z type checkers (e.g., ZTC [27] and *f*UZZ [23]) and Z animation tools, such as ZANS, to analyze models. In our experimentations, we used ZTC, *f*UZZ and ZANS and found that doing such analyses can reveal additional problems with the Fusion models (as well as the formalization of the problem).

From the above, it should be clear that the process of formalizing an informal OOM model is an iterative process. Formalization can help identify inadequacies in the informal model, which results in changes being made to the models. Formalization of the changed models is then carried out, and the process is repeated until a formalization that is consistent with the intent captured in the informal models is obtained.

It can be argued that an object-oriented version of Z such as Object-Z [22], MooZ [15] or SP-Z[19], would be a more appropriate formalism to integrate with an OOM. Unlike Z, the object-oriented versions of Z do not have sufficient tool support as yet. One of the reasons we chose Z is the availability of analysis tools. A goal of our research in this area is the development of a CASE tool supporting the creation and analysis of analyzable Fusion analysis models. It is important that the formal notation we use is adequately supported by analysis tools.

We anticipate that tools for analyzing object-oriented versions of Z will soon be available. For this reason we are currently defining rules to guide the integration of Fusion models with object-oriented versions of Z. One of the formalisms that we are looking at is Hall's object-oriented style [9]. Our derived Z specification has some common points with Hall's style, for example, our treatment of identity is based on ideas from Hall's approach. We should point out that it is not clear to us at this time whether there is a significant advantage in using an object-oriented style of Z with Fusion. The integrated approach described in this paper has been adequate for the problems we applied them to. One the objectives of our work on integrating Fusion with an object-oriented style of Z is to determine whether the object-oriented Z concepts have a significant impact on formalizing and analyzing Fusion models.

[3] see [1] for a fuller account of our experiences

References

1. Brian W. Bates, Jean-Michel Bruel, Robert B. France, and Maria M. Larrondo-Petrie. Experiences with Formalizing Fusion Object-Oriented Analysis Models. FAU Technical Report TR-CSE-95-44, Department of Computer Science & Engineering, Florida Atlantic University, Boca Raton, FL-33431, USA, November 1995.
2. G. Booch. *Object-oriented analysis and design with applications.* Benjamin/Cummings, 1994.
3. Robert H. Bourdeau and Betty H.C. Cheng. A formal semantics for object model diagrams. *IEEE Transactions on Software Engineering,* 21(10):799–821, October 1995.
4. D. Coleman, P. Arnold, S. Bodoff, C. Dollin, H. Gilchrist, F. Hayes, and P. Jeremaes. *Object-Oriented Development: The Fusion Method.* Prentice Hall, 1994.
5. T. DeMarco. *Structured Analysis and System Specification.* Prentice-Hall, 1978.
6. R. France and M. M. Larrondo-Petrie. A two-dimensional view of integrated formal and informal specification techniques. In *ZUM'95, Lecture Notes in Computer Science 967.* Springer-Verlag, 1995.
7. R. France and M. M. Larrondo-Petrie. Understanding the role of formal specification techniques in requirements engineering. In *in Proceedings of The 8th SEI Conference on Software Engineering Education, Lecture Notes in Computer Science 895.* Springer-Verlag, 1995, pages 207-222.
8. R. B. France and M. M. Larrondo-Petrie. From structured analysis to formal specifications: State of the theory. In *Proceedings of the 1994 ACM Computer Science Conference.* ACM, 1994.
9. J. A. Hall. Using Z as a specification calculus for object-oriented systems. In D. Bjørner, C. A. R. Hoare, and H. Langmaack, editors, *VDM and Z – Formal Methods in Software Development,* volume 428 of *Lecture Notes in Computer Science,* pages 290–318. VDM-Europe, Springer-Verlag, 1990.
10. T. C. Hartrum and P. D. Bailor. Teaching formal extensions of informal-based object-oriented analysis methodologies. In *Proc. Computer Science Education,* pages 389–409, 1994.
11. I. J. Hayes, editor. *Specification Case Studies.* Prentice Hall International Series in Computer Science, 2nd edition, 1993.
12. I. Jacobson. *Object oriented software engineering.* Addison-Wesley, 1992.
13. R. B. Jones. ICL ProofPower. *BCS FACS FACTS,* Series III, 1(1):10–13, Winter 1992.
14. K. C. Mander and F. Polack. Rigorous specification using structured systems analysis and Z. *Information and Software Technology,* 37(5):285–291, May 1995.
15. S. L. Meira and A. L. C. Cavalcanti. Modular object-oriented Z specifications. In Nicholls [17], pages 173–192.
16. John Murphy and Jane Grimson. The Jupiter System: A Prototype for Multidatabase Interoperability. In *Proceedings of the 12th British National Conference on Databases, BNCOD-12,* Lecture Notes in Computer Science. Springer-Verlag, 1994.
17. J. E. Nicholls, editor. Workshops in Computing. Springer-Verlag, 1991.
18. J. Rumbaugh, M. Blaha, W. Premerlani, F. Eddy, and W. Lorensen. *Object-Oriented Modeling and Design.* Prentice Hall, 1991.
19. S. A. Schuman, D. H. Pitt, and P. J. Byers. Object-oriented process specification. In C. Rattray, editor, *Specification and Verification of Concurrent Systems,* Workshops in Computing, pages 21–70. Springer-Verlag, 1990.
20. Lesley T. Semmens and Pat M. Allen. Using Yourdon and Z: An approach to formal specification. In Nicholls [17], pages 228–253.
21. S. Shlaer and S. J. Mellor. *Object lifecycles: Modeling the world in states.* Prentice Hall, 1992.
22. Graeme Smith. *An Object-Oriented Approach to Formal Specification.* PhD thesis, Department of Computer Science, University of Queensland, St. Lucia 4072, Australia, October 1992.
23. J. M. Spivey. *The fUZZ Manual.* Computing Science Consultancy, 34 Westlands Grove, Stockton Lane, York YO3 0EF, UK, 2nd edition, July 1992.
24. J. M. Spivey. *The Z Notation: A Reference Manual.* Prentice Hall International Series in Computer Science, 2nd edition, 1992.
25. I. Toyn. *CADiZ Quick Reference Guide.* York Software Engineering Ltd, University of York, York YO1 5DD, UK, 1990.
26. R. Wirfs-Brock and B. Wilkerson. *Designing object oriented software.* Prentice-Hall, 1990.
27. Xiaoping Jia. *ZTC: A Type Checker for Z – User's Guide.* Institute for Software Engineering, Department of Computer Science and Information Systems, DePaul University, Chicago, IL 60604, USA, 1994.
28. E. Yourdon. *Modern Systems Analysis.* Prentice-Hall, 1989.
29. E. Yourdon and L. Constantine. *Structured Design: Fundamentals of a Discipline of Computer Program and Systems Design.* Prentice-Hall, 1979.

Techniques for Process Analysis and Unification

Silvana Castano[1] and Valeria De Antonellis[2]

[1] University of Milano, ITALY
e-mail: castano@dsi.unimi.it
[2] University of Ancona and Politecnico di Milano, ITALY
e-mail: deantone@elet.polimi.it

Abstract. Information system reengineering activities are strongly related to a deep understanding of processes and related data in the organizations. This paper addresses problems related to the development of techniques and tools for process analysis and for the construction of a unified process architecture where semantic correspondences between processes are identified on the basis of their similarity. Unification of similar processes is considered a basic step for information system interoperability.

Index Terms - Process reengineering, Process analysis, Data Similarity, Process unification, Legacy systems, Interoperability.

1 Introduction

Many of the major organizations, both in the private and public environments, are characterized by the presence of heterogeneous information systems. Heterogeneity is generally related to application contexts, evolution strategies and support technologies. In fact, continuous developments and modifications of information systems to meet over the years changing requirements, and the rapid advances in information technology have lead to a proliferation of information system architectures with partially overlapping data and processes.

Actually, the availability of advanced information technology, together with the need of enhancing efficiency and quality of services promote activities for restructuring existing legacy Information Systems and, possibly, integrating information systems in different contexts. In particular, restructuring of information systems that are obsolete from the technological point of view requires methodological approaches apt to guide the transformation with the aim of preserving and reusing knowledge and existing applications [12]. Integration of autonomous, heterogeneous information systems emphasizes interoperability aspects [19,13]. In this framework, a basic starting point to obtain valuable results is represented by a deep understanding and reengineering of processes in legacy systems. Two levels of intervention can be distinguished: i) a conceptual level, where methods and tools are devoted to modeling, analysis and unification of processes and related data [2]; ii) a technological level, where methods and tools are devoted to the transformation and migration of existing software systems [10] and to the interconnection of existing databases with a federation approach [19,14].

In the paper, we focus on the conceptual level and provide techniques for process analysis in view of reengineering activities. For process analysis, we propose techniques with criteria and metrics based on similarity properties. In particular, we propose a methodological framework and accompanying tools to support the process unification activity, devoted to the definition of semantic correspondences between processes in different contexts, to make feasible Information System interoperability.
Process unification exploits the analysis techniques and the availability of a semantic dictionary where inter-process knowledge is properly organized.

The paper is organized as follows. In Section 2, characteristics of process specifications are given on the basis of our experience with the Information Systems Authority for Public Administration (AIPA in Italy), which is responsible for co-ordinating, planning and controlling the Public Administration Information Systems. In Section 3, the techniques we propose for the construction of the semantic dictionary are illustrated. In Section 4, the similarity techniques for process evaluation are discussed. In Section 5, we describe a methodological framework for process unification. In Section 6, we illustrate the tools supporting our approach. In Section 7, the comparison with related work is presented. Finally, in Section 8, concluding remarks are stated.

2 Process specifications

In the paper, we refer to information on work processes and information systems that has been collected by the Italian Information Systems Authority for Public Administration (AIPA in Italy) in the framework of a large project aiming at building an inventory of information systems, and at pursuing a deep revision and redesign of work processes of the Public Administration, to meet growing and changing needs of clients and the general public. A detailed characterization of Public Administration processes is presented in [6]. The following high-level specification is available for each process:

- The name of the process, univocally identifying the process within the Organizational Unit to which it pertains. The name is composed of an *identifier* $\langle OU\_ID, P\_ID\rangle$, and of a *title*. In the identifier, OU_ID is the identifier of the Organizational Unit to which the process pertains and P_ID is the process identifier. The process title is a string describing the name of the process.
- An Entity-Relationship (ER) conceptual schema, describing the characteristics of the data manipulated by the process, in form of entities and relationships among entities.
- A textual information, which provides a general description of the process and its functionality. It is a natural language description of the input/output entities (among the ones specified in the associated ER schema), the starting/ending events, the type of the process (e.g., management, administration), and possible supporting application program(s).

Process specifications have been defined by AIPA, on the basis of the data collected through a set of properly defined questionnaires released to users of various Organizational Units of the Public Administration. The questionnaires were designed in order to acquire as much information as possible on process functionalities and on data circulating among them. Process specifications are currently available in electronic format for 2203 work processes selected by AIPA for analysis and reengineering interventions. These interventions aim at achieving the following main goals:

- Reconstruction of information flows between work processes of different Divisions or Ministries, based on the similarity of the data used by processes.
- Reconstruction of macroprocesses, that is, complex activities with a well defined objective achieved by means of the coordinated execution of the constituent processes. Reconstruction of macroprocesses is based on the information available on process functionality and data interactions among different processes.
- Reengineering of work processes and macroprocesses, by optimizing their execution to improve the quality of the offered services.

These activities can result very complex, due to the fact that thousands of processes must be analyzed, spread among heterogeneous information systems [2]. In addition, processes were not always documented, and the personnel with the knowledge required to understand processes and how they work is no longer available, causing data standardization and process reengineering to become crucial activities to be performed with available specifications.

In order to perform process analysis in a semi-automatic way on this large set of specifications, we provide techniques based on the information contained in the specifications, limiting as far as possible the human intervention. In particular, we provide techniques for classifying processes by means of descriptors (Section 2.1), and similarity techniques to compare different processes on the basis of their descriptors, to support the reconstruction of information flows and macroprocess (Section 4).
Examples of applying the proposed techniques on a sample of 149 process specifications related to the Labour Ministry are illustrated, which allows us to evaluate similarity and unification for processes of different Divisions and Offices of the same Ministry. The analysis is being extended on a second sample of 240 specifications related to process of different Ministries of the Public Administration, to evaluate process similarity and unification across different Ministries.

2.1 Process descriptors

In this section, we present the technique we propose for classifying processes by means of *descriptors*, defined starting from the information contained in the process specifications. A descriptor provides a high-level formal description of the characteristics of a process. A process descriptor is a 6-tuple of *features*:

$$\langle \textit{F-Area}, \textit{I-Object}, \textit{O-Object}, \textit{Operation}, \textit{Const-Object}, \textit{Circ-Object} \rangle$$

obtained by extending the technique presented in [8] for disciplined description of process functionality, with capabilities to describe process characteristics related to input/output data. In general, the number and the type of features to be included in a descriptor depends on the type of analysis to be performed on the processes. In our case, to support similarity-based analysis, we represent the following process characteristics:

1. The functional area to which the process pertains within the organization (feature *F-Area*), in order to support cross-functional process unification.
2. The data manipulated by the process, in order to evaluate data similarity between different processes. We distinguish between input entities (feature *I-Object*), representing the entities required in input by the process to start its execution, and output entities (feature *O-Object*), which are the entities produced as the result of the process execution. One or more entities of the ER schema associated with the process can be specified in these features.
3. The functionality of the process, in order to evaluate the similarity of performed operations. Process functionality is described by means of the performed operation (feature *Operation*), the mandatory constitutive entities required by the operation (feature *Cons-Object*) and the optional circumstantial entities involved in the operation (feature *Circ-Object*).

For example, let us consider the process `Labour Inspectorate Employee Retirement`, which establishes the retirable employees of the Labour Inspectorate by evaluating the contributions they paid. This process is described by means of the descriptor shown in Fig. 1.

Labour Inspectorate Employee Retirement

⟨Functional area⟩:	General Management of General Affairs and Personnel
⟨I-Object⟩:	{ Employee of Labour Inspectorate }
⟨O-Object⟩:	{ Employee of Labour Inspectorate, Retirable Employee of Labour Inspectorate }
⟨Operation⟩:	Retire
⟨Cons-Object ⟩:	{ Employee of Labour Inspectorate }
⟨Circ-Object⟩:	{ Employee dossier }

Fig. 1. An example of process descriptor ($D(P_1)$)

In our approach, process descriptors are semi-automatically constructed, by analyzing the specifications associated with processes. In particular, when possible, features are automatically filled in with information extracted from the ER schemas (e.g., entity names in features concerning objects); if necessary, features are filled in with names manually extracted from textual information in process specifications (e.g., operation names).

A feature *f* has a set of related names, which are the names used to classify the processes with respect to the feature. Two sets of names are defined for features, namely entity names and operation names.

3 Techniques for terminological analysis

In order to evaluate process similarity, we need to compare the names specified in the features of their descriptors and determine their degree of similarity, that we call *affinity*. To evaluate name affinity, we construct a *semantic dictionary* where entity and operation names are organized into a *concept hierarchy*, as shown in Fig. 2. Two names have affinity if they refer to the same concept or to concepts that are close in the semantic dictionary hierarchy.

The hierarchy is incrementally constructed. First, we define the bottom level concepts for groups of names corresponding to entities and operations that are similar in process descriptors. Then, we abstract higher-level concepts starting from the bottom level concepts, by means of the generalization and aggregation abstraction mechanisms. In this way, we provide the process analyst with a complete overview at different levels of abstraction of the data and functionalities of the Public Administration processes.

To identify entities and operations that are similar in process descriptors, we exploit the information contained in process specifications. In particular, for entities we analyze the ER schemas associated with processes, while, for operations, we perform a categorization based on the features describing functionality in process descriptors. To evaluate entity similarity, we construct a Thesaurus, where the semantics of entities in the ER schemas is described by means of proper terminological relationships. Issues related to Thesaurus construction are discussed in Section 3.1. In Section 3.2, we provide methodological indications for the definition of the concept hierarchy in the semantic dictionary, while in Section 3.3, we discuss name affinity evaluation using the semantic dictionary.

3.1 Thesaurus construction

A Thesaurus is a dictionary storing terms that are relevant for a given application domain, and a set of relevant terminological relationships to manage synonyms and semantically related terms, to support, for example, classification and retrieval of unstructured information, such as documents [16]. The construction of a Thesaurus is based on the analysis of a set of documents and on the identification of the relevant terms and relationships for the domain of interest. In our case, we exploit the available ER schemas to define a Thesaurus specifying the terminological relationships between entity names that are relevant for evaluating entity similarity, in view of defining the bottom level concepts in the semantic dictionary.

Two entities in different schemas are similar if they describe the same or similar real-world objects. To evaluate entity similarity, we consider both the

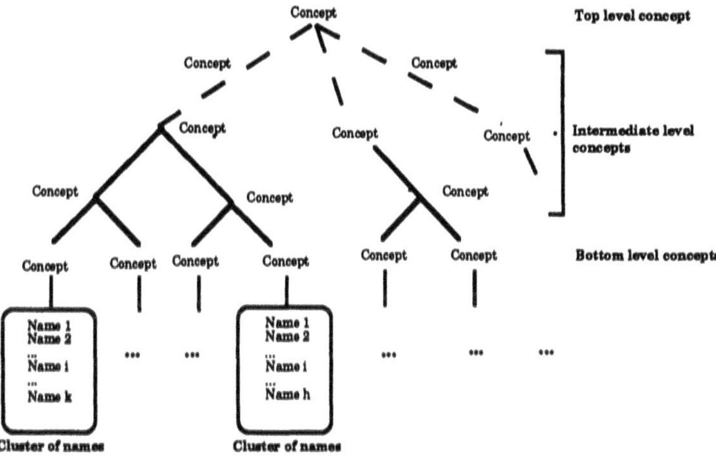

Fig. 2. Architecture of the semantic dictionary

synonymy relationship between their names (*lexical knowledge* on entity similarity) and the structural relationships in which the entities participate in the ER schemas (*schema knowledge* on entity similarity), that is, "is-a" links and relationships. In fact, two entities related by means of an "is-a" link in a generalization hierarchy have a certain degree of similarity due to the semantics associated with generalization hierarchies in conceptual schemas (i.e., inheritance mechanism, subset relationship). Two entities participating in a relationship have a degree of similarity as well, due to the semantics of the relationship in conceptual schemas (i.e., aggregation semantics). To take into account all explicit relationships and "is-a" links defined between entities in ER schemas, we construct the Thesaurus directly from available schemas.

For Thesaurus construction, difficulties are related to the fact that a high number of ER schemas is involved, and the same entity name can have been used to denote different real-world object classes (homonym problem [3]), or different names can have been used to denote the same object class (synonyms problem [3]). While synonyms do not cause problems in view of similarity evaluation, the presence of homonym can lead to the evaluation of undesirable similarities. To exclude homonym in the Thesaurus, we require normalization of the specifications; in fact, repeated entity names are proposed to the process analyst who disambiguates them, if necessary.

In the following, n_i denotes the name associated with entity e_i. Lexical and structural relationships between entities are captured in our Thesaurus by means of the following conventional binary terminological relationships between entity names:

- *USE*, defined between entity names that are considered synonyms because they represent the same class of real-world objects across schemas. We consider as synonyms: an acronym entity name and its expansion, singular entity names and their plural, an entity name and its incorrectly spelled occurrences in different schemas (e.g., ⟨*Emp. USE Employee*⟩).

- *BT* (Broader Terms), defined between names of entities participating in generalization hierarchies in the ER process schemas. In particular, $\langle n_i BT n_j \rangle$ is defined for a pair of entities such that e_i is the generalization of e_j in a schema (e.g., ⟨*Person BT Employee*⟩).
- RT (Related Terms) defined between names of entities participating in a relationship in the ER process schemas (e.g., ⟨*Employee RT Department*⟩).

These binary relationships have an inverse relationship implied by them, which is also stored in the Thesaurus, to keep the Thesaurus consistent and complete. In particular, the inverse of BT is the NT (Narrower Terms) relationship, defined between a specialization entity and its corresponding generalization, that is, $\langle n_i BT n_j \rangle \rightarrow \langle n_j NT n_i \rangle$; the inverse of the *USE* relationship is *UF* (Used For) relationship defined between synonym names, that is, $\langle n_i USE n_j \rangle \rightarrow \langle n_j UF n_i \rangle$. The inverse of the *RT* relationship is *RT* itself, that is, *RT* is symmetric.

To evaluate entity similarity, we consider:

- *Explicit relationships*, that are defined in the Thesaurus.
- *Implicit relationships*, that can be derived from the explicit ones. They capture the paths of relationships and/or "is-a" links between entities in ER schemas involving at most three entities. In fact, we assume that some degree of affinity exists between two entities due to the fact that they participate in relationship with a third entity, or to the fact that they have a common father in a generalization hierarchy, or a mixed situation (a relationship and an "is-a" link with a common entity). Longer paths are not considered for similarity purposes, because too weak affinities can be generally inferred from them, specially when paths are composed of relationships for which no inheritance semantics holds along the path.

Since, in general, these relationships can occur more than once in the whole set of analyzed schemas, we distinguish also:

- *Homogeneous multiple relationships*, (either explicit or implicit), that is, relationships of a given type with k occurrences in the Thesaurus.
- *Heterogeneous multiple relationships*, (either explicit or implicit), that is, relationships of any type with k occurrences in the Thesaurus.

To quantify the similarity between a pair of entities, we weight terminological relationships in the Thesaurus. We assign a strength $\sigma_{\Re} \in [0,1]$ to each type $\Re$ of terminological relationship, to capture its implication for entity similarity, with $\sigma_{USE/UF} \geq \sigma_{BT/NT} \geq \sigma_{RT}$. The higher the strength, the higher the similarity implication of a given terminological relationship. During experimentation, we used $\sigma_{USE/UF} = 1$, $\sigma_{BT/NT} = 0.8$, and $\sigma_{RT} = 0.5$.

The similarity between two entities e_i and e_j belonging to different ER schemas is computed by means of a similarity coefficient, $Sim(e_i, e_j) \in [0,1]$, which takes into account the type and the strengths of the explicit and implicit relationships of e_i and e_j in the Thesaurus. The higher the number of relationships for two entities in the Thesaurus, the greater the similarity coefficient computed for them. The similarity metrics are detailed described in [7].

Definition 1 Entity similarity. Two entities e_i and e_j are similar, denoted by $e_i \sim e_j$, if their similarity coefficient $Sim(e_i, e_j)$ is greater than or equal to an imposed threshold $\alpha > 0$, that is, $e_i \sim e_j \leftrightarrow Sim(e_i, e_j) \geq \alpha$.

3.2 Semantic dictionary construction

In building the semantic dictionary, we start from the concepts at the bottom level of the hierarchy, which are defined as representative of entities and operations that are similar.

To identify groups of similar entities on the basis of the similarity coefficients computed for pairs of entities, we apply the *complete link* clustering technique [9]. This technique is generally used in information retrieval to classify documents according to similarity levels [16]. It is a hierarchical agglomerative technique which produces as the output a tree of entity clusters; each cluster has associated a similarity coefficient that holds for all possible pairs of entities belonging to the cluster.

To identify groups of similar operations, we stay on a categorization based on the triplet ⟨*Operation*, *Cons-Object*, *Circ-Object*⟩, that provides indications for classification according to [8]. In particular, the following clusters of similar operations are identified:

1. "Exchange of objects with outside" (other processes, users). Operations pertaining to this cluster deal with information, documents and/or material exchange, such as "Send retirement dossier to Administrator". Examples of operation names (i.e., verbs) occurring in process specifications are 'communicate', 'deliver', 'display', 'distribute', 'give', 'obtain', 'present', 'receive', 'show'.
2. "Creation of objects". Operations pertaining to this cluster deal with generation of objects, such as "Define a retirement dossier". Examples of verbs occurring in process specifications are 'compile', 'construct', 'define', 'make a draft of', 'make', 'prepare', 'produce', 'retire'.
3. "Transformation of objects". Operations pertaining to this cluster deal with changes to objects, varying their identity, such as "Compose retirement requests". Examples of verbs occurring in process specifications are 'compact', 'compose', 'cut', 'decompose', 'divide', 'join', 'merge', 'record', 'split'.
4. "Modification/Observation" of the status of input objects. Operations pertaining to this cluster deal with modifications of objects while preserving their type, such as "Examine requests". Examples of verbs occurring in process specifications are 'check', 'choose', 'dismiss', 'examine', 'fill in', 'list', 'protect', 'retrieve', 'select', 'sign', 'test', 'update'.
5. "Deletion or removal of objects". Operations pertaining to this cluster are operations destroying objects, such as "Annul dossier". Examples of verbs

occurring in process specifications are 'annul', 'cancel', 'delete', 'eliminate', 'erase'.

The names of entities and operations in defined clusters constitute the starting point for defining the concept hierarchy in the semantic dictionary. In particular, a bottom-level concept is defined for each cluster of names, on the basis of the characteristics and semantics of the entities/operations within the cluster. The concept defined for a cluster is the generalization of the entities/operations associated with the cluster's names. Responsible for concept definition is the process analyst, who examines the clusters and identifies a suitable concept name to represent all the cluster members. Concept hierarchies are defined separately for entities and operations. The main methodological suggestions for concept definition are the following:

- Entity name clusters: the concept name can be selected starting from the names of the entities belonging to a given cluster, or can be defined from scratch on the basis of the semantics of the entities within the cluster. The following cases can occur:
  1. Multi-term names.
     For entities with multi-term names, one (or more than one) term is (are) common to all the names belonging to the cluster, and the common term(s) denote a concept. This means that the entity names are specialization of a common generic entity. The common term(s) is (are) extracted to become the name of the concept representative of the cluster, as illustrated in the example of Fig. 3. Here the concepts `Employee of Labour Ministry`, `Employee of Labour Inspectorate`, and `Employee` are defined for each respective cluster, since they are common to all the names in each cluster. These concepts are at different levels of abstraction in the hierarchy.
  2. Single-term names.
     For single-term names, if one name denotes an entity which is a generalization of the entities represented by the other cluster's entities, the process analyst selects this name to become the concept name associated with the cluster. Otherwise, the process analyst selects a new generic name for the cluster's concept.
  3. Mixed names.
     This is a mixed situation, and the process analyst proceeds as in cases 1 and 2, by considering the common term(s) of multi-term names and the single-term names as candidates for the definition of the concept name.
- Operation name clusters: the concept defined for a cluster corresponds to the type of the operation associated with the cluster. As a consequence, the concepts `Exchange`, `Creation`, `Transformation`, `Modification /Observation`, and `Deletion` are defined, as illustrated in Fig. 4.

Higher-level concepts in the hierarchy are incrementally abstracted, if necessary, starting from the bottom level concepts, by means of the generalization and

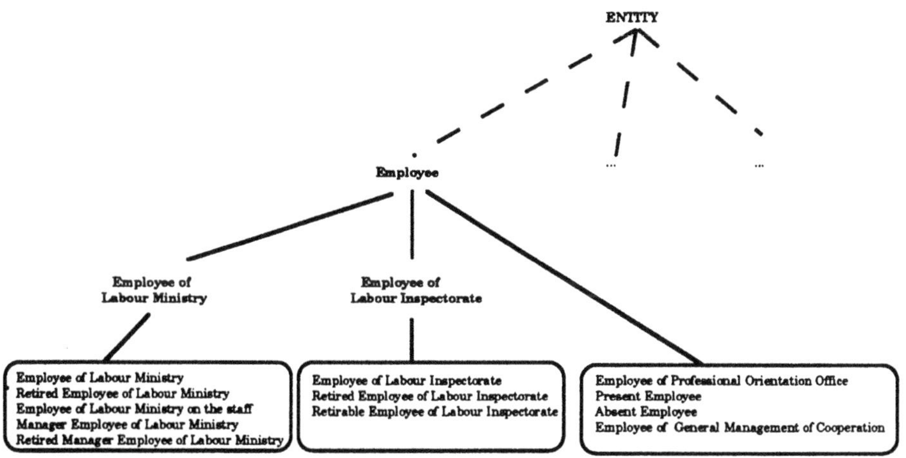

Fig. 3. An example of concept hierarchy for entities

the aggregation abstraction mechanisms, taking into account also the knowledge about the standards, rules and conventions adopted in the Public Administration.

3.3 Accessing the semantic dictionary

Concepts in the semantic dictionary are connected by means of links with other concepts in the hierarchy. Moreover, bottom level concepts are connected by means of links with corresponding clusters of names. To operationally evaluate name affinity, we assign a strength σ to links in the semantic dictionary (e.g., in our experimentation, we used $\sigma = 0.8$).

The affinity of two names depends on the length of the path between them in the semantic dictionary. The higher the number of links in the path between two names, the lower the affinity of the involved names. A path between two names in the semantic dictionary is denoted by the symbol "$\Rightarrow^l$", where $l > 0$ is the length of the path. The strength of a path "$\Rightarrow^l$" is computed as the combination of the strength of the involved links, using the monotonic function $\tau^N : N \times [0,1] \rightarrow [0,1]$, with $\tau^N(l, \sigma) = (\sigma)^l$.

Definition 2 Name Affinity Coefficient. The Affinity Coefficient $A(n_i, n_j)$ between two names n_i and n_j is the measure of their affinity in the semantic dictionary computed as follows:

$$A(n_i, n_j) = \begin{cases} 1 & \text{if } (n_i = n_j) \\ \tau^N(l, \sigma) & \text{if } n_i \Rightarrow^l n_j \\ 0 & \text{otherwise} \end{cases}$$

According to this definition, $A(n_i, n_j)$ is a numerical value in the range $[0, 1]$; it is 1 if the names are identical, is the τ^N strength of the path between them in

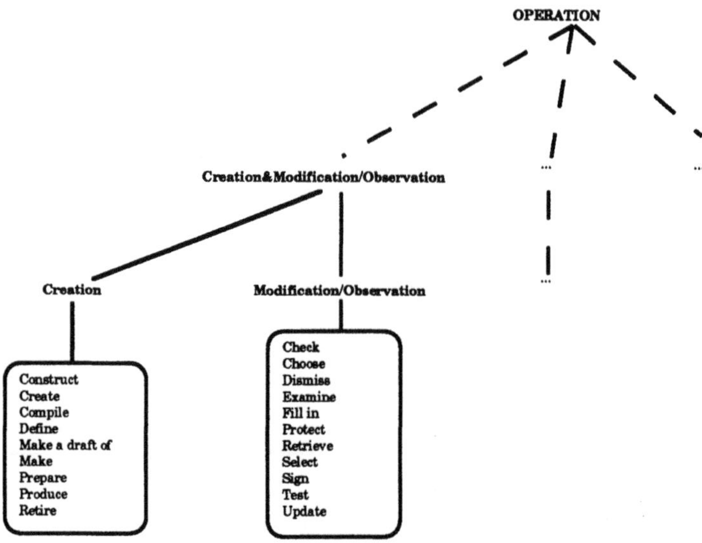

Fig. 4. An example of concept hierarchy for operations

the semantic dictionary, and is 0 otherwise. An affinity threshold can be imposed to filter out the names with affinity.

Definition 3 Name Affinity. Two names n_i and n_j have affinity, denoted by $n_i \sim n_j$, if their affinity coefficient is greater than or equal to an imposed threshold $\beta > 0$, that is, $n_i \sim n_j \leftrightarrow A(n_i, n_j) \geq \beta$.

4 Techniques for process similarity evaluation

Process similarity is evaluated on the basis of the descriptors associated with them, by comparing the involved features. Before illustrating how to measure process similarity, let us describe how feature similarity is determined for process descriptors.

Two features f and f' are *comparable* if they refer to the same set of names (i.e., entity names, operation names). The similarity between a pair of comparable features in different process descriptors is a function computed on the names they contain. Let P_i be a process specification, and $D(P_i)$ its corresponding descriptor. The notation $D(P_i).f$ indicates the name n or the set of names $n_1, \ldots, n_q$ specified in the feature f of descriptor $D(P_i)$.

Definition 4 Feature similarity. The *feature similarity* of a pair of comparable features f and f' of process descriptors $D(P_i)$ and $D(P_j)$, denoted by $Sim(D(P_i).f, D(P_j).f')$, is the measure of the affinity between their names, computed as follows.

$$Sim(D(P_i).f, D(P_j).f') = \begin{cases} A(n,n') & \text{if } f, f' \text{ are single-name} \\ & \text{and } n \sim n' \\ \frac{2 \cdot |F|}{|D(P_i).f| + |D(P_j).f'|} & \text{if } f, f' \text{ are multiple-name} \\ & \text{and } F \neq \emptyset \\ 0 & \text{otherwise} \end{cases}$$

where $F = \{\langle n, n' \rangle \mid n \in D(P_i).f, n' \in D(P_j).f', n \sim n'\}$ is a set composed of the pairs of names of $D(P_i).f$ and $D(P_j).f'$ that have affinity, and notation $\mid D(P_k).f \mid$ indicates the number of names contained in feature f of the descriptor $D(P_k)$.

Definition 4 states that the similarity of two comparable features is the affinity coefficient of their names in the semantic dictionary, if both features contain only one name, is the number of their names that have affinity multiplied by two and divided by the total number of their names (Dice's metric [16]), if features contain more than one name, and is 0 otherwise. According to the Dice's metric, an affinity mapping Φ is defined between the names of two compared features $D(P_i).f$ and $D(P_j).f'$. We require a $1-1$ mapping, that is, each $n \in D(P_i).f$ is mapped into at most one name $n' \in D(P_j).f'$ and vice versa. The set F is composed of the pair of names $\langle n, n' \rangle$ participating in the affinity mapping Φ. The mapping Φ can be total or partial. Φ is total if for each name $n \in D(P_i).f$ there exists a corresponding name $n' \in D(P_j).f'$ with affinity, and vice versa. Φ is partial if some name in $D(P_i).f$ or in $D(P_i).f'$ is left unmapped. The greater the number of pairs that participate in Φ, the higher the feature similarity.

The similarity between two process specifications is computed with respect to the involved entities (entity-based similarity) and to the performed functionality (functionality-based similarity), by means of proper *similarity coefficients*.

4.1 Entity-based similarity

Definition 5 Entity-based similarity coefficient. The *Entity-based similarity coefficient* of two process specifications P_i and P_j having descriptors $D(P_i)$ and $D(P_j)$, denoted by $ESim(P_i, P_j)$, is the measure of the similarity of their comparable and equal features related to input and output entities:

$$ESim(P_i, P_j) = \sum_{f \in \Im} Sim(D(P_i).f, D(P_j).f)$$

where $\Im$={I-Object,O-Object}.

Definition 5 states that the entity-based similarity of two process specifications is the sum of the similarity of their comparable and equal features related to the input and output entities. According to what stated for name affinity coefficients, $ESim(P_i, P_j)$ can assume values in the range $[0, 2]$. It has value 0 when all features $f \in \Im$ are not similar; it has value 2 when both features *I-Object* and *O-Object* have similarity equal to 1.

4.2 Functionality-based similarity

Definition 6 Functionality-based similarity coefficient. The *Functionality -based similarity coefficient* of two process specifications P_i and P_j having descriptors $D(P_i)$ and $D(P_j)$, denoted by $FSim(P_i, P_j)$, is the measure of the similarity of their comparable and equal features related to functionality:

$$FSim(P_i, P_j) = \sum_{f \in \Im} Sim(D(P_i).f, D(P_j).f)$$

where $\Im$ = {Operation, Cons-Object, Circ-Object}.

Definition 6 states that the functionality similarity of two process specifications is the sum of the similarity coefficients of their comparable and equal features used to describe process functionality. This coefficient returns a similarity value in the range range $[0, 3]$, depending on the number of features that have similarity, and on the feature similarity value Sim.

5 A methodological framework for process unification

The term "unification" is used to denote the combination of process specifications by identification of semantic correspondences between them, as inspired by literature on semantic heterogeneity [14].

The goal of our work is to facilitate Information Systems interconnection and interoperability by constructing a unified process architecture. In the proposed approach, we distinguish two steps. First, naming and structural conflicts between process specifications must be detected and resolved with the help of the semantic dictionary. Second, semantic correspondences between process specifications must be identified for their combination.

5.1 Conflict resolution

Conflicts have been widely studied in schema integration literature [3]. They are generally classified as follows:

- *Name conflicts.* These conflicts arise in presence of homonym and/or synonyms.
- *Structural conflicts.* They are distinguished in *type conflicts* and *link conflicts.* The former arise when the same concept has been modeled using different constructs. The latter arise when the same entities are related through different types of links, or through links having different integrity constraints (e.g., relationships with different cardinalities).

In our approach, the availability of the semantic dictionary allows the schema analyst to properly handle the problems to gain good resolution. In particular, the semantic dictionary allows the normalization of entity and operation names used for semantically similar processes, according to the concept hierarchy therein contained. In addition, for structural conflicts, the process analyst examines the ER schemas associated with the entity names contained in the same cluster in the semantic dictionary, and decides how to resolve them on the basis also of his own experience and knowledge on the Public Administration rules. In general, structural conflicts are resolved by selecting one representation as the reference representation for the involved similar process specifications, as described in [5].

5.2 Semantic correspondences

Semantic correspondences are established between processes on the basis of their level of similarity. Given two process specifications P_i and P_j with associated descriptors $D(P_i)$ and $D(P_j)$, three significant cases can be identified:

1. *Semantic equivalence.* This is the strongest measure of similarity between two processes, and indicates that P_i and P_j represent the same real-world activity. With respect to our similarity coefficients, two processes are semantically equivalent if:
   (a) $ESim(P_i, P_j) = 2$ and $FSim(P_i, P_j) = 3$ and
   (b) a total $1-1$ mapping Φ is defined for names of each comparable feature of $D(P_i)$ and $D(P_j)$ and all names in the affinity pairs are equal.

   As a consequence, two semantic equivalent processes present the same involved objects and the same functionality.
2. *Semantic relationship.* This is a weaker measure of similarity between two process specifications than semantic equivalence, and indicates that P_i and P_j represent partially overlapping real-world activities, that is, activities performing similar functionalities on similar data. With respect to our similarity coefficients, two processes have a semantic relationship if:
   (a) $1 \leq ESim(P_i, P_j) \leq 2$ and $2 \leq FSim(P_i, P_j) \leq 3$ and
   (b) a $1-1$ mapping Φ, either partial or total, is defined for names of each comparable feature of $D(P_i)$ and $D(P_j)$.

   As an example of processes with semantic relationship, let us consider the processes P_2 and P_3, recording the absences of employees, whose descriptors $D(P_2)$ and $D(P_3)$ are shown in Fig. 5 and in Fig. 6, respectively. We have that $ESim(P_2, P_3) = 2$ because Φ is total for both features *I-Object* of P_2 and P_3 and *O-Object* of P_2 and P_3. In fact, `Employee of General Management of Cooperation` of P_2 and `Employee of Professional Orientation Office` of P_3 have affinity, because they refer to the same concept `Employee` in the semantic dictionary, while remaining entity names in the considered features are equal in both descriptors $D(P_2)$ and $D(P_3)$. $FSim(P_2, P_3) = 3$ because both process operations refer to the `Transformation` concept in the semantic dictionary, the circumstantial objects have affinity in the semantic dictionary, and the constitutive objects are equal in both descriptors.
3. *Commonality.* This is the weakest measure of similarity between two process specifications, and indicates that P_i and P_j represent overlapping real-world

Personnel Absence Recording

⟨Functional area⟩: General Management of Cooperation
⟨I-Object⟩: { Employee of General Management of Cooperation, Present Employee }
⟨O-Object⟩: {Employee of General Management of Cooperation, Absent Employee }
⟨Operation⟩: Record
⟨Cons-Object ⟩: {Employee of General Management of Cooperation }
⟨Circ-Object⟩: { Presence Card }

Fig. 5. An example of process descriptor ($D(P_2)$)

Absence Recording

⟨Functional area⟩: Central Office for Professional Education and Orientation
⟨I-Object⟩: {Employee of Professional Orientation Office, Present Employee }
⟨O-Object⟩: {Employee of Professional Orientation Office, Absent Employee}
⟨Operation⟩: Record
⟨Cons-Object ⟩: { Employee of Professional Orientation Office }
⟨Circ-Object⟩: { Presence Card }

Fig. 6. An example of process descriptor ($D(P_3)$)

activities, with respect to their manipulated data and/or functionality. With respect to our similarity coefficients, two processes have commonality if they do not fall in the categories 1. and 2. and if $ESim(P_i, P_j) \geq \alpha$ and/or $FSim(P_i, P_j) \geq \beta$, where α and β are similarity thresholds defined by the process analyst to filter out similar processes. This means that a partial $1-1$ mapping Φ is defined for names of a subset comparable features of $D(P_i)$ and $D(P_j)$. As an example of processes with resemblance, let us consider the processes P_1 and P_2, whose descriptors $D(P_1)$ and $D(P_2)$ are shown in Fig. 1 and in Fig. 5, respectively. For them we have that $ESim(P_1, P_2) = 1.66$, since similarity of features $D(P_1)$.*I-Object* and $D(P_2)$.*I-Object* is 0.66 because the entity **`Employee of Labour Inspectorate`** of P_1 has affinity with **`Employee of General Management of Cooperation`**, while similarity of features $D(P_1)$.*O-Object* and $D(P_2)$.*O-Object* is 1 because the two entities specified in $D(P_1)$.*O-Object* have affinity with the two entities specified in $D(P_2)$.*O-Object*. Moreover, $FSim(P_1, P_2) = 0.512$. In fact, operations of P_1 and P_2 do not have affinity since they refer to different operation concepts in the semantic dictionary (i.e., **`Creation`** for P_1 and **`Transformation`** for P_2, supposing an affinity threshold $\beta = 0.5$ for operations). The similarity between features $D(P_1)$.*Cons-Object* and $D(P_2)$.*Cons-Object* is 0.512, which is the affinity value of **`Employee of Labour Inspectorate`** and **`Employee`**

of General Management of Cooperation in the semantic dictionary. Finally, the similarity of features $D(P_1).Circ\text{-}Object$ and $D(P_2).Circ\text{-}Object$ is 0 because **Employee dossier** and **Presence card** do not have affinity in the dictionary.

5.3 Process unification

Once naming and structural conflicts have been resolved, it is possible to proceed to the construction of a unified architecture of semantically related processes. Depending on the type of semantic correspondence, the following cases are identified:

1. *Process paradigm.*
   For semantic equivalent processes, we say that a "process paradigm", i.e., a standardized definition of the process can be defined. Process paradigms are reference specifications that can be reused in developing new applications similar to existing applications, and can guide maintenance and evolution strategies.
2. *Process hierarchy.*
   For semantically related processes (e.g., P_2 and P_3), we say that a "process hierarchy", i.e., an "is-a" hierarchy, between them can be defined, over the involved functionalities and, possibly, the objects. According to "is-a" hierarchies, features of supertype and subtype are properly distributed. Use of process hierarchies is the basis for accommodating multiple user perspectives on comparable, semantically related processes.
3. *Process cluster.*
   For processes with commonality (e.g., P_1 and P_2), we say that a "process cluster", i.e., a group of processes related by a similarity value, can be defined. Clusters are useful to facilitate browsing of domain knowledge by classification for significant features. For example, rather high entity similarity and low functionality similarity coefficients for processes in a cluster can indicate the existence of information flows between the processes in the cluster, which can be examined to possibly reconstruct macroprocesses. Identification of information flows between processes and reconstruction of macroprocess is discussed in [6], where suitable *Closeness* coefficients are described for this purpose.

6 Supporting tools

An environment to support the process analysis techniques previously illustrated has been developed, based on a repository developed by the AIPA for storage of the ER schemas and the information in process specifications. The implementation environment is PC-based, using Access 2.0. The AIPA repository provides functionalities for visualization of schemas and associated information, both with textual information format and with a simple graphical editor for ER schemas.

Concerning process analysis support, the following functionalities have been implemented:

- Definition of process descriptors; the tool extracts features related to objects (i.e., *I-Object, O-Object, Cons-Object* and *Circ-Object*) directly from the schemas stored in the repository; the *Operation* feature is interactively specified by the process analyst on the basis of the process specifications retrieved from the repository.
- Construction and consultation of the Thesaurus. The Thesaurus is automatically constructed in form of Access tables, by analyzing the ER schemas stored in the repository. A separate table is defined for the *USE* relationship for optimization purposes; spelling checker tools are employed to identify equivalent entity names. The tables for *BT/NT* and *RT* relationships are constructed by inserting a row for each pair of entities connected by means of an "is-a" link or participating in a relationship, and by inserting the corresponding σ value for the involved relationship. Functionalities for the consultation of the Thesaurus have been implemented to support:
  1. the selection of a pair of entities and the computation of their similarity coefficient;
  2. the selection of an entity e_i and the retrieval of the entities that are similar to e_i, with a similarity coefficient *Sim* greater than or equal to a (interactively set) threshold;
  3. the section of an entity and the retrieval of the entities of the Thesaurus that have a relationship with e_i in the Thesaurus.
- Grouping of similar entities into clusters, using the complete link clustering technique. Entities are submitted to pairwise similarity comparisons, and the similarity matrix is generated for the complete link clustering algorithm. The entity clusters obtained with the technique are presented to the process analyst as a tree of entities, similarly to the interface presented in [17]. Starting from the defined clusters, it is possible to interactively extract the corresponding concepts, on the basis also of the structure of names included in the cluster. Defined concepts are automatically associated with the cluster from which they are extracted. Clusters for operation names are interactively defined for each category of operations, and the type of operation becomes the concept associated with the corresponding cluster. A graphical interface is under development, to show the clusters of similar names and their corresponding abstract concepts.
- Process similarity evaluation, based on the entity similarity and the functionality similarity coefficients. The process analyst can select from a menu the coefficient(s) to be used for similarity computation, and a reference process for similarity evaluation. The user of the process analyzer can also choose to produce reports retrieving all processes related to the reference process in decreasing order of similarity, which are the basis for the unification strategies.

Retrieval and graphical presentation functionalities have been realized using the development environment provided by Access.

7 Related work

The problems discussed in the paper are related to researches concerning semantic heterogeneity in multidatabases and process reengineering.
Semantic heterogeneity.
Techniques to identify semantic similarity between data are essential in federated database systems, in view of schema integration and query processing activities [19]. Recent approaches to deal with semantic heterogeneity suggest the use of advanced data dictionaries, where taxonomies for the data in the federation are defined to provide flexible query processing facilities. In [4], a hierarchical data structure called "Summary Schema Model" is proposed, where concepts represented in the federation schemas are mapped to a pre-defined taxonomy, organized at different levels of abstraction according to linguistic relationships. Here, a manual activity is required to map concepts of local databases into a corresponding taxonomy term. In [15], fuzzy techniques are discussed to evaluate the semantic similarity between classes in different conceptual schemas. The proposed techniques exploit both an associative network of terms and the knowledge about the semantic relevance of attributes to classes, which are properly combined by means of similarity functions. In [14], a semantic dictionary architecture is proposed for multidatabase systems, where federated generic knowledge is organized according to pre-defined semantic relationships, which provide support for retrieval of information similar or related to the information managed in a local database. Also in this case, a manual activity is required to specify the relationships for the objects of different local schemas in the dictionary. Our approach tries to limit the manual activity required to build the semantic dictionary for the ER schemas, by identifying concept hierarchies from the Thesaurus, instead of referring to pre-existing taxonomies. Thesaurus relationships are automatically extracted from the ER schemas available in the repository. The concept hierarchy obtained in this way is more specific than a pre-defined taxonomy, but has the advantage of capturing similarities between entities on the basis of their actual use. However, a manual support is required to the process analyst to abstract higher level concepts in the hierarchy. The development of a semi-automatic technique for the semantic dictionary construction has been an essential requirement of our work, due to the large number of conceptual schemas and process descriptors to be analyzed.
Process reengineering.
In the area of process reengineering, workflow specifications are studied to provide formal descriptions of processes of an organization and workflow management systems for their implementation are available to facilitate process analysis and reengineering [11]. A conceptual description of tasks, executing entities, and task coordination constraints for business processes of an organization facilitates process understanding, evaluation and redesign to optimize existing processes

and adapt them to changing requirements. In reengineering processes at the technological level, new software lifecycles are required, to adequately represent reengineering processes in the lifecycle and support software development based on existing legacy software, to acquire and (re)use the domain knowledge therein contained [1]. In [2], data reverse engineering techniques are discussed, to support reengineering and cross-functional integration of information systems in the Public Sector, focusing on techniques to address data disintegration problems in large organizations. In this framework, our similarity techniques constitute a support to perform process analysis in view of reengineering. Process descriptors provide a high-level description of processes, pointing out the interaction aspects between processes in form of data exchanges. Similarity techniques help the process analyst in identifying groups of processes manipulating the same or similar data, and groups of processes that are candidate to constitute a macroprocess, which are a good basis to evaluate data distribution strategies and process optimization interventions during reengineering.

8 Concluding remarks

In the paper, we have presented an approach to support information system process reengineering at a conceptual level, by addressing issues related to process specification comparison and unification. In particular, we have proposed: i) techniques for analyzing a large set of process specifications, based on the construction of formal descriptors, providing a high-level characterization of the processes in terms of manipulated data and performed functionality in a given functional area; ii) techniques for evaluating data and functionality similarity between different processes, based on the construction of a Thesaurus, capturing the semantics of the ER schemas associated with processes, and of a semantic dictionary, where a concept hierarchy is introduced to provide the process analyst with aggregated and generalized knowledge for entities and operations; iii) a methodological framework for process unification, to identify groups of semantically related processes that can be considered together in reengineering interventions, because they perform similar operations and/or involve similar data.

Actually, entity attributes are not considered for entity affinity evaluation, because they are specified only for a restricted number of ER schemas in process specifications. However, the approach can be easily extended to include attributes. One way to extend the approach is to define a terminological relationship in the Thesaurus representing the attributes of an entity (e.g., CT, Component-Terms), which is used to determine the affinity coefficients together with existing terminological relationships. A second way is to apply the present approach to attribute names separately, that is, a Thesaurus of attribute names is constructed and clusters of similar attributes are derived on the basis of the affinity coefficients computed on the Thesaurus. An attribute hierarchy can be defined for attribute clusters similarly to the approach for schema integration presented in [18]. Entity affinity is then evaluated on the basis also of the attribute hierarchy. The presented tools are being experimented and their extension is under investigation.

Acknowledgements
Part of this work has been supported by the Information System Authority for Public Administration (AIPA). The authors thank Dr. P. Giani and Dr. S. Konstadopulu who developed the process analysis support tools, and the AIPA for providing the process specifications.

References

1. J.D. Ahrens, N.S. Prywes, "Transition to a Legacy- and Reuse- Based Software Life Cycle", *IEEE Computer,* October 1995.
2. P. Aiken, A. Muntz, R. Richards, "DoD Legacy Systems - Reverse Engineering Data Requirements", *Communications of the ACM,* vol.37, no.5, May 1994.
3. C.Batini, M. Lenzerini, S. Navathe, "A Comprehensive Analysis of Methodologies for Database Schema Integration", *ACM Computing Surveys,* September 1986.
4. M.W. Bright, A.R. Hurson, S. Pakzad, "Automated Resolution of Semantic Heterogeneity in Multidatabases", *ACM Transactions On Database Systems,* vol.19, no.2, June 1994.
5. S. Castano, V. De Antonellis, "Reference Conceptual Architectures for Reengineering Information Systems", *International Journal of Cooperative Information Systems*, vol.4, nos.2 & 3, 1995.
6. S. Castano, V. De Antonellis, "Reengineering Processes in Public Administrations", in *Proc. of OO-ER'95, Int. Conf. on the Object-Oriented and Entity-Relationship Modeling,* Gold Coast, Australia, December 1995, Springer Verlag.
7. S. Castano, V. De Antonellis, "A Systematic Approach to Process Analysis for Reengineering", Technical Report, Politecnico di Milano, 1996 (in preparation).
8. V. De Antonellis, B. Zonta, "A disciplined Approach to Office Analysis", *IEEE Transactions on Software Engineering,* vol.16, no.8, August 1990.
9. B. Everitt, *Cluster Analysis,* Heinemann Educational Books Ltd, Social Science Research Council, 1974.
10. D. H.C. Gall, R.R. Klosch, R.T. Mittermeir, "Object-Oriented Re-Architecturing: An Approach to Long-Term Information Systems Evolution", in *Proc. of the ICSE'95, Int. Conference on Software Engineering Conference,* Seattle, USA, April 1995.
11. D. Georgakopoulos, M. Hornik, A. Sheth, "An Overview of Workflow Management: From Process Modeling to Workflow Automation Infrastructure", *Distributed and Parallel Databases,*, Kluwer Academic Publishers, Vol.3, 1995.
12. I. Jacobson, *Object-Oriented Software Engineering - A Use Case Driven Approach,* ACM Press, Addison-Wesley, 1992.
13. W. Kim, I. Choi, S. Gala, M. Scheevel, "On Resolving Schematic Heterogeneity in Multidatabase Systems", *Distributed and Parallel Databases,* vol.1, no.3, 1993, and in *Modern Database Systems-The Object Model, Interoperability and Beyond,* W. Kim (Editor), ACM Press, 1995.
14. J. Hammer, D. McLeod, "An Approach to Resolving Semantic Heterogeneity in a Federation of Autonomous Heterogeneous Database Systems", *International Journal of Intelligent and Cooperative Information Systems,* vol.2, no.1, June 1993.

15. P. Fankhauser, M. Kracker, E.J. Neuhold, "Semantic vs. Structural Resemblance of Classes", *SIGMOD RECORD*, vol.20, no.4, December 1991.
16. G. Salton, *Automatic Text Processing - The Transformation, Analysis and Retrieval of Information by Computer*, Addison-Wesley, 1989.
17. G. Salton, J. Allan, C. Buckley, "Automatic Structuring and Retrieval of Large Text Files", *Communications of the ACM*, vol.37, no.2, February 1994.
18. A.P. Sheth, S.K. Gala, S.B. Navathe, "On Automatic Reasoning For Schema Integration", *International Journal of Intelligent and Cooperative Information Systems*, vol.2, no.1, June 1993.
19. A.P. Sheth and J.P. Larson, "Federated Database Systems for Managing Distributed, Heterogeneous, and Autonomous Databases," *ACM Computing Surveys*, vol. 22, no. 3, September 1990.

Handling Conceptual Model Validation by Planning

Dolors Costal, Ernest Teniente, Toni Urpí and Carles Farré

Universitat Politècnica de Catalunya
LSI, Facultat d'Informàtica
Pau Gargallo 5. E-08028 Barcelona -- Catalonia
e-mail: [dolors | teniente | urpi]@lsi.upc.es, farre@goliat.upc.es

Abstract. An important amount of research has been devoted to conceptual model validation, that is, to check whether a conceptual model correctly and adequately describes the users' intended needs and requirements. In this paper we present a new approach to model validation. We define a set of desirable properties that a conceptual model should satisfy and we show how the accomplishment of all these properties can be checked in a uniform way by means of planning. Our approach is independent of any particular planning method and it extends the facilities of the methods developed so far.

1 Introduction

This paper describes an approach for validating conceptual models of information systems. By validation we mean the process of checking whether a conceptual model correctly and adequately describes the users' intended needs and requirements [ABC82]. This is one of the most important and crucial problems in information systems engineering. Indeed, detecting possible problems during information systems specification time will prevent possible errors during the following stages.

The validation task is not fully formalizable and it is based on intuition. Then, it is desirable to provide the designer with the maximum set of tools that assist him in the validation process [Bub86]. Among the support capabilities that have been proposed there are: infological simulation [VF85, CO92], paraphrasing specifications in natural language [RP92, Dal92], generation of abstractions and abstracts of specifications [JC92], animation and symbolic execution [LL93], explanation generation [GW93, OS95] and semantic prototyping [LTP91, LK93].

One of the proposed approaches for validating conceptual models consists of defining a set of desirable properties that the model should satisfy and to provide methods for checking these properties [Kun84, Kun85]. However, this proposal has several drawbacks. First, it deals only with a reduced set of properties. Second, it does not take into account the presence of the operations of the conceptual model in both the definition and the validation of the properties. Finally, it lacks of a uniform treatment of the properties in the sense that they are checked using different techniques. The work that we present in this paper extends previous research in this direction.

In our approach, the checking of the considered properties will be performed by using plan generation techniques. We define for each property (e.g. satisfiability of a conceptual model, redundancy of integrity constraints or executability of an operation) an initial state and a final state such that if there exists a plan, that is, a sequence of operations able to perform the transition between both states, the conceptual model satisfies that property. The use of planning allows us to check the whole set of properties in a uniform way. Moreover, it allows us to easily consider additional desirable properties and to guarantee that their checking is performed correctly, due to the existence of adequate planning methods.

We would like to point out that the generality of our approach allows us to be independent of the concrete planning method used for checking the properties. This facilitates the application of the improvements in the planning research area to our approach.

Furtado et al. [VF85] proposed a concrete planning method for reasoning about conceptual models. In their approach, the designer is provided with a tool that obtains a sequence of operations able to perform the transition between a given initial and target states. Therefore, the success of validation relies only on the designer's intuition and experience when defining the initial and target states. Moreover, Furtado et al. do not consider the integrity constraints when reasoning about conceptual models.

Recently, Feenstra and Wieringa [FW95] have also outlined a method for reasoning about conceptual models specified in a language less expressive than ours which does not consider derived predicates, in a similar way than the proposed by Furtado et al.. They propose a system able to answer reachability queries which permits to express some properties similar to ours. Their method is based on extending planning techniques with a satisfiability tester [BDM88]. However, as we will show in this paper, these properties can be checked by using some of the current planning methods.

This paper extends our previous work on validation in the context of databases [DTU96], which focused on the use of view updating for validating a database schema, without taking the predefined transactions or operations into account. It also extends our work reported in [CO92], where we proposed a concrete planning method for explaining the reachability of a final state, departing from a given initial state. As for [VF85], the success of validation relied only on the designer's intuition and experience when defining the initial and target states.

This paper is organized as follows. Next section reviews basic concepts of usual conceptual models, which are based on the concept of operation. Section 3 reviews the main planning concepts and identifies the features of planning methods able to handle the validation tasks considered in this paper. Section 4 defines a set of desirable properties that a conceptual model should satisfy and shows how the checking of these properties can be handled using planning. Section 5 illustrates how to apply our approach by using two existing planning methods. Finally, section 6 presents our conclusions and points out further work.

2 Conceptual models

In this section we review usual conceptual models of information systems and we introduce our notation for describing them. Most conceptual models are based on the concept of operation. We want to be general, and therefore we use a simple formalism, based on the concept of operation, and easily adaptable to many conceptual modelling languages.

Each conceptual modelling language provides a set of concepts and syntactic features to define the structure of the Information Base: the Information Base schema. In general, we may assume that the Information Base (IB) consists of two parts: *Base* and

Derived. The Base part includes all facts that are inserted and deleted directly by the operations, while the Derived part includes all facts that are derived from base and/or derived facts, by means of some kind of deductive rules.

We will assume the IB contains facts of a given set of *predicates* . Each predicate consists of a name and a set of arguments. Facts of base predicates are updated by operations while the existence of facts of derived predicates is defined declaratively by *deductive rules*. We will use the clausal form of logic, augmented with negation, to define deductive rules.

Many conceptual modelling languages provide some constructs for the definition of integrity constraints. For the sake of uniformity, we define the constraints in denial form by means of integrity rules which have the same form as the deductive rules. Any integrity constraint can be represented in this form as described in [LT84].

Below, we show an example of an IB schema:

emp(employee,department)
dept(department)
manager(employee,department)
works-for(e,m)← emp(e,d) ∧ manager(m,d)
ic1 ← emp(e,d) ∧ ¬dept(d)

There is a single derived predicate: works-for. Its deductive rule indicates that an employee E works for another employee M if E is an employee of a department D and M is the manager of that department. Note that we also include an integrity rule. It states that all employees must belong to an existent department.

It can be seen that there is a straightforward correspondence between our IB schema and that of ER [Che76], SDM [HM81], NIAM [NH89], and many others. Note that not all of them include a derived part in the IB. Our model is even adaptable to languages based on the relational data model. In such case, views are derived predicates and their definition is a deductive rule.

A conceptual modelling language has also to provide the definition of the transitions between different states of the Information Base: the transition schema. Most conceptual modelling languages define the transition schema in terms of operations. Application of an operation induces a transition from the current state of the IB to a new state.

We describe operations by: its name, its parameters, a precondition that must hold in the state of the IB in which the operation is applied, facts to be added to the IB by the operation and facts to be deleted from the IB by the operation.

Preconditions are expressed as first order formulas. In order to guarantee domain independence, range-restrictedness of the formulas is required. We use the common definition of range-restrictedness as introduced in [Nic82]. Additions and deletions can be expressed as sets of base facts.

In this paper, we assume that the specified precondition guarantees that facts to be deleted hold in the IB state in which the operation is applied and facts to be added do not hold in that IB state. However, our approach could also be applied if this requirement was not considered. Below, we show the transition schema for the IB schema described.

New-dept(D)	**Rem-dept(D)**
prec: $\neg$ dept(D)	prec: D$\neq$Staff $\wedge$ dept(D)
add: {dept(D)}	add: {}
del: {}	del: {dept(D)}
Hire(E,D)	**Fire(E)**
prec: $\neg$ $\exists$d' emp(E,d')	prec:$\exists$d emp(E,d)$\wedge\neg$manager(E,d)
add: {emp(E,D)}	add: {}
del: {}	del: {emp(E,d)}
New-manager(E,D)	**Rem-mgr(E)**
prec: $\neg\exists$d' manager(E,d')	prec:$\exists$dmanager(E,d)
add: {manager(E,D)}	add: {}
del: {}	del: {manager(E,d)}

The execution of an operation is *valid* only if its precondition holds in the IB state in which the operation is applied and the resulting IB state obtained after its execution is consistent, i.e., integrity constraints are satisfied in it. Otherwise, the operation can not be performed.

For example, the execution of operation Hire(John,Marketing) is not valid when applied to an IB state where base fact dept(Marketing) does not hold. In this case, emp(John,Marketing) would hold in the resulting state and dept(Marketing) would not. Thus, integrity constraint ic1 would be violated in the resulting state of the IB and this resulting state would be inconsistent.

Similarly, a sequence of operations is valid only if the execution of each operation of the sequence is valid. Moreover, an IB state is *reachable* only if it can be obtained by a valid sequence of operations.

In our example, the IB state: {dept(Marketing), emp(John,Marketing)} is reachable due to the following sequence of operations: New-dept(Marketing), Hire(John,Marketing)

As it happens with our IB schema, there is a straightforward correspondence beetween our transition schema and the transition schema of many conceptual modelling languages, such as that of Taxis [MBW80] and the one introduced by Furtado et al. in [VF85].

3 Planning

In this section we present classical planning problems and we identify the features of planning methods able to handle the validation tasks considered in this paper.

A classical planning problem can be stated as follows: given a description of the world or domain of the problem, given an initial state of that world and given a goal to accomplish at a final state, obtain one or several plans able to perform the transition between the initial state and a final state in which the desired goal holds. The obtained plans have to be consistent with respect to the world description. Note that, in particular, the obtained plan may be empty which means that the initial state already satisfies the goal.

A planning method has to provide both a way to *represent* a planning problem and a mechanism to *generate* plans for the planning problems it is able to represent.

The representation used by a planning method is important because it characterizes the planning problems it is able to solve. Actually, the representation of a planning problem is strongly related with conceptual modelling of information systems. In both cases, it is necessary to represent static and dynamic knowledge about a domain that evolves through several situations or states.

In order to use a planning method for the validation of the conceptual models described in section 2, it must provide a representation of a planning problem in terms of those conceptual models either directly or through an automatic transformation.

Using this representation the planning problem can be formulated more concretely as: given an IB schema and a transition schema, given an initial state of the IB expressed as a set of base facts[1] and given a goal expressed as a range-restricted first order formula to accomplish at a final state of the IB, obtain one or several valid sequences of operations able to perform the transition between the initial state of the IB and a final state of the IB where the desired goal holds.

For example: given the planning problem domain described by the IB schema and transition schema examples of section 2, given the initial state: {dept(Marketing), emp(John,Marketing)} and given the goal: ∃d emp(Peter,d) ∧ ∃e works-for(e,Peter), a possible plan to obtain is the valid sequence of operations: Hire(Peter,Marketing), New-mgr(Peter,Marketing).

We also have a requirement on the plan generation mechanism. It must obtain at least a solution plan for a given planning problem if any solution plan for the planning problem exists. The need of this requirement will become clear in section 4 when defining the properties to validate in terms of planning.

4 Using Planning for Validating Conceptual Models

In this section we define a set of desirable properties that a conceptual model should satisfy and we show how the checking of these properties can be handled by using planning. The main idea is to define for each property an initial state and a goal to accomplish at a final state such that if there exists a sequence of operations able to achieve the goal departing from the initial state, the conceptual model satisfies that property. If a property is not satisfied, the conceptual model is ill-specified and its specification should be changed. In general, this may be due to the specification of the deductive rules, integrity constraints, operations or even due to a combination of them.

In sections 4.1 and 4.2 we deal respectively with the properties related to the validation of the IB schema and to the validation of the operations.

4.1 Checking of Properties of the IB Schema

In this section we will define three properties related to the Information Base schema: satisfiability, liveliness of a predicate and redundancy of a constraint. We will

[1] Note that we only need the base facts of the IB to describe the initial state because the derived facts may be derived using the deductive rules. In particular, this set of base facts may be empty and we will call empty initial state its corresponding initial state

also show how these properties can be uniformly handled using planning. As a related work, we would like to mention the methods for handling satisfiability proposed in [Kun84, Kun85] and [Lun82]. These methods are only concerned with finding a model that satisfies all the integrity constraints since they do not take the operations into account in both the definition and the verification of the property. In the database field, three different methods [BDM88, LMSS93, GSUW94] have been proposed that handle respectively satisfiability, liveliness and redundancy. Besides the non uniformity of the way in which these properties are handled, again the main difference relies on the fact that these methods do not consider the operations.

4.1.1 Satisfiability

A fundamental property that a conceptual model should satisfy is satisfiability. Intuitively, a conceptual model is satisfiable if there exists a state of the IB satisfying all the integrity constraints which can be obtained by a sequence of operations. If there is not such a state then the entire conceptual model becomes useless since no operation can be executed. To illustrate this property, consider a subset of the conceptual model defined in section 2 with the additional integrity constraint ic2, stating that it must exist the employee Joan assigned to the department Staff:

emp(employee,department)	
dept(department)	
ic1 $\leftarrow$ emp(e, d) $\wedge$ ¬dept(d)	
ic2 $\leftarrow$ ¬emp(Joan, Staff)	
Hire(E, D)	**New_dept(D)**
prec: ¬ $\exists$ d emp(E, d)	prec: ¬ dept(D)
add: {emp(E, D)}	add: {dept(D)}
del: { }	del: { }

This conceptual model is clearly unsatisfiable. Satisfaction of integrity constraint ic2 would require a state in which at least emp(Joan, Staff) was true, which could be achievable by the operation Hire(Joan, Staff), however the execution of this operation would violate ic1 since the department Staff would not exist. Thus, it would be necessary to execute previously the operation New_dept(Staff) that can not be executed since this execution would violate ic2.

Satisfiability in this example could be achieved, for instance, by removing integrity constraint ic2, in which case the conceptual model becomes satisfiable since the empty state satisfies all the integrity constraints. Satisfiability could also be achieved by proposing a new transaction that inserts at the same time an employee and a department.

More precisely, a conceptual model M is *satisfiable* if there exists a reachable state of the Information Base.

Satisfiability of a conceptual model M is equivalent to the planning problem of finding a plan for the goal TRUE where the description of the world is given by the conceptual model M and the initial state is empty. The tautology TRUE is the least restrictive possible goal. Thus, if it does not exist a plan for that goal, the integrity constraints can not be satisfied and therefore the conceptual model is unsatisfiable. On the other hand, if there exists at least a plan for that goal, then there exists a valid sequence of operations that leads the Information Base to an state in which all the integrity constraints are satisfied and therefore the conceptual model is satisfiable.

Note that, if the operations of the conceptual model are not taken into account, the state {emp(Joan,Staff), dept(Staff)}, for instance, would satisfy all the integrity constraints and therefore the previous conceptual model would be satisfiable according to the definition of satisfiability considered in [Lun82, Kun84, Kun85]. However, as we have seen, this state is not reachable by the operations of the model.

4.1.2 Liveliness of a Predicate

A desirable property for base and derived predicates is that they can have non empty extensions. Effectively, a predicate that has an empty extension in each reachable state of the IB is clearly a useless predicate and probably the conceptual model in which it is defined is ill-specified. As an illustrative example, consider again a subset of the conceptual model defined in section 2:

emp(employee,department)
dept(department)
ic1 $\leftarrow$ emp(e, d) $\wedge$ ¬dept(d)
Hire(E, D)
prec: $\neg \exists$ d emp(E, d)
add: {emp(E, D)}
del: { }

Clearly, both predicates dept and emp are not lively. The first one, dept, is not lively since there is no operation to insert a department and consequently it will have an empty extension in each possible state. The second one, emp, is also not lively since even though there is an operation to insert an employee this operation may never satisfy the integrity constraint ic1 that requires the existence of the department when inserting an employee. If we assume a new operation:

New-dept(D)
prec: ¬ dept(D)
add: {dept(D)}
del: {}

then both predicates become lively: predicate dept due to the presence of this new operation and predicate emp due to the fact that the sequence of operations: New_dept(Dept), Hire(Emp, Dept) leads to an state of the Information Base in which emp has the fact emp(Emp,Dept). Note that the inverse sequence Hire(Emp, Dept), New-dept(Dept) is not a valid sequence since the execution of the first operation would violate ic1.

More precisely, a predicate p is *lively* in a conceptual model M if there is a reachable state of the Information Base in which at least one fact about p is true.

The problem of finding out whether a predicate $p(\mathbf{x})$[2] is lively in a conceptual model M is equivalent to the planning problem of finding a plan for the goal $\exists\mathbf{x}\ p(\mathbf{x})$ where the description of the world is given by the conceptual model M and the initial state is empty. If there is at least a plan for such a goal then the plan will contain a valid sequence of operations that leads to a reachable state in which p has a non empty extension and thus, predicate p is lively. Otherwise p is not lively.

4.1.3 Redundancy of a Constraint

Intuitively, a constraint is redundant if integrity does not depend on it. Clearly, such a redundancy should be detected by the validation process and the designer should be informed in order that s/he could take the opportune decisions. Redundancy of a constraint may be due to several reasons. For instance, a constraint may be a tautology, it may be redundant because it is enforced by the specifications of the operations, by other integrity constraints or due to a combination of these reasons. To illustrate this property, consider a subset of the conceptual model defined in section 2 with two additional integrity constraints:

```
emp(employee,department)
dept(department)
ic1 ← emp(e, d) ∧ ¬dept(d)
ic2 ← emp(Joan, d) ∧ ¬dept(d)
ic3 ← emp(e, d1) ∧ emp(e, d2)  ∧  d1≠d2
Hire(E, D)                      New-dept(D)
  prec: ¬∃d emp(E, d)             prec: ¬ dept(D)
  add: {emp(E, D)}                add: {dept(D)}
  del: { }                        del: { }
```

Integrity constraint ic2 is redundant, since it is entailed by ic1 and therefore it can not be violated without violating ic1. Moreover, integrity constraint ic3 is redundant since the precondition of the operation Hire forbids to have an employee assigned to more than one department. Thus, the integrity of the conceptual model does not depend on ic2 neither ic3, in the sense that they could be removed and the resulting conceptual model would admit the same reachable states than the original one.

More precisely, let M be a conceptual model and let I be an integrity constraint in M, I is *redundant* if it is satisfied in each reachable state of M - {I}.

Satisfiability and liveliness can be checked by showing the existence of some reachable state. As opposed to that, the definition of redundancy of a constraint requires something for *each* state. Hence, redundancy of a constraint is best checked by verifying or falsifying the lack of redundancy, which can be done by attempting to construct *one* state which would show that the constraint under investigation can be violated and hence that is not redundant. Thus, the non redundancy of a constraint I of the form ic ← Body in a conceptual model M is checked by showing the existence of a plan for the goal $\exists\mathbf{x}$ Body, where $\mathbf{x}$ are the variables in Body, with M - {I} as a

[2] Note that here and in the following bold lowercase letters stand for vectors of variables

description of the world and with an empty initial state. If it does not exist such a plan then the integrity constraint is redundant.

In our example it does not exist any plan for the goal $\exists$ d emp(Joan, d) $\wedge$ ¬dept(d) in the world corresponding to the original conceptual model except ic2. The same happens with goal $\exists$ e,d1,d2 emp(e,d1) $\wedge$ emp(e,d2) $\wedge$ d1≠d2 in the world corresponding to the original conceptual model except ic3. Thus, both ic2 and ic3 are redundant. Instead, since the plan Hire(Peter,Marketing) is a possible plan for the goal $\exists$ e,d emp(e, d) $\wedge$ ¬dept(d) in the world corresponding to the original conceptual model except ic1, ic1 is not redundant.

4.2 Checking of Properties of the Operation Specifications

In addition to the checking of properties of the Information Base, the designer may also be interested in the checking properties of the operations of the conceptual model. For instance, s/he could be interested on checking whether the precondition of each operation is correctly specified or whether it will be possible to execute the specified operations at execution time. These properties, i. e. the applicability of an operation and the executability of an operation, are defined in this section.

Similar properties to our applicability and executability of an operation were defined in [Kun84, Kun85]. Besides the non uniformity of the way in which these properties are handled, again the main difference relies on the fact this approach does not take account of the presence of the other operations in both the definition and the verification of the properties related to an operation.

4.2.1 Applicability of an Operation

Intuitively, an operation is applicable if there exists a reachable state where its precondition holds. If an operation is not applicable, it will never be possible to execute it because its precondition may never be true. As an example, consider the following conceptual model:

emp(employee, department)
manager(employee, department)
dept(department)
has-emp(d) ← emp(e,d)
has-emp(d) ← manager(e,d)
has-mgr(d) ← manager(e,d)
ic1 ← dept(d) ∧ ¬ has-mgr(d)

Hire(E,D)	**New-mgr(E,D)**
prec: ¬ ∃d' emp(E,d')	prec: ¬ ∃d' manager(E,d')
add: {emp(E,D)}	add: {manager(E,D)}
del: {}	del: {}
New-dept(D)	**Rem-dept(D)**
prec: ¬dept(D)	prec: dept(D) ∧ ¬has-emp(D)
add: {dept(D)}	add: {}
del: {}	del: {dept(D)}

At a first glance, it may seem that all the operations of this conceptual model are applicable. However, consider the operation of removing a department: Rem-dept(D). The satisfaction of the first part of the precondition, dept(D), requires the previous execution of the operation New-dept(D). Moreover, because of the integrity constraint ic1, the operation New-dept(D) can only be executed if department D has some manager, which in turn requires the previous execution of the operation New-mgr(E,D) to add the information manager(E,D) to the IB. By the second derivation rule, manager(E,D) implies has-emp(D) and, since there is no possible way to remove this information, it cannot be achieved a state where the precondition of the operation Rem-dept(D) holds. Therefore, we have that this operation is not applicable. Several ways of making operation Rem-dept(D) applicable exist, for instance by changing its precondition, by changing the deductive rules or integrity constraints of the IB or by considering additional operations.

More precisely, an operation Op is *applicable* if there is a reachable state S where, for some instantiation of the parameters of Op, the precondition of Op holds in S.

As with the other properties, the problem of deciding whether an operation is applicable may also be handled by means of planning. In this case, we have that an operation Op, with parameters **x** and precondition Prec, will be applicable if there exists a valid sequence of operations that, starting from an empty initial state, leads to a final state of the IB that satisfies the goal: ∃**x** Prec. In the previous example, since the operation Rem-dept(D) is not applicable, no plan exists that satisfies the goal: ∃d dept(d) ∧ ¬has-emp(d). However if, for instance, we remove the second deductive rule, the following sequence of operations would be a solution plan: New-mgr(Peter,Sales), New-dept(Sales). Therefore, the operation Rem-dept(D) would be applicable.

4.2.2 Executability of an Operation

Even though an operation is applicable, it may be the case that it may never be executed because the result of applying this operation to each of the states that satisfy its precondition leads to an inconsistent resulting IB state. Detection of non-executable operations is also an important task in conceptual model validation. This is illustrated in the following example.

```
manager(employee, department)
dept(department)
has-mgr(d) ← manager(e,d)
ic1 ← dept(d) ∧ ¬ has-mgr(d)
New-dept(D)       New-mgr(E,D)              Rem-mgr(E)
  prec: ¬dept(D)  prec: ¬ ∃d' manager(E,d')  prec:∃d manager(E,d)
                    ∧ ¬ ∃e' manager(e',D)      ∧ dept(d)
  add: {dept(D)}  add:{manager(E,D)}         add: {}
  del: {}         del: {}                    del: {manager(E,d)}
```

Consider the previous conceptual model, where all the operations are a subset of the operations of the example considered in section 2, except that we have slightly changed the precondition of the operation New-mgr(E,D) by requiring also that it may only be applied if D has no manager, and the precondition of the operation Rem-mgr(E) by requiring that E must be the manager of some known department.

Rem-mgr(E) is an applicable operation because there exists a reachable state, obtained by the execution of the operations: New-mgr(E,D), New-dept(D), that satisfies its precondition. However, it will never be possible to apply it because its execution always leads to an inconsistent IB state. It is not difficult to see that the reason why Rem-mgr(E) is not executable lies on the fact that the integrity constraint ic1 requires all departments to have a manager and that the precondition for applying New-mgr(E,D) requires that no manager exists for D. Therefore, in this conceptual model a department may never have two managers and, then, the application of the operation Rem-mgr(E) will always result in a state that violates ic1.

More precisely, an operation Op is *executable* if there exists a valid sequence of operations that contains Op.

Checking the executability of an operation Op by means of planning has to deal with the problem of finding a plan that contains Op and that satisfies certain conditions of the IB. Unfortunately, most of the known planning methods do not allow the specification of conditions that the plan to obtain must satisfy. However, if the IB keeps trace of the executions of Op it is also possible to check the executability of an operation Op with usual planning methods. In conceptual models, this can be done by including in the specification of Op a new information to be added to the IB: Executed-Op, where Executed-Op is a distinguished predicate which does not occur elsewhere in the IB. Then, the executability of the operation Op is checked by showing the existence of a valid plan for the goal Executed-Op, starting from the empty initial state. If some plan exists, it must necessarily contain Op since the execution of this operation is the only possible way to add Executed-Op to the IB, and thus Op will be executable; otherwise it will not.

In the previous example, the operation Rem-mgr(E) should be described as:

Rem-mgr(E)
prec: $\exists$d manager(E,d) $\wedge$ dept(d)
add: {Executed-Rem-mgr}
del: {manager(E,d)}

and since no plan exists that satisfies the goal Executed-Rem-mgr the operation Rem-mgr(E) is not executable. Note that if we remove the second part of the precondition of New-mgr(E,D) then Rem-mgr(E) would be executable since: New-mgr(Sue,Sales), New-dept(Sales), New-mgr(Mary, Sales), Rem-mgr(Sue), would be a valid plan for the goal Executed-Rem-mgr.

5 Using Planning Methods for Conceptual Model Validation

In this section we illustrate our approach to tackle conceptual model validation by using some of the actual planning methods.

In order to use a planning method for the validation of the conceptual models described in section 2 (operational conceptual models in the following), it must provide a representation of a planning problem in terms of those operational conceptual models. This representation may be provided either directly or through an automatic transformation.

We will consider two planning methods: CDP [DMMP91] and our planning method [CO92, Cos95]. CDP will illustrate the case in which the required representation is directly provided while our planning method will illustrate the case in which the representation is provided by using an automatic transformation. This automatic transformation will show that a planning method using a representation not based on the concept of operation but only based on deductive rules can also be used for our validation tasks.

We also have a requirement on the plan generation mechanism. It must obtain at least a solution plan for a given planning problem if any solution plan for the planning problem exists. Note that this requirement is less restrictive than obtaining the complete set of solution plans. Both CDP and our planning method fulfill this requirement.

5.1 CDP [DMMP91]

CDP uses deductive databases for modelling states of the planning problem world and it uses operation specifications to model transitions between those states.

CDP obtains a complete set of correct minimal solution plans for a given planning problem. A solution plan is minimal if none of its subsequences of operations is also a solution plan. Therefore, CDP obtains at least a solution plan for a given planning problem if any solution plan for the planning problem exists.

Components of planning problems represented by CDP have a direct correspondence to a planning problem represented in terms of our operational conceptual models. We will illustrate this direct correspondence by using the example presented in section 4.2.1 to check the applicability of operation Rem-dept .

The kind of deductive databases treated by CDP can be viewed as an IB of an operational conceptual model. The IB schema with some syntactic changes will be a deductive database schema of CDP. In our example, rules corresponding to predicate has-emp after the syntactic changes will be: $\forall$e,d emp(e,d)$\rightarrow$has-emp(d), $\forall$e,d manager(e,d)$\rightarrow$has-emp(d)

Operation specifications consist of: a head, $op(x_1,...,x_n)$, where op is the operator name and the parameters $x_1,...,x_n$ are variables, a precondition and a postcondition. Preconditions are range-restricted first order formulas which define the database state where the operation is applicable. Postconditions describe the additions and deletions of base facts that must be performed to obtain the operation resultant database state. Additions are described by positive literals and deletions are described by negative literals. Therefore, a simple rewriting will turn our operations into CDP operations. In our example, the rewriting of operations New-dept(D) and Rem-dept(D) is:

New-dept(D)	**Rem-dept(D)**
prec: ¬dept(D)	prec: dept(D) ∧ ¬has-emp(D)
post: dept(D)	post: ¬ dept(D)

The initial state of the planning problem world is described as the deductive database initial state. This deductive database initial state can be seen as the initial state of the

IB of an operational conceptual model. In our example, the empty initial state will correspond to a deductive database with an empty set of base facts.

The planning problem goal G is defined as a set of range-restricted first order formulas. For uniformity reasons, it is assumed that a goal G implicitly introduces an operation *goal()*. The precondition of *goal()* is G and its postcondition is empty. Again, a simple rewriting will turn our goal into the CDP operation *goal()*. In our example, for applicability of operation Rem-dept we will have:

goal()
prec: $\exists$d dept(d) $\wedge$ $\neg$has-emp(d)
post:

A plan for a planning problem is described as a sequence of operations where the last operation is *goal()*. A plan is a solution for a planning problem if for all operations in the plan: its precondition is satisfied at the database state where the operation is applied and the database state resulting from the operation application is consistent, that is, integrity constraints are satisfied in it. Therefore, this sequence of operators will be a solution plan for the planning problem. In our example, no sequence is obtained which shows that operation Rem-dept is not applicable.

5.2 Our Planning Method [CO92, Cos95]

In [CO92, Cos95] we defined a planning method which uses a representation of the planning problem in terms of deductive conceptual models. Deductive conceptual models differ mainly from usual operational conceptual models of information systems in that they do not use the concept of operation and the transitions of the IB schema are entirely described in terms of deductive rules.

Our planning method obtains a complete set of correct minimal solution plans for a given planning problem. A solution plan is minimal if none of its subsets is also a solution plan. Therefore, our planning method obtains at least a solution plan for a given planning problem if any solution plan for the planning problem exists.

In deductive conceptual models time is a key concept. The passing of time is considered as an external event (or operation occurrence) as any other entry to the system. Consequently, there exists a state of the IB for each time point. Each possible information has an associated time point. The Information Base (IB) consists of two parts: *Base* and *Derived*. In deductive conceptual models the Base part at a time point t corresponds to the information of all the external events (or operation instances) that have occurred at time point t. As the passing of time is an external event, the Base part contains facts of an standard predicate time(t). A fact time(T) holds if T belongs to the life span of the system. The rest of the information, that is, the Derived part, can be deduced from the Base part by means of deductive rules. At a given time point t, the IB contains all the informations known until t. In deductive conceptual models the transition schema is embedded in the deductive rules.

In the following, we describe how to transform each of the components of an operational conceptual model in order to obtain a deductive conceptual model. We will illustrate this transformation by using the example presented in section 2.

For each operation Op(**x**) we define a corresponding base predicate op(**x**,t) of the deductive conceptual model. Note that we have an additional time term t to indicate its time of occurrence. In our example, we will have the following five base predicates: new-dept(d,t), rem-dept(d,t), hire(e,d,t), fire(e,t), new-manager(e,d,t), rem-mgr(e,t). The knowledge represented in the body of operations will be transformed in deductive rules as we will see in the following paragraphs.

For each base predicate p(**x**) we define a corresponding derived predicate p(**x**,t) of the deductive conceptual model. Again, the additional time term t indicates the time of occurrence of the associated information. In our example, we will have that emp(e,d,t), dept(d,t) and manager(e,d,t) are derived predicates.

We have to define deductive rules for these derived predicates. These deductive rules will represent the knowledge that in our previous operational conceptual models was described by operations. For each base predicate p(**x**) of our previous model whose facts are added by operations $a_1,...,a_n$ and deleted by operations $d_1,...,d_m$ we will define the following deductive rules in our deductive conceptual model: add-p(**x**,t)← $a_1(\mathbf{y_1},t)$ ∧ prec-a_1, ..., add-p(**x**,t)← $a_n(\mathbf{y_n},t)$ ∧ prec-a_n, del-p(**x**,t)← $d_1(\mathbf{y_1},t)$ ∧ prec-d_1, ..., del-p(**x**,t)← $d_m(\mathbf{y_m},t)$ ∧ prec-d_m, p(**x**,t)← add-p(**x**,t1) ∧ t1≤t ∧ ¬ ∃t2 del-p(**x**,t2) ∧ t2>t1 ∧ t2≤t.

We have defined auxiliary derived predicates add-p and del-p which indicate the addition and deletion of predicate p by an operation, respectively. Rules for these predicates permit to deduce a fact of them at a time point T if the operation that performs the addition or deletion has occurred at time T and the precondition of the operation held at the previous time T-1. We assume that if F is the precondition of the operation Op then prec-op stands for the formula F with the addition of a time term t-1 to each predicate of the formula. Then, it is easy to define a rule for predicate p which states that a fact of this predicate holds at a time T if it has been added at a time T1 before T and has not been deleted at a time T2 between T1 and T.

In our example we will have the following rules for predicate emp(e,d,t):

add-emp(e,d,t)← hire(e,d,t) ∧ ¬∃ d' emp(e,d',t-1)
del-emp(e,d,t)← fire(e,t) ∧ ∃d emp(e,d,t-1)∧ ¬manager(e,d,t-1)
emp(e,d,t)← add-emp(e,d,t1) ∧ t1≤t ∧ ¬ ∃t2 del-emp(e,d,t2) ∧ t2>t1 ∧ t2≤t

Previous deductive rules have to be allowed and in normal form [LT84]. This may require a transformation of the rules using the procedure described in [LT84]. This is also applied to the rules that we describe in following paragraphs.

For each derived predicate p(**x**) we define a corresponding derived predicate p(**x**,t) of the deductive conceptual model. In our example, we will have that works-for(e,m,t) is a derived predicate.

For each deductive rule p(**x**)← $L_1(\mathbf{x_1})$ ∧ ... ∧ $L_n(\mathbf{x_n})$ we define a corresponding deductive rule p(**x**,t)← $L_1(\mathbf{x_1},t)$ ∧ ... ∧ $L_n(\mathbf{x_n},t)$ of the deductive conceptual model. In our example we will have the rule: works-for(e,m,t)← emp(e,d,t) ∧ manager(m,d,t).

For each integrity constraint ic(**x**) we define a corresponding integrity constraint ic(**x**,t) of the deductive conceptual model. The time term t indicates the time of occurrence of the integrity constraint violation. In our example, we will have the integrity constraint ic1(t).

For each integrity rule ic(**x**)← $L_1(\mathbf{x_1})$ ∧ ... ∧ $L_n(\mathbf{x_n})$ we define a corresponding integrity rule ic(**x**,t)← $L_1(\mathbf{x_1},t)$ ∧ ... ∧ $L_n(\mathbf{x_n},t)$ of the deductive conceptual model. In our example we will have the integrity rule: $ic1(t) \leftarrow emp(e,d,t) \wedge \neg dept(d,t)$.

In operational conceptual models a transition of the IB is induced by the occurrence of a single operation and more than one operation can not occur simultaneously. In a deductive conceptual model transitions of the IB are induced by the passing of time and several external events or operation instances may occur at the same time. Therefore, in the deductive conceptual model, it will be necessary to forbid explicitly simultaneous operation occurrences by means of additional integrity rules.

For each operation Op(**x**) we define an integrity constraint ic(t) with the following integrity rule: $ic(t) \leftarrow op(\mathbf{x},t) \wedge op(\mathbf{y},t) \wedge \mathbf{x} \neq \mathbf{y}$. This integrity constraint will forbid two different instances of operation Op to occur at the same time. In our example, one of these integrity constraints will be the following: $ic2(t) \leftarrow$ new-dept(d1,t) $\wedge$ new-dept(d2,t) $\wedge$ $d1 \neq d2$.

For each pair of operations $Op_i(\mathbf{x_i})$, $Op_j(\mathbf{x_j})$ we define an integrity constraint ic(t) with the following integrity rule: $ic(t) \leftarrow op_i(\mathbf{x_i},t) \wedge op_j(\mathbf{x_j},t)$. This integrity constraint will forbid two instances of operations Op_i and Op_j to occur at the same time. In our example, one of these integrity constraints will be the following: $ic3(t) \leftarrow$ new-dept(d,t) $\wedge$ hire(e,d1,t).

Besides transforming the conceptual model that describes the planning problem world, we also have to transform accordingly the initial state, the goal to achieve and the solution plans.

The initial state has to be described as a set of base facts of the deductive conceptual model that represent the operations that have occurred before the planning problem is stated. In the case of an empty initial state the corresponding set of base facts will be empty.

A goal described by a formula F will be defined by a new derived predicate G(t) with a deductive rule: $G(t) \leftarrow F'$ where F' stands for the formula F with the addition of a time term t to each predicate of the formula. For example, the goal $\exists e,d\ emp(e,d)$, will be transformed into: $G(t) \leftarrow \exists e,d\ emp(e,d,t)$. The description of the goal is completed with a final time T_f in which it has to be achieved.

The plan will be obtained in terms of base facts which represent the operations that must occur. The time term of the base facts will give the order of execution of the events. For example, if we have the empty initial state and the goal $G(t) \leftarrow \exists e,d\ emp(e,d,t)$ which has to be achieved at a time 2, one of the plans we will obtain will be the following: P={new-dept(Marketing,1), hire(John,Marketing,2)}

6 Conclusions and Further Work

In this paper we have presented an approach to the validation of conceptual models. We have defined a set of desirable properties that a conceptual model should satisfy (satisfiability of a conceptual model, liveliness of a predicate, redundancy of integrity constraints, applicability and executability of an operation) and we have shown how these properties can be checked by using plan generation techniques.

The use of planning allows us to check the whole set of properties in a uniform way. The generality of our approach allows us to be independent of the concrete planning method used to check the properties. This facilitates the application of improvements in the planning research area to our approach.

We have illustrated how to apply our approach by using two concrete planning methods, one proposed for operational conceptual models and the other for deductive ones. In this sense, we have also shown how a method for planning in deductive conceptual models can be used for planning in operational ones.

As further work, we would like to extend our approach by providing explanations when a certain property is not satisfied. In this direction, we believe that by refining the definition of the properties the designer could also be informed about which part of the conceptual model should be changed to satisfy the property. We would also like to define similar properties in a framework where the operations are automatically generated (see e.g. [PO95]) and to study whether they can be validated by planning.

Another extension of our work would be to adapt it to the validation of object-oriented specifications. This can be done by extending current planning methods to the use of object-oriented representations.

We also plan to develop a tool for validating conceptual models following this

[DTU96] Decker, H.; Teniente, E.; Urpí, T. "How to Tackle Schema Validation by View Updating", *To appear in proc. of the EDBT'96*, Avignon, France, 1996.

[FW95] Feenstra R.; Wieringa R. "Validating Database Constraints and Updates Using Automated Reasoning Techniques", in B. Thalheim (ed): *Proc. of the workshop on Semantics in Databases,* 24-32, TR Univ of Cottbus, 1995.

[GSUW94] Gupta, A.; Sagiv, Y.; Ullman, J.D.; Widom, J. "Constraint Checking with Partial Information", *Proc. 13th PoDS*, 45-55, ACM Press, 1994.

[GW93] Gulla, J.A.; Willumsen, G. "Using Explanations to Improve the Validation of Executable Models", *Proc. of the CAiSE-93 Conference*, 118-142, Paris, 1993.

[HM81] Hammer, M.; McLeod, D. "Database Descritpion with SDM: a Semantic Database Model", *ACM TODS*, Vol. 6, No. 3, 351-386, 1981.

[JC92] Jesus, L.; Carapuça, R. "Automatic Generation of Documentation for Information Systems", *Proc. of the CAiSE-92 Conference*, 48-64, Manchester, 1992.

[Kun84] Kung, C.H. *A Temporal Framework for Information Systems Specifications and Verification*, PhD Thesis, Univ. of Trondheim, Norway, 1984.

[Kun85] Kung, C.H. "A Tableaux Approach for Consistency Checking", In Sernadas, A.; Bubenko, J.; Olivé, A. (Eds.) *Information Systems: Theoretical and Formal Aspects*. Elsevier Science Publishers, North-Holland, 191-207, 1985.

[LMSS93] Levy, A.; Mumick, I.S.; Sagiv, Y.; Shmueli, O. "Equivalence, Query-reachability, and Satisfiability in Datalog Extensions", *Proc. 12th PoDS*, 1993.

[LK93] Lindland, O.I.; Krogstie, J. "Validating Conceptual Models by Transformational Prototyping", *Proc. of the CAiSE-93 Conference*, 165-183, Paris, 1993.

[LL93] Lalioti, V,; Loucopoulos, P. "Visualisation for Validation", *Proc. of the CAiSE-93 Conference*, 143-164, Paris, 1993.

[LT84] Lloyd, J.W.; Topor,R.W. "Making Prolog more expressive", *Journal of Logic Programming*, No.3, 225-240, 1984.

[LTP91] Loucopoulos, P.; Theodoulidis, B.; Pantazis, D. "Business rules modelling: conceptual modelling and object-oriented specifications", In Van Assche, F.; Moulin,B.; Rolland,C. (Eds.) *Object Oriented Approach in Information Systems*, North-Holland, 323-342, 1991.

[Lun82] Lundberg, B. "On Correctness of Information Models". *Information Systems*, Vol. 8, No. 2, 87-93, 1983.

[MBW80] Mylopoulos, J.; Bernstein, P.A.; Wong, H.K.T. "A Language Facility for Designing Database-Intensive Applications", *ACM TODS*, Vol. 5, No. 2, 185-207, 1980.

[NH89] Nijssen, G.M,; Halpin, T.A. *Conceptual Schema and Relational Database Design. A Fact Oriented Approach*, Prentice-Hall, 1989.

[Nic82] Nicolas, J.M. "Logic for improving integrity checking in relational databases", *Acta Informatica*, 18, 227-253, 1982.

[OS95] Olivé,A.; Sancho,M.R. "A Method for Explaining the Behaviour of Conceptual Models", *Proc. of the CAiSE-95 Conference*, 12-25, Jyväskylä, 1995.

[PO95] Pastor, J.A.; Olivé,A. "Supporting Transaction Design in Conceptual Modelling of Information Systems", *Proc. of the CAiSE-95 Conference*, 40-53, Jyväskylä, 1995.

[RP92] Rolland, C.; Proix, C. "A Natural Language Approach for Requirements Engineering", *Proc. of the CAiSE-92 Conference*, 257-277, Manchester, 1992.

[VF85] Veloso, P.A.S.; Furtado, A.L. "Towards simpler and yet complete formal specifications", *Proc. of the IFIP Working Conference on Theoretical and Formal Aspects of Information Systems*, 175-189, 1985.

Database Design Recovery[1]

J-L. Hainaut, J. Henrard, J-M. Hick, D. Roland, V. Englebert[2],

ABSTRACT

The design of a software component, such as a database, is the trace of all the processes, products and reasonings that have led to the production of this artifact. Such a document is the very basis of system maintenance and evolution processes. Unfortunately, it does not exist in most situations. The paper describes how the design of a database or of a collection of files can be recovered through reverse engineering techniques. Recording the reverse engineering activities provides a history of this process. By normalizing and reversing this history, then by conforming it according to a reference design methodology, one can obtain a tentative design of the source database. The paper describes the baselines of the approach, such as a wide spectrum specification model, semantics-preserving transformational techniques, and a design process model. It describes a general procedure to build a possible DB design, then states the requirements for CASE support, and describes DB-MAIN, a prototype CASE tool which includes a history processor. Finally it illustrates the proposals through an example.

KEYWORDS

design recovery, database reverse engineering, database evolution, transformational approach, process modelling, CASE tool

1. Introduction

> *[...] **design recovery** must reproduce all of the information required for a person to fully understand what a program does, how it does it, why it does it, [...].*
>
> [BIGG,89]

History and Design

The history of a complex process, whatever its nature and its objective, is the trace of all the operations that have been carried out in order to complete it. This definition stands for program execution for exemple, but it is also applicable to human activities, such as information system engineering. The *design* of an information system, or of a part thereof, is the history of the processes through which the system was built, together with the various specification products (schemas, documentation, operational code) used and produced by these processes. The design also includes the requirements that the system was to satisfy and the reasonings (also called the *rationale*) according to which the processes and the decisions were carried out. The design of an existing system should be available, not only as the core documentation, but also as the basis for further system

---

1 This research is a part of the DB-MAIN project, which is partly supported by ACEC-OSI (Be), ARIANE-II (Be), Banque UCL (Lux), BBL (Be), Centre de recherche public H. Tudor (Lux), CGER (Be), Cockerill-Sambre (Be), CONCIS (Fr), D'Ieteren (Be), DIGITAL (Be), EDF (Fr), EPFL (CH), Groupe S (Be), IBM (Be), OBLOG Software (Port), ORIGIN (Be), Ville de Namur (Be), Winterthur (Be), 3 Suisses (Be). The DB-PROCESS subproject is supported by the *Communauté Française de Belgique.*

2 Institut d'Informatique, University of Namur, rue Grandgagnage, 21 - B-5000 Namur - jlh@info.fundp.ac.be

maintenance and evolution. Ideally, this design should be recorded in the repository of a CASE tool which supports these maintenance and evolution processes.

The concept of *history* is broader than suggested above. Indeed, any system engineering activity can be described by its history. Such is the case for system reverse engineering, system migration, system evolution, and system integration to mention only some examples. In the following, we will often make use of the more general term *history* instead of *design.*

The role of histories in system evolution

One immediate application of a history is to *explain* how and why the system has been developed in this way some years ago. Another important usage of a history is its *replay*. For instance, let us consider that we are provided with the history of the development of a database. This history is supposed to be the trace of all the activities of the conceptual design, of the logical design, of the physical design, and to include all the schemas which have been elaborated during these activities. Let us now suppose that we have to make a minor change in the conceptual schema of a database, such as adding a simple attribute. Ideally, all we should have to do is to carry out this change in the conceptual schema, then to *replay* the former history. If this history has been recorded in the repository of a CASE tool, this second operation can be carried out automatically, and can produce new versions of the logical and physical schemas. Of course, if the change is deeper, merely replaying the former design activities could prove insufficient since the conceptual change could imply a revision of the former decisions. The concept of history replay must be refined in order to cope with these more complex situations. Anyway, considering both applications of histories, it appears clearly that this concept must play a central role in computer-supported system evolution [BIGG,89] [HAI,94].

Unfortunately, in the current state of development practices, all this discussion may appear as basically theoretic, and far from the reality. Indeed, most systems have been (and still are) designed without any methodological concern, and consequently without CASE support. Consequently, many systems have no decent documentation, and when it exists and is up-to-date and usable, the history is unknown. In conclusion the design of most legacy systems is absent, or, at best, degenerates into a collection of hopefully correct and consistent schemas.

Reverse engineering

Trying to make a legacy information system evolve implies first to recover a possible design, i.e. a possible history together with its various (inherited or recovered) schemas and other documents. When no documentation is available for such a system, it is possible to rebuild it, at least partially, through a process called *reverse engineering*. For instance, successfully reverse engineering an existing database or a collection of files (i.e. the *physical* system) yields plausible logical and conceptual schemas for this database. It can be shown [HAI,93b] [HAI,95c] that most system forward and reverse engineering activities are transformational by nature, i.e. that they can be modelled as chains of schema transformations. Indeed, they most generally appear as processes which transform one specification product into another one. In addition reverse engineering can be described as a suite of processes, each of which is the inverse of a definite forward engineering process [HAI,93a].

Design recovery

We can record the activities which are carried out during reverse engineering. This history will be made of a sequence of elementary transformations. This is a free, but extremely valuable by-product of the process. Indeed, reversing this history, i.e. reversing the order of the operations, and replacing each of them by its inverse, should provide a way to get back the physical system from the abstract specification just recovered through the reverse engineering process. In this perspective, reverse engineering seems to be a realistic way to recover a possible design of the system.

This is precisely the idea developed in this paper, applied to database design recovery.

About this paper

The paper is organized as follows. Section 2 shortly describes the data structure specification model which will be used to illustrate the concepts developed. Section 3 defines the concept of schema transformation. Section 4 discusses the notion of history and relates it to that of methodology. Section 5 proposes a general methodology for database reverse engineering. Section 6 presents the principles of database design recovery. In section 7 we discuss the role of CASE technology in design recovery, while an example is developed in section 8.

2. A data structure specification model

Database design and reverse engineering are concerned with building, converting and transforming database schemas at different levels of abstraction, and according to various paradigms. Elaborating DMS-independent techniques and reasonings that support these activities requires the availability of a set of models to express all these schemas. Due to the transformational approach adopted in this presentation, and due to the large scope of the proposal that encompasses all the traditional levels of abstraction, it has been found essential to base it on a unique wide spectrum schema specification model. This model and its transformational operators are intended,

- to support forward as well as reverse engineering,
- to express conceptual, logical and physical schemas, as well as their manipulation,
- to support any DMS model and the production and manipulation of their schemas.

In short, conceptual schemas as well as physical schemas are expressed into a unique, generic, *extended entity-relationship model.*

In this model, a *schema* is a description of the data structures to be processed. It is made up of specification constructs which can be classified into the usual three abstraction levels, namely conceptual, logical and physical (*Fig. 1*). We will enumerate the main concepts in each level :

conceptual constructs
entity types (with/without attributes; with/without identifiers), super/subtype hierarchies (single/multiple inheritance, total and disjoint properties), relationship types (binary/N-ary; cyclic/acyclic), roles of relationship type (with min-max cardinalities; with/without explicit name; single/multi-entity-type), attributes (of entity and relationship types; multi/single-valued; atomic/compound), identifiers (of entity type, relationship type, attribute; comprising attributes and/or roles), constraints (inclusion, exclusion, coexistence, at-least-one, etc);

logical constructs
record types, fields, foreign keys, redundancy, etc;

physical constructs
files, access keys (abstracting index, calc key, etc), physical data types, bag and list multivalued attributes, and other implementation details.

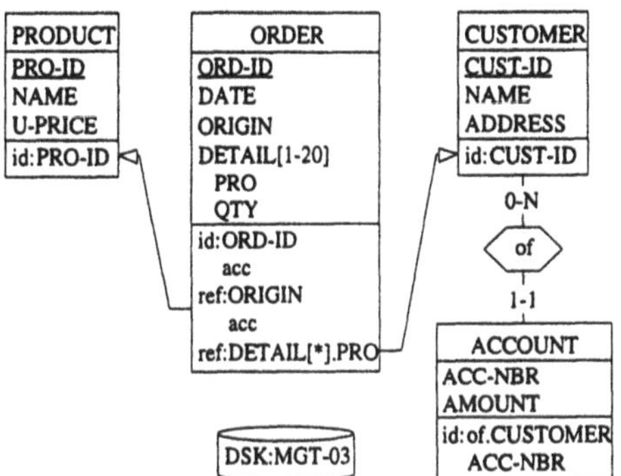

Figure 1 - A typical hybrid schema that could appear during reverse engineering. This schema includes conceptual objects (PRODUCT, CUSTOMER, ACCOUNT, of), logical objects (record type ORDER, with single-valued and multivalued foreign keys) and physical objects (access keys ORDER.ORD-ID and ORDER.ORIGIN; file DSK:MGT-03).

In database engineering, a schema describes a fragment of the data structures at a given level of abstraction. In reverse engineering, an *in progress* schema may even include constructs at different levels of abstraction. *Fig. 1* illustrates this fact through a schema which includes conceptual, logical and physical constructs. Ultimately, this schema will be completely conceptualized through processing of the remaining logical and physical constructs.

Note
A schema can be defined as a set of constructs, or specification objects. Therefore, set-theoretic relations and operators apply on schemas. For instance, a schema can be declared a subset of another one ($S_2 \subseteq S_1$) or can be defined as the union of other schemas ($S_3 = S_1 \cup S_2$). However, a proper subset of a valid schema is not necessarily a valid schema : a relationship type with one role only can be a subset of a valid relationship type, but is not valid itself.

3. Schema transformation

In general, a schema transformation consists in deriving a target schema S' from source schema S by some kind of local or global modification. Adding an attribute to an entity type, deleting a relationship type, and replacing a relationship type by an equivalent entity type, are three examples of schema transformations. Several authors postulate that producing a database schema from another schema can be carried out through selected *transformations*. For instance, normalizing a schema, optimizing a schema, producing an SQL database or COBOL files, or reverse engineering standard files and CODASYL databases can be described mostly as sequences of schema transformations. Some authors propose schema transformations for selected design activities [NAVA,80] [KOBA,86] [KOZA,87] [ROS,88] [BATINI,92] [HALPIN,95] [RAUH,95]. Moreover, some authors claim that the whole database design process, together with other related activities, can be described as a chain of schema transformations [BATINI,93] [HAI,93b] [HAI,95c][3].

---

[3] It is interesting to note that this approach has long be considered in pure software development. According to [BALZER,81] and [FICKAS,85] for instance, *the process of developing a program [can be] formalized as a set of transformations*.

Schema transformations are essential to formally define forward and backward mappings between schemas, and particularly between conceptual structures and DBMS constructs. In addition, they provide a concise and precise trace of any engineering activity, and will be the building blocks of histories.

The notion has been defined in [HAI,91] and [HAI,95c], and can be summarized as follows.

3.1 Principles

A **transformation** Σ consists of two mappings **T** and **t** :

- **T** is a *structural mapping* that replaces source construct C in schema S with construct C'; C' is the target of C through T, and is noted **C' = T(C)**. In fact, C and C' are classes of constructs that can be defined by structural predicates. T is therefore defined by a *minimal precondition* ***P*** that any construct C must satisfy in order to be transformed by T, and a *maximal postcondition* ***Q*** that T(C) satisfies. **T** specifies the *syntax* of the transformation.
- **t** is an *instance mapping* that states how to produce the T(C) instance that corresponds to any instance of C. If c is an instance of C, then c' = t(c) is the corresponding instance of T(C). **t** specifies the *semantics* of the transformation. Its expression is through any algebraic, logic or procedural language.

According to the context, Σ will be noted either **<T,t>** or **<P,Q,t>**.

3.2 Reversibility

In terms of semantics-preservation, some transformations appear to augment the semantics of the source schema (e.g. adding an attribute), some remove semantics (e.g. removing an entity type), while others leave the semantics unchanged (e.g. replacing a relationship type with an entity type). The latter are called *reversible* or *semantics-preserving*. If a transformation is reversible, then the source and the target schemas have the same descriptive power, and describe the same universe of discourse, although with a different presentation (or syntax).

- A transformation $\Sigma 1$ = <P1,Q1,t1> = <T1,t1> is *reversible*, *iff* there exists a transformation $\Sigma 2$ = <P2,Q2,t2> = <T2,t2> such that, for any construct C, and any instance c of C: P1(C) $\Rightarrow$ ([T2(T1(C))=C] and [t2(t1(c)=c]). $\Sigma 2$ is the inverse of $\Sigma 1$, but, surprisingly, not conversely. For instance, an arbitrary instance c' of T(C) may not satisfy the property c'=t1(t2(c')).
- If $\Sigma 2$ is reversible as well, then $\Sigma 1$ and $\Sigma 2$ are called *symmetrically reversible*. In this case, $\Sigma 2$ = <Q1,P1,t2>, and both transformations can be defined through the unique notation Σ = <P,Q,t1,t2>. It is called an *SR-transformation*. This is the most desirable form. However, in database design, and particularly at the implementation level, non fully reversible transformations may be used due to the unavailability of SR-transformations.

Similarly, in the pure software engineering domain, [BALZER,81] proposes the concept of *correctness-preserving* transformation aimed to compilable and efficient program production.

Remark.

We have discussed the concept of reversiblity in a context in which some kind of instance equivalence is preserved. However, the notion of inverse transformation is more general. Any transformation, be it semantics-preserving or not, can be given an inverse. For instance, `del-ET(CUSTOMER)`, which removes entity type CUSTOMER from its schema, clearly is not a semantics-preserving operation, since its mapping `t` has no inverse. However, it has an inverse transformation, namely `create-ET(CUSTOMER)`. Since only the T part is defined, this partial inverse is called a *structural inverse* transformation. We will discuss these operators in more detail in the next sections.

3.3 Notation

Though these definitions do not depend on any specific data structure model, we will concentrate on ER schemas. A PROLOG-like specification of `T` through the expression of its components `P` and `Q` is suggested in [HAI,92]. However, we will use a more readable expression in which generic versions of `C` and `T(C)` are represented through ER graphical convention. As an illustration, figure 2 describes how a *many-to-many* rel-type (i.e. C) can be replaced by a new entity type, by two *one-to-many* rel-types, and by an identifier (i.e. `T(C)`). The `t` part of the transformations will be ignored from now on.

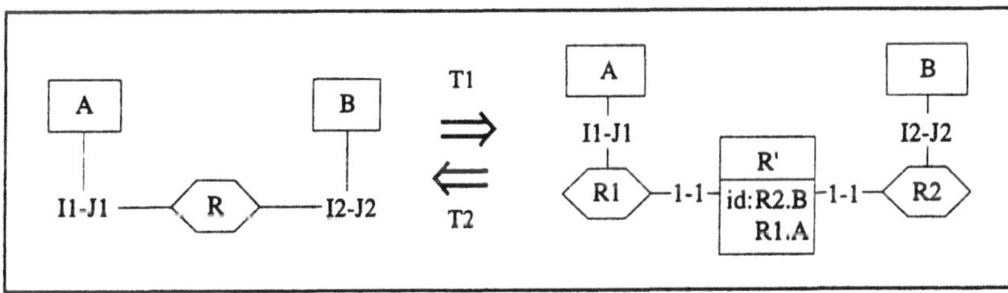

Figure 2 - Representation of structural mapping T1 (from left to right) & T2 (from right to left) of a typical SR-transformation.

This transformation is generic since the names `A, B, R, R1, R2, I1, J1, I2, J2` must be replaced by actual values (e.g. `CUSTOMER, PRODUCT, order, .., 1, 1`) in order to get an instantiated transformation acting on an actual schema.

3.4 Stuctural analysis of a transformation

A transformation is known to replace construct C with construct C' in schema S, to yield new schema S'. The effect of transformation T in schema S can be precised as follows. Let us consider the structural functions C_-, C_+ and C_0 :

$C_-(T) = S - S'$ returns the objects of S that have disappeared;
$C_+(T) = S' - S$ returns the new objects that appear in S';
$C_0(T)$ returns the objects of S that are concerned by T, but that are preserved from S to S' (the *catalytic* constructs of T).

We also have :

$$C(T) = C_0(T) \cup C_-(T)$$
$$C'(T) = C_0(T) \cup C_+(T)$$
$$S' = (S - C_-(T)) \cup C_+(T)$$

These concepts are illustrated in the following scenario, in which an instance of the rel-type/entity type transformation of Figure 2 is applied on rel-type R, and in which every object has been given a denotation :

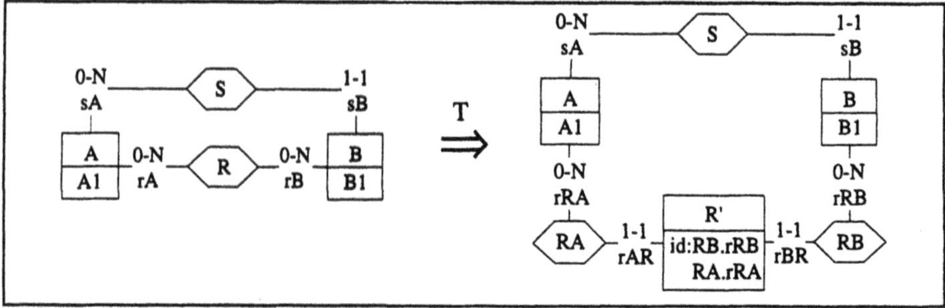

The structural functions evaluate as follows :

$C_-(T)$ = {R, rA, rB}
$C_+(T)$ = {R', RA, RB, rRA, rAR, rRB, rBR, id(R')}
$C_0(T)$ = {A, B}
S = {A, B, A1, B1, S, sA, sB, R, rA, rB}
S' = {A, B, A1, B1, S, sA, sB, R', RA, RB, rRA, rAR, rRB, rBR, id(R')}
C(T) = {A, B, R, rA, rB}
C'(T) = {A, B, R', RA, RB, rRA, rAR, rRB, rBR, id(R')}

3.5 Signature of a transformation

In a history, a transformation will be specified through its **signature**, that states the name of the transformation, the names of the concerned objects in the source schema, and the names of the new objects in the target schema. For example, the signatures of the transformations T1 and T2 in Fig. 2 are as follows[4] :

T1 : (R', {(A,R1), (B,R2)}) ← RT-to-ET(R)

T2 : R ← ET-to-RT(R')

The first one is interpreted as "*when applying RT-to-ET to relationship type R, the new entity type is called R', the rel-type involving A is called R1 and that involving B is called R2*". The second one must read as follows : "*when applying ET-to-RT to entity type R', the new rel-type is called R*". The objects which are involved in the operation, but that can be identified in the schema from the names mentioned in the signature, are not specified. In the signature of T2 for instance, entity types A and B are not mentioned since they can be deduced as "*all the entity types linked to R' in the source schema*". A signature alone does not comprise the C_-, C_+ and C_0 structural components, but it can be used to identify them in the source and target schemas. In addition, the format of a signature is not unique, but depends, a.o., on the default naming conventions. For instance, the roles are given default names in transformations T1 and T2 described above.

4 Fixed-length lists are enclosed into parentheses, while variable-length lists are enclosed into curly brackets.

Just like transformations, signatures can be generic or instantiated. For instance, the generic signature

`(R',{(A,R1),(B,R2)})` ← `RT-to-ET(R)`

could be instantiated, in an actual schema, into

`(ORDER,{(CUSTOMER,from),(PRODUCT,of)})` ← `RT-to-ET(order)`

From these examples, we can observe an essential property of the signatures : their *reversibility*. Being provided with the right-side schema and the signature of T2, we can derive the signature of T1, and conversely. In other words, the signature provides enough information, not only for *redoing* the operation, but also to *undo* it.

This property is less obvious for some non-SR-transformations. Let us consider the example of the `del-ET` operator, which removes an entity type from a schema. It can be illustrated as follows.

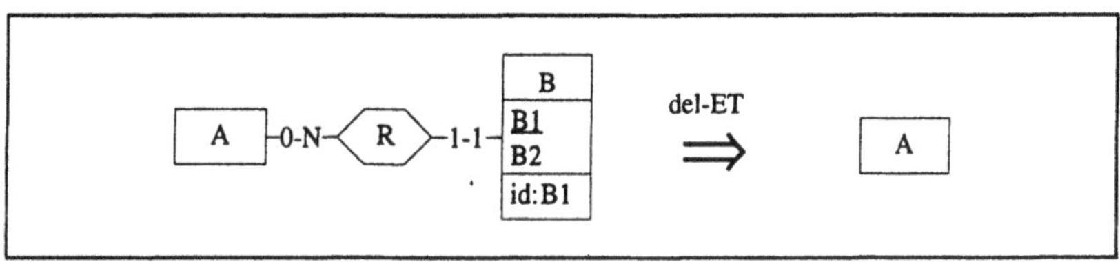

At first glance, it seems that the following signature could be quite right :

`()` ← `del-ET(B)`

Unfortunately, the problem is that, though we can redo the transformation, we are unable to undo it. Of course, we are informed that entity type B was removed, but we have lost information about its structure : what were its attributes, its roles, its constraints, etc ?

In this case, we must augment the signature with those of the derived operations. We consider that removing B consists in removing its constraints (e.g. identifiers), then its attributes and its roles, then the inconsistent relationship types, and finally B itself :

```
() ← del-ID(B,{B1},δ)
() ← del-Att(B,B1,δ)
() ← del-Att(B,B2,δ)
() ← del-Role(R,B,δ)
() ← del-Role(R,A,δ)
() ← del-RT(R,δ)
() ← del-ET(B,δ)
```

In these signatures, the symbol δ stands for any kind of additional information needed to create the object, e.g. value type, value length, cardinality constraint, narrative description, etc. Now the signature of the `del-ET` operation is reversible, though the operation itself is not.

3.6 Some examples of reversible transformations

A realistic toolset aimed at building complex database schemas would include several dozens of schema transformations. We will briefly specify some of the most popular techniques for which only the graphical expression of mapping T will be given. Some examples of usage are proposed, together with the signature of the direct and inverse transformations. A more comprehensive development will be found in [HAI,91], [HAI,93b] and [HAI,95c] for instance.

3.6.1 Transformation of a relationship type into an entity type

Any relationship type R can be expressed by an entity type E, and as many one-to-many relationship types R1, R2, .., as there are roles in R. The transformation preserves the cardinality constraints, the possible attributes as well as the identifiers. It is an SR-transformation.

This generalization of the transformation depicted in *Fig. 2* will be used to reduce complex relationship types, such as those with more than 2 roles, or with attributes. It can also be used to get rid of many-to-many or recursive relationship types.

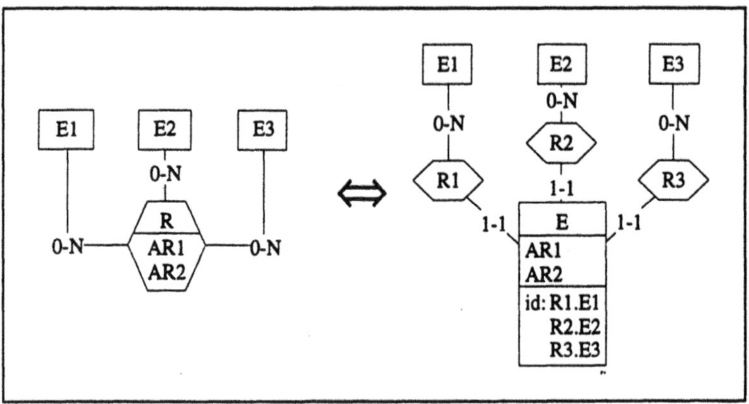

Signatures : `(E,{(E1,R1),(E2,R2),(E3,R3)})` ← `RT-to-ET(R)` *(direct)*
R ← `ET-to-RT(E)` *(inverse)*

3.6.2 Transformation of a relationship type into a foreign key

This one replaces a one-to-many relationship type R with a *foreign key*, which can be either multivalued or single-valued according to the cardinality of R. It is the main operator to produce relational schemas, but also standard file structures.

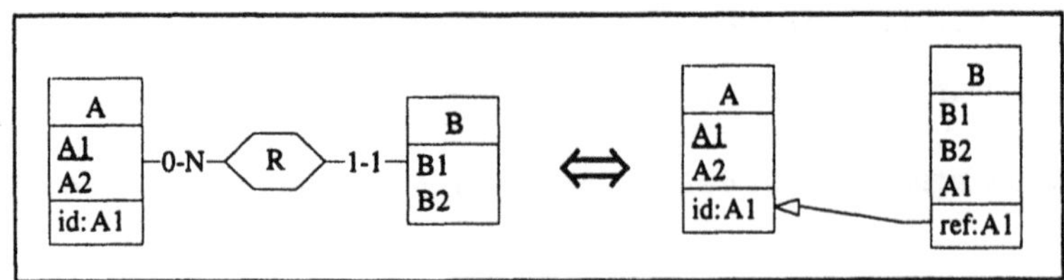

Signatures : `{A1}` ← `RT-to-FK(R,B)` *(direct)*
R ← `FK-to-RT(B,{A1},A)` *(inverse)*

3.6.3 Transformation of an attribute into an entity type

Transforming an attribute into an entity type is another common technique. It comes in two variants, namely **value representation** (above), in which each distinct value of A2, whatever the number of its instances, is represented by a distinct EA2 entity, and **instance representation** (below), in which each instance of A2 in each E entity is represented by a distinct EA2 entity. There are many applications of these techniques : eliminating multivalued attributes, eliminating optional attributes, eliminating compound attributes, extracting long attributes, defining dictionaries, promoting attributes (in conceptual analysis), normalizing entity types, etc.

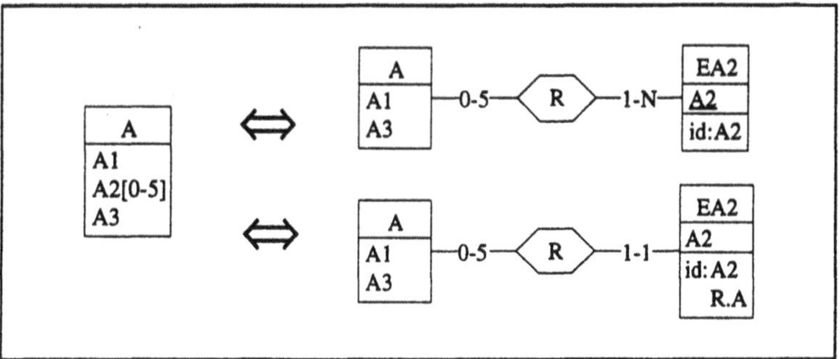

Signatures : (EA2,R) ← Att-to-ET/Value(A,A2) *(direct)*
(EA2,R) ← Att-to-ET/Instance(A,A2) *(direct)*
A2 ← ET-to-Att(EA2) *(inverse)*

3.6.4 Transformation of a multivalued attribute into serial attributes

This technique is often used to represent multivalued attributes while avoiding building an additional table, which would in turn imply costly joins in application programs. Each instance of A2 is represented by a single-valued attribute. Unfortunately, this is an R-transformation only. Indeed, the right version will allow situations which are not permitted by the left schema. For instance, the uniqueness of the A2 values is no longer ensured (the serial attributes implement a bag and not a set) and an implicit order is defined on the value set.

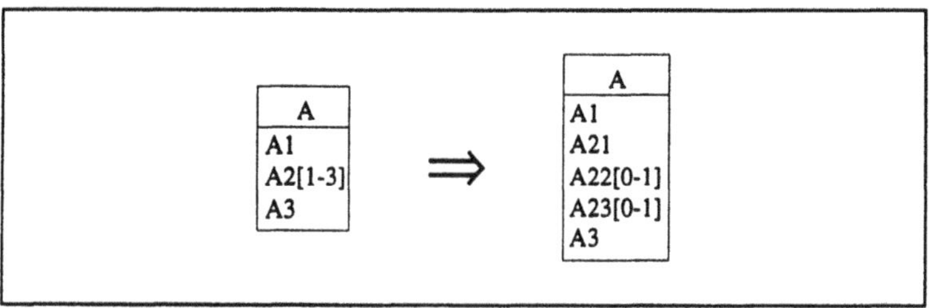

Signatures : {A21,A22,A23} ← MultiAtt-to-SerialAtt(A,A2) *(direct)*
A2 ← SerialAtt-to-MultiAtt(A,{A21,A22,A23}) *(inverse)*

4. Methodologies and histories

4.1 Modelling methodologies and histories

A history is not an arbitrary sequence of operations. It should obey to a structured way of proceeding called a *methodology*[5]. A methodology specifies the products and the processes that appear when carrying out any instance of a general engineering activity. For instance, several database design methodologies have been proposed so far, ranging from standard ERA-based approches to the more recent OO approaches. Less common activities such as database reverse engineering [HAI,93a] or schema integration [SPACCA,92] have been formally described through specific methodologies as well.

Describing methodologies relates to *(software/design) process modelling*, a discipline that is concerned with the understanding, representation and computer-based support of the software engineering activities [POTTS,88], including the development of data structures in data-centered applications. Such activities can be modeled as a set of documents, or products (schemas, programs, specifications, etc) and a set of engineering processes that transform input products into output products according to specific requirements to satisfy. For instance, in the database realm, conceptual user's views are integrated into the unique conceptual schema by an integration process, the conceptual schema is normalized into a canonical conceptual schema through a normalization process, this schema is translated into an SQL schema by a DBMS-oriented translation process, the latter schema is then optimized, and finally coded by other ad hoc processes. Each process in turn can be decomposed into a local set of products and processes, until primitive processes can be described.

The model we have developed derives from proposals such as [POTTS,88] and [ROLL,93], extended to all database engineering activities. This model describes quite adequately not only standard design methodologies, such as the Conceptual-Logical-Physical approaches [TEOREY,94] [BATINI,92] but also any kind of heuristic design behaviours, including those that occur in reverse engineering. A fairly comprehensive specification of the model has been given in [HAI,94], but we will shortly recall the elements which will be used in the following (*Fig. 3*).

Product and product instance. A product instance is any outstanding specification object that can be identified in the course of a specific design. A conceptual schema, an SQL DDL text, a COBOL program, an entity type, a table, a collection of user's views, an evaluation report, can all be considered product instances. Similar product instances are classified into products, such as CONCEPTUAL_SCHEMA, NORMALIZED_ BINARY_SCHEMA, SQL_DDL_SCHEMA.

Process and process instance. A process instance is any logical unit of activity in a history which transforms a product instance into another product instance. Normalizing schema S1 into schema S2 is a process instance. Similar process instances are classified into processes. NORMALIZATION is a process. There are two categories of processes, namely engineering processes and primitives. An *engineering process* is a goal-oriented process that is intended to make its input product satisfy specific requirements. NORMALIZATION, TIME_ OPTIMIZATION and REVERSE_ ENGINEERING are examples of design processes. On the contrary, a process is a *primitive* if it is a deterministic atomic operation. Generally, a primitive is neutral w.r.t. the requirements (it has no goal). Another difference is that the strategy of a primitive is encapsulated and is carried

---

5 We should have used the term *method*.

out by the CASE tool, while the strategy of a design process is visible, and has to be carried out by the designer, or at least under its control. The creation of an entity type and the transformation of a attribute into an entity type are examples of primitives.

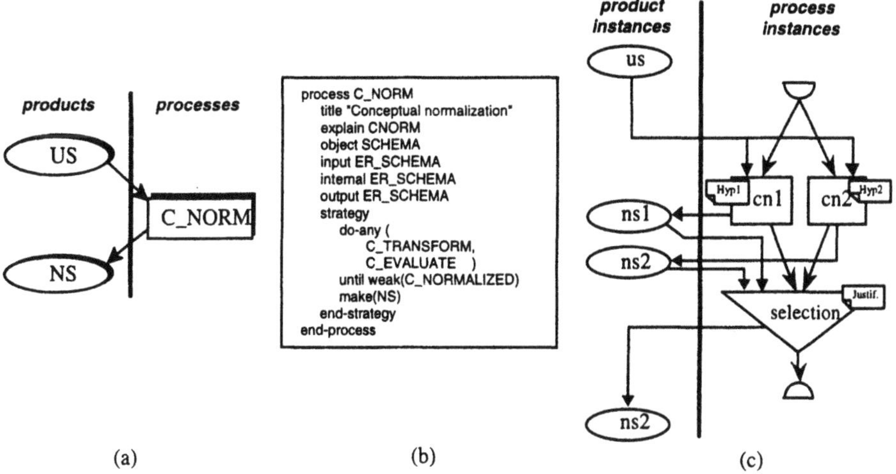

Figure 3 - Graphical representation of some aspects of the process model. (a) a process `C_NORM` is defined as a transformation of product `US` (un-normalized schema) into `NS` (normalized schema). (b) this text specifies the process, a.o. by declaring its strategy as a script ("carry out transformations and evaluations until the current schema satisfies - preferably [weak] - the submodel `C_NORMALIZED`"). (c) a history that shows two instances `cn1` and `cn2` of `C_NORM`, carried out on product instance `us`, and yielding instances `ns1` and `ns2` of `NS`. Hypotheses have been associated with each of these process instances. One of these product instances is selected, and this decision is justified. The histories of `cn1` and `cn2` would show instances of `C_TRANSFORM` and `C_EVALUATE`.

Process strategy. The strategy of a process is the specification of how its goal can be achieved, i.e. how the process must be carried out. A strategy can be deterministic, in which case it reduces to an algorithm (and can often be implemented as a primitive), or it can be non-deterministic, in which case the exact way in which each of its instances will be carried out is up to the designer. The strategy of a design process is defined by a *script* that specifies, a.o., what lower-level processes must/can be triggered, in which order, and under which condition. The control structures in a script include *action selection* (at most one, one only, at least one, all in any order, all in this order, at least one any number of times, etc.), *alternate actions*, *iteration*, *parallel actions*, *weak condition* (should be satisfied), *strong condition* (must be satisfied), etc.

Decision, hypothesis and rationale. In many cases, the engineer/designer will carry out an instance of a process with some hypothesis in mind. This hypothesis is an essential characteristics of this process instance since it implies the way in which its strategy will be performed. When the engineer needs to try another hypothesis, (s)he can perform another instance of the same process, generating a new instance of the same product. After a while (s)he is facing a collection of instances of this product, from which (s)he wants to choose the best one (according to the requirements that have to be satisfied). A justification of the decision must be provided. Hypothesis and decision justification comprise the design rationale [MYLO,92]. The decisional aspects of process modeling are particularly addressed in [POTTS,88] (through the concept of *deliberation*) and in the NATURE project [ROLL,93]. In our model, the decision is a built-in primitive process.

History. The history of a process instance is the recorded trace of the way in which its strategy has been carried out, together with the product instances involved and the rationale that has been formulated. Since a project is an instance of the highest level process, its history collects all the design activities, all the product instances and all the rationales that appeared, and will appear, in the life of the project. The history of a product instance P (also called its *design*) is the set of all the process instances, product instances and rationales which contributed to P. For instance, the design of a database collects all the information needed to describe and explain how the database came to be what it is.

4.2 Structure of a history

Depending on the complexity of the engineering process, and on the intelligence (e.g. the methodology-awareness) of the recorder, the history can be available in different formats. We will describe two dimensions according to which histories can be classified.

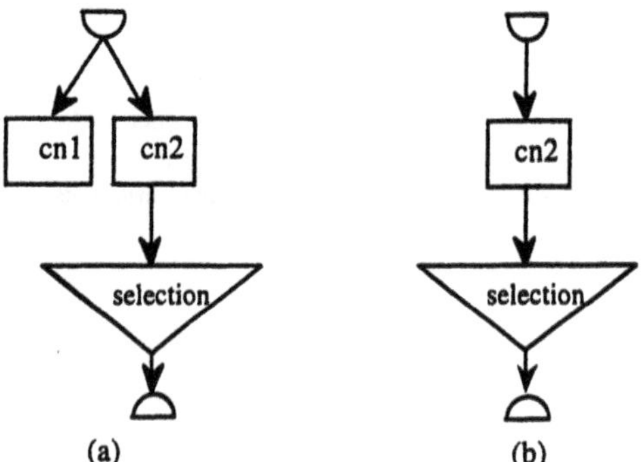

Figure 4 - The history of Fig. 3c has been restructured as a tree structure (a), and as a linear structure (b). The product instances have been hidden.

4.2.1 History topology

Technically speaking, a history can be materialized by a sort of *log file*, and therefore is a pure sequence of operations. However, if we consider multi-hypotheses approaches and decision processes, this sequence can be interpreted as a more complex graph. In general, a history has a directed acyclic graph structure, as illustrated in *Fig. 3c*. We can simplify an arbitrary history by associating every decision process instance with the successful branch, as suggested in *Fig. 4a*. In this way, a history appears as a **tree**.

Now, let us consider the successful branches only. We remove all the branches corresponding to hypotheses which have not been retained, and whose end products have been discarded. Keeping the live branches only produces a **linear** history (*Fig. 4b*). This derived history is important since it describes the way the final products could have been obtained should the engineer have proceeded without any hesitation : replaying this history on the source products will yield the same output products as the actual process did.

This classification can be generalized to methods comprising parallel branches, but this case is beyond the scope of this paper.

4.2.2 Level of aggregation

A history can be presented at different levels of detail. *Fig. 3* and *4* describe instances of C_NORM only, i.e. cn1 and cn2. In a more detailed presentation, the history of cn1 and cn2 would have been described as well, showing instances of C_TRANSFORM and C_EVALUATE. Developing in this way all the instances of engineering processes produces a complete history that can be given two extreme presentations.

- A **structured history**, which appears as an ordered tree in which each node represents a process instance. Leaves are primitive process instances, and non-leaf nodes are engineering process instances. The immediate children of node N represent instances of the processes mentioned in the script of the process of N. The root represents the instance of the main process, i.e. the project.
- A **flat history** shows the primitive process instances only. This concept is interesting because it is the easiest form of history to record. Indeed, since it represents no engineering processes, it is methodology-neutral, and can be built by simple CASE tools. In some situations, it could be the only form of history available. Such could be the case for loosely structured activities, such as some scenarios of reverse engineering.

A CASE tool must be able to present a history at various levels of aggregation.

4.2.3 Additional definitions

A history H_p is a subset of history H_n ($H_p \subseteq H_n$) if all the process instances of H_p appears in H_n, in the same order.

A history H can be sliced into sequences of process instances h_1, h_2, h_3, etc. We will note this decomposition $H = \langle h_1 \ h_2 \ h_3 \ \ldots \rangle$, where h_1 h_2 h_3 are *history slices*.

Let us consider history slice $h \subseteq H$, which starts at a time point where product instance p_1 is known to be available. h can be seen as the history of a process instance, possibly fictive, which produces product instance p_2. We can write : $p_2 = h(p_1)$.

Due to the transformational interpretation of engineering processes, a history slice can be considered as a transformation. Therefore, the structural functions are valid as well, and we can use the expressions $C_-(h)$, $C_+(h)$, $C_0(h)$.

4.2.4 Independent history slices

Let us consider history $H_0 = \langle .. h_1 .. h_2 .. \rangle$, in which we identify slices h_1 and h_2. The question addressed is : does the execution of h_2 depend on the execution of h_1, or are they independent, in which case they can be (or could have been) executed in any order, or even in parallel ? First, we define the partial order relation $\mathrm{before}(h_i, h_j)$, that states that slice h_i must be performed before h_j. This relation is defined as follows[6] :

$$\mathrm{before}(h_i,h_j) \quad \Leftrightarrow \quad C_0(h_i) \cap C_-(h_j) \neq \emptyset \vee C_+(h_i) \cap C(h_j) \neq \emptyset$$

Intuitively, h_j must follow h_i if h_j deletes *catalytic* elements of h_i, or if h_j uses constructs created by h_i. Then we define tr-before, the transitive closure of before :

6 This relation is called the *precedence* relation in [BATINI,93].

$$\texttt{tr-before}(h_i, h_j) \Leftrightarrow \texttt{before}(h_i, h_j) \vee (\exists h \subseteq H : \texttt{tr-before}(h_i, h) \wedge \texttt{before}(h, h_j))$$

Finally, h_1 and h_2 are independent in H_0 *iff*

$$\neg\, \texttt{tr-before}(h_1, h_2) \wedge \neg\, \texttt{tr-before}(h_2, h_1)$$

4.2.5 Equivalent histories

Two histories (or history slices) H_0 and H_1 are equivalent *w.r.t.* product instance p *iff*

$$H_i(p) = H_j(p).$$

Let us consider history H_0, which is expressed as a sequence of four subsequences :

$$H_0 = <h_1\ h_2\ h_3\ h_4>,$$

where h_1 and h_4 are (possibly empty) sequences of operations and h_2 and h_3 are two (non empty) history slices.

If we can prove that h_2 and h_3 are independent slices, then they can be swapped in H_0, leading to history $H_1 = <h_1\ h_3\ h_2\ h_4>$. Therefore, H_i is equivalent to H_j *iff* H_j can be built from H_i through a sequence of swap operations applied to independent slices.

Let us consider history H, which transforms the schema of Figure 1 into a relational schema : multivalued attribute DETAIL is transformed into entity type DETAIL and one-to-many rel-type from, then the latter and rel-type of are expressed as foreign keys.

```
H ≡ h1: (DETAIL,from) ← Att-to-ET/Value(ORDER,DETAIL)
    h2: {ORD-ID} ← RT-to-FK(from,DETAIL)
    h3: {CUST-ID} ← RT-to-FK(of,ACCOUNT)
```

The graph of tr-before is as follows :

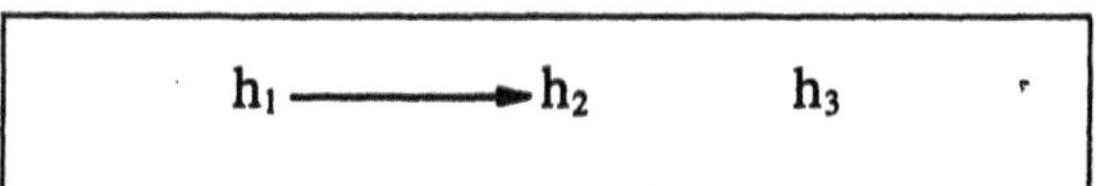

Therefore, <h2,h3> and <h1,h3> are independent and swappable. According to the definition, <h3,h1,h2> and <h1,h3,h2> are equivalent to H, while <h3,h2,h1> is not equivalent.

4.2.6 Minimal history

The history of a design process records the results of the decisions, be they right or wrong, of trials, errors, backtrackings, undos and redos which shape all the exploratory human activities. Histories generally have a complex structure including several branches which materialize the exploration of concurrent hypotheses (see *Fig. 3c* for instance), of which one only led to the discovery of a target concept, the other ones being abandoned. Cycles of *doing*, then *undoing*, and finally *redoing*, are not uncommon either. Such structures must be simplified : multiple branches must be reduced to the only one that has proved useful, useless loops must be discarded. Hence the concept of **minimal history**, which can be defined as follows :

history H is minimal w.r.t. product instance p
iff for any $H' \subset H$, $H'(p) \neq H(p)$

In other words, there is no proper subsets of H which still are equivalent to H. Given history H, H_m is a *minimal version* of H if H_m is minimal, and H_m is equivalent to H.

5. Database reverse engineering

Both reverse engineering and design recovery must be defined against a reference forward engineering approach. Indeed, reverse engineering can be modeled as the reverse of designing a database, and design recovery consists in developing a plausible history of a definite design methodology.

5.1. The reference database design methodology

In this section, we draw the main principles of standard database design methodologies as described in [TEOREY,94] and [BATINI,92] for instance. Traditionally, database design can be described as made up of a sequence of four specific processes, namely CONCEPTUAL DESIGN, LOGICAL DESIGN, PHYSICAL DESIGN and VIEW DESIGN.

- The CONCEPTUAL DESIGN process is aimed at producing the *conceptual schema*, a computer-independent representation of the information to be stored into the future database. Among others, this representation is to be given such desirable qualities as normality, minimality, clarity, that can be considered as provided through a specific sub-process called CONCEPTUAL NORMALIZATION.
- Through the LOGICAL DESIGN process, the conceptual schema is transformed into a *DMS-compliant optimized logical schema* with the following three characteristics :
  - *equivalence* : it expresses the same semantics as the conceptual schema,
  - *DMS-compliance* : it follows the data model of the chosen DMS[7],
  - *efficiency* : it satisfies operational or technical criteria such as space and time performance.

  This process can be considered as being refined, at least conceptually, into three subprocesses : schema simplification, schema optimization and DMS-translation (*Fig. 5*).

  - SCHEMA SIMPLIFICATION replaces *advanced constructs* such as IS-A hierarchies, N-ary rel-types by equivalent basic constructs. The simplified conceptual schema is perceived as an adequate medium for logical reasonings when traditional DMS are considered.
  - SCHEMA OPTIMIZATION modifies the schema in order to give it better performances.
  - SCHEMA TRANSLATION converts the schema into data structures that are compliant with the model of the DMS. The result consists into two complementary parts : the DMS constructs, that can be controlled by the DMS, and the non-DMS constructs, most often integrity constraints, that will be ignored by the DMS.

---

[7] A DMS is a Data Management System. It is either a File Management System, or a Database Management System.

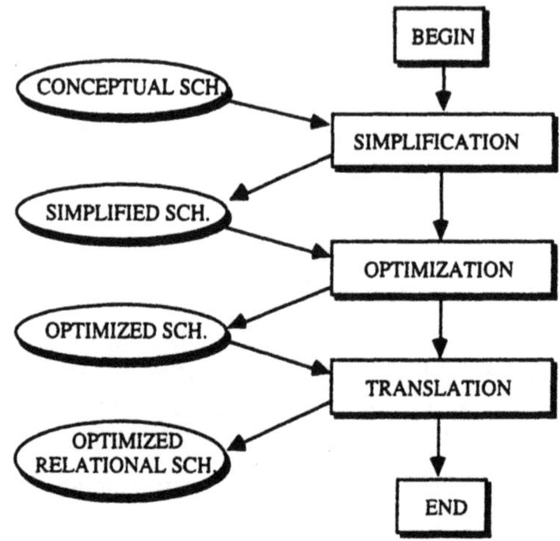

Figure 5 - Development of the Logical Design process of the reference design methodology.

- The PHYSICAL DESIGN process translates the DMS constructs of this schema into a DMS-DDL text, and the non-DMS constructs into, e.g., procedural sections or local variables of the application programs. In addition, through physical tuning, technical parameters are set and physical constructs are built, such as indexes and clusters.
- The VIEW DESIGN process builds the external views required by users and programs, and translates them in DMS-DDL and application programs fragments in the same way as for the global schema.

Most of these processes can be in turn refined, directly or indirectly, into lower-level processes or operators that are primitive schema transformations as defined in *Section 3*.

5.2 Database reverse engineering

Grossly speaking, this process transforms input products, that mainly consist of source code texts, into schemas of the database. Two schemas are of particular interest, namely the *logical schema of the database* according to the DMS model, and a possible *conceptual schema*. The main input products consist in DMS-DDL description of the global schema and of the views, either in text format, or as data dictionary contents. Essential information, for instance on untranslated integrity constraints, can be found in the source text of the application programs (DML queries, procedure and data structures), in screen layout and procedural components of the user interface and in database checking procedures (e.g. triggers, check clauses). The physical schema may yield useful hints concerning the logical schema (indexes suggesting foreign keys, join-based clusters, etc). File/database contents analysis may provide strong hints, or validate hypotheses, on the presence of such constructs as identifiers, foreign keys, field layout and value domains.

In [HAI,93a] and [HAI,95a], a general procedure is proposed for reverse engineering any database or collection of files. It consists into two major processes, namely DATA STRUCTURE EXTRACTION and DATA STRUCTURE CONCEPTUALIZATION (*Fig. 6*).

- DATA STRUCTURE EXTRACTION produces a complete description of the data structures according to the model of the DMS, e.g. COBOL file structures, CODASYL schema, relational schema, etc. In addition, the non-DMS parts of the schema have been elicited from, a.o. the procedural parts of the applications or database contents. According to the DMS, the process can be more or less easy. For instance, the DMS part of COBOL data structures can be difficult to discover while CODASYL or relational schemas can be analysed more easily. DATA STRUCTURE EXTRACTION appears as the inverse of the PHYSICAL DESIGN forward process.

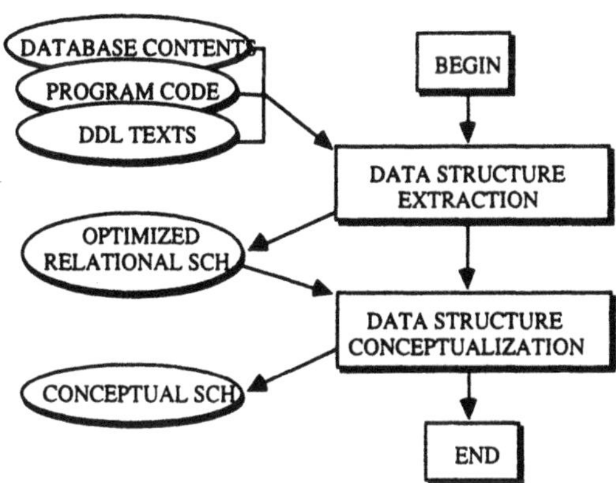

Figure 6 - Database Reverse Engineering : the major processes.

- DATA STRUCTURE CONCEPTUALIZATION tries to make the semantics of the logical schema explicit by recovering the intention of the optimized DMS data structures. This process is to a large extent the reverse of the LOGICAL DESIGN forward process, and can be decomposed into three subprocesses (*Fig. 7*).

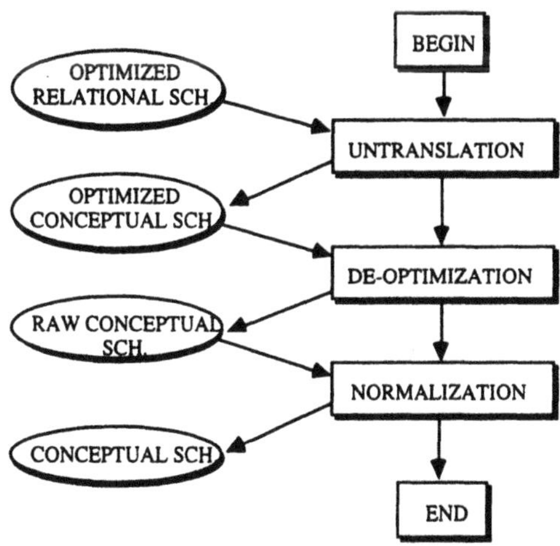

Figure 7 - Database Reverse Engineering : Development of the Data Structure Conceptualization process.

- UNTRANSLATION detects DMS-compliant constructs and replaces them by their DMS-independent equivalent. This process appears as the inverse of the SCHEMA TRANSLATION forward process.

- DE-OPTIMIZATION detects and removes the non-semantic constructs from the logical schema, and particularly the optimization structures. This process appears as the inverse of the SCHEMA OPTIMIZATION forward process.
- CONCEPTUAL NORMALIZATION has the same objectives as its forward engineering counterpart such as minimality, clarity and corporate standard compliance. In particular, it is intended to recover the high-level structures transformed by the SCHEMA SIMPLIFICATION.

According to this approach, each DBRE process is either a forward process or the inverse of a forward process. Consequently, they can be based on basic schema transformations that are either forward transformations or the inverse thereof.

6. Database design recovery

In this section, we suppose that we have been provided with the history of a reverse engineering process which has led to a correct, coherent and validated conceptual schema of a legacy system. We will shortly describe a general procedure to built in a systematic way a possible design history of this system.

6.1 Normalizing the DBRE history

The objective is to produce a correct and minimal DBRE history which complies with the standard way this process should have been carried out. The normalization includes two processes, namely minimizing and restructuring the history.

A **minimal** history is first extracted. Indeed, database reverse engineering basically is an exploratory process, and quite naturally, its history will include useless loops and dead branches. Getting rid of these structures produces a minimal history, as defined in *Section 4.2.6*. We give some detail about this minimization process.

- Removing dead branches provides a history in which only the branches and products that contribute to the final product (the conceptual schema) are kept. It consists in parsing the history backward, from the final product toward the input products, and marking the process instances and product instances examined. The unmarked instances are discarded. This process is fairly easy and can be automated.
- Detecting and reducing useless sequences, and particularly useless loops are more complex problems. Though the problem has not been completely formalized yet, we can propose the following heuristics :

  we consider history H, which is expressed as a sequence of transformations :

  $$H = \langle T_1\ T_2\ T_3\ T_4 \rangle,$$

  We denote by Σ_T the generic transformation of which $T \in H$ is an instance. If all the following properties stand in H, then H and $\langle T_1\ T_4 \rangle$ are equivalent :

  $$\Sigma_{T2} = \Sigma_{T3}^{-1}$$

  $$C_-(h_3) = C_+(h_2)$$

  $$\neg(\exists T \in H: \ (T \neq T_3) \wedge C_+(T_2) \cap C(T) \neq \emptyset)$$

  $$\neg(\exists T \in H: \ C_+(T_3) \cap C(T) \neq \emptyset)$$

  In short, we can remove any pair of transformations which prove to be the inverse of each other, and whose target objects are not used in any other transformations. This heuristics is still valid when the T's are history slices instead.

Then this history is **restructured** according to the reference RE methodology. In particular, the operations are swapped, provided they are independent, and reclassified into the reference engineering process instances in which they best fit, and the sequences are sorted in order to produce clusters of similar operations. These manipulations must preserve the equivalence of the source and final histories, according to the definitions in *Section 4.2.*

6.2 Replacing each operation with its inverse

Each operation of the normalized history is replaced by its inverse. Two cases will occur. The first one concerns primitive process instances. For each of them, there exists at least one inverse operation (e.g. *transforming an entity type into an attribute* has at least two inverse transformations, as illustrated in *Section 3.6.3*). The most adequate among them is chosen.

The second case regards the engineering process instances. According to the way in which the reference DBRE methodology has been designed (*Section 5.2*), most of its processes are, at least partially, the inverse of a forward process. Therefore, each reverse process instance is replaced, possibly after some redistribution of its contents, by its inverse forward process instance. Let us consider some representative examples :

parsing	→	code generation
conceptualization	→	logical design
normalization	→	simplification
untranslation	→	translation
un-optimization	→	optimization
remove redundancies	→	introduce redundancies

6.3 Reversing the order of the operations

In each engineering process instance, whatever its level of aggregation, the order of the operations is reversed.

6.4 Normalizing the design history

The result of the preceeding processes is a correct design history. If the DBRE history has been correctly normalized, the resulting design history should enjoy the same minimality properties. However, when compared with the history of a native design project, it will generally appear as somewhat ackward. The objective of this normalization is to produce a more natural design history according to the corporate methodology standards, i.e. the *reference methodology*. This will be obtained by reordering, sorting and grouping the operations in each engineering process instance. For instance more than one instance of the optimization process can appear in the history. They should be merged in order to group them in one contiguous slice. In addition, several similar operations in the same engineering process instance can be grouped if they have the same objective. For instance, all the *transform-rel-type-into-foreign-key* operations are packaged into one contiguous sequence.

Informal or linguistic information is associated with the important objects of the history. For instance, each data object must be given a semantic description, and for each important process instance the rationale must be documented [BIGG,89]. Recovering the rationale of the decisions is a hazardous task. However, it can be improved by the context provided by the reference methodology. In each engineering process of this methodology, several ways of working are generally proposed, each driven by specific design criteria, such as space optimization, time optimization, normality, etc. By comparing the history profile with each of these suggested way of working, we can more easily guess what were the design criteria the developer had in mind when (s)he built the legacy system. For instance, transforming a multivalued attribute into serial attributes (3.6.4) suggests access time minimization, while transforming it into an entity type (3.6.3) suggests that readability and maintainability have been given higher priority.

6.5 Generalizing the design history

As it is described so far, a history traces elementary transformations only, be they primitive or enginering process instances. Indeed, each operation specifies the application of a generic transformation to an individual specification object : *transform attribute PUBLISHER into an entity type, transform entity type BUYS into a relationship type*, and so on. This has some important consequences, of which we will mention two.

1. Such a detailled history does not help much in understanding the reasonings underlying the (hypothetical) design of the system, in the same way as reading the log of the elementary manipulations performed by a surgeon during an operation does not inform much a medical student on the objectives and on the strategies used.

2. Replaying this history works fine on the recovered abstract specifications, since it yields exactly the source logical schema, but it can lead to unsatisfying results when applied on modified abstract specifications, a scenario that is common in database maintenance and evolution.

The problem can be stated as *trying to recover the specific strategy used to perform each process*. This problem has been tackled in the software engineering domain, where researches have been conducted in recovering a possible program from traces of its execution.

These problems can be solved, at least partially, by **generalizing** the history, i.e. by replacing some sequences of similar individual operations by higher-level rules of which these sequences are the trace. For example, let us suppose that the schema on which engineering process instance `I` is performed includes relationship types `R1`, `R2` and `R3` which all satisfy predicate `P` (e.g. `is_N-ary`), and that no other objects satisfy `P`. Let us also suppose that, in `I`, transformation `RT-to-ET` is applied on `R1`, `R2` and `R3` :

```
E1 ← RT-to-ET(R1)
E2 ← RT-to-ET(R2)
E3 ← RT-to-ET(R3)
```

Technically speaking, we can replace this sequence with the *predicate-driven global transformation* :

for each rel-type R_i such that `is_N-ary`(R_i) do : $E_i \leftarrow$ `RT-to-ET`(R_i)

When generalized in this way, the history is much shorter, it provides a clearer and more explicit specification of the reasonings driving the process instance (e.g. the intention of the origin history fragment obviously was to *transform all N-ary rel-types into entity types*), and it makes the history applicable to modified versions of the abstract specifications. For instance, let us consider that, due to changes in the user requirements, a new N-ary relationship type `R4` has to be added to the conceptual schema. Replaying the first version of the history of process `I` will leave `R4` unchanged, while applying the generalized version will process `R4` as well, therefore complying with the intention of `I`.

As for most inductive reasonings, this process cannot be fully automated. Indeed, only a skilled designer can validate such a generalization. However, detecting similar transformation patterns, grouping them, and suggesting candidate generalizations can be described by formal rules, and supported by knowledge-based CASE functions.

Once again, generalization is a complex process that can be made much easier and more deterministic if a precise reference design methodology is available. Indeed, each way of working proposed to solve the problem addressed in the current process should be supported by some standard transformations plans. The problem now reduces to identifying the most appropriate plan, and trying to map sequences of individual transformations to predicate-driven global transformation.

7. CASE support of design recovery

Histories are the baseline of design recovery. Recording, managing, and processing engineering histories requires strong CASE support. From the discussion developed in this paper we can lay down the main requirements such tools should satisfy. We will mention some of them, then describe shortly a prototype CASE tool intended to support history management and design recovery.

7.1 Requirements for CASE support of design recovery

An environment that is to assist developers in design recovery of database should include some important functions.

1. The repository of the tool must accomodate specification products at various levels of abstraction, and according to various common representation paradigms.
2. Semantics-preserving transformations are the building blocks of history formalisation. Therefore, the tool must support some kind of transformational approach.
3. The tool must provide the basic functions for reverse engineering.
4. The tool must be methodology-independent : it will allow various engineering strategies, ranging from disciplined and formal approaches to informal, pragmatic and experimental ones.
5. However, the tool must be methodology-aware, and include an active method model. It must also include a method specification language, a compiler for this language, and a method engine which provide method enactment to ensure that the actions performed by the developers comply with the current method
6. The method engine must include a history recorder coupled with the current method.
7. It must include various functions for history management : viewing at different aggregation levels, restructuring, reversing, pruning, analysing, updating, annotating.
8. Finally, it must include a replay processor.

7.2 The DB-MAIN CASE tool

DB-MAIN is both a toolset to support system engineering, and a CASE tool development environment (i.e. a *Meta-CASE* or a *CASE tool factory*).It is one of the main products of the DB-MAIN project, dedicated to database applications engineering, and more particularly to the problems that arise when such applications evolve and have to be maintained. Its basic principles and its architecture have been described in [HAI,95b] and [HAI,96b]. DB-MAIN Version 1.0 offers both basic and sophisticated services for database forward and reverse engineering. Though coping with the very problem of database application evolution and maintenance in a significant way is due to 1997, the current version, and the current developments comprise important aspects that are to satisfy the requirements mentioned above.

In its first version (October 1995), the tool offers support for most forward and reverse engineering activities. More specifically, it includes the following functions and components : specifications management; representation of all the project products through a generic, wide-spectrum, representation model for conceptual, logical and physical objects; multiple views of the specifications (4 hypertexts and 2 graphical views); a toolbox of more than 25 semantics-preserving transformational operators, allowing to carry out in a systematic way such activities as conceptual normalization, or the development of optimized logical and physical schemas from conceptual schemas, and conversely (i.e. reverse engineering); code generators and parsers; interactive and programmable source text and name analysers and processors.

It also includes a history manager which records the engineering activities of the analyst, and which allows their further automatic or assisted replay; this manager can also reverse an existing history. A series of assistants (problem-driven expert modules) have been developed to assist the analyst in frequent, tedious, knowledge-based or complex tasks.

The tool also allows the development of *specialized CASE tool*, either according to specific methodologies, or by adding new concepts and new functions to the basic toolset.

The current version of the history manager, despite its early prototype state, already provides us with an experimental workbench to study the assisted building of forward histories from reverse histories. Developing an improved history manager is one of the objectives of Version 2 of DB-MAIN.

DB-MAIN have been developed in C++ for PC/Windows workstations. It is currently used by several industrial partners, mainly in reverse engineering, redocumentation, reengineering and migration projects. An education/evaluation version[8] is used in an increasing number of schools and universities, and can be obtained free of charge by non-profit organizations.

8. A short case study

Let us consider the relational schema in *Fig. 8*, which could be the result of carrying out the *Data Structure Extraction* process on the DDL and procedural texts of an application.

Interpreting this schema, i.e. rebuilding a possible conceptual schema, is the job of the *Data Structure Conceptualization* process. This process comprises three main subprocesses : *Untranslation*, *De-optimization* and *Normalization*. The first two ones can be conducted in parallel, while the third one will generally be carried out as the finishing touch. Let us imagine the following scenario, immediately translated into its history :

- we express the first foreign key, RNAME, as the relationship type `from`; we start the history with an *Untranslation* action :

  A1: `from` ← `FK-to-RT(CUSTOMER,{RNAME},REGION)`

8 Fully functional, but limited to 1000-object projects.

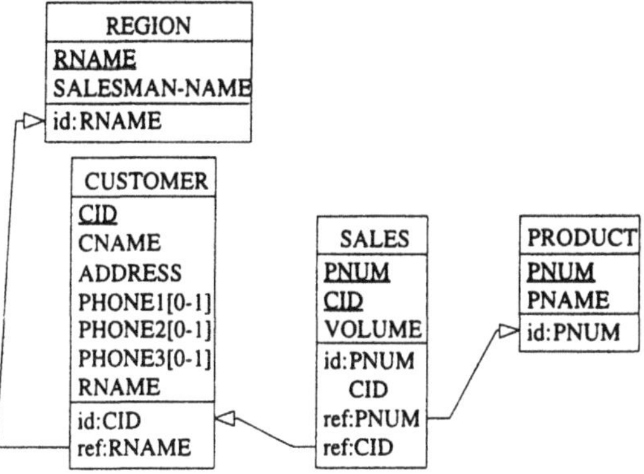

Figure 8 - The logical schema of a relational database

- we then observe the structure of serial attributes {PHONE1, PHONE2, PHONE3} in the CUSTOMER table; we know it as a common low cost implementation of a multivalued attribute; we express these attributes as the multivalued attribute PHONE :

  A2: PHONE ← SerialAtt-to-MultiAtt(CUSTOMER, {PHONE1, PHONE2, PHONE3})

  This action obviously relates to the *De-optimization* process.

- the schema includes two other foreign keys, which are known to express many-to-one relationship types; we augment the history with two *Untranslation* actions :

  A3: r1 ← FK-to-RT(SALES, {CID}, CUSTOMER)

  A4: r2 ← FK-to-RT(SALES, {PNUM}, PRODUCT)

- the attribute SALESMAN of REGION is perceived as a low-level representation of an important concept, salesmen, that will feel better as an entity type. This attribute is transformed into an entity type :

  A5: (SALESMAN, in) ← Att-to-ET/Value(REGION, SALESMAN-NAME)

  The representation seems clearer and more readable. This is a *Normalization* transformation.

- the SALES entity type is perceived as the representation of a relationship type. This decision belongs to the *Normalization* process :

  A6: SALES ← ET-to-RT(SALES)

- finally, the idea to express salesmen as an entity type is not a so good one, because it makes the schema more complex without any profit. We choose to transform this entity type into an attribute. This still is a *Normalization* operation :

  A7: SALESMAN-NAME ← ET-to-Att(SALESMAN)

The actions are classified according to the process to which they are most relevant. The history of the conceptualization process of this reverse engineering project is summarized as follows.

Untranslation

A1: `from ← FK-to-RT(CUSTOMER,{RNAME},REGION)`

A3: `r1← FK-to-RT(SALES,{CID},CUSTOMER)`

A4: `r2 ← FK-to-RT(SALES,{PNUM},PRODUCT)`

De-optimization

A2: `PHONE ← SerialAtt-to-MultiAtt(CUSTOMER,{PHONE1,PHONE2,PHONE3})`

Normalization

A5: `(SALESMAN,in) ← Att-to-ET/Value(REGION,SALESMAN-NAME)`

A6: `SALES ← ET-to-RT(SALES)`

A7: `SALESMAN-NAME ← ET-to-Att(SALESMAN)`

A graphical view of this history is proposed in *Fig. 9.* The instances of the primitive processes are represented by their labels.

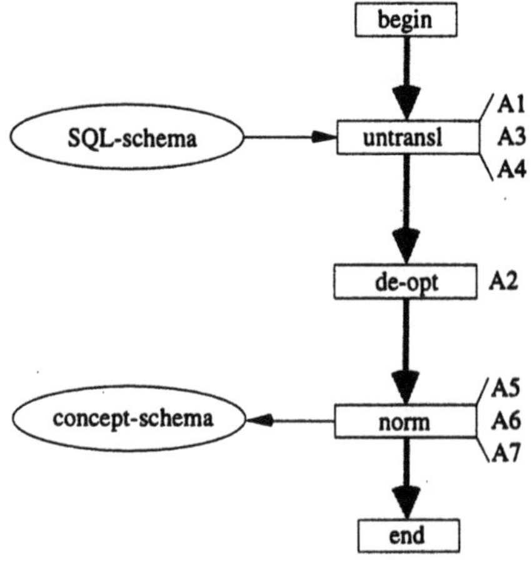

Figure 9 - The history of the reverse engineering of the relational schema of Fig. 8

The resulting conceptual schema appears in *Fig. 10.*

Building a possible design history

Let us consider the standard database design methodology whose *Logical design* phase is described in *Fig. 5.* It is obvious that following this strategy, it should be possible to produce a large variety of equivalent logical relational schemas. One of them is the source schema of *Fig. 8.* The objective is to build the unique history that produces exactly this logical schema from the recovered conceptual schema. As proposed in *Section 6*, we apply the 5-step strategy :

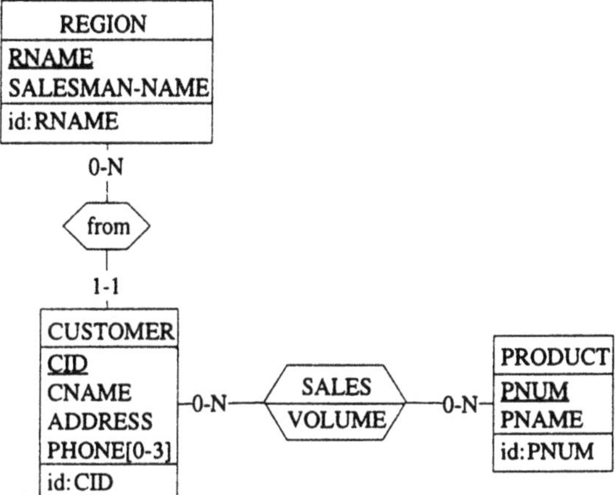

Figure 10 - A possible conceptual schema for the relational schema of Fig. 8.

1. *Normalizing the DBRE history*

   Despite its simplicity, this history need be normalized. It appears that operations A5 and A7 form a useless loop. Indeed, we have :

   - `Att-to-ET/Value = ET-to-Att`$^{-1}$
   - C_-`(A7)` = {`SALESMAN, SALESMAN-NAME, in, in.REGION, in.SALESMAN, id(SALESMAN)`} = C_+`(A5)`
   - no transformations use C_+`(A5)` = {`SALESMAN, SALESMAN-NAME, in, in.REGION, in.SALESMAN, id(SALESMAN)`}, but A7
   - no transformations use C_+`(A7)` = {`SALESMAN-NAME`}

   Therefore A5 and A7 can be removed.

2. *Replacing each operation with its inverse*

   Both engineering and primitive operations have direct inverse :

Translation

`{RNAME}` ← `RT-to-FK(from,CUSTOMER)`

`{CID}` ← `RT-to-FK(r1,SALES)`

`{PNUM}` ← `RT-to-FK(r2,SALES)`

Optimization

`{PHONE1,PHONE2,PHONE3}` ← `MultiAtt-to-SerialAtt(CUSTOMER,PHONE)`

Simplification

`(SALES,{(CUSTOMER,r1),(PRODUCT,r2)})` ← `RT-to-ET(SALES)`

3. Reversing the order of the operations

Simplification

`(SALES,{(CUSTOMER,r1),(PRODUCT,r2)}) ← RT-to-ET(SALES)`

Optimization

`{PHONE1,PHONE2,PHONE3} ← MultiAtt-to-SerialAtt(CUSTOMER,PHONE)`

Translation

`{PNUM} ← RT-to-FK(r2,SALES)`
`{CID} ← RT-to-FK(r1,SALES)`
`{RNAME} ← RT-to-FK(from,CUSTOMER)`

4. Normalizing the design history

Due to its simplicity, this history need not be normalized.

5. Generalizing the logical design history

The **Simplification** process includes one operation only. However, it is an instance of a standard way to get rid of N-ary relationship types, a typical complex construct. Therefore it is reasonable to generalize this instance into the *transformation of all the N-ary relationship types into entity types.*

The **Translation** process includes a sequence of similar operations which are good candidates for generalization : *express all functional relationship types into foreign keys.*

The **Optimization** process is much more difficult to generalize. Indeed, it often relies on complex reasonings strongly linked with the developer's skill, the technology state at development time, and with the data statistics and of the application requirements at the same time. These conditions may have changed since then. For these reasons, and in the absence of additional information, we propose not to generalize the operation(s).

The result is presented in Fig. 11.

9. Conclusion

We have shown in this presentation that database design recovery can be tackled through reverse engineering techniques which are now fairly well understood and mastered. We have also shown that the proposed approach can be formalized thanks to the concept of semantics-preserving transformation. Moreover, this formality provides a sound basis for CASE support, as illustrated by the DB-MAIN CASE tool, where prototype functions of history recording and management have been implemented. It must be admitted, however, that design recovery, as interpreted by [BIGG,89], generally goes beyond purely formal treatment. In particular, explaining why some decisions have been taken, and declaring how the reconstructed artifacts relate with the application domain is up to the analyst, who is supposed to elicit such reasonings and relations from the technical traces which (s)he faces during reverse engineering activities.

Logical design
Simplification for each rel-type R such that (R = R(E1,..,Ei) & ¬ (R is functional)) do : `(R,{(E1,r1),..,(Ei,ri)}) ← RT-to-ET(R)`
Optimization `{PHONE1,PHONE2,PHONE3} ← MultiAtt-to-SerialAtt(CUSTOMER,PHONE)`
Translation for each rel-type R such that (R = R(E1,E2) & id(E1) = A) do : `A ← RT-to-FK(R,E2)`

Figure 11 - A possible design history for the relational schema of Fig. 8.

An immediate question arises when a correct, concise and documented design is available: what to do with it ? For instance, how can we use this product to carry out system maintenance and evolution in a more systematic way than we now do ? This problem is beyond the scope of this paper, but a partial answer can be found in [HAI,94].

The data structure domain is fairly well formalized, and has long led to models and tools which are both formal and intuitive (and therefore used by practitioners). The domain of software engineering is much larger, and far less formalized, at least as far as practice is concerned. Hence a second question which can be asked at this stage : can these principles be generalized to help recover the design of other aspects of a legacy system, and in particular of the programs ? A tentative positive answer has been developed in [HAI,95a] for reverse engineering, but the question is open as far as history recovery is concerned.

9. References

[BALZER,81] Balzer, R., Transformational implementation : An example, *IEEE TSE*, Vol. SE-7, No. 1, 1981

[BATINI,92] Batini, C., Ceri, S., Navathe, S., B., *Conceptual Database Design*, Benjamin/Cummings, 1992

[BATINI,93] Batini, C., Di Battista, G., Santucci, G., Structuring Primitives for a Dictionary of Entity Relationship Data Schemas, *IEEE TSE*, Vol. 19, No. 4, 1993

[BIGG,89] Biggerstaff, T., J., Design Recovery for Maintenance and Reuse, *IEEE Computer*, July 1989

[FICKAS,85] Fikas, S., F., Automating the transformational development of software, *IEEE TSE*, Vol. SE-11, pp1268-1277, 1985

[HAI,91] Hainaut, J-L, Database Reverse Engineering, Models, Techniques and Strategies, in *Proc. of the 10th Conf. on Entity-Relationship Approach*, San Mateo (CA), E-R Institute, 1991

[HAI,92] Hainaut, J-L., Cadelli, M., Decuyper, B., Marchand, O., Database CASE Tool Architecture : Principles for Flexible Design Strategies, in *Proc. of the 4th Int. Conf. on Advanced Information System Engineering* (CAiSE-92), Manchester, May 1992, Springer-Verlag, LNCS, 1992

[HAI,93a] Hainaut, J-L., Chandelon M., Tonneau C., Joris M., Contribution to a Theory of Database Reverse Engineering, in *Proc. of the IEEE Working Conf. on Reverse Engineering*, Baltimore, May 1993, IEEE Computer Society Press, 1993

[HAI,93b] Hainaut, J-L, Chandelon M., Tonneau C., Joris M., Transformational techniques for database reverse engineering, in *Proc. of the 12th Int. Conf. on ER Approach*, Arlington-Dallas, ER Institute, 1993

[HAI,94] Hainaut, J-L, Englebert, V., Henrard, J., Hick J-M., Roland, D., Evolution of database Applications : the DB-MAIN Approach, in *Proc. of the 13th Int. Conf. on ER Approach*, Manchester, Springer-Verlag, 1994

[HAI,95a] Hainaut, J-L, *Database Reverse Engineering - Problems, Techniques and Tools*,Tutorial notes, CAiSE'95, Jyväskylä, Finland, June 1995 (available at jlh@info.fundp.ac.be)

[HAI,95b] Hainaut, J-L, Englebert, V., Henrard, J., Hick J-M., Roland, D., Requirements for Information System Reverse Engineering Support, in *Proc. of the 2nd IEEE WC on Reverse Engineering*, Toronto, July 1995, IEEE Computer Society Press, 1995.

[HAI,95c] Hainaut, J-L, *Transformation-based database engineering*,Tutorial notes, VLDB'95, Zürich, Switzerland, Sept. 1995 (available at jlh@info.fundp.ac.be)

[HAI,96] Hainaut, J-L, Specification preservation in schema transformations - application to semantics and statistics, *Data & Knowledge Engineering*, Vol. 11, No. 1, 1996.

[HAI,96b] Hainaut, J-L, Englebert, V., Henrard, J., Hick J-M., Roland, D., Database Reverse Engineering : from Requirements to CASE tools, *Journal of Automated Software Engineering*, Vol. 3, No. 1, 1996

[HALPIN,95] Halpin, T., A., Proper, H., A., Database schema transformation and optimization, in *Proc. of the 14th Int. Conf. on ER/OO Modelling (ERA)*, Dec. 1995

[KOBA,86] Kobayashi, I., Losslessness and Semantic Correctness of Database Schema Transformation : another look of Schema Equivalence, in *Information Systems*, Vol. 11, No 1, pp. 41-59, January, 1986

[KOZA,87] Kozaczynsky, Lilien, An extended Entity-Relationship (E2R) database specification and its automatic verification and transformation, in *Proc. of Entity-Relationship Approach*, 1987

[MYLO, 92] Mylopoulos, J., Chung, L., Nixon, B., Representing and Using Nonfunctional requirements : A Process-Oriented Approach, *IEEE TSE*, Vol. 18, No. 6, June 1992

[NAVA,80] Navathe, S., B., Schema Analysis for Database Restructuring, in *ACM TODS*, Vol.5, No.2, June 1980

[POTTS,88] Potts, C., Bruns, G., Recording the Reasons for Design Decisions, in *Proc. of ICSE*, IEEE, 1988

[RAUH,95] Rauh, O., Stickel, E., Standard Transformations for the Normalization of ER Schemata, in *Proc. of the CAiSE•95 Conf.*, Jyväskylä, Finland, LNCS, Springer-Verlag, 1995

[ROLL,93] Rolland, C., Modeling the Requirements Engineering Process, in *Proc of the 3rd European-Japanese Seminar in Information Modeling and Knowledge Bases*, May 1993, Budapest (preprints)

[ROSE,88] Rosenthal, A., Reiner, D., Theoretically sound transformations for practical database design, in *Proc. of Entity-Relationship Approach*, 1988

[ROSE,94] Rosenthal, A., Reiner, D., Tools and Transformations - Rigourous and Otherwise - for Practical Database Design, *ACM TODS*, Vol. 19, No. 2, June 1994

[SPACCA,92] Spaccapietra, S., Parent, C., View Integration : A Step Forward in Solving Structural Conflicts, *IEEE Trans. on Knowledge and Data Engineering*, October, 1992

[TEOREY,94] Teorey, T. J., *Database Modeling and Design : the Fundamental Principles*, Morgan Kaufmann, 1994

The World-Wide Web As A Platform For Supporting Interactive Concurrent Engineering

Martin Hanneghan[†] Madjid Merabti[‡] Gary Colquhoun[†]

[†] School of Engineering and Technology Management
[‡] School of Computing and Mathematical Sciences
Liverpool John Moores University, Byrom Street, Liverpool, L3 3AF, UK.

E-mail: {m.b.hanneghan, m.merabti, g.j.colquhoun}@livjm.ac.uk

Abstract

This paper describes the use of the Internet and World-Wide Web (WWW) as a means for disseminating information and enabling collaborative working in a Concurrent Engineering (CE) environment. It discusses the authors architecture for a concurrent engineering support environment, the CONCERT environment, and describes the implementation of a WWW-based interface to this environment.

1. Introduction

Concurrent engineering (CE) has been described in the literature under a number of synonyms including: simultaneous engineering, integrated product development, concurrent product and process design, life-cycle engineering, design for production, design for assembly, integrated and co-operative design, design fusion and producibility engineering. It now has the almost universally accepted definition of: "... a systematic approach to the integrated concurrent design of products and their related processes, including manufacture and support. This approach is intended to cause the developers, from the outset to consider all elements of the product life-cycle from conception through disposal, including quality, cost, scheduling and user requirements" (Winner et al. 1988).

Changes are inevitable during the design and development of any product. In a traditional sequential product development process, up-stream problems are fed back to the previous development phase to be corrected in an iterative fashion. The cost of this reworking can amount to a substantial proportion of the total development cost — (Sheldon and Perks 1990) report that around 80% of the total cost of a product is committed during the design and planning stages. Therefore, consideration of potential up-stream problems at this stage can help reduce costs. Concurrent engineering aims to eliminate the possibility of costly design errors by utilising multi-discipline or cross-functional teams, i.e. teams with members from each functional area of the product's life-cycle — from conception to disposal. Improved communications and dramatic changes in working practices (Nickerson 1990; Trapp et al. 1992) have led to large reductions in product development lead time and overall cost (Coupland 1992; Dowlatshahi 1994).

Recent developments have led to a number of computer-based support environments to enable Computer-Aided Concurrent Engineering (CACE). These environments attempt to provide shared access to a common product information model over a computer network and so enable collaborative working.

We believe that concurrent engineering support environments should provide at least the following functionality:

- Allow transparent access to all the necessary tools and applications needed throughout the development process, e.g. CAD, CAM and project administration
- The ability to treat geographically dispersed resources as though they were local
- A communication sub-system for effective participation between all people involved in the project
- Facilities for controlling and tracking the project tasks and resources including people
- A consistent user interface even across multiple computer platforms and architectures
- The ability for the environment to be extended to include further tools and technologies as and when they become available

With these issues in mind we have proposed an architecture for a CE support environment which we have called the CONCERT (CONCurrent Engineering suppoRT) environment (Hanneghan et al. 1995b).

Organisations employing a CE strategy usually have team members and resources who are geographically dispersed throughout the company (or even the World) yet these people need to collaborate on projects and communicate on a regular basis. These people have a clear need to share information and making this process as efficient as possible can lead to significant cost savings.

The CONCERT environment attempts to address these problems by providing three fundamental components or *support services*. These are:

1. *A distribution support service* — this is to accommodate problems of geography and allow team members to co-operate in a distributed, client-server fashion

2. *A repository support service* — this is to enable team members to share a common repository (database) for any items (objects) created during the life-cycle of the product (this involves both storage and retrieval of objects within the repository)

3. *A Computer Supported Co-operative Working (CSCW) support service* — this allows collaboration and communication between team members.

The remainder of this paper describes the use of the World-Wide Web as a means of implementing the CONCERT environment and discusses some of the issues raised as a result of using the WWW for distributed, interactive client-server applications. Section 2 discusses our rationale for using the WWW while section 3 details the role of communication within a CE environment. A description of our implementation is given in section 4 and we give some conclusions about WWW-based development in section 5. Finally we describe some areas for future research in section 6.

2. Rationale for Using the World-Wide Web

The WWW is a relatively mature networked hypertext system. It is a distributed architecture on which to base simple client-server applications and a number of novel WWW-based applications are currently being used and developed to exploit this. Examples include on-line insurance quotations, credit ratings, stocks and share prices, Internet home shopping malls and even the purchasing of a new car.

The Internet is an exponentially growing global network which can be accessed relatively easily and cheaply by both large and small companies. There is no discrimination against who can join the Internet — it is not owned by any single organisation. This may be of special importance to companies in third world and developing countries who wish to use the Internet to apply a Concurrent Engineering strategy.

(Ellsworth and Ellsworth 1994) lists ten reasons why businesses are using the Internet and it is clear that these reasons have a lot in common with the goals of a CE strategy:

- Communication (internal and external)
- Corporate logistics
- Levelling the playing field — globalisation
- Gaining and maintaining competitive advantage
- Cost containment
- Collaboration and development
- Information retrieval and utilisation

- Marketing and sales
- Transmission of data
- Creating a corporate presence

The WWW can be considered as a medium for delivering *requested* information. In a CE environment, multiple members of a design team (also described as a virtual team) *produce* and *consume* documents: designers and engineers create new designs or proposals and submit them into a repository where they can be viewed, commented upon and reviewed or modified by other team members. These team members also need to communicate with each other to share and discuss ideas and problems (Siemieniuch and Sinclair 1994).

By enabling the Internet to be used as a collaborative design and working media we believe there is an opportunity to:

- Increase the level of co-operation through the greater awareness of the information that is available
- Increase the level of understanding of data through the use of hyperlinks to related documents
- Increase the ease with which support applications can be developed and then subsequently distributed and made available to team members within the given environment.

We have therefore produced the following set of design requirements for any application designed to support a concurrent engineering strategy:

1. The application should be distributed over the Internet using the World-Wide Web or other such mechanism
2. Documents and displays should be formatted, where possible using a dynamic hypertext-based interface such as that provided by HyperText Mark-up Language (HTML)
3. Documents should be automatically generated from source objects in an Object Database Management System (ODBMS) repository
4. Documents should be content-rich (i.e. they should accommodate the acts of navigation, searching and browsing) to enhance the understanding and reduce the complexity of the data in the repository
5. The application should have an appealing, intuitive user interface.

By fulfilling these requirements, we hope to provide a better environment for companies employing a Concurrent Engineering strategy.

2.1 Client-Server Development over the WWW

Traditional WWW-based applications operate in a client-server fashion. A client (also known as the browser software) will request information from a server machine using HyperText Transfer Protocol (HTTP). The server will then deliver a specific document to that client (see Figure 1).

In more detail, the process is as follows:

1. The client software requests a specific item of information (the *document*).

2. The server then processes the request and either delivers the document or executes a Common Gateway Interface (CGI) compliant script program that will generate the document. In this way, CGI scripts can be used to provide pseudo-dynamic documents on-the-fly. These documents are pseudo-dynamic because even though they are created dynamically their content is strictly of a static nature i.e. the document does not have the ability to change its own content as time progresses[1].

3. Documents are delivered in either one of a number of predefined Multipurpose Internet Mail Extension (MIME) types (Borenstein and Freed 1993) or some *undefined* type. If the browser software is capable of displaying the document MIME type (e.g. it is HTML or ASCII format) it will do so. Otherwise it may be able to launch an auxiliary application to view the document[2].

The link between the server and the user is terminated when the document has been delivered. This means that a user cannot modify a document and return the modified document to the server for other users to view.

In this type of WWW-based application, CGI server scripts need to optimised so that they run either as fast as possible or use as few resources as possible depending on whether priority should be given to the user or the server load. If the server machine is also serving other requests such as mail and printing, it may be more desirable to have the server scripts use as few system resources as possible therefore reducing the response times to user requests.

As a result of this, it has become apparent that there is a need for more control and processing responsibility to be on the client side thus reducing the load on the server.

---

[1] This shortcoming has been addressed by Netscape Communications Corporation who have implemented a non-standard way of making HTML documents automatically refresh their contents (i.e. request that the server re-send the document) by using a meta-command such as <META HTTP-EQUIV="Refresh" CONTENT=5>. When used in conjunction with a CGI script, this technique can deliver documents with changing content.

[2] This is dependent on the browser software and each user's local configuration of that browser — two separate users can safely and legally use different applications to view a given document type.

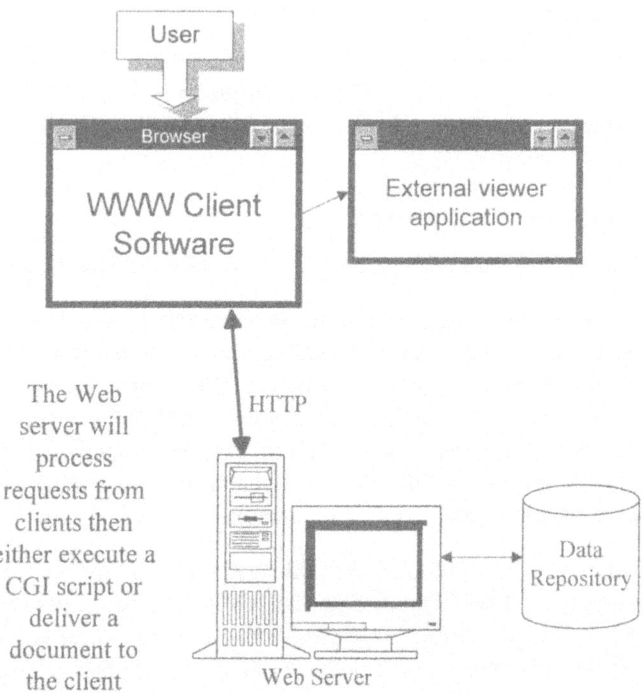

Figure 1. Client-server applications using the World-Wide Web

Clients typically use powerful machines anyway, so we can harness that power to improve productivity and increase resource utilisation.

The WWW therefore provides us with support for distribution in its present form but has no in-built support for co-operative working or the submitting of documents from the client to the server. It is therefore unsuitable for developing interactive and dynamic environments without first extending the means by which clients interact with the server. This is a recognised problem and a number of solutions have been proposed to address this.

2.2 Alternative Methods for Applications on the WWW

A number of new technologies have recently emerged to enable WWW clients to accept processing responsibility and provide interactive WWW-based applications. These technologies typically achieve this by extending standard HTML with new tags. If an existing (or new) WWW browser does not understand the new tag it will ignore it by default and hence the new tag will have no effect. This type of transparency is essential for open systems but it also means that WWW-based application developers who use these techniques have to ensure that the client software accessing their WWW-based system must be capable of supporting the new tag. Examples of these technologies include Java applets, Weblets, JavaScript and Hush Tcl / Tk.

- *Sun Microsystems Java™ applets*

Java (Sun Microsystems 1995) is a dynamic, object-oriented language and environment. At the time of writing, a number of WWW browser applications including Sun's HotJava and Netscape's Navigator provide support for Java applications via a non-standard extension to HTML: the `<APPLET>` tag. This allows small applications (or applets) to be delivered over the WWW to be executed on the client machine.

Java applets are sent to the client by the server at run-time ensuring that each user has the same revision of the software at all times thereby creating an environment that has truly pervasive applications (see Figure 2). This improves the level of standardisation and allows a quicker route for application developers to distribute new versions of software or new prototypes.

- *Eòlas Technologies Weblets™*

This technology uses a technique similar to Java applets which the developers call Weblets (Eòlas Technologies 1995). Weblets are self-contained applications like applets but can be run either entirely on the client machine (i.e. local

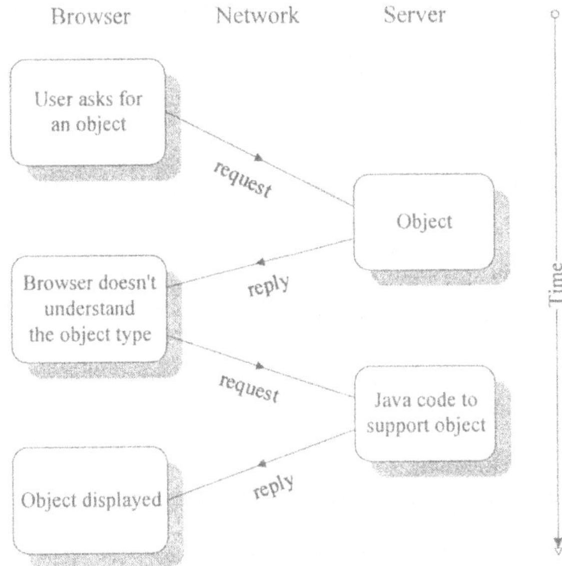

Figure 2. Java™ applet communication

processing) or on the server machine (remote processing) in client-server fashion. This technology utilises a non-standard <EMBED> HTML tag.

- *The JavaScript scripting language*

Netscape Communications Corp. in conjunction with Sun Microsystems has developed JavaScript to support the Netscape Navigator WWW browser (Netscape Communications Corporation 1996). This is an application programming interface (API) that allows scripting of events, objects and actions. It allows the WWW application developer to detect and act upon events such as start-ups, exits and user mouse clicks. The scripting language is based on Sun's Java language and can be used to glue HTML, special auxiliary plug-in applications and Java applets to each other. The syntax for this language extends HTML to include a new <SCRIPT LANGUAGE="JavaScript"> tag.

- *Hush Tcl / Tk*

In common with the other techniques described here, this system (van Doorn and Eliëns 1995) defines a new <HUSH> HTML tag which allows the application developer to embed Tcl / Tk program code (Ousterhout 1994) into a WWW page. It provides the application developer with a simple WWW browser window in as little as four lines of Tcl code.

3. Communication in a CE Environment

We have already mentioned the need for support for communication and collaborative working within virtual teams but to fully describe the types of communication methods that are needed between team members in a CE environment we need to think in terms of life-cycle time scales. The time scale we are concerned with refers to the length of time that it takes to produce a finished product from its initial conception. The time taken will, to a large extent, dictate the level and speed of communication needed within the environment.

This can be clarified with some real life examples:

- In the production of a *daily newspaper* there is a very short life-cycle (typically less than 24 hours)
- In the production of *high street fashion clothing* there is a short life-cycle (typically measured in weeks — from *catwalk* to *shop*)
- In the development of *software* there is a medium to long life-cycle (typically in the region of months to years)
- In the development and production of a new *space shuttle* there is usually a long to very long life-cycle (typically many man-years).

In very short production life-cycles, there is an obvious need for immediate (i.e. synchronous) communication between team members. In longer production cycles, communication can be less immediate (i.e. asynchronous).

3.1 Computer-Mediated Communication Methods

Computer-mediated communication methods can be sub-divided into two classes: synchronous and asynchronous. Synchronous methods provide *immediate* feedback between two or more people. Examples include:

- Direct video link (videoconferencing)
- Direct voice link (audioconferencing)
- Telephony
- Direct text-based conferencing (terminal / teletype text link)

Note that these communications can be of a *one-to-one* or *one-to-many* nature.

Asynchronous methods provide *delayed* feedback between two or more people. Examples are:

- Electronic mail
- Bulletin boards (organisation wide)
- USENET News group (organisation wide or global)

Again, these communications are of a *one-to-one* or *one-to-many* nature.

The importance of computer-mediated communication should not be underestimated: results of recent studies have shown that electronic brainstorming is superior to traditional verbal brainstorming for large groups involved in exchanging ideas (Aiken et al. 1994).

4. The Concurrent Engineering Web Workbench

We have created a WWW interface to our concurrent engineering support architecture (the CONCERT environment highlighted earlier) which we have called the Concurrent Engineering Web Workbench (CEWW) (Hanneghan et al. 1995a). The CEWW uses NCSA's WWW server software running on a Sun Microsystems SparcStation 4 with Solaris 2.4. Storage within the environment is provided by the Postgres95 Object-Relational Database Management System (Yu and Chen 1995). We use the Java language to implement special applications within the environment and these will be discussed in this section. The environment therefore requires access to WWW browser software that supports Java applets.

4.1 Facilities Available in the Environment

This section describes the types of WWW-based application that are currently available within the CEWW. Java applets are very dynamic in nature unlike the largely static format of HTML. In practice this means that we can use Java to produce applications that are capable of responding to requests and actions in real time, thus giving the user immediate feedback using dynamic data.

The facilities that are currently available or targeted for implementation include:

- group decision support
- user-definable bulletin-board systems (information notice boards)
- user tracking (information-rich equivalents of the UNIX `finger` and `who` commands)
- multi-user synchronous text conferencing
- one-to-one user text communication
- electronic mail

These activities fall mainly into the area of CSCW tools. In addition to this we have support for WWW-based document editing. This allows a user to download a document and edit the contents on their local workstation. They then have the ability to re-submit the document to the server machine for subsequent re-editing[3] by themselves or other users.

4.1.1 Group Decision Support

In concurrent engineering teams group consensus is often used to solve problems. A facility is available the CEWW for team members to express a problem as a statement and have other team members electronically vote (i.e. agree, disagree or abstain) on the statement. The system can automatically collate results and display the outcome in the form of a graph. This information is retained within the repository for the life-time of the project.

4.1.2 Project-wide Publishing via Bulletin boards

The CEWW has facilities for team members to post information to a project bulletin board. Team members are notified of any new messages on the bulletin board when they login to a project. Information in the bulletin board has a finite lifetime and will

---

[3] To accommodate multiple users, we enforce a version control system on documents so that the user is always editing a new version of an existing document. When editing is complete, the new version is checked into the object repository and its availability is publicised to all users.

expire after a given date[4]. It can therefore be used to provide notification of forthcoming events and other temporal information.

4.1.3 Identifying Users on the WWW

It is possible using a suitable WWW server to force users to authenticate themselves using a username and password combination before delivering a requested document. This provides the server with the following details (amongst others):

- the designated username of the user (this is not the person's login username for the system from which they are accessing the WWW page but an agreed and known username used solely for accessing the WWW service.)
- the name and Internet Protocol (IP) address of the client machine which is attempting to access the WWW page, e.g. `ace.cms.livjm.ac.uk` and `150.204.51.2`. These two values can be used interchangeably since the machine name can be determined from the IP address using a Domain Name Service (Hunt 1993).
- the client software[5] (agent) that is attempting to access the WWW server.

When we force CONCERT users to login, we can retrieve the IP address and machine name, software agent name and their username and password. We also need to ascertain which project the user wishes to work on since the CONCERT environment supports multiple projects running concurrently so we request this information from the user by means of a drop-down list of all available projects. Using all these details, the database relation in Table 1 is populated.

Table 1. Database relation for login information

Username	*IP address*	*Login Date*	*Project title*	*Client software agent*
martin	150.204.51.2	31/3/96	Computer	BrowserX

[4] The information is not deleted from the repository. It will simply not be shown when the user requests a list of current notices. Notices can easily be made visible for long periods by setting a long expiry date for the message.

[5] It is important to know what this is because there are applications within the environment which run as Java applets and therefore require the client software to be a Java-capable browser. If the client software accessing the CEWW system is not Java-capable then we need to take some other appropriate action (at present we inform the user that they should upgrade their browser software before continuing and provide a list of prescribed browsers which are suitable for use.)

This information is logged in the database for the entire session, i.e. until the user logs out of the workbench.

4.1.4 User tracking

One of the aims of the CONCERT environment is to increase awareness and improve the level of knowledge about other users in the environment. Finding out where a particular user is at any given time is extremely important in a multi-user collaborative environment. Each user accesses the system from a unique terminal. Each terminal has characteristics such as:

- the building / city / country that the terminal is situated in
- the organisation or company which owns the hardware
- the number of the nearest telephone to the terminal

The CONCERT system collects details of all the terminals that access the system in order to populate a database of this information. When a user logs in to the system from a terminal that the system doesn't know about, the CONCERT system will interrogate the user to determine information about the terminal from which they are accessing the system.

Within the system database is a relation holding the personal details of all team members including such information as name, job title and organisation, office address, electronic mail name, telephone and fax numbers and a graphic image. There is also a record of which project and task a given team member is currently working on. In addition to this we determine information about the terminals connecting to the system can therefore locate a particular team member logged onto the system. This information is available to all team members and, of course, the project leader in order to track, co-ordinate and exercise control amongst the team.

4.1.5 Multi-User Synchronous Text Conferencing

This applet allows multiple users to broadcast text messages among a group of their co-workers. The following points summarise its functionality:

1. The applet starts up a separate conference application window (in addition to the normal browser window, to allow participants to access other data during the conference). This conference application then repeatedly interrogates the repository looking for new messages and displays them in the window.
2. Each conference has a unique title since there may be multiple conferences taking place at any one time.
3. Users specify which conference they wish to contribute to before submitting any messages. When a person joins a conference, details of *who* and *when*

are logged for future reference e.g. "*John Doe* has joined the conference *at 10:21am.*"

4. Any person can initiate a new conference but only the person who started a conference has the ability to terminate it, i.e. a given user will own the conference. When a conference is started, a message is broadcast to all users of the environment informing them that the conference is about to begin. The date and time that the conference began is logged for future reference.

5. The applet allows users to view a log of all messages sent by all users in the form of a scrollable text window.

6. Any messages submitted to a conference automatically includes the name of the sender and the data and time of the message.

7. Every message submitted is stored in a temporary file space on the server until the conference has concluded. All the messages are then collated together, formatted and logged into the repository as the minutes for the on-line meeting. This can then be retrieved by users within the environment at any time for consulting.

4.1.6 One-to-one User Communication

This is a similar applet to the one described above except that communication is between two team members only and the messages that are sent are not logged within the repository. It allows private discussion to take place in a synchronous manner. In addition to this there is access to electronic mail to allow asynchronous communication with team members who may be temporarily unavailable.

4.2 Working on Objects

Objects (or items) within the repository can be anything that can be created during the entire life-cycle of the product. In the CONCERT environment, users need to submit new items and work on existing items already placed into the repository. Since the WWW does not provide us with a method of submitting objects from a client to a server, we have devised the following methods to accommodate this service.

Working with existing objects

The technique we use for allowing objects to be transferred from the server to the client and back to the server again is shown in Figure 3. The process is as follows:

- a team member requests an existing object
- the server checks out a copy (new version) of the object from the repository and places it into a known file space where the client can access it
- the client then retrieves the object into its local file space where the team member can edit it

- when the team member has finished editing the object it is transferred back to the server and checked back into the repository under version control

In Figure 3 we have shown the repository residing on the server machine. In practice, the repository may be distributed on another remote machine (as is the case in our implementation) but the same principal applies.

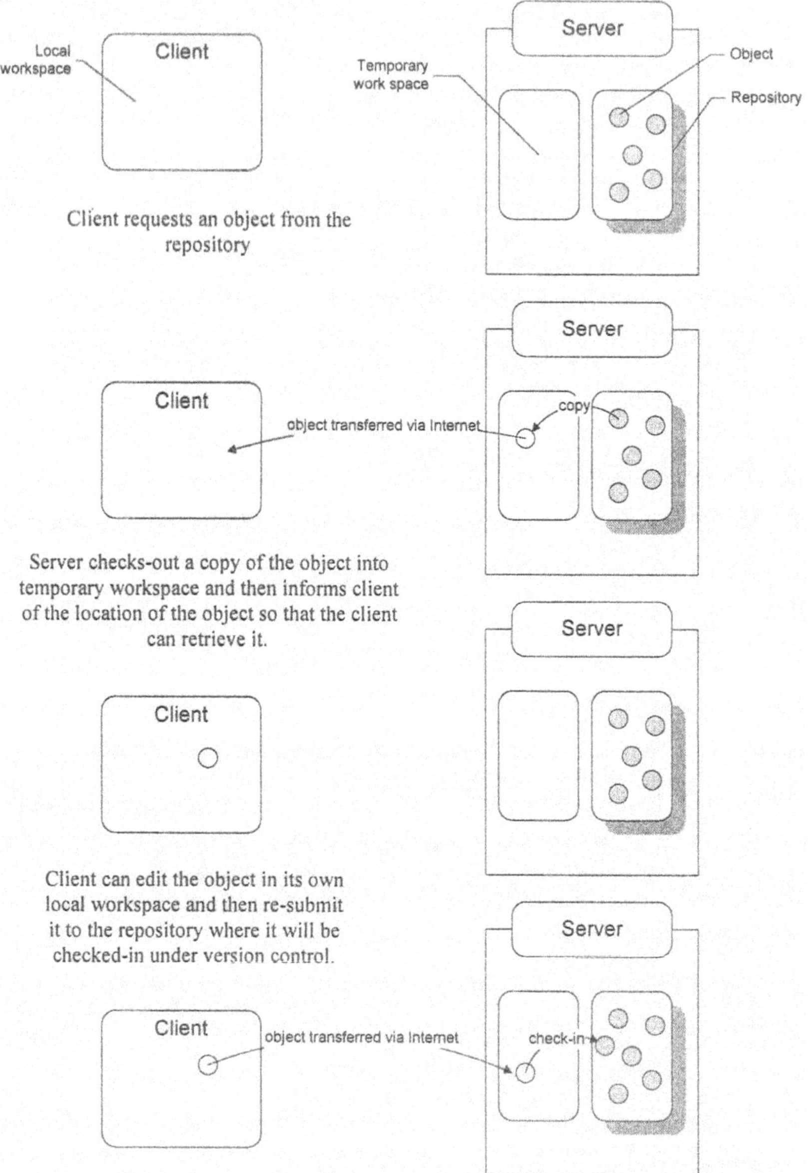

Figure 3. Working on existing objects within the repository

There is much debate over the security aspects of WWW-based transactions at present. Encryption and firewalling offer two approaches to security. In the highly competitive design and manufacturing world, organisations do not want their new designs being stolen by their competitors before they are released and so encrypting the data that is sent via the Internet is considered as a prerequisite for any environment. Firewalling sensitive data (i.e. the repository) is another technique that can be used to exclude access from outside organisations or only allow specific network sites to access the system. Since the CEWW controls how data is transferred between the user and the environment, it is relatively easy for us to incorporate a level of security into the data transfer process.

Creating new objects

The creation of new objects uses a similar technique to that described above:

- a team member will create an object (either on their own local machine in private file space or on some remote machine) that they wish to store in the repository
- the team member notifies the system that the new object exists and transfers it to the server machine's temporary file space
- the server will then log the new object into the repository under version control and then publicise the fact to all team members working on the same project.

5. Conclusions

This paper has described a WWW-based application to support organisations employing a concurrent engineering strategy. The Concurrent Engineering Web Workbench provides facilities for enabling virtual teams composed of all the people associated with the design of a product to collaborate and share information using the World-Wide Web.

Although the Internet is set to be important in all areas of industry, it is not without its faults. The biggest concern at the moment is that of Internet security. The British Computer Society Security Committee has summarised some of the key security issues as the fact that there is no strong central control, service availability guarantees do not exist, delivery guarantees are not available and there is no native confidentiality (BCS Security Committee 1995). Delivery guarantees require some method of hand-shaking so that each party acknowledges receipt of information. The CSCW service within the CONCERT environment provides a mechanism for this protocol. Confidentiality is catered for by an separate two-stage encoding-decoding process. Any data that is submitted to the central repository first has an encoding process applied and is transferred over the Internet in encrypted form. The CEWW server then decodes and verifies the data upon arrival. If the Concurrent Engineering Web Workbench is applied to an *Intranet* or private internal network then the issue of central control can also be addressed.

Another problem we have found is with authentication. WWW servers currently authenticate users based on a username and password combination and a unique IP address. This brings with it the requirement that users should not leave their terminals unattended once they have logged in since the only way of validating a user is by determining their machine address. Once a valid link has been established, the terminal is open to abuse or misuse from third parties. One way to overcome this would be to periodically force users to re-authenticate themselves although this may prove to be a distraction to most users.

In this paper we have described our use of the Java language for delivering applications over the Internet. Since this is a relatively new language it is therefore subject to change and revision. The success of Java as a standard Internet programming language is not guaranteed and as we described, there are other languages available that are poised to take its place if it fails.

We believe that the Internet provides a medium on which to build portable, client-server applications on a global scale. By allowing controlled access from clients, who may be on opposite sides of the globe, we hope that an improved level of co-operation can be achieved. Engineering information is typically locked into the organisation's Local Area Network and is forced to undergo conversions and translations whenever data is needed outside the organisation for example by external consultants. By allowing the consultants to become clients to the CEWW, the data can be accessed remotely with relative ease.

6. Future Work

The CEWW is an ongoing research project and the authors would welcome any comments about the system or requests for additional features within the environment. In particular, there are a number of areas which we would like to address in the near future.

We intend to conduct performance tests to evaluate the rate at which team members can retrieve objects from the repository. This is a function of the repository management service, the network traffic and the server / client load. We will also look into replicating the repository on a number of network sites to improve access times to items within the database. This will mean incorporating complex replication controls to ensure that data is consistent between users.

The CSCW tools available in the environment are only a small section of the range of CSCW tools currently available elsewhere. In particular we believe that screen sharing tools and non-destructive collaborative authoring tools would be beneficial to a virtual design team. We would also like in the future to be able to introduce a facility to enable videoconferencing between team members using the environment. Developments in the field of WWW-based video transfer, such as the work undertaken as part of the *VideoMosaic* project (Campbell et al. 1995) and the wider availability of broadband networks could provide progress in this area.

Other areas of interest that could be incorporated into this research in the future includes the use of VRML (Virtual Reality Modelling Language). VRML (Bell et al. 1995) is a language designed to enable 3-dimensional worlds to be composed and displayed on-screen. Users can fly-through and navigate around these virtual worlds and point and click on hyperlinked objects. In its most basic form, this technology could be utilised by members of a design team to visualise and interactively review CAD data models. A more dynamic use would be the visualisation and navigation of complex data structures such as the data stored in the concurrent engineering repository that is described in this research. With the ever increasing processing power available to end-users nowadays, VRML is poised to become the standard way of navigating though objects on the Internet. However, the widespread adoption of VRML amongst the CAD community seems unlikely until there is a greater availability of CAD data model to VRML translation tools.

7. References

Some of the works referenced in this paper can be found on the World-Wide Web. Where this is the case, the Uniform Resource Locator (URL) for the document is given in the form: *http://website/document.*

Aiken, M., Krosp, J., Shirani, A., and Martin, J. (1994). "Electronic Brainstorming in Small and Large Groups." *Information & Management*, 27(3), 141-149.

BCS Security Committee. (1995). "Internet Security." *The BCS Computer Bulletin*, 7(6), 16-17.

Bell, G., Parisi, A., and Pesce, M. (1995). "The Virtual Reality Modeling Language: Version 1.0 Specification." , http://vrml.wired.com/vrml.tech/vrml10-3.html.

Borenstein, N., and Freed, N. (1993). "MIME (Multipurpose Internet Mail Extensions) Part One: Mechanisms for Specifying and Describing the Format of Internet Message Bodies." , http://www.oac.uci.edu/indiv/ehood/MIME/1521/rfc1521ToC.html.

Campbell, R. H., Tan, S., Chen, Z., Li, Y., and Xie, D. (1995). "VOSAIC: Continuous Media Browser." , http://choices.cs.uiuc.edu/Vosaic/Vosaic.html.

Coupland, J. W. (1992). *Concurrent Engineering: An Information Pack*, IEE Technical Information Unit, London.

Dowlatshahi, S. (1994). "A Comparison Of Approaches to Concurrent Engineering." *International Journal Of Advanced Manufacturing Technology*, 9(2), 106-113.

Ellsworth, J. H., and Ellsworth, M. V. (1994). *The Internet Business Book*, John Wiley & Sons, New York.

Eòlas Technologies. (1995). "Eòlas Technologies Home Page." , http://www.eolas.com/.

Hanneghan, M., Colquhoun, G., and Merabti, M. (1995a). "The Concurrent Engineering Web Workbench." , http://ace.cms.livjm.ac.uk:1995/.

Hanneghan, M., Merabti, M., and Colquhoun, G. (1995b). "The Design Of An Object-Oriented Repository To Support Concurrent Engineering." OOIS'95 - Proceedings of the 1995 International Conference on Object-Oriented Information Systems, J. Murphy and B. Stone, eds., Springer-Verlag, London, 200-215.

Hunt, C. (1993). *TCP/IP Network Administration*, O'Reilly & Associates, Sebastopol, CA.

Netscape Communications Corporation. (1996). "JavaScript Authoring Guide." , http://home.netscape.com/eng/mozilla/Gold/handbook/javascript/index.html.

Nickerson, D. P. "Introduction to Concurrent Engineering in Design." *Electro/90 Conference*, 174-179.

Ousterhout, J. K. (1994). *Tcl and the Tk Toolkit*, Addison Wesley Publishing Company.

Sheldon, D. F., and Perks, R. (1990). "Designing for Whole Life Cycle Costs." *Journal of Engineering Design*, 1(2).

Siemieniuch, C. E., and Sinclair, M. A. (1994). "Concurrent Engineering and CSCW: The Human Factor." Computer Support for Co-operative Work, K. Spurr, P. Layzell, L. Jennison, and N. Richards, eds., John Wiley and Sons Ltd, Chichester, 111-125.

Sun Microsystems. (1995). "Java (TM) - Programming for the Internet." , http://java.sun.com/.

Trapp, G., Lawson, M., and Burkett, B. "Workshop on Concurrent Engineering." *CAD and Engineering Workstations '92 and Business Graphics '92 Conference and Exposition*, 766-792.

van Doorn, M., and Eliëns, A. (1995). "Integrating Applications and the World-Wide Web." *Computer Networks and ISDN Systems*, 27(6), 1105-1110.

Winner, K. E., Pennell, J. P., Bertrand, H. E., and Slusarzuk, M. M. G. (1988). "The Role of Concurrent Engineering in Weapons System Acquisition." *R-338*, Institute for Defense Analysis, Alexandria, Virginia.

Yu, A., and Chen, J. (1995). "The POSTGRES95 User Manual Version 1.0." , Computer Science Division, Dept. of EECS, University of California at Berkeley.

Context-Driven Information Base Update

Panos Constantopoulos and Yannis Tzitzikas

Department of Computer Science, University of Crete
and
Institute of Computer Science,
Foundation for Research and Technology - Hellas
email : {*panos* | *tzitzik*}@*ics.forth.gr*

Abstract. A major issue in information management is information update. In this paper we address this problem within the framework of a fairly general information model incorporating notions of context as a way to control and drive the update operations. We introduce three kinds of contexts: role,task and focus context. *Role context* relates users with update tasks, *task context* restricts the scope of updates and *focus context* is used to guide the user at run-time. In particular, we focus on issues regarding the expressive power of contexts, the consistency of context declarations with the contents of the information base, flexibility and brevity of context declaration and management and utilization of contexts. An implementation is proposed as part of a specific system, the Semantic Index System.

1 Introduction

It might be common place to claim that building and managing very large information bases is an activity of ever growing importance. By *information bases* we refer collectively to the various kinds of databases (relational, object-oriented, deductive, etc.), knowledge bases, hypermedia bases, etc. There seems to be a clear need emerging for heterogeneous information bases, obtained from disparate sources, to be managed in an integrated way and to be accessed by a range of applications and tools. Another clear trend appears to be the management of metadata. This has been particularly established for information bases on engineered artifacts, in which case *repository systems* have been proposed as a framework for metadata management [5]. However, metadata management is essentially a ubiquitous problem : legal databases, historical documentation, medical databases, educational and research information bases are but a few examples where metadata can be used to advantage besides engineering databases.

Two necessary ingredients of a general approach to information base management are [5, 21]: (i) a common information model and (ii) contexts, as meaningful decompositions of information. In this paper we address the problem of updating an information base. This is done within the framework of a fairly general information model, enabling uniform treatment of data and metadata and using notions of *context* to control and drive the update operations.

The information base management system must at least support a set of *primitive update operations* and an *update process*. The latter involves update transactions which are sequences of primitive operations. These sequences can be (i) predetermined, automatically executable or requiring some user input, or (ii) they may be dynamically generated. Dynamic update sequences are mostly the case in creative and judgemental applications, e.g. CAD. It is this class of applications that also call for metadata update and evolution, which we are primarily concerned with.

We introduce three kinds of *context* for driving the update process : *role* context, *task* context and *focus* context. Users assume roles, to which update tasks are assigned. The role context relates a user with his/her roles and the corresponding tasks. The task context restricts the scope of the updates to a subset of the information base, defined according to various criteria (filtering, authorization). The focus context finally guides the user to execute the primitive update operations needed by the current task.

A metamodeling approach is taken for defining the update contexts. This yields significant benefits in terms of maintaining context consistency with the information base contents. Positive and negative declarations (exceptions) are supported, as well as configurable composite declaration types and reuse of declarations, thus offering flexibility and efficiency.

Section 2 reviews the framework used for information representation and management. Section 3 introduces the primitive update operations. Section 4 discusses the issues of information update which motivate our work. Section 5 presents the update contexts and their use. Section 6 discusses implementation aspects. Section 7 reviews related work, while section 8 draws some conclusions.

2 Information Representation and Management

The information representation framework we adopt is the language Telos [20], an object-oriented knowledge representation language that supports a number of structuring mechanisms as well as an assertional and temporal reasoning sublanguage. In particular we confine ourselves to a version of the structural part of the Telos language, which we have implemented into a system for the management of very large collections of highly interrelated information objects with evolving structures, called the Semantic Index System (hereafter SIS) [10, 9]. This system is especially well suited for use as a repository system, providing metadata management and the kernel of an integrated environment of a dynamic collection of tools [5].

2.1 The SIS Data Model

The SIS data model complies with the structural part of the Telos language, which offers mechanisms analogous to those supported by semantic networks and semantic data models.

An information base consists of structured objects built from two kinds of primitive units: individuals (I) and attributes (A) . Individuals represent entities while attributes represent binary relationships from individuals or attributes to individuals. Individuals and attributes can be concrete or abstract, and they are commonly referred to as objects (O). They have unique system (internal) identifiers and they can be named.

Objects are organized along three dimensions : attribution, classification and generalization [2, 7, 16, 20]. A distinctive feature of Telos and, consequently, of the SIS data model, is the uniform treatment of individuals and attributes. This allows attributes to be organized in classification and generalization hierarchies and to have attributes of their own, which provides great expressive power and flexibility.

Multiple classification is allowed, supporting the separate representation of multiple modeling aspects. An open-ended classification hierarchy is possible. Atomic objects, that is, objects which cannot have instances are called tokens. These are instances of classes which are instances of meta-classes and so on. Every object must be declared as an instance of one system class. System classes (O_{sys}) are special classes which partition the information base according to two criteria: (i) instantiation level and (ii) object type (individual,attribute).

Classes within a given instantiation level are also organized in terms of generalization (or isA) relationships. These can be multiple and give rise to hierarchies that are directed acyclic graphs. They induce strict inheritance of attributes, in the sense that inherited attributes cannot be overridden but only restricted by the definition of the subclass.

Figure 1 gives a graphical example of a SIS-Telos information base.

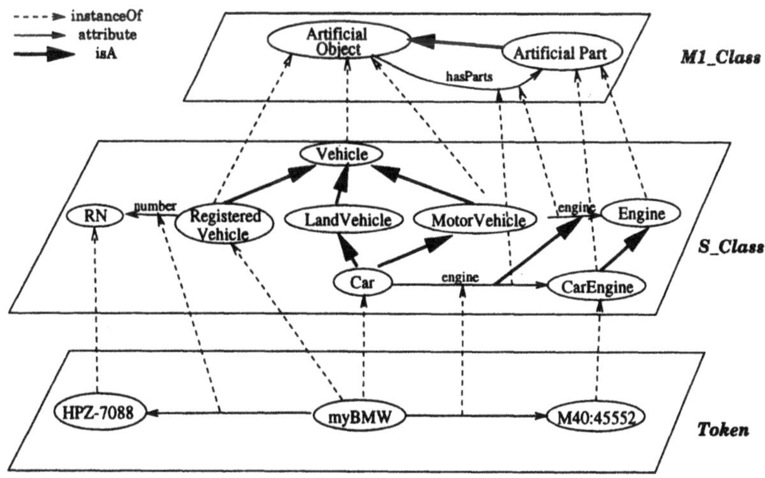

Fig. 1. A SIS-Telos information base

2.2 The Semantic Index System

The Semantic Index System (SIS) is a tool for describing and documenting large evolving varieties of highly interrelated data, concepts and complex relationships, as opposed to large homogeneous populations in fixed formats (handled by traditional DBMS). As such, it is suited for the representation of scientific knowledge and engineering designs or constructs. These kinds of data are also characterized by relative stability, i.e. they undergo fewer updates than, say, administrative, financial or observational data, which give rise to continuously changing sets of uniform items.

The SIS persistent storage mechanism is based on the SIS-Telos data model described in section 2.1 and supports transactions and concurrency control.

The user interface supports menu-guided and form-based query formulation with graphical and textual presentation of the answer sets. It also supports graphical browsing and navigation in a hypertext-like manner. A hypertext annotation mechanism is also provided. Menu titles, menu layout and domain-specific queries are user-configurable. Thus, the user interface can be customized to the application without changing the executable code.

A form-based interactive data entry facility is provided. It allows for entering data and schema information in a uniform manner. By employing the schema information, it automatically adapts itself to the structure of the various classes and subclasses. Furthermore, it is customizable to application-specific tasks, such as classification of items, addition of descriptive elements, etc.

An API for communication with other tools is provided.

So far, SIS has been used as the kernel for various applications, such as the Software Static Analysis and Class Management System [9], the CLIO Cultural Documentation System [8], and prototype systems for hypermedia presentations [11], thesaurous management and mechanical fault documentation and diagnosis.

3 Primitive Update Operations

Each field of the SIS storage structures is subject to one or more *generic update actions* (add, delete, change, create, destroy). For each field and its related generic update action(s), we assign an identifier. These identifiers constitute the set of *elementary action identifiers*, EA, and are listed in table 1 together with their meaning.

We call *primitive update operations* (PUO) the finest update operations that leave the base consistent (according to our data model). These are listed in table 2, while examples of their use are drawn in figure 2.

Each primitive update operation causes one or more elementary update actions on the objects it takes as arguments. This mapping is shown in table 3. If U is the set of all primitive update operations of a base, table 3 essentially defines the function $ea : U \to 2^{O \times EA}$ which, for each $u \in U$, returns the pairs (object, elementary action identifier) of the corresponding elementary actions.

EA	Storage Field	Meaning
REN	Name	object renaming
DEL	Internal ID	object deletion
AddAF	AttrsFrom	addition of an attribute
DelAF	AttrsFrom	deletion of an attribute
AddAT	AttrsTo	addition of an attribute reference
DelAT	AttrsTo	deletion of an attribute reference
AddIn	Instances	addition of an instantiation link
DelIn,	Instances	deletion of an instantiation link
AddClass	Classes	addition of a classification link
DelClass	Classes	deletion of a classification link
AddSub	Subclasses	addition of a generalization link
DelSub	Subclasses	deletion of a generalization link
AddSup	Superclasses	addition of a specialization link
DelSup	Superclasses	deletion of a specialization link
CrObj	systemclass.insts	creation of a new object
DelObj	systemclass.insts	deletion of an object

Table 1. The set of elementary action identifiers

4 Issues of Information Update

Information bases for creative and judgemental applications present in particular the following requirements of the update operations : (i) *schema evolution* at run-time in order to capture new designs, concepts, aspects or changes thereof ; (ii) *update control* as a way to secure data and facilitate interactive updates (filtering), taking account of the application domain, user and task ; (iii) *update process driving*, for user guidance ; (iv) *combination of browsing and update* at run-time. Thus, it should be possible to answer efficiently questions of the form: "does this primitive operation belong to an update task of the current user ?" (update control), or "which primitive update operations are related to the current object, current user and current task?" (guidance).

Schema evolution at run-time is supported directly by the SIS data model and system. Therefore we focus on issues concerning update control and update process driving. Update control capabilities depend mainly on the way that constraints are represented. Below we discuss some existing approaches and present our proposal through an example.

Consider a base with the schema shown in figure 3 and assume that **Manos** is the database administrator and **Charoula** is an ordinary user. We want to allow **Charoula** to update all the instances of the base, except for the attributes of class **born** . We will refer to this part of the base as **Charoula** 's context.

(I) One approach is to define a virtual class by a query [14, 4] and attach it to a real class. The definition could be :

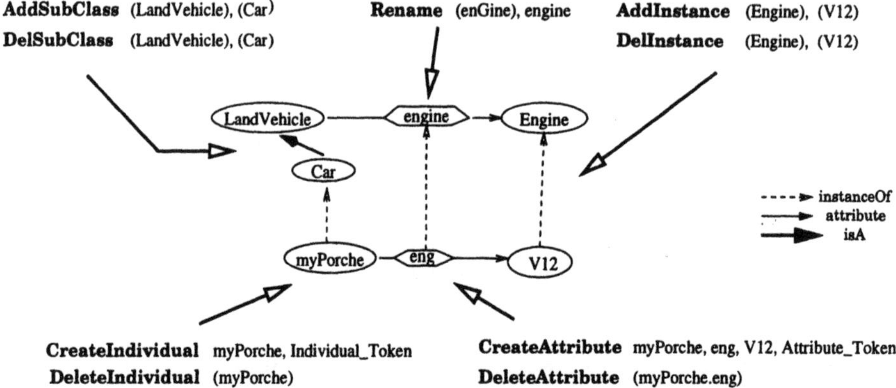

Fig. 2. Examples of primitive update operations

A parenthesized logical name stands for the internal identifier of the object with that logical name.

Prim. Update Op.	Arguments	Description
CreateIndividual	SysClass,name	Creates an individual object
CreateAttribute	from, name, to, SysClass	Creates an attribute object
DeleteIndividual	o	Deletes an individual object
DeleteAttribute	a	Deletes an attribute object
Rename	o,*name'*	Renames object o as *name'*
AddInstance	a,b	Makes b an instance of a
AddSubClass	a,b	Makes b a subclass of a
DeleteInstance	a,b	Deletes b from the instances of a
DeleteSubClass	a,b	Deletes b from the subclasses of a

Table 2. The primitive update operations

SysClass represents a system class identifier, *name* a logical name, *o, from* are object identifiers, *to* is either an object identifier or a primitive value (int,float,char*) and *a, b* are object identifiers which are both either individuals or attributes.

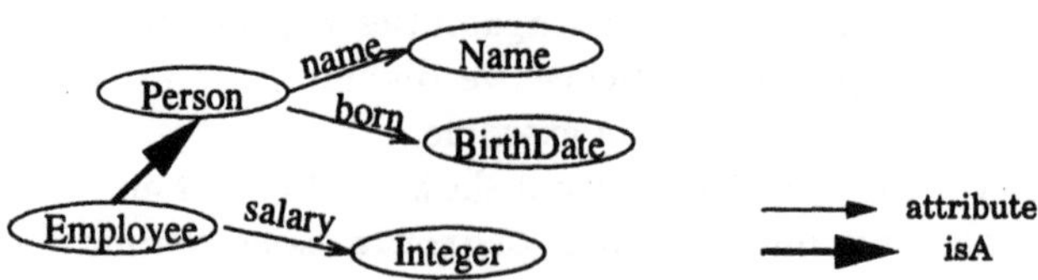

Fig. 3. Example schema

Primitive Update Operation	Elementary Actions
CreateIndividual n, S	$(S, CrObj)$
CreateAttribute *from* , *to* , n, S	(*from* , $AddAF$), (to , $AddAT$), $(S, CrObj)$
DeleteIndividual o	$(o, DEL), (sys(o), DelObj)$
DeleteAttribute a	$(a, DEL), (from(a), DelAF),$ $(to(a), DelAT), (sys(a), DelObj)$
Rename o , *newname*	(o, REN)
AddInstance a , b	$(a, AddIn), (b, AddClass)$
DeleteInstance a , b	$(a, DelIn), (b, DelClass)$
AddSubClass a , b	$(a, AddSub), (b, AddSup)$
DeleteSubClass a , b	$(a, DelSub), (b, DelSup)$

Table 3. Analysis of primitive update operations to elementary actions

The function $sys(o)$ returns the system class of object o, while the functions $from(a)$ and $to(a)$ return the starting and the ending point of an attribute a respectively.

DEFINE VIEW `EmployeeSecr` **AS**
SELECT [`Person.name, Employee.salary`]
FROM `Employee` [1]

Only the definition, i.e. the query string, is stored by the DBMS. This approach introduces some problems : If `Manos` decides to delete or rename the attribute `salary` as `Salary` , then `EmployeeSecr` loses its integrity, hence it needs redeclaration. Moreover, `Manos` does not get any warning about this. Additionally, a virtual class cannot be used for the definition of other virtual classes and in order to reference a virtual class through an attribute, we have to define a virtual class of the referencing type, too . In general, the management of virtual classes is neither flexible, nor uniform with the management of real classes.

Continuing with the example, in order to prevent `Charoula` from updating a specific person, say `Anna` , we have to redeclare `EmployeeSecr` as follows :

DEFINE VIEW `EmployeeSecr` **AS**
SELECT [`Person.name, Employee.salary`]
FROM `Employee`
WHERE [`Person.name` <>"`Anna`"]

Finally this approach requires `Manos` to learn and use a query language.

(II) A second approach is to define a view class by a query, which is now embodied in the schema of the base as an ordinary class [23, 1, 19]. This results in schema reorganization. For example, the following declaration will make the schema look as in figure 4.

[1] Virtual classes of only one class are supported.

```
DEFINE VIEW EmployeeSecr AS
SELECT [ Person.name, Employee.salary ]
FROM Employee
```

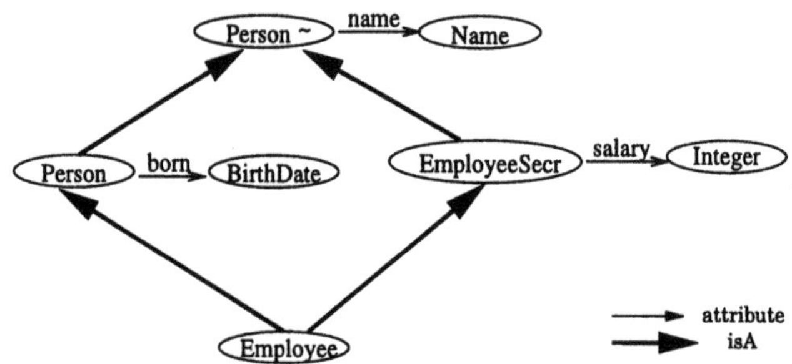

Fig. 4. View EmployeeSecr is embodied in the schema as a class

In particular, the projection of a class is represented as a superclass of that class containing only the attributes to be projected. Now, **Manos** can rename/delete attributes without causing any problem to **Charoula** 's context. Unfortunately, other problems appear : the schema is extended (fragmented) very much (imagine defining many different contexts) and no symmetrical operation is proposed for contracting the schema (UNDO is not supported). In addition naming problems appear : how to name the new automatically constructed classes (eg: Person˜)?. Moreover, **Manos** will be confused when trying to add a new person (which class to choose), or delete one (in which class to search).

Here, the protection of **Anna** from **Charoula** ‘s updates requires the definition of a new view class :

```
DEFINE VIEW EmployeeSecr2 AS
SELECT *
FROM EmployeeSecr ,
WHERE [ name<> "Anna" ]
```

resulting in the schema shown in figure 5. A new view class was created (`EmployeeSecr2`) which became subclass of the class `EmployeeSecr` . Although this is a simple case, if we want more than one selection views, the problem of predicate subsumption arises, which is undecidable in general.

(III) A third approach is to use an authorization control mechanism. In order to define the desired context, a number of grant/revoke commands must be executed. Usually such mechanisms store ownerships in the actual data. This, apart from large storage requirements, sometimes makes the context hard to define: eg. the population of **Employee** may be owned by many different users, therefore **Manos** will have to execute a number of granting commands.

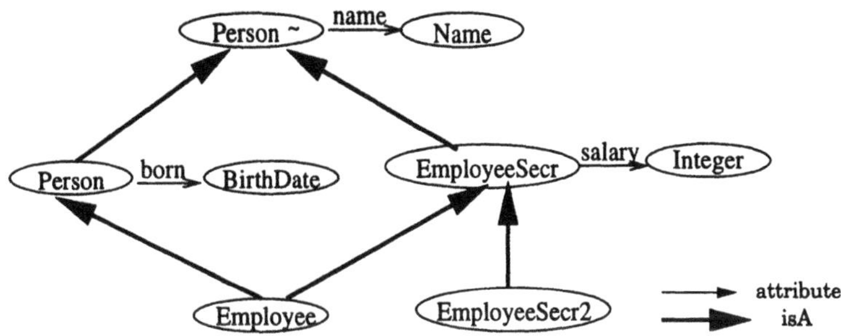

Fig. 5. View `EmployeeSecr2` further extends the schema

Furthermore, these mechanisms usually organize hierarchically operation types, authorization objects and users [22, 25, 28]. This is not what we need because we may want to define a context containing only a part of the schema but not the corresponding data (instances). This is desired in cases that we want to define a context to act as a filter and not as an authorization constraint. Since a user can be assigned to more than one role contexts or update tasks, we can assign him/her a context permitting updates on the corresponding data, too.

(IV) Here we propose a different approach : we use a metamodel to represent update contexts. Context definition requires a set of declarations (metadata) which are relationships between objects (belonging to the application domain) and metadata types. The metamodel, the corresponding metadata and the relationships between data and metadata (declarations) are represented in the information base itself. We support a set of metadata types which allow fine grain, dynamic and flexible context definitions and can be used in declarations concerning individuals, attributes, tokens or classes.

The key point is that declarations are represented as Telos attributes belonging to a special class of attributes, *contextDeclaration*, defined for this purpose [2]. This results in improved metadata management (e.g. efficient context utilization during browsing) and data-metadata consistency. Storing metadata (declarations) as data also results in implementation benefits (usage of the existing mechanisms to represent/store/query/visualize metadata) and ease of use (`Manos` is not required to learn a query language). Furthermore, update context definitions leave the information model unchanged.

Returning to our example, the declaration of `Charoula` 's context looks like figure 6. Declaration `a1` defines that `Charoula` can update instances of the specialization hierarchy, while declaration `a2` represents the constraint concerning `born` attributes and `a3` represents the constraint concerning `Anna` . Thus, `Charoula` 's context maintains its integrity when `Manos` renames any at-

[2] SIS allows the definition of attribute classes which can be used (instantiated) from any object of the base.

tribute class (including `born`). Besides, **Manos** cannot delete attribute `born` , because that would violate a structural constraint of Telos (he should delete link `a2` first). Furthermore, if we filter out the attributes belonging to the special attribute class for declarations, we will get the original information model.

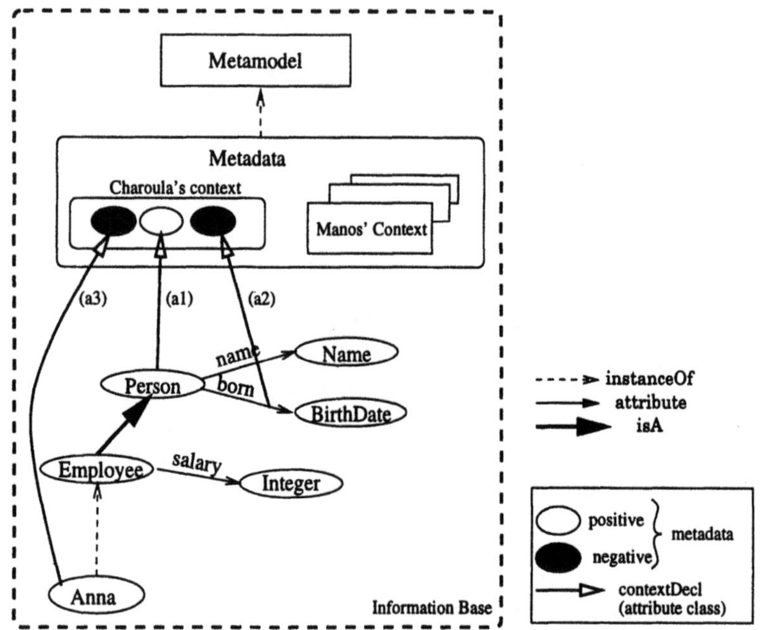

Fig. 6. Context-driven update

5 Update Contexts

The *role, task* and *focus* contexts are presented in detail in this section. The basic concepts underlying the update metamodel are shown in figure 7.

Users are classified in one or more groups. User groups are assigned Update Tasks (for short, Tasks) which are defined via Update Declarations (for short, Declarations) and are related to some Usage Info (user preferences, guidance comments and starting points).

5.1 Role Context

The users of the information base are represented in the information base itself as objects and are organized in groups. User groups correspond to *roles* and are related with update tasks. A user may belong to more than one group. We define as *role context* of a particular user, the set of roles that are assigned to

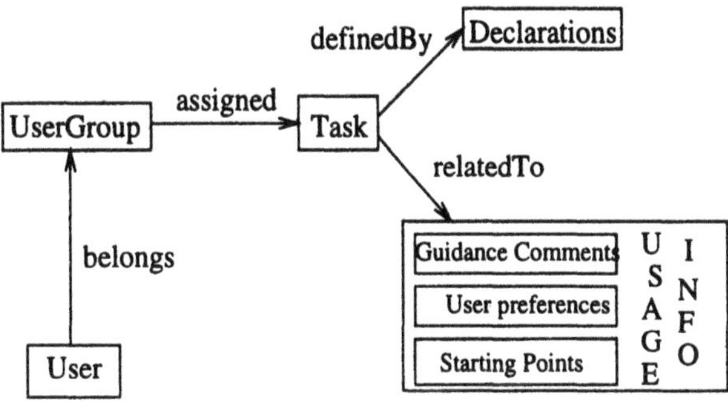

Fig. 7. Basic concepts underlying the update metamodel

that user. User groups are organized in a specialization hierarchy, so we may have "subgroups". A subgroup inherits all the tasks assigned to its supergroups. An example is shown in figure 8.

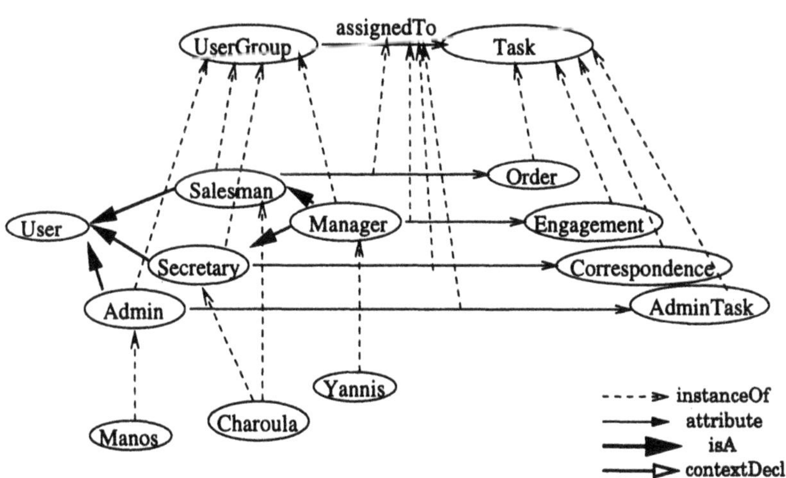

Fig. 8. User context example

These declarations permit Charoula, the secretary, to work also as a salesman (in the afternoon), and Yannis can also replace his secretary or salesmen (on weekends).

5.2 Task Context

Update tasks are special objects stored in the base itself. These objects constitute the class *Tasks.*

Definition.

Each task is defined as a set of primitive update operations. This definition permits fine grain tasks which update data and/or schema. To define tasks we have to specify (via declarations) a function *contents* which returns the primitive update operations of each task :

$$contents : Tasks \rightarrow 2^U$$

To define a task t, we assign (via declarations which are presented next) elementary update action identifiers (EA) to objects. Let $Pred(t)$ be such an assignment ($Pred(t) \subset O \times EA$). This is construed as permissions regarding the execution of the participating pairs of objects and elementary actions. Obviously, $Pred(t)$ implicitly defines primitive update operations, since (as explained in section 3) each primitive update operation causes the execution of one or more elementary actions. Therefore, a primitive update operation u , is included in a task t , if the corresponding elementary update action identifiers ($ea(u)$) are members of $Pred(t)$. Thus, we define :

$$contents(t) = \{u \in U \mid ea(u) \subseteq Pred(t)\} \tag{1}$$

The multitude of elementary action identifiers is a measure of the level of detail of the possible task definitions. We could have used only two identifiers : one for schema update and one for data update.

Declarations.

Tasks are defined through declarations. We call $Decl$ the set of all possible declarations in a base. Each set of declarations is interpreted (mapped) to a subset of $O \times EA$ which defines primitive update operations.

Let I be the interpretation function $I : 2^{Decl} \rightarrow 2^{O \times EA}$ and $decl$ the function that for each $t \in Tasks$ returns the related declarations $decls$: $Tasks \rightarrow 2^{Decl}$. Therefore we can rewrite equation 1 as :

$$contents(t) = \{u \in U \mid ea(u) \subseteq I(decls(t))\}$$

Decl consists of binary relationships between *objects* and *Declaration Types* (for short *Types*) :

$$Decl = \{(o, t) \mid o \in O, t \in Types\}$$

Types are 3-tuples, consisting of an EA, a *target identifier* and a *state identifier* :

$$Types = \{(id, targ, st) \mid id \in EA, targ \in Target, st \in State\}$$

State is the set {POS, NEG} and its members are used to distinguish positive (state=POS) from negative (state=NEG) types, hence positive from negative declarations. Using combinations of positive and negative declarations offers flexibility as illustrated in figure 9.

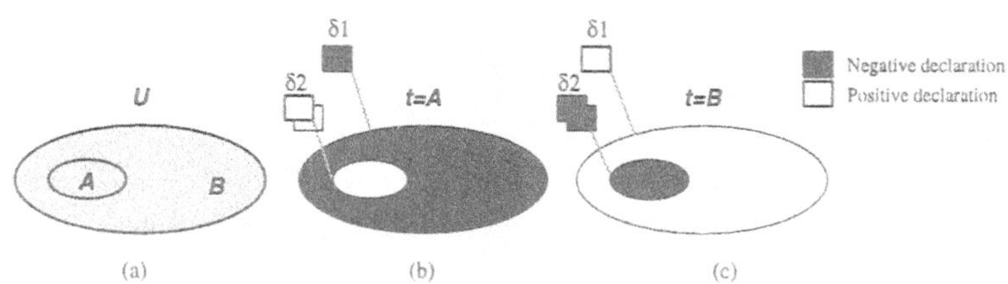

Fig. 9. Combining positive and negative declarations

The sets A and B constitute a partition of U (a). The definition of a task containing only operations on set A (b) requires a negative declaration δ1 concerning the whole set U and some positive declarations δ2 concerning set A (they are exceptions to the declaration δ1). The opposite case is shown in (c).

Target is the set $\{onObj, onAttr, onInst\}$ and its members are used in order to characterize the declarations with respect to the declaration object. *Declaration object* is the object in reference to which the declaration is made. A declaration with target *onObj* concerns the declaration object itself (see fig. 10(a)), with *onAttr* it concerns all the attributes of the declaration object including inherited ones (see fig. 10(b)), and with *onInsts* it concerns the instances of the declaration object (see fig. 10(c)).

Now, we present the *interpretation function,* $I : 2^{Decl} \rightarrow 2^{O \times EA}$, which determines the semantics of the declarations. Function I is the projection of a function I' which is a composition of other functions :

$$I' = I_{sys} \circ I_{sys_{onAttr}} \circ I_{onAttr} \circ I_{onInst} \circ I_{isa}$$

I_x are functions from 2^{Decl} to 2^{Decl}. If $A \subseteq Decl$ then

$$I'(A) = I_{sys}(I_{sys_{onAttr}}(I_{onAttr}(I_{onInst}(I_{isa}(A)))))$$

The composition order of functions I_x determines (implicitly) the prevalence among opposite declarations. For example, if $A \subseteq Decl$, then $I_x(A)$ does not contain any declaration opposite to a declaration belonging to A. Actually, these functions combine positive and negative declarations, introduce inheritance rules and interpret target identifiers, in order to define finally a subset of $O \times EA$.

The declaration of a task, t, must be complete. Completeness is expressed by the following axiom :

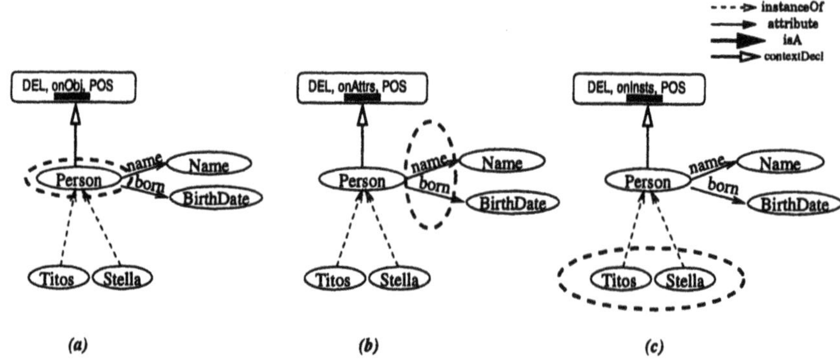

Fig. 10. Interpretation of *Target* identifiers

$$\forall o \in O,\ id \in EA\ \ \exists d \in I'(decls(t)) : d = (o, (id, onObj, st))\ ,\ st\ \in State$$

Practically this axiom is satisfied by making a declaration for each $id \in EA$ and assign it to the system class *Object*. As this will be explained while describing the function I_{sys}, such a declaration concerns all the objects of the base, thus makes a task declaration complete.

Function I is a projection of I' :

$$if\ \ A \subseteq Decl\ then\ I(A) = \{(o, id) \mid\ (o,\ (id, onObj, \mathrm{POS}))\ \in\ I'(A)\}$$

The description of functions I_x, follows :

• I_{isa}

If $A \subseteq Decl$, then $I_{isa}(A)$ includes besides A , declarations inherited through generalization (isA) relationships. The inheritance rules of Telos (and SIS) are modified in order to support negative, in addition to positive, information. The rules of $I_{isa}(A)$, illustrated in figure 11, are :

- A declaration is inherited to all subclasses (see nodes *h,i,j*).
- An explicit declaration is stronger than an inherited one (see nodes *a,c*).
- If an object inherits two opposite declarations (see *node j*), then the declaration of the more special class (*h* is a subclass of *g*) prevails. This rule is called *inferential distance ordering* [29, 24] and is used by systems which support positive and negative attributes.
- If an object inherits two opposite declarations and the previous rule does no apply (see node *e*), then the negative declaration prevails.

• I_{onInst}

Each declaration with target *onInst* is analyzed (at run-time) in a set of declarations with target *onObj* , which concern the instances of the declaration object. If $A \subseteq Decl$, then $I_{onInst}(A)$ contains the declarations of A with target $\neq$ *onInst*, plus declarations which are deduced from the declarations of A with target = *onInst* and are not already in A. In case of conflicts, for example an

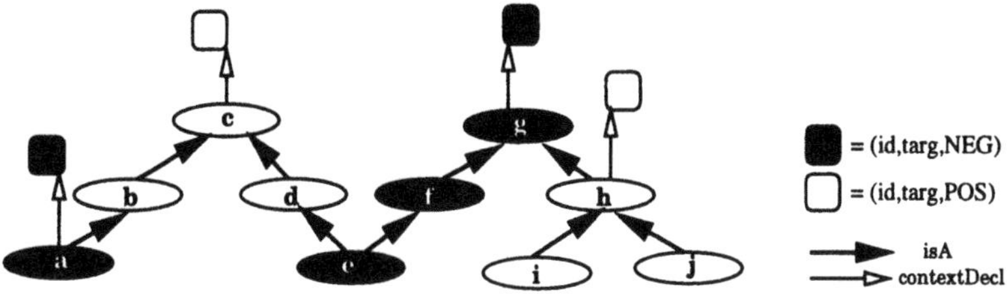

Fig. 11. Inheritance of declarations

Black and white rectangles indicate two declarations with the same *id, target* , but with opposite *states* (negative and positive, respectively). Classes have been colored according to the declaration they inherit.

object classified to two or more classes on which opposite declarations have been made, the negative one prevails.

- I_{onAttr}

Each declaration with target *onAttr* is analyzed in a set of declarations with target *onObj* , which concern the attributes (including inherited ones) of the declaration object. If $A \subseteq Decl$, then $I_{onAttr}(A)$ contains the declarations of A except those with declaration object $\in (O - O_{sys})$ and target $=$ *onAttr*, plus declarations which are deduced from the excepted declarations and are not already in A.

- $I_{sys_{onAttr}}$

Each declaration on a system class (O_{sys}) with target *onAttr* is analyzed in a set of declarations with target *onObj* which concern the attributes (including the inherited ones) of objects which belong to that system class. If $A \subseteq Decl$, then $I_{sys_{onAttr}}(A)$ contains the declarations of A except those on system classes with target $=$ *onAttr*, plus declarations which are deduced from the excepted declarations and are not already in A.

These declarations offer coarse grain specifications which facilitate the definition of tasks. For example, in order to forbid the deletion of any attribute of a metaclass (regardless of the instantiation level of the attribute) we only have to make the declaration $(Individual\_M1Class, (DEL, onAttr, NEG))$.

- I_{sys}

Each declaration on a system class (O_{sys}) is analyzed in a set of declarations concerning the objects which belong to that system class. If $A \subseteq Decl$, then $I_{sys}(A)$ contains the declarations of A plus the ones deduced from declarations in system classes in A , which are not already in A.

These are also coarse grain declarations which contribute to task definition brevity. For example, to define a task which permits changes (e.g. deletion) of tokens only, we simply have to make two declarations :
$(Object, (DEL, onObj, NEG))$ and $(Token, (DEL, onObj, POS))$. The second declaration is an exception (concerning the Token level) of the first (which con-

cerns all the objects of the base) [3].

Some indicative examples of the declarations usage are presented in figures 12, 13 and 14.

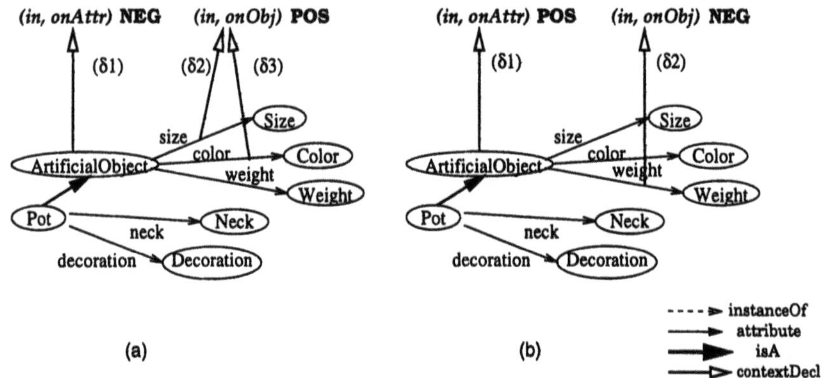

Fig. 12. Declaring class projections

Identifier *in* stands for the identifiers *AddIn* and *DelIn*. Declaration δ1, in (a), forbids the instantiation of all attributes classes of `ArtificialObject` . Due to inheritance, the same holds for the attributes of `Pot` . Declarations δ2,δ3 define the instantiation of classes `size` and `color` respectively. The latter prevail so the example defines the instantiation of a projection of the whole hierarchy, consisting of the attributes `size` and `color` . Figure (b) shows the opposite case. Here, declaration δ2 forbids the instantiation of class `weight` . Example (b) defines different projections from (a) because in (b) any new attribute, instead of (a), will be a member of the updatable projection.

Composite declaration types: Since our types offer fine grain definitions, often more than one declarations are made in reference to the same object. In order to reduce the effort of the user, we support composite declaration types. A composite declaration type consists of a number of types with different pairs of elementary update action identifiers and target identifiers , and can be created by the user according to need. The combination of declarations with composite and simple types make the task declaration process efficient and effective. Some frequently used composite types are those which define: (i) specialization hierarchies with invariant instances, (ii) specialization hierarchies used to classify objects, (iii) evolvable specialization hierarchies , (iv) specialization hierarchies whose population is used only as attribute values. An example is shown in figure 15.

Context Synthesis: Each task is related to a class whose extent are the declara-

[3] This holds since SIS system classes are organized in a specialization hierarchy : e.g. *Token* isA *Object*.

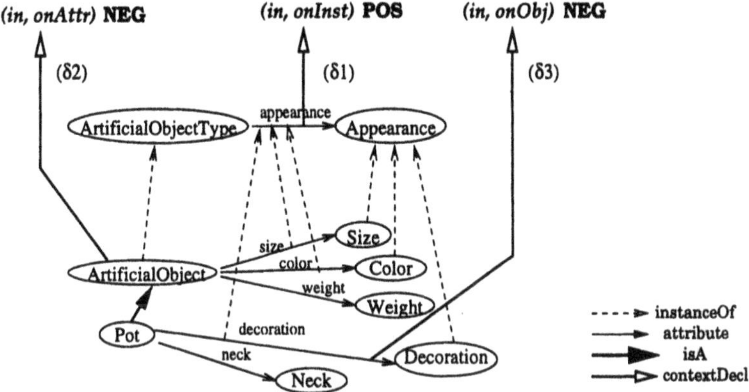

Fig. 13. Declaring class projections via metalevel

Instantiation levels are exploited to provide efficient and dynamic definitions of updatable projections. Declaration δ1 concern the attributes `size,color` and `decoration`. This declaration prevails the negative declaration δ2, so any new attribute classified in the attribute metaclass `appearance` will be a member of the projection. Finally, declaration δ3 forbids the instantiation of class `decoration` (it prevails declaration δ1).

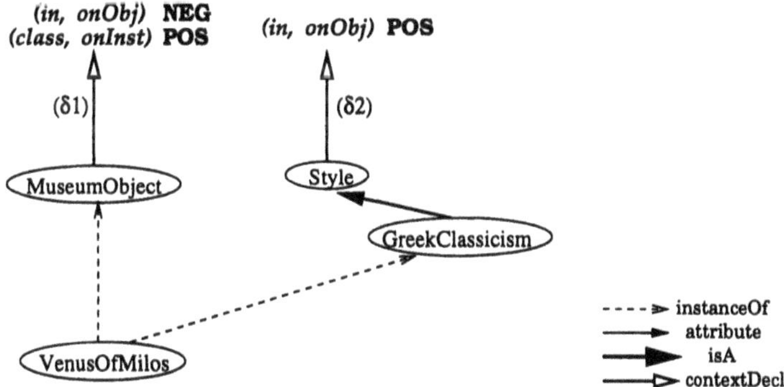

Fig. 14. Declaration examples

Identifier *class* stands for the identifiers *AddClass* and *DelClass*. Declaration δ1 forbids the instantiation of `MuseumObject` but also permits the classification of its instances. This means that for the instances of `MuseumObject` the deletion of the classification links to class `MuseumObject` is forbidden, but the classification to other classes, e.g. the subclasses of `Style` (see declaration δ2), is possible.

Controlled_Attribute_Values			
EA	*onObj*	*onAttr*	*onInst*
AddIn, DelIn	NEG	NEG	
AddAT, DelAT	POS		POS
AddAF, DelAF	NEG	NEG	NEG
AddSub, DelSub	NEG	NEG	NEG
AddSup, DelSup	NEG	NEG	NEG
AddClass, DelClass	NEG	NEG	NEG
REN	NEG	NEG	NEG
DEL	NEG	NEG	NEG

Fig. 15. A composite declaration type

This type marks specialization hierarchies whose extent should remain invariant and are used as attribute values

tions of that task. By organizing these classes in a specialization (isA) hierarchy we can reuse sets of declarations, obtaining fast task declarations.

Representation.

Each declaration relates an object with a *Type*, according to the model shown in figure 16. Although this is not the unique way to model the ternary relation (*object, task, type*), the key point is that it is represented by links which are stored bidirectionally. This permits efficient deductions from any point : from *Object* (updatability checking), from *Task* (declaration analysis) or from *Type* (usage examples). The representation of declaration types is shown in figure 17. Finally figure 18 presents the whole metamodel.

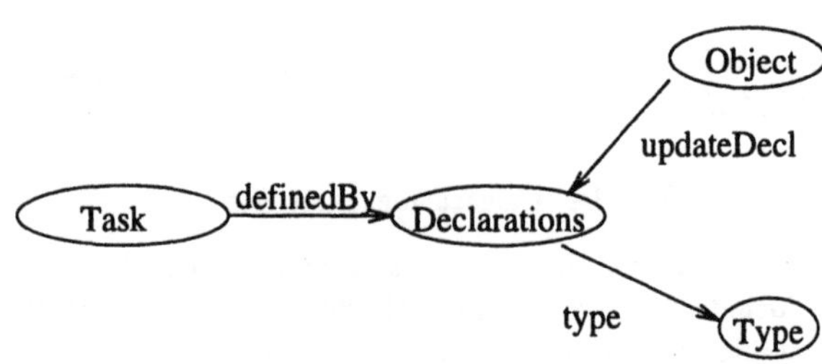

Fig. 16. Declaration representation

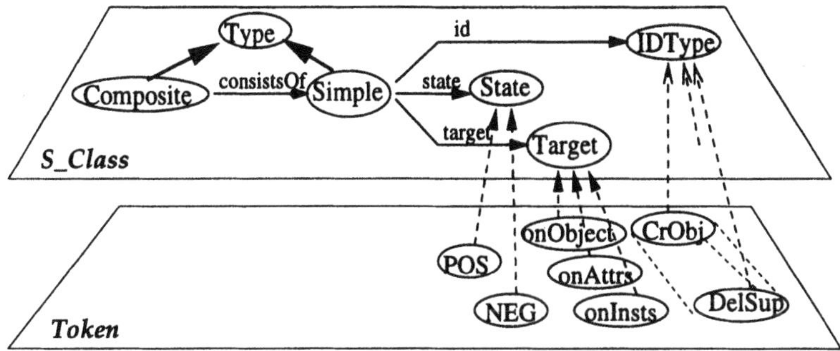

Fig. 17. Representation of declaration types

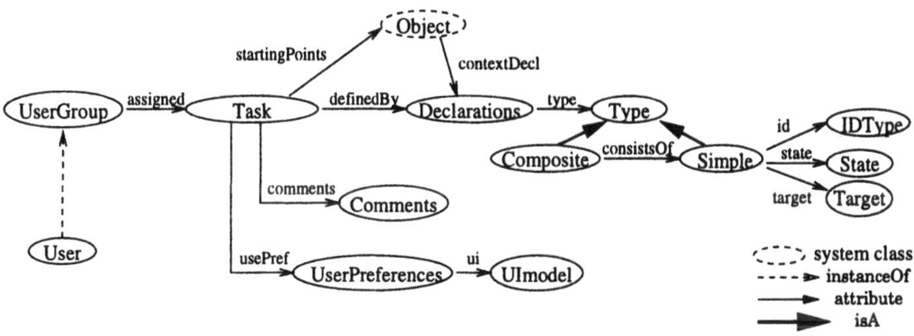

Fig. 18. The task context metamodel

5.3 Focus Context

The interactive user interface (UI) of an information management system should include concurrent browsing, presentation, modification and updating. Commonly, the development of such a UI is done using a toolkit, a graphical editor and a lot of programming effort. In order to reduce that cost, tools that map object structures to widget structures resulting in automatic UI construction, have been proposed and implemented (e.g. O_2Look [6]). In order to refine and customize (including information update restriction) these ready-made mappings, special tools have been developed (e.g. *ToonMaker* [6]). Similarly, object display definition systems ([13]) and data-oriented UIMS have been proposed [15, 17].

We believe that, in addition, tools should take into account the role/task contexts in order both to control and guide/facilitate (customize) the interaction. Because the interaction is normally held on a per object basis, in this section we introduce the *Focus Context* as a concept which facilitates the interactive updates concerning one object, the focal point (or, simply, *focus*). The interactive mechanism we propose, which exploits the focus context, is described in section 6.

The focus context is implemented by a set of procedures which, assuming the *user* has selected a *task* and is focusing on one *object* , determine the set of candidate next primitive update operation. In order to compute that set, they take into account (i) the focus, (ii) the data model (and the corresponding modeling guidelines) and (iii) the current task [4]. Actually, they compute the set of all primitive update operations which (i) take the focus argument, (ii) are semantically correct [5] and (iii) belong to the contents of the current task.

Assume that t is the current task, f is the focus, U is the set of all syntactically correct PUO, and $U_{sem}(f)$ is the set of semantically correct PUO which take f as argument. The set of candidate next update operations is :

$$CN = contents(t) \cap U_{sem}(f)$$

The data model of SIS-Telos and the representation of role/task contexts allows the efficient computation of the above set. When f is an attribute, CN is small, but when it is an individual, there are cases where it is too big to be practically useful. In such cases some common modeling guidelines based on the data model are used in order to restrict this set. Alternatively, the user can provide additional information for filtering this set.

An interesting extension of the focus context concerns the facilitation of creating composite objects or objects which satisfy some desired and predefined conditions (predicates). To face this need, we propose a high-level update operation, makecopy. *Makecopy* is able to produce copies of the focus (which can be a composite object), which users can subsequently differentiate [6]. This is a quite natural manner of evolution. It relies on detecting analogies between the intended new object (a mental conception) and an existing object (the focus). Parts of the structure and the contents of the existing object are preserved (reused) while the different elements are introduced, thus creating the new object. The rising problems concern the range of copying (an object may be connected with many others), and the copying process (is the value-object of a copied attribute the same as the original value, a new one automatically generated, or a user supplied value ?). To address the first problem we believe that *makecopy* should take into account the context of the current task and objects which can act as copy templates. To address the latter, makecopy should take into account the cardinality/dependency constraints of relationships (in order to face the problem concerning the attribute values) and could exploit the context-based naming mechanism (to name the automatically generated objects) which have been proposed for SIS-Telos by Theodorakis [27, 26]. An example is shown in figure 19.

Makecopy can also be used in order to facilitate the creation of objects which satisfy a desired condition. This can be achieved by copying an object which satisfies that condition.

We are currently working on all these issues concerning the focus context.

---

[4] or more generally the role context

[5] Although the SIS executes only semantically correct updates, focus context procedures precompute the set of all semantically correct updates in order to prevent the user from making wrong, hence rejected, requests.

[6] There are occasions where *makecopy* asks the user to make some decisions in order to drive the execution.

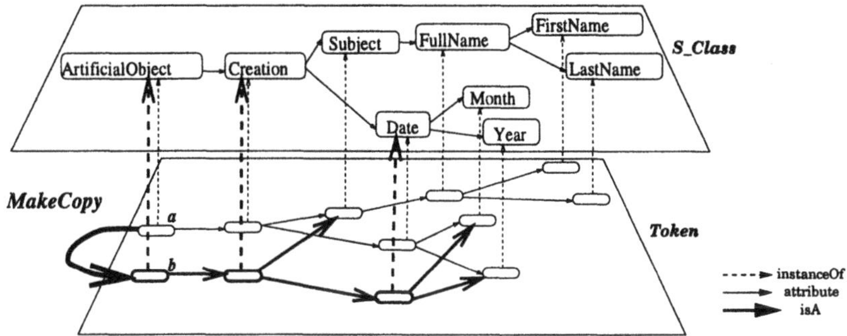

Fig. 19. An example of *makecopy*

6 Implementation Aspects

Choosing a metamodel to represent role and task contexts, results in a number of implementation benefits: usage of existing mechanisms to represent, store, query and present the corresponding data.

As contexts are utilized at run-time, the speed of the corresponding deductions (regarding task contexts) is crucial [7]. The representation of declarations allows efficient deductions since SIS-Telos links are stored bidirectionally and SIS-Telos if very fast in link traversals. The interpretation algorithm comprises steps of determining explicit and inherited declarations. In terms of complexity the latter are the more significant. The average complexity of determining inherited declarations can be shown to depend on the average depth of generalization hierarchies and the average number of classes of an object. These average numbers are in practice bounded by small numbers, less than 10. Therefore, the average complexity of the interpretation algorithm is practically constant, independent of the size of the information base.

In order to optimize performance we propose the usage of a *cache* in order to reuse deductions (fig. 20 describes the cache elements). As the consistency of its contents is indispensable we must store deductions whose invalidation can be checked efficiently. Therefore we propose a cache to store the declarations inherited from superclasses. This reduces the cost of interpretation I_{isa}.

The interactive mechanism we propose which exploits role/task/focus contexts is described schematically in figure 21. A prototype which implements role/task contexts, enriched with some extra operations for context administration and supervision (user role tree, declarations tree, examples of type usage, composite type analysis), not shown in fig 21, has been implemented using the customizable user interface of SIS.

---

[7] Speed requirements would be greater if trying to implement read contexts, since they would affect the query speed.

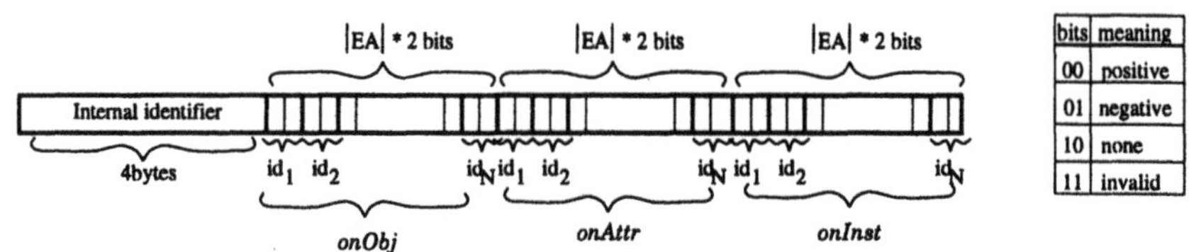

bits	meaning
00	positive
01	negative
10	none
11	invalid

Fig. 20. Cache element structure

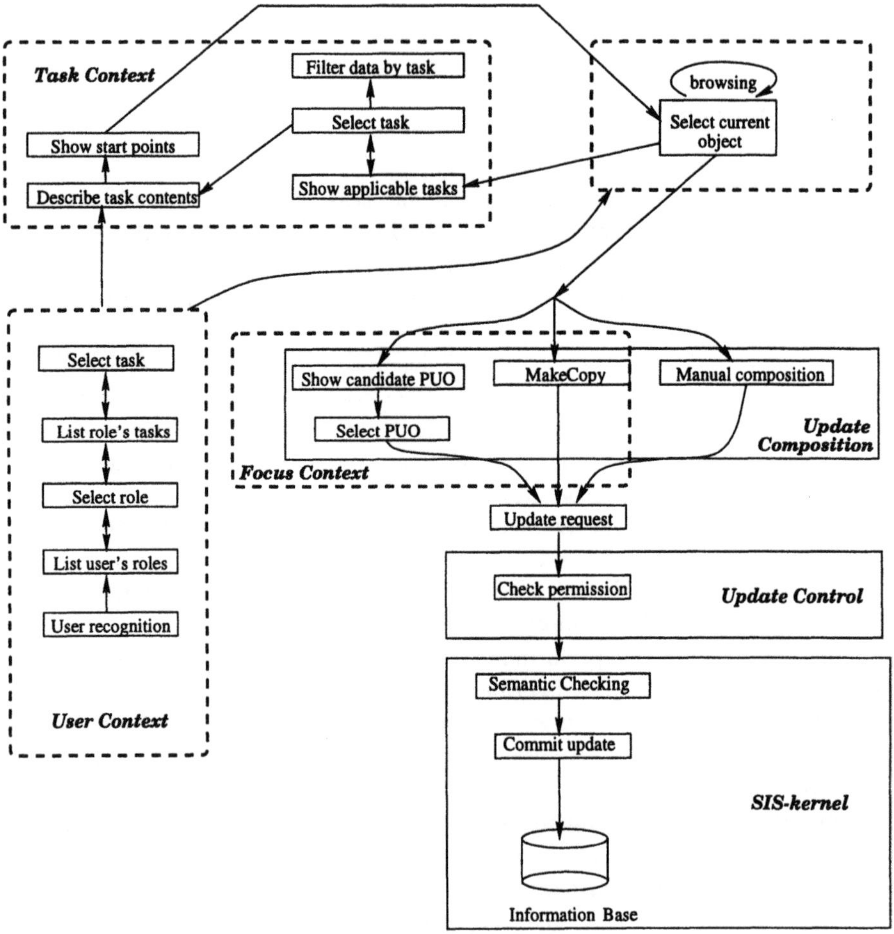

Fig. 21. An interactive mechanism for context-driven update

7 Related Work

Related work is found in many research areas including database views and authorization mechanisms. Below we draw comparisons to our work with regard to certain aspects, namely expressive power, flexibility, representation, and utilization.

Expressive power

View mechanisms commonly define update contexts which concern only the data of the base [14, 23, 4]. They support dynamic definitions through the use of a query language.

We provide a uniform way to define tasks concerning data and/or schema. We support dynamic definitions, through (i) special dynamic declaration types, (ii) inheritance and (iii) instantiation levels (e.g. we exploit the attribute metaclasses to provide very efficient declaration of projection classes). We also support fine grain definitions and role/task context declaration reusability since one role or task context can be exploited for the declaration of other contexts.

Flexibility

To define a context, positive declarations are commonly used [25, 14]. Using combinations of positive and negative declarations offers flexibility and brevity in task declarations [22]. Combining positive and negative declarations may result in ambiguities which require time consuming search to detect [22].

We support combinations of positive and negative declarations which do not need checking since all ambiguities that can appear, are resolved. In order to speed up task declaration we support user-configurable composite declaration types which can be combined with simple types. This suites our needs better than organizing hierarchically the operation identifiers, as used by authorization mechanisms [22, 25]. Moreover, declarations do not pose any extra cognitive requirement to the administrator, since they are constructed using the existing structuring mechanisms.

Representation

Representing views as stored query strings results in contexts which are not easily supervised, maintained and utilized [14, 4]. On the other hand, embodying views in the schema results in schema fragmentation and ambiguities [23].

We use a metamodel to model context definitions (metadata). Work concerning the usage of metamodels can be found in [12, 18, 3]. Metadata are stored as attribute relationships between objects and metadata types. This enhances the concept of contexts because their declarations are subject to semantic checking, remain consistent with the base and can be utilized efficiently. In addition, they do not affect the information model.

Utilization

We relate each context with usage information (starting points, user preferences, comments) as proposed in [5]. In addition, we propose the focus context which exploits the role/task contexts and facilitates the interactive updates. It includes a high level update operation, *makecopy*, which helps creating composite objects. In [4], views which define virtual paths are proposed in order to face this process. Our proposal is simpler and requires less effort. Makecopy also facilitates the creation of objects which are supposed to satisfy predefined conditions (predicates). Some existing systems can specify such sets of objects (which satisfy a predicate) with the notion of selection view, but regarding the addition of new objects to these sets, they deal only with the dilemma of acceptance or rejection of the request for creating an object which does not satisfy the corresponding predicate (some permit it [23], some do not [14, 4]). They do not provide any user support.

8 Conclusion

In this paper we address the problem of information base update by introducing three kinds of contexts: *role,task* and *focus* context. *Role context* is used to relate users with update tasks, *task context* restricts the scope of updates to a subset of the information base, according to various criteria posed by actual tasks (filtering) or authorization constraints, and finally, *focus context* is used to guide the user at run-time, by exploiting the focus and the corresponding roles and tasks of the user.

We focus on issues regarding the enhancement of the notion of context in information bases. In particular, we offer a uniform way of defining tasks which concern the data or the schema, which also permits fine grain and dynamic definitions. We represent contexts in a way that ensures the consistency of its declarations with the contents of the information base, thus minimizing the maintenance cost. We believe that flexibility and brevity of context declarations are important qualities, therefore we support combinations of positive and negative declarations, as well as coarse grain declarations and declaration reuse. Our metamodel in conjunction with the adopted information representation framework offers efficient utilization of update contexts. Moreover, we make suggestions regarding further optimization. At last, we describe briefly the general interactive mechanism which exploits contexts, including a high level update operation, *makecopy*, which help users in creating objects which satisfy desired predicates and can be composite.

We are currently working on extensions concerning the expressive power of our metamodel, such as declarations inherited by attributes and the flexibility of task declarations (improved context synthesis). There are also open issues concerning the efficiency of task utilization, e.g. the implementation of declaration types in the kernel of our repository system, testing of cache, and focus context. In addition, for better context utilization, special user interface operations must be implemented.

Acknowledgements

We wish to thank the members of the Information Systems and Software Technology Group at ICS-FORTH for their explicit and implicit contribution to this work, in particular Dr. Martin Doerr, George Georgiannakis, Polivios Klimathianakis, Manos Theodorakis and Athena Trapsioti.

References

1. Rakesh Agrawal and Linda G. DeMichiel. "Type Derivation Using the Projection Operation". *Information Systems*, 19(1):55–68, 1994.
2. G. Attardi and M. Simi. "Completeness and Consistency of OMEGA, A Logic for Knowledge Representation". In *Proceedings of International Joint Conference on Artificial Intelligence*, Vancouver, 1991.
3. Z. Bellahsene. "An Active Meta-Model for Knowledge Evolution in an Object-oriented Database". Technical report. LIRMM UMR CNRS/Montpellier II, 1992.
4. Z. Bellahsene. "The Point of View Notion for Defining and Updating Views in an Object-oriented Database". Technical report. LIRMM UMR CNRS/Montpellier II, 1992.
5. Philip A. Bernstein and Umeshwar Dayal. "An Overview of Repository Technology". In *Proceedings of the 20th VLDB Conference*, pages 705–713, Santiago, Chile, 1994.
6. P. Borras, J.C. Mamou, D. Plateau, B. Poyet, and D. Tallot. "Building User Interfaces for Database Applications : The O2 experience". *SIGMOD RECORD*, 21(1):32–38, March 1992.
7. M. Brodie, J. Mylopoulos, and J. Schmidt, editors. *"On Conceptual Modeling: Perspectives from Artificial Intelligence, Databases and Programming Languages"*. Springer-Verlag, 1984.
8. Panos Constantopoulos. "Cultural Documentation: The CLIO System". Technical Report 115, Institute of Computer Science Foundation for Research and Technology Hellas, January 1994.
9. Panos Constantopoulos and Martin Doerr. "Component Classification in the Software Information Base". in O.Nierstrasz and D.Tsichritzis, eds.,Object-Oriented Software Composition, Prentice-Hall,1995.
10. Panos Constantopoulos and Martin Doerr. "The Semantic Index System : A brief presentation". Institute of Computer Science Foundation for Research and Technology Hellas, May 1994. (http://www.ics.forth.gr/proj/isst/Systems/sis/).
11. Panos Constantopoulos, Manos Theodorakis, and Yannis Tzitzikas. "Developing Hypermedia Over an Information Repository ". to appear in the 2nd WorkShop on Open Hypermedia Systems at Hypertext'96, Washington, DC, USA,March 16-20, 1996.
12. Oscar Diaz and Norman W. Paton. "Extending ODBMS Using Metaclasses". *IEEE Software*, pages 40–47, May 1994.
13. Belinda B. Flynn and David Maier. "Supporting Display Generation for Complex Database Objects". *SIGMOD RECORD*, 21(1):18–24, March 1992.
14. Andreas Geppert, Stefan Scherrer, and Klaus R. Dittrich. "Derived Types and Subschemas : Towards Better Support for Logical Data Independence in Object-Oriented Data Models". Technical Report 93.27, Institut für Informatik, Universität Zürich, June 1993.
15. S. Hudson and R. King. "Semantic Feedback in the Higgens UIMS". *IEEE Transactions of Sortware Engineering*, August 1988.
16. Richard Hull and Roger King. "Semantic Database Modeling". *ACM Computing Surveys*, 19(3):202–260, September 1987.
17. Michel Kuntz. "The Gist of GIUKU. Graphical Interactive Intelligent Utilities for Knowledgeable Users of Data Base Systems". *SIGMOD RECORD*, 21(1):58–64, March 1992.

18. Leo Mark and Nick Roussopoulos. "Metadata Management". *IEEE Computer*, pages 26–36, December 1986.
19. M. Missikoff and M. Scholl. "An Algorithm for Insertion into a Lattice: Application to Type Classification". In *Proceedings 3nd International Conference on Foundations of Data Organisation and Algorithms - FODO*, pages 64–82, Paris, June 1989. Springer-Verlag.
20. John Mylopoulos, Alex Borgida, Matthias Jarke, and Manolis Koubarakis. "Telos : Representing Knowledge about Information Systems". *ACM Transactions on Information Systems*, 8(4), October 1990.
21. John Mylopoulos and Renate Motschnig-Pitric. "Partitioning Information Bases with Contexts". In *Proceedings of Conference on Cooperative Information Systems, CoopIS-95*, pages 44–54, Vienna, Austria, May 1995.
22. Fausto Rabitti, Elisa Bertino, Won Kim, and Darrell Woelk. "A Model of Authorization for Next-Generation Database Systems". *ACM Transactions on Object Oriented Database Systems-TODS*, 16(1), March 1991.
23. Marc H. Scholl, Cristian Laasch, and Markus Tresch. "Updatable Views in Object-Oriented Databases". In *Proceedings of the 2nd International Conference on Deductive and Object-Oriented Databases*, pages 189–207, 1991.
24. Lokendra Shastri. "Default Reasoning in Semantic Networks: A Formalization of Recognition and Inheritance ". *Artificial Intelligence*, 39:283–355, 1989.
25. Gerhard Steinke. *"Task-Based Security for Knowledge Base Systems"*. PhD thesis, University of Passau, July 1992.
26. Manos Theodorakis. "Context-based Naming in Semantic Networks". to appear in the 3rd Doctoral Consortium on Advanced Information Systems Engineering, Heraklion, Crete, Greece, May 20-21, 1996.
27. Manos Theodorakis. "Name Scope in Semantic Data Models". Master's thesis, Department of Computer Science - University of Crete, September 1995. (in Greek).
28. M.B. Thuraisingham. "Mandatory Security in Object-Oriented Database Systems". In *Proceedings of Object-Oriented Programming, Systems, Languages and Applications - OOPSLA*, pages 203–210, October 1989.
29. David Touretzky, John Horty, and Richmond Thomason. "A Clash of Intuitions : The Current State of Nonmonotonic Multiple Inheritance Systems". In *Proceedings of the 10th IJCAI, Milan, Italy*, pages 476–482, 1989.

Managing Overlapping Transactional Workflows *

Juha Puustjärvi[1], Henry Tirri[1] and Jari Veijalainen[2]

[1] Department of Computer Science
P. O. Box 26 (Teollisuuskatu 23)
FIN-00014 UNIVERSITY OF HELSINKI
Finland
e-mail: {puustjar, tirri}@cs.helsinki.fi
[2] VTT Information Technology
Multimedia Systems
P.O. Box 1203
FIN-02044 VTT
Finland
e-mail: Jari.Veijalainen@vtt.fi

Abstract. Workflow management techniques have become an intensive area of research in information systems. In large scale workflow systems modularity and reusability of existing task structures with context dependent (parametrized) task execution are essential components of a successful application. In this paper we study the issues related to management of overlapping transactional workflows, i.e., workflows that share component tasks and thus avoid redundancy in design. The notion of parametrized transactional properties of workflow tasks is introduced and analyzed, and the underlying implementation mechanism based on Event/Condition/Action (ECA) rules is discussed.

1 Introduction

Workflow management techniques have become one of the most exciting areas of research in information systems. The underlying concepts have been around in various forms for a long time, however, only recently the know how to implement commercial systems has been available.

Modern business applications are usually composed of independently designed components which are accessed concurrently by a large set of users. Workflow management can be seen as central techniques to coordinate and streamline *business processes*, which themselves are represented as *workflows*. On the other hand current organizational investments into data processing equipment and software are significant, and there is a growing interest to benefit as long as possible from the existing "legacy systems". In large scale workflow systems with 10,000 users linking together several thousand geographically distributed sites, modularity

* This work was done in ESPRIT LTR project TransCoop (EP8012), which is partially funded by the European Commission. The partners of TransCoop are GMD (Germany), University of Twente (The Netherlands), and VTT (Finland).

of design, reusability of existing task structures and context dependent (parametrized) task execution are essential components of a successful application. It is within this framework of efficient business process re-engineering that our research is inscribed.

Mohan et el [21] listed several key aspects in large scale workflow management design: failure handling, availability, navigational flexibility, replication and distributed coordination. Such aspects are clearly in the realm of *transactional workflows* where the application execution has to conform to a set of correctness constraints derived from the application domain. Since workflow management systems have become the top layer in the corporate information system architecture, we would like to add to this list of issues *modularity* and *task reusability* and focus here on mechanisms achieving these goals.

Workflow task reusability is an essential feature of real life workflow systems, and should be taken into account also in the development of such systems. Reusability allows one to avoid redundant design, which is an important aspect as large workflow applications are typically defined by combining existing applications. Consequently management of *overlapping workflows*, i.e., workflows that share one or more tasks, is an important topic to be addressed in transactional workflows.

Workflow management research is clearly related to the work done in developing advanced transaction models, especially for cooperative environments. Cooperative transaction models have been discussed in [18, 19, 26, 24, 15, 23] in the centralized case, and in order to better match the requirements of various modern database applications, more general transaction frameworks are developed in [9, 22, 33]. The ASSET system [3] provides transaction primitives for the specification of extended and cooperative transaction models. Some of the recent work also makes direct connections between workflow management systems and advanced transaction processing: workflows are treated as extended transactions in DOM systems [4, 13], and the Contract model [31, 32] provides task reusability and application specific concurrency control.

In this paper we will study the design of workflow management systems that support modular, overlapping workflows. In order to achieve this goal of increased task reusability we introduce *task execution modes* and the notion of *task integration*, i.e., we rely on *context-dependent, parametrized transactional properties* of the workflow tasks. By using different execution modes it is possible to combine tasks located at different sites to compose appropriate transactional units. In addition, by task integration we can bind together tasks executed at the same site to comprise appropriate units of atomicity or isolation. In this way we incorporate workflow notions similar to multilevel atomicity [20], and increase task reusability and workflow system throughput. As far as we are aware of, this notion of parametrized transactional properties to increase reusability of tasks has not been addressed before. The mechanisms to implement such properties are based on Event/Condition/Action rules (ECA rules) [5] which are defined on the global workflow schema (i.e., task parameters). The ECA rules are used to specify which synchroniztion operations are needed. Such rules are given as part of the workflow specification, and used by the global level workflow manager module during the execution phase.

The remainder of this paper is organized as follows. In Section 2 we will introduce the components of workflow specification, and describe the underlying workflow system architecture. In Section 3 we illustrate our concepts through an extensive example by considering five workflows in a banking domain. These workflows are used through the paper as an example to demostrate our approach. Section 4 discusses the management of concurrent execution of interfering workflow tasks with ECA rules. The use of parametrized transactional properties for task execution modes and task integration issues are introduced in Section 5. Section 6 concludes the discussion.

2 The TransCoop Workflow architecture

2.1 Workflow specification and task variations

Full specification of a workflow (scenario) is a complex task.For our purposes only the following workflow specification components need to be described:

- The tasks T_i involved in a particular workflow.
- The transactional requirements of the workflow.
- The data flow between the workflow tasks.
- The execution structure of the workflow.

In this paper we are focusing on the first two aspects since they are directly related to task reusability. Data flow between tasks is determined by specifying the input and output parameters of the tasks, and the execution structure specifies the ordering constraints for the executions of the tasks, e.g., a task may not begin before a particular previously started task commits. Such constraints can be specified e.g., by triggers [7, 6] of which the ECA rules are a special case, by Petri nets [16] or by finite state automaton [1]. In the following, we will make no assumptions of the method the execution structure is specified with. For a detailed discussion on inter-task dependency enforcement in workflow context see [27].

In our terminology a *task* defines some unit of work to be done, which can also be shared by several different workflows. A task may be specified in a number of ways. However, we model only the aspects which are relevant from task's reusability point of view. In order to maximize task reusability a task is allowed to have several *task variations*. Task reusability and task variations can be illustrated by the component structure given in Figure 1.

The component structure consists of the two levels: *workflow level* and *component level*. The overlapping tasks in the *component set* represent the variations of tasks. The tasks of a workflow comprise a subset of the overall *component set*.

We make the distinction between a *basic task* and *task variations*. Basic tasks can be used by the workflow designer to integrate tasks in order to compose appropriate transactional units (e.g., for atomicity or isolation). This issue will

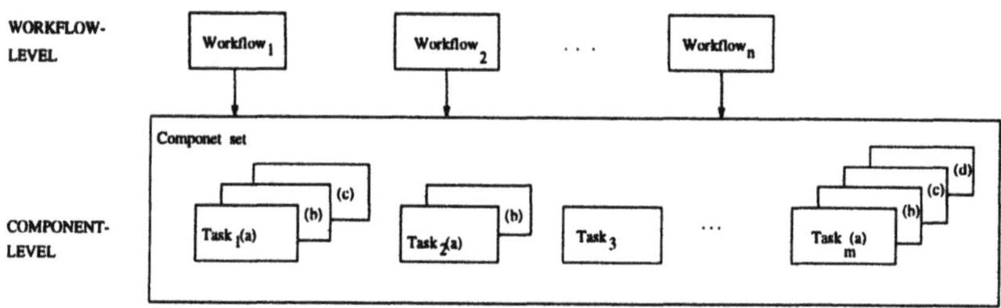

Fig. 1. Workflow component structure.

be discussed more detail in Section 5.1. *A task variation* is a modification of a task which matches better the requirements of a particular workflow. Task variation can be seen as a logical concept in the sense that the variation is specified as a parameter in the task call itself. In principle a task variation can be understood as workflow's view of the basic task, and it is analogous to view definitions in a traditional database setting. In addition task variations can also be used to compose appropriate units of atomicity or isolation. As an example consider a case where two tasks located at different sites will be integrated to compose a unit of atomicity. In such situation one uses task variations that provide the prepared state as an external state. We will return to these execution mode issues in Section 5.2.

2.2 Architectural considerations

Our architectural views for the workflow environment are influenced by the general reference architecture under development in the TransCoop project [8]. The TransCoop architecture is intended to provide a platform for transaction management support for cooperative applications in general. The architecture consists of both a specification environment (TSE) and a run-time environment (TRE) which use the services of an object server (TOS). Since we are concerned with a particular application domain, workflow management, the architecture presented is more specific than the original generic architecture. The overall modified architecture is illustrated in Figure 2.

We assume that the workflow environment consists of a global and a local level. The global level supports the overlapping workflows whereas the local level supports existing legacy applications and databases. Here we focus on the global level workflows only, and discuss briefly those architectural issues that are related to the topic of the paper, specification and execution of concurrent overlapping workflows. For more detailed discussion on architectural questions see [8].

A workflow designer specifies system supported workflows as well as the consistency constraints of the system. The *Workflow Specification Environment (WSE)* analyzes the specifications to determine whether such a workflow can be implemented. For example, if the specification includes a reusable task but such

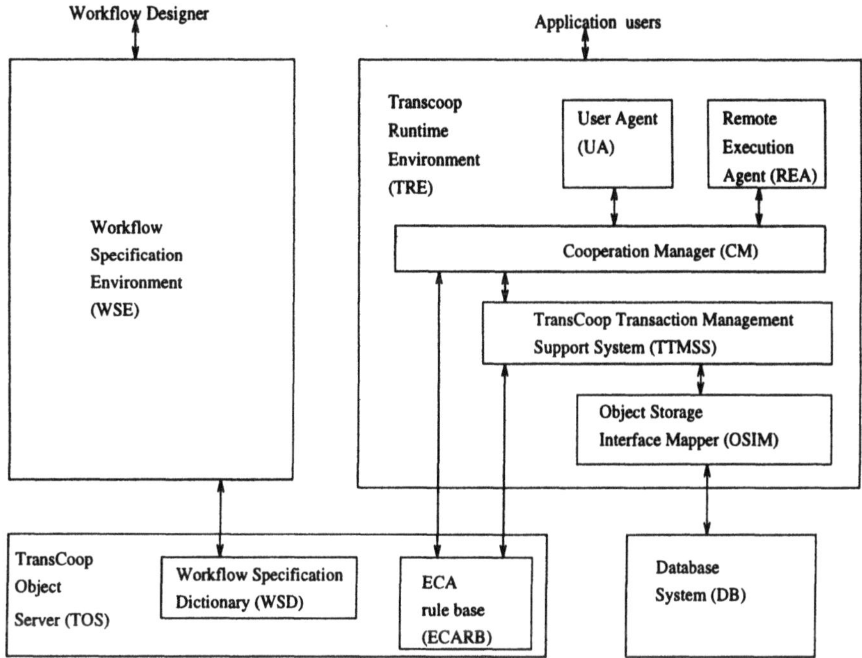

Fig. 2. Workflow system architecture.

a task is not found from the *Workflow specification dictionary* stored in the TOS object server, then the mismatch is reported to the workflow designer. If there are no mismatches the specification is stored in the *Workflow Specification Dictionary.* In addition to the individual workflow specifications a workflow designer can specify consistency constraints of the system. To enforce such a constraint WSE compiles the necessary set of Event/Condition/Action (ECA) rules which are stored in the *ECA rule base* in the object server. In a distributed case the ECA rules (and the possible locking data structures) are stored at the sites where the tasks in question are executed.

The *User Agent (UA)* module provides the interface between the users and the system. A user may be a human, an application program or a remote workflow or task request. When it receives a workflow call, it generates a *workflow specification* based on the *Workflow Specification Dictionary.* Then it sends non-local task requests to the UA's of the appropriate sites via the *Remote Execution Agent (REA).* Local workflow specifications are passed to the *Cooperation Manager (CM)*, which is responsible that the execution is compatible with its specification. WM uses the services of the *TransCoop Transaction Management Support System (TTMSS).* It can enforce correct sequencing of the tasks.

To ensure correct interleaving of concurrent workflows and that predefined constraints are not violated, the Cooperation Manager uses the ECA-rule base generated in the specification phase. If CM will not delay the operation or a task the necessary operations will be performed by the TTMSS.

3 An example of a set of overlapping workflows

As an illustrative example we will consider the following five workflows in a banking environment: *Client Credibility, Credit Account Request, Credit Card Request, Loan Request* and *Bill request.* In the figures describing these workflows we have denoted subworkflows (i.e., the tasks which may also be executed as an independent workflow) by double outlines, and shared tasks by rounded rectangles (i.e., tasks that can be included as components in more than one workflow).

The workflow *Client Credibility* can be executed as an independent workflow or as a subworkflow in other workflows. Its modular task structure and task execution ordering constraints are presented in Figure 3.

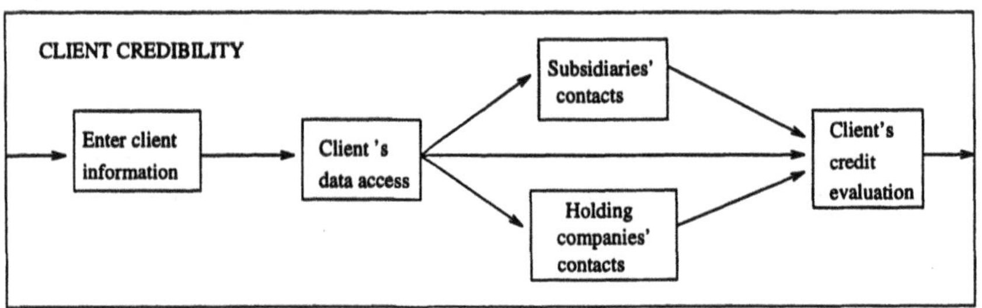

Fig. 3. Execution precedence graph for the workflow *Client Credibility.*

The task *Enter client information* accepts the information of the client. Based on this information the task *Client's data access* retrieves from the bank's database the relevant client information. This information includes the amount of the loan the client has in the bank, the names of the subsidiaries and the holding companies where the client has liabilities. If such liabilities exist the subsidiaries or holding companies are contacted to get their assessment of the client. These are performed by the tasks *Subsidiaries contacts* and *Holding companies' contacts.* The task *Client's credit evaluation* decides the credibility of the client.

The workflows *Credit account request* in Figure 4 and *Credit card request* in Figure 5 have the subworkflow *Client Credibility* as a second task, and share the last task *Client data update* which updates client's data by the given limit if the request has been accepted. In practice, however, these workflows are quite different in nature as the task *Enter credit account decision* is processed by the bank while the task *Enter credit card decision* is processed by the credit company. Hence, the former is typically a short duration activity, while the latter tends to become a long lasting workflow.

The workflow *Loan request processing* is presented in Figure 6. The first task *Enter loan request* accepts the amount and the information of the client. Based on the client information the subworkflow *Client Credibility* is processed which gives input for the task *Risk evaluation.* The risk evaluation task computes the interest

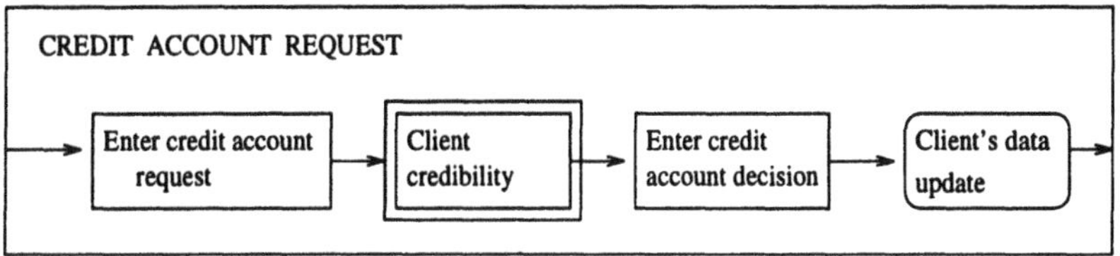

Fig. 4. Execution precedence graph for the workflow *Credit account request.*

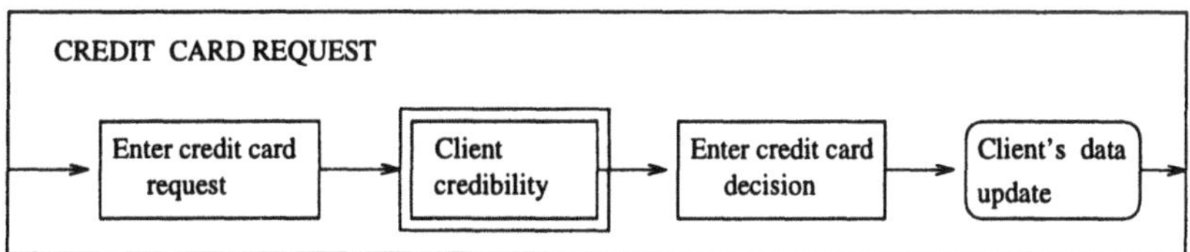

Fig. 5. Execution precedence graph for the workflow *Credit card request.*

for the loan request based on the amount of the loan and client credibility. The task *Enter loan decision* makes the decision to either grant or refuse the loan request. Before the loan can be granted the task *Bank's liability update* checks that the bank does not exceed its liability limit, and if the limit will not be exceeded, bank's total liability will be increased by the amount of the loan. If the loan is granted the task *Client's data update* adds the information of the granted loan to client's data, and if the loan request is refused the task *Bank's liability decrement* compensates the increment of bank's total liability.

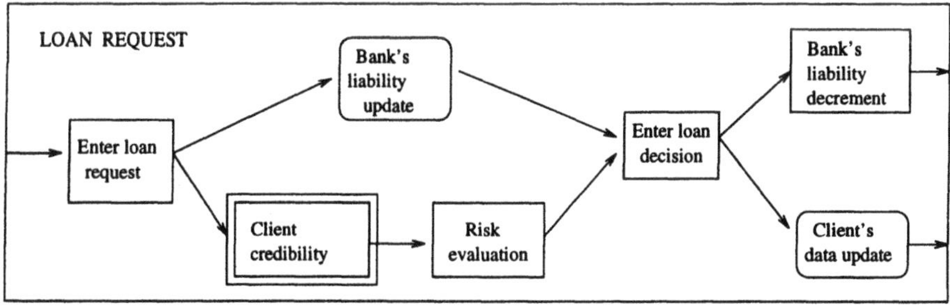

Fig. 6. Execution precedence graph for the workflow *Loan request processing.*

A bill is a special type of loan which differs from other loans in that the capital involved is usually smaller, and no pledges are used. The task *Bank's liability update* is shared by both the workflow *Bill request* (Figure 7) and the workflow *Loan request.* In these workflows, however, the task has different execution requirements: in the former it is executed as a traditional ACID transaction and in the latter as a semantically atomic transaction, i.e., it can be compensated by the task *Bank's liability decrement* if necessary.

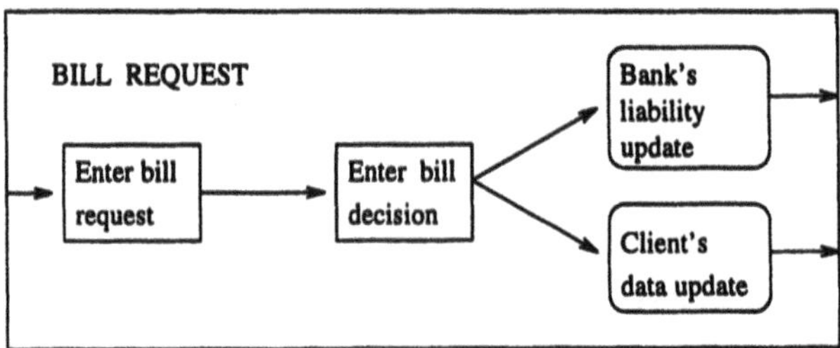

Fig. 7. Execution precedence graph for the workflow *Bill request processing.*

The simplified example above was chosen only for illustrative purposes. In our analysis of real workflow processes, one example being Telecom Finland [28], we have encountered numerous examples of overlapping workflows. From these studies it is evident that there are tasks which can be used as part of different workflows. For example the customer credibility check can be used in several different service workflows, whenever a new customer is added into the set of serviced customers (a new mobile unit, a new "101-service" etc.). In principle the same task can be used, but the credibility requirements might differ due to the differences in tariffs. The same holds for the customer billing base creation. In such a case different type of tasks or task variation is needed, because mobile customer records and practices differ from those of a 101 customer. Otherwise, the overall process specifications of customer insertion into these service processes are different and non-overlapping (in fact they are handled by separate units).

The reusability of the tasks is naturally closely linked to their definition. It is evident that the processes supported by workflows are changing. Consequently the tasks and their signatures change according to the changing functions of the organization. Methodically, whenever a new workflow specification is being developed, the existing tasks are checked and compared against the emerging needs, and the new workflow is based on a modification of existing ones, assuming that close enough match can be found. This way the best fitting set of tasks for the organizational needs will be adopted.

4 Managing overlapping concurrent workflows

4.1 Event/Condition/Action rules and markers

When several related workflows are executed concurrently, the interference of their tasks has to be controlled. The problem is naturally related to traditional transaction concurrency control [2]. A trivial approach to this problem (as well as to all concurrency control problems) would be to treat each workflow as a single monolithic transaction and require the execution of workflows to be serializable. The problem is that the workflows are prime examples of long lasting activities which cannot be handled using traditional concurrency control methods without heavy penalties to the overall system performance. For example, if straight-forward locking is used for concurrency control, the task *Client credibility* would lock client's data until the end of the workflow. Such a lock would then hold for many days preventing client's data to be updated, which clearly is not an acceptable alternative. In the other extreme are the s-transaction model [30] and the Sagas [12], where the local subtransactions (including the compensation transactions) are run in a serializable manner together with other subtransactions and local transactions, without global level restrictions on the order of the subtransactions (for more discussion on the topic see [29]).

We use *ECA rules* [17] and *markers* as mechanisms to control the interference caused by several tasks (from different workflows) executing concurrently. ECA rules with the related marker conditions are defined at the global schema level, since in the general case it is not possible to control the data modification at the underlying "legacy system level". In this respect our ECA rule mechanism is similar to, but more general than predicate locking [10] or escrow locking [25]. Unlike these locking methods our ECA rules are based on a predefined set of markers. In principle, the more marker types we have, the more application semantics we can utilize in our workflow concurrency control. An additional benefit in using ECA rules is that they conform nicely to the work done in active database area, and can reuse (at least part of) the implementation mechanisms available [5].

In general, an ECA rule is of the following form:

```
DEFINE RULE <rule_name>
    CALLED BY <ctask_id>
    IF <marker_condition> THEN
    EXECUTE <control_operation>
ACTIVATED FOR <workflow_id,task_id>
```

For our purposes the ECA rules can be viewed as predicates that should be satisfied by the system in order to guarantee that the workflows work correctly. It should be pointed out that ECA rules (unlike 2-phase locking) do not aim at ensuring that the execution history will be serializable. In managing concurrent workflows ECA rules are activated by tasks. Therefore the workflow designer determines the constraints that the tasks have to follow in order to ensure that the workflow behaves correctly.

In our example bank application case the following ECA rules are introduced:

```
DEFINE RULE upperlimit(x,l)
    CALLED BY <ctask_id>
    IF value(x) > l  THEN
    EXECUTE suspend(ctask_id)
ACTIVATED FOR <workflow_id,task_id>
```

```
DEFINE RULE bottomlimit(x,l)
    CALLED BY <ctask_id>
    IF value(x) < l  THEN
    EXECUTE suspend(ctask_id)
ACTIVATED FOR <workflow_id,task_id>

DEFINE RULE value(x,S)
    CALLED BY <ctask_id>
    IF value(x) NOT IN S  THEN
    EXECUTE suspend(ctask_id)
ACTIVATED FOR <workflow_id,task_id>

DEFINE RULE variation(x,S)
    CALLED BY <ctask_id>
    IF value(x) NOT IN [x-s,x+s], s IN S  THEN
    EXECUTE suspend(ctask_id)
ACTIVATED FOR <workflow_id,task_id>
```

The ECA rule **upperlimit(x,l)** prevents other workflows from updating a data object **x** such that the new value would be greater than **l**. Respectively **bottomlimit(x,l)** prevents other workflows of updating **x** in such a way that the new value would be smaller than **l**.

A **value(x,s)** prevents other workflows from updating the data object **x** in such a way that the new value would not be included in the value set **S**. The value set may be an interval or a finite set of values. Setting a value lock does not require that the current value of **x** is included in the value set. This is necessary if value rules are used as dynamic consistency constraints. A related rule type is **variation(x,S)**, which allows other workflows to update **x** only if the new value of **x** deviates from its old value by the value which is an item of the set **S**. In all these ECA rules the execution condition "suspend" implies that the task attempting to violate the constraint is suspended to wait the removal of the activation of the rule. This corresponds to traditional locking. ECA rules offer also other possibilities, for example the execution of the calling task can be continued with a notification that the attempted modification of the data object was not allowed.

As an example of the use of an ECA rule consider the workflow *Client credibility* of Figure 3. The correctness of the workflow requires that data on which the evaluation is based on should be valid at the end of the execution of the workflow. For example, the loans the client has should not have essential increments during the process. Minor increments could be allowed as they may be resulted from interest additions. Such a constraint can be forced by activating in the task *Client's data access* the rule **upperlimit(client_loan,l)**, where the value of **l** is e.g., five percent greater than the value of client's current loan. The rule may be deactivated at the end of the workflow or at the end of the workflow which called *Client credibility* as a subworkflow. In general, the moment when the rules are deactivated may be a parameter of the task or a workflow call.

4.2 Managing static consistency constraints

As an example of the use of the **upperlimit** ECA rule to maintain a consistency constraint assume that there is a consistency constraint stating that a fixed limit **maxliability** exists for the bank's liability. To ensure this consistency constraint the workflow designer defines the ECA rule **upperlimit(bank's liability, maxliability)**, after which workflows can be processed concurrently as long as the validity of the constraint is not challenged. Evidently this is a more liberal approach than testing the validity of the consistency constraint in each transaction program updating bank's liability and setting a traditional "data lock" on bank's liability. It should be observed that activating an upperlimit rule does not require reading the state of the object **x** itself. This is important as the workflow management system is a global system constructed on top of possibly autonomous applications, and thus has no way of controlling the modification of the data objects used by the applications.

4.3 Managing dynamic consistency constraints

By activating more than one ECA rule on a single data object it is possible to utilize more application semantics in the synchronization. For example, by activating rules **upperlimit(x,10)** and **variation(x,1)** we can enforce that data item **x** can only grow in increments of one from it's current value up to value 10.

By allowing ECA rules to invoke other ECA rules we can also support dynamic consistency constraints. To illustrate this assume that the workflow system supports the states **(hand-in, in-processing, granted, rejected)** of the "request" workflows such that the state transitions have dynamic consistency constraints (Figure 8).

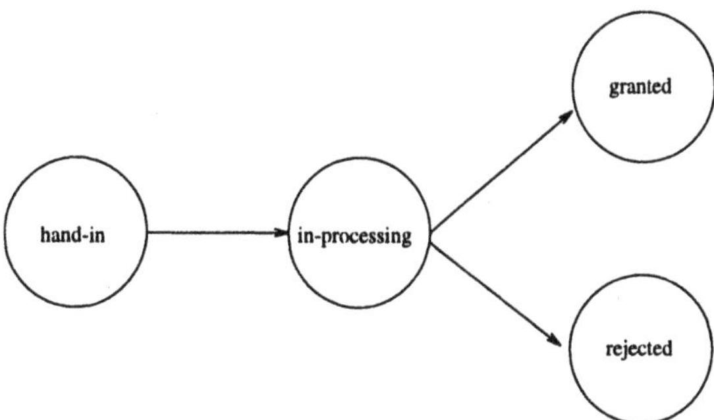

Fig. 8. A graphical presentation of a dynamic consistency constraint.

For example assume that the marker object is **loan-request-status** having the value **hand-in**. Then the ECA rule **value** with the value set **S = {in-processing}** would only allow the modification **hand-in → in-processing**. If such a modification activates a value rule with the value set consisting of the items **granted** and **rejected**, the dynamic consistency constraint stating the intended legal state transitions is enforced.

4.4 Ensuring compensations

The use of the traditional transaction models would require that a whole workflow or a workflow task constitutes an atomic unit. In fact we argue that atomicity, i.e., a workflow being always run into a successful or a non-successful completion, is in many cases a useful transactional property for users. Unfortunately, if "too much" autonomy is left for the local legacy systems, atomicity cannot be fully guaranteed. Some tasks do not, even in principle, have a compensating task, and even if they had, the compensating task cannot always be completed without violating the local database consistency. This can easily be illustrated by a simple example. Let us assume that a task transferring an amount consists of an action which performs a withdraw on bank account **account_9** and an action which deposits into account **account_1** the same amount. Assume now that the withdrawal fails and the deposit succeeds, and immediately after the successful deposit an action succeeds to withdraw the whole account **account_1**. As a result the compensation, i.e., the withdrawal from account **account_1** will not succeed anymore.

To prevent the above described situations from happening, we can use previously described ECA rules. For example, one only needs to activate a rule which prevents withdrawals in the above example case. However, this is overly conservative as withdrawals have to be prevented only if the balance of the account is less than the amount to be withdrawn. This can be enforced by activating a rule **bottomlimit(account_1,amount)** in the withdrawing task.

5 Task reusability

We have already argued above that workflow task reusability is an essential feature of real life workflow systems. However, task reusability introduces the problem that the task variations appearing in different workflows may require different transactional properties (e.g., isolation or atomicity requirements). This leads us to consider parametrized transactional properties which reflect the application dependent variations in the workflow tasks. We will address the reuse issues by introducing the concepts of *task integration* and *task execution modes*, implemented by the ECA rule mechanism.

5.1 Task integration

ECA rule based mechanisms are very suitable for providing less restrictive properties than the traditional ACID-properties. For example, the traditionally used *consistency degrees* [14] from degree 0 to degree 3 provide various atomicity and isolation levels, and for each of the levels there is a corresponding ECA rule[3]. Such rules differ in their execution policies described in their action parts. In particular the "degree 3 consistency" provides traditional serializable and recoverable executions, while other levels weaken these criteria.

It should be noted, that theoretically task integration with ECA rules is akin to multilevel atomicity [20], which weakens the usual notion of serializability by permitting controlled interleaving among transactions. Multilevel atomicity in the general transactional context, analogously to our workflow task integration, is based on the observation that there are different purposes for grouping the steps into transactions (transaction forms a unit of atomicity, or a unit of serializability).

A simple example illustrates the notion of task integration. Let us assume that the basic tasks T_1 and T_2 are units of serializability, while their compound execution $T' = T_1 T_2$ should only be a unit of atomicity. In our example domain, banking environment, transfer of money (i.e., withdrawing an account followed by the deposit of another account) can be seen as a compound transaction T'.

If the workflow tasks T_1 and T_2 are units of serializability and they are to be integrated into one unit of serializability, we have to address three things:

- First, as the integrated task T' is a unit of serializability the operations of the basic tasks T_1 and T_2 should not cause any conflicts.
- Second, there must be a moment during the execution of T' when both T_1 and T_2 have an exclusive access to all the data objects they need. Such a moment corresponds to the traditional serialization point [2] and thus guarantees serializable behavior.
- Third, either both T_1 and T_2 commit or neither of them will.

The first of the above aspects can be enforced by creating an equivalence class for the task identifiers **task_id**(T_1) and **task_id**(T_2) used in the "**ACTIVATED FOR**" component in the ECA rule. For ECA rules it is assumed that the rule conditions are not checked for equivalent **task_id** identifiers. The second aspect can be enforced by using markers **rel_an_object**(T_1) and **rel_an_object**(T_2) which test the signal that the corresponding basic task has acquired access to all necessary data objects, and is ready to share an object value with others. These markers are tested in a single ECA-rule **all_accesses_acquired**(T') and the access decision in the action part for other tasks will then depend on the result of this conjunctive condition. The third condition, commit is handled analogously.

The three most straight-forward task integration choices can be specified e.g., by the following specification primitives, which the specification environment then tranlates into a set of ECA rules:

[3] In the most degenerate case ECA rules can be used to implement traditional locking policies to achieve the various degrees of consistency defined by Gray. However, in the general case the flexibility of the action part in an ECA rule allows us a more fine-grained scale of consistency degrees.

- **DEFINE task-atomicity**($T_1, ..., T_n$)
- **DEFINE task-serializability**($T_1, ..., T_n$)
- **DEFINE task-transaction**($T_1, ..., T_n$) (corresponding to degree 3 consistency)

Naturally this set of task integration primitives is open in the sense that new primitives can be introduced if needed, e.g., the integration primitives corresponding degree 1 and degree 2 consistency could be introduced.

5.2 Task execution modes

Coming back to our example, we have seen that the task *Bank's liability update* is included in the workflows *Loan request* and *Bill request*. In the former it can be compensated by the task *Bank's liability decrement* if necessary. In the latter it is not executed until the bill is granted, and thus its execution requirement matches more to that of the traditional transaction without any requirement for compensation. This example suggests that analogously to the different isolation modes discussed in the context of basic task integration, a variation task may also require different modes for atomicity. This situation is analogous with nested transactions [22, 11, 12] where typically subtransactions have to satisfy ACID properties when executed alone, but the nested transaction does not necessary have to be fully isolated.

To capture the facility of varying execution requirements of a task we introduce the following execution modes:

- **DEFINE serialization-mode**(T)
- **DEFINE prepare-mode**(T)
- **DEFINE compensation-mode**(T)
- **DEFINE independent-mode**(T)

The **serialization mode** is the strictest way to execute a task. A task is in a serialization mode if it is in a prepared mode [14] and it has not released access to any data object it requires. If several tasks $T_1, T_2, ...T_n$ are executed in serialization mode then the commit protocol (e.g., the 2PC-protocol [2]) implies that this set of tasks can be combined into one transaction. Executing the transactions $T_1, T_2, ...T_n$ in the **prepare mode** ensures only the atomicity of the combined task. In many workflow application domains even prepare mode is too strict or cannot be used as no commit protocol is available (e.g., due to local autonomy). In such cases a more liberal way to execute a task is to use application semantics and execute a task in **compensation mode** , i.e., to enforce semantic atomicity. Compensation mode is particularly useful in the execution of distributed workflows as it allows one to preserve the autonomy of local systems. Executing a task in a **independent mode** means that no assurance of ACID properties of a task execution is needed. In such cases it is assumed that the workflow itself restarts the failed task.

6 Conclusions

Modern business applications are usually composed of independently designed components which are accessed concurrently by a large set of users. Workflow techniques can be seen as techniques to coordinate and streamline such business processes. We have discussed here several key aspects in the development of large scale workflow management systems based on the notion of transactional workflows, where the application execution has to conform to a set of correctness constraints derived from the application domain.

One salient feature of a real workflow system is its dynamicity. New workflow definitions and the modifications of existing workflow specifications occur frequently. We argue that to avoid redundant design and maintenance it should be possible to produce new specifications by using existing specifications, i.e., workflow task reusability should be possible. Consequently management of overlapping workflows, i.e., workflows that share one or more tasks, is an important issue in transactional workflows. Our work presented relies on the observation that there is no reason to bind the specification of a task to any particular set of transactional properties (atomicity and isolation requirements) since these requirements may vary in different workflows. Consequently in our approach transactional properties are not fixed until a specification is linked to a workflow.

Our goal has been to address issues related to concurrent execution of overlapping workflows and to provide concepts for managing tasks with transactional properties in such contexts. In particular we have introduced the novel idea of parametrized transactional properties of task specifications with the related notions of task integration and task execution modes. Our approach is based on the use of the ECA rule mechanism at the global schema level in the TransCoop architectural framework described in Section 2. Evident topics for future work are twofold: formalization of the parametrization concepts introduced, and application of the techniques in the real life cases available in the TransCoop project.

References

1. M. Attie, M. Singh, A. Sheth, and M. Rusinkiewicz. Specifying and enforcing intertask dependencies. In *The 19th International Conference on VLDB*, 1993.
2. P. Bernstein, V. Hadzilacos, and N. Goodman. *Concurrency Control and Recovery in Database Systems*. Addison-Wesley, 1987.
3. A. Biliris, S. Dar, N. Gehani, H. Jagadish, and K. Ramamritham. Asset: A system for supporting extended transactions. *SIGMOD Record*, 23(2), June 1994.
4. Y. Breitbart, A. Deacon, H.-J. Schek, A. Sheth, and G. Weikum. Merging application-centric and data-centric approaches to support transaction-oriented multi-system workflows. *Sigmod Record*, 22(3), September 1993.
5. C. Bussler and S. Jablonski. Implementing agent coordination for workflow management systems using active database systems. In S. Chakravarthy and S. Urban, editors, *IEEE Proceedings Research Interests in Data Engineering: Active Database Systems (RIDE'94)*, 1994.

6. U. Dayal, M. Hsu, and R. Ladin. A transaction model for long-running activities. In *The 17th International Conference on VLDB*, 1991.
7. U. Dayl, M. Hsu, and R. Ladin. Organizing long-running activities with triggers and transactions. In *ACM SIGMOD International Conference on Management of Data*, 1990.
8. R. de By, A. Lehtola, O. Pihlajamaa, J. Veijalainen, and J. Wäsch. A reference architecture for cooperative transaction processing systems. Technical Report 1694, Technical Research Centre of Finland, 1995.
9. A. Elmagarmid, Y. Leu, W. Litwin, and M. Rusinkiewicz. A multibase transaction model for interbase. In *The 16th International International Conference on VLDB*, 1990.
10. K.P. Eswaran, J.N. Gray, P.A. Lorie, and I.L. Traiger. The notions of consistency and predicate locks in a database system. *Communications of the ACM*, 19(11), November 1976.
11. H. Garcia-Molina, D. Gawlick, J. Klein, K. Kleissner, and K. Salem. Modeling long-running activities as nested sagas. *IEEE Data Engineering Bulletin*, 14(1), March 1991.
12. H. Garcia-Molina and K. Salem. Sagas. In *ACM SIGMOD International Conference on Management of Data*, 1987.
13. D. Georgakopoulos and M. Hornick. A framework for enforceable specification of extended transaction models and transactional workflows. *Journal of Intelligent and Cooperative Information Systems*, September 1994.
14. J. Gray and A. Reuter. *Transaction Processing: Concepts and Techniques*. Morgan Kaufmann, 1993.
15. W. Harrison, H. Ossher, and P. Sweeney. Coordinating concurrent development. In *Proceedings of the Conference on Computer-Supported Cooperative Work*, 1990.
16. K. Jensen. *Colored Petri Nets*. Springer-Verlag, 1991.
17. S. Joosten. Trigger modeling for workflow analysis. In *Proceedings of CON'94: Workflow Management, Challenges, Paradigms and Products*, 1994.
18. G. Kaiser. Flexible transaction model for software engineering. In *Proceedings of Sixth International Conference on Data Engineering*, 1990.
19. G. Kaiser and C. Pu. Dynamic restructuring of transactions. In A.K. Elmagarmid, editor, *Database Transaction Models for Advanced Applications*, chapter 8. Morgan Kaufmann Publishers, 1992.
20. N.A. Lynch. Multilevel atomicity - a new correctness criteria for database concurrency control. *ACM Transactions on Database Systems*, 8(4), December 1983.
21. C. Mohan, G. Alonso, R. Günthör, and M. Kamath. Exotica: A research perspective on workflow management systems. *Bulletin of the IEEE Technical Committee on Data Engineering*, 18(1), March 1995.
22. J.E.B. Moss. *Nested Transactions: An Approach to Reliable Distributed Computing*. PhD thesis, Massachusetts Institute of Technology, 1985.
23. K. Narayanaswamy and K. Goldman. "Lazy" consistency: A basis for cooperative software development. In *Proceedings of the Conference on Computer-Supported Cooperative Work*, 1992.
24. M. Nodine, S. Ramaswamy, and S. Zdonik. A cooperative transaction model for design databases. In A.K. Elmagarmid, editor, *Database Transaction Models for Advanced Applications*, chapter 3. Morgan Kaufmann Publishers, 1992.
25. P.E. O'neil. The escrow transactional method. *ACM Transactions on Database Systems*, 11(4), December 1986.

26. C. Pu and N. Hutchinson. Split transactions for open ended activities. In *The 14th International Conference on VLDB*, 1988.
27. J. Tang and J. Veijalainen. Enforcing inter-task dependencies in transactional workflows. In *Proceedings of the the Third International Conference on Cooperative Information Systems (CoopIS-95)*, 1995.
28. T. Tesch and P. Verkoulen. Transcoop deliverable ii.2. Technical Report TC/REP/GMD/D2-2/207, ESPRIT Basic Research Action 8012, 1995.
29. J. Veijalainen. Heterogeneous multilevel transaction management with multiple subtransactions. In *Proceedings of the DEXA '93*, 1993.
30. J. Veijalainen, F. Eliassen, and B. Holtkamp. The s-transaction model. In A.K. Elmagarmid, editor, *Database Transaction Models for Advanced Applications*, chapter 12. Morgan Kaufmann Publishers, 1992.
31. W. Wächter. Contracts: A means for improving reliability in distributed computing. In *IEEE COMPCON*, 1991.
32. H. Wähter and A. Reuter. The contract model. In A.K. Elmagarmid, editor, *Database Transaction Models for Advanced Applications*, chapter 7. Morgan Kaufmann Publishers, 1992.
33. G. Weikum and H. Schek. Concepts and applications of multilevel transactions and open nested transactions. In A.K. Elmagarmid, editor, *Database Transaction Models for Advanced Applications*, chapter 13. Morgan Kaufmann Publishers, 1992.

Shared Data Management Mechanism for Distributed Software Development Based on a Reflective Object-Oriented Model

Masakazu Hori[1], Yoichi Shinoda and Koichiro Ochimizu[2]

[1] INTEC Systems Laboratory Inc.
ISL Bldg., 3-23, Shimoshin-Machi, Toyama 930, Japan
[2] School of Information Science,
Japan Advanced Institute of Science and Technology
Asahidai 15, Tatsunokuchi, Ishikawa 923-12, Japan

Abstract. In this paper, we propose a new object-oriented mechanism to manage shared data in distributed software development with following features.

1. *Workspace Manager Object* and *Artifact Object* manage the range of responsibility for a software engineer's task and control data sharing.
2. *Autonomous Mediator Object* supports negotiation relevant to the modification of shared data and coordination for the negotiation.
3. Each object has a meta-object. By the mechanism, it is possible to dynamically select available actions based on a variety of situations.

In the software development environment having these features, a software engineer can work having the only knowledge about the range of responsibility for his task and the relationships with other engineers who share data with him. In addition, the environment provides a mechanism to change policies flexibly in a cooperative work style for data sharing and modification of shared data.

1 Introduction

Shared data plays an important role at cooperative works in distributed software development. A software engineer uses shared data to form a common understanding with other engineers for the completion of his task. The way how to support data sharing and modification of the shared data is one of the key factors that affect the progress of engineers' task. Therefore we should analyse an actual work style and reflect it to a software development environment.

In a distributed software development, we should guarantee each software engineer[3] to work independently, and coordinate their works if necessary. If an engineer must understand all the details of the development, the overhead of the extra work would become extremely large. Therefore, we need a model and an environment to support cooperative work such that an engineer can work having the only knowledge about the range of responsibility for his work and

[3] We call software engineer as engineer in short from here.

the relationships with other engineers who share data with him. Based on this idea, we propose a new architecture to manage shared data.

In the present style of distributed development, an engineer spends considerable time for managing shared data as well as completing his work. For example, assume a designer asks a programmer to develop a program with a given program specification. Then, the specification becomes a shared data between them. The specification is likely to receive continuous modifications, for example, to correct a bug in the module interface. These modifications must be approved by all the members under the influence. This work style increases the overhead, particularly in a distributed environment.

We take into account the following three points to manage shared data.

1. Shared data changes as time passes.
   When an engineer asks another engineer for a development task, some data, for example, specification, is shared. The contents and the range of shared data change subsequently according to the progress of the development. We need a mechanism that detects such modifications and provides support for the engineer to correctly perform the development task regardless of the modifications.
2. Modification requests on shared data are processed by a human engineer.
   If an engineer requests to modify shared data, related engineers should decide how to deal with the modification through negotiation. We therefore need a mechanism to support such negotiation, and then reflect the results to the shared data. Unlike a strict transaction system, it is seldom that multiple engineers request modifications of a same data simultaneously. In this sense, we need a mechanism to control the modification of the shared data that is biased toward the better human-computer interaction, rather than the control based on a serializability theory [1].
3. We need to select a proper method for the modification of shared data according to the work status of relevant engineers at the time of modification.
   A method to modify shared data changes according to the degree of the influence to other engineers. For example, we may need only to notify how to modify a specification if the modification is to take place at the beginning of a development, because the modification yields little or no influence to programmers' task. However, at the end of the development, a designer and programmers must need to discuss whether they should modify it, and in some case, they might put it off. We therefore need a mechanism to select a proper method from multiple candidates to deal with a modification request.

To summarize, the three issues in the management of shared data in a distributed software development environment are: (1) the contents and the range of shared data change dynamically and frequently, (2) we should consider a human factor when we modify shared data, and (3) the work style of an engineer depends on various situations during development.

In this paper, we propose a set of solutions for these issues.

1. We introduce a concept of a *distributed workspace* managed by the corresponding *workspace manager object*. Here, by object we mean a software module which has an internal state, and performs an operation on the state by the acceptance of a message in a form of method invocation. The distributed workspace corresponds to the range of responsibility for an engineer's work. We define *shared workspace* as the space overlapped by several distributed workspaces.
2. An *autonomous mediator object* supports negotiation related to the modification of shared data and coordination for the negotiation.
3. Each object has a meta-object. By the mechanism, it is possible to dynamically invoke required actions when changes in work style are introduced. These actions include modification of shared data, modification in range of sharing, and selection of engineer's activity based on his work status.

We use *computational reflection* [2] to realize dynamic change and selection of a method invocation. A system with a reflective architecture is capable of computing the configuration and the process of computation of itself. Many works have been reported on mechanisms to change the configuration of basic system dynamically, for example, in operating systems [3, 4, 5, 6, 7]. In this paper, we show that the computational reflection is also useful for a mechanism to change policies flexibly in cooperative work style (Figure 1).

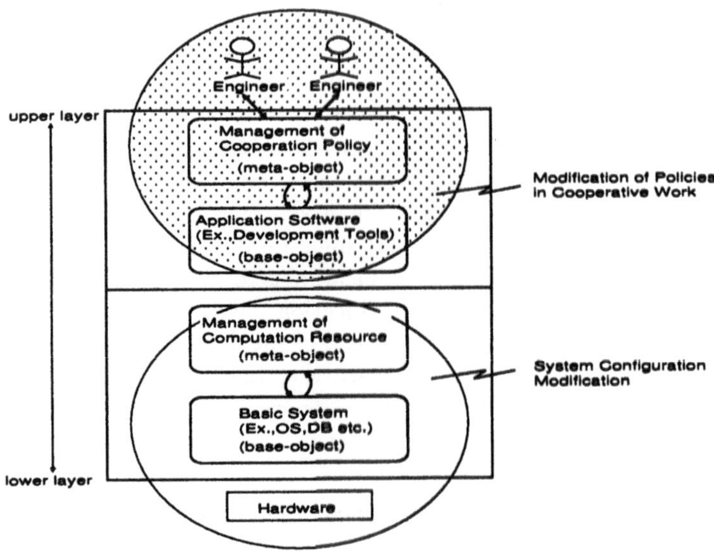

Fig. 1. Computational Reflection Applied to Modification of Policies in Cooperative Work

This paper is organized as follows. Section 2 gives the outline of the proposed object-oriented model for a distributed software development environment that concentrates on control of data sharing. We define distributed workspace as an engineer's responsibility for development, and then define a shared data as a component in a product of distributed workspaces. Based on these definitions, we introduce workspace manager, artifact object and autonomous mediator object. We will also describe roles of each object and interrelations between them. In Section 3, we analyze requirements in functionality for the workspace manager object and the artifact object which are the components of the distributed workspace. In Section 4, we consider the type of negotiation observed when an engineer requests to modify a shared data. We will elaborate the functionalities of autonomous mediator that supports negotiation based on the negotiation types considered above. Section 5 gives practical example of "*Cooperative Write*" in detail. Section 6 exhibits the outline of prototype implementation that we build to verify the feasibility of the model. Section 7 gives concluding remarks.

2 A Distributed Software Development Model for Data Sharing

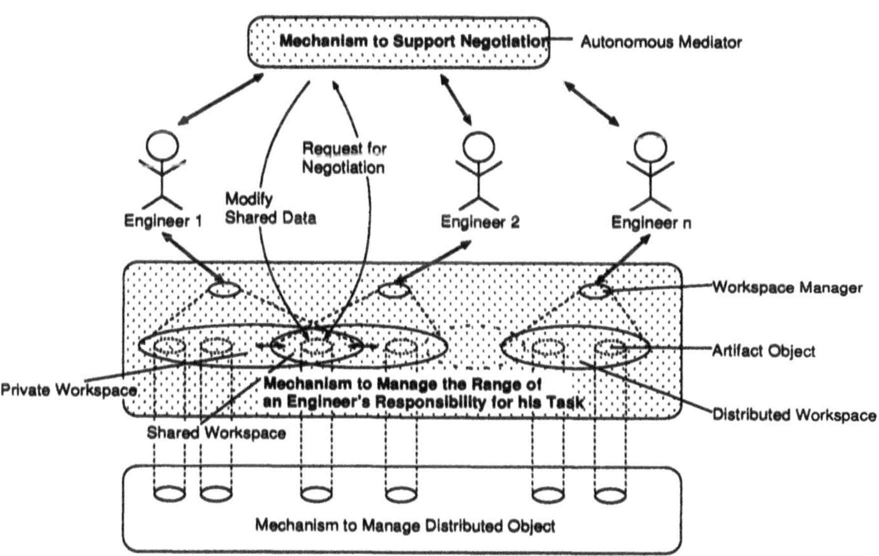

Fig. 2. The Outline of a Distributed Software Development Environment for Data Sharing

Figure 2 summarizes our view of how data should be shared, and how mechanisms to support the sharing should be placed. A mechanism for distributed object management [3, 9, 10], which guarantees distributed transparency [8], is located in the lowest layer. The two mechanisms that we are going to propose in this paper are located above this layer. The first mechanism's role is to manage the range of responsibility for engineer's task, and another mechanism's role is to support negotiation concerning a modification of shared data. These two mechanisms are briefly discussed in the following two subsections.

2.1 Management of the Range of Responsibility for Engineer's Task

Let us consider that an engineer's task is to develop a requested intermediate artifact. We define a range of engineer's responsibility by a set of intermediate artifacts relevant to the engineer's current task. We call this range as *distributed workspace*. An *artifact object* manages a corresponding artifact that is a component of the distributed workspace. Each engineer has his own *workspace manager*, which manages his distributed workspace and controls access to artifacts in the workspace.

We define a *shared workspace* as an intersection of multiple distributed workspaces and a *private workspace* as the difference between a distributed workspace and shared workspaces.

Since an artifact object in a shared workspace is accessed from multiple engineers, the object performs user-wise access control on each method invocation. An engineer accesses the artifact object through his workspace manager to cope with possible sharing situations. The workspace manager then selects a proper method for an actual access to the artifact object based on current activity status of the engineer and through negotiation of other workspace managers which shares the artifact object with.

2.2 Negotiation Support for Shared Data Modification

Shared data is modified after all the engineers, whose workspace contains a shared workspace[4] in which the shared data resides, agree with a modification request. We need not only to make a negotiation by collecting their opinions about the request, but we also have to perform a processing based on the result of the negotiation. Autonomous mediators are generated by meta of each relevant workspace manager when shared data is requested to modify, and they establish a necessary environment to support negotiation among relevant engineers. One engineer may act as a coordinator who detects a problem and coordinates relevant members if necessary. In such case, rest of the members act as negotiators to exchange their opinions.

The relationship between the mechanism described in this section and the mechanism described in Section 2.1 is as follows: (1) When an engineer requests a modification to shared data, a request to begin a negotiation is generated and sent to the mechanism that support negotiation. (2) After the negotiation completes, a method of a processing the shared data is notified to the shared artifact object to carry out the actual modification.

[4] A shared workspace and distributed workspaces which configure it change as time passes.

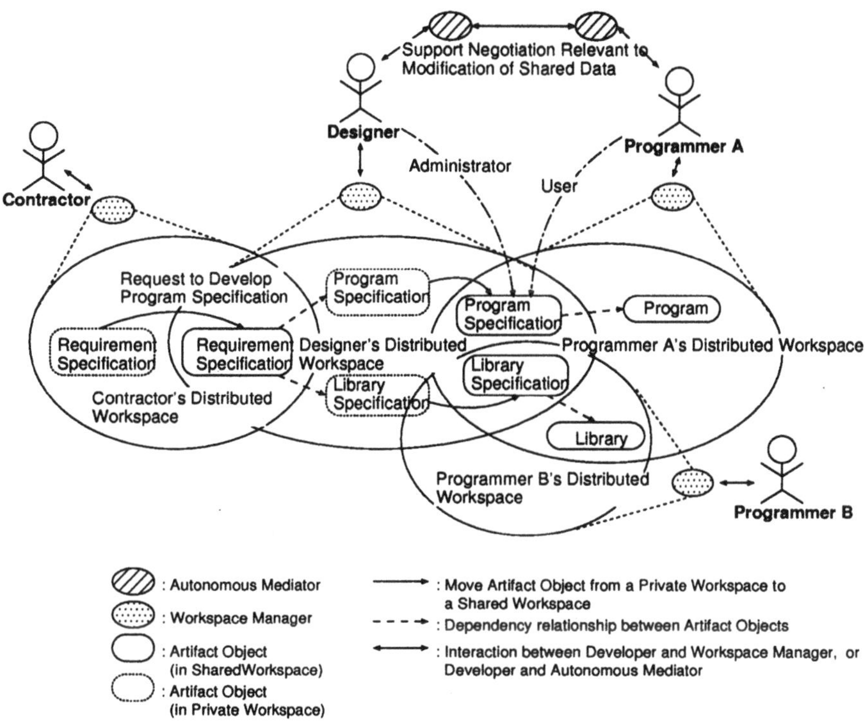

	Base-object	Meta-object
Autonomous Mediator	1. Ask a Question to a Developer 2. Invoke a Method in Other Object	1. Control a Method Invocation to the Base-object by a Half Protocol (State Transition Diagram)
Workspace Manager	1. Manage Artifact Objects in Workspace(Move between a Private Workspace and a Shared Workspace, and Change the Access Right at the Same Time) 2. Accept the Access to an Artifact Object from an Engineer	1. Ask the Meta-object of an Administrator's Workspace Manager for the Right to Modify an Artifact Object in a Shared Workspace 2. Generate an Autonomous Mediator to Support Negotiation
Artifact Object	1. Manage an Intermediate Artifact	1. Control a Method Invocation to the Base-object

Fig. 3. The Roles of Each Object

2.3 Dynamic Change of Work Styles by Computational Reflection

In this section, we show the role of each meta-object concerning the following two issues.

1. Dynamic change of access rights for shared data.
2. The way to deal with a request from an engineer who is not allowed to modify shared data.

Let us now explain about an assumption for the application of computational reflection to these issues.

To reflect the change of the range of engineer's responsibility for his work to an environment, we need to change access rights dynamically. In addition, we allow only one engineer to modify shared data simultaneously. This condition is considered not too restrictive, since simultaneous requests of modification of a single data by multiple engineers is a rare case in the distributed development.

We summarize the assumption about a typical work style to modify shared data in this paper.

We assume that there exists an administrator for each shared data who has an exclusive modification access to the data. Other engineers do not have the right to modify the shared data. If they want to modify the data, they notify the administrator, and then they begin negotiation for permission of modification.

Our understanding is that it is more important to change access rights timely for an engineer who needs to modify shared data. That is, access control mechanism we discuss here has a policy that guarantee the soundness of the work performed by the engineer as much as possible. For example, if we receive a modification request from an engineer who can not be granted for immediate access, the engineer may be notified of the time when he will be granted, or the access may be granted through negotiation.

Based on these work styles, we explain the way how shared data is generated and modified according to Figure 3. The upper part of Figure 3 shows the outline of interrelations between objects. The table at the lower part summarizes the major roles for each base-object and meta-object.

- **Generation of a shared data**
  Shared data is generated when a development is requested. For example, when "designer" requests "programmer A" to develop a program, "designer" requests the base of his workspace manager to move a program specification from his private workspace to the workspace shared with "programmer A". The base of the workspace manager also notifies access right for "programmer A" to the meta of the artifact object.
- **Modification of a shared data**
  Meta of workspace manager snoops method invocations at base of the workspace manager. If a base's first attempt to modify a shared artifact object is refused by the object, meta of the workspace manager will contact the meta of the workspace manager which is owned by the administrator of the artifact object for the grant to execute the modification. For example, when programmer A requests the base of his workspace manager to modify program specification which is shared with designer, the meta of the workspace manager receives a message that the request is refused. Therefore the meta of programmer A's workspace manager asks the meta of designer's workspace manager for his right for the modification of the program specification. The

```
[object meta-workspace-manager
 (state [queue := [queue-gen <== :new]] ;;  a message queue
        [scriptSet := scripts]          ;;  a set of scripts
        [mode := ':dormant]              ;;  an execution mode
        ... )
 (script
  (=> [:message M R S] ;;  an arrival of a message & receiving it
     [queue <= [:enq [Message Reply Sender]]]
     (when (eq mode ':dormant)
       [mode := ':active]
       [Me <= :begin]))
  (=> :begin ;;  acceptance of a message & script execution
     ;;  dequeue one triple [M R S] from a queue
     (match [queue <== :deq]
      (is [M R S]
         (match (find-script M R S scriptSet)
           (is [Bindings ScriptBody]
               ;;  Start a script evaluation
               [evaluator
                 <= [:do ScriptBody [env-gen <==
                  [:new Bindings state]] Me Group-manager evaluator]
                 @ [cont ' [Me <= :end]]]])
           (otherwise
            (warn "~S cannot handle the message ~S" [den Me] M))))))
  (=> :end ;;  after a script execution
     (if (not [queue <== :empty?])
       [Me <= :begin]
       [mode := ':dormant]))
  (=> [:reject owner time M R S]
     (match M
      (is [:set-artifact a-obj a-data]
          [[meta owner] <= [:want-to-modify a-obj a-data]]))
      ...)
  ... )]
```

Fig. 4. Example Definition for Meta of Workspace Manager in ABCL/R2

meta of designer's workspace manager deals with the situation by selecting one of the prepared procedures. A result may vary. The modification might be allowed at the specific time, or the meta-object might prompt the designer for human intervention. If the designer judges that negotiation is necessary, the meta of his workspace manager generates an autonomous mediator which implements a protocol for the negotiation concerning the modification of the program specification.

3 Distributed Workspace

3.1 Workspace Manager

Workspace manager manages distributed workspace composed of a set of artifact objects, and it accepts requests from its owner to invoke a method in artifact object.

Several reports are published concerning a mechanism to deal with multiple objects, for example, a mechanism to invoke methods in multiple objects by one invocation [11, 12] and a mechanism to change the behavior of objects dynamically [4]. Techniques to manage a single object belonging to several different groups by group-wise methods are also reported [3, 13]. Based on these studies, the workspace manager is designed to be capable of dealing with multiple objects for implementation of distributed workspace. That is, shared artifact object is managed by multiple workspace managers with the different policy depending on each engineer's work style.

An engineer's workspace manager keeps an attribute which indicates "*role*" of the engineer in addition to information to manage artifact objects in the workspace. It determines the range of responsibility for the engineer's work. The "*role*" can be expressed as follows:

$$role = ((artifact_1, work_1), \cdots, (artifact_n, work_n)) \tag{1}$$

where *role* means the role of an engineer, *artifact* is the name of an artifact and *work* is an operation performed on the artifact by him. Examples of *work* are "*edit*", "*modify*", "*test*", etc. We use an attribute "*role*" for access control of shared data. When we ask an engineer for a development, we submit a pair "(*artifact, work*)" to the base of his workspace manager. At the same time, the workspace manager notifies the kind of work and name of the engineer to meta of the artifact object for an establishment of access control.

We show an example for a typical role made by meta of workspace manager. Described below is a 4-step behavior of meta of workspace manager when an engineer does not have right to modify a shared data.

1. *Meta of workspace manager asks meta of an administrator's workspace manager for permission to modify.*
   When an engineer requests to modify an artifact object in a shared workspace even though he does not have the right to modify it, the meta of the artifact object notifies the meta of his workspace manager of the refusal. Then, the meta of the workspace manager requests the meta of an administrator's workspace manager to acquire the right to modify.
   Figure 4 is an example implementation of meta of workspace manager written in a concurrent reflective object-oriented language ABCL/R2 [5, 6]. The intended behavior of the meta of workspace manager is to detect a request to modify, and then asks the meta of an administrator's workspace manager for permission to modify.
   (a) Meta of workspace manager dequeues one triple [*M R S*] from the message queue(line 14). *M* is a message sent to base of workspace manager, *R* is the reply destination for *M*, and *S* is the sender object identity of *M*.
   (b) Meta of workspace manager creates a new environment, and then evaluates the body of the script[5] under the new environment by "evaluator" object (line 16 - 21).

[5] In ABCL/R2, implementation of method is called script.

(c) When the script is executed normally, a message *:end* is sent to meta of the workspace manager (line 22). However, if the method invocation is refused by an artifact object, meta of the workspace manager receives a message [*:reject* ...] from meta of the artifact object (line 29). Then, meta of workspace manager sends a message [*:want-to-modify* ...] to meta of the administrator's workspace manager to acquire the permission to modify.

2. *Meta of an administrator's workspace manager judges whether it should notify the administrator of the arrival of inquiry.*
The administrator sets a necessary condition for this decision to meta of his workspace manager in advance. Some of the possible actions are: (1) If the request is for a specific artifact object that does not accept the negotiation, the request is immediately turned down, (2) a negotiation request will be accepted at the specified date, or (3) the negotiation will begin immediately.
3. *Meta of the workspace manager presents the request to the administrator.*
It presents the request by the output format which the administrator chooses. For example, it displays the difference between the original data and the requested one (for example, output format from *diff* command in UNIX). Nature of the modification may also be presented at this point.
4. *Meta of the workspace manager follows an instruction of how to deal with the request given by the administrator.*
The administrator instructs meta of workspace manager how to deal with the request based on the information presented at the previous step. Examples of instructions are *"begin negotiation"*, *"allow modification"*, *"reserve modification "*, and etc.

3.2 Artifact Object

An artifact object corresponds to each artifact produced during software development life cycle. In this paper, we treat a coarse grained object for artifact object such as specification sheet, source program, and etc. Artifact object has methods to handle artifact data, for example, generation, modification, and etc. We define artifact object as an abstract class which represents artifact. Each artifact object is defined as a subclass of the artifact object class. We treat the data of artifact as an attribute of the artifact object.

In general, we should consider the management of shared data from the views of concurrency control [1], access control [14], version control [15, 16], and configuration management [17]. Since we restrict one person at a time to modify shared data, we do not have to consider concurrency control.

Meta of artifact object controls a method invocation to the base-object. If an invocation is refused, it provides the following data to the client: (1) the name of an administrator for this object, and(2) the date if an administrator accepts a negotiation request in the future.

Figure 5 illustrates an example of access control by meta of artifact object. Meta of artifact object sends a message to "acl" object to verify if a method

```
1. [object meta-artifact-object
2. (state ...
3.        [acl := nil] ;; an object to manage access rights control list
4.        [owner  := nil] ;; an owner of this object.
5.        [time   := nil]) ;; time to accept negotiation
6. (script
7.  (=> [:message M R S]
8.      ... )
9.  (=> :begin
10.     (temporary right)
11.     (match [queue <== :deq]
12.       (is [M R S]
13.         ;; get the access right for a message M from acl
14.         [right := [acl <== [:check-right (second M) (first M)]]]
15.         (cond ((right)
16.           (match (find-script M R S scriptSet)
17.             (is [Bindings ScriptBody]
18.                ...)
19.             (otherwise
20.              (warn "~S cannot handle the message ~S~%" [den Me] M)
21.               [Me <= :end])))
22.          ((t [[meta S] <= [:reject owner time M R S]]
23.               [Me <= :end]))))
24.     (otherwise
25.      [Me <= :end])))
26.  ...)]
```

Fig. 5. Example Definition for Meta of Artifact Object in ABCL/R2

invocation is allowed for a client before it is executed (line 14). If it receives the reply of acceptance, it evaluates the message and executes the script as normal(line 17 and 18). Otherwise it does not execute it and notifies the time to accept a negotiation request to the meta of client's workspace manager. The merit of access control by meta-object is that we can localize the control in a meta-object rather than scattering it around the methods in base-objects.

4 Negotiation Support for Modification of Shared Data

4.1 Requirements for a Mechanism to Support Negotiation

We specifically address the following two requirements concerning the negotiation[6] support for modification of shared data.

1. An ability to support negotiation with a half protocol and change it dynamically.
   According to our experiences that we took part in several software development projects, we believe that we can formalize the process of the negotiation to some extent, and, thus, we should provide a mechanisms to support it. For example, we can specify the order of messages exchanged between the

[6] In this section, negotiation corresponds to one relevant to the modification of shared data.

relevant engineers, the way to acquire necessary information, the way to process the acquired data, and so on[7]. A half protocol refers to such process, and specifies the flow of an engineer's behavior depending his role during negotiation. It is a "*half*" protocol because a protocol generally specifies the flow of messages between two sites. An actual protocol is formed when two half protocols actually exchange messages during a negotiation.
In Section 4.2, we formalize the aspects of negotiation as the type of negotiation. We also present the way of dynamically replacing the half protocol in Section 4.4.

2. An ability to support coordination according to the progress state of negotiation.
Since several engineers in distributed sites negotiate, we need a coordinator, who detects a problem and coordinates engineers for it. That is, a coordinator needs to detect who meets trouble and help him to promote the progress. In Section 4.4, we will show an example that supports coordination by a progress state of negotiation and a negotiation history, which are specified by a series of state transitions.

4.2 Types of Negotiation

In this section, we investigate the type of negotiation, which corresponds to a unit in a half protocol.

We assume that a negotiation consists of the three steps: (1) gathering the necessary information for decision, (2) making a decision, and (3) post-processing that depends on the decision. We denotes the type of such negotiation by eight tuple.

$$\langle S, G, I, R, O, gather, decide, action \rangle \quad (2)$$

S is a set of negotiation states. When all the necessary data in a state is gathered, negotiation moves to a new state. G denotes a set of possible selections for decision. For example, when we are to vote for "*admit*" or "*reject*", these two items become the elements of G. I is a set of information gathered to make a decision. We can either ask an engineer or invoke a method of the object in order to acquire the information. R is a set of decisions. For example, when we select our opinion from G, the selected elements from G become elements of R. O is a set of messages which are sent as a result, for example, "*notify result*", "*begin other type of negotiation*", "*execute a tool*", and etc. A function "*gather*" gathers the necessary data to specify the subject of decision. It is invoked after the data for S and G are determined.

$$gather : S \times G \rightarrow I \quad (3)$$

The decision R is determined by function "*decide*" with inputs I and G.

$$decide : I \times G \rightarrow R \quad (4)$$

[7] We do not consider formalization of the decision process itself in this paper.

O is generated by function "*action*" with input R. After the O is generated, the negotiation moves to a new state.

$$action : R \times S \rightarrow O \times S \tag{5}$$

During the evaluation of these three functions, an engineer may intervene with the process. For example, an engineer may select his choice from presented candidates to make a decision.

4.3 Autonomous Mediator

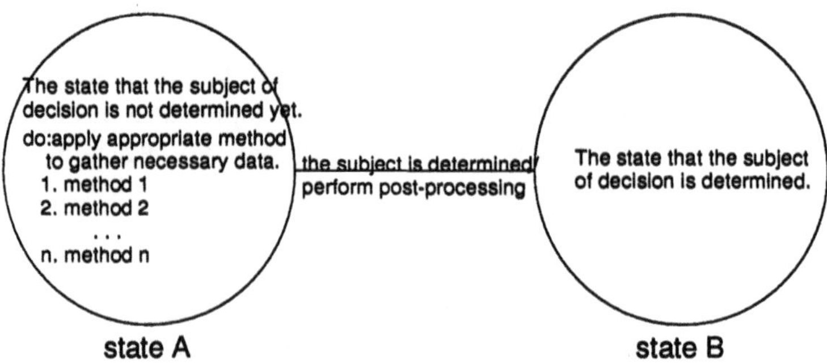

Fig. 6. The Notation of a Half Protocol Managed by Mediator

We refine autonomous mediator[8] as a model for implementation of the negotiation types that contains half protocols based on the type of negotiation discussed in the previous section.

By "*autonomy*", we mean that the mediator is capable of automatically selecting new method of execution from a set of prepared methods if a previous method fails. By this autonomy, mediator deals with an abnormal situation, for example, when it could not get the reply from an engineer or an environment by a deadline.

Mediator autonomously performs a processing by a state transition based on the rule in Figure 6. It moves from state A to state B via three steps: (1) applying a selected method i. If it fails, another method is selected and applied, (2) making a decision based on the gathered data, (3) performing a post-processing according to the decision. These three steps correspond to evaluating the three functions "*gather*","*decide*", and "*action*" in order.

Let us now examine the role of base and meta of the mediator. Base of the mediator implements all the necessary methods to act autonomously. It interacts with outside by an inquiry of an engineer and the method invocation of other object. Meta of the mediator controls autonomous processing by the base-object

[8] We call mediator in short from here.

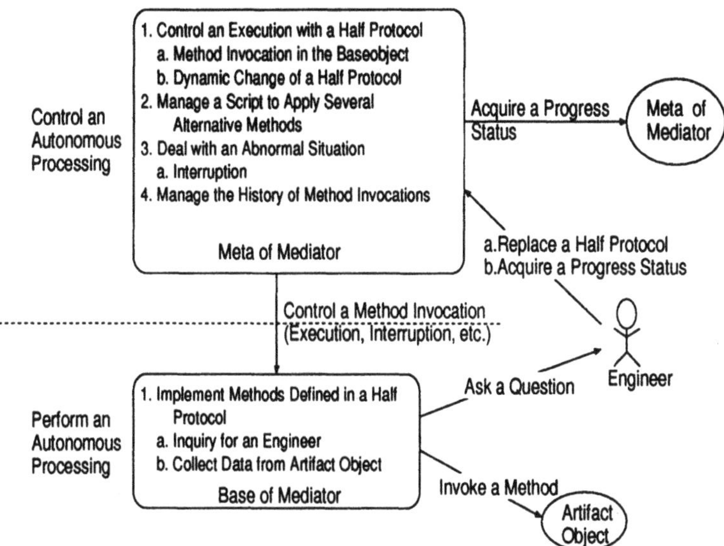

Fig. 7. Reflection Mechanism for Mediator

from the following four points. (1) It manages a half protocol implemented as a state transition diagram. It controls an execution in the base-object. It can change a half protocol dynamically by exchanging the state transition diagram. (2) It manages a script to apply several alternative methods prepared for an error. (3) When it is interrupted, it performs various processing depending upon the situation. (4) It manages a history of method invocation to supply the necessary data for the support of coordination.

4.4 The Internal Mechanisms of Autonomous Mediator

A Mechanism for Dynamic Replacement of Half Protocol The reason to replace a half protocol dynamically is that we probably come across the situation different from which we anticipate at the beginning of negotiation. One of the possible cause for this is that we insufficiently specify each parameter for the type of negotiation defined by tuple (2) in Section 4.2. We suppose the following situation as for the insufficiency of each parameter. For example, S may not include a necessary state, or items in G may not be sufficient, or O might include an undefined post-processing.

The Mediator contains a mechanism for dynamically changing half protocol by one of two ways. Each case is described below using the code fragment for meta of the mediator in Figure 8.

```
1. [object meta-mediator
2.   (state ...
3.    [abuf := nil] ;; associated list for mem-no
4.    [c-state := ':get-decision] ;; current state
5.    [c-func  := ':gather]        ;; current function
6.    ;; state transition diagram
7.    [state-trans
8.     := '((:get-decision ((:gather ((:set-reply mem-no)))
9.                          (:decide :get-decision)
10.                         (:action ((yes  :change)
11.                                   (no   :nochange)))
12.                         (:next-state ((yes  :end)
13.                                       (no   :end)))))))])
14.  (script
15.   (=> :end
16.      (cond ((equal c-func ':gather)
17.             ( ... )) ;; process for ':gather function
18.            ((equal c-func ':decide)
19.             ( ... )) ;; process for ':decide function
20.            ((equal c-func ':action)
21.             ( ... ))) ;; process for ':action function
22.      (if (not [queue <== :empty?])
23.          [Me <= :begin]
24.          [mode := ':dormant]))
25.   (=> [:exchange-state-trans new-st]
26.      ...
27.      [state-trans := new-st]) ;; set a new state transition diagram
28.   (=> [:add-user new-user]
29.      [users := (append users (list new-user))]
30.      (rplacd (assoc 'mem-no abuf) (1+ (cdr (assoc 'mem-no abuf)))))
31.   (=> [:start-new-mediator mediator-type]
32.      [[mediator-gen <= [:new mediator-type Me]]]) ;; generate a new mediator
33.   ...)]
```

Fig. 8. Dynamic Replacement Mechanism of a Half Protocol for Meta of Mediator

1. Replacement of a half protocol

This method also accompanies of data used in the half protocol. A variable "*state-trans*" in line 7 - 13 denotes a state transition diagram which defines a half protocol. A variable "*:get-decision*" in line 8 represents the name of a state, and the method name for the functions "*gather*"," *decide*", and "*action*" are specified.

Mediator exchanges a half protocol when the method [*:exchange-state-trans* ...] in line 25 is invoked. After it verifies that no other method is executing, it sets new state transition diagram as the half protocol (line 27)[9]. As an example of accompanied data modification, we use the case that the participants of the negotiation increases. This case is notified to the mediator by the message [*:add-user* ...] in line 28, which increments the number to wait for the end of *:set-reply* method in "*gather*" function by one.

---

[9] Note that, in our research, we aim to realize a mechanism that meta of mediator reuses the history of negotiation and changes the structure of a state transition diagram dynamically, when it changes a half protocol. However, at the current implementation, meta of mediator exchanges a half protocol and retries negotiation from the beginning.

```
1. [object meta-mediator
2.   (state
3.     [c-state := ':get-decision] ;;  current state
4.     [c-func  := ':gather]       ;;  current function
5.     [monitor-obj := [monitor-gen <== :new]])
6.   (script
7.     (=> :begin
8.         (match [queue <== :deq]
9.           (is [M R S]
10.              [monitor-obj <= [:monitor Me :begin [M R S]]]
11.              (match (find-script M R S scriptSet)
12.                (is [Bindings ScriptBody]
13.                    [evaluator
14.                     <= [:do ScriptBody [env-gen <== [:new Bindings state]]
15.                         Me Group-manager evaluator]
16.                    @ [cont ' [monitor-obj <= [:monitor Me :end [M R S]]]
17.                            [Me <= :end]]]))))))
18.    (=> :current-status?
19.        !(list c-state c-func))
20.    (=> :access-history? @ R
21.        [monitor-obj <= :access-history? @ R])
22.    (=> :abort
23.        ...
24.        [c-state := ':end])
25.   )]
```

Fig. 9. Mechanism to Support Negotiation Coordination

2. *Delegation to other types of mediators*
   It is often the case that we need an assistance from other types of mediators. As the subject of negotiation is analyzed in detail, we often come across the situation which we do not anticipate before negotiation. For example, we may have an obscure point about the modification. We deal with this situation by the method [:*start-new-mediator* ...] (line 31) to delegate to other type of mediator to solve it.

A Mechanism to Support Coordination for Negotiation In this section, we discuss a mechanism to support an engineer, acting as a coordinator, to coordinate a negotiation according to Figure 9. The coordinator needs to gather the necessary information to know the progress status of negotiation. The coordinator assists an engineer if he is in trouble. For this purpose, meta of mediator keeps track of a progress status in a variable "*c-state*" and a history of method invocation in "*monitor-obj*" object. The history is taken before and after the execution of the main method (line 10 and 16). We can retrieve the history by invoking the method ":*access-history?*" (line 20). By examining the history, we can obtain the knowledge about the progress of negotiation. We can also detect whether negotiation is moving towards affirmative or negative side in a total at the time. In addition, we perceive the possibility of an engineer in a trouble if we detect unnecessary repetition and stagnant at the same state. In this case, a coordinator inquires the status for the engineer and knows his situation in more detail in order to give some advice. However, if a coordinator judges that they cannot continue the negotiation, he requests all meta of mediators to interrupt the negotiation, or initiate replacement of a half protocol.

5 Practical Example: Cooperative Write

5.1 The Situation of Cooperative Write

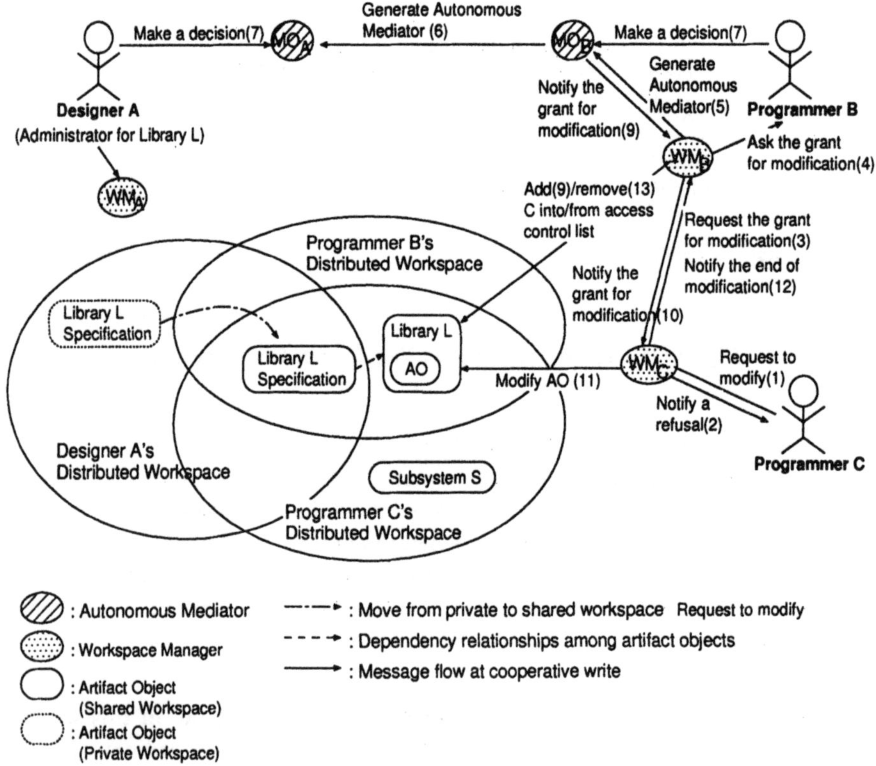

Fig. 10. Cooperative Write

We assume a project whose members develop a software in distributed places using C++ language. Consider the situation that a designer A and two programmers B and C in this project work cooperatively(Figure 10). A designer A designed the specification of library L and asked B to develop a program according to the specification. A programmer B develops library L. A programmer C develops sub-system S and uses L for his development. That is, B has the right to modify L, but C does not. In this situation, let us assume that C notices a problem in an interface of a class "*libclass*" in L. The programmer C will begin negotiating with A and B to modify the interface.

5.2 Scenario of Cooperative Write

A typical scenario of the Cooperative Write is as follows. The number in parentheses corresponds to the number in a message flow in Figure 10.

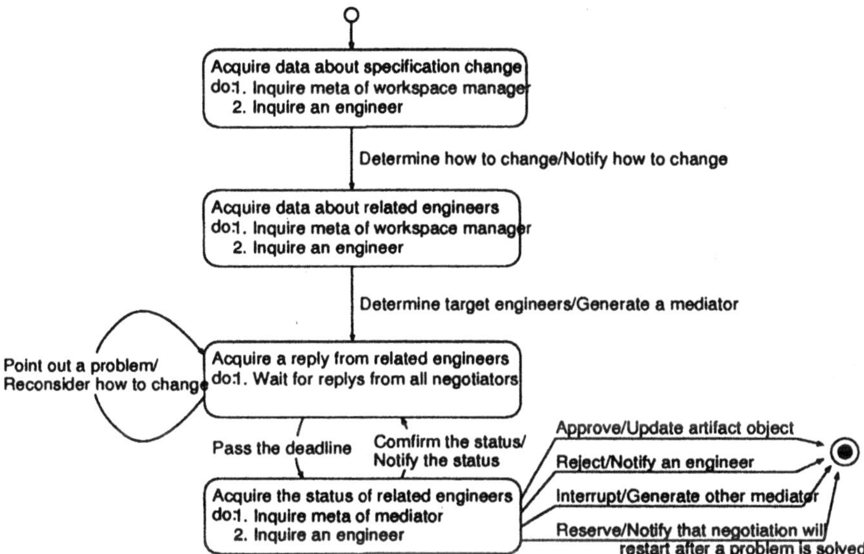

Fig. 11. A State Transition Diagram for the Mediator to Support a Coordinator

1. C reads an artifact object AO which defines the interface of "*libclass*", and then sends the modification request with a new interface to C's workspace manager WM_C (1).
2. Meta of C's workspace manager MWM_C notifies C that the modification request is rejected because C has no right to modify AO (2). MWM_C requests B, who is an administrator of AO, to allow to modify AO (3).
3. MWM_B reserves the modification request and asks B if he permits the modification (4).
4. If B permits the modification, MWM_B starts MO_B to negotiate with A because A designs the specification of AO (5). B takes a role of coordinator and MO_B assists B during negotiation. Figure 11 shows the state transition diagram in MWM_B.
5. MO_B generates MO_A to ask A's opinion (6). Figure 12 shows a state transition diagram on MWM_A. The goal for the execution by MO_B is to select a decision from 1) approve, 2) reject, 3) interrupt, or 4) reserve.
6. A and B negotiate each other through MO_A and MO_B, and finally select a decision from the four candidates described in the step 5 above (7).
7. A result of selection is notified to MWM_B (8). If the is "approve", MWM_B temporary adds C into the access control list for modification in MAO until he completes the modification (9).

8. MWM_B notifies MWM_C that C can modify AO (10), and then C modifies AO[10] (11).
9. MWM_C notifies MWM_B that C has finished the modification (12). C is removed from the access control list in MAO (13).

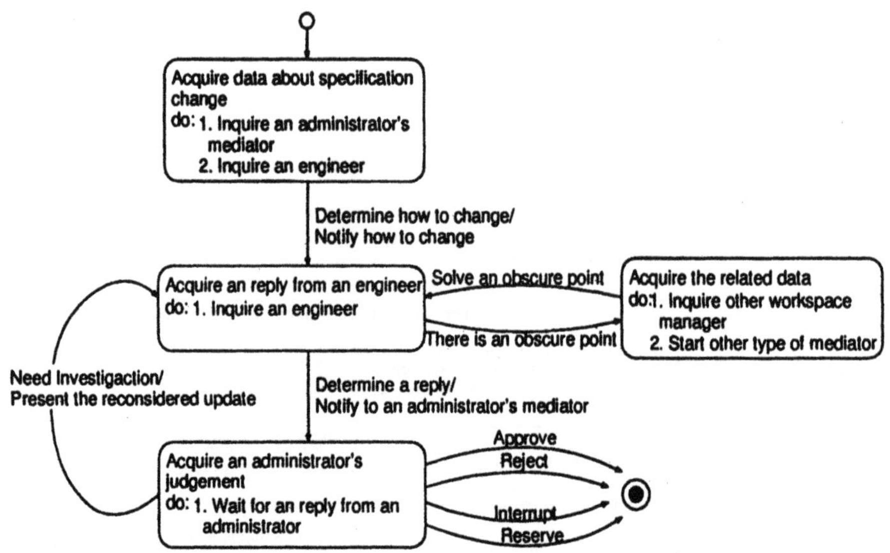

Fig. 12. A State Transition Diagram for the Mediator to Support a Negotiator

6 Prototype System Implementation

We implemented a prototype system and investigated the feasibility of the model. In this section, we report the result.

We can easily implement base/meta of object in ABCL/R2 because it is an object-oriented concurrent reflective language. ABCL/R2 is a public domain software and it runs on Sun SparcStation and SONY NEWS in our environment. Since ABCL/R2 does not provide a mechanism for (1) access to distributed object (2) object migration between different workstations, we implemented these functionalities on ABCL/R2.

7 Conclusion

We have proposed an object-oriented architecture for data sharing and modifications of the shared data in a distributed software development environment.

[10] Note that in this scenario, we dropped the following details: (1) the case that the result of negotiation between A and B is not "approve" (2) the case that C is allowed and delegated the right for modification.

Since shared data generated during distributed software development are considerable source of cooperative works, a mechanism to support the data sharing must consider human-computer interaction. We modeled a distributed workspace as a range of responsibility for an engineer's work. We have proposed a mechanism to present and modify shared artifact object jointly by the workspace manager and the object. We have also proposed a mechanism to support negotiation required for modification of shared data. We have analyzed the types of negotiation and introduced the autonomous mediator for an implementation model of the type.

We have used computational reflection to modify policies in cooperative work style. This approach has two advantages: (1) We can customize an environment dynamically according to the change of the work style, because we can select a proper method from ones which are prepared in advance, and (2) We can select a method to deal with an abnormal situation if the first method did not finish normally.

We should notice that the computational reflection is indistinguishable in the design of workspace manager and mediator object. Workspace manager changes access method to shared data and mediator collects data by multiple substitute methods.

Currently we have a plan of an experiment to apply our result to a real distributed environment. We are going to investigate the way to deal with more complex situations [19]. The model and system which we propose in this paper is considered to be a sub-system of *CSCSD* (*Computer Supported Cooperative Software Development*) "*JIZAI*" [20]. *JIZAI* integrates the support of software development and communication among engineers.

8 Acknowledgments

We thank to Hidehiko Masuhara for his kind advice for the implementation issues by ABCL/R2.

References

1. Bernstein,P.A., Hadzilacos,V., and Goodman,N.: Concurrency Control and Recovery in Database Systems. (1987), Addison-Wesley Publishing Company.
2. Maes,P.: Concepts and experiments in computational reflection. Proc. of OOPSLA'87, (1987), pp. 147-155.
3. Yokote,Y.: The Apertos Reflective Operating System: The Concept and Its Implementation. Proc. of OOPSLA '92, (1992), pp. 414-434.
4. Watanabe,T. and Yonezawa,A.: An actor-based metalevel architecture for groupwide reflection. Proc. of the REX School/Workshop on Foundations of Object-Oriented Languages (REX/FOOL), (1990). (Also in LNCS No. 489, 1991).
5. Masuhara,H., Matsuoka,S., Watanabe,T. and Yonezawa,A.: Object-Oriented Concurrent Reflective Languages can be Implemented Efficiently. Proc. of OOPSLA '92, (1992) pp. 127-144.

6. Matsuoka,S., Watanabe,T., and Yonezawa,A.: Hybrid Group Reflective Architecture for Object-Oriented Concurrent Reflective Programming. Proc. of ECOOP '91, LNCS No. 512, (1991), pp. 231-250.
7. Okamura,H., Ishikawa,Y., and Tokoro,M.: Metalevel Decomposition in AL-1/D. LNCS No. 742, (1993), pp. 110-127.
8. Rodden,T., Mariani,J.A. and Blair,G.: Supporting Cooperative Applications. Computer Supported Cooperative Work, No. 1, (1992), pp. 41-67.
9. Mullender,S.J., Rossum,G.van, Tanenbaum,A.S., Renesse,R.van, and Staaveren,H.van: Amoeba A Distributed Operating System for the 1990s. Computer, May (1990), pp. 44-53.
10. OMG: The Common Object Request Broker: Architecture and Specification. OMG Document Number 1991.12.1, Revision 1.1, OMG, Draft 0, Dec. (1991).
11. Pardyak,P.: Group Comminication in an Object-Based Environment. Proc. of International Workshop on Object-Orientation in Operating System, (1992), pp. 106-116.
12. Black,A.P. and Immel,M.P.: Encapsulating Plurality. Proc. of ECOOP '93. LNCS No. 707, (1993), pp. 57-79.
13. Belkhatir,N., Estublier,J. and Melo,W.L.: Software Process Model and Work Space Control in the Adele System. Proc. of 2nd ICSP, (1993), pp. 2-11.
14. Hailpern,B., and Ossher,H.: Extending Objects to Support Multiple Interfaces and Access Control. IEEE Trans. on Soft. Eng., Vol. 16, No. 11, (1990), pp. 1247-1257.
15. Adams,E.W., Honda,M., and Miller,T.C.: Object Management in a CASE Environment. Proc. of 11th ICSE, (1989), pp. 154-163.
16. Katz,R.H.: Toward a Unified Framework for Version Modeling in Engineering Databases. ACM Computing Surveys, Vol. 22, No. 4 (1990), pp. 375-408.
17. Gallo,T., Serrano,G. and Tisatu,F.: ObNet: An Object Oriented Approach for Supporting Large, Long-Lived, Highly Configurable Systems. Proc. of the 11th ICSE, (1989), pp. 138-144.
18. Yonezawa,A., editor. ABCL: An Object-Oriented Concurrent System. Computer Systems Series. (1990), The MIT Press.
19. Araki,K., Okamura,K., Saeki,M., Miura,N., Ochimizu,K., Sinoda,Y., and Kaiya,H.: Supporting Cooperative Works Through Computer Network. Summer Workshop in Tateyama, IEICE, Vol.95, No.1, (1995-07), pp.105-112 (in Japanese).
20. Ochimizu,K., Kadowaki,C., Fujieda,K., and Hori,M.: Design of A Software Development Environment JIZAI for Distributed Software Development. Technical Report of IEICE, SS94-18, (1994) (in Japanese).

Agent-Based Tool Integration for Distributed Information Systems

M. C. Norrie, M. Wunderli

ETH (Swiss Federal Institute of Technology)
Institute for Information Systems,
ETH-Zentrum, CH-8092 Zurich, Switzerland.
email: {norrie,wunderli}@inf.ethz.ch

Abstract. We present an approach for the integration of existing tools into higher-level application systems such as is required for workflow management, computer integrated manufacturing and computer-assisted software engineering. Tool integration is achieved through the introduction of agents which monitor and control the operation of the tool and provide an abstract view of the local data and operations. Then the management of data is distributed among the local tools and a central coordination system. Agent functionality is described in terms of both a general architecture and an examination of two specific agents — one for a revision control system and one for a CAD system. Following this, we present a general scheme for agent construction based on tool classification.

1 Introduction

Advanced application systems for business processing, computer integrated manufacturing (CIM) and computer-assisted software engineering (CASE) are all concerned with the integration of new and/or existing tools to achieve the coordination of high-level user and application tasks. A variety of technologies have been proposed to support such systems and these include workflow management systems [GHS95], repository systems [BD94] and product data management systems for CIM [CADIM, Sherpa]. These technologies vary in terms of their intended functionality, application domain and approach to coordination. However, what they have in common is the necessity to interface to existing tools to gain the required level of control over their operation and data.

Many of these systems assume that the information flow that controls coordination is either based on email messages or a shared database. In the former case, it is assumed that users notify some form of central coordination system when certain actions have been completed and, as a result, other users will be requested to perform certain other actions. In this way, the tools are actually integrated into the system via the users. This approach has been adopted in some workflow management systems (see [GHS95] for an overview of existing products).

Alternatively, a central integrated database may be used to store all data objects and also rules which can trigger the system operations necessary for coordination. This approach is used in many repository-based systems for CASE [BD94]. In such cases, it is usually assumed that the tools are open systems to which external control and data access are provided. This may be the case with tools developed as part of such advanced application systems or according to new interoperability standards such as CORBA [OMG91] or STEP [STE92]. However, many existing tools, such as CAD systems, are large, complex systems which support limited forms of external access and cannot be easily replaced. Data is stored locally, usually not under the control of a DBMS, and using internal formats that frequently vary between system versions.

Current product data management systems [CADIM, Sherpa] can be considered as combining these two approaches in the sense that data is stored in a central integration database, but the information and control flow between this database and the tools is performed through the users by means of explicit check-in/check-out mechanisms.

In this paper, we address the specific issue of how to integrate existing tools into distributed information systems in such a way that the information and control flow is automated as far as possible. We achieve such integration by means of tool-specific agents which monitor their operation and can invoke local operations.

We are not concerned here with a particular architecture or application domain. Most of the discussion is therefore independent of whether data resides only locally or is stored in a central integration database. However, we note that the approach described here has been adopted in a system for CIM tool integration which stores only coordination data in a central repository. Details of this coordination approach are given in [NW95, NSSW94, NWM+94].

In section 2, we discuss the need for such agent-based tool integration and the general requirements for such agents in terms of the functionality they must support. A general agent architecture is presented in section 3. In sections 4 and 5, we give overviews of two specific agents that we have developed. The first is a relatively simple agent which was developed for the revision control system, RCS. The second agent is for the CAD system, Pro/ENGINEER [Par93], and it exhibits many of the features typical of agents required for the integration of existing, complex design tools. Section 6 examines the various categories of tool architectures with respect to the required integration approach and effort and presents a general tool classification scheme. The resulting classification scheme is useful, not only in understanding the various issues and approaches, but also in enabling someone to construct an agent for a particular tool by identifying similar tool architectures and reusing implementation technique and code.

2 Agent Requirements

We assume an advanced application system built on top of existing tools which store and manipulate local data. Coordination of activities is achieved through some form of central coordination system which manages certain metadata and data. The extent to which data is managed, or replicated, centrally is not of importance to this discussion. Likewise, the precise nature of the coordination system and the forms of coordination supported is not significant here. Rather, we focus on the issue of how the coordination system interfaces to the tools in order that it knows that certain tool activities have been performed and, further, can initiate local actions.

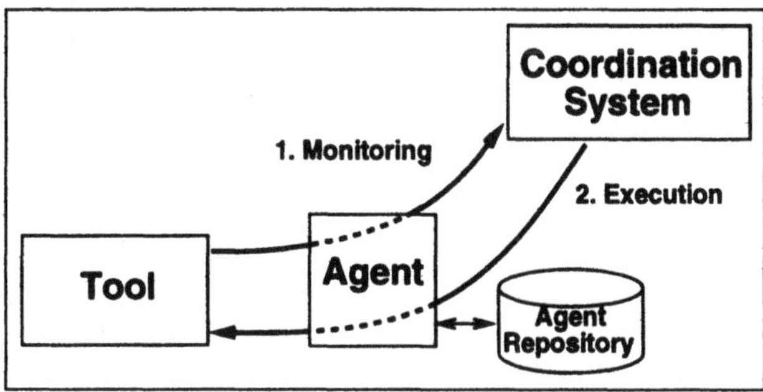

Fig. 1. Agent main tasks

The interface between a tool and the coordination system is realised by an agent as shown in figure 1. The two main tasks of an agent are to monitor the tool and keep the coordination system informed of any operations of global interest, and, to ensure that the tool performs operations necessary to the coordination process. It is not always the case that the tool operations can be invoked automatically as it may be necessary for a user to be involved in taking decisions or supplying information. In such cases, a message may be sent to the relevant users requesting that they take some action. However, it should not be the case that all tool operations have to be initiated by a user as is the case in some workflow management systems where all information and control flow is by means of email to users.

The agent must provide an abstract view of the tool's data and operation that corresponds to that of the coordination system. For example, for a CAD system, the abstract view of data and operations would be at the level of design objects and save operations on these objects rather than at the lower levels such as individual edit operations on a drawing. Likewise, the coordination system may not require knowledge of the object structure and value but rather only of its existence and relationship to objects operated on by other tools. Thus, for coordination in a CIM system, it may be required to know that a particular design object is related to a particular document object, but it is not necessary to know about the geometry of a drawing.

The abstract view of a tool's data and operation is provided by a mapping between the model of the coordination system and that of the tool. This mapping information is stored in the agent's repository. The coordination process must be subject to transaction management to ensure global consistency. The agent's repository therefore also stores log information about the coordination process and possibly even about the local tool data and operations in order that certain recovery actions may be supported.

The abstract view, as well as the model of the coordination system, are expressed in terms of a global data model. In the examples of this paper, we assume the semantic model NIAM [VB82] as the global data model. However, the general approach is independent of a specific data model.

3 Agent Architecture

In order to encapsulate tool-specific aspects into distinct components of an agent, and for the sake of reusability, we have split the agent architecture into modules. A schematic overview is shown in figure 2. In this section, we describe each of the four modules.

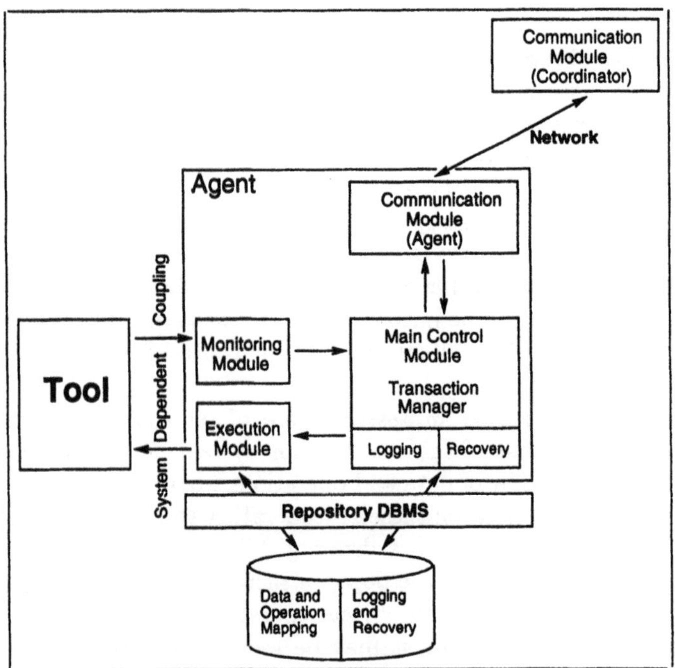

Fig. 2. General agent architecture

3.1 Communication module

The communication module deals with the input and output of messages between the agent and the central coordination system which would have a similar communication module. In the systems we have built, the communication module is based on a socket library as is available on major operating systems such as Unix, MVS, MacOS and Windows. The advantage of choosing such a low-level of communication is that it ensures independence of both the nature of the tool and the platform on which it runs.

The communication modules exchange information by means of a network transfer language that specifies the format of messages. A message comprises a header part and a data part. The header gives information such as the message source, the associated global and local transaction identifiers and the requested operation. The data part consists of any data objects to be transferred. Messages may be either control messages where the requested operations are related to transaction management or data messages where the requested operations are related to the creation, deletion and update of data objects.

3.2 Main control module

The main control module of an agent schedules local operations initiated by a tool and requests from the central coordination system. The operation and complexity of this module varies greatly according to the nature of the tool, especially in terms of the notions of atomicity and concurrency that it supports. Generally, there are two fundamental categories of tool systems. One category consists of those such as CAD systems which have low concurrency, long-running transactions and frequently a check-in/check-out mechanism for control of shared access to data. The other category consists of those with high-concurrency and short transactions such as might be found in a resource management system; these systems are often implemented on a DBMS.

In the former category, a simple scheduler will suffice whereas, in the latter case, the scheduler must be more complex to ensure efficiency of operation. For example, for a CAD system, a scheduler may simply serialise incoming requests and interact with the user to ask for the release of locks on objects in order that the processing of these requests may proceed.

3.3 Execution module and monitoring module

The remaining two modules are the monitoring module and the execution module which are responsible for the monitoring of tool operations and initiation of externally requested actions, respectively. It is these modules that map between tool data and operations and those of the centralised coordination system. Their operation is very specific to the tool architecture. Thus, while the communication and control modules can be generalised, the execution and monitoring modules are tool specific. However, by recognising similar classes of tools, it is possible to reuse design, and even code, in the development of particular agents.

As stated, the monitoring and execution modules require a mapping between tool data and operations and those of the central coordination system. The overall coordination of the distributed information system is expressed in terms of a basic set of operations on objects such as *insert*, *delete* and *update*. These operations are interpreted locally by mapping them into a number of tool specific operations. Note that these operations may include requests and notifications to users as well as the direct invocation of tool operations. For example, the update of a new design document by a CAD tool may ultimately result in an email message to another user requesting that they create a corresponding update in the design documentation using a text editing tool. Such a user notification, however, should always be coupled with a monitoring component which detects whether a user has at least done *something*. Whether he did the right thing, of course, cannot be checked by the tool's agent.

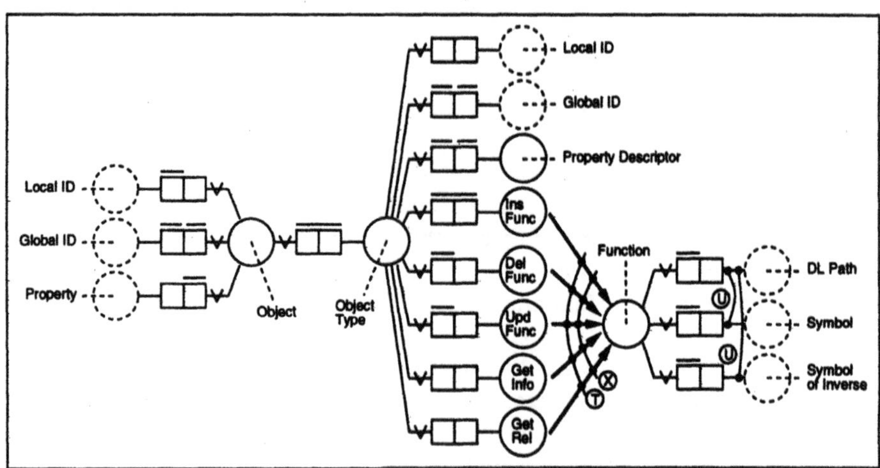

Fig. 3. Metamodel for data model mapping

Figure 3 is a NIAM representation [VB82] of the agent's metamodel for this mapping. The metamodel shows the mappings between the global and local objects and object types. Solid circles represent NIAM object types, dashed circles stand for attributes. Attributes and object types are connected by the same construct, the NIAM fact type, which is graphically represented as a box. Cardinality constraints are imposed on fact types by an existing or non-existing V (lower boundary 1 resp. 0) and an existing or non-existing bar (upper boundary 1 or *). For the sake of simplicity, we have omitted here the attributes associated with certain object types, e.g. **Property Descriptor**.

Global operations, such as *update* on object types are represented in the metamodel as object types describing the location of their implementation. We use the concept of dynamic linking and loading (DLL) to avoid the hard-coding of implementation of the global functions; the functions are dynamically loaded at the start-up time of an agent, thereby permitting flexible customisation. The function DDL paths and symbols are stored in the agent's repository.

Additionally, we have inverse functions corresponding to inverse global operations on the object types. These inverse functions implement compensating actions in the event that operations stemming from requests from the central coordination system have to be undone because a global coordination operation failed.

The mapping between global operations and local functions also provides operations to support the agent's task. The *GetInfo* operation allows it to retrieve information about objects from the local tool dataset in order that it may, for example, be included in the data part of messages and possibly used in other tools. The *GetRel* operation is used to get information about the relationships in which an object participates in order that insert or delete operations on objects can cater for any such dependencies and ensure that local consistency is not violated.

The mapping between local and global operations is directly implemented in functions of the monitoring module, and therefore is not visible in the meta schema. However, the concept of dynamic loading and linking (DLL) is applied too to avoid hardcoding of monitoring functions.

Since the monitoring and execution modules are tool specific, we discuss two particular instances in the following sections. The first is for the Revision Control System, RCS and the second is for the CAD system Pro/ENGINEER [Par93]. These two agents illustrate the differences that can arise in both tool characteristics and, correspondingly, the complexity and detailed architecture of their agents. Following on from the description of these two specific agents, we generalise to consider the various forms of agents corresponding to the various classes of tools.

4 RCS Agent

The revision control system, RCS (produced by the Free Software Foundation), supports shared access to documents by means of version management together with check-in/check-out mechanisms.

RCS is in fact a collection of small application programs which together form the complete system. Each application program performs a specific task such as checking-in a version or displaying log tables. These application programs can be used either directly by a user in interactive text mode, or, by other higher-level application systems, such as a document management system (e.g. Framemaker) in batch mode.

A tool, such as RCS, implemented as a number of user-task-specific programs and with a batch interface is amenable to the use of wrapper programs to realise the monitoring and execution modules of an integration agent. This is illustrated in figure 4. Each wrapper program has the same interface as the original application program, but, in addition to performing the user-task by means of a call to the original program, they perform the monitoring task of the agent. In this way, information flow from the tool to the agent is guaranteed and is at the logical level of user operations. The execution module of the agent is easily realised by directly calling the programs.

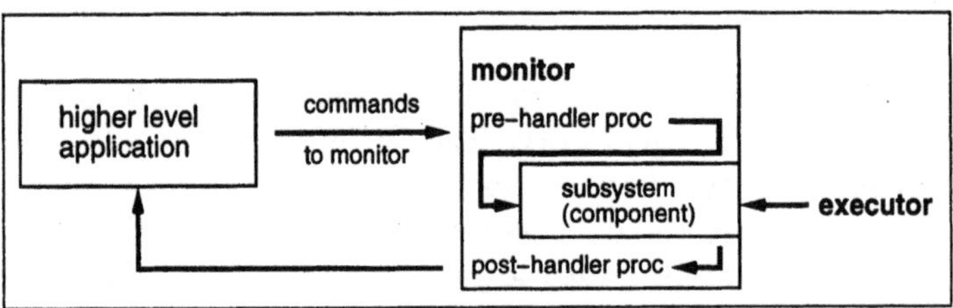

Fig. 4. Monitoring and execution by wrappers

Concurrency of operations on files controlled by RCS is managed by the RCS system itself by means of lock files. However, atomicity is more of a problem as it is possible to lose the whole version tree of a document due to a system failure. We therefore regard RCS as not providing atomicity of operations.

We now describe in detail how the RCS agent realises the abstract interface and the monitoring and execution modules.

4.1 RCS abstract interface

As RCS files are plain UNIX files, they reside in the UNIX filesystem. The RCS files of our example scenario are located on the account `cimdoc` in folders grouping them according to their purpose as illustrated in figure 5. Multiple occurrences of a file in more than one folder is implemented using links, however this is not supported by the RCS system itself and has to be done by an account administrator.

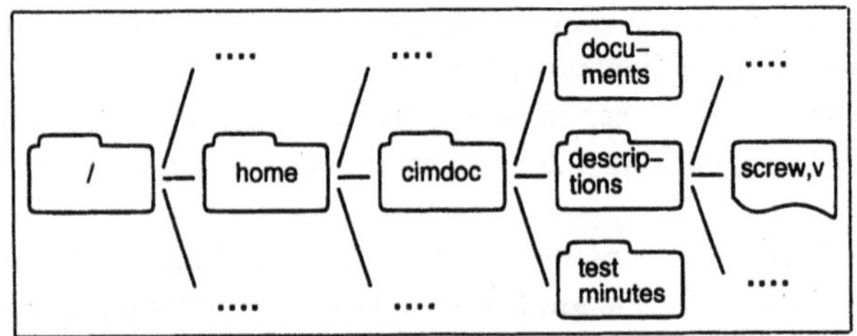

Fig. 5. The RCS document management system's schema

The description of the local data in terms of the global data model is quite straightforward as shown in figure 6: The mapping between the local and the global description of object types is a 1:1 mapping. The abstract interface models a subset of the RCS system's data on each file representing attributes considered to be of global importance. These are the attributes which will be sent in the object information part of a request to the coordination system and which are required by other tools.

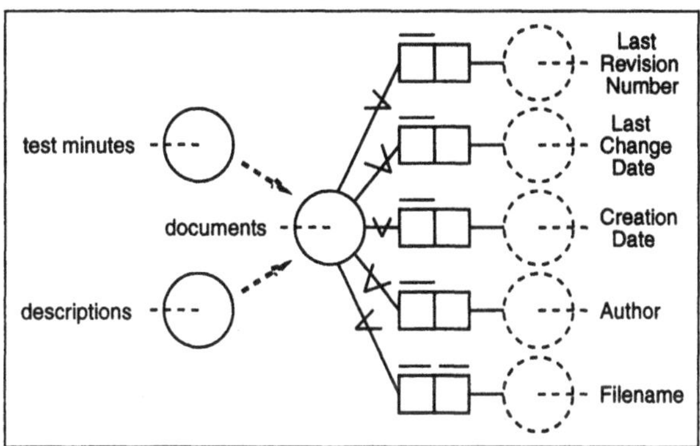

Fig. 6. RCS abstract interface

Although the notion of a transaction is not present in the RCS system, a call to an RCS component can contain more than one RCS file as its parameters. In order to maintain this grouping in the coordination system, we group these multiple operations into a single (sub-)transaction. The mapping of the most important RCS operations to transactions is shown in table 1.

It is important to note that most tools have no transaction support. Such a feature normally has to be provided by the agent of a tool, a fact which is reflected in the state transitions of a user-involved and a coordination-system-involved (local) subtransaction. We will show this in the next subsection.

4.2 Monitoring module

Since the monitoring is based on wrapper programs around the tool operations `ci`, `co`, `rcsdel` and `rcsinit`, each tool operation (program call) can be mapped to a single transaction for which confirmation has to be requested from the coordination system.

Figure 7 shows the possible state transitions of a transaction corresponding to a user operation. A subtransaction is started before the tool operation takes place in order to prepare the global transaction and the transaction associated logging. We then wait until the tool operation has completed successfully before sending the complete request to the coordination system (EoST: End of SubTransaction).

tool operation	induced transaction
co (check-out read)	snapshot operation, not relevant to coordination
co -l (check-out write)	start of (update) transaction
ci (check-in)	end of transaction, send update request to coordination system
rcsdel	transaction requesting the deletion of one or more RCS files
rcsinit	transaction requesting the creation of one or more RCS files

Table 1. RCS operations and their impact on the coordination system

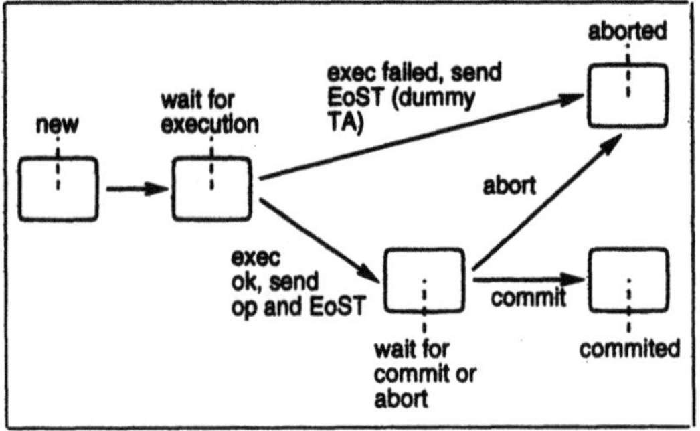

Fig. 7. Performing a user operation

If the tool operation fails, an empty transaction is sent which does no harm. If it succeeds, we are sure that we are really in a ready-to-commit state and therefore are really authorised to send such a request.

4.3 Execution module

The implementation of the execution module of the RCS agent is straightforward. In the case of delete and create requests, the corresponding operations `rcsdel` and `rcsinit` can be called by the execution module in the same way as they would be called by a user and therefore can be handled automatically. However, in the case of update requests, we have chosen an interactive approach. An email message is sent to the last author of a document requesting the update. If this user then performs a check-in operation (`ci`) of the file for which the update was requested, the requested operation is regarded as being fulfilled.

Figure 8 shows the state transitions of a request received from the coordination system. The agent starts a new transaction if it receives such a request. It

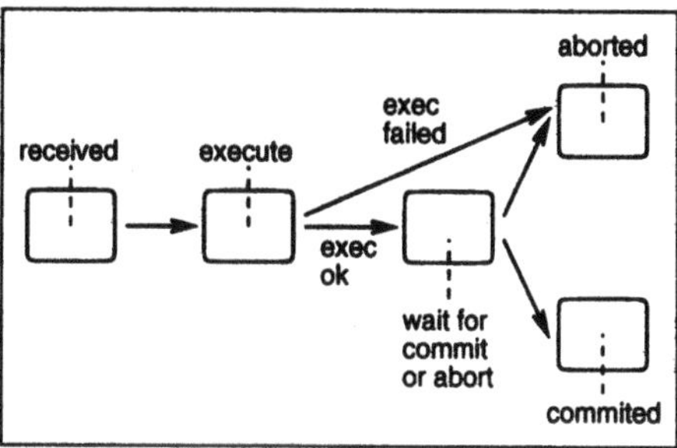

Fig. 8. A request received from the coordination system

then waits until the execution module reports success or failure of the requested operation and afterwards goes into the state 'aborted' or 'wait for commit/abort'. The latter wait state is left depending on the answer of the coordination system as to the outcome of the associated global transaction.

5 Pro/ENGINEER Agent

Pro/ENGINEER [Par93] is a modern CAD system both in terms of its design paradigm based on feature modelling and its extensibility. The system stores its data in files with each design version stored in a separate file. Therefore, while it does not support atomicity directly, its storage of version data does facilitate support for atomicity as provided by the agent. The system does not control concurrent access to data, a feature which has to be supplied by the agent.

5.1 Application Programming Interface Pro/DEVELOP

Pro/ENGINEER provides the developer with an Application Programming Interface called Pro/DEVELOP. This interface allows external applications to execute operations on Pro/ENGINEER's data (both in memory and on disk) and monitor user functions such as "save a drawing" using pre- and post-handlers. These pre- and post-handlers provide the basis for information flow to an agent. Figure 9 illustrates the interfacing concept in the case of Pro/ENGINEER.

Through its application programming interface, Pro/ENGINEER can be enhanced with procedures that are triggered whenever the associated operation is executed. Such a procedure sends a notification message containing the name of the operation to a program which is defined in a Pro/ENGINEER configuration file.

In order that user actions can be monitored, event-handlers have to be installed for all the relevant Pro/ENGINEER operations. An event is the execution of a Pro/ENGINEER operation. It can be fired either before or after the execution of the operation, and, correspondingly, we speak of before-events

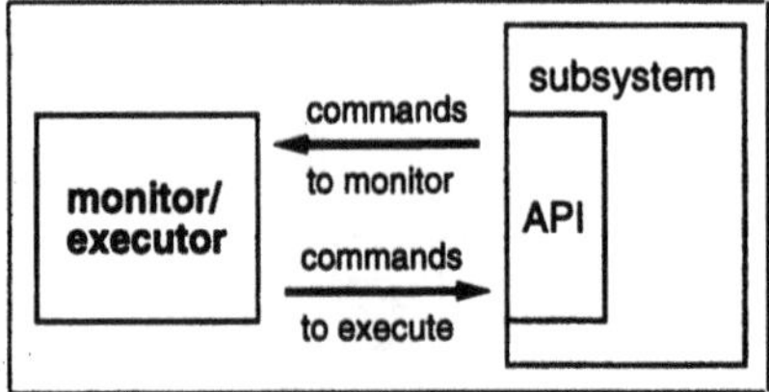

Fig. 9. Monitoring and execution by API

and after-events. When the event is fired, the corresponding handlers will call procedures running in a separate process using the Pro/DEVELOP library.

The Pro/ENGINEER operations we want to monitor are the so-called dbms-operations. These operations include all the operations for file handling, e.g. the storing of the CAD objects. The label 'dbms' should not mislead: The dbms-operations are just plain file operations and have nothing to do with a DBMS nor do they implement anything of the well-known transaction properties of a DBMS.

The central procedure for the installation of handlers is the Pro/DEVELOP function `prodev_notify`. This function gets a label representing the monitored operation, a switch whether it is the before- or the after-event and the name of the procedure to be called if the event occurs. For example,

```
prodev_notify("menu_dbms_create_object", "begin", NotifyPreInsert);
```

will called the procedure `NotifyPreInsert` before an operation to create an object is executed.

In order to receive acknowledgements that Pro/ENGINEER has completed its task, handlers can be installed which are called *after* the tool's operation has taken place. The form of the installation is analogue to the installation of the before-event handlers.

We have seen in this subsection what possibilities Pro/ENGINEER supplies to monitor its actions. We will now have a closer look at the problems associated with this approach and how we solved them.

5.2 Monitoring module

In theory, it would be very convenient if knowledge about a user action would be obtained before it actually takes place. As we have seen, Pro/ENGINEER supports pre-handlers for the dbms-operations which could do the required task. However, these handlers can only be installed for events fired as a result of the *selection of a menu entry* for a given operation, not the final execution of the requested operation.

This apparently minor difference causes a lot of problems. After the selection of a menu entry, it is not yet clear on which object the requested operation will be performed. Pro/ENGINEER only proposes a default value to the user which is usually the document name of the active window, or, a system-generated name if the object has not yet been saved. This default value can be requested by the before-event handler. It would be possible for that handler to restrict the selection of the object to be saved to exactly the default value. However, this would restrict a user and would change the functionality of the Pro/ENGINEER interface.

Another problem lies in the hierarchical organisation of designs into assemblies and parts. A before-event handler gets only the name of the root assembly if an assembly has to be saved. In order to determine which subordinate assemblies and parts will also be saved, it has to parse the corresponding assembly file and detect which elements have been changed. Since Pro/ENGINEER designs can be very complex, this takes a considerable amount of time. Furthermore, exactly the same action is performed by Pro/ENGINEER itself afterwards, when the real save operation takes place and it passes the names of the saved parts to the after-event handler.

For these reasons, we decided not to use the pre-handlers for the monitoring module. Fortunately, this decision does not impose large problems on the agent because the before-images of the saved objects, i.e. the files with a lower version number attached, are available for a potential compensating operation should the operation have to be undone.

monitored	action	
dbms-operation	pre-handler	post-handler
create, retrieve	—	requests locks, prepare undo
delete	—	buildup delete request
save	—	new object: buildup insert request existing object: buildup update request
copy	—	buildup insert request
rename	—	update repository (the local id)
purge	—	maybe save second-newest version

Table 2. Mapping of operations

Table 2 shows how we map the user operations in Pro/ENGINEER to actions in the agent. The mapping of the **purge** and the **save** operations may require further explanation.

Purge will delete all old versions of a certain object, i.e. all files with the same name but not having the highest version number. In the case of `screw.part;1`, `screw.part;2` and `screw.part;3`, the operation **purge** consequently would delete `screw.part;1` and `screw.part;2`. As there are cases where `screw.part;2` could be required for a compensating operation, we may first have to save it elsewhere.

In the case of the **save** operation, only one insert or update request is generated in a transaction. This is due to the fact that, for coordination with other tools, only the fact that an update or an insert has occurred is important, and not the possibly numerous intermediate steps created by repeated saves.

5.3 Execution module

We have so far described how operations from Pro/ENGINEER can be monitored and how confirmation is requested for them from the coordination system. In this subsection, we consider the opposite direction concerning requests from the coordination system to execute actions on Pro/ENGINEER data files.

During the development of the execution component, we discovered that very few actions can be performed automatically in theory, and even less in practice. If we regard the three basic global operations insert, delete and update, we can state the following:

insert: Although a CAD design normally cannot be created automatically, one could create an empty file without user interaction. This, however, is not very useful and we therefore did not choose that solution. We decided to inform the user about the necessity to create a new design and leave the rest to him (although certain transaction support is given as we will show later in this subsection).

update: In case of an update request, the situation is quite clear. A user must be involved and no action can be taken automatically by the execution module. User notification is the only possibility.

delete: The deletion of a part or an assembly is the only operation where an automatic approach could be employed. The choice would be to either physically delete the file or move it to another location and inform the user. Unfortunately, there is no Pro/DEVELOP function to remove a part or an assembly (although there is the possibility to monitor the deletion of an object if the user does it interactively). Because of the references of files into other files, it is not possible just to execute a move operation on the operating system level. Therefore, even the delete operation had to be implemented as a request to the user.

There are two ways in which user notification is performed. Firstly, the user who last accessed the relevant object is sent an email message containing the request. Secondly, notification messages are additionally displayed in a special message window attached to Pro/ENGINEER. Of course, a request to the Pro/ENGINEER system is not regarded as being fulfilled simply by sending the notification message. The monitoring module will detect that the requested action has been performed and passes on the information to the main control module.

Consider the case of an `insert` request. The control module checks every insertion message sent by the monitoring module to determine whether it is for an object (id) with an outstanding execution request. If this is the case, the transaction manager in the control module will remove the insertion operation from the tool request and unifies it with the corresponding one from the execution request. Therefore a user can react on an insertion request by saving a new object with the same local identifier as mentioned in the request message. The same mechanism applies for the delete and update operations requested by the coordination system.

In summary, although execution requests sent by the coordination system cannot be performed automatically, we have found an efficient and elegant way to create a semi-automatic solution.

We can contrast Pro/ENGINEER with the classic CAD system, CATIA. CATIA is a monolithic CAD system built by IBM [CATIA] and its age is very much reflected in its architecture. Atomicity of operations is not guaranteed at all and the execution of actions by external programs — although it is possible — has to take care of concurrency itself.

In the case of CATIA, the aspect of information flow to an external program is a bit more difficult to classify. Strictly, the operation of a tool should be unaffected by the integration process — at least if no user interaction is necessary for re-establishing global consistency. The user interface consequently has to remain the same. If this condition were to be satisfied, there is no straightforward way for an agent to monitor a user's actions. However, it is possible to extend the CATIA function menus using Application Programming Interfaces (API) such as GII and CATGEO [GII88, CATGEO92] which allow the call of CATIA internal data management functions. Using these APIs, a completely new function-menu structure can be built which enables the monitoring of all relevant user actions by providing the necessary hooks. But note that existing menus cannot be disabled and therefore bypassing the agent is theoretically possible.

6 Tool Classification

The ease with which an existing tool can be integrated into a distributed information system and the extent to which a full and seamless integration can be achieved depends on the nature of the tool. If the tool is based on an open, extensible architecture and supports distribution standards such as CORBA [OMG91], then the task is reasonably straightforward. However, as discussed, many existing application tools are actually complex systems with a fairly closed architecture and with little or no support to aid the integration process.

We base our classification of tools on three characteristics:

1) The form of communication supported between the tool and an external system.
2) The means by which tool data can be updated.
3) The extent to which the atomicity and durability of updates on data is supported.

Property 1) determines how the agent can obtain information about local operations and further how the agent can influence and control these operations.

Property 2) is concerned with how an agent can initiate local operations. Property 3) is concerned with the extent to which the operation of the tool may be considered reliable in terms of ensuring the consistency and currency of its stored data.

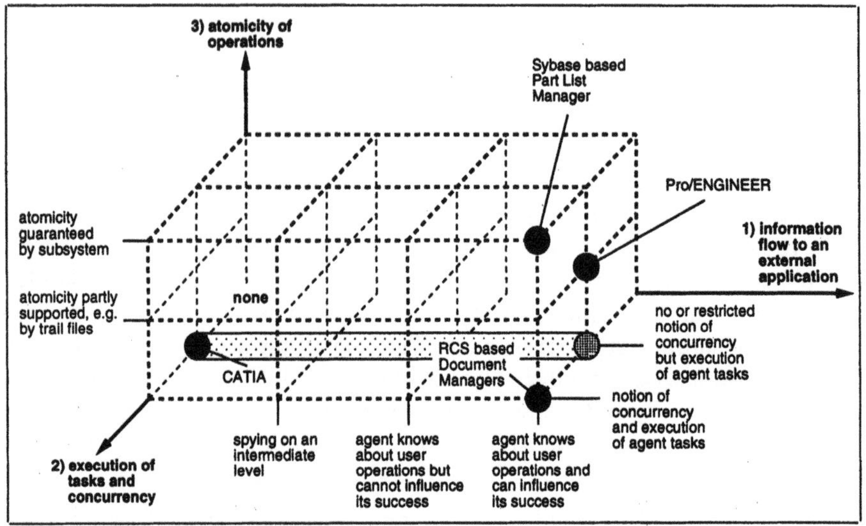

Fig. 10. Classification scheme for tools

To show the variety of tools and how they may be classified according to these characteristics, we illustrate a classification scheme in figure 10. Each axis corresponds to one of the above characteristics as indicated by the labels. In particular, we show the classification of the RCS and Pro/ENGINEER tools which were described in the previous sections. We will now describe the classification scheme in detail.

6.1 Information flow to an agent

For axis 1), we indicate four possible levels of information flow from the tool to an external application. The worst case scenario is that of a closed tool which provides no information on operations performed and does not permit foreign control over its data and operations. An example of such a tool might be a word-processing system with its data in files. In such a case, the agent might have to resort to monitoring file sizes and modification timestamps combined with tool version dependent knowledge of internal file structures to obtain information about user operations.

At the second level of information flow, we assume that it is possible to obtain information about operations and data at an intermediate level, i.e. at a higher level than sequences of bytes, but a lower level than the tool and user's model of data. An example of such a tool is a CAD system which manipulates geometrical objects such as cylinders but stores the data as sequences of lines, points etc. in a relational database system. In such a case, it may be possible to introduce a layer between the client and server which can monitor and interpret sequences of SQL statements.

A preferred situation is that of being able to obtain information about the tool's operations at the same logical level as that of the user operation. Assuming that information at this level is provided, we can further distinguish the case of obtaining the information *after* the operation has been performed from that where the information is obtained *before* the operation is performed. In the former case, there is no possibility to influence the outcome whereas in the latter case, it is possible to first seek authorisation from the central coordination system before any updates are committed. In the event that a tool supports some form of *undo* actions such that committed actions can be compensated, then the tool can be considered at the preferred level of information flow equivalent to the case where information is obtained about operations before they are committed.

6.2 Execution of external tasks and concurrency

The second aspect used to classify a tool into our framework is important in order that an agent can initiate an operation in its tool in response to a request by the coordination system.

It is preferred that a tool allows external triggering of operations. For example, the automatic creation of part lists, or the setting up of initial frames for technical manuals, are cases where it is desirable that an action can be initiated by an agent. Because a request submitted by the coordination system is not synchronised with any user action, it is important for the construction of an agent whether a tool supports concurrent or quasi concurrent access to its data. If not, the agent has to take care of the concurrency management.

6.3 Atomicity of operations

The third aspect of how a tool can support the construction of an agent and its integration into a distributed information system has to do with system failures. In an ideal world with no system failures, the aspects of information flow to an agent and the triggering of actions, as described in the previous two subsections, would be sufficient to classify a tool. Unfortunately, a tool failure, which results in a loss of data integrity, can occur due to either hardware or software problems. In the case of a stand-alone system, i.e. an application not integrated in a coordinated system, the worst result of a failure would be a full or partial loss of data which, hopefully, would be reduced by restoring data from a backup. However, in the case of a tool integrated in a coordinated system, the state of a tool is at least partially known outside the application, and we must guarantee that all state information made persistent in the coordination system truly reflects the current situation in the tool. This requirement can be fulfilled if the tool guarantees atomicity of operations and data durability together with a way to query its state.

If a tool does not completely provide such a notion, then the agent, with the help of the tool, has to provide it. It may be the case that the tool has some form of log files or trail files, which the agent can use to guarantee durability and atomicity. These files would be used for redoing failed operations or undoing partially performed operations. If the tool does not provide any support, the agent will have to perform all the logging and recovery itself.

In all three degrees of atomicity support described in this subsection, the atomicity related actions of an agent are isolated from the rest of the coordinated system so that the coordination system can deal with a component system (a tool plus its agent) as a database management system. In case of recovery from a crash, however, the coordination system has to be incorporated into the process to obtain necessary knowledge about the state of a component system. Further details on this topic are discussed in [Sch96].

7 Conclusions

We have shown that it is possible to integrate existing tools into distributed information systems by means of agents capable of monitoring and controlling tool operations. While the nature of such agents is tool-specific, it is possible to identify certain classes of tools which determine the appropriate agent architecture. As a result, general guidelines for the development of agents can be produced which, in many cases, facilitate the reuse or adaptation of existing agent modules.

Our experiences in building such agents bring out some interesting points concerning the nature of both the agents and the coordination of tasks in specific application domains.

Contrary to our initial expectations, we could not generally exploit the capability of tools to install pre-handlers for user operations, thereby enabling confirmation from the coordination system to be obtained before execution of the operation. Rather, these pre-handlers were typically used only to prepare a potential compensation of the operation. This was due to the fact that, with these pre-handlers, it is not certain whether the operation will in fact execute and, further, exactly what the operation will be as parameters may be unspecified at this point. For this reason, in both of the agents described in this paper, the transmission of the final user operations was performed in the post-handler part of the monitoring component.

In terms of the nature of task coordination, we found it rare that fully automatic execution of coordination requests is possible, or even desirable. Instead, we discovered that, in most cases, the best solution was some form of semi-automatic execution in which the user receives request notification, either by email or via the message window, and the system then monitors whether the user acts on this request. This approach allows the user to decide what happens to their data, while at the same time automatically detecting that the required task coordination happens.

References

[BD94] P. A. Bernstein and U. Dayal. An Overview of Repository Technology. In J. Bocca, M. Jarke, and C. Zaniolo, editors, *Proc. 20th Intl. Conf. on Very Large Databases (VLDB'94)*, pages pp 705–713. Morgan Kaufmann, September 1994.

[CADIM] Eigner+Partner GmbH, Ruschgraben 133, D-76139 Karlsruhe, Germany. *CADIM/EDB.*

[CATGEO92] IBM Corporation, Department 34CA, Neighbourhod Rd., Kingston, NY 12401, USA. *CATIA Base - Geometry Interface Reference Manual, SH50-0091-04*, 1992.

[CATIA] IBM Corporation, Marketing Publications, Department 824, 1133 Westchester Avenue, White Plains, NY 10604, USA. *The CATIA CAD system.*

[GHS95] D. Georgakopoulos, M. Hornick, and A. Sheth. An Overview of Workflow Management: From Process Modeling to Workflow Automation Infastructure. *Distributed and Parallel Databases*, 3:119–153, 1995.

[GII88] IBM Corporation, Marketing Publications, Department 824, 1133 Westchester Avenue, White Plains, NY 10604, USA. *CATIA - Graphics Interactive Interface (GII) Reference Manual, SH50-0020-0*, 1988.

[NSSW94] M. C. Norrie, W. Schaad, H.-J. Schek, and M. Wunderli. Exploiting Multidatabase Technology for CIM. Technical Report 219, Department of Computer Science, ETH Zurich, July 1994.

[NW95] M. C. Norrie and M. Wunderli. Modelling in Coordination Systems. *Intl. Journal of Cooperative Information Systems*, 4:189–211, 1995.

[NWM+94] M. C. Norrie, M. Wunderli, R. Montau, U. Leonhardt, W. Schaad, and H.-J. schek. Coordination Approaches for CIM. In *Proc. European Workshop on Integrated Manufacturing Systems Engineering*, Grenoble, France, December 1994.

[OMG91] OMG. The Common Object Request Broker: Architecture and Specification. Object Management Group and X/Open, Document Number 91.12.1, Rev. 1.1, 1991.

[Par93] Parametric Technology Corporation, 128 Technology Drive, Waltham, MA 02154, USA. *Pro/ENGINEER User Manuals*, 1993.

[Sch96] W. Schaad. *Transaktionsverwaltung in heterogenen, föerierten Datenbanksystemen.* PhD thesis, ETH Zürich, ETH Zentrum, CH-8092 Zürich, 1996.

[Sherpa] Sherpa Corporation, 611 River Oakes Parkway, San Jose CA 95134, USA. *Sherpa: DMS/PIMS.*

[STE92] STEP. *ISO DIS 10303, Product Data Representation and Exchange.* International Standard Organisation, Technical Committee 184, 1992.

[VB82] G. M. A. Verheijen and J. Van Bekkum. Niam : An information analysis method. In T. W. Olle, H. G. Sol, and A. A. Verrijn-Stuart, editors, *Information Systems Design Methodology*, pages 537–589. North-Holland, 1982.

When Parents Need Not Have Children -- Cognitive Biases in Information Modeling

Keng Siau, Yair Wand, Izak Benbasat

Faculty of Commerce & Business Administration
The University of British Columbia
2053 Main Mall , Vancouver, B.C.
Canada V6T 1Z2

Abstract

Cognitive biases associated with human judgment and choice are widely studied, recognized, and documented in behavioral decision research. It is also well accepted that an understanding and acknowledgment of these biases are vital to mitigate their effects. However, research into cognitive biases in information modeling is virtually lacking. Lest one assumes that research on cognitive biases is irrelevant to the field, information modeling is a cognitively intensive activity and is, thus, highly susceptible to such biases. There is a pressing need then, to identify and understand these human biases in order to lessen their effects. This paper describes an experiment designed to investigate the use of syntactic and semantic information by modeling experts. The experimental results indicate that when interpreting information models, modeling experts tend to focus on the syntactic aspects of information and totally ignore the semantic information, even in situations where the semantic information is clearly more representative of the real world situation. These biases exhibited by modeling experts are explained using the learning paradigm in cognitive psychology.

1.0 Introduction

An expert is one who does not have to think. He knows.

-- *Frank Lloyd Wright*

Information modeling can be defined as "the activity of formally describing some aspects of the physical and social world around us for the purpose of understanding and communication" (Mylopoulos 1992). Information modeling involves investigating the problems and requirements of the user community, and from that, building a requirements specification for the desired system (Rolland & Cauvet 1992, Kangassalo 1990). The product of the information modeling process is an information model which serves as the link between requirements specification and systems development.

The information model plays two important roles. First, it provides the basis for communicating and thinking about information systems during the analysis phase (Willumsen 1993). Second, it serves as the foundation for tools and techniques employed in the development of information systems (Kung & Solvberg 1986). The importance of a correct information model cannot be overemphasized. Boehm (1976) made this point clearly when he stated:

> *It is estimated that the relative cost of fixing problems detected during final testing or operation is 50-100 times greater than for problems detected during requirements specification.*

To achieve accurate information systems requirements, the analysts and end users must understand and communicate with one another effectively (Holtzblott & Beyer 1995). However, information requirements specification is no easy task. Brooks (1987, p. 16) writes "the hardest part of the software task is arriving at a complete and consistent specification." Gladden (1982) estimated that information systems failures run as high as 70% of all information systems projects and Boar (1984) reported that 60-80% of these failures result from poor requirements specification. Also, research (e.g., Lientz & Swanson 1980, Ramamoorthy *et al.* 1984) has shown that about two-thirds of the maintenance cost can be attributed to misconception -- not identifying the real needs, or improper conceptual design.

Misunderstanding and miscommunication result from the different views of the analysts and end users. Because of the differences in background and training, the analysts and end users have very different perspectives. End users are experts in the application domain, but are usually untrained in the application of modeling techniques. It is plausible that, therefore, they will tend to focus on the semantic information depicted in the information models. Analysts, on the other hand, are experts in the modeling techniques, but unaware of the requirements of the organizations. Thus, it is likely that they will pay more attention to syntactic information in the models and less to the semantic information. To use the "blind men and the elephant" analogy, the one who felt the elephant's tail had quite a different view of the elephant from the one who felt its trunk. Therefore, the analysts and end users, during the information modeling phase, might be looking at the same information models, but reach different conclusions eventually. For example, the study by Curtis *et al.* (1988) showed that the modeler may became trapped in initial representations of the information model and failed to see alternative representations. Such biases are collectively known as cognitive biases (Tversky & Kahneman, 1982)

Because information modeling is a cognitively intensive activity, such an activity is susceptible to cognitive biases. Thus, there is a need for us to identify and understand these sources of biases in order to recognize and control them. Researchers such as Stacy (1995), and Stacy and MacMillian (1995) have also argued for the importance of understanding cognitive biases in software development. They argued that the awareness of these human biases will lead to better software engineering practice, and better understanding between the analysts and end-users.

1.1 Cognitive Biases

Cognitive biases associated with human judgment and choice are extensively researched in behavioral decision making arena (see Baron, 1988, Hogarth, 1980; Tversky & Kahneman, 1982). It is widely acknowledged that these biases can interfere with decision making processes and affect the quality of the decisions. The majority of these biases arise as a result of limitations in human information processing capability (Newell & Simon, 1972). Despite the acceptance and recognition of cognitive biases in human decision making, few researchers of information modeling have attempted to investigate the effect of cognitive biases in information modeling. Information modeling, nonetheless, is susceptible to cognitive biases of analysts and end-users because models are abstractions of the real-world (Holland *et al.* 1986). In constructing and interpreting information models, analysts and end-users are likely to use their own common sense knowledge, domain knowledge, heuristics, and rules-of-thumb to assist them in their tasks. Such personalized knowledge and heuristic are highly subjective and may be detrimental to the understanding and communication aspects of information models which are the fundamental goals of information modeling.

1.2 Outline of the Paper

In this paper, we report an experimental study which clearly demonstrates the biases of modeling experts when they are given contradictory syntactic and semantic information in information modeling. The findings are discussed and the theoretical explanations from cognitive psychology suggested.

2.0 Research Framework

2.1 Research Question

Two types of information are represented in any modeling technique: syntactic and semantic information. Syntactic information is defined as the order of language units, as specified by the grammatical rules of the modeling techniques (Mayer 1983). Semantics information, on the other hand, refers to the meaning or referents represented in the information model. As an example, consider the information model given below.

An Information Model

The rules and notations governing the use and interpretation of entities, relationships, and structural constraints (i.e., (1,*)) in the model represent the syntactic information. On the other hand, the idea that "parents have children" is the semantic information.

In our previous study (Siau *et al.* 1995), we investigated the use of relationship concept by modeling experts. The results show a predominant use of optional over mandatory relationships by expert users for both familiar and unfamiliar domains. This raises the question of whether modeling experts pay attention to the semantic information depicted by the information models.

The objective of this research is to extend our precious study and analyze the use of syntactic and semantic information by modeling experts. The main difficulty in this study is to separate the syntactic from the semantic information. Without a clear separation, the research question could not be investigated because of the confounding effect of one type of information on the other. How could we separate the syntactic from the semantic information ?

One good way to differentiate the two is to introduce a conflict in the syntactic and semantic information. For example, we could use the idea "Parents have children" and then introduce a conflict into the information model by presenting a syntactic information that "Parents need not have children." In other words, the semantic information and the syntactic information are now in contradiction. This design enables us to investigate the use of the two types of information by the subjects.

The conflicting syntactic information is manipulated using structural constraints. Structural constraint is defined as the cardinality ratio and participation constraints taken together (Elmasri & Navathe 1994). It is represented by a pair of integer numbers (min, max) with each participation of an entity type E in a relationship type R, where $0 \leq \text{min} \leq \text{max}$ and $\text{max} \geq 0$. The numbers mean that for each entity e in E, e must participate in at least min and at most max relationship instances in R at all time.

Broadly speaking, structural constraints can be classified into two categories: optional and mandatory. If the minimum participation is 0, it is an optional relationship and if the minimum participation is greater than 0, it is a mandatory relationship. In our study, the mandatory constraint is depicted using the notation (1, *) whilst the optional constraint is shown using the notation (0, *). The structural constraints can be used to create a conflicting information model. For example, the first model below is conflicting since the semantic information tells us that parent must have children (i.e., knowledge from real world) but the syntactic information (i.e., depicted by the structural constraint -- (0, *)) suggests an optional relationship. The second diagram, however, is non-conflicting because the conflicting structural constraint is absent.

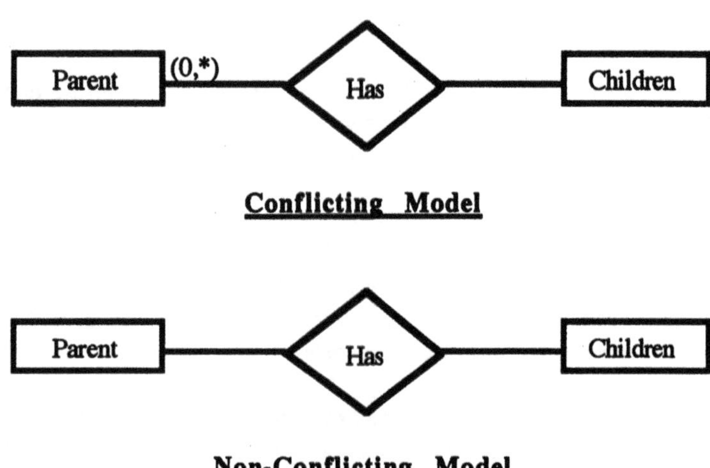

The experiment consists of two groups of subjects. The first group is exposed to information models that have a conflict between the syntactic and semantic information. The second group is exposed to information models that do not have such a conflict. The research framework for the study reported in this paper is summarized below.[1]

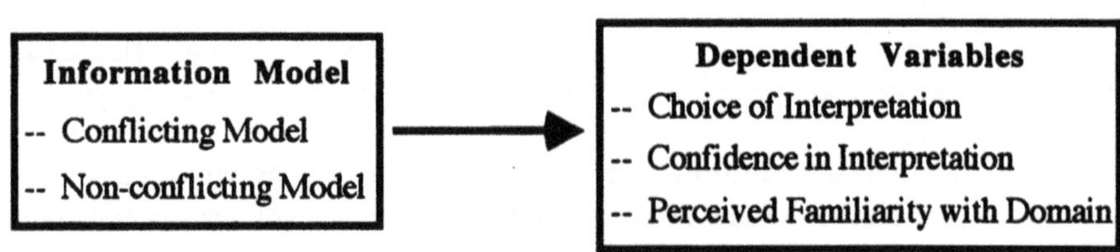

Experimental Framework

---

1 The entire design of the experiment consists of 3 cells. The first cell consists of models with conflicting syntactic and semantic information. The models in the second cell have no structural constraints and therefore no such conflict. The third cell contains models with structural constraints but there are no conflict between the syntactic and semantic information. For simplicity and lack of space, we only report on the comparison of the first two cells in this paper. This comparison is also the most interesting and enlightening.

2.2 Independent Variable

The independent variable in this study is the information model and it consists of two levels -- conflicting model versus non-conflicting model. Conflicting model means that the syntactic information and the underlying semantic information depicted by the model are in contradiction. For non-conflicting models, there is no conflict between the syntactic and semantic information because the structural constraint is absent. The subjects in the experiment were randomly assigned to either the conflicting or non-conflicting group. The two groups received exactly the same set of models except for the presence or absence of structural constraints.

2.3 Dependent Variables

The dependent variables in this study are the choice of interpretation, confidence level, and perceived familiarity with domain. The choice of interpretation was captured using multiple-choice questions. Subjects were presented with a choice of Must or May (i.e., mandatory or optional) to categorize the information models. These two choices (i.e., Must and May) were randomly ordered to counter a possible order effect. The confidence of interpretation and perceived familiarity with domain have values ranging from 1 to 7, with 1 indicating the lowest and 7 indicating the highest. An example of the question is shown in Appendix A.

2.4 Task Characteristics

The study uses familiar problem domains such as university course selection and enrollment. These familiar domains were chosen to allow subjects to use common sense reasoning to help them interpret the information models. The domain characteristics are controlled by giving the two groups the same set of models. The subjects received either 8 conflicting models or 8 non-conflicting models. The models were randomly ordered so that each subject received a uniquely ordered questionnaire. Again, this is to counter any possible order effect. The same training set that describes the basic information modeling constructs (e.g., entity, relationship, structural constraints) and some examples was provided to both groups of subjects. They were asked to read the training set prior to answering the questionnaire. No formal training or discussion was conducted.

The experimental task required the subjects to select the appropriate interpretation (i.e., mandatory or optional) for a set of information models. They were also asked their confidence level and their perceived familiarity with the domain. The use of interpretation task for the study is explained below.

2.5 Use of Interpretation Task

There are two task categories in information modeling -- model interpretation and model construction. Model interpretation involves interpreting or validating the information given in the information model, whereas model construction requires the subjects to construct an information model from a given case description. Interpretation task was selected for this research.

Interpretation task is an important aspect of information modeling for several reasons. Despite the popularity of end-user computing, large scale information models are still been developed by analysts and validated by end-users (Kim 1990). Thus, the ability of the end-users to correctly understand and validate an information model is important to the success of systems development. Secondly, we strongly believe that information models, as a communication vehicle in information modeling, should be end-user driven rather than analyst driven. As professionals, analysts could afford the time and energy to learn the modeling techniques, whereas the same could not be said about end-users. Therefore, modeling constructs and construct representations that facilitate validation by end-users may be more appropriate and important than constructs that directly correspond to subsequent design techniques or programming languages. Thirdly, even for analysts, there is the constant need to review current and old information models for modification and maintenance purposes. In other words, model interpretation is a task that is common to both analysts and end-users, whereas model construction is mainly done by analysts.

Model interpretation is also a task that is reasonably within the range of the analytic tools we have available from behavioral research. It is a task of considerable but manageable complexity. Because of the intrinsic importance of the task itself, and the tractable complexity of the task, studies on information model interpretation are a natural starting point in the behavioral study of information modeling.

3.0 Experimental Results and Discussions

3.1 Subject Characteristics

A total of 24 subjects participated in this experiment. The number of subjects and the number of observations for each group are summarized as follows:

Group	No. of Subjects	No. of Questions Per Subject	No. of Observations
Conflicting	13	8	104
Non-Conflicting	11	8	88

The subjects in this study were MIS graduate students and faculty. The experiment was conducted at one of the weekly MIS workshops. This group of workshop participants was randomly assigned to the two groups. One group received information models with no conflict and the other group received information models with conflicting syntactic and semantic information. The randomization ensures that user characteristics are controlled. A demographic information sheet was completed by each subject prior to the experiment. The subjects' expertise in information modeling are measured using a scale of 1 to 5 (1 -- Totally unfamiliar, 5 -- Very familiar). The following table summarizes their expertise with the modeling technique and constructs:

Technique/Constructs	Mean	Std. Dev.
ER Model	4.17	0.92
Entity	4.33	0.70
Relationship	4.21	0.72
Cardinality	3.67	1.31
Average	*4.10*	

Based on the demographic information given, we consider this group of subjects as modeling experts. They were very comfortable with the various modeling constructs with an average familiarity score greater than 4 (out of a full score of 5). This was not surprising since most of the subjects had extensive training in data modeling techniques from the courses they had taken (or taught). Some of the subjects also had industrial experience.

3.2 Choice of Interpretation

For this analysis, we are comparing the choice of interpretation between the conflicting and non-conflicting groups. The responses of the non-conflicting group serve as a "benchmark" for the conflicting group. In other words, the answers from the non-conflicting group allow us to evaluate the semantic information without the interference of structural constraints. These answers can then be compared to the conflicting group.

	Conflicting Group			Non-Conflicting Group	
	Syntactic Information Depicted	Number of Must Choice	Number of May Choice	Number of Must Choice	Number of May Choice
Q1	(0,*)	1	*12*	*8*	3
Q2	(1,*)	*12*	1	0	*11*
Q3	(0,*)	1	*12*	4	*7*
Q4	(0,*)	2	*11*	*6*	5
Q5	(0,*)	2	*11*	*10*	1
Q6	(1,*)	*12*	1	0	*11*
Q7	(1,*)	*13*	0	1	*10*
Q8	(0,*)	0	*13*	2	*9*

The table above depicts the choice of interpretation for the two groups. The majority's choice for each question is emphasized. There are two interesting observations in the table. First, consider the choices of the conflicting group. Notice that for all of the 8 questions, the choices of the majority in this group are consistent with the syntactic information depicted in the information models. For example, Q7 has a structural constraints of (1,*) and all the subjects in the conflicting group selected Must as their choices whereas Q8 has structural constraints of (0,*) and all the subjects selected May as their choices. Second, most of the majority's choices in the non-conflicting group are the exact opposite of those in the conflicting group. Take Q6 for example; all the subjects in the non-conflicting group selected May as their choices whereas all, except 1, in the conflicting group selected Must as their choices.

The findings, thus, seem to indicate that the syntactic information presented by structural constraints had a strong impact on the way information models were interpreted. When structural constraints were given, almost all the subjects followed the structural constraints depicted and ignored the underlying semantics of the information models. The following diagrams depict the number of May choices and Must choices for the two groups.

From a psychological point of view, these subjects exhibited ***attentional bias***. They attended only to the syntactic information depicted by the structural constraints when they should have been attending to both the syntactic and semantic information. We use the term ***attentional bias*** here to mean the failure to consider alternative possibilities or the failure to look for evidence against an initial possibility based on structural constraints. This behavior can also be known as "***semantic fallacy***"[2] ***or semantic negligence*** which means that the subjects ignore the underlying semantics depicted by the information models and focus mainly on the structural constraints given, even for models that had *obvious contradiction* between the structural constraints and the underlying semantics. A discussion with two of the

---

2 This can be compared to the "***base rate fallacy***" coined by Tversky and Kahneman (1982) in the decision making literature.

subjects in the conflicting group after the experiment revealed that they simply looked at the structural constraints to determine the interpretation. They did not even bother to look at the wordings for the entities and relationships depicted in the information models.

3.3 Confidence Level and Perceived Domain Familiarity

The confidence level and perceived domain familiarity for the two groups were analyzed using General Linear Models (GLM) (SAS 1985). The statistics show that there are significant differences between the conflicting and non-conflicting groups for confidence level and domain familiarity (i.e., $p < 0.0001$ and $p < 0.0028$ respectively). The results are summarized in the table below (DF -- Degree of Freedom; SS -- Sum of Square; MS -- Mean Square; F -- F Statistic).

Measure	DF	SS	MS	F	Pr > F
Confidence Level	1	76.26	76.26	24.09	0.0001
Domain Familiarity	1	21.82	21.82	9.17	0.0028

GLM statistics for Confidence Level and Domain Familiarity

The means and standard deviations for both group are summarized in the table below. To our surprise, the conflicting group rated confidence level and perceived domain familiarity significantly higher than the non-conflicting group.

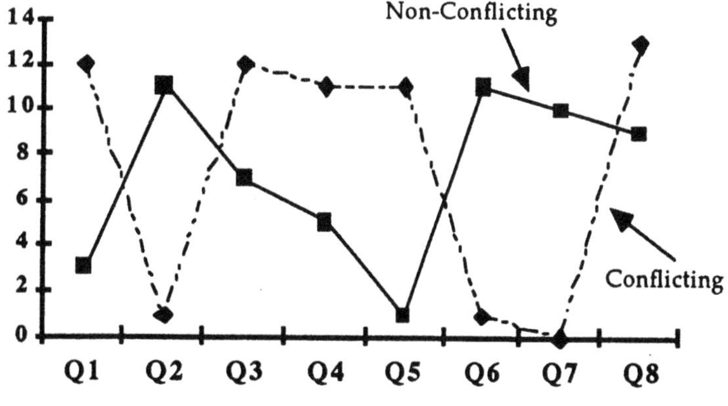

Number of May Choices for the Two Groups

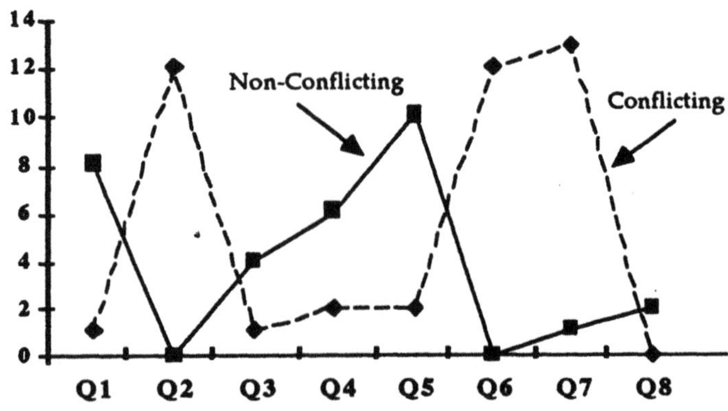

Number of Must Choices for the Two Groups

As can be seen, most of the choices of interpretation for the two groups are directly opposite of one another. The results indicate that those subjects that were not given the structural constraints interpreted the information models based on the underlying semantics. However, subjects who were given the structural constraints (even though they were in conflict with the underlying semantic information), simply followed the structural constraints in their interpretation.

Group	Confidence Level Mean (Std. Dev.)	Domain Familiarity Mean (Std. Dev.)
Conflicting	6.23 (1.28)	5.78 (1.17)
Non-Conflicting	4.97 (2.23)	5.10 (1.89)

Means and Standard Deviations for the Two Variables

The results were puzzling. Not only does the existence of syntactic information (i.e., structural constraints) had a significant effect on the interpretation of the information models, but it also increased the subjects confidence and perceived familiarity of the domain. How could these subjects who are trained and experienced in information modeling rate the confidence level and domain familiarity of clearly conflicting information models higher than those that are non-conflicting ? To fully understand the puzzle, we analyzed the phenomena at the individual question level. The detailed statistics (i.e., mean and standard deviation) for each question are summarized in the table below.

	Confidence Level Mean (Std. Dev.)	Domain Familiarity Mean (Std. Dev.)
	Conflicting Group	
Q1	6.38 (1.12)	6.15 (0.80)
Q2	6.38 (0.87)	6.46 (0.52)
Q3	6.54 (0.66)	6.00 (0.82)
Q4	6.08 (1.66)	6.38 (0.77)
Q5	5.92 (1.75)	5.85 (0.90)
Q6	5.77 (1.88)	4.46 (1.66)
Q7	6.31 (1.11)	5.38 (1.33)
Q8	6.46 (0.66)	5.54 (0.97)
	Non-Conflicting Group	
Q1	4.82 (2.18)	5.27 (1.90)
Q2	5.45 (2.46)	5.45 (1.92)
Q3	4.91 (2.30)	4.91 (1.70)
Q4	5.18 (2.44)	6.18 (1.60)
Q5	5.27 (2.37)	5.45 (1.86)
Q6	5.00 (2.32)	4.18 (2.27)
Q7	4.55 (2.25)	4.36 (1.96)
Q8	4.55 (2.07)	5.00 (1.67)

The question by question analysis of the study reveals more surprises. The confidence level for every question in the conflicting group is higher than the corresponding question in the non-conflicting group. Similarly for domain familiarity, all the conflicting questions have a higher perceived domain familiarity than their corresponding non-conflicting questions.

The table also shows strong differences between the two groups in terms of confidence level. The lowest confidence level in the conflicting group (i.e., 5.77) is still higher than the highest confidence level in the non-conflicting group (i.e., 5.45). One probable explanation is that the subjects treated structural constraints as part of the information and felt more comfortable with its presence. This is not surprising as these subjects are all experts in the information modeling technique. It is, therefore, likely that the additional information provided by the structural constraints increased their confidence level. Another possibility is that, with the missing cardinality, the subjects have to retrieve and apply their domain assumptions. This forces them to review and question their domain knowledge, which leads to a lower confidence level.

The following diagrams depict the confidence level and perceived domain familiarity for each of the questions.

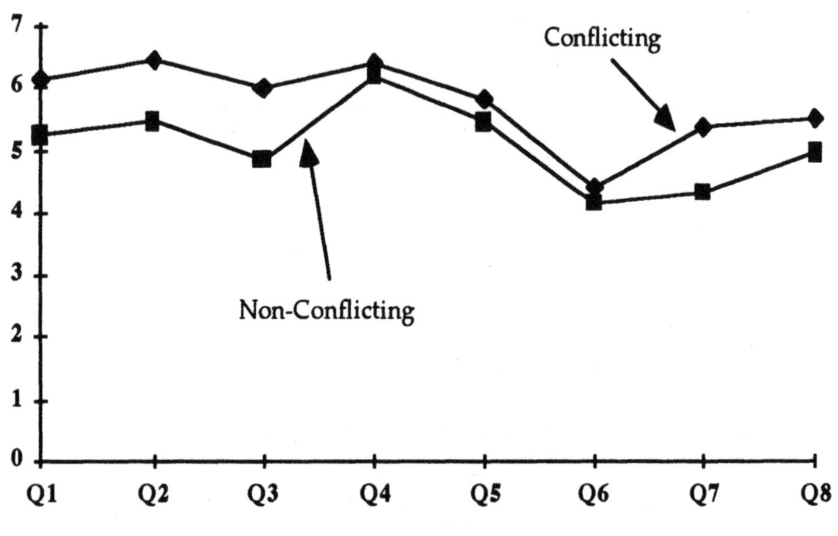

Domain Familiarity for Each Question

Although the effect on confidence level can be explained by the additional information provided by the structural constraints, the impact on domain familiarity is harder to explain. How could the perceived domain familiarity be higher in the conflicting group ? Perceived domain familiarity is determined by the entire information model (i.e., entities, relationship, and structural constraints (if present)) and how closely the information conveyed by the model fit the reality. One possible explanation is that these subjects placed too much faith on the structural constraints. They made up scenarios (however far-stretched that might be) to convince themselves that the structural constraints were correct. Another plausible explanation is that the subjects did not even realize the conflict. This again goes back to the notions of attentional bias and semantic negligence. They looked at the information models but they did not see the conflicts. How could these phenomena be explained from a theoretical perspective ?

4.0 Theoretical Explanation of Results

Trying to make sense of the results, we reviewed the cognitive psychology literature. The learning paradigm in cognitive psychology provides a plausible theoretical explanation for the results. First, a few words on learning.

Minsky (1986) defines learning as "an omnibus word for all the processes that lead to long-term changes in our minds." Similarly, Thorpe (1963) defines learning as "that process which manifests itself by adaptive changes in individual behavior as a result of experience," and Wingfield (1979) defines it as "a relatively permanent change in behavior or knowledge brought about by practice or experience."

Despite the proliferation of theories, various attempts by psychologists to divide the process of skill learning into stages have been remarkably similar (Fitts 1964, Fitts & Posner 1967, Anderson 1983, 1995). The three main stages are: cognitive stage, associative stage, and autonomous stage.

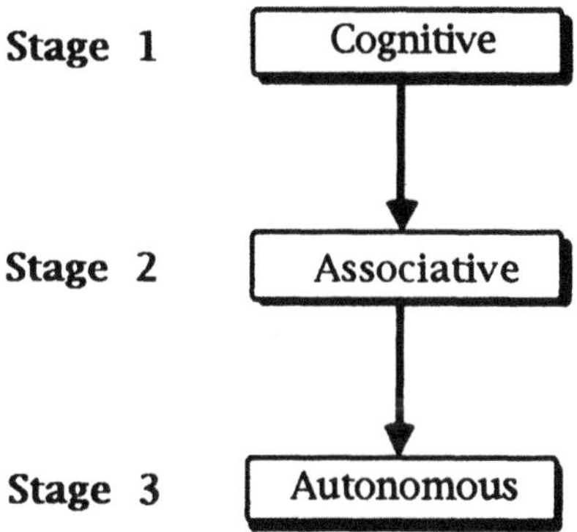

The first phase, cognitive stage, is characterized by discovery of the relevant aspects of the task and the storage of declarative knowledge[3] about the skills. During the associative stage, the skill are chunked, or compiled, into procedural knowledge[4]. In the final or autonomous stage, the procedures undergo a process of continual refinement (i.e., tuning) and strengthening, which results in increased speed and accuracy in performance of the skill. As an example of this transformation, let us take the case of a golfer. A novice golfer, in preparing to hit the ball, may verbalize, "Bend your knees," "Head down," "Keep your left arm straight,", and so on. However, an expert golfer could execute these processes in split seconds and without conscious awareness.

Because the subjects in this experiment are modeling experts, they are most likely to be at the automatic stage in their learning curve for information modeling. At the automatic stage, processes are run without any conscious allocation of attention (Best 1992). Gagne *et al.* (1993) stated that automated skills are executed almost unconsciously when certain conditions are met. Logan (1988) also stressed that automation is "fast, effortless, autonomous, stereotypic, and unavailable to conscious awareness." Thus, these modeling experts, who are used to interpreting information

3 Declarative knowledge is knowing that something is the case. It is knowledge of facts, theories, events, and objects.

4 Procedural knowledge comprises the skills to perform something. It includes motor skills, cognitive skills, and cognitive strategies.

models and who have formed highly-specialized modeling-domain-specific strategies, simply attended to the structural constraints depicted in the information models, as they usually do, and ignored the semantic information depicted by the models.

Automaticity of the processes also explains the attentional bias and semantic negligence exhibited by the modeling experts. In other words, those subjects in the conflicting group simply looked at the structural constraints to decide on the Must or May choice and unconsciously ignored the semantic information in the models. Subjects in the non-conflicting group, on the other hand, are exposed to information models that were incomplete (i.e., missing structural constraints). For these information models, the subjects could not activate the automatic skill because certain conditions (i.e., structural constraints) were not met. They were, therefore, forced to evaluate the models based on the semantic information. Thus, differences arose between the two groups.

5.0 Conclusions

> *An individual's use of multiple decision strategies in different situations, including various simplifying methods or choice heuristics, is an adaptive response of a limited-capacity information processor to the demands of complex decision tasks.*
>
> -- *Payne, Bettman and Johnson, 1993, p. 2*

The objective of this research is to understand human cognition in information modeling. The goal is to bridge the gap between behavioral studies and the technical research in information modeling. In this study, we investigated the behavior of modeling experts when given conflicting semantic and syntactic information. The findings of this study indicate that modeling experts are highly biased towards syntactical aspects of the models. When structural constraints were not included in the information model, the subjects based their interpretation on the semantic information. However, when structural constraints were given and presented in a way that contradict the semantic information, almost all of the subjects based their interpretation on the structural constraints depicted and ignored the underlying semantics of the information models. Considering the fact that information model is a communication vehicle during systems analysis, such biases might be detrimental to the information systems projects. The experimental results also show that the existence of structural constraints in the information models significantly increased both the confidence level of the subjects and their perceived familiarity of the domain.

We believe this research has significance implications for both academic and practitioners. The cognitive biases exhibited by the subjects are important issues that need to be addressed. For example, a recent Delphi survey of senior IS executives conducted by Niederman *et al.* (1991) showed that IS executives were concerned with data-related issues. In fact, they listed information architecture and data resource as their top two concerns. Approaches to resolving these issues include education and training of the existing and future IS professionals. Documenting such incidents in text books and training materials serve as important reminder to readers.

Our next experiment will investigate the cognitive differences between modeling experts and modeling novices. With this stream of work, we are not attempting to formulate a complete explanatory model for human behavior in information modeling. We are instead making the point that human cognition is an important dimension in information modeling.

Acknowledgments. The authors would like to thank the anonymous referees for their many valuable comments. Many thanks also to the participants of the MIS Workshop for taking part in the study. This research was supported in part by the Natural Sciences and Engineering, and Humanities and Social Sciences Research Councils of Canada.

References

1. Anderson, J.R. (1983), The Architecture of Cognition, Cambridge, MA: Harvard University Press.
2. Anderson, J.R. (1995), Learning and Memory: An Integrated Approach, John Wiley & Sons, 1995.
3. Baron, J. (1988), Thinking and Deciding, Cambridge, Cambridge University Press.
4. Best, J.B. (1992), Cognitive Psychology, Third Edition, West Publishing Company.
5. Boar, B.H. (1984), Application Prototyping: A Requirements Definition Strategy for the 80's, New York, John Wiley & Sons.
6. Boehm, B.W. (1973), Software and Its Impact: A Quantitative Assessment, Datamation, 19, 5, pp. 48-59.
7. Brooks, F.P. (1987), No Silver Bullet: Essence and Accidents of Software Engineering, IEEE Computer, pp. 10-19.
8. Curtis, B., Krasner, H., and Iscoe, N. (1988), A Field Study of the Software Design Process for Large Systems, Communications of the ACM, Vol. 31, No. 11, pp. 1268-1287.
9. Elmasri, R. and Navathe, S. B. (1994), Fundamentals of Database Systems, Second Edition, Benjamin/Cummings.
10. Fitts, P.M. (1964), Perceptual-motor Skill Learning, in: A.W. Melton (ed.), Categories of Human Learning, New York: Academic Press.

11. Fitts, P.M., and Posner, M.I. (1967), Human Performance, California: Brooks-Cole.
12. Gagne, E.D., Yekovich, C.W., and Yekovich, F.R. (1993), The Cognitive Psychology of School Learning, Harper Colins.
13. Gladden, G.R. (1982), Stop the Life Cycle, I Want to Get Off, Software Engineering Notes, Vol. 7, No. 2.
14. Hogarth, R.M. (1980), Judgment and Choice: The Psychology of Decision. Chichester: John Wiley & Sons.
15. Holland, J.H., Holyoak, K.J., Nisbett, R.E., and Thagard, P.R. (1986), Induction: Processes of Inference, Learning, and Discovery, MIT Press.
16. Holtzblott, K., and Beyer, H.R. (1995), Requirement Gathering: The Human Factor, Communications of the ACM, Vol. 38, No. 5, pp. 31-32.
17. Kangassalo, H. (1990), Foundations of Conceptual Modeling: A Theory Construction View, In: Information Modeling and Knowledge Bases, Amsterdam, IOS Press, pp. 20-29.
18. Kim, Y.G. (1990), Effects of Conceptual Data Modeling Formalisms on User Validation and Analyst Modeling of Information Requirements, Unpublished Dissertation, University of Minnesota.
19. Kung, C.H., and Solvberg, A. (1986), Activity Modeling and Behavior Modeling, in: Information Systems Design Methodologies: Improving the Practice, Olle T W, Sol H G and Verrijn-Stuart (eds.), Amsterdam: Elsevier Science Publishers B.V. (North-Holland), pp. 145-172.
20. Lientz, B.P., and Swanson, E.B. (1980), Software Maintenance Management, Addison-Wesley. Reading, Mass.
21. Logan, G.D. (1988), Toward an Instance Theory of Automatization, Psychological Review, Vol. 95, No. 4, pp. 492-527.
22. Mayer, R.E. (1983), Thinking, Problem Solving, Cognition, Freeman and Company.
23. Minsky, M. (1986), The Society of Mind, Simon & Schuster.
24. Mylopoulos, J. (1992), Conceptual Modeling and Telos, in: P. Loucopoulos and R. Zicari (Eds.), Conceptual Modeling, Databases and Case, New York, John Wiley & Sons, pp. 49-68.
25. Newell, A., and Simon, H.A. (1972), Human Problem Solving, Englewood Cliffs, New Jersey: Prentice Hall.
26. Niederman, F., Brancheau, J.C., and Wetherbe, J.C. (1991), Information Systems Management Issues for the 1990's, MIS Quarterly, pp. 475-500.
27. Payne, J.W., Bettman, J.R., and Johnson, E.J (1993), The Adaptive Decision Maker, Cambridge: Cambridge University Press.
28. Ramamoorthy, C.V., Prakash, A., Tsai, W., and Usuda, Y. (1984), Software Engineering: Problems and Perspectives, Computer, Vol. 17, No. 10, pp. 191-209.
29. Rolland, C., and Cauvet, C. (1992), Trends and Perspectives in Conceptual Modeling, In: P. Loucopoulos and R. Zicari (Eds.), Conceptual Modeling, Databases and Case, New York, John Wiley & Sons, pp. 27-32.
30. SAS (1985), SAS User's Guide: Statistics, Version 5, SAS Institute Inc.

31. Siau, K., Wand, Y., Benbasat, I., A Psychological Study on the Use of Relationship Concept -- Some Preliminary Findings, in: Iivari, J., Lyytinen, K., Rossi, M. (eds.), Lecture Notes in Computer Science, Vol. 932, Springer-Verlag, pp. 341-354.
32. Stacy, W. (1995), Cognition and Software Development, Communications of the ACM, Vol. 38, No. 6, pp. 31.
33. Stacy, W., and MacMillian, J. (1995), Cognitive Bias in Software Engineering, Communications of the ACM, Vol. 38, No. 6, pp. 57-74.
34. Thorpe, W.H., (1963), Learning and Instinct in Animals, Second Edition, London: Methuen.
35. Tversky, A. and Kahneman, D. (1982), Judgment Under Uncertainty: Heuristic and Biases, in: Judgment under Uncertainty, Cambridge University Press, pp. 3-20.
36. Willumsen, G. (1993), Conceptual Modeling in IS Engineering, In: Executable Conceptual Models in Information Systems Engineering, Trondheim, pp. 11-21.
37. Wingfield, A. (1979), Human Learning and Memory: An Introduction, New York: Harper & Row.

Appendix A

Circle one of the following two options that more correctly reflects the participation of the Shareholder entity type in the Owns relationship type:

1. may own
2. must own

What is your confidence level in the above choice?

No confidence 1 2 3 4 5 6 7 Absolute confidence

What is your familiarity with the domain depicted in the diagram?

Not familiar at all 1 2 3 4 5 6 7 Very familiar

The Role of Benchmarking in Information System Development

M. Daneva
Institut für Wirtschaftsinformatik
at the University of the Saarland
Altenkesseler str. 17/B2, D-66 115 Saarbrücken, GERMANY
E-mail: maya@iwise1.iwi-uni.sb

Abstract. This paper highlights the importance of benchmarking for fitness and enhancement of quality and productivity in IS development life cycle. We introduce a pragmatic approach to IS improvement based on continuos learning from best-in-class achievements. We also report a benchmarking case study that illustrates the application of the method during the requirements analysis and the development of requirements specification.

1 Introduction

Controlling quality and productivity is a critical success factor for today's software projects [13]. The importance of IS controlling increases when the projects deal with the development or the customization of business/engineering applications, and are essential parts of a business process reengineering initiative. To get some insight in IS-controlling, software engineering people from the industry, the government and the academia have developed numerous measurement approaches and assessment frameworks that should serve as a basis for enterprise-wide metrics programs capable of guiding quality improvement efforts. In a lot of cases, these schemes are too complex to use and difficult to learn; their application has a significant duration and require costly data collection procedures and expensive IS-staff training. Unfortunately, it is very easy to specify an improvement conceptual model that does not work for most practical purposes [14].

The main objective of this work is to advise the IS-development community of how to benefit more from software metrics technology in terms of efficiency and effectiveness. We deliver a pragmatic tool to IS organizations together with practical guidelines how and when to use it.

The remainder of this paper is organized as follows: Section 2 presents how the concept of benchmarking fits with IS-improvement. Section 3 overviews our benchmarking method. Section 4 provides some guidelines for conducting benchmarking studies easily. Section 5 reports a comparative study on IS requirements definitions.

2 Benchmarking: a feasible path to IS-enhancement

Competency and knowledge in controlling IS productivity are considered as a key strategy for dominating the global information technology market in the next century [13]. Surprisingly, recent research on the deployment of quality control mechanisms revealed that the actual use of controlling procedures is generally poor and lower than organizations claim [10]. It also is surprising that the IS-practitioners and academicians have devoted much efforts to develop new measurement and improvement frameworks, and very few works have dealt with the effectiveness and efficiency of these mechanisms [10]. Although the lack of reliable quantitative information about the usefulness of the current measurement and assessment methods, the existing experience helps us identify some serious drawbacks of these improvement schemes:

1. Quality programs based on Capability Maturity Model [15], Bootstrap method, or the SPICE Standard are too expensive and implementationally difficult [3, 14]. Getting organization's staff involved in the assessment team and training them in assessment technique proved too costly and disruptive for small and middle-sized enterprises.
2. The assessment models completely disregard company's specific improvement objectives [18]. Major efforts are required to customize these frameworks to the organization's circumstances and needs. As the size of the IS-organization shrinks, the assessment methodology becomes increasingly informal. In such situations the existing models fail in formulating improvement advice which maximizes the returns on investments for small companies.
3. The current assessment practices mainly address the question *where* to improve, but not *how* and *how much*. As Zultner writes [20], they are extremely weak on what to do after the assessment. The software metrics technology itself does not add value to a company; its use makes sense only when this leads to implemented improvement actions.

To counteract these difficulties, we propose an approach to IS-enhancement based on the concept of software benchmarking [6]. This is a process of continually searching for the best software experience, indicating software standards to be achieved in day-to-day company's operations, adopting or adapting the best-in-class practices, and implementing them to become the best of the best. We believe, the above three points referring to the current assessment methods can be handled by means of IS benchmarking in the following manner: First, our intention is to provide both large companies and small IS organization with an instrument for deriving comprehensive and effective software metrics programes that contribute significantly to successful improvement initiatives. Second, our approach is context-based what means we regard the fact that software practitioners usually set their own quality priorities according to their own development environments [10]. Moreover, IS-benchmarking is aimed at giving starting point to analyze how well a straight transplant of somebody else's solution fits with the own organization. This ensures the holistic view to the questions *where*, *how* and *how much* to improve.

3 An overview of the approach

3.1 Preliminaries

The present approach is based on the idea that a software organization could and should learn about its own technological and marketing opportunities by learning about other's similar operations and processes. We do not see benchmarking as a competitive study, „number crunching“, spying or stealing, but organizational learning. This hypothesis is directly derived from our previous work on the problem of software quality ranking [5] and software benchmark design and use [6]. We have developed a holistic view of software benchmarking, whose focus was on the key steps of the benchmarking process and how they are to be performed. We also determined systematic procedure for software controlling together with a generic benchmarking model explaining the software enterprise items in benchmarking terms [4].

The approach we present here, is anchored on management by metrics [7], which uses high-level quantitative indicators for the manager to control software projects and products. We also follow the AMI tradition [1] and Basili's framework [2] to goal-driven derivation of software metrics, whose focus on goals leads to focus on what actions can be taken.

3.2 The benchmarking process

This section summarizes our benchmarking method. The approach includes the following steps:

1. Clarify the goal. Formulate the software bottleneck and identify decisions which would be made on the base of IS-benchmarking results. Derive a *benchmarking goal* that refers to the specific aspects of company's competitive agenda: increasing customer satisfaction, shortening time-to-market, improving service quality.
2. Operationalize the benchmarking goal. Identify interest groups, i.e. the IS-staff-members who are interested the most in benchmarking information. Express the benchmarking goal in a hierarchy of measurement goals. These help us determine that the benchmarks reflects what they are presumed to measure. Begin with an analysis of what information the benchmarking study has to reveal, e.g. current productivity level, current schedule ranges, probabilities of achieving significant recognition (European Quality Award, ISO 9000 Certification, CMM Level 3, 4 and 5 [15]). This analysis delivers a top level measurement goal that is further broken down into a set of primitive measurement goals which are easily expresses by software attributes.
3. Select competitors. These are software objects from one of the following groups: (i) *work products* - any artifact, produced as a part of defining, maintaining, or using software process, which may or may not be intended for delivering to the customers or end users [15], (ii) *processes* - any means by which people, procedures, methods, equipment, and tools are integrated to produce a desired end results, and (iii) *resources:* i.e. teams, hardware, CASE tools, etc. The software objects candidates for benchmarking should be prioritized by experts or by using some heuristic procedures or formal decision making techniques.

   Establish best-in-class object which one can learn from. This can be either an object which embodies somebody else's practice recognized as a best-in-class one, or a preliminary defined model whose values are numerical quality or productivity thresholds.

4. Specify IS benchmarks. Define two major benchmark components - the domain specification and the measurement (or assessment) specification. The first one describes completely the IS-quality or productivity aspects the benchmark should deal with and the second specification establishes the relevant IS-characteristics to be measured or assessed.
5. Collect benchmarking data. Implement the measurement specification by constructing a set of measured functions. Carry out the measurement, i.e., assign actual values to characteristics involved in benchmarking. The benchmarking data can be classified as follows:
   - *expert judgments.*
   - *elementary metrics:* these are numbers derived from facts [1]. For example, marketing indicators, such as market share, sales volume, or engineering indicators, such as lines of code, elapsed time, cyclomatic complexity.
   - *assessments:* these can be done using either predefined calculation rules (Halstead's software science, Function Point Analysis [13], etc), or questionnaires in the software enterprise (CMM, BOOTSTRAP).
   - *profile charts:* these are sets of expert judgments and assessments relevant to a certain software characteristics which can not be quantified directly (for example, maintenance).
   - *competitive figures:* these are sets of software characteristics and their competitive levels revealing the position of the company with respect to its competitors.
6. Compare software objects. Given objects' measurements/assessments, determine some superiority and inferiority criteria that help the benchmarker rank objects according to their capability to support the benchmarking goal. The ranking points out where a company is in both developmental and quality terms.
7. Decide on learning strategy. Project future quality and productivity levels. Check to what extent it is possible to implement a solution already used in another IS-organization. Prioritize strategies how to implement the best-in class experience in home. Make decisions on course of improvement actions.
8. Develop and implement an action plan. Establish functional improvement goals and identify steps that systematically lead to goal achievement.
9. Re-evaluate. Check how well the best-in-class practice is incorporated into home. Continue through conducting a new benchmarking study.

It is worth stressing that IS-benchmarking is rarely a strictly linear process. It is possible to re-define benchmarking goal after defining precisely measurement goals, or after identifying the best-in-class achievements.

3.3 The instrumentation

An IS-benchmarking study has to be aware of the software objects' characteristics submitted as benchmarks as well as the possible ways the benchmarks are quantified and interpreted. To provide the benchmarker with guidance to successful benchmarking studies we propose an instrumented scheme that consists of a benchmarks model and operations permitted on it. The scheme ensures a common understanding of benchmarking and provides a mechanism for structuring the information about benchmarking practices. The scheme is based on the ISO Standards as well as the STEP standard [19] that suggest to organize software characteristics according to an hierarchical quality model flexible enough to be customized to the needs of any benchmarker. We refine this idea by developing three level scheme for IS-benchmarks. It consists of categories, indicators and metrics. The categories provide a high level view to the types of benchmark measurements performed on software objects. The indicators are measurable aspects of the quality/productivity for any given category. The indicators are quantified by assessing one or more facts about an software object. Each fact to be assessed is called a metric. The benchmarker can investigate objects at any of these levels.

Generally, a benchmarking procedure defines six operations over a quality model:

- derivation: given a set of categories, generate a set of indicators, and a set of metrics to be considered, trying to minimize the measurement costs.
- integration: given a set of measurements, generate relevant set of indicators and categories, and construct objects' benchmarking profiles.
- auditing: given a preliminary established model recognized as a best-in-class one, compare a set of target objects against the best-in-class assessments.
- visioning: given a benchmarking goal, rank target objects with respect to their capability of supporting the predefined objective.
- interpreting: given a model benchmarking profile, map objects' values (e.g. the function point number is 107) onto merit values (e.g. 1.5 on a scale from 0.0 (low complexity) to 10.0 (highest complexity)).
- reasoning: given a model benchmarking profile, explain why the measurements produced this profile.

4 Benchmarking case study

This section summarizes some results of a benchmarking initiative undertaken at the University of the Saarland. Our benchmarking approach was applied to the life cycle phase of requirement analysis. The objective with this study was twofold: (1) to control the process of requirement gathering, and to ensure the quality of IS-requirement specifications in efficient and effective way, and (2) to anticipate pitfalls in integration of submodels and/or customization of IS reference models.

The benchmarked IS-requirement definitions were represented in form of business process models by using the specification language of event-driven process chains (EPC) [17]. Any EPC specifies details of the modes of operation which a system can be in, as well as the interface between the system and entities beyond the scope of the system. The formalism comprises three basic elements: functions, events, and logical operators (*and*, *or*, and *exclusive or*). The functions are considered as time-consuming activities that create or modify objects. The events are both conditions for the execution of functions, and results. The events refer to points in time and are defined as data items that should be available at the start and at the end of functions' execution. In the EPC-schemes, the functions are represented by rounded boxes and the events as hexagons. An example of an EPC-scheme is given in Fig. 1.

We operationalized the benchmarks model so as to use it in benchmarking studies dealing with the complexity. A set of appropriate complexity indicators has been defined as well. For any indicator we explained how it helps us improve the IS-requirements specifications and how it would be more difficult to make improvements without the indicator. Finally, the indicators were specified by following AMI metrics description guidelines [1].

In the next section, we review some complexity indicators. We suggest to present the benchmark definitions together with an illustrative example.

4.1 An illustrative example

To show how metrics data are collected we use the EPC in Fig. 1 which depicts the high level definition of the process „Bid preparation“ developed by the ESPRIT BIDPREP Consortium [11]. Due to space limitations we present a part of benchmark specifications only (namely, the reference object and the integration rules).

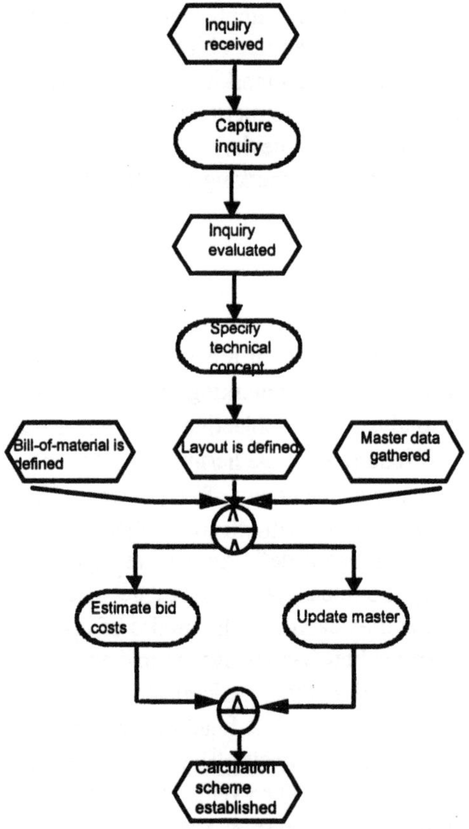

Figure 1. A part of BIDPREP Specification.

4.2 Function Cohesion (FC)

Reference Object: Function

Integration Rules: $FC = (FC_{inp} + FC_{out})/2$

where FC_{inp} und FC_{out} are the input and output function cohesion measures. These are defined as follows:

$FC_{inp}(0) = k_0 N_0$

$FC_{inp}(i) = k_i.(FC_{inp}(i-1) + N_i)$ $i=1,..,n$

$FC_{out}(0) = k_0 N_0$

$Fc_{out}(i) = k_j.(FC_{out}(i-1) + N_j)$ $i=1,..,l$

where i and j are levels of nesting, k_i and k_j are weights, and N_i and N_j are the numbers of the input and output events with respect to the function under consideration.

The numbers k_i and k_j are defined by modifying Rechenberg's weighting scheme [10]:

Type of Event	Weight	Type of Event	Weight
AND-Event	3	OR-Event	2
XOR-Event	3	Single Events	1

Table 1.

Examples:

FC (Capture inquiry) = (1+1)/2 = 1

FC (Estimate bid costs) = (3x3 + 1x1)/2 = 5

4.3 Data Item Cohesion (DIC)

Reference Object: Event

Integration Rules: $DIC = DIC_{inp} + DIC_{out} + c.NF$

where DIC_{inp} and DIC_{out} are the input and output data item cohesion cohesion measures, c is an event cohesion class, and NF is the number of functions affected by the event under consideration. These are defined as follows:

$DIC_{inp}(0) = k_0 NE_0$

$DIC_{inp}(i) = k_i.(DIC_{inp}(i-1) + NE_i)$ $i=1,..,n$

$DIC_{out}(0) = k_0 NE_0$

$DIC_{out}(i) = k_j.(DIC_{out}(i-1) + NE_j)$ $j=1,..,l$

where i and j are levels of nesting, k_i and k_j have the above meaning, NE_i is the number the of co-items, with which a data item acts together as an input to a function, and NE_j is the number the of co-items, with which a data item acts together as an output from a function.

The cohesion class c defines the role of an event. It characterizes the decision power of the event and reflects the way in which the event affects the functions related to it. We established the following rules for defining the cohesion class of an event:

1. An event has a cohesion class 1 when it is produced by only one function and is an input to only one function.
2. An event has a cohesion class 2 when it is produced by more than one functions but is an output to only one function.
3. An event has a cohesion class 3 when it is produced by only one function and is an input to more than one functions.
4. An event has a cohesion class 4 when it is produced by more than one functions and is an output to more than one functions.

Example:
DIC (Inquiry is evaluated) = 0+0+2x1= 2
DIC (Layout is defined) = 0 + 2x3 +3x3 = 6 + 9 = 15

4.4 Validation of complexity benchmarks

To investigate the expressive power and the adequacy of the developed benchmarks, we followed Fenton's guidelines [8] for software metrics validation. The operationalized benchmarks models were applied to representative sample of EPC-schemas produced. The results were compared with expert evaluations referring to the same models. We refined benchmark calculation rules every time when our method did not come to the same conclusion as the experts. Finally, the conformity between expected and effective benchmark values has been checked through estimating Kendal's concordance coefficient. This study pointed out the strong correlation between expert opinions and the quantified indicators.

We have also studied the statistical independence among the benchmarks. The benchmark values exhibited a low correlation, what pointed out that they characterize distinct aspects of business process models.

4.5 Benchmarking profiles

To illustrate how our solution strategy works, we report here a summary of a comparative study on the model complexity. We evaluated and benchmarked a model produced by IDS Prof Scheer GmbH, Saarbrücken, Germany, for the process „Human resource administration" at the enterprise X, an electric company in Eastern Europe, with an optimized model that represents the same process. The latter was recognized as a best-in-class one. The considered benchmarks are: Function Cohesion, Data Item Cohesion and Cohesion of Logical Connectors. Figure 2. represents the average benchmark values. The complexity evaluations of the model of company X exceed those of the best-in-class model.

To define corrective actions, the modellers needed a roadmap and guideline where to begin from. Therefore, we focused our further investigation on each particular benchmark. To identify which objects contribute the most to the average benchmark

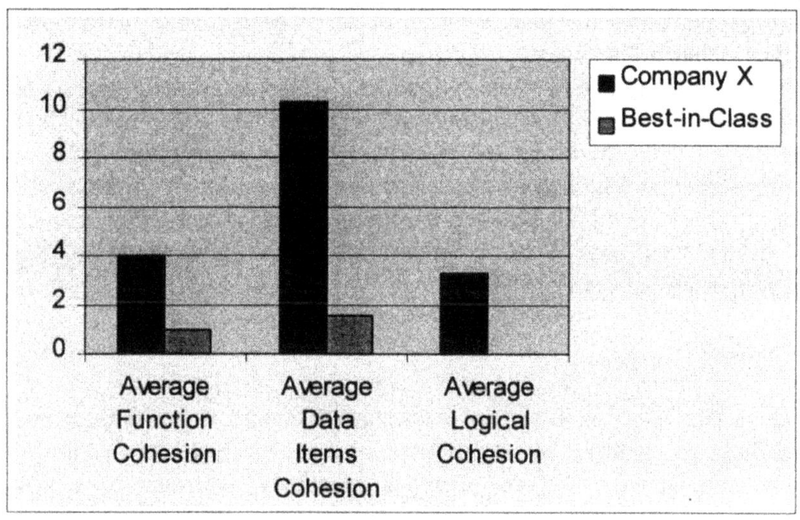

Figure 2. Benchmarking profiles.

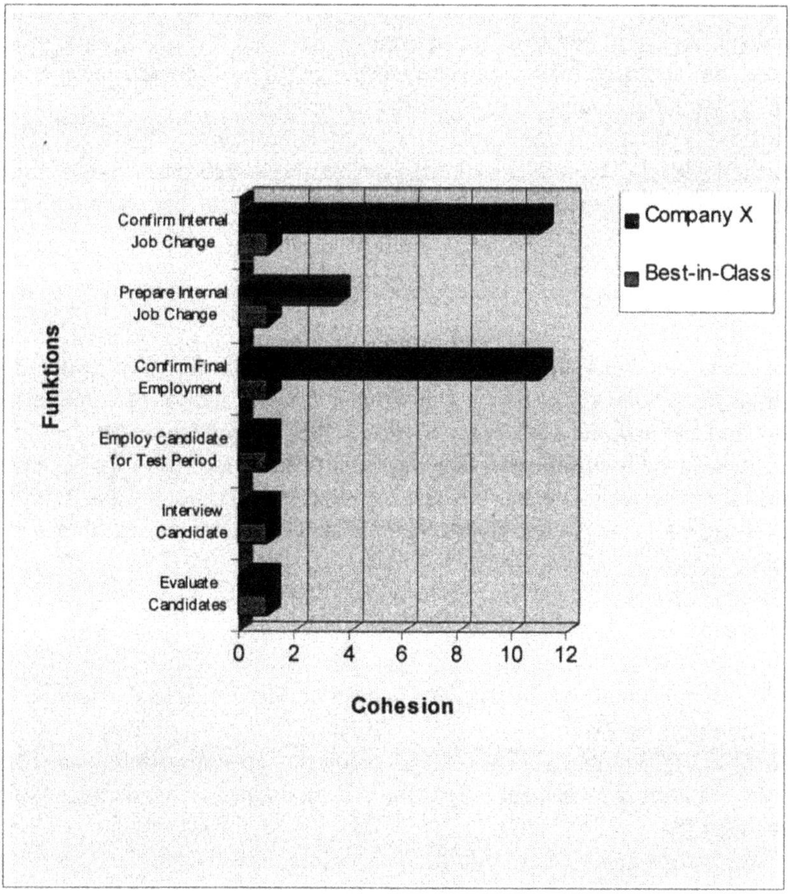

Figure 3. A comparison on function-by-function basis.

values we compared the models on an object-by-object basis. Let us analyze the benchmark function cohesion.

Figure 3 represents a function-by-function comparison. The functions, which both models have in common are compared with respect to their FC values. As it is evident from the data, the high average function cohesion is attributed to the functions „Confirm internal job change“, „Confirm final employment“, „Prepare internal job change“. These can be submitted to the modellers for further enhancement. Thus, it was pointed out how a benchmarking study can deliver a basis for model improvement initiatives.

5 Conclusions

Benchmarking expertise is a set of knowledge and skills which support modellers in controlling IS quality. Our experience has shown how the quality issues in requirements analysis can be mastered effectively according to a documented procedure that makes the quality of produced specifications quantitatively known. Our approach is very different from the existing improvement schemes in the following three ways: First, its focus is on identifying after-assessment actions. The main point in IS-benchmarking is how to add value to the IS-organization by using software metrics technology, instead of how to get assessment.

Second, the approach places the comparison against best-in-class achievements as a starting point in developing an IS-improvement program.

Third, the approach is applicable to support improvement efforts initiated at any organization level. The method allows even the least ambitious IS-staff member to develop useful benchmarks and to compare the results of his own job against the excellent ones.

6 Acknowledgements

I would like to thank the colleagues from the Institut für Wirtschaftsinformatik, Saarbrücken, for many stimulating conversations on the subject. I would also like to thank Thomas Geib and Karl Wagner from IDS Prof Scheer GmbH for the fruitful discussions on enterprise-model-benchmarking. My thanks also go to the friends Mathias Krömker from Bremen Institute for Industrial Technology and Applied Work Science, and Christian Rose from Software Union GmbH, for the use of their reference models.

7 References

1. AMI: Application of Metrics in Industry, Metrics Users' Handbook, AMI Consortium, 1992.
2. Basili,V., H.Rombach, The TIME Project: Towards Improvement-oriented Software Environments, IEEE Transactions on Software Engineering, 14(6), 1988, pp 758-773.

3. Brodman, J.G., D.L.Johnson, What Small Business and Small Organizations Say About the CMM, Proc. of the 17th International Conference on Software Engineering, Sorento, 1994, pp. 331-340.
4. Daneva, M., Benchmarking Practice for Software Quality Achievement, Proc. of the 5th International Conference on Software Quality, Austin, 1995, pp. 443-457.
5. Daneva, M., Knowledge-based Approach to Software Marketing Modelling and Support, Ph.D. Dissertation, BAS, Institute of Mathematics, 1994.
6. Daneva, M., Software Benchmark Design and Use,.Reengineering the Enterprise, Galway, Ed. J. Brown and D. O'Sullivan, Chapman and Hall, New York, 1995, pp. 20-29.
7. ESPRIT Project 2151: „SCOPE - Technology for Evaluation and Certification of Software Product Quality", Project Brochure, November, 1992.
8. Fenton, N., Software Metrics: A Rigorous Approach, Chapman&Hall, 1991.
9. Fenton, N.E., S. Pfleeger, R. Glass, Science and Substance: a Chalange to Software Engineers, IEEE Software, July, 1994, pp. 86-95.
10. Hall, T., N. Fenton, Software Practitiones and Software Quality, Proc. of the 5th International Conference on Software Quality, Austin, 1995, 313-324.
11. Hirsch, B.E, K.-D., Thoben, M. Krömker, A. Wickner, Benchmarking in BidPreparation for Capital Goods, Proc. of IFIP WG 5.7 Workshop on Benchmarking - Theory and Practice, Trondheim, 1994.
12. Jones, C., Global Software Quality in 1995, Proc. of the 5th International Conference on Software Quality, Austin, 1995, pp. 283-290.
13. Jones, C., Patterns of Software Systems Failure and Success, International. Thomson Computer Press, Boston, 1996.
14. Paulk, M.C., A Perspective on the Issues Facing SPICE, Proc. of 5th International Conference on Software Quality, Austin, 1995, pp. 416-425.
15. Paulk. M., C.Weber, B. Curtis, M.B.Chrissis, The Capability Maturity Model: Guidelines for Improving the Software Process, Addison-Wesley Publ Co., Redings, MA, 1995.
16. Rechenberg, P., Ein neues Mass für die Softwaretechnische Komplexität von Programmen, Informatik Forschung und Entwicklung, 1986, pp. 26-37.
17. Scheer, A.-W., Wirtschaftsinformatik, Referenzmodelle für industrielle Geschäftsprozesse, 6.Ed., Springer-Verlag, Berlin et all, 1995.
18. Strigel, W., Assessment in Small Software Companies, Technical Report, Software Productivity Centre, Vancouver, 1995.
19. Tyler, J., Models, Managing Modekls, Quality Model: an Example of Quality Management, U.S. Department of Commerce, National Institute of Standards and Technology, NISTIR 4738, December, 1991.
20. Zultner, R., The Deming Way to Software Development, Proc. of the 5th International Conference on Software Quality, Austin, 1995, pp. 457-470.

User-Enhanceability for Organisational Information Systems through Visual Programming

Nikolay Mehandjiev[1] and Leonardo Bottaci[2]

[1] Dept. of Management Systems and Sciences
University of Hull
HULL HU6 7RX, England.
[2] Dept. of Computer Science
University of Hull
HULL HU6 7RX, England.

Abstract. Organisations that adapt rapidly require flexible software systems. Conventional system development methods are too slow for these organisations. One way to alleviate these problems is to empower members of the organisation, domain experts, to directly control and modify such systems (user enhanceability). This paper considers the applicability of visual languages as an enabling tool for user enhanceability. Previous systems in this area have succeeded only for narrow application domains and have failed to scale up. This paper highlights some major problems in such an endeavour, presents a generic architecture that addresses these problems and discusses a user enhanceable system for workflow applications that was implemented using this architecture.

1 Introduction

1.1 Why We Need User Enhanceability

Information systems for the support of organisational group activities (e.g. office and workflow systems) are notoriously difficult to build and maintain due to the speed of organisational changes and the complex social aspects of group work and organisational processes. These systems must support higher-level organisational coordination activities such as activity management, task scheduling and workload distribution, but these high-level activities are quite vulnerable to organisational change and their social context makes them inherently difficult to capture and formalise. As a result, frequent modifications are needed to either reflect organisational changes (often known as adaptive maintenance) or to better match the system to the organisational and user needs (part of perfective maintenance).

The large costs and time-scales involved in modifying software are often attributed to the necessity of translating user requirements to code modifications. This translation is generally performed by software professionals and, as Poo and Layzell state in [27], the process is 'often fraught with misunderstanding and poor translation, which result in unwanted changes, and so the process repeats, adding to the total maintenance costs'. The general reasons for miscommunication between software professionals and end users are summarised by Novick in [25].

Software professionals play a vital role during development by ensuring that the system is based on a well structured architecture. However, during maintenance their role (assuming that they have indeed produced a good design) is less strategic and for most modifications they are acting simply as translators or programmers. Some researchers and practitioners believe that domain experts would be more effective than software professionals in performing the majority of the needed enhancements [18, 22, 1]. Enabling these domain experts, which we call *application managers*, to perform a large subset of the information systems enhancements with little or no help from software professionals is known as *user enhanceability*. Other names for user enhanceable systems are 'radically tailorable systems' [23] and 'configurable systems' [7]. Although we assume that application managers are computer literate, they are not expected to know a conventional programming language, nor be familiar with programming techniques and algorithms. Apart from helping to keep information systems up-to-date, user enhanceability [16] will also give application managers a powerful instrument to explore different processes and to introduce organisational transitions in a gradual way.

1.2 Our Approach to Achieving User Enhanceability through Visual Programming

Visual programming languages describe a program through graphical or spatial expressions rather than through character sequences as in conventional programming languages. They are generally considered to have potential for user-level programming [30, 24], but if a visual language is to be suitable for application managers then it should not be simply a programming language which has a diagrammatic as opposed to a textual representation. Such a language solves none of the problems of programming except perhaps difficulties with syntax. Instead, a visual language must render irrelevant the low-level problem solving activities of conventional programming [12, 28, 30, 29, 19].

The visual language must exploit, as far as possible, the fact that these application managers will not be tackling general purpose programs but will be solving problems that are specific to their particular domain, for example constructing a depreciation formula in a spreadsheet, or describing the route of an electronic form throughout an office. The visual language should thus provide task-specific programming constructs, i.e. constructs that represent concepts from the application domain. The graphical dimension of the visual programming language can be exploited to present these concepts effectively. Such a visual language is often called a task-specific or domain-oriented visual programming language. An extended argument for the benefits of task-specific programming is contained in Nardi's book [24].

Unfortunately, a number of problems have prevented the successful application of domain-oriented visual programming in complex domains [8, 5], and they have so far been successful only for comparatively simple target domains, for example spreadsheets [23] for accounting and statistics, form painters for database access, LabView for signal processing, Khoros for image processing. The failure of visual languages to scale up has been recognised and some problems of the general-purpose visual languages have been investigated in a recent article by Burnett *et al* [5]. However, the problems faced by domain-oriented languages are rather different than the problems of general-purpose ones.

In the remainder of this paper we discuss the problems of applying domain-oriented visual languages for user enhanceability of organisational information systems and then we describe a novel architecture that addresses these problems and achieves enhanceability at two levels:

- User enhanceability, where application managers modify application functionality to reflect changing organisational requirements
- Meta-enhanceability, where software professionals modify enhanceability facilities to reflect changes in the enhanceability requirements.

The paper concludes with a brief report about experiences from ongoing tests of ECHOES, and with a review of the relevant research work, where the novel aspect of the proposal are identified.

2 Applying Visual Languages to Complex Information Systems

2.1 Management of Complexity

One of the first problems we face when applying visual languages to organisational information systems is one of complexity. We need to find a compromise between hiding complexity from the application manager and providing an expressive visual language. Four strategies for complexity management are appropriate in this context:

Multiple Descriptions Since a well designed domain-oriented visual description should employ only a small number of high-level abstractions [24], complex concepts are often best presented by using multiple descriptions, For example, organisational structure should have a different description from that used for information processing and different yet again from the structure of the information. Also, by having a choice of different enhanceability formalisms and facilities, there is no need to treat all organisational processes in the same way.

These multiple descriptions must of course be integrated to help application managers to comprehend and navigate between them. The descriptions thus form a visual language, where each description communicates to the application manager a small coherent aspect of the application.

Assumptions The descriptions employed by domain experts are often informal and incomplete in the sense that a lot of detail is not articulated but taken for granted. This is inevitable and indeed a desirable consequence of abstraction. For example, the activity of sending a form to a specific office worker could be easily presented in a visual language as the dragging of a form icon to an office worker icon. However, this representation hides many details. For example, office workers receive many forms and so they must be queued in some way. What is the queue discipline? One assumption may be that all queues are served in first-in first-out (FIFO) manner.

Often, as in fourth-generation languages (both visual and textual), the software designers bury these assumptions deep in the code, hoping that they match user's expectancies and "common sense". Unfortunately, when an application manager tries to comprehend and modify the system, his or her expectations may be quite different from the assumptions made by the designers. For example, the application manager may rely on priority-based queue processing, and would therefore expect a form or letter, marked "Urgent" to be processed immediately.

We argue that such assumptions are a part of the application domain and therefore they should be explicit. They should be available on request to the application manager. Hopefully, the application manager will not need to modify assumptions, but if this proves necessary, assumptions can be replaced by visual descriptions, thus enhancing the visual language. Assumptions have well defined interfaces to facilitate replacement by a visual description.

Exploratory Enhancements In any complex system it is difficult to predict all the consequences of a specific enhancement. Therefore, in an ideal user enhanceable system it should be possible to perform modifications in an exploratory style. That means that the boundaries between modification and execution must be removed and rich animation and feedback techniques provided. The application manager should directly manipulate the application system through its domain-level representations, thus fully exploiting user-level metaphors for domain concepts. Visual languages that provide this style of working are referred to as *responsive* visual programming languages [5], or as visual languages with a high degree of *liveness* [33]. In these languages there is no separate compilation step, instead the user actions are immediately executed and their effects shown. Examples of such visual languages are spreadsheets, Forms/3 [4], OVAL [23] and HI-VISUAL [14].

Modifications Support Whenever possible, important consequences and side-effects of a change should be pointed out to the application manager, even if they do not belong to the visual description where the change is performed. For example, when an office worker is deleted from the organisational description, the description that shows flow of work between activities should also be updated to exclude the deleted worker. This update should then be brought to the application manager's attention, since the deletion may affect other activities.

2.2 Changing Enhanceability Requirements (Meta-Enhanceability)

Enhanceability requirements cannot be guaranteed to be stable and there is sometimes a necessity for software designers to change the manner in which the application is modified (meta-enhanceability). Indeed, very high level, application specific languages are more vulnerable to such changes since they typically lack the universality of conventional programming languages.

A substantial meta-enhancement would be to substitute one visual description with an alternative. For example, when describing the personnel of an organisation, we may substitute a taxonomy that is based on specialising job descriptions, to an organisational chart, which shows the authority structure. The most radical enhancement would be to develop a new visual description to control some previously unvisualised aspect of the domain, for example a visual description to interact with a queue of forms. Providing facilities for such meta-enhancements while preserving the underlying application is one of the problems addressed by our architecture.

3 An Instantiation of the Proposed Architecture

A crude description of the proposed architecture of pluggable visual descriptions is presented in Figure 1. It consist of a number of visual descriptions and assumption modules, which interface to an application system. However, the best way to present the architecture is to understand the motivation behind it. This motivation is illustrated below in an extended use scenario within ECHOES *(Easily CHangeable OfficE Systems)*. ECHOES is a prototype system, implemented in Smalltalk-80 with VisualWorks and HotDraw — a generic drawing editor described in [17]. ECHOES instantiates the architecture to provide a user enhanceable workflow system that may be used for order and invoice processing, insurance application approval, etc.

3.1 The Visual Language

The domain is abstracted into the following user-level visual descriptions: information flow, service definition, organisational structure, information taxonomy and information appearance description.

Information Flow Visual Description ECHOES is a general purpose architecture for end-user development systems but to explain ECHOES we will use an example workflow system. This kind of system is likely to be familiar to readers and the particular system we describe is part of the processing of university undergraduate applications within a particular department. As shown on Figure 2, the application forms are initially checked for completeness, then some of the applicants are selected for interviewing and others are rejected. After the interview an offer is decided for the particular applicant, the case is filed and

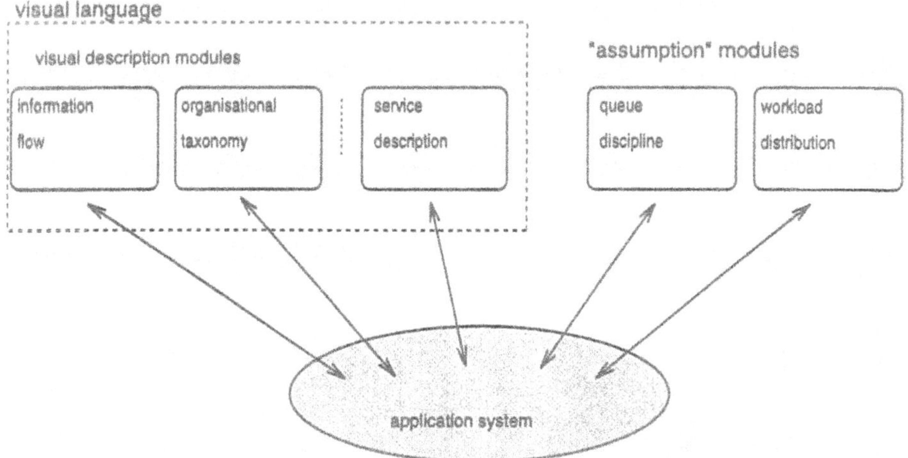

Fig. 1. A crude description of the architecture behind ECHOES

letters are sent as appropriate. The results are sent to the university admissions system for processing.

The flow of information between office clerks is represented as an information flow diagram. It is based on the data flow paradigm and, as shown on Figure 2, the diagram shows the flow of information and control messages between the services that constitute the application system. A service is an information processing activity performed by a participant in the workflow, a clerk.

A service is represented as an unobscured rounded rectangle, all the clerks that perform the particular service are represented as rounded rectangles that are stacked behind it. The message flows are represented as arrowed lines that connect the source and the target of the message. To reroute messages the application manager may directly move the message arrows to new source or target services.

If the application manager, for example, needs to add a new service to the system, he or she selects the appropriate service symbol from the palette on the right and places it on the diagram as shown with the dashed arrow. The dashed lines have been superimposed on the screenshot to show the interaction dynamics. The visual description will convert the application manager's action into a sequence of "low-level" commands that add a new service to the application system.

When the application manager adds a new service to the information flow diagram, he or she should also specify who may perform the service. The application system knows that each service is performed by one or more office clerks, and therefore detects the need for additional information. The application broadcasts a request for this information to all modules currently plugged to

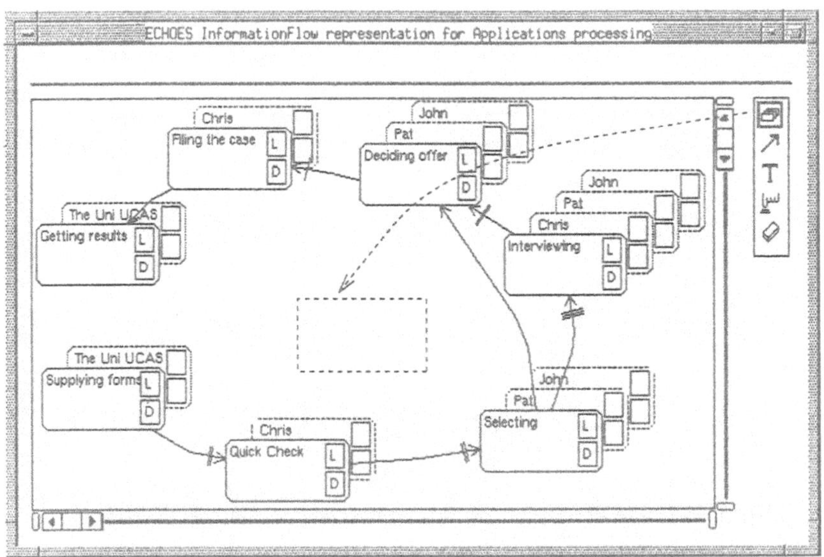

Fig. 2. Example information flow visual description for university admissions

the application system, regardless of whether they are visual description modules or "assumption" modules.

Organisational Visual Description In ECHOES, the assignment of services to office clerks is performed via the organisational description. It groups services into "job descriptions" and then classifies clerks in a prototype inheritance taxonomy, based on their job descriptions. An example is shown on Figure 3 ('Academic' is the job description, 'John' and 'Pat' are the office clerks that have this job description).

Continuing the example from the previous section, in response to the broadcast request for which office clerks are to perform the new service, the organisational description module responds to supply this information. It opens the window on Figure 3, which shows the organisational taxonomy, and asks the application manager to select either a group of people, linked by a common job description such as "Employee" or an individual office clerk such as "Pat". If, as shown on the Figure, the application manager selects 'Pat', the description module will ask him or her to confirm whether the new service will be added only to Pat's job description or to the job descriptions of all "Academic" staff. Confirmation is necessary since, if the answer is 'just Pat', a new job description will be specialised for her (as shown on Figure 5).

Now the system has all the necessary information to create a new service as a part of the application. After the service is created, the application system will notify all "plugged in" modules. In response, some of the visual description

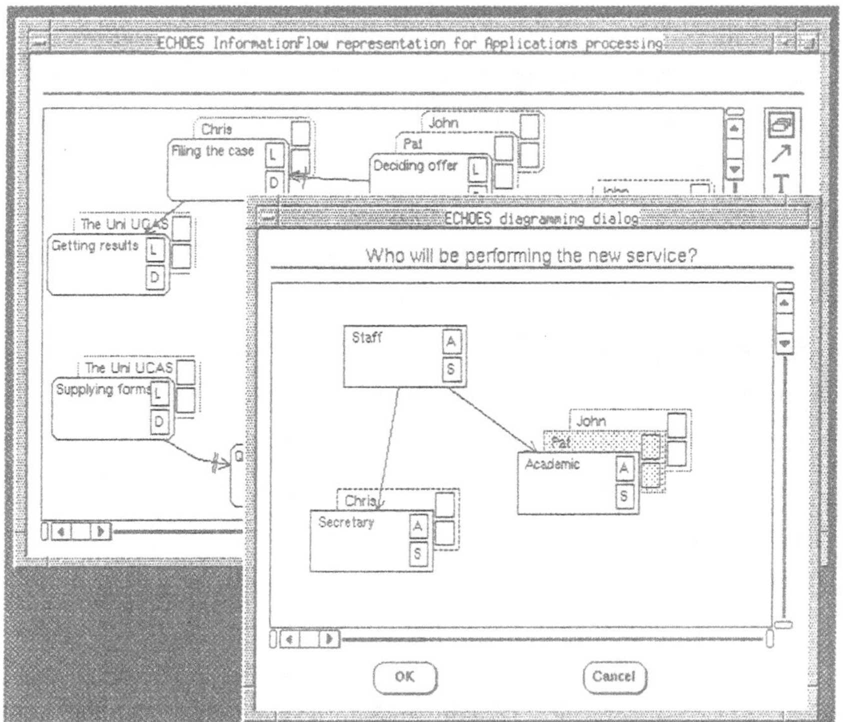

Fig. 3. Organisational description module responds

modules will update their representation of the application system. For example, the information flow module will place the new service on the information flow diagram as shown on Figure 4, and stack Pat's oval behind the service's symbol, since it has read the current configuration from the application system.

The new service will initially appear with a default name and priority. The application manager can rename it and change its priority by clicking on the "S" button of the relevant job description as shown on Figure 5.

The application manager may then proceed to connect the new service to other services with message flows. When a new flow is created on the diagram, the system needs to know the type of information on this flow and this request is answered by the information descriptions, the subject of the next section.

Information Descriptions In ECHOES, information is modelled in terms of forms. On the information taxonomy visual description, the type of each message flow is specified in a hierarchy which defines specialisation and composition relationships between these forms. Manipulating this taxonomy is performed in a similar manner to manipulating job descriptions on the organisational taxonomy.

The structure and the appearance of each form is controlled by the applica-

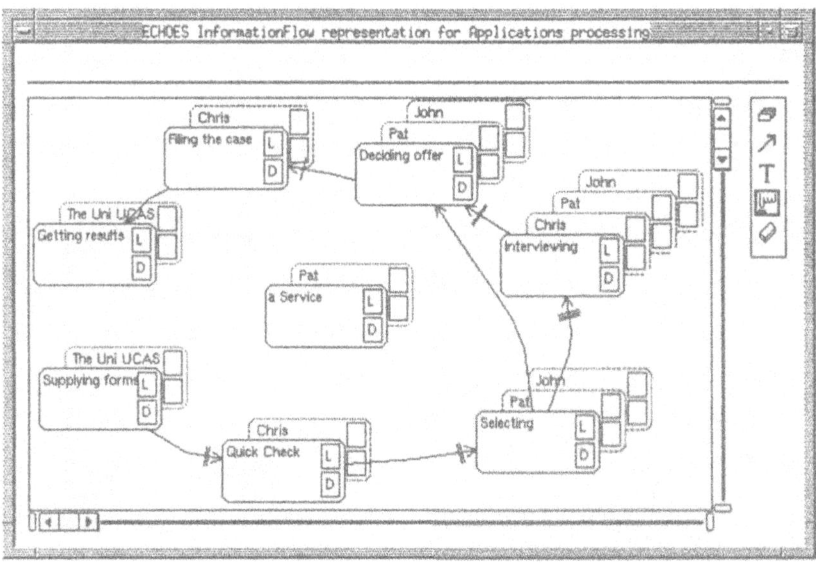

Fig. 4. The new service appears on the information flow description

tion manager directly manipulating the form's elements (*i.e.* input fields, menus, formulae) as in a standard form painter. Indeed, the standard form painter supplied by the implementation platform VisualWorks was used in ECHOES, since form painters are not novel.

Service Visual Description When the new service "Selecting Disabled Applicants" is created in our example, a default process description is associated with it. In its simplest form, the service will simply present forms that arrive on incoming flows to the office worker. The worker can process the form and then press the 'OK' button, then the service will send the result to an output flow. This default service description is shown on Figure 6. Four dashed arrows have been added to the screenshot to show the dynamics of the interaction.

The visual description of the processing that takes place in services, integrates the event-driven and the procedural elements of a service in a single visual description. As shown in Figure 6, a template-like frame surrounds the description. Events that control the processing are listed on the top of the frame. The input flows are listed on the left of the frame and given names, the output flows are listed on the right. Interaction with users is also modelled in terms of form-based messages exchanged between the service and the office worker, but in this case the form is displayed on the screen to both present output and gather input from the office worker. These interaction flows are designated with a computer terminal icon and do not appear on the information flow diagram.

The service description has highlighted the second output flow with a ques-

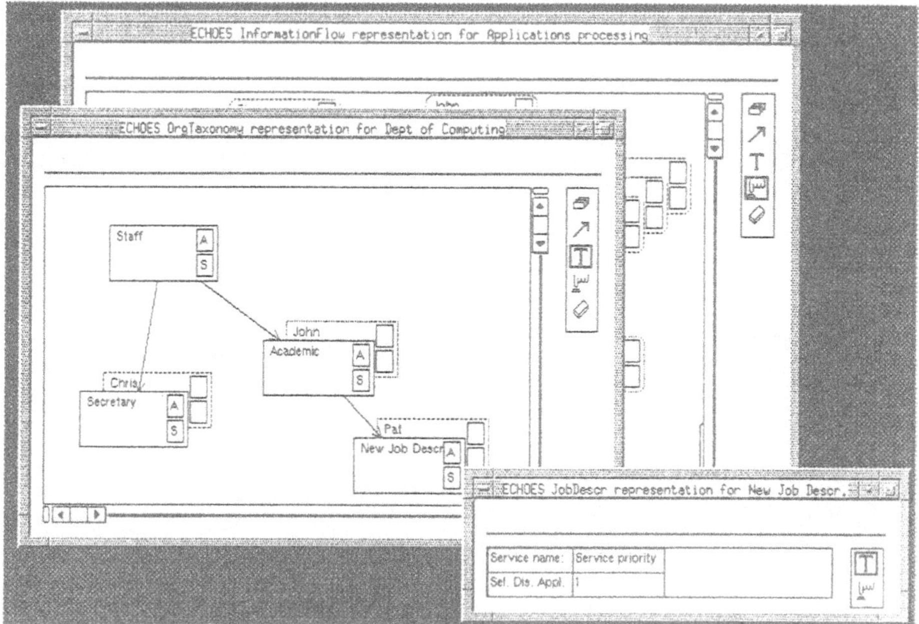

Fig. 5. The new job description has been created

tion mark, because it is not yet assigned. This prompts the application manager to modify the description to take this flow into account. Indeed, if the default service processing is not satisfactory, the application mãnager has to modify the service processing description. A description could be copied from another service and then modified to reflect the new functionality required.

Processing control flow is animated. The current state of the processing is represented as a token moving through a network of states. The triggering events are shown to control the opening and closing of switches that in turn control the movement of the token by enabling and disabling certain transitions. On its way through the network the token passes through the so-called action blocks, where it triggers a simple sequence of actions by stepping through them. The sequence of actions in each action block is represented in a separate window, as shown on Figure 6.

3.2 Assumption Modules

After the newly created service 'Selecting disabled applicants' is connected with information flows to the rest of the diagram, forms will start queueing on the input flow of the service. When Pat comes to work and opens her 'To Do' list, the new service will appear. If Pat activates the new service, the service object within the application system will try to get the first item on the incoming queue

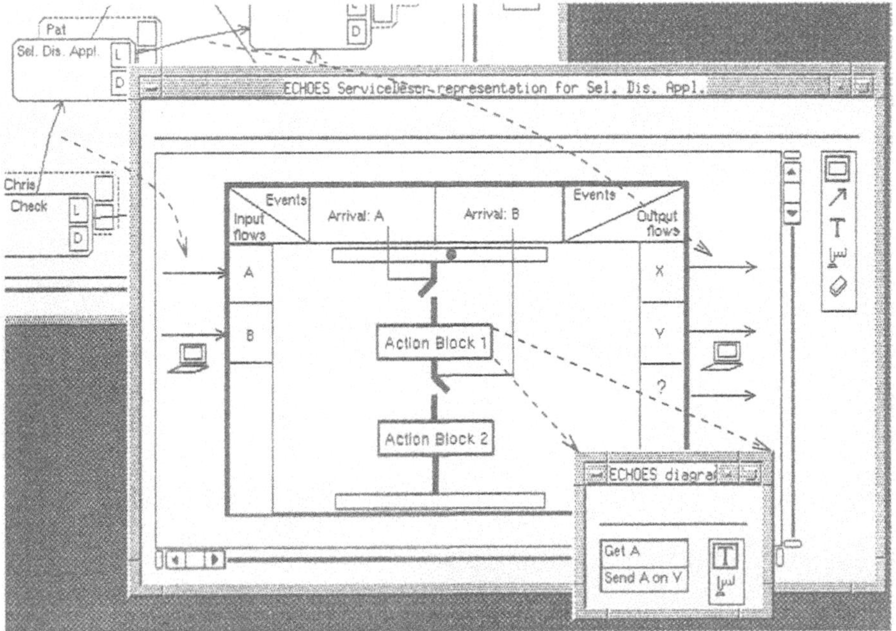

Fig. 6. The default visual description of the new service

from a special coordination object. This coordination object is shared between all the clerks that perform a given service. It distributes their workload and manages their incoming queues. This coordination object contains the scheduling algorithm for retrieving the next item on the queue for a particular clerk.

Currently there is no visual description in ECHOES, whereby the application manager can specify this algorithm. In a traditional fourth generation language this algorithm will have been buried in the implementation code of the coordination object. In ECHOES, however, the specification of this algorithm is encapsulated into an assumption module, which is integrated into the system in an identical manner to all other visual description modules.

When the new service was created by the application manager, the corresponding coordination object was also created, and the specification for its queue discipline was defined by the assumption module. The current specification in the assumption is that all queues are served in 'first-in first-out' fashion.

So, like visual description modules, assumption modules supply application-specific information. However, unlike the visual description modules, the assumption modules obtain the necessary information by performing a pre-specified algorithm that can not be visually manipulated by the application manager.

However, in our scenario, the application manager may wonder why a certain form that was marked 'Urgent' has not been processed immediately by Pat, but has been waiting on the queue together with all other forms. In this case the application manager may try to open the queue in the way he or she would open any other element on the diagram that has a visual description (e.g. a service symbol expanded into a service definition diagram). The architecture does not distinguish between visual descriptions and assumptions but simply propagates an "open description" request for the relevant application aspect. Since our queue assumption module does not have a visual description, it will instead open up a text window containing a explanation of the assumption that is coded in the algorithm of this module. In our case this would read "All information items on a queue are processed in a first-come first-serve basis".

So, although the application manager cannot, at this level, control the assumption contained in the corresponding assumption module, he or she can at least be made aware of it.

4 Pluggable Visual Descriptions Architecture

In this section we will describe the architecture of pluggable visual descriptions, which underlies ECHOES. This architecture allows an application system to be controlled through multiple visual descriptions. The use of multiple descriptions of a single application system is similar in concept to the model-view-controller paradigm used in Smalltalk and described in [11]. An outline of the proposed architecture of "pluggable visual descriptions" is presented on Figure 7.

In this architecture the domain model encodes the facts that hold all applications in the target domain of organisational systems. This model provides a language for controlling the application system.

A higher level domain-oriented visual language, consisting of several visual descriptions, is used to construct and modify application systems. Each description presents a coherent aspect of the application to the application manager in high-level task-specific concepts. The assumptions made when creating the visual language are made explicit in "assumption" modules.

4.1 Visual Description Modules

Each visual description module is composed of two parts as shown on Figure 8. The graphical interface part enables the application manager to directly manipulate diagrammatic, table-based or some other graphical representation of a part of the system. The second part is the translator, which links graphical actions and graphical entities to operations and entities in the application. In one direction, it transforms the application managers' manipulations of diagram symbols into operations performed over application-level objects. In the other direction, it maps the application objects to concepts and symbols on the diagram. The translator ignores the irrelevant and cosmetic user gestures such as moving a node in a graph-based diagram.

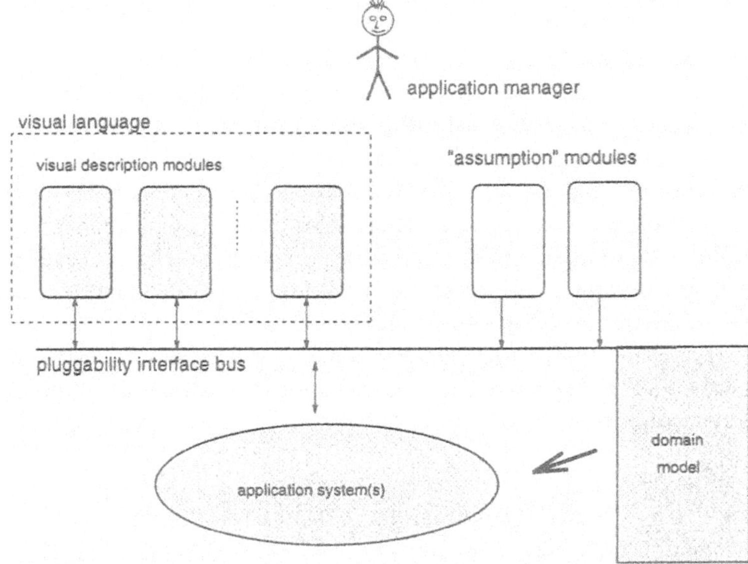

Fig. 7. Generic architecture for user enhanceability — "pluggable visual descriptions"

For example, when a new symbol representing a service was added by the application manager to the diagram in the scenario of Section 3, the graphical interface passed the event on to the translator, which translated the event as a request to the application to generate all corresponding application object(s) that implement this service. After the application objects were generated, all translators were notified that the application has changed. The information flow description then translated the new application objects to a high-level representation of a service, which was displayed by the graphical interface part. Some other visual descriptions also added the new service, the rest ignored the notification.

Similar mechanisms of interaction between the application system and a translator are also used in the following two cases:

prompting for information needed to complete a change Often, as in the case of adding a new service above, the application manager has to supply additional information. The application will then broadcast a request for this additional information to all modules. Then the translator of the first relevant visual description module will arrange for the description to prompt the user for this information and will supply it to the application. The other relevant modules will not be activated.

implementing hypertext-style links To support modifications, concepts from different visual descriptions are linked with hypertext-style links. These links

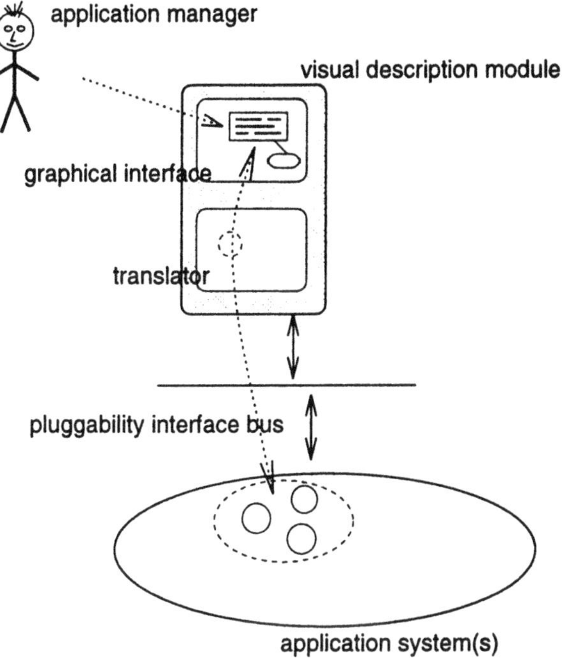

Fig. 8. Structure of a visual description module

serve as navigation paths and as change propagation links. For example, when a high-level concept has been modified, or even just selected, in one visual description, the application manager should be demonstrated the effects on all relevant concepts from other visual descriptions. This is implemented by the following mechanism. When application manager selects a high-level concept, its translator will "flag" the corresponding application objects. This event will be propagated to all other translators, and some of them will in turn highlight the high-level concepts that are linked to some of the "flagged" application objects.

For a given domain model, and, indeed, even for a given application, various descriptions may be added or removed (i.e. "plugged" in and out of the system), thus catering for cases when the requirements for enhanceability change. i.e. for "meta-enhanceability". An example of a meta-enhanceability scenario is given later.

The key feature that enables such plugability is that a visual description does not contain any information that is necessary for running the application, such as the state of the application objects, their functionality or the relations between them. A visual description only keeps representational information such as the position of a symbol in the diagram. Indeed, a completed application system should still run even after all visual descriptions are detached from it.

4.2 Assumption Modules

Assumption modules implement aspects of the domain that need to be available for inspection, but hopefully should not require modification. Thus an assumption module does not need a visual representation, but it should be narrated to the application manager on request, possibly by devising a "help"-style textual description. If later, as a result of accumulated experience in using the software, an assumption turns out to be inappropriate, it can be modified by software professionals. If the application manager wants to control the assumed aspect, then it can be replaced by a visual description. This will expand the visual language.

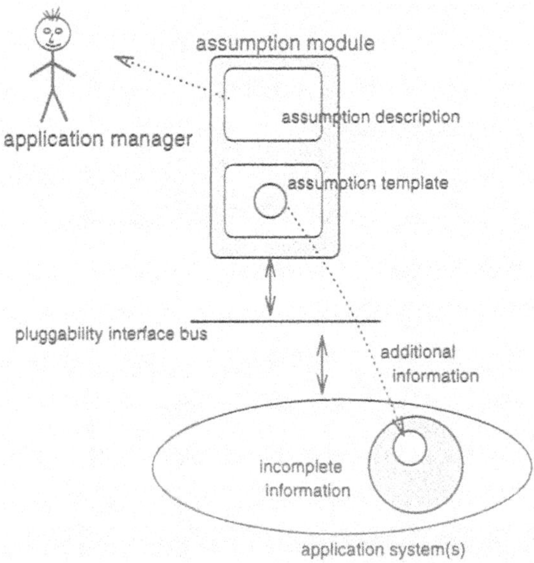

Fig. 9. The structure of an assumption module

Handling these requirements is best performed by separating the assumption in a separate assumption module as shown on Figure 9. In our extended ECHOES example we have encapsulated in such a manner the template algorithm dealing with the discipline of message queues. An assumption module also contains the text describing the algorithm, and behaves in a similar way to the visual description modules:

- It supplies the design assumption contained in its software template to the application. This assumption will then be used when formally interpreting the informal concepts and commands within the visual descriptions
- It displays the textual description of this assumption to the application manager on request.

Since assumption descriptions are explicit and available for inspection by the application manager, we overcome the problems with the fourth generation languages, where, for example, the design assumption about how users would do a search through a data table is hidden in the code of the language interpretor. All the user of such a system would see is the FIND command, which may not operate in the desired manner.

In essence, the assumption description modules complement the current set of visual descriptions and serve as place-holders for future visual descriptions to be added to the visual language. These novel assumption descriptions are a major factor that enables our user enhanceability approach.

4.3 Meta-Enhanceability

Meta-enhanceability is the facility to change the means and ways in which a system can be enhanced. In this section we will extend the scenario from Section 3 in order to demonstrate how building ECHOES using the "pluggable visual descriptions" architecture extends what is enhanceable by adding a visual description that controls the queue discipline instead of the current assumption module. Similarly, one type of visual description could be substituted for another by unplugging the relevant visual description module and plugging a new one in its place.

For this scenario, let us suppose that the queue discipline for all queues in the system is 'FIFO', and that this is unsatisfactory. The discipline is implemented as an assumption, but a more flexible arrangement is required, where the application manager can control the queue discipline. We decide to develop a new visual description to allow the application manager to see the status of each queue and to manually re-arrange the order of the items on the queue as required.

This visual description module incorporates a modified version of the algorithm from the old assumption module. The information items on the queue are ordered first-in first-out within two subsections — urgent and non-urgent, the items from the urgent subsection are processed first. The visual descriptions shows the information items ordered in the two subsections of the queue, but also allows the application manager to manually override this ordering at will by directly moving items.

The old assumption module is then removed from the system and the new visual description module is plugged in its place. The new module also specifies the queue ordering algorithm as did the old one, but in addition it can issue requests for the coordination object to override this algorithm and to re-arrange the default order.

5 Discussion and Limitations of the Proposed Approach

5.1 Discussion of the Coherence Problem

To allow different visual descriptions to be easily plugged in and out of the application, which is essential for meta-enhanceability, we require that each visual description should be directly connected only to the application and comparatively independent from the others for its operation. Also, the application should not be dependent on the visual descriptions for its execution. However, a problem exists with this architecture. One visual description may put the application system into a state that has not been anticipated by another visual description, and the latter then becomes invalid.

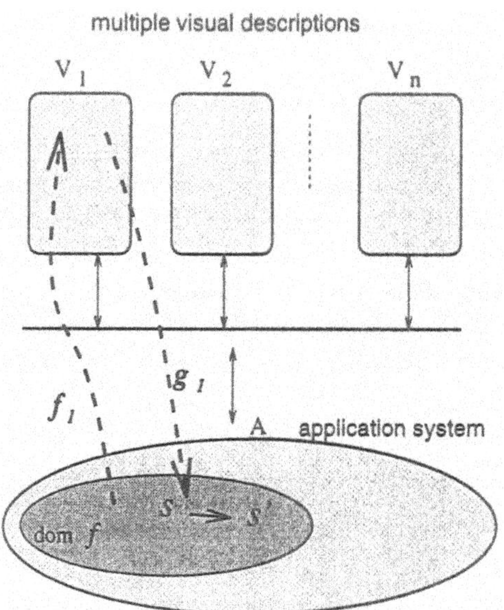

Fig. 10. The pluggable visual descriptions idea

In Figure 10, V_1, V_2 and V_n denote different visual descriptions, attached to the application system A. Creating and maintaining a particular description V_i could be presented as a partial view function f_i from the set of all application system states S_A to the set of corresponding visual description states S_{V_i}, so that for any $s_A \in S_A$ either there exists $s_{V_i} \in S_{V_i}$, such that:

$$s_{V_i} = f_i(s_A)$$

or:

$f_i(s_A)$ is undefined.

For example, such a view function will convert the state "snapshot" of a workflow application system to a description that shows the workload of every worker involved. Implementing the view function is the responsibility of the visual description, since the application system should not be dependent on any visual description.

If visual descriptions are to be used for modifying the application, our visual description V_i should also transform user operations within the visual description into commands requesting modifications of the application. In other words, the description should implement a control function g_i from a set of user operations O_{V_i} to a set of corresponding sequences of commands for modifying the application O_A. For example, if a user adds a new service to the information flow visual description, the visual description should generate a sequence of commands that generates a new service in the application system. There exists $o_A \in O_A$ for every $o_{V_i} \in O_{V_i}$, such that:

$$o_A = g(o_{V_i})$$

Since a single visual description deals with only one aspect of the domain, it is highly likely that any view function f_i is not defined for all application states:

$$\text{dom } f_i \subset S_A,$$

i.e. that exists s_A, such that $s_A \in S_A$, and $s_A \notin \text{dom } f_i$

This means that visual descriptions will be undefined for some application states. However, undefinedness is not the real problem since a visual description can alert the application manager by showing a special message instead of a diagram, but detecting undefinedness is. There are two alternative solutions to this potential problem. The first alternative is to ensure that the application state stays always within the definition domain of the visualisation function f_i, and indeed, considering the definition domains of all visual descriptions as shown on Figure 11, that the application state stays always within the intersection of the definition domains of all visualisation functions *i.e.* for all s_A, for which $s_A \in S_A$, we have

$$s_A \in \bigcap_{i=1}^{n} \text{dom } f_i$$

Enforcing such a solution, however, contradicts the "independence" of visual descriptions, a basic principle of the architecture, since, if the visual descriptions are indeed independent of each other, there are no means to ensure that this union in not an empty set, as illustrated on Figure 11(a).

Even if the visual descriptions have been designed to work together and therefore their definitional domains overlap as shown on Figure 11(b), keeping the application state within the area of overlap would again contradict to the principle that the application system should execute independently from the visual descriptions. Indeed, the transitions between application states are based on the application's internal logic. If the application is independent from its visual descriptions and the translator functions are defined within the visual descriptions, the application can not possibly detect whether a state transition will take it out of the definitional domain of a description, so it can not stop the transition from happening nor issue a warning. And since the application is the only one to approve changes of its state, the visual descriptions can not prevent these transitions either.

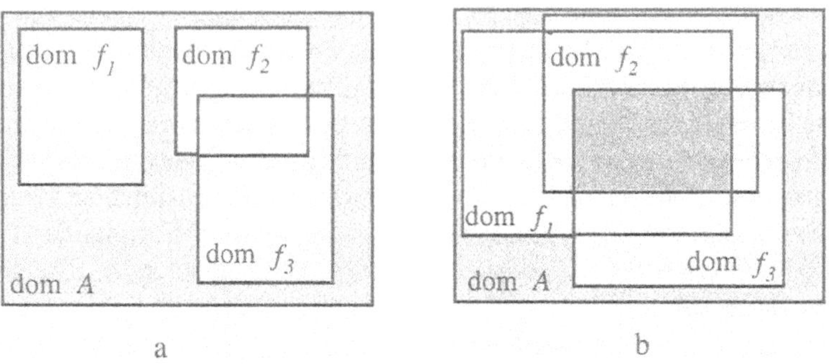

Fig. 11. Two cases of visual description definition domains

The second alternative is to not limit the state of the application system. In this alternative, each view function f_i should be constructed in such a way that it can detect when the application is in a state for which the function is not defined, *i.e.* $s_A \notin \text{dom}\, f_i$, by testing some pre-conditions. If the test fails, the visualisation function will issue a warning to the user instead of creating a visualisation.

Indeed, testing for pre-conditions is now encouraged as a good software implementation practice. Furthermore, in most practical cases the view function will perform this testing as a part of its algorithm, and therefore this solution will not bring about a big increase in the development efforts and costs.

This solution could be used to add functionality to the visualisations of the application. For example, different users may be allowed to see or modify only certain visual descriptions according to their authority. Also, the users of a workflow application system, for example, may want to see different visual descriptions in different business situations.

5.2 Other Issues

limits of meta-enhanceability Another technological issue to consider is the limits of meta-enhanceability for a given domain model. The variety of concepts and paradigms used within the visual language is constrained by the semantics of the underlying domain model, since each high-level concept or an operation from a visual description corresponds to a set of objects or operations from the domain model. Therefore the level of abstraction in this model should be carefully selected, if a large variety of user-level visual languages are to be mapped onto the model.

applicability to other domains The architectural framework presented in this article does not seem to contain domain-specific constructs, and several similar architectures as I-CASE, C-CASE[31] and MVC, are deemed applicable for professional software development in a variety of domains. However, our practical experiences of applying the framework are narrow, since ECHOES targets only the domain of workflow application systems. Therefore, the architecture's applicability to other organisational and non-organisational domains can not be tested without substantial further investigations.

organisational factors Different organisational factors play an important role for the success or failure of user enhanceability. For example, the application manager should be someone with time to devote to maintaining the application, and with the power to implement the necessary changes in work patterns. Also, some of the participants in the system may see the application manager's role as holding too much power, and may obstruct the process of implementing changes. Another danger is that, when the application manager leaves the organisation, the system could be left in a poorly documented state, after a large number of modifications have caused design deterioration.

system design deterioration It is widely accepted that any software enhancements cause deterioration of the system design[3, 20]. This factor is particularly important in an user enhanceability scenario, where application managers lack training in software design principles. Hopefully, since application managers are domain experts, working with domain-oriented model of the application will help them to avoid changes that cause deterioration of this model and of the design structure of the application.

risks of end user development Allowing end users to create and modify applications software, can lead to a large number of errors if appropriate support is not provided. For example, Panko in [26] points that some consultants' personal experiences show that something like a third of all operational spreadsheet models contain errors. One consultant from Price Waterhouse reported 128 errors within four large spreadsheet models[6]. To alleviate these problems, application managers need to be supported not only with better tools, but also with better training and professional help.

6 Our Experiences so Far

We are still at early stages of testing ECHOES, so the experiences reported here should be treated as preliminary first results only.

Implementing ECHOES in Smalltalk did not require departures from the architectural framework outlined here. The Smalltalk dependency mechanism was used to implement the plugability bus. The number of visual descriptions turned out to be high, since attribute tables, action block descriptions and other auxiliary windows were implemented in a way identical to the major visual descriptions described in the paper.

We have used ECHOES to develop two workflow applications. The first is a simplified version of departmental system for processing student applicants, which was used in section 3 to present ECHOES. The second one is a workflow system to support production of a central university timetable. The first system was used as a case study at early stages of the project, and its requirements were captured using a structured analysis method. They were recently converted into a workflow application, which was used to test ECHOES on several scenarios. The feedback was used to appropriately modify ECHOES. The requirements of the second application were captured using the ECHOES language as a requirements formalism, and this seemed to work well for this limited size project. When showing diagrams to the University timetabling administrator, we were surprised to find out the large extend to which her domain expertise did reduce the necessity for training in the ECHOES formalisms.

We have designed, but have not yet implemented, two pilot experiments, where ECHOES will be used by two domain experts to perform enhancements in the two applications developed. While the first experiment will involve a departmental administrator who has not taken part in the development of the university applicants processing application, the second one will involve the domain expert who was helping us to develop the timetabling system. On these experiments we hope to obtain feedback comments that will help us develop better appreciation of how well does the tool and the architecture support user enhancements.

We should stress here that we do not currently plan to conduct statistically reliable evaluation studies for three main reasons. Firstly, such studies will require a large number of participants to take into account diversity of programming backgrounds, aptitudes and abilities. Secondly, the software is still a "proof-of-concept" prototype and is not stable enough for usability evaluation. Finally, good evaluation of enhanceability will require long-term observation of enhanceability practices by real application managers.

7 Related Work

Multi-description Based Visual Languages Multi-description based visual languages are presented in [2] and [13]. Indeed, Visual Toolset [2] and MViews [13] do exploit the idea of handling domain complexity by using a multiple visual and text descriptions as a part of a multi-paradigm language. However, they are not oriented to a particular application domain and as a result they take different considerations into account. For example, Visual Toolset is oriented towards general programming. Therefore, while the elements of the specialised visual language in our paper map directly to the domain concepts and to the model structures, the users of Visual Toolset have to perform this mapping themselves for each particular application domain, which requires a higher level of programming expertise and familiarity with the programming language concepts such as data structures, functions and procedures.

MViews is a model for general-purpose software development environments, where the main concern is integrating the different views and the change propagation. It has evolved in the domain of Prolog programming, and therefore lacks these elements of our architecture that support organisational and office domain specifics such as the assumption modules.

Visual Languages for Organisational and Office Systems Some visual languages that address the domain of organisational and office systems are "Officeaid VPE"[10], HI-VISUAL[14] and Regatta VPL[32].

"Officeaid VPE" and HI-VISUAL have a restricted scope in the sense that they are used for the description of single office tasks only, without integrating them in an office processing framework. The first of them is based on a flowchart representation of office activities, partly built by programming-by-example techniques, the second one exploits the object semantics of overlapping iconic representations of office concepts.

Regatta VPL, on the contrary, targets the overall work process in an office or organisation. It allows end-user modification of process descriptions through the use of a graphical planning tool, thus evolving and improving the process description on-the-fly. It is a representative of a subclass of the workflow systems described in [15]. The systems from this subclass are used to visually describe organisational workflows. However, these systems tend to take a single, highly abstract view of the organisational processes, and are not designed to accommodate radical meta-enhancements.

Enhanceable Systems Oval[23] and of Cosmos[7] are concerned with the user enhanceability of office systems for cooperative work. Oval aims to allow users to modify their applications, but users are meant to develop their system from scratch. The system does not offer visual programming tools as such, nor support for coordination activities in its user-level language.

Cosmos, on the other hand, does provide higher-level coordination support, but the model is be configured by using two text-based languages - a scripting language and a communication structure definition language. The authors of this paper believe that making the system configurable by ordinary users could be achieved on a textual level with the help of good textual editors as opposed to developing diagrammatic versions of languages.

A third system, proposed by Oei *et. al.* in [9] handles not only enhanceability, but also meta-enhanceability. Starting from an empty system, the application evolves as a result of a stream of update requests that are processed and then validated. However, the provided enhanceability facilities are not targeted to the level of computer expertise that domain experts are expected to have.

8 Summary and Conclusions

If visual languages are to be effective in building user enhanceable information systems, then one must address the complexity of the domain, the specific requirements of user-level programming and meta-enhanceability.

This article proposes a novel conceptually integrated approach to these problems, the generic architecture of 'pluggable visual descriptions'. In this approach application managers control an application system by directly manipulating high-level domain concepts within a changeable set of visual descriptions. A set of novel assumption modules encapsulate those aspects of the domain that are currently not enhanceable. These assumption modules, together with the visual descriptions, can be replaced to achieve meta-enhanceability. An expanded scenario is used to present ECHOES, which is an application of this approach to workflow systems.

Our experiences from implementing ECHOES are positive in regard to the functionality and expressive power of the proposed architecture and ECHOES. However, further research is needed to identify some usability characteristics of ECHOES, the applicability of the architecture for other application domains and the limits of meta-enhanceability for a particular domain model.

There are some important limitations to user enhanceable systems, which have been outlined in section 5. However, our limited experiences with ECHOES have supported the position [24, 21] that tapping into the domain expertise of the users can help to overcome most of these limitations, so that domain experts do not only achieve satisfactory results in software modifications, but they often tailor the software in novel and creative ways.

References

1. Jon A. Barrett. User Enhanceable Systems. Talk synopsis handed out on the User Enhanceable Systems : Enabling Technologies — JFIT preliminary proposals workshop, 18 Nov 1992, DTI, London, November 1992. Digital Equipment Corporation.
2. Jose A. Borges and Ralph E. Johnson. Multiparadigm visual programming language. In *Proceedings of the 1990 IEEE Workshop on Visual Languages*, pages 233–240, IEEE Service Center,Piscataway, NJ, USA, Oct 4-6 1990. IEEE Computer Soc and Univ of Pittsburgh and Knowledge Systems Inst and VL Foundation, IEEE. IEEE cat n 90TH0330-1, ISBN: 0-8186-2090-0.
3. Frederick P Brooks Jr. *The Mythical Man Month*. Addison-Wesley, London, 1975.
4. M. Burnett and A. Ambler. Interactive visual data abstraction in a declarative visual programming language. *J. Visual Languages and Computing*, 5(1):29–60, March 1994.
5. Margaret M. Burnett, Marla J. Baker, and Pieter van Zee. Scaling up visual programming languages. *IEEE Computer*, 28(3):45, March 1995.
6. S Ditlea. Spreadsheets can be hazardous to your health. *Personal Computing*, pages 60–69, January 1987. Cited in [26].
7. Jean Dollimore and Sylvia Wilbur. Experiences in building a configurable CSCW system. In J.M. Bowers and S.D. Benford, editors, *Studies in Computer Supported Cooperative Work*, pages 173–181. Elsevier Science Publishers B.V. (North-Holland), 1991.
8. Jr. F. P. Brooks. No silver bullet. *IEEE Computer*, 20(4):10–19, April 1987.
9. E.D. Falkenberg, J. L. H. Oei, and H. A. Proper. A conceptual framework for evolving information systems. In H. G. Sol and R. L. Crosslin, editors, *Dynamic Modelling of Information Systems, II*, pages 353–375. North-Holland, Elsevier Science Publishers B.V., 1992.
10. Paolino Di Felice, Frederick L. Lochovsky, and Thierry Mosser. Officeaid VPE: a visual programming with examples system for specifying routine office tasks. *Journal of Visual Languages and Computing*, 2(3):275–296, 1991.

11. Adele Goldberg and David Robson. *Smalltalk-80: The language.* ParcPlace Systems Inc., 1989.
12. Robert B. Grafton and Tadao Ichikawa. Visual programming (guest editors' introduction). *IEEE Computer*, 18(8):6–9, August 1985.
13. J.C. Grundy and J.G. Hosking. Constructing multi-view editing environments using MViews. In *Proceedings of the 1993 IEEE Symposium on Visual Languages*, IEEE Service Center,Piscataway, NJ, USA, August 1993. IEEE Press.
14. Masahito Hirakawa, Minoru Tanaka, and Tadao Ichikawa. An iconic programming system, HI-VISUAL. *IEEE Transactions on Software Engineering*, 16(10):1178–1184, October 1990.
15. Stefan Jablonski. Workflow management systems — modelling and architecture. Tutorial notes on CAiSE*94, June 1994. Utrecht, the Netherlands.
16. JFIT. User enhanceable systems : Enabling technologies. JFIT preliminary proposals workshop, 18 Nov 1992, DTI, London.
17. Ralph E. Johnson. Documenting frameworks using patterns. In *Proceedings OOPSLA '92, ACM SIGPLAN Notices*, pages 63–76, October 1992. Published as Proceedings OOPSLA '92, ACM SIGPLAN Notices, volume 27, number 10.
18. Phil Jones. Editorial. *Informatics*, 15(6):3, June 1994.
19. Gabor Karsai. A configurable visual programming environment: A tool for domain-specific programming. *IEEE Computer*, 28(3):36, March 1995.
20. M M Lehman and L A Belady, editors. *Program Evolution: Processes of Software Change.* Academic Press, London, 1985.
21. Wendy E. Mackay. Beyond iterative design: User innovation in co-adaptive systems. Technical Report EPC-1991-130, Rank Xerox Research Centre, Cambridge Laboratory, 61 Regent Street, Cambridge CB2 1AB, 1991.
22. V.A.J. Maller. User enhanceable systems. an outline proposal for a new DTI/SERC advanced technology programme in IT. distributed on User Enhanceable Systems : Enabling Technologies — JFIT preliminary proposals workshop, DTI, London, 18 Nov 1992.
23. Thomas W. Malone, Kum-Yew Lai, and Christopher Fry. Experiments with Oval: A radically tailorable tool for cooperative work. In Jon Turner and Robert Kraut, editors, *Proceedings of the ACM CSCW'92 Conference on Computer-Supported Cooperative Work: Emerging technologies for Cooperative Work*, pages 289–297, POB 64145, Baltimore, MD 21264, 31 October - 4 November 1992. ACM, ACM. ACM Order Number: 612920.
24. Bonnie A. Nardi. *A Small Matter of Programming: Perspectives on End User Computing.* Massachusetts Institute of Technology, Cambridge, Massachusetts, USA, 1993.
25. D Novick and E Wynn. Participatory conversation in PD. *Communications of the ACM*, 36(4):93, June 1993. Note.
26. Raymond R. Panko. Introduction to the minitrack on risks in end user computing. In *Proceedings of the Twenty-Ninth Hawaii International Conference on System Sciences*, January 1996.
27. CCD Poo and PJ Layzell. Enhancing software maintenance through explicit system representation. *Information and software technology*, 32(3):176–186, 1990.
28. Georg Raeder. A survey of current graphical programming techniques. *IEEE Computer*, 18(8):11–25, August 1985.
29. Alexander Repenning and Tamara Sumner. Agentsheets: A medium for creating domain-oriented visual languages. *IEEE Computer*, 28(3):17–25, March 1995.

30. Nan C. Shu. *Visual Programming.* Van Nostrand Reinhold Company Inc., New York, 1988.
31. L. Slusky. Modelling of I-CASE platform. *Information and Software Technology,* 33(8):547–558, October 1991.
32. Keith D Swenson, Kent T Irwin, Robin J Maxwell, Toshikazu Matsumoto, and Bahram Saghari. A business process environment supporting collaborative planning. *Journal of Collaborative Computing,* 1(1):15–34, March 1994.
33. S. Tanimoto. Viva: A visual language for image processing. *Journal of Visual Languages and Computing,* 1(2):127–139, June 1990.

An Integration Method for Design Schemas

Isabelle Mirbel and Jean-Louis Cavarero

Laboratoire I3S, CNRS-URA 1376
250 Avenue Albert Einstein
Sophia-Antipolis 06560 Valbonne
France

Abstract. The complexity of databases is increasing continually. The work of several designers become necessary. Therefore it is interesting to improve the design process with a new phase devoted to information integration, in order to take into account the designers'viewpoints. In this paper, we present an integration process which allows similarities to be discovered between the schemas under study. It works on object-oriented schemas. Whenever possible, we propose several results for the integration of two given schemas. This then makes it possible to choose the one which is the best adapted to the working context, amongst the result schemas. When design schemas are being integrated, the structural, but also and above all, the semantic part of the schemas are studied. To represent the semantic of the words which are used in a schema, we have defined a model of thesaurus drawn from the domain dealing with the meaning of words : linguistics.

1 Introduction

The complexity of information systems is increasing continually. The work of several designers become necessary. Therefore, during the design phase, several views of the information system are described by various designers belonging to different domains. So, it is necessary to improve the design process with a new phase devoted to information integration, in order to take into account the designers'viewpoints. Moreover, any enterprise needs to evolve in time. This evolution must be passed on to the underlying information systems. So with time, it is necessary to integrate changes resulting from this evolution into the existing design schemas.

The schema-integration process satisfies this dual goal. It allows a federative framework to be given to the designers, and the schema evolution to be taken into account .

In this paper, we present our integration process. The schema comparison is based on the structural, and above all, the semantic aspects of the schemas. We show the richness of these kinds of comparison and how we use them in other phases of the process.

In the next section, we briefly present the existing works on design-schema integration. Then we describe the most important phases of our process, that is to say the comparison phase, the conflict-solving phase and the result-presentation phase. After that, we indicate the strategies for using this process. In the last section, we conclude.

2 Existing Work

A lot of different work has been done on schema integration. This goes from works on the tools to help the designer to get two schemas without conflicts [1], to work on the formal presentation of the integration rules [2]. An overview of the variety of existing work can be found in [3].

Generally, the integration process is divided in four phases. The first phase is the pre-integration one. It consists in translating the schemas under study into a same formalism, and/or into a canonical form [4]. The next phase is the comparison one. It consists in discovering existing similarities and conflicts between the two schemas to be integrated. This is the most difficult part of the integration process [5]. The fundamental problem is that the universe of discourse (UoD) can be modeled in different ways. The same phenomenon of the real word can be described by using different abstraction levels, different properties. These differences react on the structure chosen to represent the phenomenon, but also on the terminology used to name it (homonymy and synonymy conflicts). The less recent approaches describe how to merge several schemas with regard to a set of correspondences between the schemas under study [1, 6, 4]. These approaches were based on relational, functional and entity-relationship models. The inter-schema assertions had to be supplied by the designer, and the conflict solving depended on the designer's common sense. Some recent approaches, in most cases based on object-oriented models, proposed tools to find the likeness between the schema elements with regard to structural criteria [7], behavioral criteria [8] and semantic criteria [9].

The next phase is the conflict-solving phase. This consists in making the schemas compatible, that is to say without conflicts, by applying structural-changing rules to them. The object of this phase is to be able to integrate the schemas [10]. Lastly, the merging phase consists in building a result schema by merging the schemas under study. Several approaches exist. Each of them presents structural-merging rules. Generally, these rules are model dependent [11].

3 The Integration Process

Our integration process allows similarities to be discovered between the schemas under study. The designers do not need to enter the equivalence before doing the integration, as is required in a lot of existing works [6].

The process works on object-oriented schemas. These schemas do not have to be expressed in a particular formalism among existing models, but rather on all the object-oriented concepts used in most of the existing object-oriented design methods [12, 13]: that is to say, concepts of attribute, method, class and reference-and-inheritance links.

The structural, but also and above all, the semantic part of the schemas are used when design schemas are being integrated. The semantic part is used especially when design schemas are being compared, but also when conflicts are being solved and when the result schema is being presented.

Whenever possible, we propose several results for the integration of two given schemas. This then makes it possible to choose the one which is the best adapted to the working context, amongst the result schemas. One could, for example wish to integrate the schemas in order to enrich an existing library of design schemas. In this case, one could compare the result schemas obtained, in accordance with re-use criteria such as those presented in [14].

We will now present the comparison criteria used when design schemas are being compared.

3.1 The Semantic Similarities

To represent the semantics of the words used in the schemas, we have defined a model, drawn from a domain dealing especially with the meaning of words: linguistics [15]. In our data structure, we differentiate words (or terms) from concepts (or meanings), following Quillian's works; he was the first to make this distinction [16]. Each concept is represented by a sentence, the most explicit one, which can be sometimes a definition. We make the distinction between words and concepts so that we can work at a level (the concept level) where knowledge can be defined very precisely, without ambiguity, without synonym and homonym problems. Concepts are linked together by conceptual relationships of a semantic type. Some interpreting relationships between words and concepts allow the expression of meanings given to words.

We define two kinds of relationships in our thesaurus: conceptual relationship of a semantic type, that links concepts together; and interpreting relationship, that links words and concepts together in order to explain their meanings. We will present each of them.

The conceptual relationship of a semantic type: we use two kinds of conceptual relationships which are the generic relationship and the aggregation relationship. These are the relationships most often used. There exists a lot of other relationships linking concepts together[17]. But keeping them inside our thesaurus will bring nothing more, because we cannot exploit them, when design schema are being integrated.
In order to capture more semantics, we graduate the membership in these relationships with likelihood degrees, varying between 0 and 1. So we can represent some categories with ill-defined boundaries, situations between everything and nothing, like the quasi-generic relationship [17], or the fact that a component is optional or not [17].

We differentiate several kinds of aggregation relationships. D. A. Cruse [15] and J. Lyons have shown in their works the existence of transitive and non-transitive aggregation relationships [18], that is to say the preservation, or not, of the part features. (This feature will be used in the thesaurus exploitation phase.)

The interpreting relationships: interpreting relationships make it possible to link words and concepts together. As was done previously, to have a better representation of the real world, we define them like fuzzy relationships which indicate the probability for the concept to be a meaning for the word.

The thesaurus exploitation allows us to know which words are ambiguous, when they can be used with different meanings. It also makes it possible to detect similar words in the schemas under study. Two lexical relationships often appear in linguistic papers: the synonym relationship and the homonym relationship [19]. In our structure, lexical relationships do not appear explicitly, because they can be deduced from interpreting relationships. Moreover, in order to capture more semantics, we speak more globally about semantic likeness and ambiguity. We deduce weighted knowledge from conceptual and interpreting relationships.

The ambiguous word treatment: to know if a word is likely to be ambiguous, we must worry about its connection to several concepts, that is to say to several meanings. In this case, it can be considered as ambiguous. But, we think it will be more interesting to qualify this ambiguity. A word is linked to concepts by an interpreting relationship which has a probability coefficient, varying between 0 and 1, and indicating how much the word is linked to the concept. We can use the information provided by these coefficients to detect words which are likely to be ambiguous. That is why, we compare the probability coefficients of all the interpreting relationships connected to the word. If the coefficients have close values, the different meanings are used as often as each other. If the values are very different, some meanings are used more than others. In this last case, the word is less ambiguous than in the first one. That is why a word's degree of ambiguity is defined by the formula written by Shanon in information theory. So, when we find a same word in several design schemas, we are able to know its ambiguity degree, and make it easier to carry out the schema integration. It will avoid integrating a word used in different meanings in the different schema.

The semantic likeness of word treatment: to know if two words have semantic likeness is more difficult than to determine some ambiguity of one of them, because it requires considering the concepts linked to the two words under study. The most interesting case is when the first word has some concepts which are not directly linked to concepts linked to the second word. In this case, we must first value the proximity between concepts linked to the words under study. That is why we will present the cases where transitivity is admitted. In the next table, we recapitulate the different cases of succession of different relationships: Let c_a,

c_b and c_c be the concepts under study, such as $\exists f_l(c_a, c_b)$ and $f_j(c_b, c_c)$. In lines, we find the different kinds of relationships that can link c_a to c_b. In columns, we find the different kinds of relationships that can link c_b and c_c.

Table 1. The different cases of succession of different relationships

		generic relationship		aggregation relationship			
		$f_{jS^{-1}}$	f_{jS}	$f_{jA_{not}}$	$f_{jA_{(e,s)}}^{-1}$	$f_{jA_{not}}$	$f_{jA_{trans.}}$
ge. rel.	$f_{iS^{-1}}$	f_S^{-1}	•	•	•	$f_{A_{not\ tr.}}$	$f_{A_{not\ tr.}}$
	f_{iS}	•	f_S	$f_{A_{not\ tr.}}^{-1}$	$f_{A_{not\ tr.}}^{-1}$	•	•
aggr. rel.	$f_{iA_{not\ tr.}}^{-1}$	•	$f_{A_{not\ tr.}}^{-1}$	•	•	•	•
	$f_{iA_{trans.}}^{-1}$	•	$f_{A_{trans}}^{-1}$	$f_{A_{not\ tr.}}^{-1}$	$f_{A_{trans}}^{-1}$	•	•
	$f_{A_{not\ tr.}}$	$f_{A_{not\ tr.}}$	•	•	•	•	•
	$f_{A_{trans}}$	$f_{A_{trans}}$	•	•	•	$f_{A_{not\ tr.}}$	$f_{A_{trans}}$

When we substitute two relationships by a single one, one must assign a fuzzy coefficient to it, calculated from the two initial ones. That is why, we have differentiate several cases: let c_a and c_c be the two concepts under study, and c_b be the concept linked to c_a and c_c.

1. If the three concepts are linked together with a same type of relationship, then the semantic distance between the two concepts is:

$$dist = f(c_a, c_b) \times f(c_b, c_c)$$

2. If two relationships are transitive, we see that the aggregation relationship carries more semantics than the generic one. That is why, the semantic distance depends on the aggregation coefficient:

$$dist = 0.9 \times f(x, y),$$

   where $f(x, y)$ represents the aggregation relationship.

Now, we can compute the degree of likeness of the two words from the deduced relationship between them. Let m_a and m_b be the two words under study. Let $C_a = \{c_{a1}, c_{a2}, ..., c_{am}\}$ be the set of concepts linked to m_a, and $C_b = \{c_{b1}, c_{b2}, ..., c_{bm}\}$ the set of concepts linked to m_b. In C_a and C_b, concepts from m_a and m_b are directly linked two by two by the new deduced relationships ($\forall k \in [1, m], \exists f = f_S(c_{ak}, c_{bk})$ or $\exists f = f_S^{-1}(c_{ak}, c_{bk})$ or $\exists f = f_A(c_{ak}, c_{bk})$ or $\exists f = f_A^{-1}(c_{ak}, c_{bk})$). We define the semantic likeness degree D between m_a and m_b by:

$$D(m_a, m_b) = max_{c_{ak} \in C_a, c_{bk} \in C_b} min(f_{Cpt}(m_a, c_{a_k}), f(c_{a_k}, c_{b_k}), f_{Cpt}(m_b, c_{b_k}))$$

where f_{Cpt} represents the interpreting relationship, and f the deduced one.

And we are also able to qualify this likeness by a type of likeness which could be: synonym, but also generalization, specialization, composed or component. More information about this thesaurus can be found in [20].

Thanks to the thesaurus, we are able to know the likeness between two words, and the ambiguity of a given word. Moreover, in design schemas, we note that some words are used more frequently than others. They are used in a more general way, without being attached to a particular domain. They provide less semantics than the others. That is why for example, in order to avoid considering as close (and merge) two classes whose only common elements are *number* or *name*, we have defined the notion of semantic weight. This weight is attached to each word placed inside the thesaurus. The word's semantic weight varies in inverse proportions to the word's rate of appearance in all the design schemas (all domains mixed together). It is updated each time the integration process is used. Let $Nb_A(w)$ be the number of appearances of the word w in the already-studied schemas, n be the total number of already-studied schemas and $P_S(w)$ the semantic weight of the word w,

$$P_S(w) = \frac{n}{Nb_A(w)}$$

3.2 The Structural Similarities

Structural similarities which may exist between two elements depend on the type of elements examined.

At attribute level: similarities deal with the domains (identical, included in one another, intersecting or disconnected), and with the units (identical, compatible or incompatible).

At method level: similarities deal with the attributes used by the methods, and the way they are used (instantiation, modification, consultation). The attribute lists have to be identical or different.

At class level: similarities deal with the attributes and methods included in the classes. The percentage of similar elements, the semantic weights of the similar elements and the semantic weights of the non-similar elements are also considered. The algorithm is as follows:

1. If the average semantic weight of the similar elements is high (higher than the threshold defined by the user)
   (a) If the average semantic weight of the non-similar elements is high
      i. If the percentage of similar elements is high, then the two classes are considered to be similar.

   ii. If the percentage of similar elements is not high, (lower than the threshold defined by the user), the two classes are not considered to be similar.
  (b) If the average semantic weight of the non-similar elements is not high, then the two classes are considered to be similar.
2. If the average semantic weight of similar elements is not high
  (a) If the average semantic weight of non-similar elements is not high
   i. If the percentage of similar elements is not high, then the two classes are not considered to be similar.
   ii. If the percentage of similar elements is high, then the two classes are considered to be similar.
  (b) If the average semantic weight of the non-similar elements is high, then the classes are not considered to be similar.

At link level: the similarities deal with arrival and departure classes (similar, inverted or different), the intervals defined by the minimal-and-maximal cardinality (equal, included in one another, intersecting or disconnected) and the type (weak, if the object instances can be shared or strong, if the object instances cannot be shared). The links may be identical or different.

3.3 The Comparison Phase

In the comparison phase, especially in structural comparison, knowledge about incorporated elements is needed in order to compare the incorporating elements. For example, knowledge about attributes and methods is needed to compare classes. That is why the comparison order is: first, attribute comparison, then method comparison, then class comparison and last link comparison.

It is possible that two designers may have represented the same concept of the real word by using different structures in their schemas. All the cases are possible. So, we also look for comparisons between attributes, methods, classes and links. Of course, these comparisons are limited to a semantic examination, because the element structures are different.

The comparison phase is divided into two parts where similar and conflicting pairs of elements (one of each schema) are detected and memorized.

Part 1: semantic-privileged examination

Step 1: examination of pairs of elements where the structures are different and incompatible: attribute/method, method/class and method/link. Pairs where names are strictly identical are detected and memorized : they are conflicting.

Step 2: examination of pairs of elements where the structures are different but compatible: attribute/class, attribute/link and class/link. Pairs of this type in which there are some semantic similarities (with regard to the criteria defined above) and where the semantic likeness is higher than the threshold defined by

the user are detected and memorized.
This allows the desired semantic-proximity degree to be given for carrying out the integration.
As the examination is only semantic here, pairs whose degree of ambiguity is higher than the threshold defined by the user, are eliminated.
The attribute/link pairs where semantic likeness is of a composed/component type are also eliminated, because they are useless.

Step 3: examination of pairs of elements where the structures are identical: attribute/attribute. Attribute pairs with semantic similarities (with regard to the criteria defined above) and where the semantic likeness is lower than the threshold defined by the user are detected and memorized.
Then, structural similarities are looked for only among the pairs resulting from the semantic examination. Structural similarities between two attributes not having semantic similarities are not sufficient for the attributes to considered as similar. Moreover, there is no point in examining the structural similarities (i.e. the domains) of two attributes, if their semantic likeness is of the composed/component type.
Then, amongst the pairs obtained, pairs whose similarities are only semantic and where at least one of the two words appears with an ambiguity higher than the threshold defined by the user, are eliminated.

Step 4: building the solution tree: some elements of the first schema may be close to several elements of the second schema, and the other way round. It is impossible to merge one element of the first schema with several elements of the second schema, and the other way round. At this stage of the process, we are not capable of choosing the likeness which will allows the best integration, we keep them all and build a result from each one of them. A tree is built. Each node corresponds to a possible choice between several likeness for a given element. In each path which leads from the tree root to one of its leaves, an element only appears once. At the leaf level, several sets of likeness are obtained. The solution tree is built on the pairs obtained through the steps 2 and 3. We call them coherent sets. The likeness related to the pairs where the names are identical, obtained through the step 1, are added in order to solve the homonym conflicts they represent, whatever the coherent set is.

Part 2: structure-privileged examination

When attributes are being examined, the semantic examination prevails over the structural examination. Indeed, a similarity between the domains of two attributes does not imply a similarity between the two attributes. On the contrary, a similarity between the names of two attributes implies a similarity between these attributes. This explains why we first try to find semantic similarities amongst the attributes, before trying to find the structural ones. When method, class and reference links are being examined, it is the opposite, the structural examination prevails over the semantic examination. For example, two classes with only one name in common can not be considered as similar; whereas two classes with only one structure in common must be considered as similar classes. This involves an inversion in the examinations carried out on methods, classes and links: the structural examination precedes the semantic examination. This inversion necessitates adding a new step to try to find elements which are strictly identical from a semantic point of view, but structurally different, and which represent an homonym conflict.

Step 1: examination of the likeness between methods, classes and links: the structural-similarity examination is carried out according to the criteria defined in Sect. 3.2. Then, the semantic examination consists in trying to find the likeness between the names of the elements found during the structural examination. As at the attribute/attribute level, semantic likenesses lower than the threshold defined by the user, are eliminated.
The link/link pairs having a component/composed type of semantic likeness are also eliminated, as they cannot be used during integration of design schemas.
At the class level, our approach consists in examining the different possible combinations between the concept provided by the class (the structural part) and the name given to it (the semantic part), in order to detect any possible conflicts. For that purpose, we consulted the works of B.R. Gaines and M.L.G. Shaw [21] which were carried out in the knowledge acquisition domain. This helped us to show different cases encountered when classes of design schemas are being integrated. They are:

1. Case 1: two classes have the same name; they are composed of the same elements.
2. Case 2: two classes have the same name and they have some common elements (a not insignificant part).
3. Case 3: two classes have different names; they are composed of the same elements.
4. Case 4: two classes have different names but they have some common elements (a not insignificant part).

Step 2: The method/method, class/class and link/link pairs having identical names and different structures are detected and memorized, because they represent homonym conflicts. At the class level (classes having the same name but no common elements), it is a new case, called case 5, in addition to the for cases presented above.

Step 3: building the solution tree: if the elements under study (method, class, link) are close to elements which are already in the solution tree (through the step 4 of the part 1), we continue building the solution tree, by adding this new choice discovered in part 2. Otherwise, it is not possible to build the solution tree. There is simply an enrichment of the existing coherent sets. Indeed, inside

each set, either there are all the necessary likenesses for the new pairs of likeness (attributes and methods for the classes, classes for the links) in which case we add the new likeness to the set; or not all the necessary likenesses are there and we do not add the new likeness to the set.
We also add likeness related to pairs of elements with strictly identical names and different structures (step 2) to each coherent set, in order to solve the homonym conflict they represent, whatever the set.
When classes are being examined, in addition to the presence of attributes and methods in the coherent sets, the following rules have to be respected. The object here, is that the elements of a given class are not involved in more than one likeness, at the same time allowing a class from one schema to be merged with several of the other schema.

1. If the type of likeness between two classes is 1 or 3, no other likeness involving these two classes is allowed in the same branch;
2. If the type of likeness between the two classes is 4, and if other likeness involving these classes exist, the type of likeness must be 4 and/or only one case 2 for each class involved; the likeness between classes must involve different attributes and methods;
3. If the type of likeness between the two classes is 2, and if other likenesses between the two classes exist, the type of these likeness must be 4 and must involve different attributes and methods.

3.4 The Conflict-solving Phase

One concept of the real world can be represented in several ways in two different schemas. It is a conflict between the two schemas. In order to solve this conflict, we must choose one of the two representations. In order to know which representation must be chosen, we assign a credibility coefficient (varying between 0 and 1) to each schema. It represents the expert credibility. Its value is propagated on each attribute, each method, each class and each reference link of the schema. If a conflict between two elements is encountered, we know which representation must be chosen upon the others, by comparing the credibility coefficients of the elements. Each time a choice has to be made, if one schema has to be privileged, the structure of the privileged schema is chosen and used to express similar information in the other schema. If there is no schema to privilege, the richest structure is always chosen.

Each time a conflict is solved, the maximum of the values of the two credibility coefficients of the two structures under studies is assigned to the credibility coefficient of the structure of the result schema.

This way of proceeding, added to the fact that the order of rule-application is well defined, makes it possible to justify the unicity of the integration result. In addition, because the integration is carried out from coherent sets, and because these sets are strictly identical whether they are the result of the comparison of schema 1 with schema 2 or whether they are the result of the comparison of schema 2 with schema 1, there is commutativity.

Part 1: conflict solving of pairs of elements with different and incompatible structures

Here we examine the attribute/method, method/class and method/link pairs, resulting from step 1 of part 1 of the comparison phase. At least one of the two names has to be changed, in order to eliminate the homonymy conflict existing between the two elements. If one of the two schemas has to be privileged, the name of the element of the other schema is changed; otherwise, the names of the two schemas are changed for different names. Then the likeness between the two elements is eliminated, because they are now different elements.

Part 2: conflict-solving in pairs of elements with different but compatible structures

Step 1: attribute/link, attribute/class and class/link pairs: If one schema has to be privileged, the structure of the element of the other schema is changed for the element structure of the privileged schema; otherwise the structures are modified as shown in Fig. 1, 2 and 3 .

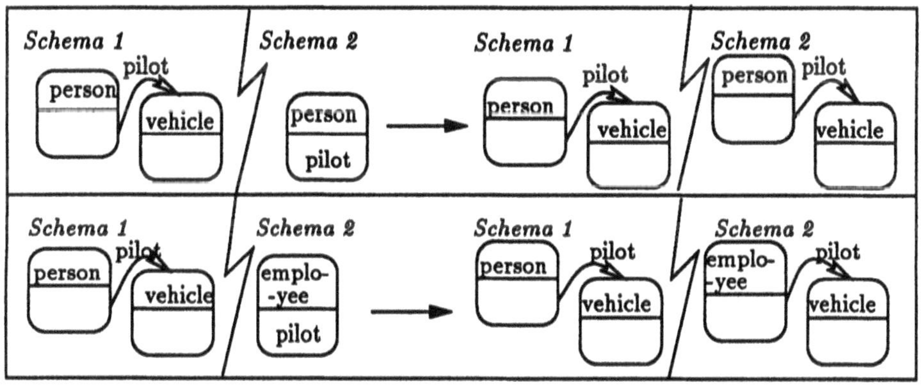

Fig. 1. Conflict-solving in attribute/link pairs

Part 3: conflict solving in pairs of elements with similar structures

Conflict solving dealing with attributes and methods is done through the step 3 of this part of the conflict-solving phase, except the method homonym conflicts, solved here.

Step 1: methods: if the two methods have identical names and different struc-

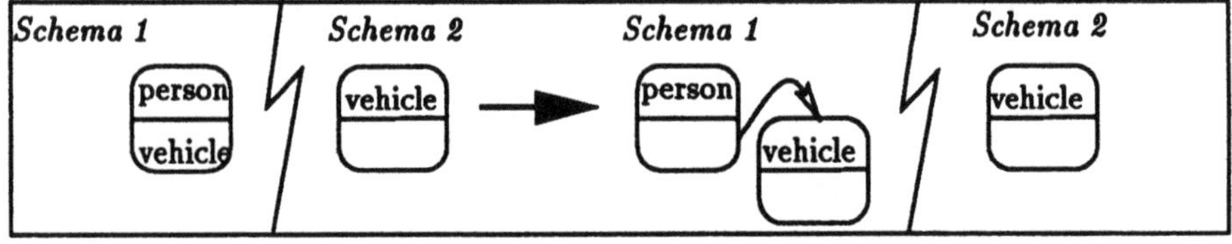

Fig. 2. Conflict-solving in attribute/class pairs

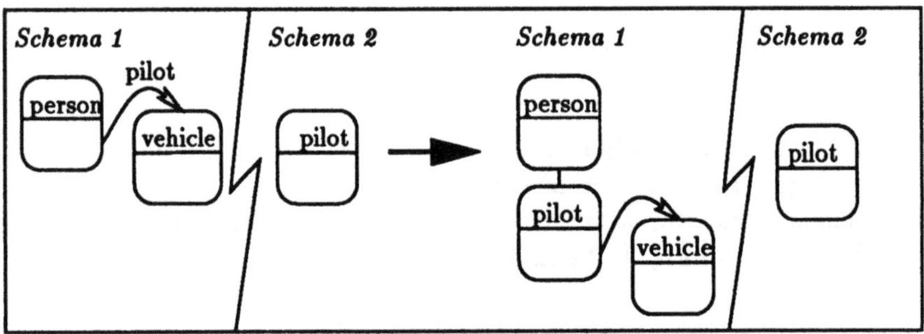

Fig. 3. Conflict-solving in classes/links pairs

tures, at least one of the two names must be changed, in order to eliminate the homonymy conflict that they represent. If one schema has to be privileged, the name of the method of the other schema is changed; otherwise the two names are changed for different names. Then the likeness between the two methods is eliminated, because it has no more reason to exist.

Step 2: classes:

1. case5 : at least one of the two names has to be changed, in order to eliminate the homonymy conflicts existing between these two classes. If one of the two schemas has to be privileged, the name of the class of the other schema has to be changed; otherwise the names of the two classes has to be changed. Then the likeness between the two classes has to be eliminated, because they are now different classes.
2. case 3 : at least one of the two names has to be changed, in order to solve the synonymy conflict existing between the two classes. If one of the two schemas has to be privileged, the name of the class from the other schema is changed for the name of the element of the privileged schema; otherwise the name of the two classes are changed for a common name. The nearness kind of the two classes is changed to case 1.

At this stage, two classes are either identical (with regard to their names and contents) (case 1); or close with regard to their contents (some common elements) but different with regard to their names (case 4); or close with regard to their contents (some common elements) and similar with regard to their names (case 2).

The rules for solving conflicts, according to the different cases are as follows:

1. case 1 : the two classes are strictly identical. There is no conflict between these classes. Only the conflicts between the attribute-and-method descriptions have to be solved.
   (a) Attribute conflict-solving: if the domains are compatible, the union of their intervals is made. If the domains are incompatible, one of them is chosen (the one from the privileged schema if it exists, otherwise the largest one).
   (b) Method conflict-solving: if the two methods have different names but strictly identical structures, they represent a synonymy conflict which must be solved. If one of the two schemas has to be privileged, the name of the method of the other schema is changed for the name of the method privileged schema; otherwise the two names are changed for an identical name.
2. case 2 : our idea is to assume that the two designers have seen the same reality, but from two different points of view. So, we must enrich each point of view with the other one in order to obtain the same class representing the same concept in the most complete way (see Fig. 4).

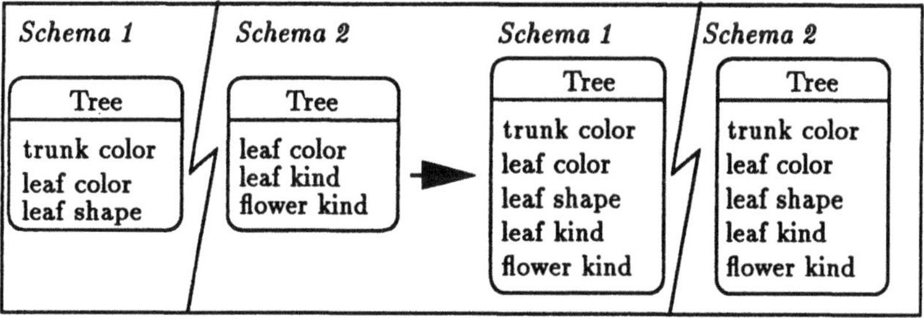

Fig. 4. Example (Case 2)

3. Case 4: the changes to be made in order to resolve conflicts are not the same, depending on whether the class belongs to a inheritance hierarchy or a reference hierarchy. If the two classes belong to inheritance hierarchies, we can think that one or several common abstraction levels have been omitted in the two schemas (see Fig. 5). If the two classes belong to reference hierarchies, it is a the decomposition level which is missing.

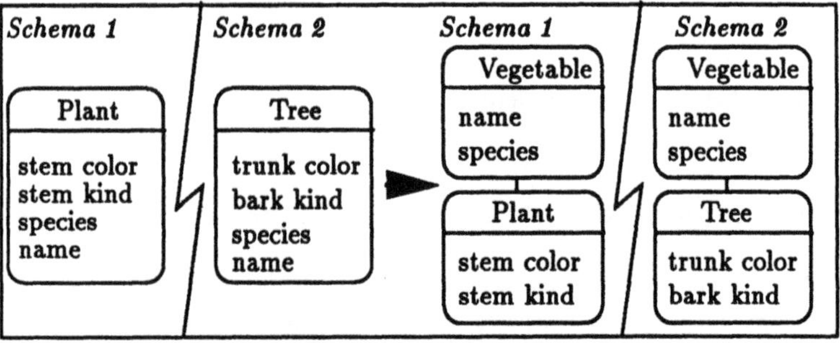

Fig. 5. Example (Case 4a)

What makes our approach worthy of interest is the discovery of dependencies (through references) and generalization/specialization relationships (through inheritance) between elements of the two schemas, even if there are no equivalent classes in the two schemas.

Step 3:links.
The algorithm for solving conflicts between reference links is as follows:

1. the two links have identical names and different structures: one of the two names has to be changed in order to eliminate the homonymy conflict existing between the two classes. If one the two schemas has to be privileged, the name of the other schema is changed; otherwise, the names of the two schemas are changed for two different names. Then the likeness between the two links is eliminated, because they are no longer similar.
2. the two links have different names but similar structures : the following changes must be done.
   (a) change at least one of the two names, in order to solve the synonymy conflict they represent. If one of the two schemas has to be privileged, the name of the link from other schema is changed for the name of the link from the privileged schema; otherwise, the two names are changed for a common one.
   (b) if the departure and arrival classes are inverted and one schema has to be privileged, then its departure and arrival classes are chosen and the reverse-link created.
   (c) if the cardinalities are different and if one schema has to be privileged, then the cardinality of the privileged schema is chosen for the two schemas, otherwise
      i. if there is an inclusion, the largest interval is chosen,
      ii. if there is an intersection or a disjunction, the union of the two intervals is chosen.
   (d) if the types are different and if one schema has to be privileged, the type of the privileged schema is chosen, otherwise the weak type is chosen.

Now that the conflicts are solved we are able to merge the two schemas at the link level, that is to say to superpose the link hierarchies. This step is not explain here, because it is only structural. More information about this step can be found in [22].

3.5 Choice of the Result Schema

One of the advantages of proposing several schemas as result of the integration process, is the possibility of choosing the best schema according to the use one has for it. For example, with regard to quality criteria [23] or re-use criteria [14], if the integration has been carried out with a view to enriching an existing library of design schemas.

3.6 Presenting the Result

At this stage of the process, we superpose a vocabulary level over each result schema, in order to present it to each designer in his own vocabulary when there is a difference in words used from one designer to another.

We will now present strategies for using the integration process, when more than two design schemas are being integrated.

4 Integration Strategies

Two contexts exist when more than two schemas are being integrated. When we need to integrate a schema into a set of already-integrated schemas, it is the incremental context; and when we need to integrate more than two schemas at any given time, it is the multi-expertise context. We will present the integration strategies in both contexts.

4.1 The Incremental Context

In the incremental context, at a given time t, we try to integrate a new schema with a set of already-integrated schemas, which was carried out at time $t-1$. To integrate the schemas in the right way, it is necessary to take into account the time passed between $t-1$ and t, as well as the evolution of the information system represented by the schemas to be integrated. This is done by a robustness coefficient, k. When k leans towards 0, the system is not considered as a robust one, and the new schema is privileged compared to the schema resulting from the previous integration. On the other hand, when k tends to 1, the system is considered to be robust and is privileged compared to the new schema. Therefore, as time goes by, a convergence may be found, a stable schema may be obtained as the result of the incremental integration of different expertises, and of the stability of the information system observed. But this stability also depends of the time elapsed between the two integrations under study. The system can be stable for a while, and then become unstable because of the deep modifications of the information system in question.

The conflict solving is local : if the starting coefficients of the elements have all the same value defined at the schema level, these values will become different one from the others while several integrations are being processed, because they change with regards to the encountered local clashes. The comparison is based on the coefficients assigned to the elements of the conflicting schemas (attributes, methods, classes and links). The weighting by the robustness coefficient k (which is a global coefficient) is done on each local coefficient. The robustness coefficient is assign to the schema which is the result of the already-integrated schemas.

Let S_r be the result schema of the already-integrated schemas at $t-1$, S_n be the schema integrated with S_r at t, E_r be an element of S_r clashing with an element E_n of S_n, C_{E_r} be the credibility coefficient of E_r in S_r, C_{E_n} be the credibility coefficient of E_n in S_n, and k be the robustness coefficient assign (globally) to S_r, then the weights P_{E_r} and P_{E_n} respectively assigned to the elements E_r and E_n in order to know which one must be privileged when conflicts are being solved are as follows :

$$P_{E_r} = C_{E_r} * k \text{ and } P_{E_n} = C_{E_n}$$

Each time a conflict is solved, the value of the maximum of the credibility coefficients of the structures of the elements under study is assigned to the credibility coefficient of the structure of the element of the result schema. It is important to emphasize that it is the maximum between C_{E_r} and C_{E_n} which is kept, and on no account the maximum between P_{E_r} and P_{E_n}.

Is is important also to observe that when the value of C_{E_r} is very low, compared to the value of C_{E_n}, even a high value of k will not allow C_{E_r} to be privileged on C_{E_n}; and it seems to be reasonable. A very-low local credibility cannot be privileged on a very-high local credibility, even if the schema is globally robust. In the same way, if the value of C_{E_r} is very high, compared to the one of C_{E_n}, even a low k will not enable C_{E_n} to be privileged on C_{E_r}.

Lastly, we can see the interest of local work: the choice of the privileged structure is more precise. And while several integrations are being processed, it allows to improve the credibility of a given representation for a given concept. In addition, it allows to distinguish several sub-schemas inside the result schema, each of them having a different credibility level. We can, for example, distinguish a stable and very-credible kernel.

4.2 The Multi-expertise Context

There exists two strategies [3]: the ladder strategy and the balanced strategy. The first one consists in the integration of two schemas, then the result of the integration with a third one and so on until all the schemas have been integrated. The second consists in a parallel integration of pairs of schemas, then a parallel integration of pairs of result-schemas, and so on until a single schema is obtained. The latter strategy does not correspond to a natural process. Moreover, it seems difficult to choose (and to justify) which pairs of schemas to start with. That is why we have chosen the ladder strategy.

The integration process in a multi-expertise context is equivalent to the integration process in a incremental context but without taking time into account, that is to say without using a robustness coefficient. Integrations are made at the same time (the incremental context corresponds to a multi-expertise context in which we have decided to delay the integration). In this case, the weights assigned to the elements through the integration are the credibility coefficients.

Let S_r be the result schema of the integration of n schemas, let S_n be the $n+1$st schema to be integrated, let E_r be an element of S_r clashing with an element E_n of S_n, let C_{E_r} be the credibility coefficient of E_r in S_r and C_{E_n} the credibility coefficient of E_n in S_n, then the weights P_{E_r} and P_{E_n} respectively assigned to the elements E_r and E_n, in order to know which one will be privileged when conflicts are being solved are defined as follow:

$$P_{E_r} = C_{E_r} \text{ et } P_{E_n} = C_{E_n}$$

5 Conclusion

We have presented a process which allows to perform the integration of object-oriented schemas. This process is based on comparison rules, conflict-solving rules and superposition rules. The integration is structural but essentially semantic. To take into account the semantics provided by the design schemas, a tool like the fuzzy thesaurus is quite a valuable asset at all the process levels, because it makes it possible to find similarities between the schemas, but also to solve conflicts and to present the result schema.
This process also propose several solutions to the integration of two given schemas, in order to allows the choice of the best result, with regards to context-dependent criteria, like the reuse criteria for example.

A prototype of this integration method is under development.

We would like to improve our thesaurus by taking into account domain applications, during the acquisition phase, but also during the exploitation phase. We also would like to complete our integration process with specific modules, each on dedicated to one existent object-oriented model (like OMT or MCO). First, it will allow to integrate schemas expressed with one of these formalisms, and it will then become a federated framework for all these formalisms.

References

1. A. Motro. Superviews : virtual integration of multiple databases. *Transaction on software engineering*, SE-13(7):785–798, July 1987.
2. S. Navathe, R. Elmasri, and J. Larson. Integrating user views in database design. In *IEEE Computer*, pages 50–62, January 1986.
3. C. Batini, M. Lenzerini, and S. Navathe. A comparative analysis of methodologies for database schema integration. *ACM Computing Surveys*, 18(4):323–364, December 1986.
4. P. Johannesson. Schema transformations as an aid in view integration. In *Advanced information systems engineering : proceedings of the 5th international conference on advanced information system engineering (CAISE'93), June 8-11, 1993*, volume 685 of *Lecture Notes in Computer Sciences*, pages 71–92. Springer Verlag, 1993.
5. P. Johannesson. Supporting schema integration by linguistic instruments. In *First workshop on applications of natural language to data bases(NLDB'95)*, pages 41–55, Versailles, France, 28-29 June 1995.
6. S. Spaccapietra, C. Parent, and Y. Dupont. Model independent assertions for integration of heterogeneous schemas. *Very Large Data Bases Journal*, 1:81–126, 1992.
7. I. Comyn-Wattiau. *L'intégration de vues dans le système SECSI.* PhD thesis, Université Paris VI, France, Octobre 1990.
8. C. Thieme and A. Siebes. An approach to schema integration based on transformations and behaviour. In *Advanced information systems engineering : proceedings of the 6th international conference on advanced information system engineering (CAISE'94), June 6-10, 1994*, volume 811 of *Lecture Notes in Computer Sciences*, pages 297–310. Springer Verlag, 1994.
9. P. Fankhauser, M. Kracker, and E.J. Neuhold. Semantic vs. structural resemblance of classes. *Sigmod record*, 20(4):59–63, December 1991.
10. C. Thieme and A. Siebes. Schema integration in object-oriented databases. In *Advanced information systems engineering : proceedings of the 5th international conference on advanced information system engineering (CAISE'93), June 8-11, 1993*, volume 685 of *Lecture Notes in Computer Sciences*, pages 54–70. Springer Verlag, 1993.
11. P. Buneman, S. Davidson, and A. Kosky. Theorical aspects of schema merging. In *International conference on extending database technology (EDBT'92), Vienna, Austria, March 23-27, 1992*, volume 580 of *Lecture Notes in Computer Sciences*, pages 152–167. Springer Verlag, 1992.
12. J. Rumbaugh, M. Blaha, W.Premerlani, F. Eddy, and W. Lorensen. *Object-oriented modelling and design.* Prentice Hall, New Jersey, 1991.
13. X. Castellani. *MCO, méthodologie générale d'analyse et de conception des systèmes d'objets.* Masson, 1993.
14. S. Castano and V. De Antonellis. Reuse in object-oriented information systems development. In *Object-oriented methodologies and systems, International symposium (ISOOMS'94), Palermo, Italy, September 1994*, volume 858 of *Lecture Notes in Computer Sciences*, pages 346–358. Springer Verlag, 1994.
15. D.A. Cruse. *Lexical semantics.* Cambridge textbooks in linguistics. Cambridge university press, 1986.

16. M. W. Evens. Relational models of the lexicon : introduction. In M. W Evens, editor, *Relational models of the lexicons*, pages 1–37. Cambridge university press, 1988.
17. J.C. Sager. *A practical course in terminology processing*. John Benjamins, 1990.
18. M. A. Iris, B. E. Litowitz, and M. W. Evens. Problems of the part-whole relation. In M. W Evens, editor, *Relational models of the lexicons*, pages 261–288. Cambridge university press, 1988.
19. G. Hirst. *Semantic interpretation and the resolution of ambiguity*. Cambridge University Press, 1987.
20. I. Mirbel. A fuzzy thesaurus for semantic integration of design schemes. In J. Sharpe, editor, *AI System Support for Conceptual Design (LIWED'95)*, pages 319–335, Ambleside, United Kingdom, 27-29 March 1995. Springer.
21. B.R. Gaines and M.L.G. Shaw. Comparing the conceptual systems of experts. In *International Joint Conference on Artificial Intelligence (IJCAI)*, pages 633–638, Détroit, 1989.
22. A. Cavarero and E. Vittori. COD, un système de définition de classes d'objets. In *Inforsid*, Lille, France, Mai 1993.
23. S.R. Chidamber and C.F. Kemerer. A metrics suite for object-oriented design. *IEEE Transactions on software engineering*, 20(6), June 1994.

Advanced Primitives for Changing Schemas of Object Databases

Philippe Brèche*

Projet VERSO - INRIA Rocquencourt
BP. 105 78 153. Le Chesnay Cedex - France
Philippe.Breche@inria.fr

Abstract. Currently, existing Object Database Systems (ODBSs) perform schema changes by means of primitives closely related to their respective data model. Software Engineering (SE) applications, Object Methodologies (OM) and designers building up object database schemata require a more abstract level. This paper addresses new facilities for updating a schema filling the gap between object design and object programming.
A set of advanced primitives, so-called "High Level Primitives", is presented to cope with these requirements. The semantics of these new primitives and how to maintain a schema consistent after such a schema update are the main contributions of this paper.
We discuss issues on implementation on top of the commercial ODBS $O_2$and consider related work.

1 Introduction

In the last decade, the object paradigm beneffited from a great success, successively covering the various steps of the software life cycle, from analysis to testing, and various software domains, in particular the database system field. Object technology, particularly (but not exclusively!), aims at producing software that is easy to understand and to re-use. Fully enabling these properties, requires more flexible and more powerful means of accessing, interpreting and evolving software modules. Regarding this latter point, achieving more flexibility on evolving software depends on two main parameters of software engineering:

- *change management*, which facilitates the changes occurring in the object software life cycle, and
- *reuse*, encouraging people to re-use and to integrate software modules already developed.

Change Management is the focus on this article. In the ODBS field, this topic referred to as Schema Change Management [4, 10, 25, 27], is widely addressed.

* On leave from DBIS department at the J.W. Goethe University, Frankfurt/Main, Germany. Partially supported by Esprit III project Goodstep.

Currently, most existing ODBS products and prototypes do not allow free and dynamic changes to the schema. They merely allow the performance of schema changes by means of primitives (from here on called *LLPs — Low Level Primitives*) close to the respective underlying data model. Taxonomies of such schema update primitives can be found in [4, 10, 15, 26, 16]. They deal with the creation, deletion or modification of the schema definitions of the data model, classes and properties (attribute and method) and some additional concepts specific to the ODBS. They may also differ regarding the level of integration between the data, the schema and the meta-schema, if any [26]. These primitives are considered as a first level of schema update primitives.
In contrast to this, Software Development Environments (SDE) should support more declarative complex/advanced operations occurring in the design process such as *generalization* or *merge* of definitions. Most of the object methodologies, such as OOSE [2] [9], OOSA[2][18], OOD[2][6], RDD[2], OMT[2][5]) highlight the need for designers to build information models and their corresponding database schemas at such an abstract level through all the incremental and spiral design process. The designer has to fill the gap between the functions currently provided by ODBS environments and the design requirements. For example, to generalize classes and to insert the class of generalization in the hierarchy, a designer usually spends time collecting the required information, and thus to find, group and order the appropriate basic primitives *LLPs* changing the schema. To do it properly, the designer has to be aware of the rules which maintain the consistency of the ODBS data model. To find the right *LLPs* accordingly, the designer has to foresee and to solve the intermediate conflicts which appear. Moreover, functions have to be written and run against the base to propagate the structural changes to the data and views. Application programs have to be checked and eventually changed to run against the new schema. All these maintenance operations are time expensive and error prone. New declarative complex schema change primitives (hereafter *HLPs – High Level Primitives*) are developed to free the designer from performing mundane tasks.
Schema changes are strongly related to the notion of correctness. Our approach of *HLPs* amounts to facing classical problems of schema change: specify the *semantics* of the new primitives and accordingly, specify *rules* to preserve the *consistency* of the resulting schema (the database consistency is not addressed hereafter). These two items are the main contributions of this paper.
This work was partially funded by the broader GOODSTEP project [30] under the ESPRIT III program. The baseline of the project is an existing commercially available ODBS, O_2.
The rest of the paper is organized as follows. Section 2 gives an overview of the *HLPs* semantics. Section 3 shows how to preserve a schema consistent after a schema update. Section 4 finally concludes on related work and points to future developments.

---

[2] OOSE: **O**bject–**O**riented **S**oftware **E**ngineeering, OOSA: **O**bject–**O**riented **S**ystems **A**nalysis, OOD: **O**bject–**O**riented **D**esign, RDD: **R**esponsability–**D**riven **D**esign and OMT: **O**bject **M**odeling **T**echnique.

2 High Level Primitives for Changing a Schema

The *HLPs* library we have implemented aims at providing the designer with new schema update facilities. It is based on the existing O_2 schema update primitives. The *HLPs* can be used in application program or interactively, through a GUI, by a schema designer.
We first detail the current O_2 *LLPs* for changing a schema. The general semantics of the newly developed primitives, *HLPs*, together with a revised taxonomy for schema modification, complete this Section.

2.1 Taxonomy of Current Schema Updates in O_2

In order to assess the level of schema change facilities offered by O_2, we have defined a taxonomy of its available basic update operations. The classification differentiates updates concerned with class structure, method or class hierarchy. Such a taxonomy gives an indication of the underlying data model. At this stage, the O_2 schema update facilities [19] (the *LLPs*) cover the taxonomy found in Figure 1.
So far, the O_2 *LLPs* are used by a designer either interactively by means of an O_2 shell interpreter, a class browser GUI, or embedded in C/C++ alike programs (calls to O_2API functions).

2.2 The New O_2 Schema Modification Primitives

In this section, we define the semantics of the set of *HLPs* that have been added to the O_2 database for changing the schema. The choice of such primitives is motived by a detailed analysis of schema update operations occurring in schema design. They are inspired from our practice of OMT, Booch and Schlaer & Mellor methodologies. Together with general definitions of these primitives, we present the important steps that occur when running them. These steps approximate the equivalent ordered set of *LLPs* that a designer should apply to perform an identical schema change. Intuitive definitions often give way to more formal definition for clarification. After such a schema change, the O_2 invariants hold. Rules of interest that preserve these invariants and allow a consistent target schema to be attained after the update are detailed in Section 3.
The mode which promotes interactions with the designer directed our attention, enabling us to seek solutions for the undecidable cases of certain schema changes. In such cases, further information provided by the designer avoid having to abort the update or to degrade the target schema.
These definitions extend the taxonomy of Section 2.1 to a new one discussed in Section 2.3.

Abstraction–Generalization of Classes As opposed to the specialization facility [3] which allows a designer to refine general concepts to reach a "solution", an

[3] This is usually provided in most of the ODBS.

1. Changes to the structure of a class (node)
   1.1. Changes to the type of a class
   1.2. Changes to attributes (in case of type `tuple`)
      1.2.1. Add a new attribute to a class
      1.2.2. Delete an existing attribute
      1.2.3. Change the name of an existing attribute
      1.2.4. Change the type of an existing attribute
      1.2.5. Change the visibility of an attribute (public/read/private)
      1.2.6. Change the inheritance (parent) of an attribute
      1.2.7. Rename an inherited attribute
   1.3. Changes to visibility of a class type (encapsulation – public/read/private)

2. Changes to the behavior of a class (node)
   2.1. Add a new method
   2.2. Delete an existing method
   2.3. Change the name of an existing method of a class
   2.4. Change the code of a method in a class
   2.5. Change the visibility of a method (public/private)
   2.6. Refine the code of an inherited method
   2.7. Change the inheritance (parent) of a method
   2.8. Rename an inherited method

3. Changes sub/superclass relationship (edge)
   3.1. Add a new superclass
   3.2. Delete an existing superclass

4. Changes to the class hierarchy (node and edge)
   4.1. Add a new class
   4.2. Drop an existing class
      4.2.1. a leaf class in the DAG
      4.2.2. a class and all its subclasses
   4.3. Change the name of a class
   4.4. Change a class share-ability (export/import)

Fig. 1. Current O_2 Taxonomy of Schema Updates

essential facility is being able to generalize information from existing concepts, that is, to factor information. This allows the improvement of classifications and the gaining in generality and modularity for further reuse purpose. This operation occurs in bottom up approaches in a design life cycle.

For example, a designer generalizes class **`Employee`** and class **`Client`** into class **`Person`**. This is performed factoring out the common properties of the source classes **`Employee`** and **`Client`**. The factorization is based on the (user–defined) names of the properties. Renamings are emphasized and lead to interaction with

the designer. A factorization of methods' implementations is performed following an interactive process only, due to the well-known non-safe use of polymorphism [11]. The source classes are kept and re-connected to the newly created class of generalization, C_g . They are refined accordingly.
Two main steps occur in this process:

- *How to construct the content of the class* C_g
  The specification of the features of the class is performed by means of two operators which generalize the source class types and the source classes methods. They look for *common names* and *intersect* the types (class types, attribute types and method signatures) following the covariance. The encapsulation (rights) is constructed, keeping in mind that a class should be only less "visible" than or equal to its subclass.
  Thus, further information has to be inferred to complete the class specification, namely:
  - the location of the class in the hierarchy, that is, the list of super-classes and subclasses of C_g . This location is such that C_g subsumes (directly) the two source classes whereas the lowest common super-classes of the source classes subsume it.
  - those properties that are inherited and locally defined in the class,
  - the list of inheritance links starting from the source classes; they have to be updated (deleted),
  - the list of properties to be deleted in the source classes,
  - the various conflicts to be solved in the source classes and their subclasses: name conflicts, eventual attributes/methods precedence, repeated inheritance conflicts and property identity conflicts.
- *How to realize the class* C_g *through a set of LLPs*
  Once the information dealing with the specification of the class is computed, the class is created and inserted in the hierarchy throughout an ordered set of basic updates. Hereafter, we simulate the order that a designer would follow to reach the target schema, applying the set of *LLPs* according to the information collected in the previous steps:
  1. create an empty class directly under the lowest common super-classes,
  2. fill the class with the locally defined properties,
  3. store and drop those properties in the source classes and their subclasses that create further conflicts in step 4, as well as the common properties already factored in the class of generalization,
  4. delete the inheritance links between the source classes (or eventually intermediate classes in between the source classes and the lowest common super-classes) and their lowest common super-classes,
  5. re-connect the two source classes (or the intermediate classes according to 4) to the generalization class,
  6. re-create eventual properties of the source classes and their subclasses concerned by step 3, filtering those of the properties of the source classes which are already present in the generalization class.

The corresponding synopsis of the **Generalize** primitive is expressed by:

> **generalize [classes]** *Class_name* [,[*Class_name*]...]
> **into class** *Superclass_name*

Abstraction–Specialization of Classes This primitive specializes one source class into one, two or several classes, which become subclasses of the source class. For example, designing figures, with class **Figure**, currently sub-classed with **Point**, **Line**, **Spline**, **Polygon** and **Circle**, a further classification is performed regarding the dimensions of the figures. Class Dim_0, Dim_1 and Dim_2 are inserted for this purpose.
This primitive completes the specialization usually found in the basic ODBS updates under class inheritance declarations (bottom–up approach). In the design process, this new facility is suitable while mixing bottom–up and top–down approaches.
A class existing in the class hierarchy is specialized into new classes inserted in the hierarchy. The location of these specialized classes might be constrained specifying super-classes and subclasses.
The consistency of the newly created inheritance links in the class hierarchy is the main point addressed in such a schema update. First, each specialized class is proven to be in a good sub-classing/super-classing relationship with its declared subclasses and super-classes. Then, the class of specialization is built up taking care of restructuring of properties in subclasses of the class of specialization, before and after the insertion of the classes in the hierarchy. Just as for generalization, these steps entail resolving renaming and repeated inheritance conflicts.
The specialization is addressed by the following declaration:

> **specialize [class]** *Class_name* **into classes**
> *Subclass_name* [**super**(*Class_name* [[, *Class_name*]...])]
> [**sub**(*Class_name* [[, *Class_name*]...])]
> [[, *SubClass_name* [**super**(*Class_name* [[, *Class_name*]...])]
> [**sub**(*Class_name* [[, *Class_name*]...])]]...]

Accordingly, the following declaration maps the schema update proposed in our example with figures:

specialize class *Figure* **into classes**
Dim_0 **sub**(Point), Dim_1 **sub**(Line , Spline), Dim_2 **sub**(Polygon , Circle)

Abstraction–Merge Classes Merging classes allows the refinement class hierarchy, changing generality, modularity and granularity of the model. This occurs both in a bottom up and top down approaches in a design process.
This primitive merges several source classes into one new class definition, deleting the source classes and consequently restructuring the class hierarchy. Options enable the specification of the kind of strategy carried out while merging the source

classes. *Union*, *intersection* or *difference* operators applied to the properties of the source classes are available. The primitive restructures the hierarchy, usually replacing the source classes to be merged by the class of merge.

Remark: regarding the chosen option and due to covariance constraints, it is not always possible to delete the source classes and to reconnect their subclasses to the class of *merge*. In this case, the class of *merge* is merely created and well–located in the class hierarchy whereas the source classes are kept unchanged.

To illustrate this notion, the classes **`Employee`** and **`Client`** are merged into the class **`Person`** with a criterion of properties generalization. The intention is to preserve the common information from the source classes, removing these classes in the target schema. Similarly to class generalization, this is performed by factoring the common properties (attributes and methods' signatures) of the source classes **`Employee`** and **`Client`**. The source classes are removed, their subclasses are re–connected to class **`Person`** and refined consequently. One might also choose to keep all the information from the source classes through a *union* option or to retain only information that distinguishes the source classes through a *difference* option.

The merge process carries on a new class creation and its insertion in the class hierarchy. This entails first building up the content of the virtual class of merge according to a criterion. Then, according to the properties of the class, one has to "classify" this class in the class hierarchy. The last step is to materialize the class and to restructure the source classes (and their subclasses) through a set of ordered *LLPs*.

The corresponding synopsis of the **Merge** primitive is expressed by:

> **merge [class] [– i | u | d]** *Class_name* [[, *Class_name*] ...]
> **into** *Class_name*

where *i, u, d* stand for intersection, union and difference (resp.).

Remove a Class The primitive *remove* deletes a class anywhere in the class hierarchy. The class hierarchy then has to be reorganized.

Let C_{del} be a class located in the middle of the class hierarchy (C_{del} has super-classes and subclasses). In addition, C_{del} has specific features specified as properties locally defined in the class.

Assume now that the class C_{del} is to be deleted. The policy of the designer is to retain in subclasses of C_{del} information specific to class C_{del}. This information was previously inherited. To be preserved, this information should be locally redefined in the direct subclasses of C_{del}. The designer has to *propagate* the properties locally defined in C_{del}.

At the same time, the designer decides that the subclasses of C_{del} should also preserve the information coming from the super-classes of C_{del}. Another designer argues that the classification of the class hierarchy should remain "similar" after the class deletion. Direct sub-classes of C_{del} should therefore be reconnected to the direct super-classes. This is called *reconnection*.

The previous examples attempt to illustrate the various options that might be required when deleting a class. This can be summarized with the willingness of preserving or losing information captured in a class C_{del}. It includes information about static (attributes) and dynamic (methods) properties and, at the same time, locally defined or inherited properties. Thus, deleting a class C_{del}, a designer may choose different options, combining *reconnection* to the super-classes of C_{del} and *propagation* of properties local to C_{del}, as follows:

1. propagation and reconnection preserves information locally defined and inherited through C_{del}. Properties locally defined in C_{del} and not locally redefined in the sub-classes are propagated. All sub-classes of C_{del} are reconnected to every super-class of C_{del}. This leads to information redundancy but retains the information.
2. no propagation, no reconnection loses information captured by C_{del}. The subclasses are not re–connected to the super-classes and the properties locally defined in C_{del} are not propagated to its subclasses.
3. propagation, no reconnection preserves the information locally defined in C_{del}. Information inherited from the super-classes through C_{del} is lost but the one locally defined in C_{del} is preserved. This is performed propagating (copying) the properties into the direct sub-classes of C_{del} unless the direct sub-classes redefine them. This may lead to a waste of information or to information redundancy.
4. no propagation, reconnection loses information locally defined in C_{del} but does preserve the one inherited from C_{del}. Properties locally defined in C_{del} are not propagated but each direct sub-class of C_{del} is reconnected to each super-class of C_{del}.

Performing such a class deletion amounts to find out an ordered set of *LLPs*. These *LLPs* delete inheritance links and create properties, taking into account name conflicts, repeated inheritance conflicts and property identity conflicts. This is further detailed in the example in Section 3.3.
The corresponding synopsis of the **Remove** primitive is expressed by:

remove [– p|–r|– pr] [class] *Class_name*

where *-p* propagates the properties locally defined in C_{del} whereas *-r* reconnects all the subclasses of C_{del} to its super-classes.
Readers interested on more details are referred to [8].

Abstraction–Aggregation This primitive creates an *aggregation* class which is built up out of several source classes. The designer can specify properties of aggregation links (e.g. cardinalities) and can establish *part_of* reverse–links (see the *composite* objects in [4]). For example, starting from class definitions for `Monitor`, `System_Box`, `Mouse`, `Keyboard`, etc, one can introduce the class `Micro -computer` with the attributes `Mouse`, `Keyboard` ...

Its representation is a one level–tree in which all nodes are classes. Figure 2 illustrates the example of the **Microcomputer**. The root of the tree represents the class produced by as the aggregation of classes at the leaves. Each arc in the tree, states that a leaf class is a part of the root class.

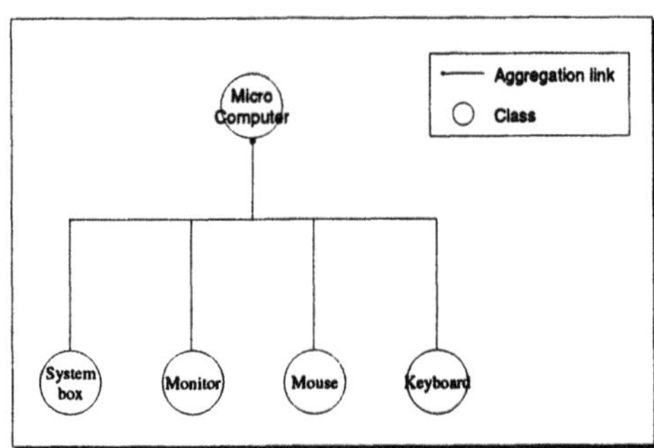

Fig. 2. Aggregation abstraction: the Microcomputer example.

The corresponding synopsis of the **Aggregation** primitive is expressed by:

aggregate [class] [[–r][–b|l|s]] *Class_name* [[, [[–r][–b|l|s]] *Class_name*]...]
in [class] *Class_name*

The option *-r* specifies a reverse link creation in the aggregated class. the options *-b|l|s* specify the cardinality of aggregation through constructors *b*ag, *l*ist or *s*et (resp.). By default, a one to one aggregation is constructed.
The following declaration updates the schema

aggregate –r–b Monitor, –r System_Box, Mouse, Keyboard
in class Microcomputer

creating class **Microcomputer** with the attributes of types bag of **Monitor**, **System_Box**, **Mouse** and **Keyboard**.
This primitive does not lead to unsual difficulties regarding either the schema consistency maintenance or regarding the set of *LLPs* and the order of application.

Abstraction–Decomposition This primitive acts in a way opposite from the way the aggregation primitive acts. It creates classes out of decomposition from a set of attributes addressed in a source class [4]. The reverse link *is_a_part_of* is automatically created in these classes. Only those attributes which are specified together with a class generate a class of decomposition. A *-s* option allows switching an attribute type specification to a newly created class type. The name of the new class is declared together with the name of the attribute addressed

[4] The source class is assumed to be of type *tuple*.

by this change. The "deepest" type specification of the attribute is taken into account while converting the type.
In addition, the source class may be preserved or dropped.
Accordingly, the corresponding synopsis of the **Decomposition** primitive is expressed by:

decompose [-d] [class] *Class_name*
[**into** [-s] *attribute_name Class_name*] [, [[-s] *attribute_name Class_name*]] ...]

The option *-d* deletes the source class whereas, by default, the class of decomposition is preserved. The *-s* option switches the attribute type.
For instance, class *Car* is decomposed into classes *Color*, *Company*, *Motor* and *Price* as in Figure 3 by means of a simple decompose statement.

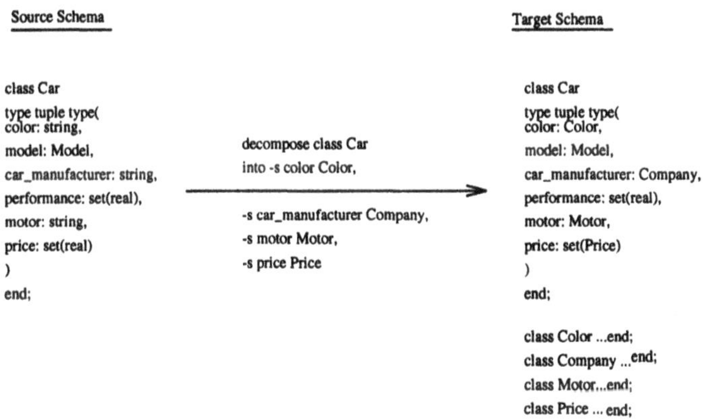

Fig. 3. Decomposition abstraction: the Car example.

2.3 A Revised Taxonomy for Schema Update Primitives

Consequently, we have revised the O_2 taxonomy for schema update primitives found in Section 2.1 as in Figure 4, including the new complex schema changes. In addition, these new facilities are available via an interactive GUI which helps the designer while performing schema change.

3 Schema Consistency and Schema Change

A schema update should result in a new schema with no inconsistencies. Moreover, the consistency of the other elements relying on a schema also have to be maintained. Potentially, a schema update may make the database(s) instance(s) of the schema inconsistent, as well as the view(s) based on the schema and some

4. Changes to the class hierarchy (node)
   4.2. Drop an existing class
      4.2.3. remove a class in the middle of the hierarchy
      4.2.4. remove a class in the middle of the hierarchy – propagate
      4.2.5. remove a class in the middle of the hierarchy – reconnect
      4.2.6. remove a class in the middle of the hierarchy – reconnect and propagate

   4.6. Change to a set of classes
      4.6.1. Generalization of classes
      4.6.2. Specialization of classes
      4.6.3. Merge two classes
         4.6.3.1. Merge–Unify classes
         4.6.3.2. Merge–Intersect classes
         4.6.3.3. Merge–Subtract classes

5. Changes to the class hierarchy and classes
   5.1. Aggregate classes into an attribute of a class
   5.2. Decomposition of an attribute into a set of classes

Fig. 4. Revised Taxonomy of Schema Updates

application programs running on top of the schema/base. Strictly relating to the schema, to preserve the consistency following an alteration of the schema relates to both the structural aspect and the behavioral aspect of the schema. This depends on the consistency definitions or *invariants* of a given ODBS and its peculiar rules to preserve this consistency.

Therefore performing any kind of *HLP* update should preserve as well the O_2 invariants. Hereafter we apply to the O_2 data model the methodology used in [4, 22] to specify the formal framework for schema evolution. Like ORION, the O_2 model incorporates all the basic object concepts. Data might be *values* or *objects*. The classes encapsulate the data defined by an underlying class type (the atomic types, the constructors list, set and bag and the class type are possible types) together with methods that operate on the data. A class might inherit from different super-classes (multiple inheritance). The inheritance mechanism is defined on a covariant sub-classing relationship and is carried out with *late binding*.

An O_2 class is roughly a quadruple c =(name, vis, type, methods), with a name, an access right *vis* (hereafter called visibility) that may be public, read or write, visibility defined on the global type *type*, and a set of methods. An attribute is quadruple a = (pid, name, vis, type) with an *pid* that identifies uniquely the property along an inheritance path, a name, an access right and a type (signature). Similarly, a method is a quintuple m = (pid, name, vis, si, body), with a pid, a name, an access right, a signature (typed arguments and result) and an implementation.

Readers are encouraged to have a look at [3, 1, 20] for more details. The O_2 features lead to set of invariants a slightly different from that of ORION or Gemstone, but to different rules to preserve these invariants. In a first attempt, schema change focuses on preserving the structural consistency of the schema.

3.1 O_2 Invariants

The structural consistency is specified through the constraints listed bellow, so–called invariants of the database system, to be preserved after each schema update.
Hereafter, *property* denotes the notion of both *attribute* and *method* of a class. *Node* and *edge* in a graph representation of the class hierarchy stand respectively for a class (labeled with its name) and an inheritance link between two classes (labeled by the name of the classes).

1. **I1** Class Hierarchy Invariant
   The class hierarchy is a rooted (the O_2 root class is called *Object*) and connected (there is no isolated node) Acyclic Directed Graph (DAG) with named nodes and labeled edges.
2. **I2** Distinct Name Invariant
   All classes of a schema have distinct names (unique label for the nodes in the DAG).
   All properties of a class (locally defined or inherited) have distinct names.
3. **I3** Distinct Identity Invariant
   All the properties of a class have distinct identity (also referred to as *origin* or *pid*).
4. **I4** Full Inheritance Invariant
   A class inherits all properties (except the method *init*) from each of its superclasses unless there are conflicts related to invariants 2, 3 and 4. There are of two kinds of conflicts: name conflicts and values conflicts.
5. **I5** Domain Compatibility Invariant
   If a property p_2 of a class C is inherited from a property p_1 of a super-class of C, then the domain of p_2 is either the same as that of p_1 or a subtype of p_1 (covariance redefinitions).
   The number of parameters of the signature of p_2 and p_1 has to be the same.
   The default value of an attribute must be an instance of the type that is the domain of this attribute.
6. **I6** Access Compatibility Invariant
   If an entire type t_1 (tuple or non–tuple) of a class C is inherited from a super-class of C, then the visibility of t_2 is either the same as that of t_1 or more visible than that of t_1.
   An attribute p of a class C may have a specific visibility that is either the same as that of the entire type of the class C or more visible.
   If a property p_2 of a class C is inherited from a property p_1 of a super-class of C, then the visibility of p_2 is either the same as that of p_1 or more visible as that of p_1.

7. **I7** Class Specification Invariant
   An object is an instance of a class determined by its class specification. A class specification requires a class name, and optionally, a class type together with its visibility, a set of class methods together with their visibilities, a set of parent classes (inheritance) and a set of property renamings.

3.2 Rules to Preserve Schema Consistency

To preserve these invariants, O_2 rules are defined which cope with potential conflicts. We address hereafter only those rules that are relevant regarding our examples in Section 3.3, and which are different from the rules solving similar conflicts in *ORION* or *Gemstone*.

- **R1**: rules to preserve the Class Hierarchy Invariant
  R1.1. Node deletion
  Only those nodes that are leaves classes might be deleted.
  A node together with all its subclasses can always be deleted.
  R1.2. An edge BA might be defined (A direct super-class of B) unless BA already exists, B is imported or covariance, compatible visibilities, names and distinct identities conflicts appear because of *I4*. Thus A is added in the class inheritance of B, A becoming a direct super-class of B.
  R1.3. Acyclicity
  A partial ordered sub-typing relationship is defined on the O_2 types (set–inclusion semantics).
  A strict partial ordered sub-classing relationship, based on the sub-typing relationship, is defined on the O_2 class types. Thus a class cannot be a super-class of itself.
- **R2**: rules to preserve Distinct Names Invariant
  R2.1. If a class C is defined and its name is the same as that of an existing class in the current schema, the new class is selected over that existing unless the invariant *I5* is violated. This is, if the new specification is not a covariant re–definition of the existing C, or if the existing class C is imported, the new class creation is rejected.
  R2.2. If an attribute is defined within a class C and its name is the same as that of an attribute of one of its super-classes, the locally defined attribute is selected over that of the super-class.
  The same holds for a method.
  R2.3 If an attribute p_2 in C is specified with the same name, a compatible signature and visibility as a method p_1 in a super-class of C, then p_2 overrides the definition of p_1 in C.
  The same holds if the attribute p_2 is inherited and re-defined in class C (in that case p2 should be of the same origin as p_1 to avoid the automatic renaming).
  The reverse case does not hold. A method cannot override an attribute.
  This rule preserves as well *I4*.

R2.4. Multiple inheritance
If two or more super-classes of a class C have a property which appears with the same name but distinct super-class origins, the property is automatically renamed in class C, as many time as the property is present among all the conflicting direct super-classes. This is the *automatic renaming.*
This renaming is propagated going down in the class hierarchy from C.
This might occur while adding a property in a class or adding an edge between classes.
This rule also preserves *I3.*
R2.5. Repeated inheritance
If two or more super-classes of a class C have a property with the same name and the same super-class origin, and none of the classes on the different inheritance paths have redefined the property definition, the property is inherited only once from the class origin.
As a corollary, if on one path the property has been redefined, the property has to be locally re-defined in class C.
This rule preserves as well *I4.*
R2.6. Scope of a property
When a property in a class C is changed (visibility, name, type(s)), the changes are propagated to all of the subclasses of C that inherit them unless these properties have been re-defined within the subclass or name conflicts appear.
This does not hold from the method *init.*
This rule preserves as well *I4.*

- **R3**: rules to preserve Distinct Identity Invariant
  R3.1. If a property is created in class C not inherited from one of its super-classes, this property has a new unique distinct identity (pid).
  R3.2. If a property p_2 of a class C is inherited, renamed or not, locally re-defined or not, from a property p_1 of a super-class of C, its identity is the same as that of p_1.
  R3.3. The same holds if the property is inherited, locally re-defined or not, from two or more super-classes of the class C, with the same origin (the latter is a *repeated inheritance* case).
  R3.4. Deleting an edge BA (A direct super-class of B) is not allowed if there is at least one property p_2 locally re-defined in B or in one of its subclasses that is inherited only through this edge from a property p_1 of A or one of its super-classes. The property p_2 has to be deleted first. This avoids having properties p_1 and p_2 with a same pid in two non related (through inheritance link) classes after the schema change.
- **R4**: rules to preserve the Full Inheritance Invariant
  R4.1 A property inherited can be only re–defined through a creation in a subclass (including type and/or visibility and renaming).
  Explicit property "renamings" updates work both on inherited and locally defined properties.
  "Method body" updates work on inherited properties (it is well known to be unsafe).

- **R5**: rules to preserve Domain Compatibility Invariant
  _R5.1._ Covariance
  The domain of a property can be generalized or specialized. The domain of an inherited property cannot be generalized beyond the domain of the property origin and specialized beyond the domains re–defined in the subclasses.
- **R6** rules to preserve the Access Compatibility Invariant Since they are not used in the following sections, these rules are not detailed for simplification.
- **R7** rules to preserve the Class Specification Invariant
  These rules are not detailed herein.
  _R7.1._ Each type name provided in a type specification must be defined before use. If not, the forward reference becomes an *undefined* type.
  This is an interesting O_2 feature which enables incremental design.

Each *HLP* update, u_{hlp}, should preserve the invariants of the schema. Our general policy is to foresee whether the consistency is sound before applying u_{hlp} to a schema. For that purpose, an ordered set of *LLPs* u_i is generated, if any. In intention, we declare u_{hlp}, which is replaced by the equivalent set of basic updates $< u_1, \dots, u_n >= u_{hlp}$ to attain the target schema s_n from the source schema s_o. Each basic update u_i such as $< u_i : s_{i-1} \rightarrow s_i >$ starts from a consistent schema s_{i-1} and proves the intermediate schema s_i to be consistent. That is, the u_i preserve the invariants.
Hereafter, following complex update declarations, two examples explain how to check and collect information and the way to perform the update through an ordered set of *LLPs*.

3.3 Examples of Methods Preserving the Consistency for HLP Updates

Hereafter, class generalization and class removal in particular, show how to keep a schema consistent, avoiding conflicts and preserving the invariants with the application of well–ordered set of *LLPs*.

Class Generalization: Domain Compatibility and Set of LLPs
When generalizing two classes, the content of the newly created class and its location in the class hierarchy have to be found.
In the first step, we built up the new class type from the source classes, focusing on preserving the Domain Compatibility Invariant, this is the *covariance*.
The type of the class of generalization, deduced from the types of the source classes, is constructed as the lowest super-type (lowest upper bound) of the source types, according to the O_2 sub-typing definition.
Informally, let T_1 and T_2 be the respective types of the source classes c_1 and c_2. The type T_g of the new class c_g is achieved "intersecting" the structure of T_1 and T_2. The operator $\sqcap_t$ is specified for that purpose and summarized in Figure 5, where T_1 , T_2 , t_1 and t_2 are types in the O_2 type set. The cases of the array

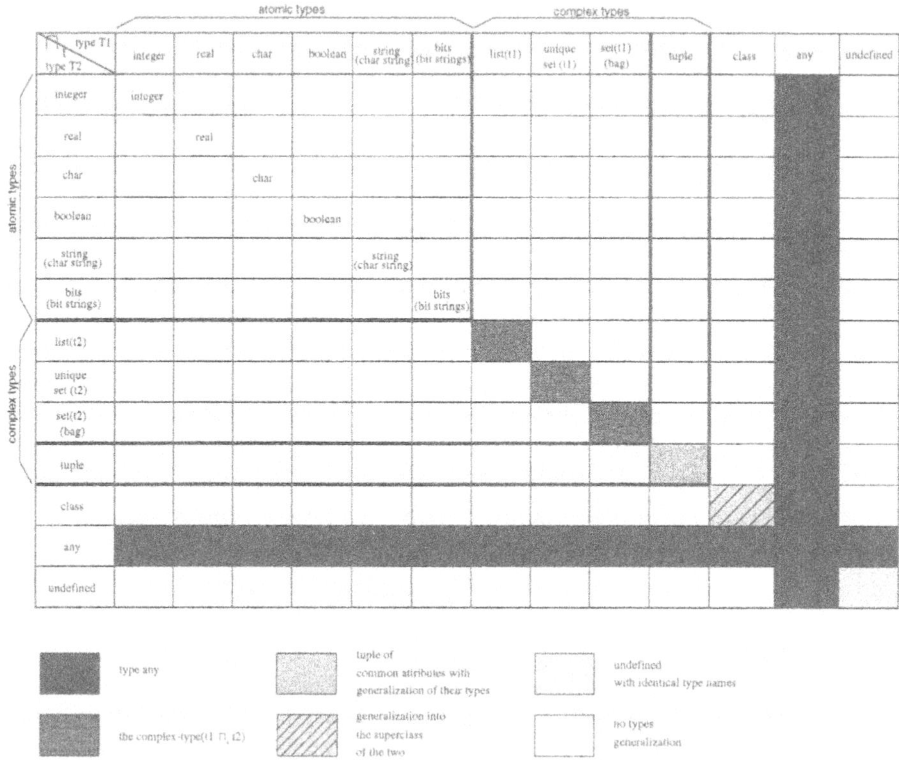

Fig. 5. Class types generalization: operator type intersection $\sqcap_t$.

highlight with different colors, together with certain type definitions, the type being attained through the $\sqcap_t$ operator.
Accordingly, $T_g = T_1 \sqcap_t T_2$ and the following relationships hold between the new type T_g and its source types T_1 and T_2:
$T_1 \leq_{ty} T_1 \sqcap_t T_2$ and $T_2 \leq_{ty} T_1 \sqcap_t T_2$
where $\leq_{ty}$ denotes the sub-typing relationship.
Moreover, $T_1 \sqcap_t T_2$ is the lowest common super-type of T_1 and T_2. That is, for all c_{cs}, common super-class of the source classes, of a structure T_{cs}, the following sub-typing relationships holds:
$T_1 \sqcap_t T_2 \leq_{ty} T_{cs}$
This definition also is not a sufficient condition to attain a singular generalization. Further arbitrary choices complete these conditions to make the generalization unique.
The following four cases then are distinguished regarding the $\sqcap_t$:
$T_1 \sqcap_t T_2 = any$, $T_1 \sqcap_t T_2 = T_1$, $T_1 \sqcap_t T_2 = T_2$ and $T_1 \sqcap_t T_2 \notin \{T_1, T_2, any\}$
This results in different placements of the resulting type $T_1 \sqcap_t T_2$ in the type hierarchy. The latter case only is of interest, when types are *type incompatible* but

are *type comparable*. For example T_1 and T_2 have common type information (e.g. type **tuple** with common attributes names) and, in addition, have information that differentiates them. The set of the lowest common super-classes of the source classes is then computed in order to locate the class c_g in the class hierarchy.

The above solution is proved to follow the covariance required by the *Domain Compatibility Invariant* (this has to be restricted in specific cases of renamings in between the lowest common super-classes of the source classes and the source classes).

When all the informations is collected, we can create and insert the class c_g in the class hierarchy following invariant *I7*. A first *LLP* creates a class together with its properties defined locally. The class is located under the lowest common super-classes of the source classeswith creations inheritance links. In the following step, *LLPs* delete inheritance links between the source classes and the lowest common super-classes. According to rule *R3.4.*, this is preceded by the deletion of those properties that are locally redefined in the source classes and their subclasses, and properties which are already factored in the class of generalization.

Two *LLPs* recreate the inheritance links between the source classes and c_g (this is restricted in some cases of intermediate classes existence). Finally, a set of *LLPs* refine properties in the source classes and their subclasses concerned with the factoring.

We showed how to preserve the covariance of the type between the classes and we verified the set of *LLPs*and their order of application enabling the creation of generalization class.

Class Removal: Property Identity and Order of LLPs

Removing a class in the middle of a class hierarchy involves a step where the inheritance links with the subclasses of the deleted class are removed. Because of the rules preserving the *Distinct Identity Invariant*, those of the properties that are concerned with rule *R3.4* have to be stored and deleted. Thereafter, eventually re–creating a property locally, this property receives an identical *pid* if a property with the same name still exists father up the inheritance path, a new *pid* otherwise.

Such properties may eventually solve repeated inheritance conflicts in a subclass of the deleted class. In this case, per subclass, *LLPs* that delete properties are run first, going down in the class hierarchy from the subclass, followed by *LLPs* deleting the inheritance links between the subclasses and the deleted class.

Hereafter, the option *reconnection* to the super-class(es) of the deleted class is assumed to be set. The re–definitions of the properties solving repeated inheritance are re-created in a specific order to avoid repeated inheritance conflicts, following the rule *R2.5.*. The order is bottom–up/transversal in the class hierarchy.

These methods take part in the maintenance of invariants *I2*, *I3* and *I4* while deleting a class. They are used in other *HLPs* algorithms and highlight the importance of the *LLPs order*.

4 Conclusion and Future Work

In this paper we presented new facilities for enhancing schema evolution that allow to change object database schemas in a declarative manner. We discussed issues on implementation on top the O_2 database.
At this stage, none of these new primitives are implemented in current commercial ODBSs. Related works usually address this topic through generalization, specialization or aggregation considerations [29, 17, 21, 28], general schema change management (widely addressed, [31]), view management [24] and schema change simulation through views [23, 7]. Generic and complex update operators for types are developed for this purpose. They are used to change, to extend and to integrate real or virtual schemas and bases.
The current available *HLPs* can be used interactively through an O_2 shell or a GUI. We plan to extend the *HLPs* with default behaviors and to focus on imported classes. This latter point would enhance the capacity for software reuse and schema integration.
Due to limited space, we did not address the notion of database update following a schema change. Database update is currently limited to those updates that are covered by the *conversion* and *migration functions* found in [13] and [12] and implemented in O_2. Readers interested in this aspect are referred to [8] for more details where it is explained how to perform data update following a class deletion.
As for implementation, prototypes were demonstrated at CEBIT 95 and BDA 95.
Concrete evaluation of advantages gained while designing with these primitives can be measured. The current implementation of the *HLPs* allows the designer to set options that register how many "equivalent" *LLPs* updates are called while performing an *HLP* update and what these *LLPs* are. We intend to use this reporting facilities together with specification of new metrics to evaluate schema change costs, including the database updates [14].
Since we consider simulation of schema change through views [7, 2] an important related issue for enhancing schema change, *HLPs* facilities have another potential application.

References

1. M. Adiba and C. Collet. *Objets et bases de données. Le SGBD O_2*. Traîté des Nouvelles Technologies, Série Informatique. Hermès, Paris, 1993.
2. S. Amer-Yahia. Mise à Jour des Données dans les Vues Objet. Master's thesis, Université Paris Dauphine, September 1995.
3. F. Bancilhon, C. Delobel, and P. Kanellakis, editors. *Building an Object-Oriented Database System — The Story of O_2*. Morgan Kaufmann, San Mateo, California, 1992.
4. J. Banerjee, H.J. Kim, W. Kim, and H.F. Korth. Semantics and Implementation of Schema Evolution in Object-Oriented Databases. In Umeshwar Dayal and I.rv

Traiger, editors, *ACM–SIGMOD '87 Conference on Management of Data, Conference Proceedings*, pages 311–322, San Francisco, California, February 1987. ACM Press.

5. M. Blaha, F. Eddy, W. Premerlani, W. Lorensen, and J. Rumbaugh. *Object Oriented Modeling and Design*. Prentice–Hall International Editions, 1991.
6. G. Booch. *Object Oriented Design with Applications*. Benjammin/Cummings Publishing Co., Menlo Park, California, 1991.
7. P. Brèche, F. Ferrandina, and K. Kuklok. Simulation of Schema and Database Modification using Views. *In Proceedings of the 6th International Conference and Workshop on Database and Expert Systems Applications, Conference Proceedings*, September 1995.
8. P. Brèche and M. Wörner. How to remove a class in an object database system. In *In Proceedings of the 2nd International Conference on Applications of Databases, ADB '95*, San José, California, December 1995.
9. M. Christerson, I. Jacobson, P. Jonsson, and G. Òvergaard. *Object–Oriented Software Engineering. A Use Case Driven Approach*. Addison Wesley, 1992.
10. C. Delcourt and R. Zicari. Consistency Checker (ICC) for an Object Oriented Database System. In *Proceedings of ECOOP'91, European Conference on Object–Oriented Programming*, pages 97–117, Geneva, Switzerland, July 1991. Springer Verlag.
11. S. Even and M. Sakkinen. The safe use of polymorphism in the o2c database language – 5/94. Technical report, University of Frankfurt, FB 20 – Datenbanken und Informationssysteme, University of Frankfurt, Kettenhofweg 135 , 60325 Frankfurt am Main - Germany, March 1994.
12. F. Ferrandina, G. Ferran, J. Madec, T. Meyer, and R. Zicari. Database Evolution in the O_2Database System. In *Proceedings of the 21st International Conference on Very Large Databases*, September 1995.
13. F. Ferrandina, T. Meyer, and R. Zicari. Implementing Lazy Database Updates for an Object Database System. In *Proceedings of the 20th International Conference on Very Large Databases*, pages 261–272, Santiago, Chile, September 1994. Morgan Kaufmann.
14. F. Ferrandina, T. Meyer, and R. Zicari. Measuring the Performance of Immediate and Deferred Updates in the Object Oriented Database Systems. In *OOPSLA Workshop on Object Database Behavior, Benchmarks and Performance*, Austin, Texas, October 1995.
15. Inc. Itasca Systems. OODBMS Feature Checklist. Rev. 1.1. Technical Report TM–92–001, Itasca Systems, Inc., December 1992.
16. A. Kemper and G. Moerkotte. *Object Oriented Database Management. Applications in Engineering and Computer Science*. Prentice-Hall, 1994.
17. W. Klas, E.J. Neuhold, and M. Schrefl. Metaclass in VODAK and their Application in Database Integration. Technical Report P-90–09, GMD-IPSI, GMD-IPSI, Integrated Publication and Information Systems Institute. Dolivostr. 15, D-6100 Darmstadt, Germany, Sep 1990.
18. S. Mellor and S. Shlaer. *Object Lifecycles. Modeling the World in States*. Yourdon Press Computing Series. PTR Prentice–Hall, 1992.
19. O2 Technology. *O2C Reference Manual, Version 4.5*. O2 Technology, Versailles, France, November 1994.
20. O2 Technology. *The O_2C Reference Manual. Version 4.5., Released June 1994*. O2 Technology, Versailles, France, June 1994.

21. C.H. Pedersen. Extending Ordinary Inheritance Schemes to Include Generalization. In N. Meyrowitz, editor, *Proc. OOPSLA'89, ACM SIGPLAN Fourth Annual Conference on Object-Oriented Programming Systems, Languages and Applications*, volume 24(10), pages 407–417, New Orleans, Louisiana, October 1989. ACM Press.
22. D.J. Penney and J. Stein. Class modification in the Gemstone OODBMS. In *Proc. OOPSLA'87, ACM SIGPLAN Second Annual Conference on Object–Oriented Programming Systems, Languages and Applications*, pages 111–177. ACM Press, October 1987.
23. Y.G. Ra and E.A. Rundensteiner. A transparent object–oriented schema change approach using view schema evolution. In *Proceedings of the International Conference on Data Engineering*, March 1995.
24. E.A. Rundensteiner. Multi View: A Methodology for supporting Multiple View Schemata in Object–Oriented Databases. In *Proceedings of the 18th International Conference on Very Large Databases*, pages 187–198, Vancouver, Canada, August 1992. Morgan Kaufmann.
25. B. Schiefer. *Eine Umgebung zur Unterstützung von Schemaänderungen und Sichten in objektorientierten Datenbanksystemen.* Thesis, FIZ, Forschungsbereich Datenbanksysteme. DBS. Forschungszentrum Informatik. Universität Karlsruhe. Haid-und-Neu-Str. 10-14, D-76131 Karlsruhe, Dec 1993.
26. M.H. Scholl and M. Tresch. Meta Object Management and its Application to Database Evolution. In *Proc. 11th International Conf. Entity–Relationship Approach*, pages 299–321. Springer LNCS 645, Karlsruhe, Germany, October 1992.
27. M.H. Scholl and M. Tresch. Schema Transformations without Database Reorganization. *ACM SIGMOD Record 1993*, 22(1):21–27, March 1993.
28. A. Siebes and C. Thieme. Schema Integration in Object–Oriented Databases. In *Advanced Information Systems Engineering. Proceedings of the 5th International Conference, CAiSE'93*, number 685 in LNCS. Springer–Verlag, Paris, June 1993.
29. J.M. Smith and D.C.P. Smith. Database abstractions: Aggregation and Generalization. *ACM Trans. on Database Systems*, 20(6):105–133, June 1977.
30. GOODSTEP Team. The GOODSTEP Project: General Object–Oriented Database for Software Engineering Processes. In *Proc. of the Asia–Pacific Software Engineering Conference, Tokyo, Japan*, pages 410–420. IEEE Computer Society Press, 1994.
31. R. Zicari. A framework for schema updates in object-oriented database system. Technical Report 90-025, Politecnico di Milano, Dipartimento Di Elettronica, 1990.

Views for Information System Design without Reorganization

Z. Bellahsene[1] P. Poncelet[2] M. Teisseire[1]

[1] LIRMM - UMR CNRS 9928 - Université Montpellier II
161 rue Ada 34392 Montpellier Cedex 5 FRANCE
E-mail: {bella,teisseir}@lirmm.fr
[2] LIM - URA CNRS 1787 - Université de la Méditerranée
E-mail: poncelet@lim.univ-mrs.fr

Abstract. In this paper, we propose an approach for managing structural evolutions through views. Evolutions are not actually performed but simulated, thus the database schema is preserved for both users and existing applications. Furthermore, the approach avoids costly database reorganizations. This results from the multi-schema architecture which is introduced and from the isolated management of additional data.
In our approach, the concept of virtual class is complemented through the notion of virtual schema, encompassing several classes and their possible inheritance or derivation relationships with their own properties. The inter-view visibility is enhanced with the main advantage of improving view re-use.

1 Introduction

In relational systems, views are widely used for controlling access, simplifying queries, or providing users with a mere and accurate vision of data as regards their needs.
In an object-oriented context, the application scope of views has been extended [1, 5, 14, 10, 11, 17]. In particular, some approaches consider views as a relevant mechanism when managing structural evolutions [5, 10, 17]. Actually, modifications of an Object-Oriented Database (OODB) schema can be captured through views, without altering the DB schema and thus without reorganizing the database and maintaining existing application programs. In fact, structural evolutions are simulated through views and not actually performed within the DB schema.

Views definition for OODBMS has been addressed in different approaches among which two trends can be distinguished depending on whether the views are included in the database schema or not, i.e. managed in isolation. For the first trend, considering views as parts of the DB schema means inserting new virtual classes in the inheritance hierarchy of the application [11, 10, 17]. Although base classes are preserved, the schema itself no longer reflects the real world since it is enforced with additional classes, perhaps not meaningful for users in particular if they stand for "some external vision" of data. Furthermore, these virtual class insertions complicate the inheritance hierarchy [5]. The second trend [5] diverges significantly from the first one by considering two clear cut levels: on one hand the base classes describing the application schema, and on the other hand the virtual classes representing views. This clear distinction is particularly relevant when considering the cumbersome phenomenon of view proliferation which happens over time, all along the application life.

The proposed approach is rather close to the second described trend but it boosts the separation between views and database schema by introducing a middle level, called the "*Federated Schema*", which offers an overview of both base classes of the schema and virtual classes of views. This schema provides a relevant knowledge of both structural and behavioural aspects of applications. More precisely, schema modifications are not actually performed but are captured by defining views. Thus the database schema is never altered (likely until an entire reorganization becomes necessary). We believe that in such a framework, sharing and re-using views could be significantly improved. Furthermore, views are not only derived from a single class but they could result from any query involving several classes. When additional information (i.e. non derived) is captured through the creation of new properties in a virtual class, it is not actually stored in the database. In fact, the structural enrichment is reflected in the federated schema, while inserted values are stored in the federated base. The latter base is an additional storage for data added all along the application life. With this approach, we can insert new properties in any virtual class even if it is derived from several classes.

The paper is organized as follows. Section 2 proposes an overview of our approach and focusses on the multi-level schema architecture that we define. Schema definition is also addressed. Section 3 is devoted to the manipulation language provided to handle views. An implementation experiment is described in section 4. In section 5, we give an overview of related work. As a conclusion, we compare our proposal to other approaches.

2 The Federated Approach: An overview

2.1 Preambule

In our approach, designers can handle both base classes defined in the application schema and virtual classes initially derived from the former classes. Virtual classes can capture evolutions concerning a single class, such as deletion, modification or insertion of properties which can be either attributes or methods. But they can also represent creations of new relationships between classes, with their possible own properties ("relationship" is intented in the sense of the Entity/Relationship model). In such cases, the underlying virtual classes are derived from several base classes.
Thus users can handle the virtual classes through their virtual schemas. A virtual schema is a set of virtual classes which are related by IS_A links or reference links.

Thus, such a schema captures a set of modifications applying to different classes (including references between classes) but also IS_A links. Furthermore, each virtual class in a virtual schema is associated to at least another class belonging to the base schema or being virtual, through derivation links. Inheritance and derivation hierarchies are both constrained by construction rules which avoid, in particular, cycles when defining virtual schemas.

Virtual schemas defined by designers as well as the DB schema are integrated in the federated schema. This schema offers an overview of all the available structural components of an application. Thus it provides designers with a framework in which new virtual schemas can be created. When evolutions capture new information, i.e. new properties, it is actually stored in the federated schema. The associated values are managed in isolation from the original database. In fact additional data are stored in the federated database. The possibility of including additional properties in a virtual class allows the views to be augmented independently from the base classes. Figure 1 depicts the proposed approach for managing views.

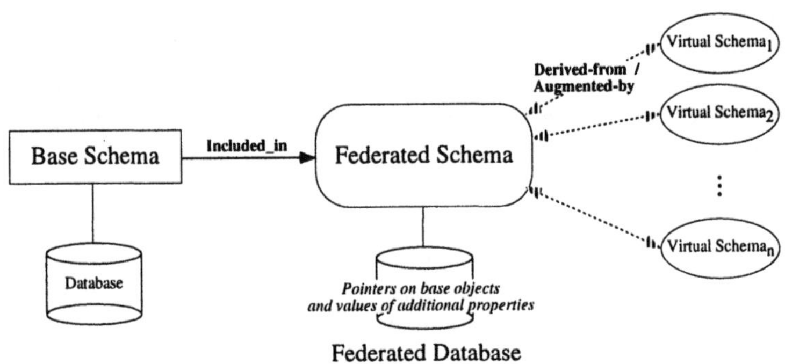

Fig. 1. The Federated Approach

2.2 Definitions

Since our approach fits in an OO context, we assume that the DB schema is an inheritance hierarchy of classes (above called base classes) with possible references between classes (expressed through attribute domains). For setting the groundwork of our manipulation language, we formally define the described concepts.

In this paper, we consider, like in [6], a typical object model: An object is defined by properties which may be either attributes or methods. Objects sharing common properties, i.e. same attributes and behaviour, are grouped into classes. Classes are related by IS_A links through an inheritance hierarchy or by reference links (an attribute with a domain being another class). Multiple inheritance is allowed but the following condition must hold: two super-classes of a class have necessarily a common super-class. A base schema, or merely a schema, is defined as follows.

Definition 1 Schema
A database schema S is defined as a directed acyclic graph $S = (C, IS\_A)$ *where* C *stands for the set of classes and* IS_A *for the IS_A links such that:*

- *there is no IS_A cycle in the graph;*
- *two directed paths of IS_A links sharing the same origin have to be extended to a common super-class.*

A virtual class is derived from one or more *source* classes which may be either base or virtual classes. Nevertheless, the derivation process is constrained according to the following definition.

Definition 2 Derivation links
The derivation links must respect the following condition:
the virtual class includes an attribute referencing each one of its source classes.

A virtual schema includes several classes possibly related by IS_A links, and initially derived from a base schema.

Definition 3 Virtual Schema
A virtual schema S_v *is defined by a triplet* $S_v = (C_v, IS\_A_v, Deriv_v)$ *such that:*

- (C_v, IS_A_v) *satisfies Definition 1;*
- $Deriv_v$ *is a set of derivation links (according to Definition 2);*
- *there is no derivation cycle in* S_v.

The federated schema is then defined from a base schema and the various virtual schemas "derived" from it.

Definition 4 Federated Schema
The federated schema $S_F = (C_F, IS\_A_F, Deriv_F)$ *of a base schema* $S = (C, IS\_A)$ *from which n virtual schemas* $S_{v_i} = (C_{v_i}, IS\_A_{v_i}, Deriv_{v_i})$ *are derived is defined by:*

$$C_F = C \bigcup_{i=1}^{n} C_{v_i},\ IS\_A_F = IS\_A \bigcup_{i=1}^{n} IS\_A_{v_i},\ Deriv_F = \bigcup_{i=1}^{n} Deriv_{v_i}.$$

3 Creating and Manipulating Views

The following section describes, in an intuitive way[3], some of the most interesting operations provided for creating and manipulating views.

Example 1 *Our illustrating example, all along the paper, is managing university students. Let us consider the following base schema, graphically described in Figure 2, and from which we will derive our view examples. It is complemented by a textual*

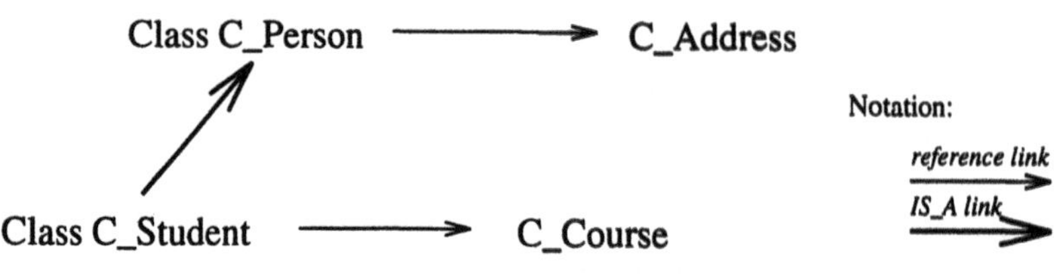

Fig. 2. The *University* Schema

description:

```
schema University;

class C_Person
type tuple (name: string,
 firstname: string,
 address: C_Address );
methods ···
end;

class C_Student inherit C_Person
type tuple (id: string,
 courses: set(C_Course));
methods ···
end;
```

```
class C_Address
type tuple (number: integer,
 street: string);
methods ···
end;

class C_Course
type tuple (title: string,
 discipline: string);
methods ···
end;
```

□

3.1 Schema Definition Language

This section is devoted to the schema definition language, provided for creating virtual schemas and classes. This language can be used by designers while end-users are provided with the manipulation language described in section 3.2.

[3] The evolution operations are fully described in [4].

Federated Schema Creation The federated schema results from the union of the base schema and its associated virtual schemas (Cf. Definition 4). Therefore, on an implementation level, the federated schema is necessarily initialized to the base schema. Then virtual schemas being derived are integrated in the federated schema. Creating a federated schema is performed through the following statement:

create federated schema *FederatedSchemaName*
from *BaseSchemaName*;

At this step, the federated schema *FederatedSchemaName* is merely the same than the base schema[4].

Example 2 *Let us consider the federated schema generated by:*

create federated schema UniversityFed from University;

where UniversityFed *is the federated schema name associated to the base schema* University. *The principle of such an initialization operation is illustrated in Figure 3. It has no effects on the base schema nor on the database where data are actually stored (*University *Base). Through the federated schema, designers can handle*

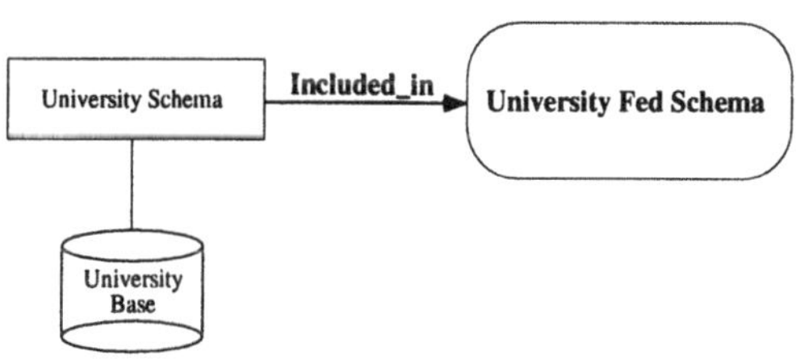

Fig. 3. The *UniversityFed* Federated Schema

the base classes and derive from them new virtual classes which enrich the federated schema: UniversityFed *Schema. When additional information is captured through virtual classes, it will be managed in isolation from the original database (as illustrated in Example 4)* □

Virtual Schema and Class Creation The federated schema provides the groundwork in which new virtual schemas can be defined, by using the following creation operation:

---

[4] In fact, on an implementation level, pointers are initialized to the base classes of the specified schema.

create virtual schema *VirtualSchemaName*
from *FederatedSchemaName*;

Example 3 *Within the* UniversityFed *Schema, we consider a virtual schema* Marks, *yielded by the operation.*

```
create virtual schema Marks from UniversityFed;
```

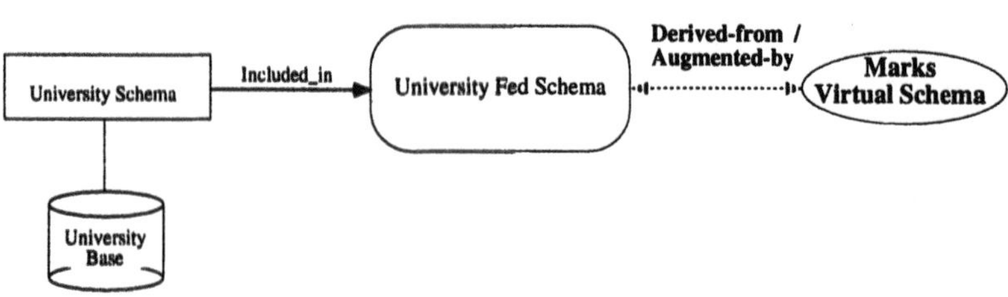

Fig. 4. The *Marks* Virtual Schema

In this virtual schema, initially empty, new virtual classes can then be created, as shown in Figure 4□

When defining new virtual classes which enrich the virtual schema, designers specify queries necessarily applying to classes in the federated schema. Thus virtual classes are provided with a structure or schema (attributes specified in the *Select* clause of the query and which reference other classes) and an extension (objects retrieved by the query). Virtual class creation is merely performed by:

create virtual class *ClassName* **from** *listofClassNames* **as** *Query*;

where *Query* is a retrieval order which could be expressed by using whatever DB manipulation language. For exemplifiying this principle, we choose a language similar to O_2SQL [16].

Example 4 *In the virtual schema* Marks, *we imagine that the designer wants to provide users with a virtual class* Student_Mark *capturing marks of each student for each taken course. For defining this virtual class, the first step necessarily specifies "what is derived", i.e. which attributes in which virtual or base classes are considered. This creation is performed as follows:*

```
create virtual class Student_Mark from C_Student, C_Course as
 (select s:C_Student, c:C_Course
 from s in C_Student, c in C_Course
 where c in s.courses);
```

Resulting from this operation, the virtual class Student_Mark *encompasses objects having their own identifier and defined as tuples of references which are stored in the database as illustrated in Figure 6. More precisely, each object captures a relation-*

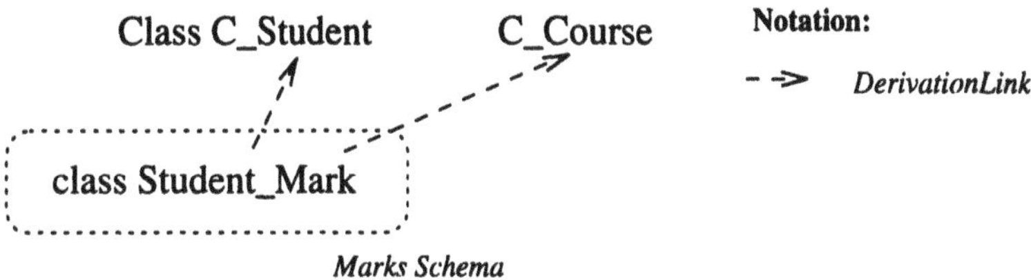

Fig. 5. The *Mark_Student* Virtual Class

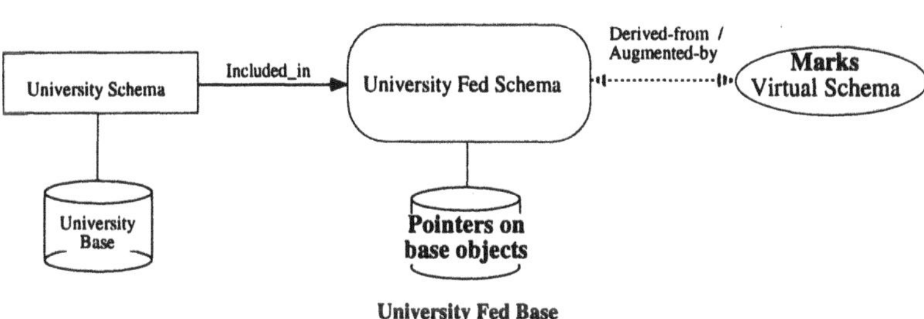

Fig. 6. The *Mark_Student* Objects in the Federated Database

ship between an existing student (for instance, object o_{s1}) and a course. For example, objects $o_{ms1} = (id_{ms1}, (*o_{s1}, *o_{c1}))$ and $o_{ms2} = (id_{ms2}, (*o_{s1}, *o_{c2}))$ capture the fact that student o_{s1} has taken the courses o_{c1} and o_{c2}. Thus objects in `Student_Mark` *are defined through their identifier and a couple of pointers referencing the classes* `C_Student` *and* `C_Course` *(Cf. Example 1). Figure 5 partially illustrates the federated schema* `UniversityFed` *as yielded by the operations described so far. For the sake of clearness, we do no fully represent the federated schema, i.e. the inheritance hierarchy and composition graph of base classes (Cf. Figure 2). We just consider the two base classes:* `C_Student` *and* `C_Course`*. The latter classes are related by derivation links to the virtual class* `Student_Mark` *which is the single class in the virtual schema* `Marks` □

Inserting additional attributes in a virtual class is the mechanism for supporting view augmentation. By this way, real world changes consisting of data enrichment are taken into consideration. The associated statement is the following:

`add attribute` *Attribute* : *AttributeDescription* `to` *ClassName*;

Example 5 *Let us resume the virtual class* `Student_Mark`*, derived in the previous example. Since no marks are stored in the original database, the virtual class must be complemented to fully capture the semantics intented by designers. Thus a new attribute marks is added by the following operation:*

```
add attribute marks: set(real) to Student_Mark;
```

Furthermore, a new method is required for getting values of the added attribute. This is done by:

```
add method getmarks (C_Student,C_Course) to Student_Mark;
```

Mark values of the virtual class are then stored in the federated database, as illustrated in Figure 7. When defining additional attributes, pointers on objects in the associated

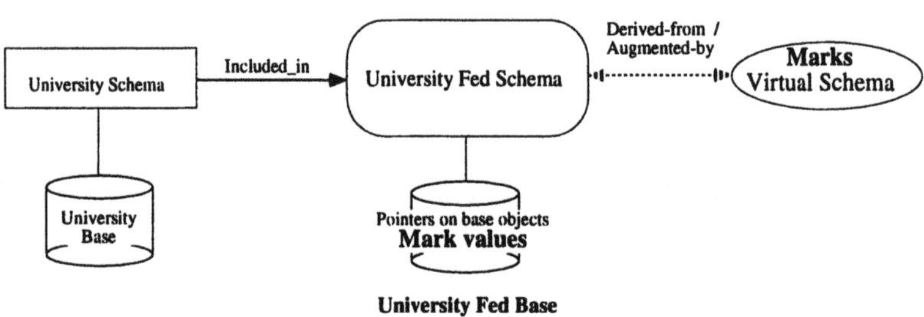

Fig. 7. Adding Values in the Federated Database

virtual class become persistent. In addition, persistency can apply to the class, merely by specifying it as a persistency root, in a similar way than in O_2 [16]:

```
name themarks: set(Student_Mark);
```

□

This approach requires an accurate management of update operations applying to the original database, because these operations must be propagated to virtual classes. When such propagations involve persistent virtual classes, it is necessary to evaluate once again the definition query of the considered class. We do not develop this aspect since the object update propagation is beyond the scope of this paper.

When attributes of referenced classes are not necessary in the virtual class, they can be hiden. Thus the designer can refine the external vision of data, offered by the new class, to fully meet user's expectations. In the associated statement, specified attributes can only be attributes of classes related by derivation links to the virtual class under examination:

`hide` *listofAttributeNames* `to Mark` *ClassName*`;`

Example 6 *When defining the virtual class* `Student_Mark`*, the designer aims to provide a mere view of student's results. In particular, attributes courses in* `C_Student` *and discipline in* `C_Course` *are not necessary and thus they are discarded from the user's view of* `Student_Mark` *by:*

```
hide (courses, discipline) to  Student_Mark;
```

□

All the operations previously described can be grouped together within a single declaration of virtual class, including the query specification, attribute and method insertion, and attribute hiding.

create virtual class *ClassName* **from** *listofClassName* **as** *Query*;
add attribute *AttributeName* : *AttributeDescription*;
add method *MethodName* : *MethodDescription*;
hide *listofAttributeNames*;
end;

Example 7 `Student_Mark` *could have been defined as follows:*

```
create virtual class Student_Mark from C_Student, C_Course as
 (select s:C_Student, c:C_Course
 from s in C_Student, c in C_Course
 where c in s.courses);
add attribute marks: set(real);
add method getmarks (C_Student,C_Course);
hide (courses, discipline);
end;
```

□

Additional Features In this section, we briefly present two additional features of our approach. The first one is the inter-view visibility. With such a capability, it is possible for a virtual schema to re-use classes defined in another virtual schema. Sharing classes is a relevant mechanism for avoiding redundant definitions of virtual classes but also for simplifying derivations.
An existing class in a virtual schema can be visible, and then used, in another schema through the following export order:

export virtual class *ClassName*;

In our approach, a second feature to be underlined is the creation of virtual attributes. Virtual attributes are just attributes of a virtual class yielded by its definition query (and not user-defined, Cf. Section 3.2). A virtual class can be complemented by inserting new virtual attributes. Let us notice that virtual attributes can merely reflect base attributes. But they can also capture additional semantics hiden in the original database, by performing calculus. In such cases, the attribute must be given a name by user.

Example 8 *We imagine that a virtual schema* `Averages`*, illustrated in Figure 8, is defined, including a single class* `Course_Average`*. This class is derived from the virtual class* `Student_Mark` *(which must be previously exported) through a query performing an object grouping. The performed orders are the following:*

```
export virtual class Student_Mark;
create virtual schema Averages from UniversityFed;

create virtual class Course_Average from Student_Mark as
 (group sm in Student_Mark
 by (t: sm.course.title));
```

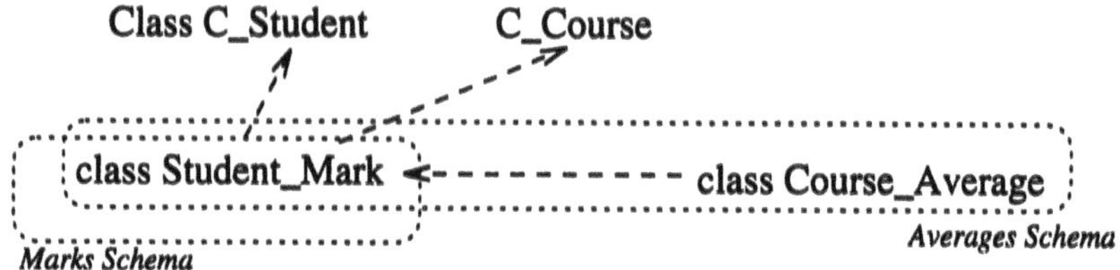

Fig. 8. Two Virtual Schemas

The class **Course_Average** *is complemented by adding a new attribute* **average** *reflecting the average marks of students for courses. This attribute is virtual since its values can be computed from* **Student_Mark** *through a mere query, as shown in the following order:*

```
add virtual attribute average as
(select avg(sm.partition.marks) from sm in Course_Average);
hide (address,name,firstname,libelle,id);
```

where partition is obtained from the previous query □

3.2 Schema Manipulation Language

For updating their virtual schemas, users are provided with evolution capabilities, enhanced through the proposed manipulation language. In fact, each DB programmer or user only accesses his own schema and update operations must not alter schemas of other users.
In an OO context, the evolution issue has been widely addressed [2, 3, 8, 9, 18]. In particular, a set of primitives proved to be minimal and complete is proposed by R. Zicari in [19]. By combining these primitives, any more complex evolution can be expressed. In our approach, we resume these basic operations and adapt them to our view context. These operations are insertion or deletion of property, class and IS_A link.
In the following sub-sections, we present, in an informal and illustrated way, the different operations provided for updating virtual schemas, along with their possible effects on other virtual schemas and the federated schema.

Adding Property Adding a property (attribute or method) in a virtual class cannot be merely seen as the modification of some class in the federated schema because such an operation can have consequences for other existing virtual schemas. Critical side-effects can occur when the updated class is exported or derived for a re-use concern. Thus it is necessary to restrict the application scope of property insertions to the single virtual schema in which the concerned virtual class is defined. With this constraint, virtual schemas using the complemented class are garanteed to be consistent. For enhancing such a constraint, our approach redefines the virtual class to be modified. In fact, the property insertion is not actually performed in the original class but in a simulated copy (by a virtual class) of it. This copy is created and managed by the system, and it is not visible for the user. From the designer's viewpoint, he is provided with an alias of the virtual class, denoted by the key word *is-used-as*.

Example 9 *Let us imagine that, for meeting an application or user need, the final marks of students for the taken courses must be captured. An attribute insertion in the virtual class* `Student_Mark` *can be performed in the following way:*

```
add attribute finalmark: real to Student_Mark;
```

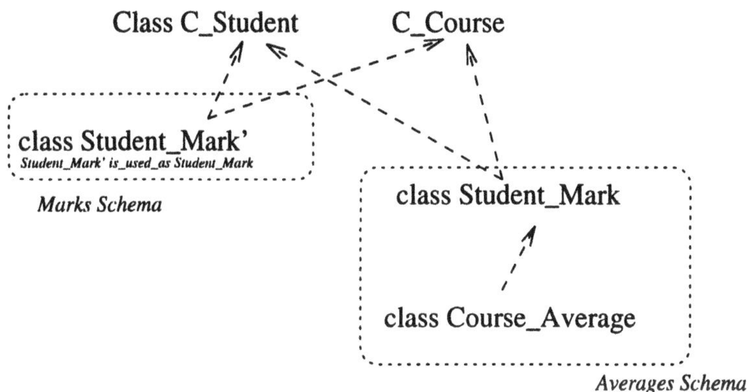

Fig. 9. The Final Virtual Schemas after an Insertion

However, since `Student_Mark` *is re-used by the virtual class* `Mark_Average`, *the insertion does not actually alter* `Student_Mark`, *but a virtual copy of it:* `Student_Mark'`. *Figure 9 proposes the low-level representation of our federated schema example, but for designers the federated schema remains the very same (apart from the provided alias)* □

IS_A Link and Class Creation New classes can be created by specifying their inheritance relationship with one or several existing classes, by using the following order:

`virtual class` *InheritedClassName* `inherit` *ClassName*;

In addition, a class can be declared as being the super-class of another one:

`virtual class` *SuperClassName* `SuperClass of` *ClassName*
`[hide` *listofAttributes* `];`

Example 10 *In Figure 10, the virtual class* `Honours_Student`, *in the virtual schema* `Marks`, *is defined as a sub-class of* `Student_Mark` *merely by specifying an inheritance link between them:*

```
virtual class Honours_Student inherit Student_Mark;
```

□

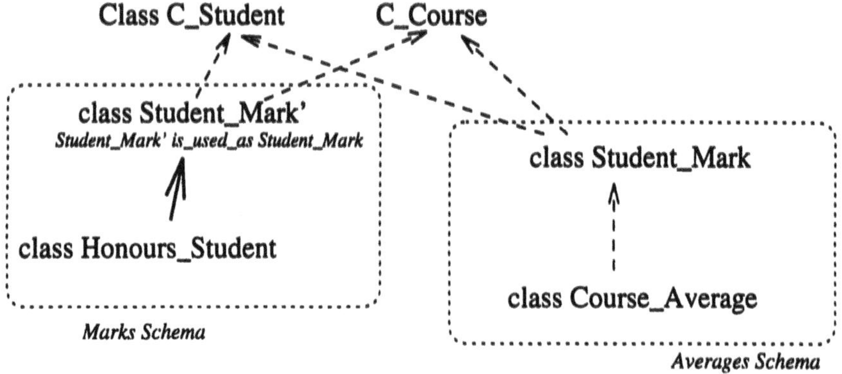

Fig. 10. The *Honours_Student* Virtual Class

Deleting a Property Deleting property from a virtual class must preserve the consistency of all the virtual schemas within the federated schema. Like for property insertion, if the virtual class is re-used, the operation is performed on a copy of the concerned class by hiding the property to be deleted. It is propagated to possible sub-classes within the considered virtual schema, once again by using the hide clause.

Example 11 *If the user wants to discard* `Address` *from the virtual class* `Student_Mark`, *he can use:*

```
hide (address) to Student_Mark;
```

As a result, the attribute is no longer visible for the user, in particular in the sub-class `Honours_Student`, *but the operation applies on the copy* `Student_Mark'`. *Thus the single virtual schema to be modified is* `Marks` □

Deleting a Class In an inheritance hierarchy, deleting a class is usually performed by removing it while relating its possible sub-classes to its super-class(es) [19]. However, in our context, class deletion must be examined by paying particular attention to derivation links. In fact, exactly like for property insertion or deletion, the operation effects must be located within the single virtual schema from which a class must be removed. In our approach, class deletions are guaranteed to be without side-effets, once again by using the copy mechanism. Now, let us consider the modified virtual schema. If the user intends to remove a virtual class having sub-classes, the deletion is necessarily propagated to the sub-classes. Actually, sub-classes cannot be preserved, since a main part of their semantics is captured through the definition query of their super-class.

Example 12 *If the user deletes the virtual class* `Student_Mark` *in the virtual schema* `Marks`, *its sub-class* `Honours_Student` *is automatically removed (Figure 11). In fact deletion applies to the virtual copy* `Student_Mark'`, *thus the virtual schema* `Averages` *is preserved.*

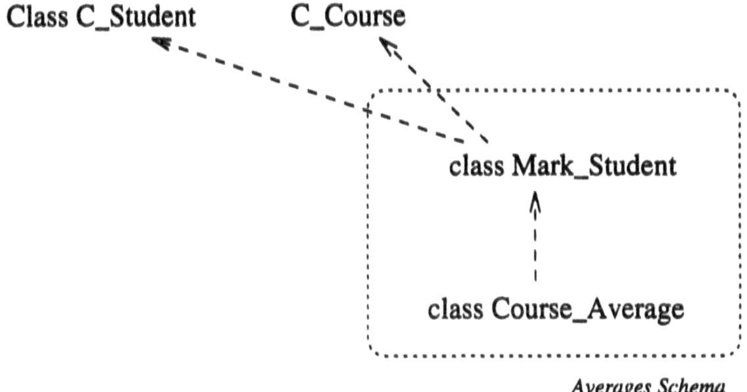

Fig. 11. Federated Schema after *Student_Mark* Deletion

4 An Implementation using the O_2 DBMS

4.1 System Architecture

Based on the approach described in this paper, a prototype [7] is currently developped on top of the O_2 DBMS: *SETV* (Schema Evolution Through Views). It provides both the view definition and manipulation languages. Figure 12 gives an overview of *SETV* architecture. Within the system, the component Virtual Object Manager maintains relationships between virtual objects and the associated base objects.

When a virtual class is derived from several classes, its objects must be provided with their own OID, created and managed by the system all along the worksession. For additional attributes added in virtual classes, values are get through an "init" method which includes a "new" operator.

There are two pure ways to perform query processing against views: materialization and query transformation. The first one is to materialize all derived classes referenced by the query. The other consists of transforming a query into an equivalent set of subqueries refering to base classes.

In our implementation, we adopt a dynamic materialization for composite virtual object. However, the materialized virtual objects must be maintained for reflecting the update operations on the database. In our system, this consistency is verified through triggers related to update actions in the same way as in [3].

4.2 System Classes

The components of *SETV* are implemented as system classes. A part of the *SETV* Meta-Schema hierarchy is presented in Figure 13. We just give an example including system classes representing a virtual class with the O_2 data definition language:

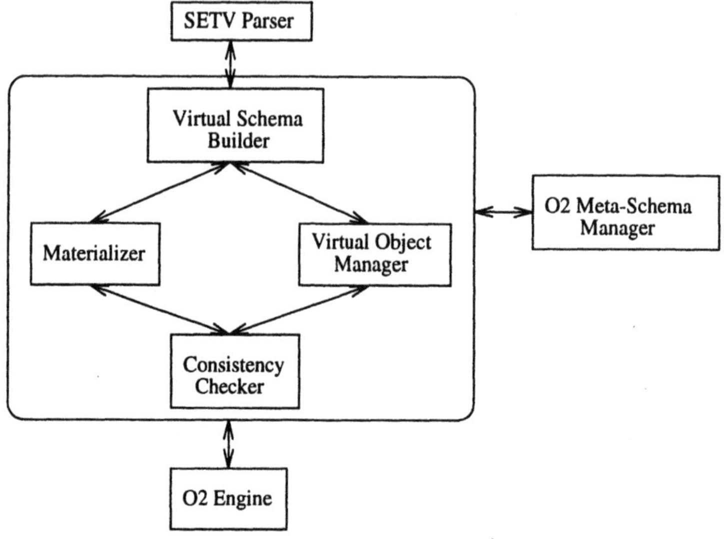

Fig. 12. The *SETV* Architecture

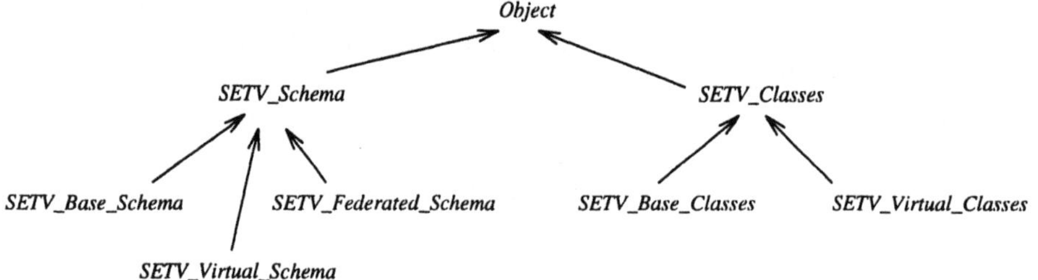

Fig. 13. The System Classes

```
class SETV_virtual_classes inherit SETV_classes
public type tuple(
range: string, /* class visibility */
from: set(SETV_base_classes), /* base class names */
extension: SETV_extensions, /* virtual class extension */
attributes: set(SETV_attr), /* virtual class attributes */
methods: set(SETV_methods), /* virtual class methods */
has_additional: integer, /* flag for additonal property */
has_init: integer) /* flag for init method */
end;

class SETV_extensions
```

```
public type tuple(
name: string, /* extension name */
class: SETV_virtual_classes, /* related virtual class name */
is_materialized: integer, /* flag for materialization */
query: string, /* for populating virtual class */
is_persistent: integer, /* flag for peristent extension */
end;
```

5 Related Work

The concept of schema virtualization is introduced by K. Tanaka et al. [15]. A more sophisticated view language is proposed in [1] for the O2 object model. It includes a set of view primitives (creation of virtual classes, imaginary classes, virtual attributes, OID creation for imaginary objects). The concepts described in [1] are extended and implemented in the prototype O2Views on top of the OODBMS O2 [13]. However, capacity augmenting views are not allowed. Therefore, O2Views cannot be used for simulating schema evolutions.
By using the view mechanism, the approach proposed in [5] enhances various DB features such as: dynamic sets, partition of classes, schema evolution and versions. The author shows how most of the schema changes can be simulated by view creation. In [17], the simulation process is enhanced and included in an external schema definition. An external schema is defined as a subset of base classes and a set of views corresponding to the schema modifications. Besides, this external schema has to be closed. More recently, the Multi-view system [12] is enhanced for supporting schema evolutions [11]. However, the issue concerning capacity-augmenting views derived from several base classes is not addressed.

A very important question to be answered concerning the simulation of schema evolution is: can all schema modifications be simulated? An answer can be found in [17] where schema modifications are classified according to their impact on the object modelling capacity. In fact, three kinds of transformations are considered depending on whether they preserve, reduce or augment capacity. All theses transformations could be simulated with views. But, when considering views as integrated in the base schema, capacity augmenting operations necessarily require a data reorganization [17, 11]. Let us notice that integrating views in the base schema reveals another defect: fully artificial classes can be necessary when a view is derived from several classes [17]. These artificial classes can be cumbersome for users since they only result from intermediary steps when computing views. By using the proposed federated approach, such problems are avoided.

6 Conclusion

In this paper, we propose an approach for managing structural evolutions through views. Evolutions are not actually performed but simulated, thus the DB schema

is preserved for both users and existing applications. Furthermore, the approach avoids costly database reorganizations. This important advantage results from the multi-schema architecture which is introduced and from the isolated management of additional data (within the federated base).
In our approach, the concept of virtual class (widely used in related work) is complemented through the notion of virtual schema, encompassing several classes and their possible inheritance or derivation relationships. Furthermore, through the concept of federated schema, the inter-view visibility is enhanced with the main advantage of improving view re-use. With the proposed clear cut separation between the federated and base schemas, none operation needs an actual database reorganization, even if it is capacity augmenting. By this way, our approach boosts the simulation capabilities when compared to [11]. Furthermore, artificial classes are not necessary for defining views.
View definition and manipulation languages are defined for designers and users. They provide the required functionalities for handling views. Furthermore when manipulating classes, modification operations are guaranteed without side-effects for other users. With this approach, each user is provided with a great autonomy for updating his virtual classes while taking advantage of other user's manipulations through the federated schema.

References

1. S. Abiteboul and A. Bonner. Objects and Views. In *Proceedings of the International Conference on Management of Data (ACM SIGMOD*, pages 238–247, Denver,USA, May 1991.
2. J. Banerjee, W. Kim, K.J. Kim, and H. Korth. Semantics and Implementation of Schemes Evolution in Object-Oriented Databases. In *Proceedings of the International Conference on Management of Data (ACM SIGMOD)*, San Francisco, USA, May 1987.
3. Z. Bellahsene. An Active Meta-Model for Knowledge Evolution in an OODBMS. In *Proceedings of the 5th International Conference on Advanced Information Systems (CAiSE)*, Lecture Notes in Computer Science, Paris, France, June 1993.
4. Z. Bellahsene. View Mechanism for Schema Evolution. Technical Report 95035, LIRMM CNRS/ University of Montpellier II, France, May 1995.
5. E. Bertino. A View mechanism fo Object-Oriented Database. In *Proceedings of the 3rd International Conference on Extending Database Technology (EDBT)*, pages 136–151, Vienne, Austria, March 1992.
6. E. Bertino and L. Martino. Object-Oriented Database Management Systems: Concepts and Issues. *Computer*, 24(4):37–47, April 1991.
7. G. Lucato. Evolution de schéma au travers des vues. Technical report, LIRMM CNRS/ University of Montpellier II, France, June 1995.
8. D.J. Penney and J. Stein. Class Modification in the GemStone Object-Oriented DBMS. October 1987.
9. P. Poncelet and L. Lakhal. Consistent Structural Updates for Object-Oriented Design. In *Proceedings of the 5th International Conference on Advanced Information Systems (CAiSE)*, Lecture Notes in Computer Science, Paris, France, June 1993.

10. Y-G. Ra, H. Kuno, and E.A. Rundensteiner. A Flexible Object-Oriented Database Model and Implementation for Capacity Augmenting Views. Technical Report CSE-TR-215-94, Electrical Engineering, Computer Science and Engineering Division, University of Michigan, Ann Arbor, May 1994.
11. Y-G. Ra and E.A. Rundensteiner. A Transparent Object-Oriented Schema Change Approach Using View Evolution. In *Proceedings of the IEEE Conference on Data Engineering(ICDE)*, Tapei, Taiwan, 1995.
12. E.A. Rundensteiner. Multiview: a Methodology for Supporting Multiple Views in Object-Oriented Databases. In *Proceedings of the International Conference on Very Large Databases (VLDB)*, Vancouver, Canada, 1992.
13. C.S. Dos Santos. Design and Implementation of an Object-Oriented View Mechanism. Technical Report GOODSTEP N-7, INRIA, Rocquencourt, March 1994.
14. C.S. Dos Santos, S. Abiteboul, and C. Delobel. Virtual Schemas and Bases. In *Proceedings of the International Conference on Extending Data Base Technology (EDBT)*, Lecture Notes in Computer Science, Cambridge, UK, March 1994.
15. K. Tanaka, M. Yoshikawa, and I. Koso. Schema Virtualization in Object-Oriented Databases. In *Proceedings of the IEEE Conference on Data Engineering(ICDE)*, February 1988.
16. O2 Technology. The o_2 User's Manual Version 3.3. Technical report, March 1992.
17. M. Tresch and M.H. Scholl. Schema Transformation without Database Reorganization. *ACM SIGMOD Record*, 22(1):21–27, March 1993.
18. R. Zicari. A Framework for O_2 Schema Updates. In *Proceedings of the 7th IEEE International Conference on Data Engineering(ICDE)*, pages 146–182, April 1991.
19. R. Zicari. Primitives for Schema Updates in an Object-Oriented Database System: A Proposal. *Computer Standards & Interfaces*, pages 271–28, 1991.

Semantics, Features, and Applications of the Viewpoint Abstraction

Renate Motschnig-Pitrik[1] and John Mylopoulos[2]

[1] Department of Applied Computer Science and Information Systems
Rathausstrasse 19/4
1010 Vienna, Austria
email: motschnig@ifs.univie.ac.at

[2] Department of Computer Science,
University of Toronto,
Toronto Canada M5S 1A4
email: jm@cs.toronto.edu

Abstract: Partitioning information bases such that their contents may be viewed from different situations and represented and processed in different contexts, constitutes a fundamental concern in various disciplines of computer science. Not surprisingly, numerous notations and techniques support certain aspects of the viewpoint abstraction. This paper motivates the use of a well defined terminology and framework regarding basic notions accompanying the viewpoint abstraction, such as contexts, perspectives, situations, and relativism. Furthermore, it establishes the cognitive and linguistic evidence on the usefulness of considering multiple views. A previous paper introduced a generic framework for contexts in order to provide a common kernel for the modelling of information base partitions. This paper demonstrates the embedding of the framework into an extensible, structurally object-oriented data/knowledge model and illustrates the applications of contexts and their accompanying mechanisms for authorization and change propagation to the modelling of (database) views, (software engineering) workspaces, and versions.

1. Introduction

Classical abstraction mechanisms have proved to be indispensable means for managing the complexity in various notations[1] employed for programming and conceptual modelling. In general, an abstraction is a simplified description, of some subject matter that emphasizes some details or properties while suppressing others [Shaw84]. As a result, the simplified description may be more easily understood and used. Previous research (e.g. [Smith 77], [Brodie84], [Hull87], [Motschnig-Pitrik92, 93] [Storey93]) has concentrated on the classical abstractions like classification, aggregation, and generalization/specialization, that by now are well-accepted semantic modelling concepts. One abstraction that is by far less well understood is that of providing partial information on conceptual entities by viewing them from different viewpoints or situations and representing them in different contexts [Mylopoulos95], [Motschnig-Pitrik95]. Nevertheless, the notion of viewpoints has been considered in quite a few

---

[1]In the following, the term notation will be used in a generic sense to subsume terms like language, diagrammatic technique, and data/knowledge model.

formal notations of computer science stemming from areas such as programming languages, software development, database modelling, and knowledge representation. In these areas, the viewpoint abstraction appears under the guises of workspaces for the support of cooperative work, views delineating data for particular user groups, or knowledge base partitions typically constraining the problem space with respect to reasoning to a manageable size. Most proposals provided in the literature and in software products, however, deal with only some of the issues of a comprehensive viewpoint mechanism. Furthermore, they use disparate terminology, such that their features can hardly be compared. Yet, as will be argued shortly, the viewpoint abstraction, like the other classical abstractions, has a common, uniform kernel whose support proves beneficial for a number of well defined tasks, such as the support of database views, software engineering workspaces, AI topics, versions, etc. .

We see *information bases* as a generalization of terms such as (object-oriented, deductive, active, multimedia, or just traditional) databases, knowledge bases, hypertext bases, etc. . The construction of such information bases assumes an *information model* which, again, is seen as a generalization of the the terms data/knowledge model, conceptual model, or knowledge representation scheme. Proper use and management of an information base is supported by an information base management system which offers an information model along with efficient query and transaction processing facilities. The exact nature of these facilities may well be influenced by structuring mechanisms such as the one proposed here.

The purpose of this paper is to embed a formal framework for the viewpoint abstraction (for more details see [Mylopoulos95], [Motschnig-Pitrik95]) into an object-oriented notation and to illustrate in what ways the framework provides a unifying notion and hence support of well known applications such as views, workspaces and versions. In addition, the paper

* motivates the consideration of viewpoints as a useful abstraction that facilitates the construction and maintenance of large information bases and leads to models that more transparently model (some aspects of) the real world. This issue encompasses the comparison of viewing with related notions;

* explores results from cognitive psychology and linguistics that point to the benefits of organizing information along contexts such that each context addresses a particular situation in the real world;

* shows some benefits of integrating the generic framework for contexts [Mylopoulos95] into a particular information model, for example an object-oriented one;

* compares our framework with related work and demonstrate how our model addresses and provides more uniform support of several features of applications of the viewpoint abstraction, in particular views, workspaces, and versions.

The paper is organized as follows: the next section introduces the viewpoint abstraction and explores its cognitive and linguistic grounding. The generic context framework ([Mylopoulos95]) is reviewed in section 3 and illustrated by a simple example. Section 4 shows the embedding of the generic framework into an extensible, structurally object-oriented language. While we use Telos, the principles and insights gained from the embedding apply to most object-oriented notations. Nevertheless, as will be shown shortly, the extensibility of Telos allows for a particularly straight-forward incorporation. Applications of the context framework, such as its use for the modelling of (database) views, (software engineering) workspaces, and major aspects of versions, are discussed in section 5. This section further compares our approach with related work. Finally, the conclusion rounds up the paper and points to issues for further research.

2 Terminology and Grounding

2.1 Terminology

In the literature, several related terms, such as perspective, view, context, vista, space, world, role, and topic are employed to capture two accompanying notions used in the context of information base partitions. In [Motschnig-Pitrik95] the terms *context* and *perspective* are introduced and it is shown how these notions relate to the application dependent terms employed in individual approaches to view modelling. In this paper we give a more detailed scenario illustrating the appliability of contexts and perspectives in an object-oriented environment. As a starting point, consider the meaning of *perspectives* as derived from Webster's Dictionary, where a perspective is described to mean: an "aspect of an object of thought from a particular standpoint". Based on this definition and on the insights gained from the meaning of synonyms and related terms listed above, let us adopt the following as a working definition on perspectives:

A *perspective* is a symbolic structure encoding information about a conceptual entity as viewed from a particular standpoint. Borrowing from [Levesque84], a standpoint, more technically, will be referred to as a *situation*. Due to the emphasis on a particular situation, the information encoded in a perspective is considered partial when compared with the representation of the conceptual entity *regardless* of that situation. Typically, *multiple* perspectives on the *same* conceptual entity coexist in one model and thereby provide alternative descriptions of that conceptual entity. This multiplicity can be ascribed to the fact that the contents of perspectives are determined by *viewing* a conceptual entity from particular situations. Moreover, not only the contents but also the most appropriate representation of a perspective may be determined by a particular situation. Thus the reason for specifying a perspective is basically extrinsic, determining the inclusion of a relevant subset of the characteristics of the entity. Note that he term *conceptual entity* is used synonymously with the 'object of thought' taken from the quote in Webster's dictionary and is intended to mean any semantically meaningful entity. The relationship between a perspective and the corresponding conceptual entity is referred to as `perspective-on` and its inverse is called `has-perspective`.

In a specific case the conceptual entity itself, without (seemingly, for the moment) any regard to a specific situation may be represented by a symbolic structure within a model. In that case the symbolic structure will be referred to as the *primary perspective*, in order to allow to distinguish it from the others. In this respect, in the above definition the term *partial* should be understood in contrast to (approachably) complete information as typically included in the primary perspective or, in the case the latter is not represented, as given by the union of all perspectives on some entity. In fact, multiple intentions behind expressing partial information can be identified, such as setting the focus by ignoring issues not relevant to a specific situation, modelling limited availability of or restricted access to certain kinds of information, describing situations with not yet established further evidence as in reasoning processes, or viewing an entity from just one instant of time as opposed to tracking it throughout its entire life cycle.

Complementary to mapping a conceptual entity into perspectives according to situations, it often appears useful to represent the situations themselves within the model. This is specifically the case if some subject matter consisting of several conceptual entities is to be viewed from the same situation. The latter then can be interpreted as a frame (space), enclosing the conceptual entities viewed. In accordance with [Schneider80], we refer to the denotation of a situation in a model as a *context*. Thus, a context typically is a meaningful slice of the model or, in a special case, represents the universal context. In fact, our usage of the term perspective corresponds to what Schneider called a view. The latter term, however, we tried to avoid since it is heavily overloaded in current approaches.

Note, that decomposing information bases with contexts is orthogonal to the classical notion of the decomposition of a system into subsystems which is driven by the goal of producing a good system's decomposition (see for example [Yordon79], [Wand91]). Indeed, contexts and subsystems differ in so far as a subsystem is it intended to provide a unique and complete specification of some part of the model, covering, at its best, the representational need of all situations. On the contrary, a context, in general, is constructed with different intents in mind, such as to provide a customized view of the system for a particular user's group, to delineate the information necessary for accomplishing a particular task, or to focus attention on a particular topic and abstract from other information.

2.2 The Cognitive Evidence for a Viewpoint Abstraction

Besides computer science, architecture, psychology and, in particular linguistics have acknowledged the importance of the viewpoint abstraction. Consider, for example, the practical utility of the traditional notion of perspective as applied by architects in the design of artifacts. In order to provide the complete picture of, say, a building, several perspectives have to be provided.

Results from cognitive psychology indicate improvements in the mental performance of humans when being confronted with information organized along situations or viewpoints. We believe that such results provide useful guidelines on the choice of semantic concepts in those situations in which understandability by humans is an issue, such as in conceptual modelling. Therefore we briefly state some findings from Cognitive Psychology [Anderson90] that offer hints on the ways perspectives and contexts support and improve human information processing.

Consider, for example, an experiment designed to test the effects of the provision of foci of attention [Rothkopf66]. In a text retrieval task, Rothkopf had three groups of subjects read a long text, each under different conditions: while the text of the first two groups contained questions interspersed every few pages and relevant to the pages following or, respectively, preceding the questions, the third group read the text without any such questions. Furthermore, the first group was advised to answer the questions after reading the pages and the second to read the text with the questions in mind. In a final test on the whole text the third group answered correctly 30% of the test items, whereas the groups whose questions previewed or reviewed the text answered 72% of the test items relevant to their questions and 29% or 42% of the irrelevant items, respectively. This indicates that considering specific standpoints or situations proves beneficial for understanding larger amounts of information.

In general, many of the effects, such as the one above, in which a more constrained situation can be mastered better than a more convoluted one can be explained by the fact that the processing of new information requires attention. The latter is defined in [Anderson90] as being a "very limited mental resource that can be allocated to at most few cognitive processes at a time." Consequently, all means of focusing attention to some specific situation--imagine to listening to only one of two people talking at once or to concentrating on a single task at a time--will improve performance in that situation. Besides being important on such a broad basis as focusing attention, the merits of constraining information to a set of facts relevant to a specific situation can equally well be ascertained at a more syntactic level. Subjects who were presented sentences on famous people could respond faster to questions about these people than subjects who, in addition to the same sentences, were also presented fancy facts about the same famous people [Lewis76]. Experiments, like the one described, directly point to the fact that information not being relevant in a situation is not simply redundant but even has deteriorating effects on the processing of the relevant fraction.

2.3 The Linguistic Evidence for a Viewpoint Abstraction

In linguistics, the notion of a context is a central one, since the context determines the meaning of expressions. For example, P. Gerstl [Gerstl93, p.82,83] writes: "The context in which an expression occurs determines its meaning. The context at a specific point of time during a discourse consists in a typically large number of factors that reflect dependensies between knowledge elements. Formally speaking, factors are partial relations that connect intermediate results of the interpretation process. ... Since factors themselves are derived from knowledge elements, they differ in the way they are represented in the system. Some are explicitely 'coded' as attributes of lexical units or concepts, others result from the application of rules. ... Besides linguistic factors due to global syntactic requirements, (...), some derive from background knowledge, others from the discourse situation or from conventions governing successful communication." This quote nicely demonstrates the analogy between the linguistic and computer science notion of relativity: the linguist's 'interpretation of expressions within a context' corresponds to the computer scientist's ' transaction execution with respect to a context'.

3. Review of an Abstract Context Model

In [Mylopoulos95] a generic framework for partitioning information bases into possibly overlapping contexts has been proposed and will briefly be reviewed in this section. The proposal makes minimal assumptions on the underlying information base model, notably that an information base consists of named, interconnected information units, operated upon by transactions that are triggered by users. The main contribution of the context model rests with the features chosen for the context mechanism, namely:

* relativism, in the sense that the same conceptual entity may have different perspectives as well as names in different contexts;

* relativized transaction execution, meaning that transactions are executed with respect to a context;

* authorization, whereby every context is associated with an authorization predicate such that both content-dependent as well as content-independent authorization is provided;

* change propagation, allowing one to define propagation channels between context and optionally to constrain these channels to transmitting changes that depend on the user and the transaction that issued the change.

3.1 Definitions and Basic Postulates

In the terminology of the abstract context model, an *information unit* (hereafter just *unit*) is the basic building block for information bases. A unit might refer to an entity, object, attribute, relationship, agent, rule, method, record, text file etc. Let `Units` be the set of all possible units. Likewise, we define `Predicates` to be a set of Boolean expressions, possibly with free variables, used as components of context definitions, while `Users` is the set of potential users who may access or operate on an information base, `Transactions` is the set of all possible atomic operations on contexts, and `PropagationLinks` are all potential interconnections between contexts along which changes may be propagated.

Contexts are special units representing a decomposition of the information base. The definition of each context includes four components which define respectively the

- *contents* of the context,
- the local names (*lexicon*) used for units in the context's contents,
- *authorization rules* based on combinations of different users and transactions, and
- *propagation links* specifying contexts which receive changes from or propagate changes to the context under definition :

$$\texttt{P(Units)} \times (\texttt{Identifiers} \rightarrow \texttt{Units}) \times \texttt{Predicates} \times \\ \times \texttt{PropagationLinks} \supseteq \texttt{Contexts}$$

The selector function `contents` takes as argument a context and returns the set of units included in that context

$$\texttt{contents: Contexts} \rightarrow \texttt{P(Units)}$$ [2]

When a unit o is an element of the contents of context c, we will say that o is *visible* in c. Note that units provide both an IB-wide unique identification of their referent conceptual entities as well as a context dependent representation of their referents, i. e. perspectives. In order to provide these two functions, each unit is constructed to consist of a locally unique identifier and a context dependent reference to a perspective. In some

---

[2] P(Set) stands for the powerset of Set.

more detail, a unit's global identifier (or a local identifier, tagged by the context name) uniquely determines the unit's referent such that within one IB no two conceptual entities are referred to by the same unit. A unit's reference to a perspective, however, is context dependent. Thus, considering the example in figure 1, `'unit3'` denotes the conceptual entity of a particular person called `chryss` which may be modelled by different perspectives in the contexts `c1` and `c2`, respectively.

Identifiers are special units consisting of character sequences used as external names for other units with respect to a given context. The selector function `lexicon` maps each context to its lexicon of identifiers and their referents with respect to that context

```
lexicon: Contexts → (Identifiers → Units)
```

Thus, `(lexicon(c))('john')` evaluates to the referent of the external name `'john'` with respect to context `c`. This referent identifies the conceptual entity called `'john'` with respect to context `c` and points to the respective perspective. In the sequel, we will use simply `john` when the context is obvious, as a shorthand for the above expression. Note that the same units may have different identifiers (i.e. external names) with respect to different contexts and, conversely, the same external name may refer to different units in different contexts. Renaming of units, though, should be done with great care since it hides the externally visible semantic ties between perspectives.

Likewise, `authorP` is a selector function which selects for each context `c` and user-transaction pair `(u,t)` a predicate which determines whether user `u` is authorized to execute transaction `t` within context `c`:

```
authorP: Contexts → (Users × Transactions → Predicates)
```

In a similar vein, `propagationFrom` and `propagationTo` are selector functions which associate each pair of communicating contexts with an authorization predicate:

```
propagationFrom: Contexts → (Contexts ×
                 ((Users × Transactions) → Predicates))

propagationTo: Contexts → (Contexts ×
               ((Users × Transactions) → Predicates))
```

`propagationFrom` indicates a communicating context that is supposed to propagate update operations to the context under definition. In analogy, `propagationTo` indicates which context shall be sent changes from the context under definition. In both cases, propagation proceeds selectively in so far as the changes to be sent or received may be filtered by an authorization predicate such that only specific changes are transmitted/accepted. As a result, a change operation in one context effects another context only if both communicating context agree on the propagation.

Figure 1 illustrates the above definitions with a simple example which contains two contexts `c1` and `c2`, each including three units, along with their respective lexicons, authorization predicates and change propagation links.

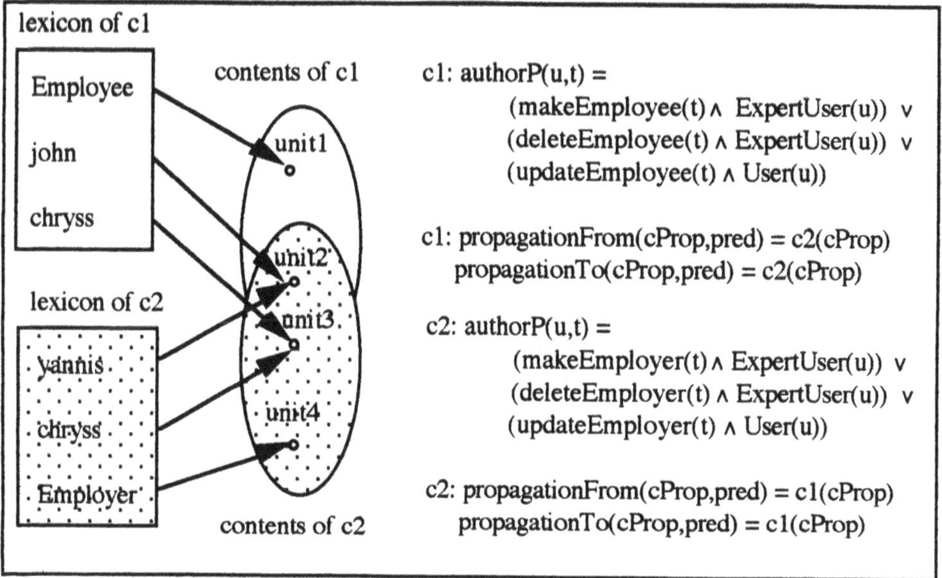

Fig. 1: Example showing the features of the context model

The contents of the context c1, for example is defined as:

```
context(c1) =
    {'Employee','john','chryss','c1',unit1, unit2,
    unit3, unit 137} .
```

The lexicon for c1 has the following name-unit identifier pairs:

```
lexicon(c1) =
    {['Employee',unit1],['john',init2],
    ['chryss',unit3],['c1',unit137]} .
```

According to the figure, '`chryss`' is used synonymously in the two contexts and so are the identifiers '`john`' with respect to context `c1` and '`yannis`' with respect to context `c2`. The authorization predicate of c1 authorizes users having the role ExpertUser to execute makeEmployee and deleteEmployee transactions, All users having the role User (or a role that implies the user role, such as ExpertUser) may execute updateEmployee transactions. A similar predicate is accociated with the context c2. Further, propagation links are specified as to allow for unconstrained bidirectional propagation of changes.

The special context `null` represents the empty context. Note that an empty context may still contain units because it includes built-in units that need not be created explicitly by users of an information base. Moreover, the only transactions that can be executed with respect to the `null` context are `Query` transactions (which retrieve information from, but don't change the contents of `null`). This means that the contents of the `null` context can't be changed:

```
authorP(null)(u,t) =  Query(t)
```

An *information base* is a collection of contexts

```
InformationBases  = P(Contexts)
```

3.2 Operations and Transactions

3.2.1 Primitive Operations on Contexts and Information Bases

Operation on Information Bases. Information bases can be treated as special contexts in the sense that their contents may only contain contexts. Like other contexts, information bases include an authorization and change propagation component. New IB's are created through the operation

```
newIB()
```

which creates and returns a new IB that contains the single context `null` which contains all the built-in units for the new IB. Note that newIB() is the only operation which is not executed with respect to a context. Thus, an *information base* is a collection of contexts

```
InformationBases  = P(Contexts)
```

Following some object-oriented notations, we also postulate that each context is an element of its own contents and can be referenced through the special local identifier self:

$$(\forall c/\mathrm{Contexts})[c \in \mathrm{contents}(c) \wedge \mathrm{self\ wrt}\ c = c]$$

Operations on Contexts. There are two sets of primitive operations on contexts. Firstly, there are operations which create new contexts from sets of units or in terms of existing contexts. Secondly, there are operations for modifying the contents, lexicon and authorization predicate of a context.

newContext(unitSet,unitPairSet,pred(u,t),chProp(c,pred(u,t)) creates a new context containing all elements of `unitSet`, having lexicon `unitPair-Set`,.authorization predicate `pred`, and change propagation `chProp`. The new context is added to the contents of the context wrt which the current transaction is executing:

$$\mathrm{newContext}: P(\mathrm{Units}) \times P(\mathrm{Identifiers} \times \mathrm{Units}) \times \times \mathrm{Predicates} \times \mathrm{PropagationLinks} \rightarrow \mathrm{Contexts}$$

clone(c) creates and returns a new context which "clones" the contents and lexicon of c, while its authorization predicate is set to true and no propagation links are defined.

Context addition (⊕). c ⊕ c' creates and returns a new context whose contents are defined as the set-theoretic union of those of c, c'. The definition of context addition [Mylopoulos95] implies that when an identifier has different referents in c, c', its referent with respect to c takes precedence within c ⊕ c'.

Likewise, the operations *context product* and *context difference* are specified as adaptations of their set-theoretic operation cousins.

The primitive operations provided for changing a context component include ones for inserting/removing entries from the contents and lexicon of a context.

insertContents(c,unitSet)	insertLexicon(c,tupleSet)
removeContents(c,unitSet)	removeLexicon(c,tupleSet)

In addition, operations are provided for assigning to and removing from a context an authorization predicate, for adding/removing a propagation link, for changing incrementally the authorization predicate and/or propagation channels, etc. Furthermore, our proposal assumes that an information base comes with two sets of operations:

* *Primitive operations* for different classes of units, including operations on contexts described above;
* *Transactions* on the information base.

3.2.2 Primitive Operations on Different Categories of Units

Primitive operations define what operations make sense for a particular unit in a particular context. Such operations are are defined along with each unit class. Note that a unit may belong to different classes in different contexts, and therefore admit different sets of primitive operations. For instance, a unit may be a text file in one context and a C++ object in another. This means that the same unit may have different associated representations in different contexts but there is an information base-wide mechanism for keeping track of corresponding representations of the same unit. One such mechanism may be to associate to each representation of a unit in a context an internal, global identifier which uniquely identifies the unit being represented. A second alternative would be to maintain tables of correspondences between the (local) internal identifiers of units in different contexts.

3.2.3 Transactions

Transactions define meaningful operations for the whole information base. They are defined in terms of primitive operations on units including contexts and compositional constructs such as sequencing, conditional, iteration. Transactions are always executed *with respect to* (hereafter *wrt*) a particular context. and can access and/or effect change only to that context.The context with respect to which a transaction execution is carried out is referred to as its *execution context*. An execution context provides, through its lexicon, the symbol table used by a transaction execution. As with other modern database transaction models, our transaction model is nested and assumes rollback if a transaction execution fails.

Transactions can be thought as classes (in the sense of object-oriented information models) and can therefore be organized in terms of a generalization hierarchy. We shall assume that this organization is based at least partly on the generalization hierarchy of their parameter lists [Mylopoulos80]. For instance, the `AssignSal(emp:Employee)` transaction might have specializations depending on whether its argument is a **Secretary, Manager, Designer** or **Receptionist** or one of the specializations of these **Employee** classes.

We may assume that there are built-in transactions which support basic query, insertion, deletion or update operations. These may be refined to form specialized query, insertion, deletion or update operations; alternatively, these may be combined to form composite transactions which carry out combinations of the primitive operations. The left part of figure 2 shows an example of such a hierarchy for the use with the Telos context framework presented in the next section. Note that the arrows in the figure point in the direction of authorization implication. Names in capitals denote operations that are predefined in Telos, while the names in small letters distinguish user defined transactions. In order to determine whether a given transaction is authorized to be executed in a given context, this context's authorization predicate is examined. The transaction is executed in the case that it is authorized explicitly by an authorization predicate, or its authorization can be derived by following the authorization implication links of the transaction lattice.

In the same spirit, we assume that users of the information base are instances of user classes (or user roles), such as SystemAdministrator, Manager, ExpertUser, User, etc. which are also organized in an authorization implication lattice.

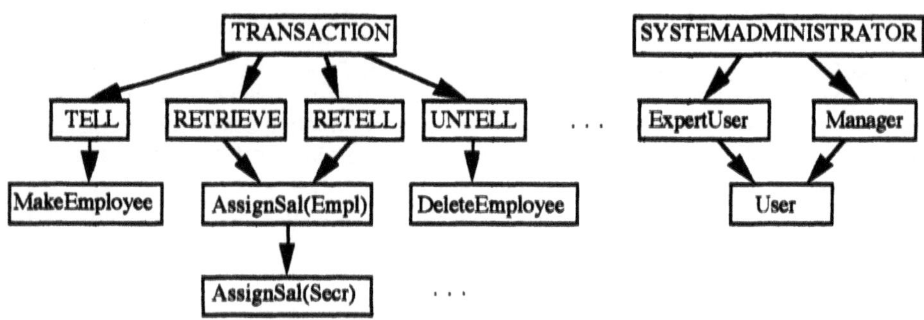

Fig. 2: Example of a transaction lattice (left) and a user role lattice (right) for authorization implication.

4. An Information Model with Contexts

In order to illustrate how existing object-oriented information models can be extended to support contexts, this section shows the embedding of contexts into the Telos framework. We chose Telos mainly due to its extensibility of language constructs (explained shortly), object-oriented nature, associated assertion language capable of expressing, for example, authorization predicates, and its transparent high-level notation having a precise, logically grounded low-level counterpart.

Telos is a knowledge representation language originally designed for information system development applications [Koubarakis89, Mylopoulos90, Jarke92]. Its representational framework is a generalization of graph-theoretic data structures used in semantic networks, semantic data models and object-oriented representations, supporting classification, generalization and attribution. The assertional component of the language includes linguistic facilities based on First Order Logic for declaring constraints and deductive rules. Its novel features include the treatment of attributes as first-class citizens, the extensibility provided through metaclasses and a powerful classification mechanism [Motschnig-Pitrik92] and the special representational and inferential facilities for temporal knowledge (which will not be dealt with in this paper). We'll introduce Telos incrementally, pointing out extensions required in order to support the context mechanism proposed here. The main objective in adopting the context mechanism has been to use as much of the basic Telos framework as possible, in order to minimize extensions to the language.

4.1. The Family Metaphor

A Telos information base consists of *propositions*, which are either *individuals* (entities) or *attributes* (named, binary relationships, represented by triples `[source, label, destination]`[3] (or `[from, label, to]`). Assertions are treated as special individuals, while `instanceOf (in)` and `isA` relationships are treated as special attributes. For purposes of introducing a context mechanism into the language, Telos information bases can be viewed at two levels of granularity, the *proposition level* and a corresponding *family level*. At the proposition level, a Telos information base is simply a collection of propositions. Moreover, *everything* is a proposition. Changes to the state of the information base simply amount to insertions/removals of propositions.

At the family level, on the other hand, an information base is viewed as consisting of several overlapping *families* of (interrelated) propositions each defined by one *parent* proposition, along with all attributes that have this proposition as source, all `instanceOf (in)` links connecting these attributes to classes and all components of attributes in the family, including instantiated classes. The contents of a family provides information on the relationship of the parent proposition to other propositions, along with instantiation information that offers possible interpretations of parents and their associated relationships. A family is intended to be a minimal meaningful collection of propositions. Families are to be seen as the molecules out of which one constructs an information base. As an example, figure 3 shows the family having the parent proposition `chryss`. Note that attributes, such as `[chryss,SI#,06061507]`, are treated as potential family parents too, whose components include instance links and attributes and attribute components representing relationships to other propositions (e.g., the attribute `[chryss,SI#,06061507]` is instance-of `[Person, SI#, Integer]`). If Telos information bases are defined at the family level, operations effecting changes may include insertions, removals of families (each involving the insertion/removal of several propositions) as well as family updates (i.e., changing the set of attributes associated with a particular family).

---

[3] Actually, propositions have a fourth component that defines the lifetime of the entity or relationship represented by the the proposition. As indicated earlier, for reasons of expediency we will ignore the temporal component of Telos.

```
{chryss,[chryss,name,Chryss],[chryss,SI#,06061507],
[chryss,sal,100000],
[chryss,in,Employee],[chryss,in,Person],
[[chryss,name,Chryss],in,[Person,name,String]],
[[chryss,SI#,06061507],in,[Person,SI#,Integer]],
[[chryss,sal,100000],in,[Employee,sal,Integer]],
100000,06061507,Chryss,Employee,Person,Integer,
'name','SI#','sal','in',
[Person,name,String],[Person,SI#,Integer],
[Employee,sal,Integer]}
```

Fig. 3: Example of a family with the parent proposition chryss.

For the rest of the discussion we focus on the family level, since it leads to a more interesting, and powerful, notion of Telos contexts. This is because sets of (related) families can be encapsulated into yet larger building blocks, referred to as *neighborhoods* and *districts*. In order to make the notion of a family and a district more precise, we introduce the function family(prop) as a special case of the function district(propSet), defined in terms of the auxiliary functions nucleus, comp and closure. district(propSet) specifies the set of all propositions constituting a Telos family with parents the elements of propSet:

```
nucleus(propSet) =def { p | p ∈ Attributes ∧ from(p)
        ∈ propSet }
     ∪{ p1 | p1 = [p,in,c] ∧ p ∈ propSet ∧ c ∈ Class}
     ∪{ p2 | p2 = [p',in,c'] ∧ c' ∈ AttributeClass ∧
        p' ∈ Attributes ∧ from(p') ∈ propSet }
     ∪{ propSet }
closure(propSet) =def { p | p ∈ comp(p') ∧
     p' ∈ propSet }
comp(propSet) =def { p |
     [(p = from(p') ∨ p = label(p') ∨ p = to(p')) ∧
        p' ∈ propSet] ∨
     (∃p'')[p'' ∈ comp(p') ∧ p'' ∈ propSet ∧
     (p = from(p') ∨ p = label(p') ∨ p = to(p'))]}
district(propSet) =def closure(nucleus(propSet))
```

According to this definition, the topology of a *district* is defined in terms of a *set* of parents, one or more classes each parent (respectively) is an instance of, and the attributes associated with the parent and these classes, as illustrated above. The definition of a *family* is derived from that of a district by having propSet contain a *single* proposition only. Thus, districts derived from a single parent proposition are called families.

Figure 4 shows several examples of family creation operations (defined through TELL), all having a single parent, namely the name of the class/token under definition. In particular, PersonClass is defined as a metaclass (whose instances are classes) and a specialization of the metaclass SimpleClass. In addition, PersonClass has an associated attribute class labelled avgAge, declared to be a single-valued, simple class (i.e., its instances are tokens, representing particular binary relationships in the application domain). Person, on the other hand, is declared to be a simple class with a name attribute class, a single-valued SI# attribute class and a avgAge attribute having the value 30. Employee and Employer are defined as specializations of Person (also instances of PersonClass) with additional attributes. Finally, chryss and john are defined as tokens, instances of Employee and Employee as well as Employer respectively, having particular attribute values for attribute classes associated with the class they are classified under. Note that the family being created in terms of TELL TOKEN chryss operation, for example, has been given in figure 3 above.

```
TELL CLASS PersonClass
   ISA SimpleClass
   IN MetaClass
   WITH
     attribute, single
       avgAge: 1..100
END Person Class

TELL CLASS Person
   ISA Token
   IN PersonClass
   WITH
     attribute
       name: String
     single, attribute
       SI#: Integer
       avgAge
       - : 30
END Person

TELL CLASS Employee
   ISA Person
   IN PersonClass
   WITH
     attribute
       sal: Integer
       avgAge
                - : 35
END Employee

TELL CLASS Employer
   ISA Token
   IN SimpleClass
   WITH
     attribute
       employee#: Integer
       empName: String
END Employer

TELL TOKEN chryss
   IN Employee
   WITH
     name
       - : Chryss
     SI#
       - : 06061507
     sal
       - : 100000
END chryss

TELL TOKEN john
   IN Employee, Employer
   WITH
     name
       - : John
     SI#
       - : 30501960
     sal
       - : 100000
     employee#
       - : 10
     empName
       - : Cognos
END john
```

Fig. 4: Telos family definitions

A final point about Telos, before returning to contexts. **Attribute** and **Single** are attribute metaclasses which are used to bestow semantics to attribute classes. **Single**, for example, can be defined as shown in figure 5. This definition declares the source, label, and destination components of **Single** and associates with it a constraint that states, in effect, that its instances are single-valued attribute classes. This class is instantiated in the definition of the attribute class **SI#** to declare that it is single-valued.

```
CLASS Single = [Class,single,Class]
   IN AttributeClass, MetaClass
   WITH
     integrityConstraint
       hasOneValue: (Forall s/Single, p,q/Attribute)
          (p in s) and (q in s) and
          (from(p) = from(q)) implies to(p) = to(q)
END
```

Fig. 5: Defining the attribute metaclass Single

4.2. Contexts as Family Homes

In order to introduce contexts in Telos, we begin by defining the class Context, which has all contexts constituting an information base as instances.

```
TELL CLASS Context
  ISA Token          /* means that Context is a simple class having
                     tokens as instances*/
  IN SimpleClass     /* SimpleClass is the immediate successor of the class
                     Token in the instance-of lattice */
  WITH
   part
         contents: Proposition
         lexicon: ExternalNameUnitIdPairList
                     /* associates external names with local unit identifiers
                     included in the contents */
         authorP: AssertionClass |
                     UserTransactionPairList
                            /* list of user-transaction pairs specifying which
                            users may execute which transactions */
         propagationFrom, propagationTo: AssertionClass |
                     ContextAuthorizationPairList
                             /* list of contextname-authorizationpredicate
                             tuples, where the contextname refers to the context
                             that propagates or receives changes, respectively */
   attribute
         owner: User
END Context
```

Fig. 6: Definition of the class Context

In addition, we assume that `Context`, like other built-in Telos classes are all in the empty context, `null`, and are therefore present in all other contexts too.

The second extension to Telos exploits the obvious correspondence between contexts and families, based on the observation that both define collections of propositions. However, a context has associated supporting structure (contents, lexicon) and offers mechanisms for encapsulation, authorization and change propagation. Families, on the other hand, are mere collections of propositions that constitute an information base neighborhood. It therefore makes sense to treat a family as a context, thereby endowing it with context-related structure and mechanisms.

As an example demonstrating the definition of a context based on a particular family, namely `family(Person)` consider the creation of the token `personContext` as an instance of the class `Context`. Assume that `personContext` is created within an enclosing context called `enterprise` as shown in figure 7.

```
TELL TOKEN personContext
   IN Context
   WITH
     contents
       - : {'Person',unit35,'personContext', unit40,
              'john',unit41}
     lexicon
       - : {['Person', unit35],
           ['PersonContext',unit40],['john',unit41]}
     authorP
       - : {[User,MakePerson],[User,RemovePerson]}
       - : $ T(x) = SetSI#(person) implies
              person = User $
     propagationFrom
       - : {[self,true],[workplace,true]}
     propagationTo
       - : {[self,true],[workplace,
           [SystemAdministrator, Transaction]]}
     owner
       - : john
END Person
```

Fig. 7: Defining `Person` as a context.

We assume that `Person` is being created within the context `enterprise`, so `self` refers to `enterprise`. Also, we will use `this` to refer to the newly created context. Note that the contents and the lexicon for family contexts are created automatically. Further, the redefinition declares authorization such that all users having the user-role `User` may execute the `MakePerson` and the `RemovePerson` transactions (regardless of the particular parameterlists). The transaction `SetSI#(person)`, however, may be executed only by users operating on their own records. In addition, the definition declares propagation channels to and from `enterprise` as well as `workplace`.

Furthermore, changes affected by transaction executions initiated by users that carry the role of `SystemAdministrator` are specified to be propagated from the `Person` context to `workplace`.

A `TELL` operation then creates a new family and (optionally) declares it to be a context. The family itself may be visible and may be changed in many other contexts. It is often useful to use the original family context as homebase (*home*) for the family, which accumulates all changes effected elsewhere thereby keeping track of the family status. In general, we envision each family having zero or more homes which are characterized by the fact that they receive change propagations effected elsewhere.

One of the advantages of assigning a newly created family to a home is that the constraints and deductive rules associated with that family may then remain private to the family home and need only be checked when the home is first created or is subsequently updated. This situation is in sharp contrast with that found in the current definition of Telos, where constraints and deductive rules are global to an information base and are therefore checked any time there is an update anywhere in the information base.[4]

4.3 Contexts Beyond the Family Home: Neighborhoods and Districts

We now turn our attention to other useful collections that might be encapsulated in terms of contexts. The definition of Telos includes functions which make it possible to fetch all instances of a class `c`, in terms of the expression `c.instances`, all classes of which a proposition `p` is an instance, `p.in`, all specializations of a class `c`, `c.spec`, and all generalizations of a class `c`, `c.isA`. The result of using any combination of these four functions as multiple parent propositions in order to derive a district is referred to as *neighborhood*. Neighborhoods being constructed such that the parents are, for example, a classname and its chain of super and/or metaclasses, are particularly useful in the construction of contexts since they encapsulate intimately related fragments of an IB. So are neighborhoods that contain as parents a classname along with subclasses and/or instances of the respective class.

In general, Telos contexts (containing more than one family) can be constructed in one of three ways: by a context operation (compare section 4), by explicitly enumerating the families or their parent propositions to be included, or by a query expressed in the Telos query language ([Koubarakis89]). In all three cases the contents of a context is specified as the value of its `contents` attribute. As an example of a context created by the context addition operation with regard to the two family contexts Employee and Employer, consider the context `workplace` given in figure 8 and assume it is created within the context `enterprise`. The contents of `workplace` is specified by context addition and hence includes the contents of its two parent contexts. In addition, `workplace` makes use of generalization hierarchies of user roles by authorizing expert users, `ExpertUser`, (assumed to be a subclass of `User`) to call the transactions `MakeEmployee, RemoveEmployee, MakeEmployer, RemoveEmployer.` Any user may call `UpdateEmployer and UpdateEmployee`. Furthermore, `workplace` declares a bidirectional propagation channel from/to `enterprise` and

---

[4] In short, homelessness is computationally (...as well as socially!) undesirable.

from/to **Employee** and **Employer**. Changes propagated from the **Test** context are specified as not to be considered within the **workspace** context.

```
TELL TOKEN workplace
      IN Context
      WITH
         contents
            - : contents(Employee  ⊕  Employer)
         lexicon
            - : /* constructed automatically by applying the definition of context
                   addition */
         authorP
            -:  { [ExpertUser, MakeEmployee],
                  [ExpertUser, RemoveEmployee],
                  [User, UpdateEmployee],
                  [ExpertUser, MakeEmployer],
                  [ExpertUser, RemoveEmployer],
                  [User, UpdateEmployer],[User, query(t)] }
         propagationFrom
            - :  {[self,true], [Employee,true],
                  [Employer,true], Test,false]}
         propagationTo
            - :  {[self,true], [Employee,true],
                  [Employer,true]}
         owner
            -: susan
END workplace
```

Fig. 8: Example of a context containing multiple families

This example demonstrated in which way the home metaphor can be extended to other useful categories of contexts. By analogy to home contexts, we defined an example of a *district* context where changes to a family's state are propagated back home. Carrying this idea further, one could define *town* contexts which are global collections of several homes, neighborhoods, and districts, having a common function within an information base.

5. Applications and Related Work

The context model presented above is intended to provide a unifying, generic framework for applications which rely on partitionings of an information base, such as (software engineering) workspaces, (database) views, (knowledge base) partitions and topics, and several aspects of versions and configurations. This section discusses related work on each of these notions along with demonstrating the ways in which contexts can be applied to support these notions. Since authorization is a key issue in all applications of contexts, we start by discussing related work on authorization models.

Authorization. The authorization model adopted for contexts follows the policy of discretionary, content-based models. Users, arranged in a role hierarchy, own contexts and may provide access authorizations to other users, contexts and transactions, based on the contents of their contexts. Our model shares essential features--most importantly the content-based nature--with the model suggested in [Bertino94]. Both models allow to express authorizations in terms of authorization predicates. This is in contrast to models that define all authorizations in the form of a matrix that does not allow one to examine the contents of an object for the purpose of deriving authorization decisions.

Like other advanced discretionary models, such as those reported in [Rabitti91] or [Jonscher93], our model is based on hierarchies of user roles (authorization subjects) as well as authorization objects. Two distinguishing features of our model are the flexible grain-size of authorization objects and the reliance on transaction hierarchies rather than on hierarchies of (primitive) access types. Since contexts themselves form units of authorization and can be constructed to contain contexts, such as those that form the components of a composite object or others that are versions, any arbitrary grain-size of authorization objects is accommodated. Note that this is not the case in authorization models designed for object-oriented data models since these employ a predefined hierarchy of authorization objects.

Workspaces. In the field of software development, commercial tools like Apollo DSEE [Leblang84] or SUN NSE [SUN88] provide basic support for workspaces. These tools, however, support authorization only at a very coarse level and are constrained to deal with change notification. In the field of object-oriented development, Wile and Allard [Wile86] propose worlds as a mechanism to combine the advantages of conventional file systems, such as the data sharing mechanisms, with object-bases. The resulting structures, worlds, describe clusters of information in an object-base. In [Motschnig-Pitrik90], perspectives have been proposed as one basic structuring and abstraction mechanism within SFW, an abstract structuring framework. Perspectives in SFW, like in the framework presented here, allow to filter out relevant information on conceptual entities while discarding irrelevant details. A recent approach to partitioning in the context of software development environments is the concept of "perspectives" as introduced in [Prevelakis93]. "Perspectives" are embedded in an object management system and come equipped with similar, powerful, set-based construction operations as do contexts.

The approach presented here, however, differs with respect to the basic data structure (called lexicon) used to keep track of information units scattered across contexts and with respect to handling authorization. Also, we suggest a generic model of change propagation that generalizes models of view updates in databases and extends change propagation facilities of workspaces models [Katz90]. Besides sharing, authorization, and change propagation, a workspace model must provide means for information hiding [Katz90]. Using the context mechanism, information hiding is achieved in one of two ways. First, authorization predicates can be used to "hide" (portions of) contexts with respect to other contexts, users, or transactions. Alternatively, users may be forced to work in contexts that have been created by a difference or masking operation thus blending out units to be hidden.

User Views. Database views constitute a well known technique of partitioning as well as integrating databases. Since the functionality of a view concept largely depends on the underlying data model, it is instructive to compare the modelling of views in the context framework with view mechanisms found in advanced data models such as those for object-oriented databases (OODBs) (see, for example [Scholl91], [Abiteboul91], [Bertino92], [Rundensteiner92], [dos Santos94], and [Motschnig-Pitrik96] for a survey). Contexts share with object preserving approaches to OO views (for example, [Scholl 91], [Rundensteiner92]) the advantage of not having to cope with the view update problem[5] [Gottlob88]. As discussed in [Scholl91], this is because objects in OO notations have an identity independent of their associated values. Thus, if the view definition language preserves object identity, view updates can unambiguously be traced back to their parent objects. It is apparent that the object preservation property holds for the operations used to create and extend contexts. This follows immediately from the fact that these operations manipulate the contents and the lexicon of contexts without ever creating new referents. The latter can only be created using operations that an information provides for the purpose of introducing objects into the information base.

In fact, views constitute but one constellation of contexts that can be developed into a pattern for designing contexts. We first suggest a basic pattern and then show along which dimensions it can be extended. According to a basic pattern, an IB includes one global context that plays the role of the global IB. GlobalCtx includes any arbitrary number of (directly or indirectly) derived contexts. Authorization predicates are specified such that the global context and all those derived contexts that model updateable views authorize any transaction to be performed on them. Derived contexts modelling non updateable views, however, are assigned an authorization predicate that only allows queries to be performed on them, i.e. `authorP(u,t) = query(t)`. Further, the owners of derived contexts modelling non updateable views must also be prevented from updating their contexts. Change propagation links are defined such that all changes from the global context are propagated to all derived contexts, but changes from contexts modelling updateable views are propagated only to the global context. An example of a global context called globalCtx and two view contexts, cv1 being updateable and cv2 not being updateable, is shown in figure 9. Variations on the basic pattern may, for example, tighten access rights. In such a case contexts modelling views could be further constrained by the authorization mechanism such as to realize the concept of view-based authorization that is known from classical database systems.

---

[5] In the relational model, views, in general, cannot be updated arbitrarily. This is because it is often ambiguous how to propagate view updates to updates on the base tuples. Thus, only views containing the key of their (single) base relation can be updated.

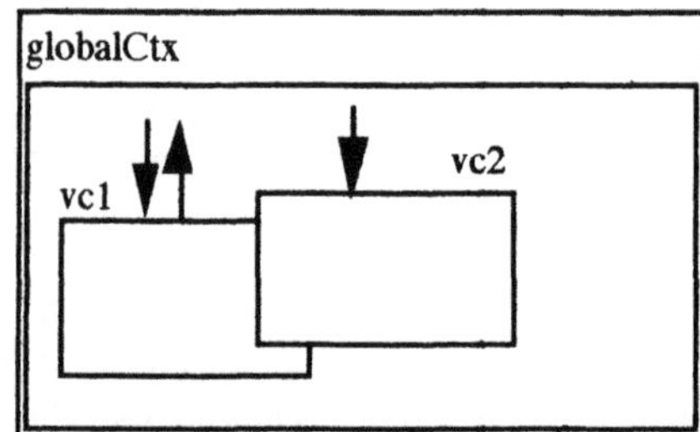

vc1: /* updateable view */
authorP(u,t) = true
vc2: /* non-updateable view */
authorP(u,t) = query(t),
authorP(owner,t) = query(t)

globalCtx:
propagationFrom(cProp,pred) = vc1(cProp)
propagationTo(cProp,pred) = cProp ∈ {vc1, vc2)

vc1:
propagationFrom(cProp,pred) =globalCtx(cProp)
propagationTo(cProp,pred) = globalCtx(cProp)

vc2:
propagationFrom(cProp,pred) = globalCtx (cProp)
propagationTo (cProp,pred) = false

Fig. 9: The use of contexts for modelling views in database systems as an example of a context-based design pattern.

Versions. The general way in which contexts serve to model versions is described in [Mylopoulos95]. In this place we would like to draw the reader's attention to the application of the particular embedding of the context mechanism into Telos. This is because advanced version modelling features tend to depend on the underlying information model [Katz90], [Ahmed91]. In order to illustrate this situation, below we show how two characteristic data model related issues can be mapped into Telos, extended to capture contexts. First recall that advanced approaches to version modelling consider the distinction of three categories of attributes:

* *invariant* attributes; these attributes may not be modified at the version level;
* *version-significant* attributes; the update of a *version-significant* attribute causes a new version of the respective object to be created;
* *nonversion-significant* attributes may freely be updated without causing a new version to be generated.

The semantics of all three attribute categories can be captured within Telos by the mechanism of attribute metaclasses. For this reason, an attribute metaclass `invariant` is defined that postulates that no authorization predicate that allows for a modification may be defined on an invariant attribute. Any attribute within a particular context that shall be classified as invariant, is then made an instances of the "invariant" metaclass by associating it with the *invariant* attribute category. In a similar vein, the metaclass `versionSignificant` is introduced to require the creation of a new version (via the `clone` operation), once an attribute assigned the `versionSignificant` category is updated. Finally, assume that the `nonversionSignificant` category is the default since it does not impose any restrictions.

Second, consider the distinction of three *version states* in terms of the manipulations allowed in each of these states [Ahmed91]:

* a version being in the *validated* state may not be updated; new versions may be derived from it;
* only nonversion-significant attributes of a version being in the *stable* state may be modified, new versions may be derived;
* all except invariant attributes may be modified in *transient* versions; new versions may not be derived.

```
TELL CLASS Versionable
   ISA Token
   IN SimpleClass
   WITH
      unique
        version#: VersioCode
        parent: VersionCode
END Versionable

TELL CLASS ValidatedContext
   ISA Context
   IN SimpleClass
   WITH
      integrityConstraint
        validated:      $ authorP(u,t): not
                        (t in UpdateTransaction) $
        noPropagation:  $ (propagationFrom(context,
            authorP(u,t)) = false) ∧
            (propagationTo(context,authorP(u,t) =
            false) $
END ValidatedContext

TELL TOKEN davidContext
   IN Versionable, ValidatedContext
   WITH
      contents
        - : {'david', unit7, 'davidContext', unit33}
      version#, versionSignificant
        - : 1.1
      parent, invariant
        - : 1.0
END david
```

Fig. 10: Example showing the realization of versionable objects via contexts in Telos

In Telos, the following restrictions, respectively, can be imposed on contexts in order to model states corresponding to those described above:

* in a *validated* context, no modifying transactions are authorized; no change propagation channels may be defined;
* in a *stable* context, modifying transactions are authorized only on nonversion-significant attributes; changes received via change propagation links may effect only nonversion-significant attributes;

* in a *transient* context, modifying transactions are not authorized on invariant attributes; transactions performing the "clone" operation are not authorized; changes received via change propagation links may not effect invariant attributes;

In order to demonstrate version modelling via contexts in Telos, figure 10 shows the class `validatedContext` as a subclass of the `Context`. Further, the class `Versionable` is introduced to allow for the instantiation of version objects with version numbers and links to their repective parents. Note that the class `validatedContext` implements constraints on authorization and change propagation. On the bottom of figure 10, the validated version of the context `davidContext` that encapsulates an instance of the class `Person` in form of a versionable context, is included in order to illustrate the interplay of the predefined classes used for the modelling of versions.

6. Conclusions

This paper suggests viewpoints as an abstraction mechanism which can be used to partition an information base into fragments, called contexts, according to varions criteria such as views, workspaces, versions and topics. This versatility of contexts is not surprising, since research in cognitive science has proved that viewing, essentially focusing on relevant information while discarding irrelevant issues, considerably aids understandability. These findings have been confirmed by linguistics. For linguists, the consideration of a context has for a long time been vital in order to allow one to derive the proper meaning of a word. The major contribution of this work has been to show that the viewpoint abstraction is amenable to sufficient formalization such as to be incorporated into current information models. In this respect it was shown how a generic framework for partitioning information bases into possibly overlapping contexts can be incorporated into the structurally object-oriented language Telos. In particular, the application of our framework to issues such as workspaces, database views, and features of version models has been discussed. It was shown in which ways these applications depend on the features designed into the context mechanism, such as operations for context construction , means to obtain relativity with respect to transaction executions, authorization and access control, encompassing the notion of privacy, and change propagation.

Furthermore, some applications of contexts were presented and illustrated by examples. In general, this work showed the feasibility of a unifying notion and accompanying support mechanisms for partitioning and focus of attention mechanisms which can be found in many areas of computer science. Further research will investigate guidelines for context construction that support the construction of pragmatically useful topologies of units that can be captured by contexts. Also, we are in the process of designing a metamodel for the viewpoint abstraction taking into account various factors that characterize viewpoints such as agents, biases, granularity levels, notations, and temporal aspects [Jarke96]. Furthermore, the adaptation of algorithms for efficient, incremental maintenance of contexts such as those proposed by [Dong92] and [Gupta93] will be addressed. We also intend to incorporate into Telos advanced, data-model dependent issues regarding version management, composite objects ([Kim89], [Ahmed91]), and authorization implication rules [Bertino94].

References

[Abiteboul91] Abiteboul, S., Bonner A.: "Objects and Views"; Proc. of ACM SIGMOD International Conference on the Management of Data, 238 - 247, 1991.

[Ahmed91] Ahmed R., Navathe S., B.: "Version Management of Composite Objects in CAD Databases"; Proc. ACM-SIGMOD Conference, 218-227, Denver, Colorado, May 1991.

[Anderson90] Anderson, J., Cognitive Psychology and its Implications, third edition, Freeman, 1990.

[Bertino92] Bertino E.: "A View Mechanism for Object-Oriented Databases"; EDBT 92'; Vienna, April 1992, Lecture Notes in Computer Science, 1992.

[Bertino94] Bertino E., Weigand H.. " An approach to authorization modeling in object-oriented database systems"; Data & Knowledge Engineering, 12 (1), 1-29, February 1994.

[Brodie84] Brodie, M.: "On the Development of Data Models"; in: Brodie, M., Mylopoulos, J., Schmidt J., W., (eds.), On Conceptual Modeling, Springer, 1984.

[Dong92] Dong G., Topor R.: "Incremental Evaluation of Datalog Queries"; ICDT 92', 1992.

[dos Santos 94] dos Santos C. S., Abiteboul S., Delobel C.: "Virtual schemas and bases"; in Jarke, Bubenko, Jeffery (ed.), Advances in Database Technology - EDBT '94, 81-94, Springer, 1994.

[Gerstl93] Gerstl P.: "Linking Linguistic and Non-Linguistic Information"; in R. P. van de Riet, R. A. Meersman, ed.: Linguistic Instruments in Knowledge Engineering", Elsevier Science Publishers, 1992.

[Gottlob88] Gottlob G., Paolini P., Zicari R.: "Properties and Update Semantics of Consistent Views"; ACM TODS, Vol.13, No.4, 486 - 521, December 1988.

[Gupta93] Gupta A., Mumick I., S., Subrahmanian V., S.: "Maintaining Views Incrementally"; SIGMOD 93', 1993.

[Hull87] Hull, R. and King, R., "Semantic Database Modelling: Survey, Applications and Research Issues", *ACM Computing Surveys 19(3),* September 1987.

[Jarke92] Jarke M., Mylopoulos J., .Schmidt J.W., Vassiliou Y.: "DAIDA: An Environment for Evolving Information Systems"; ACM Transactions on Information Systems, Vol.10, No.1, 1-15, January 1992.

[Jarke96] Jarke M., Gebhardt M., Nissen H. : personal communication.

[Jonscher93] Jonscher D., Dittrich K.,R.: "A Formal Security Model Based on an Object-Oriented Data Model"; Technical Report No. 93.41, Institut fuer Informatik, Universitaet Zuerich, November 1993.

[Katz90] Katz R., H.: "Toward a Unified Framework for Version Modeling in Engineering Databases"; ACM Computing Surveys, Vol.22, No.4, 375-408, Dec. 1990.

[Kim89] Kim, W., Bertino, E., Garza, J., F., "Composite Objects Revisited"; OOPSLA 89', 337-347, 1989.

[Koubarakis89] Koubarakis, M., Mylopoulos, J., Stanley, M., Borgida, A., "TELOS: Features and Formalization", KRR-TR-89-4, Univ. of Toronto, Feb. 1989.

[Leblang84] Leblang D., B., Chase R., P.: "Computer-aided Software Engineering in a Distributed Workstation Environment", Proc. of the ACM SIGPLAN/SIGSOFT Conf. on Pract Software Development Environments, ACM, New York, 104-112, April 1984.

[Levesque84] Levesque, H., A Logic of Implicit and Explicit Belief, Proc. of the National Conference on Artificial Intelligence, Austin, Texas, pp.198 - 202, Aug. 1984.

[Lewis76] Lewis, M., W., Anderson J., R., Interference with real world knowledge. *Cognitive Psychology*, 7, pp.311 - 335, 1976.

[Motschnig-Pitrik90] Motschnig-Pitrik R.: "A Framework for the Support of a Common Structural Level for Software, Database-, and Knowledge Based Systems"; *The Journal of Systems and Software*, North Holland, (12)12, 125-137, December 1990.

[Motschnig-Pitrik92] Motschnig-Pitrik R., Mylopoulos, J.: "Classes and Instances"; Int. Journal on Intelligent and Cooperative Information Systems, Vol.1, No.1, 61-92, 1992.

[Motschnig-Pitrik93] Motschnig-Pitrik R.: "The Semantics of Parts Versus Aggregates in Data/Knowledge Modelling"; Proceedings of the CAiSE'93, Lecture Notes in Computer Science No. 685, 352-373, Springer, 1993.

[Motschnig-Pitrik95] Motschnig-Pitrik R.: "An Integrating View on the Viewing Abstraction: Contexts and Perspectives in Software Development, AI, and Databases";.Journal of Systems Integration, Kluwer, 5 (1), 23-60, April 1995.

[Motschnig-Pitrik96] Motschnig-Pitrik R.: "Requirements and Analysis of View-Mechanisms for Object-Oriented Databases", *Information Systems,* to appear, 1996.

[Mylopoulos80] Mylopoulos J., Bernstein P., Wong H., "A Language Facility for Designing Interactive, Database-Intensive Applications"; *ACM Transactions on Database Systems*, 5(2), June 1980.

[Mylopoulos90] Mylopoulos, J., Borgida, A., Jarke, M. and Koubarakis, M., "Telos: Representing Knowledge About Information Systems", *ACM Transactions on Information Systems* , Vol.8, No.4, 325-362, Oct. 1990.

[Mylopoulos95] Mylopoulos J., Motschnig-Pitrik R.: "Partitioning Information Bases with Contexts"; Proc. of the 3rd International Conference on Cooperative Information Systems, 44-54, Vienna, May 1995

[Prevelakis93] Prevelakis V., Tsichritzis D.: "Perspectives on Software Development Environments"; Rolland C. et al. (editors), Proc. of the CAiSE '93, Paris, France, June 1993, Lecture Notes in Computer Science 685, Springer Verlag,1993.

[Rabitti91] Rabitti F., Bertino E., Kim W., Woelk D.: " A Model of Authorization for Next-Generation Database Systems", ACM TODS, 16 (1), 88-131, March 1991.

[Rothkopf66] Rothkopf E., Z., Learning from Written Instruction Materials: An Explanation of the Control of Inspection Behavior by Test-like Events, *American Educational Research Journal*, 3, pp.241 - 249, 1966.

[Rundensteiner92] Rundensteiner E.: "MultiView: A Methodology for Supporting Multiple Views in Object-Oriented Databases"; Proc. of the 18th International Conference on Very Large Databases (VLDB), Vancouver, 1992.

[Scholl91] Scholl M., H., Laasch C., Tresch M.: "Updateable Views in Object Oriented Databases"; Proc. of the 2nd Conf on DOOD, Munich, Dec. 1991.

[Schneider80] Schneider, P., F., Contexts in PSN, Proc. of the AI-CSCSI-SCEIO Conference, pp.71-78, Victoria, B.C., May 1980.

[Shaw84] Shaw M.: "The Impact of Modelling and Abstraction Concerns on Modern Programming Languages"; in: Brodie, M., Mylopoulos, J., Schmidt J., W., (ed.), On Conceptual Modeling, Springer Verlag, 1984.

[Smith77] Smith J.M., Smith D.C.P.: "Database Abstractions: Aggregation and Generalization"; ACM Trans. on Database Systems, Vol.2, No.2, 105-133, June 1977.

[Storey93] Storey V., C.: "Understanding Semantic Relationships"; in*Very Large Data Bases Journal*, Vol.2, No.4, 455-488, October 1993.

[SUN88] SUN Microsystems. "Introduction to the NSE.SUN Part No. 800-2362-1300, March 1988.

[Wand91] Wand Y., Weber R.: "A Unified Model of Software and Data Decomposition", Proc. of the 12th Annual International Conference on Information Systems, 101-110, New York, December 1991.

[Wile86] Wile, D., S., Allard, D., G., Worlds: an Organizing Structure for Object-Bases, ACM SIGPLAN Notices, Vol.22, No.1, 16-26, Jan. 1986.

[Yordon79] Yourdon E. and Constantine L.L.: "Structured Design - Fundamentals of a Discipline of Computer Program and Systems Design", Prentice Hall, 1979.

Relaxing the Instantiation Link: Towards a Content-Based Data Model for Information Retrieval

Youssef Lahlou Noureddine Mouaddib

CRIN-CNRS,
BP 239, Campus scientifique,
54506 Vandoeuvre-les-Nancy, France.
Tel : (33) 83 59 20 61.
Fax : (33) 83 41 30 79.
E-Mails : {lahlou, mouaddib}@loria.fr

Abstract

In this article, we define a semantic data model, where objects' structures are richer than those of their classes. This model is intended to be used in applications such as content-based information retrieval, whose particularity is the fact that objects do not have a predefined conceptual structure that can be fully abstracted in a class schema.

For this purpose, we relax the classical instantiation link between classes and objects, and rebaptize it the "realization" link.

Some of the problems that arise because of this relaxation are investigated, especially when it comes to querying the database. We present a query language for the model that respects the realization link.

The implementation of the model uses a class-based object-oriented model as a meta-model. All of our model concepts are classes in the meta-model, that will be instanciated, for each application of the model, into objects representing all the application features (classes, objects, attributes, queries, ...).

Key Words:

Semantic Model, Information Retrieval, Relaxed Instantiation, Realization Link, Query Language, Meta-Model.

Introduction

The present study focuses on data models for handling complex information (as commonly encountered in CAD-CAM and multimedia database systems), in comparison with Information Retrieval applications where objects are not very structured. The major task is to find a suitable mapping for information about real-world entities into machine representations which, from the user's conceptual viewpoint, ensures the least loss in expressiveness for the entities and enhances user expectations about the retrieval process.

The Relational Model [COD70] (along with its extensions [RKS88]) was the first data model to provide an efficient representation theory and a mechanism for query evaluation. It however turns out to be strongly limited when it comes to coping with complex information. One reason for this is that such a model disseminates semantic information over a large set of relations, the pertinence of which is not always obvious to the user. A second reason for this has to do with the value-based characteristic of the relational model [HUL89].

Semantic Data Models [HK87] arose as an attempt to overcome the inherent limitations of the relational theory. Their major contribution is to bridge the semantic gap between the user's perception of a real-world application and his conceptual and, to a lesser extent, physical representation of the application. Semantic models played an important role as a transition from relational models towards the new generation of object-oriented database environments [CAT94].

Unstructured objects such as texts and images handled by Information Retrieval systems cannot be modelled through only simple use of hierarchical structures, or abstraction into class structures. Common applications more often require object content indexing rather than grouping into well-structured classes. Furthermore, unstructured objects may also refer to structured objects and vice versa, especially in multimedia environments [WLK87].

The proposed model is able to cope with the representation and the manipulation of both unstructured objects as encountered in content-based models as in Information Retrieval, and structured objects as in semantic or object-oriented models.

Systems based on the relational data model and dedicated to cope with unstructured objects (such as images) are encountered in the current literature [HLMM92]. Our concern is to define a semantic data model, capable of responding to a wide range of specific problems related to data modelling in Information Retrieval. The model draws its conceptual inspiration from Semantic Data Models, and allows objects to have an individual flexible structure, rather than their classes'.

We thus relax the traditional instantiation link between an object and its class, and rebaptize it the "realization link". A class is no longer a set of objects having the same structure; it is only a minimal structure that have to be implemented by each object tied to it.

This loss of similarity between object and class structures induces some problems when it comes to querying the database. We explore such problems and show that they can be overcome by embedding our whole model into a higher (meta) level (structured) model.

Section 1 presents an overview of data models and information retrieval. Section 2 then sets out an informal definition of the concepts of our model while section 3 gives a formal specification of them. Section 4 presents the query specification language while section 5 describes an implementation of our model and an image application of it. We then conclude by setting out the future development envisaged for study.

1 Data Models and Information Retrieval

In this section, we explore the main approaches for modelling complex information in 1.1; we present the specificities of Information Retrieval applications in 1.2. This will lead us to give some motivations behind the definition of a new model, in 1.3.

1.1 Complex objects modelling

The relational model with its 1NF constraint provides a less suitable environment for handling complex information. As mentioned above, the pertinence of the associated sets of relations is not always obvious and natural to the user.

Attempts have been made to extend, improve and overcome the limitations of the relational model through the introduction of surrogates [COD79] and/or more complex data constructors than the flat classical relations [RKS88]. Advanced relational models (based on NF2 (e.g. nested) relations) provide a way of using the power of the relational calculus and algebra to deal with complex information. Such complex object models provide some abstractions for object modelling (aggregation, grouping, ...) whose effects on algebra and calculus are investigated. The inherent value-based approach does however represent a major limitation for complex modeling [HUL89].

Semantic Data Models arose as an attempt to bridge the gap between the application semantics and the logical machine representation of the data it carries. Even though every semantic model has its own concepts and characteristics, they all share some underlying concepts [HK87] such as:

- Classes of objects,
- Standard abstraction of object types (generalization, specialization, association, ...),
- Structured types of objects (aggregation, grouping),
- Semantic relationships between objects.

The Object-Oriented approach [KIM90, CAT94] combines advances in programming languages and knowledge representation in Artificial Intelligence. An object has a structure (static characteristics) and a behavior (associated procedures). These two aspects are encapsulated within the object and one can access the structure only through the associated behavior. Objects are abstracted into classes with each object being an instance of one or more classes. A class is thus a collection of objects sharing a common structure and behavior. The common structure is a collection of instance variables. An instance variable refers to an object class and has, as a value, an object of that class. The inheritance mechanism allows the transmission of structure and behavior from a generic class to specific ones. With the exception of object behavior, (the static part of) the object-oriented approach embraces the major characteristics of semantic data models.

1.2 Information Retrieval

In some applications, the manipulated objects are not easy to structure and group into classes, because of the different levels of description required and the possibility of introducing subjective descriptions. Text, image and other multimedia databases are examples of such applications.

In the preceding applications, a distinction is made between three description levels [KKL91]:

- the primitive data level: the contents of the physical representation of objects before any analysis or indexing (strings, pixel matrixes, ...),

- the contextual data level: this concerns object contexts (length or width of images, words count in texts, author name, ...),

- the semantic data level: this embraces information contained in, referenced or connotated by the objects. They are the most difficult to model and require several specific treatements. They may be distinguished into objective and subjective semantic data.

Text databases and text captioning of image databases can be indexed using key-words [HCK90, HLMM92, RS92], or subsequent to a natural language analysis step [SCH90].

Image databases contain more information than do simple text captions or key-words such as graphical items, subjective contexts (cultural connotations, ...) and so on. The authors in [HLMM92] further proposed the distinction between pre-iconographic, iconographic and iconological contents of an image. For the objective part, images can be seen [RS92] as component objects inter-linked by object-to-object relations.

In such database applications, the data model is more an indexing-retrieval model than a structuring model, inasmuch as object categorization (classification) into structures is all but feasible. Some approaches [GPVG89] try to overcome this problem by using a formal grammar instead of a structured model for the description of their objects.

1.3 Motivations

The central aim is to design a data-model capable of coping with two opposing paradigms involved in multimedia-like applications, where an object can either be structured or remain unstructured.

An image in an image database is difficult to stucture into a class (category) since it is practically impossible for the structure (contents) of an image to be totally defined at the conceptual level. All the same, an image may refer to other objects (contained therein) that are structured or need structuring simply because such objects, like cars, houses or horses are intrinsically structured.

To reach our main goal, we propose a data model which adapts to the two information retrieval contexts with facilities for representing classical paradigms of (structured) semantic data models (generalization, aggregation, ...) for the objects in the base, without necessarily imposing on the latter a predefined structure within their classes.

An object in our approach is a weak instantiation or a realization of a class, and has a specific individual structure. An image for instance, has some usual features (e.g size, photographer, date, ...) and additional individual components (e.g persons, flowers, ... whatever). Usual features are abstracted into an image class, that describes them (e.g. the size of an image is a real value). Individual features are defined within a particular image object.

2 Informal definition of the concepts

In this section, we informally present the main concepts of our model starting with object types, moving on through classes to objects. Particularly, we define our intent in relaxing the instantiation link between objects and classes.

2.1 Types and classes

According to the definitions given in [HUL89], we make a distinction between the two different paradigms of *type* and *class*.

An object type is the static definition of a structure. A structure is a distribution of data in a specific way. Each part of the distribution is in turn distributed in a certain way. A type is thus an intentional definition of objects. This definition is similar to classical definitions of object types [HUL89, AB88].

Types are organised into a lattice corresponding to a partial order; that is, a "sub-type" holds the complete definition of a "super-type" and augments it with additional features. Since types are nothing more than structure definitions, wherever a super-type can be used (in the definition of other types), it represents itself along with all its sub-types.

On the other hand, a class is usually a set of objects (instances) of the same type, that is the type of the class itself [HUL89]. In our model a class is not a set of objects. A class is the association of a class name and an object type. The definition of a class is the assignment of a name to an object type and some attribute names to each part of the static structure of the type.

Classes are organized into a lattice of generalization / specialization links. They can therefore be refined and incrementally defined using more specific constraints and new attributes.

2.2 Objects

An object is the machine representation of a real universe (of discourse) entity. It has a unique and exclusive identifier and a structure that involves other objects. This incremental definition of objects referencing each other assumes that there exists a collection of primitive objects, having no references to others and called values or terminal objects.

Realization is a mechanism that links an object to a class. In other words, an object can never exist without a class to which it is tied: in this sense the object is said to be a realization of the associated class.

The mechanism of realization can be seen as the operation of giving a value to the attributes of the class by assigning an object to each of them.

The possibility is then left for objects to have in turn other additional objects in their structure, in addition to those fixed by the class. This enables objects to have an individual composition rather than their abstraction into classes. From this comes the improved flexibility and extensiveness of the model.

Thus, the link between an object and its class is different from the traditional "instantiation" link, where an instance of a class has exactly the structure abstracted in that class.

According to the definition of super-types and sub-types, we can characterize the realization mechanism by the fact that the type of the realization (the object) is a sub-type of the class type, since it holds information and structure, additional to that of the class type.

As we stated in paragraph 1.3, an image object holds more information than does the image class, to which it is tied: flowers, hourses, ... (or whatever appears in the image), are added to the common image features e.g. size, photographer, ... etc.

2.3 Overview

It follows from the preceding presentation that our model has two related levels of abstraction, a concrete level (objects) and a conceptual level (classes, types).

For the purpose of taking the realization mechanism into account, we use a third level of abstraction called the meta-level. In this level, all the concepts of the model (classes, objects, ...) are described in terms of meta-classes, as is summarized in figure 1. This figure points out the strategy of implementation of the model within a class-based object-oriented model, such as that presented in [CAT94].

2.4 Queries

Queries are intentional expressions on the structures of objects satisfying them. For this purpose, the query specifier is aware, at query specification time, of the structures of the classes (s)he will use in his (her) query, knowing that instances

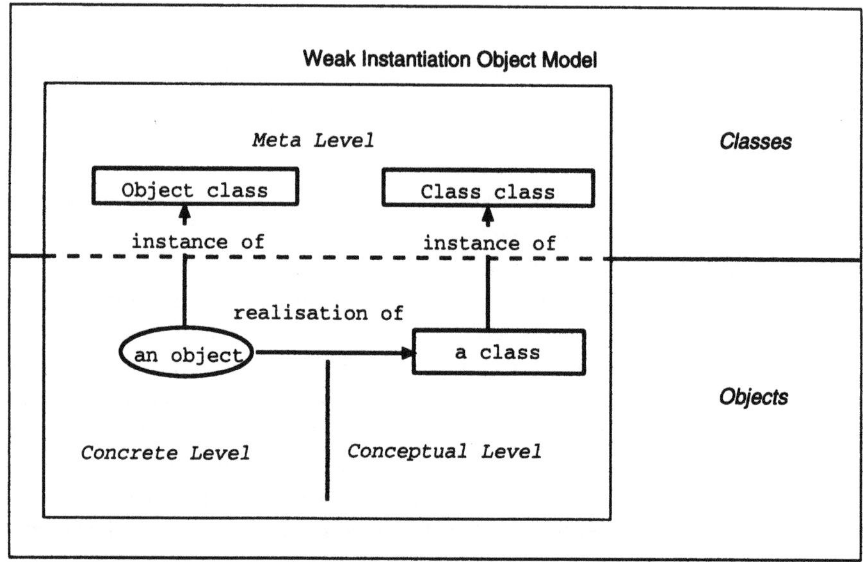

Figure 1: The realization mechanism

of those classes would have the same structure. The query only specifies some values for the structures.

In our model, little about object structures is known at the conceptual level (that of classes). Only the minimal structure of objects tied to a class (by the realization mechanism), i.e., the class structure, is known. Thus, queries have to deal with the additional structure of objects in order to fully make use of the expressiveness of the model. The query language must provide the user with features allowing her (him) to query both the class structure and the individual structure of objects.

3 Formal definition of the concepts

The main features of our model are types (cf. 3.1), classes (cf. 3.2) and objects (cf. 3.3). We give a formal definition for each of them and describe in 3.4 what a database is, according to our model. Finally, we exhibit some problems related to the flexible nature of the model.

3.1 Types

3.1.1 Definition

We assume the existence of some *terminal types*, corresponding, for example, to basic data types: integer (I), real (R), string(S), ... and a special type, called the "empty type" and noted $\top$.

We refer to $\mathcal{T}$ as the set of all object types, which are recursively defined as follows:

- terminal types and the empty type are types,
- if t is a type, then t^* is also a type, called a *set type*,
- if $t_1, ..., t_n$ are types, then $t_1 \times ... \times t_n$ is also a type, called a *tuple type*.

Examples:
Let R, S and I be terminal types.
$R \times S^* \times I$ and $(R \times I)^*$ are types.

3.1.2 Partial order on types

Assuming that its restriction to terminal types is known, we recursively define a partial order $\leq_\tau$ on $\mathcal{T}$ by:

- $\forall t \in \mathcal{T}, t \leq_\tau \top$; in other words, $\top$ is the greatest element of $(\mathcal{T}, \leq_\tau)$
- if $\exists i \in [1, n], t_i \leq_\tau t$ then $t_1 \times ... \times t_n \leq_\tau t$
- $t^* \leq_\tau t'^*$ iff $t \leq_\tau t'$
- if $t = t_1 \times ... \times t_n$ and $t' = t'_1 \times ... \times t'_{n'}$, then $t \leq_\tau t'$ iff:
  - $n' \leq n$
  - $t_i \leq_\tau t'_i$ for $1 \leq i \leq n'$

Example:
$R \times S^* \times I \leq_\tau R \times I$.
Indeed, $R \times S^* \times I = R \times (S^* \times I)$,
and we have: $R \leq_\tau R$ and $S^* \times I \leq_\tau I$.

3.2 Classes

3.2.1 Definition

Object classes, are members of the set $\mathcal{C}$; they are defined as follows:

- a *terminal class* is defined by the assignment of a class name c to a terminal type,
- a *simple class* is defined by a name c and a list $\langle a_1 : c_1, ..., a_n : c_n \rangle$, possibly empty and called the structure of c ; we note $c = \langle a_1 : c_1, ..., a_n : c_n \rangle$; a_i are attribute names while c_i are classes ; if the structure of a simple class c is empty, then c is said to be an "empty class",
- a *set class* c^* is defined for each simple class c.

We assume for the purpose of this study that the recursive definition of classes is cycle free. In other words, a class c can not refer to a class c' that is a specific class of c (in the sense of the inheritance graph defined in 3.2.3).

Examples:
$Integer, String, Real$, ..., terminal classes
$Date = \langle day : Integer, month : Integer, year : Integer \rangle$
$Person = \langle name : String, first\_name : String, age : Integer \rangle$
$Image = \langle photograph : Person,\ date : Date,\ location : String,\ characteristics : String^* \rangle$

3.2.2 Associated type for a class

To each class c, we associate an object type $[\![c]\!]$, recursively defined as follows:

- terminal classes:
  The associated type of a terminal class is the terminal type upon which the class is defined,
- simple classes:
  If $c = \langle a_1 : c_1, ..., a_n : c_n \rangle$, then $[\![c]\!] = [\![c_1]\!] \times ... \times [\![c_n]\!]$; if $n = 0$ then $[\![c]\!] = \top$,
- set classes:
  $[\![c^*]\!] = [\![c]\!]^*$.

Example:

$$
\begin{aligned}
[\![Image]\!] &= [\![Person]\!] \times [\![Date]\!] \times [\![String]\!] \times [\![String^*]\!] \\
&= ([\![String]\!] \times [\![String]\!] \times [\![Integer]\!]) \times \\
&\quad ([\![Integer]\!] \times [\![Integer]\!] \times [\![Integer]\!]) \times [\![String]\!] \times [\![String]\!]^* \\
&= (S \times S \times I) \times (I \times I \times I) \times S \times S^*
\end{aligned}
$$

3.2.3 Inheritance link between classes

The inheritance link between classes is a partial order, noted $\leq_\gamma$, such that:

- its restriction to terminal classes is deduced from the partial order on the associated terminal types: $c_1 \leq_\gamma c_2$ iff $[\![c_1]\!] \leq_\tau [\![c_2]\!]$,
- it is *user defined* for simple classes, in such a way that:
  if $c_1 = \langle a_{11} : c_{11}, ..., a_{1n_1} : c_{1n_1} \rangle \leq_\gamma c_2 = \langle a_{21} : c_{21}, ..., a_{2n_2} : c_{2n_2} \rangle$, then:
  - $n_2 \leq n_1$,
  - there exists an injection σ from $[1, n_2]$ to $[1, n_1]$, called "attributes renaming", such that $\forall i \in [1, n_2], c_{1\sigma(i)} \leq_\gamma c_{2i}$,

- $c_1^* \leq_\gamma c_2^*$ iff $c_1 \leq_\gamma c_2$.

If $c_1 \leq_\gamma c_2$, we will say that c_1 inherits from c_2.

Example:
If we have:
$Employee = \langle ssn : String, name : String, first\_name : String, age : Integer$
$salary : Real, addresses : Address^* \rangle$,
with:
$Address = \langle number : Integer, street : String, zip\_code : Integer, town : String \rangle$,
then:
$Employee \leq_\gamma Person$, given the renaming function:

$$\begin{array}{rrcl} \sigma : & [1,3] & \longrightarrow & [1,6] \\ & 1 & \longmapsto & 2 \\ & 2 & \longmapsto & 3 \\ & 3 & \longmapsto & 4 \end{array}$$

because:
$c_{1\sigma(1)} = c_{12} = String \leq_\gamma String = c_{21}$,
$c_{1\sigma(2)} = c_{13} = String \leq_\gamma String = c_{22}$,
$c_{1\sigma(3)} = c_{14} = Integer \leq_\gamma Integer = c_{23}$.

The role of the σ function is to take into account the possible renamings and reorganisations of attributes across the inheritance link, particularily in the case of multiple inheritance. For the sake of simplicity, we assume from now on, without loss of generality, that this function equals the identity function.

3.3 Objects

3.3.1 Definition

An object $o = (i, s)$, is an element of $\mathcal{O}$ (the set of all objects), and is defined by a unique and exclusive identifier $i(o) \in \mathcal{I}$ (where $\mathcal{I}$ is the set of all object identifiers) and a structure $s(o)$.

We distinguish three kinds of objets according to the nature of their structure:

- *terminal objects*, where the structure is a value associated to a given terminal type;
- *simple objects*, where the structure is a list $\langle a_1 : o_1, ..., a_n : o_n \rangle$, possibly empty, where a_i are attribute names and o_i are component objects; a special attribute name is "X", it will be used whenever no semantics can be attached to the role that the component plays in the composition of the main object; if $s(o)$ is the empty list, o is called an "empty object" ;
- *set objects*, where the structure is a set $\{o_1, ..., o_p\}$, o_i being objects.

Examples: We give some examples of objects' structures.

$s(o_1) = \langle photograph : o_2, date : o_3, location : o_4, characteristics : o_5,$
$\quad X : o_6, X : o_7\rangle$
$s(o_2) = \langle name : o_8, first\_name : o_9, age : o_{10}\rangle$
$s(o_3) = \langle day : o_{11}, month : o_{12}, year : o_{13}\rangle$
$s(o_4) = "Paris"$
$s(o_5) = \{o_{14}, o_{15}\}$
$s(o_6) = \langle name : o_{16}, first\_name : o_{17}, age : o_{18}, salary : o_{19}, addresses : o_{20}\rangle$
$s(o_7) = \langle name : o_{21}, first\_name : o_{22}, age : o_{23}\rangle$

$s(o_8) = "Martin"$	$s(o_{16}) = "Meunier"$
$s(o_9) = "Georges"$	$s(o_{17}) = "Jean"$
$s(o_{10}) = 65$	$s(o_{18}) = 50$
$s(o_{11}) = 14$	$s(o_{19}) = 7645, 34$
$s(o_{12}) = 5$	$s(o_{20}) = \{o_{24}, o_{25}\}$
$s(o_{13}) = 1968$	$s(o_{21}) = "Duchemin"$
$s(o_{14}) = "portrait"$	$s(o_{22}) = "Emile"$
$s(o_{15}) = "black \,\&\, white"$	$s(o_{23}) = 23$

$s(o_{24}) = \langle number : o_{26}, street : o_{27}, zip\_code : o_{28}, town : o_{29}\rangle$
$s(o_{25}) = \langle number : o_{30}, street : o_{31}, zip\_code : o_{28}, town : o_{29}\rangle$
$s(o_{26}) = 17$
$s(o_{27}) = "Rue\ des\ lilas"$
$s(o_{28}) = 54000$
$s(o_{29}) = "Nancy"$
$s(o_{30}) = 19$
$s(o_{31}) = "Rue\ des\ roses"$

3.3.2 Associated type for an object

To each object o, we associate an object type $[\![o]\!]$, recursively defined as follows:

- Terminal objects:
  The type associated to a terminal object o is the terminal type to which is tied the value $s(o)$.
- Simple objects:
  If $s(o) = \langle a_1 : o_1, ..., a_n : o_n\rangle$, then $[\![o]\!] = [\![o_1]\!] \times ... \times [\![o_n]\!]$. If $n = 0$ then $[\![o]\!] = \top$.
- Set objects:
  If $s(o) = \{o_1, ..., o_p\}$, then:

  $$[\![o]\!] = (\sup_{i=1}^{p}[\![o_i]\!])^*$$

  where *sup* means the upper bound in the sens of the partial order on object types ($\leq_\tau$).

Remark:
The latter definition is consistent, since $(\mathcal{T}, \leq_\tau)$ admits a greatest element: $\top$.

3.3.3 Realization link

The realization link is a binary relation, noted $\leftarrow$, defined on the set $\mathcal{O} \times \mathcal{C}$, in such a way that:

- if o is a terminal object and c is a terminal class of the same type, then $o \leftarrow c$,
- its restriction to the cartesian product of the set of simple objects by the set of simple classes, is *user defined*, in such a way that if $o \leftarrow c$ and $c = \langle a_1 : c_1, ..., a_n : c_n \rangle$, then:
  - $s(o) = \langle a_1 : o_1, ..., a_{n'} : o_{n'} \rangle$, with $n' \geq n$,
  - $\forall i \in [1, n], o_i \leftarrow c_i$,
- if o is a set object such that $s(o) = \{o_1, ..., o_p\}$, then $o \leftarrow c^*$ iff $\forall i \in [1, p], o_i \leftarrow c$,
- if $o \leftarrow c$ and $c \leq_\gamma c'$, then $o \leftarrow c'$.

If $o \leftarrow c$, we will say that o realizes c.

Assuming this definition, we can exhibit the fundamental following rule:

$$\boxed{\text{If } o \leftarrow c, \text{ then } [\![o]\!] \leq_\tau [\![c]\!]}$$

Proof:

See appendix A.

Examples:
From the previous object and class examples, we have:
$o_1 \leftarrow \mathit{Image}$, $o_3 \leftarrow \mathit{Date}$
$o_2 \leftarrow \mathit{Person}$, $o_6 \leftarrow \mathit{Employee}$, $o_6 \leftarrow \mathit{Person}$
$o_4 \leftarrow \mathit{String}$, $o_5 \leftarrow \mathit{String}^*$, $o_{10} \leftarrow \mathit{Integer}$, $o_{19} \leftarrow \mathit{Real}$
$o_{20} \leftarrow \mathit{Address}^*$, $o_{24} \leftarrow \mathit{Address}$, $o_{25} \leftarrow \mathit{Address}$

Remark:
In order to provide objects with richer structures than their classes', we separately defined the type and class paradigms. In contrast to the definition given in [HUL89], a class is not a set of objects in our model. It references a type that is more generic (in the sens of the partial order on types) than that of all its realizations (objects).

3.4 Databases

A database according to our model, is a triple $((\mathcal{C}, \leq_\gamma), \mathcal{O}, \leftarrow)$, where $(\mathcal{C}, \leq_\gamma)$ is a set of classes, latticed by a partial order, representing the inheritance link; $\mathcal{O}$ is a set of objects and $\leftarrow$ is a binary relation on $\mathcal{O} \times \mathcal{C}$ representing the realization link.

One can notice that this definition involves both the notions of database schema (in the class set and its partial order) and database instances (in fact realizations, in the object set and the realization relation).

As mentioned earlier, the user defines the classes, the objects, the partial order on simple classes and the realization link on simple objects. The remainder of the database structure is deduced, according to the previous inheritance and realization rules.

3.5 Discussion

We shall point out some advantages of the realization link in 3.5.1, but also note some drawbacks in 3.5.2.

3.5.1 Advantages from relaxing the instantiation link

- The realization link frees objects from the imposed structure constraint induced by their class.
- In modelling some kinds of applications (particularly in the Information Retrieval field), the database designer is not always able to catch the exact structure of all classes, but only a part of it, representing a minimal stable and standard structure. The advantage of the realization link resides in allowing objects afterwards to have individual structures that might be further abstracted into the class, if the designer so decides.
- When exceptions are encountered among objects, i.e. when some objects have several different properties compared to their classes, the realization link prevents users from turning to some artificial design solutions to deal with such problems, like creating lots of sub-classes, one for each exception.
- The realization link is a good "design tool" when dealing with evolutionary applications, where objects' structures are often time-changing, in a way that can not be predicted in advance (non-stable life cycle). Such phenomena are often encountered in CAD-CAM or architectural applications. The realization link allows objects to evolve quite independently from their classes.

  Besides, it provides a basis for a possible "reverse engineering", which allows one to redefine class structures, once objects have stopped evolving. This is a classical problem in evolutionary databases.

3.5.2 Some drawbacks from the realization link

The main problems arising from the model we defined earlier appear when it comes to querying the database or specifying integrity constraints among it. In classical structured models (relational, semantic, object-oriented), query formulation or integrity constraints specification are based on class structures, assuming that objects only value those structures with other objects or values.

In the remainder of this paper, we will focus on query formulation and processing, and defer integrity constraint investigation to a later study.

So, when querying a database for 50 years old employees, living in Nancy, the user is aware *a priori* of the existence of a class named *Employee*, representing employees and having an attribute giving their age (say *age*) and an other giving the town they live in (say *address*). The query can then be expressed by the set:

$$\{o \in Employee, o.age = 50 \wedge o.address.town = "Nancy"\}$$

As is the case in structured data models, this kind of query can also be specified in our model, since each object realizing the *Employee* class has an *age* attribute, and an *address* attribute, and each object realizing the class *Address* has a *town* attribute. In order to fully make use of the power of the realization link, queries have to deal also with the additional part of object structures that is not in their class structures. But this structure is not known at the conceptual level; for instance, the o_1 object, realizing the *Image* class uses, in its (additional individual) structure, the o_6 object, realizing the *Employee* class. This is not a mandatory (predictable) reference in the *Image* class.

The main question is how to make the user be able to specify such queries as images of 50 years old employees, living in Nancy?

In our opinion, an easy solution is to formulate queries the same way as objects: a part tied to class structures and an other tied to individual contents.

The first part comprises some criteria expressible at the conceptual level (i.e., involving properties from the target class). The second part is a set of sub-queries that have to be satisfied by component objects (mandatory and additional) of the main object satisfying the query. This strategy makes a good use of the expressive power of our model.

4 Queries

In this section, we define in 4.2 a model of queries suited to our data model. We first give some basic notions in 4.1.

4.1 Basic notions

For specifying queries, we need to define some preliminary notions, such as valid paths and path destinations for classes and objects.

A *path* is a list of attributes names, separated by points; e.g. *address.town* or *age.salary*.

This definition yields arbitrary paths; thus, we define valid paths for classes and objects, and along with it, we define valid path destinations, noted $Dest(c,p)$ (for a class c) and $Dest(o,p)$ (for an object o).

4.1.1 Valid paths and their destinations for a class

For obvious reasons, we define these notions only for simple and set classes (not for terminal classes).

- Simple Classes:
  - a path of length 1: $p = a$, is valid for a class $c = \langle a_1 : c_1, ..., a_m : c_m \rangle$ iff $\exists j \in [1,m], a_j = a$. Then we have: $Dest(c,p) = c_j$,
  - a path $p = a_1...a_n$ ($n > 1$), is valid for a class c, iff $p' = a_1...a_{n-1}$ is valid for c and $p'' = a_n$ is valid for $Dest(c,p')$. Then we have: $Dest(c,p) = Dest(Dest(c,p'),p'')$.
- Set classes:
  a path is valid for c^* iff it is valid for c ; and we have: $Dest(c^*,p) = (Dest(c,p))^*$.

<u>Example:</u>

$$\begin{aligned} Dest(Image, date.month) &= Dest(Dest(Image, date), month) \\ &= Dest(Date, month) \\ &= Integer. \end{aligned}$$

4.1.2 Valid paths and their destinations for an object

A path p is valid for an object o, iff $\exists c \in C$, $o \leftarrow c$ and p is valid for c. Now, let us define the destination of a valid path for an object.

- Paths of length 1:
  - Simple objects: $Dest(o,a) = o.a$: the object corresponding to attribute a in $s(o)$.
  - Set objects: $Dest(o,a) = o'$ such that: $s(o') = \{Dest(o_i,a), o_i \in s(o)\}$.
    <u>Remark:</u>
    In this case, we create a new object not already existing in the object base. It is the only case of automatic object creation.
- Paths of length $n > 1$:
  $Dest(o, a_1...a_n) = Dest(Dest(o, a_1...a_{n-1}), a_n)$.

<u>Example:</u>

$$\begin{aligned} Dest(o_1, photograph.name) &= Dest(Dest(o_1, photograph), name) \\ &= Dest(o_2, name) \\ &= o_8. \end{aligned}$$

4.2 The query model

In 4.2.1, we define the general syntax of a query, and in 4.2.2 its semantics.

4.2.1 Query syntax

A query is a quadruple $q = (c, Cl, Q, p)$ where:

- c is a class, called *target* of q,
- $Cl = \{cl_1, ..., cl_n\}$ is a set of clauses, called *criteria* of q,
- $Q = \{q_1, ..., q_m\}$, is a set of queries, called *sub-queries* of q,
- p is a valid path for c, called *projection* of q.

Criteria, sub-queries and/or projection may be empty.

A clause is a disjunction of literals: $cl_i = l_{i1} \vee ... \vee l_{iq_i}$.

A literal l_{ij} takes one of the following forms:

- $p = p'$ or $p \neq p'$, where p and p' are valid paths for c, such that $Dest(c,p) \leq_\gamma Dest(c,p')$ or $Dest(c,p') \leq_\gamma Dest(c,p)$,
- $p = o_0$ or $p \neq o_0$, where p is a valid path for c and o_0 is a terminal object, such that $o_0 \leftarrow Dest(c,p)$,
- $p \in p'$ or $p \notin p'$, where p and p' are valid paths for c, such that $Dest(c,p') \leq_\gamma (Dest(c,p))^*$ or $(Dest(c,p))^* \leq_\gamma Dest(c,p')$,
- $o_0 \in p$ or $o_0 \notin p$, where p is a valid path for c and o_0 is a terminal object, such that $Dest(c,p) = c'^*$ and $o_0 \leftarrow c'$,
- $p \subseteq p'$ or $p \not\subseteq p'$, where p and p' are valid paths for c, such that $Dest(c,p) = c'^*$ and $Dest(c,p') = c''^*$, having $c' \leq_\gamma c''$ or $c'' \leq_\gamma c'$,
- $o_0 \subseteq p$ or $o_0 \not\subseteq p$, where p is a valid path for c such that $Dest(c,p) = c'^*$, and o_0 is a set object, the structure of which is a set of terminal objects, and such that $o_0 \leftarrow c'^*$.

If $c = c'^*$, then we define: $q_* = (c', Cl, Q, p)$.

Before giving the formal semantics of such queries, we outline their informal meaning: query q looks for objects realizing class c, satisfying all clause members of Cl and referencing, for each query member of Q, at least one object resulting from this query. The result of q is the set of path p destinations for all objects satisfying those three conditions.

In consequence, as was the case for classes, the recursive definition of queries must be cycle free.

Examples:
The query $q_1 = (c_1, Cl_1, Q_1, p_1)$ looks for 50 years old employees, living in Nancy.

$c_1 = Employee$
$Cl_1 = \{age = o_{01}, o_{02} \in addresses.town\}$, with $s(o_{01}) = 50$ and $s(o_{02}) =$ "Nancy"
$Q_1 = \emptyset$
p_1 is empty.

The query $q_2 = (c_2, Cl_2, Q_2, p_2)$ looks for images of such employees.
$c_2 = Image$
$Cl_2 = \emptyset$
$Q_2 = \{q_1\}$
p_2 is empty.

The realization link is taken into account in our query specification language, within the set Q, that specifies criteria on all referenced objects of the main object. Conceptual knowledge on objects, coming from their class structure is used in the set Cl.

Thus, a query uses more structures than only those of the target class.

4.2.2 Query semantics

We define the formal semantics of a query $q = (c, Cl, Q, p)$ as being an application μ_q, defined on the powerset of $\mathcal{O}$ as follows:

$$\begin{array}{lll} \mu_q : \mathcal{P}(\mathcal{O}) & \longrightarrow & \mathcal{P}(\mathcal{O}) \\ \quad O & \longmapsto & \mu_q(O) = \{Dest(o,p), o \in O \wedge o \text{ satisfies } q\}. \end{array}$$

The satisfaction of a query by an object is defined as follows:

- A simple object o such that $s(o) = \langle a_1 : o_1, ..., a_n : o_n \rangle$ satisfies a query $q = (c, Cl, Q, p)$, iff the three following conditions are satisfied:
  - $o \leftarrow c$.
  - The evaluation of all clause members of Cl within o leads to True. This evaluation is done in an intuitive way, according to the kind of each literal in the clause. Within a literal, a path p is evaluated to $Dest(o, p)$.
  - $\forall q' = (c', Cl', Q', p') \in Q, \exists i \in [1, n], \exists o' \in \mathcal{O}$, o' satisfies $q' \wedge Dest(o', p') = o_i$.
- A set object o satisfies a query q, iff $\forall o' \in s(o), o'$ satisfies q_*.

<u>Examples:</u>
Object o_6 satisfies query q_1 and as a consequence, object o_1 satisfies query q_2.

5 Implementation

To validate our approach, we developped a prototype within the Smalltalk-80 object oriented programming environment [GR83], on a SPARC station.

Each of the model concepts (objects, classes, attributes, queries, ...) has been represented by a class in Smalltalk, that is a *meta-class* in our model. Accurate methods are attached to each class. Those methods implement the "philosophy" of our model, by describing the behaviour of each concept.

The object-oriented data model of smalltalk is then used as a *meta-model* for our model.

Each feature of our model (an object, a class, a query, ...) is represented as an object in Smalltalk, that is a *meta-object* in our model. It is an instance of the related meta-class (cf. figure 1).

To the concepts presented throughout the paper, we added two important features:

- the distinction between objects and values; that is terminal objects are treated as values (no identifiers);
- the capability to manage semantic relationships between objects; e.g. a person is *on* a boat, a house is *in the back* of an image.

Those features have not been specified in this paper, in order to define the realization mechanism (that is the main originality of our model), in a simple and clear way. But they are also integrated into the mechanism.

The prototype allows one to:

- create, modify or delete classes and relationships, within a *conceptual level browser* (cf. figure 2),
- create, modify or delete objects, within a *concrete level browser* that has the same look as the precedent,
- create, modify or delete queries, within a *query browser* that also has the same look as the conceptual browser.

In the actual version, queries are evaluated among the object base, according to the query semantics presented in 4.2.2, extended to capture relationships.

We have experimented our approach on an image database containing images of Paris in the 1900's, that has also served as an example database for the RIVAGE system, also developped in our team [HCK90]. Figure 3 gives the results of a query looking for images containing two aquatic vehicules, side by side.

When queries address images, the resulting objects (images) are visualized using an image viewer, that has been developped for the RIVAGE system [CHA93] (figure 3).

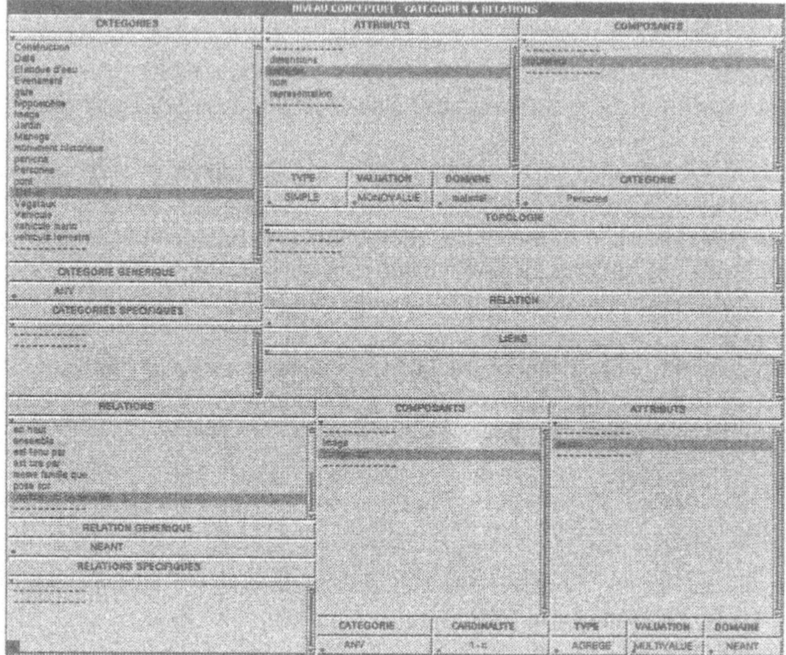

Figure 2: Conceptual browser

This experimentation clearly showed that queries on image databases can be extended to capture complex objects and semantic links in image contents, rather than the simple use of keywords.

Conclusion

We have presented a data model intended to model and query complex objects having a strong individual structure, as those usually encountered in Content-Based Information Retrieval (images, texts, ...).

One particularity of the model is to provide objects related to a given class with an extra individual structure, in addition to that of the class (common to all its related objects).

The classical instantiation link between an object and its class has been relaxed and rebaptized "realization link", in order to clearly outline the gained freedom for objects, with regard to their classes.

We have also presented a query specification language suited to our data model and showed that all the model concepts can be represented as meta-classes in a class-based object-oriented model.

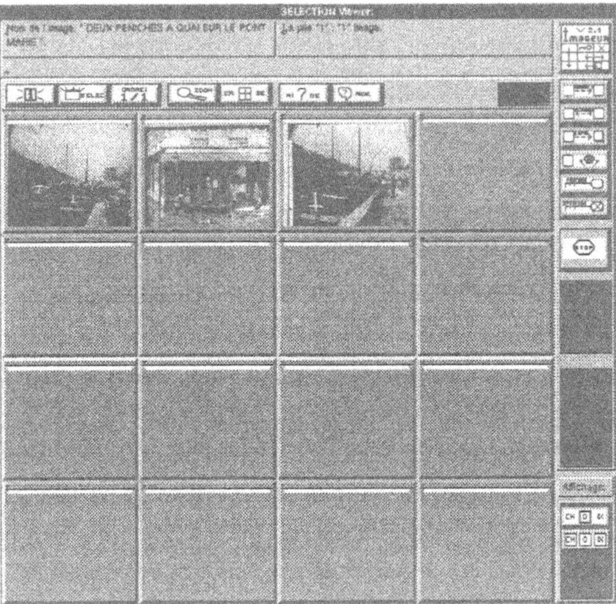

Figure 3: Image browser

The realization link shows itself particularily useful in the Content-Based Information Retrieval field, as has been stated in some of our previous research [MLH94, LAH95].

The perspectives envisaged for this work are to explore integrity constraints specification and maintainance, according to our model features. In classical databases, integrity constraint specification, like query specification, uses some conceptual knowledge about class structures, to specify criteria among objects. Since in our model, objects have richer structures than their classes, it would be interesting to use the additional individual object structures in constraint specification, as we have done for queries.

References

[AB88] S. ABITEBOUL and C. BEERI. On the power of languages for the manipulation of complex objects. Technical Report RR-0846, INRIA, 1988.

[CAT94] R.G.G. CATTELL, editor. *The Object Database Standard: ODMG-93.* Morgan Kaufmann, 1994.

[CHA93] D. CHAFFIOL. Rivage et imageur. Rapport de stage ESIAL 2, Univ. Nancy I, 1993.

[COD70] E.F. CODD. A relational data model for large shared data banks. *Communications of the ACM*, 13(6):377–387, 1970.

[COD79] E.F. CODD. Extending the relational model to capture more meaning. *ACM Transactions on Database Systems*, 4(4):397–434, 1979.

[GPVG89] M. GYSSENS, J. PAREDAENS, and D. VAN GUCHT. A grammar-based approach towards unifying hierarchical data models (extended abstract). In *ACM-SIGMOD'89*, pages 263–272, 1989.

[GR83] A. GOLDBERG and D. ROBSON. *Smalltalk80: The Language and its Implementation.* Addison-Wesley, 1983.

[HCK90] G. HALIN, M. CREHANGE, and P. KEREKES. Machine-learning and vectorial matching for an image retrieval model : Exprim and the rivage system. In *ACM-SIGIR'90*, pages 99–114, 1990.

[HK87] R. HULL and R. KING. Semantic database modelling: Survey, applications and research issues. *ACM Computing Surveys*, 19(3):201–260, 1987.

[HLMM92] J.N.D. HIBLER, C.H.C. LEUNG, K.L. MANNOCK, and N. MWARA. A system for content-based storage and retrieval in an image database. In *Image Storage and Retrieval Systems, IS&T / SPIE Symposium on Electronic Imaging - Science and technology, SPIE'92*, pages 80–92, San Jose, California, 1992.

[HUL89] R. HULL. Four views of complex objects: A sophisticate's introduction. In *Nested relations and complex objects in databases*, pages 87–116. Springer-Verlag, Lecture Notes in Computer Science, No 361, 1989.

[KIM90] W. KIM. Object-oriented databases: definitions and research directions. *IEEE Transactions on Knowledge and Data Engineering*, 2(3):327–341, 1990.

[KKL91] D.A. KEIM, K.C. KIM, and V. LUM. A friendly and intelligent approach to data retrieval in a multimedia dbms. In *Database and Expert Systems Applications, DEXA'91*, pages 102–111, Berlin, Germany, 1991.

[LAH95] Y. LAHLOU. Modeling complex objects in content-based image retrieval. In *Storage and Retrieval for Image and Video Databases III, IS&T / SPIE Symposium on Electronic Imaging - Science and technology, SPIE'95*, pages 104–115, San Jose, California, 1995.

[MLH94] N. MOUADDIB, Y. LAHLOU, and G. HALIN. Emir: A content-based data model. In *Maghrebian Conference on Software Engineering and Artificial Intelligence, MCSEAI'94*, pages 503–512, Rabat, Morocco, 1994.

[RKS88] M.A. ROTH, H.F. KORTH, and A. SILBERSCHATZ. Extended algebra and calculus for nested relational databases. *ACM Transactions on Database Systems*, 13(4):389–417, 1988.

[RS92] F. RABITTI and P. SAVINO. Automatic image indexation to support content-based retrieval. *Information Processing & Management*, 28(5):547–565, 1992.

[SCH90] C. SCHWARZ. Content-based text handling. *Information Processing & Management*, 26(2):219–226, 1990.

[WLK87] D. WOELK, W. LUTHER, and W. KIM. Multimedia applications and database requirements. In *IEEE Office Automation Symposium*, pages 180–189, 1987.

A Proof of the realization rule

Let $o \in \mathcal{O}$ and $c \in \mathcal{C}$, such that $o \leftarrow c$. We have to prove that $[\![o]\!] \leq_\tau [\![c]\!]$.

- If o is a terminal object, then c is a terminal class of the same type, and we have indeed $[\![o]\!] \leq_\tau [\![c]\!]$.
- If o is a simple object, then $s(o) = \langle a_1 : o_1, ..., a_{n'} : o_{n'} \rangle$ and $c = \langle a_1 : c_1, ..., a_n : c_n \rangle$, having:
  - $n' \geq n$,
  - $\forall i \in [1, n], o_i \leftarrow c_i$,

  The proof is done in an inductive fashion, on the component objects of $s(o)$. Assume, as induction hypothesis, that $\forall i \in [1, n], [\![o_i]\!] \leq_\tau [\![c_i]\!]$; we then have:

  $[\![o]\!](= [\![o_1]\!] \times ... \times [\![o_{n'}]\!]) \leq_\tau [\![c]\!](= [\![c_1]\!] \times ... \times [\![c_n]\!])$, coming from the definition of the partial order on tuple types.
- If o is a set object, then $s(o) = \{o_1, ..., o_p\}$ and $c = c'^*$. From the definition of the realization link, we get: $\forall i \in [1, p], o_i \leftarrow c'$.

  The proof is also done in an inductive fashion, on the member objects of $s(o)$. Assuming, as induction hypothesis, that $\forall i \in [1, p], [\![o_i]\!] \leq_\tau [\![c']\!]$, we see that $[\![c']\!]$ is greater than all the $[\![o_i]\!]$'s, in the sense of the partial order on object types; and so we induce:

  $$\sup_{i=1}^{p} [\![o_i]\!] \leq_\tau [\![c']\!]$$

  which yields:

  $$[\![o]\!] = (\sup_{i=1}^{p} [\![o_i]\!])^* \leq_\tau ([\![c']\!])^* = [\![c'^*]\!] = [\![c]\!]$$

□

Deriving Normalized Is_a Hierarchies by Using Applicability Constraints

Nadira Lammari, Régine Laleau, Mireille Jouve, Xavier Castellani
CEDRIC-IIE (CNAM) laboratory
18 allée Jean Rostand 91025 Evry - France
Phone: (33 1) 69 36 73 93
Fax number: (33 1) 69 36 73 05
Email: {lammari, laleau, jouve, castellani}@iie.cnam.fr

Abstract. The paper presents an object-oriented normalization mechanism which splits a class into an inheritance hierarchy. It defines a normal form for classes. This normal form is required if an existant factorization mechanism (which is also an object-oriented normalization mechanism) is to be used.
The proposed splitting mechanism is applied for each class of a model. It uses a set of applicability constraints defined between characteristics of a class (methods and attributes). These constraints translate part of the semantics of an application that will be expressed in the generated inheritance graph. They are supplied by the designer and are of three kinds: exclusive applicability, conditioned applicability and mutual applicability constraints.

1 Introduction

Object-oriented concepts are a good basis for data models used in next generation database applications such as CAD and CAM systems, knowledge-based systems and multimedia information systems. The concept of inheritance is one of the essential elements of the object paradigm. It provides greater expressiveness, increases the reusability and facilitates the maintenance. It can be of specialization or implementation. The implementation inheritance expresses the reusability of a super-class characteristics by its subclasses. It is useful in the object implementation stage. The specialization inheritance is a more powerful concept. It not only expresses the characteristic reusability, but it also translates the IS_A semantics.

Many research projects look into the problem of the inheritance definition. In the literature, we have registered three research directions: validation rules, optimisation rules and inheritance derivation mechanisms. The validation rules ([Gol92], [Lin92], [Wir90], etc.) help the designer (or the used CASE tool) to judge about the validity of designed inheritances (e.g. no cycles in an inheritance hierarchy). The optimization rules ([Cas93], [Lal92], [Thi94]) guide the designer to decide about retaining or not a designed inheritance. The decision is taken after computing some ratios or metrics (e.g. number of characteristics in a subclass) and comparing them to thresholds. The inheritance derivation mechanisms ([And92], [Ber91], [God93], [Lie91], [Thi93]) are processes for reorganizing classes. They are considered as object-oriented normalization mechanisms, since they aim at reducing semantic or syntactic redundancies. They are factorization mechanisms based on the analysis of syntactic and semantic similarities of classes (most of them only consider the class structure). Although dedicated to be applied in the conceptual design stage, these mechanisms derive specialization as well as implementation inheritances, in spite of the fact that implementation inheritances should not appear in this stage. Furthermore, the distinction between the two inheritance types during the process is not made and some implementation inheritances can be derived to the detriment of specialization inheritances.

One could believe that inheritances can be derived only by factorization. In reality, this is not true. Indeed, classes which, in fact, gather different entities having common characteristics hide inheritance hierarchies that must be exhibited. For example, let C be a class describing all the museums and the historic monuments of a country. Its structure is defined by the mandatory attributes *Name*, *Description*, *Address*, and *Fees* and by the optional attributes *Century* and *Specialized_Branches*. Obviously this class can be decomposed into four classes C1, C2, C3 and C4. C1 is described by the attributes *Name*, *Description*, *Address*, and *Fees*. The classes C2 and C3 are subclasses of C1. C2 has as specific and mandatory attribute *Century*. It represents the historic monuments of the country. C3 has as specific and mandatory attribute *Specialized_Branches*. It represents the museums of the country. C4 describes the set of tourist sites which are both museums and historic monuments.
Furthermore, if we try to apply the above-mentioned mechanisms to such classes (containing optional attributes), they will derive "bad" inheritances or they will deduce similarity of classes that are semanticaly different.

In this paper, we propose a mechanism that derives inheritances by splitting classes rather than factorizing them. It can be applied to each class of a model which contains optional attributes. In this way, inheritances that the factorization mechanisms cannot derive are deduced. The splitting of classes is not necessarily the ultimate goal we want to achieve. However, it allows a maximal splitting of classes according to supplied constraints. This decomposition can then be reviewed according to optimization problems. In this case, some factorizations are necessary but integrity constraints expressing the lost semantic of the decomposition will have to be added.

The proposed mechanism is based on the analysis of applicability constraints defined between class characteristics (attributes and methods). These constraints are supplied by the designer and capture part of the semantics of an application. They are of three kinds: mutual, exclusive and conditioned applicability constraints.
Conditioned applicability constraints between attributes (widely known in database literature as existence constraints) were originally studied by [Mai80], [Mai83], then by other authors such as [Atz83]. They have formally defined them (formal definition

and inference rules) and have also studied their interaction with functional dependencies. More precisely, these constraints between attributes have mainly been used to extend the relational theory to relations with null values. Another use was developed by [Halp91], [Bla94], [Kor95] and [Wei91]. Halpin [Halp91], for example, has used existence constraints as integrity constraints in order to model conceptual constraints such as subset constraints in a relational implementation. By comparison with these works, we use these three kinds of constraints between attributes (mutual, exclusive and conditioned applicability constraints) to deduce the structure of the different types of entities that are represented by a class [Lam94a]. Moreover, we have extended the formal definition of the conditioned applicability constraint to the exclusive and mutual applicability constraints. However, to our knowledge, no work, so far, defines or uses the applicability constraints between methods or attributes and methods. This paper gives only formal definitions of these constraints. Inferences rules, soundness and completeness proof of the given formal systems are presented in [Lam94a].

We finally describe the splitting mechanism. It is decomposed into three phases. The first one verifies the consistency of the set of applicability constraints. The second phase consists in deducing from the class structure the set of substructures compatible with the class applicability constraints. This phase has been completely described in [Lam94b]. It uses the applicability constraints between the class attributes. The last phase consists in defining all the classes of the inheritance graph. The classes are deduced by taking into account the applicability constraints between methods and between attributes and methods. A deduced class will have one of the structures previously defined in the second phase and its behaviour will be described by a subset of the methods of the initial class.

Our paper is organized as follows. The example to which we refer all through the paper is mentioned in Section 2. The three kinds of applicability constraints are formally defined in Section 3. In Section 4 we present the mechanism which splits a class into an inheritance hierarchy. Section 5 concludes our work.

2 Example

In this section, we present the example that illustrates the concepts we use. It concerns the class Person of the model of the information system which manages students and teachers of an university. Its attributes are: Name, First_Name, Address, Academic_Year, Academic_Cycle, Hire_Date, Function, Thesis_Subject, Firm_Name, Firm_Phone. Teachers are of three kinds: part-time lecturers, full-time lecturers and temporary assistants. Part-time lecturers are full-time workers in their company. Students are in an academic cycle (1, 2 or 3) and in an academic year. Some PhD students are hired as temporary assistants. Students cannot be part-time lecturers. The designer has defined the following methods: Change_Thesis_Subject, Hire_Teacher, Display_Students_Temporary_Assistants, Display_PhD_Students,

Display_Students_Academic_Cycle_1, Display_Students_Academic_Cycle_2, Display_Part_Time_Lecturer, Register_Student, Exclude_Student, Modify_Address, Display_Teachers.

3 Applicability Constraints

In this section we present a kind of constraints that we consider worthwhile because they allow the reorganization of a class into a set of classes related by IS_A relationships: applicability constraints between characteristics of a class. Their definition are based on the notion of applicability domain that we first outline.

3.1 Applicability Domain

According to [Cod90], a missing value for an attribute in an instance of its class, in practice, results from the fact that either the value for this attribute is temporarily unknown but applicable, or that its value can never be known because this attribute is inapplicable to this instance. In this latter case, we can define an applicability domain to each attribute of a class, that is the set of instances for which the attribute may have a value. For instance, the attributes Name, First_Name and Address are applicable to every instances of the class Person. On the other hand, the applicability domain of the attributes Academic_Cycle and Academic_Year is constituted only by instances of Person describing Students.

Each class method also has its applicability domain. It is constituted by the set of instances that can be consulted, modified, suppressed or created by this method. For example, the method Modify_Address is applicable to every instance of the class Person because every person can change his/her address. On the other hand, the applicability domain of the method Display_Teachers is reduced to the set of possible instances that describe teachers because only these can be displayed using this method.

3.2 Applicability Constraints

Our aim is to gather characteristics having the same applicability domain into the same class. However, we cannot define precisely an applicability domain at the design stage. But, we can approximate it by comparing it to other applicability domains. This is translated by the applicability constraints. They are of three kinds: mutual, conditioned and exclusive applicability constraints.

Intuitively, an exclusive applicability constraint between two characteristics X and Y of a class, denoted $X \not\leftrightarrow Y$, captures that, for each instance where X is applicable, Y is not applicable and vice versa. In other words, their applicability domains are disjoined. For example, the applicability of the attribute Academic_Cycle to an instance of the class Person excludes the applicability of the attribute Firm_Name and vice versa. This results from the fact that the first attribute is applicable to every instance describing a student, whereas the second one is applicable to every instance describing a part-time lecturer who cannot be a student.

A mutual applicability constraint between two characteristics X and Y of a class, denoted $X \leftrightarrow Y$, translates that, for each instance of the class where X is applicable, Y is also applicable and vice versa. In other words, the applicability domains of the two characteristics are equal. In the class Person, for instance, the attribute Academic_Cycle and the method Register_Student are mutually applicable. Every student who is registered is in an academic cycle and conversely every student who is in an academic cycle has previously been registered.

The conditioned applicability constraint between two characteristics X and Y, denoted $X \mapsto Y$, expresses that, for every instance of the class where X is applicable, Y is also applicable; the converse is not always true. In other words, the applicability domain of X is included in the applicability domain of Y. For example, the applicability of the method Change_Thesis_Subject implies the applicability of the method Modify_Address. Indeed, only Ph.D. students have thesis subjects and therefore can change the subject of their thesis. However, any instance of the class Person, so including Ph.D. students, can have its address changed.

Although presented between characteristics, these constraints can also be used to capture relationships between sets of characteristics. We take this into account in the following formal definitions.

Formal definitions.

Let:

- C (U, M, I) a class. U represents the set of attributes of C, M the set of methods and I the set of *all the possible* instances of C.
- X and Y two sets of $U \cup M$ composed respectively by $x_1,\ldots,x_2,\ldots,x_k,\ldots,x_n$ and $y_1,\ldots,y_2,\ldots,y_p,\ldots,y_m$.
- D_{x_k} (respectively D_{y_p}) the applicability domain of the characteristic x_k (respectively of y_p).

We say that:

- X and Y are mutually applicable or $X \leftrightarrow Y$, if and only if:

$$\forall\, x_k \in X, \forall\, y_p \in Y,\ D_{x_k} = D_{y_p}$$

- the applicability of X excludes the applicability of Y or $X \not\leftrightarrow Y$, if and only if:

$$\forall\, x_k \in X,\ \forall\, y_p \in Y,\ D_{x_k} \cap D_{y_p} = \varnothing$$

- the applicability of X depends on the applicability of Y or $X \mapsto Y$, if and only if:

$$\bigcap_{k=1}^{k=n} D_{x_k} \subseteq \bigcap_{p=1}^{p=n} D_{y_p}$$

Remark 1: let us note that $X \leftrightarrow Y \Rightarrow X \mapsto Y \wedge Y \mapsto X$. The converse is true only if X and Y are sets of only one characteristic.
Remark 2 The inference rules for each kind of applicability constraints and those expressing the interaction between them are described in [Lam94a]. The completeness and soundness proof of the formal systems expressed throughout these inference rules are also presented in [Lam94a].
Remark 3: An attribute of a class can be atomic (Boolean, Character, Integer, ...), or composite if the tuple or set constructor is used. It can also be a reference to another class. For example, we can define for the Person class, instead of Firm_Name and Firm_Phone, the attribute Person_Firm that references the Firm class. Thus the constraint "Person_Firm $\mapsto$ Name" can be stated.
Remark 4: To maintain the structure of the attributes of the initial class in the classes generated by the reorganization mechanism, among all constraints between attributes only those that are defined between attributes which are not components of other ones are considered. In the following, the word "first level attributes" is used to designate this kind of attributes.

4 Splitting Mechanism

Two splitting approaches can be considered: a structure-oriented approach and a behaviour-oriented approach. The first one aims at building a hierarchy of classes by gathering instances with "similar" structures (structures defined by attributes having the same applicability domain). It consists first in deducing the substructures included into the structure of the initial class, then in linking sets of methods to these substructures in order to construct the hierarchy classes. The second approach aims at building a hierarchy of classes by gathering instances with "similar" behaviour (behaviour described by a set of methods having the same applicability domain). It consists first in deducing sets of methods with the same applicability domain, then in associating a structure to each of these sets (the set of attributes required for the applicability of the set of methods) in order to build the hierarchy classes. In this last approach, since, generally, the user processing requirements are evolving quite rapidely [Bou94], the derived inheritance graph will need to be often remodeled. On the contrary, structures are usually far more stable. The main reason is that in a database implementation we must avoid, for performances reasons, changing too often the database structure. This does not mean that the structures of the generated classes are completely stable but that they evolve more slowly. So a graph based on structures will need less changes.This justifies our choice for the first approach which is developed in this paper.
The splitting mechanism is based on the analysis of the applicability constraints supplied by the designer and those derived by using inference rules [Lam94a]. It is decomposed into three phases (see Figure 1). The first one verifies the consistency of the set of applicability constraints. This verification is carried out according to

validation rules (such as $X \leftrightarrow Y \Rightarrow \neg(X \not\leftrightarrow Y)$) described in [Lam94a]. Incompatible constraints and violated rules are shown to the designer.

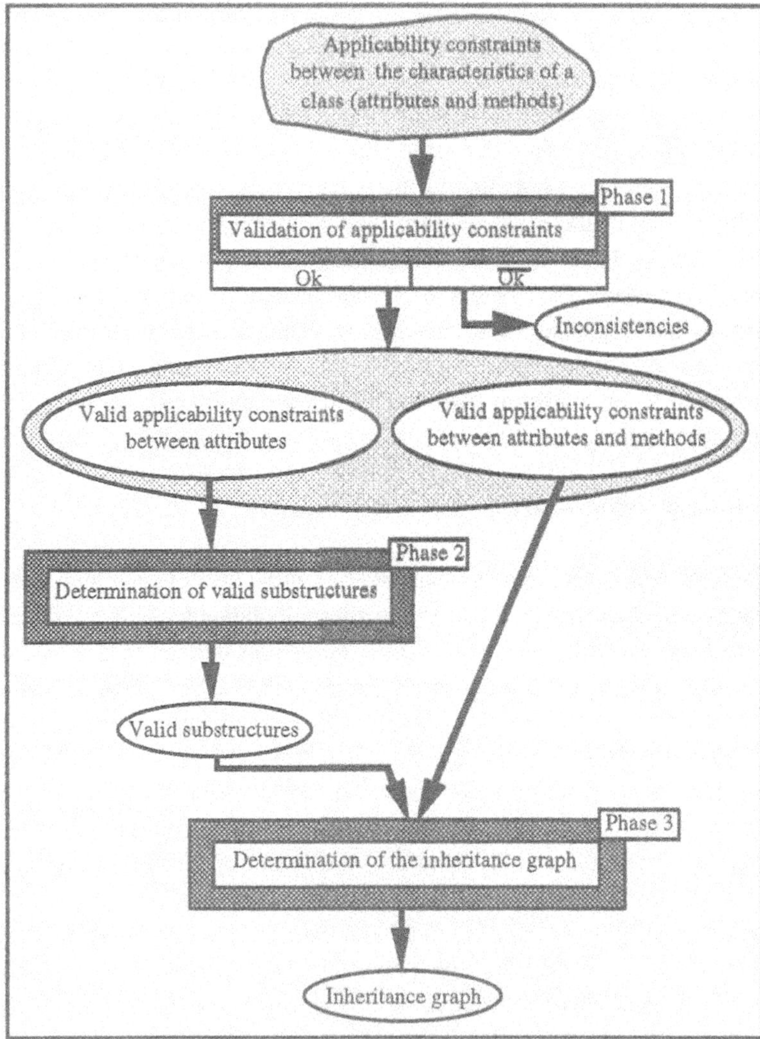

Fig. 1. Description of the reorganization process

The second phase consists in deducing from the class structure the set of substructures compatible with the applicability constraints defined between attributes. This phase is described in [Lam94b] and briefly recalled throughout the example of the class Person in the following subsection. The last phase consists in defining all the classes of the inheritance graph. The classes are deduced by taking into account the applicability constraints between attributes and methods. A detailed description of this last phase is given in Subsection 4.2.

For example, a reorganization of the class Person, taking into account the constraints presented in Figure 2 and according to the structure-oriented approach, gives the inheritance graph of Figure 3. The intermediate results will be given when we describe the second and the third phases.

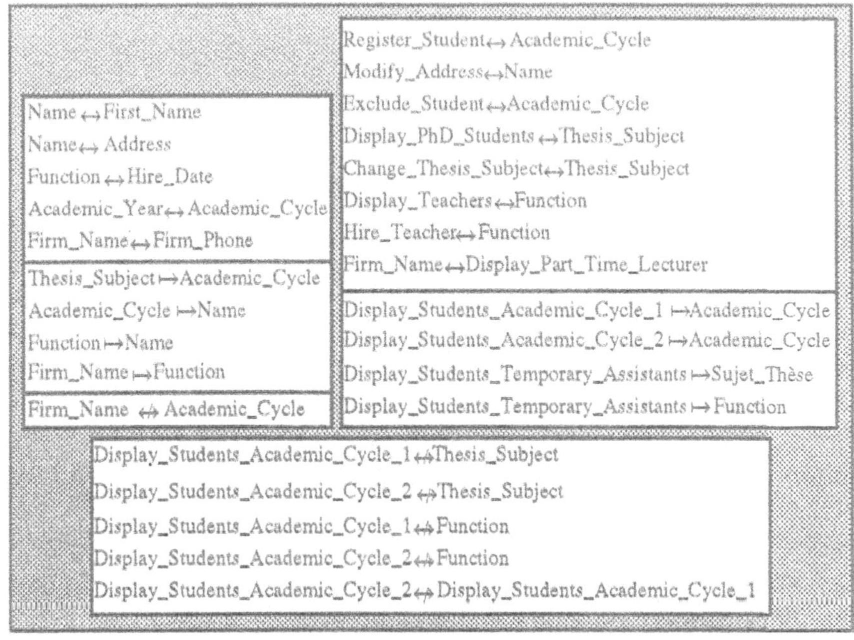

Fig. 2. Applicability constraints supplied by the designer

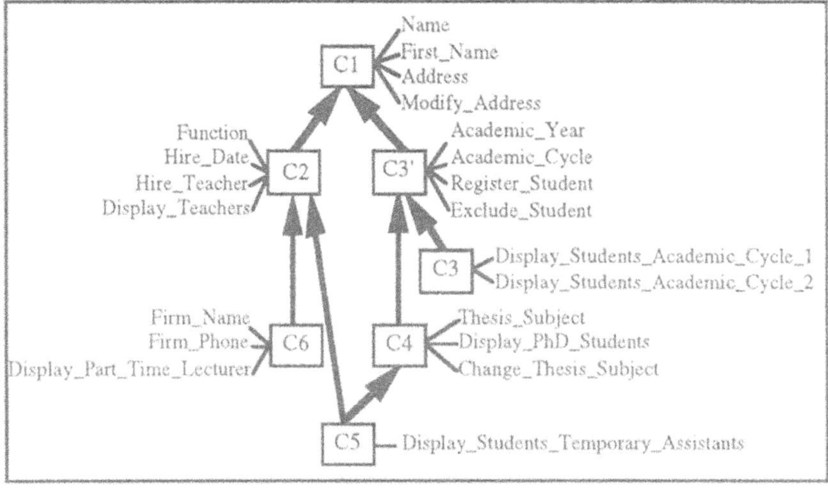

Fig. 3. Generated inheritance graph

Remark: The conditioned applicability constraints between methods and attributes could be very extensive but they can in great part be deduced from the definition of the method signatures. The deduction is further improved if the methods are expressed in a formal specification language (for example VDM or Z). This is a work we want to investigate.

4. 1 Determination of Substructures

Definition of a Substructure.

Intuitively, a substructure of a class is defined by the set of attributes describing it. It constitutes a subset of the class attributes. For instance, among substructures included in the class *Person*, we find: *Student, Teacher, etc.* For example the attributes *Name, First_Name*, Address, *Hire_Date, Function* implicitly describe a substructure that can be called *Teacher*. Among all the possible associations of the class attributes (the power set of the class attributes), only some of them are valid. The valid substructures are those which are compatible with the applicability constraints and, therefore, those to which we can associate possible instances. For example, the set of attributes Name, First_Name, Address and Hire_Date is not a valid substructure because of the applicability constraint: Hire_Date $\leftrightarrow$ Function. In fact, Person instances with only Hire_Date or only Function cannot exist.
So, if we denote $\wp(U_{first})$ the power set of U_{first} (U_{first} represents the set of the first level attributes of a class C) and if we have a set of mutual, conditional and exclusive applicability constraints then, a set p of $\wp(U_{first})$ is a valid substructure if and only if:
Rule (i): Any attribute of U_{first} which is mutually applicable with any attribute of p is in p.
Rule (ii): There are no exclusive applicability constraints between attributes of p.
Rule (iii): Any attribute of U_{first} which determines the applicability of any subset of p is in p.

Formal Definition.

Let:
- C be a class.
- U_{first} be the set of the first level attributes of U: $U_{first} = \{x_1, x_2, \ldots, x_i, \ldots\}$.
- F_{cond_app}, F_{mut_app} and F_{exc_app} be respectively the set of conditioned, mutual and exclusive applicability constraints linking the attributes of U_{first}.
- $F^+_{cond\_app}$, $F^+_{mut\_app}$ and $F^+_{exc\_app}$ be respectively the closure of F_{cond_app}, F_{mut_app} and F_{exc_app}.
- $T \in \wp(U_{first})$

We say that T is a valid substructure of C if and only if the following conditions are verified:

$$- \forall x_i \in T,\ x_i \leftrightarrow X \in F^+_{mut\_app} \Rightarrow X \subset T \qquad (1)$$

$$- \forall x_i \in T,\ \forall x_j \in T,\ x_i \not\leftrightarrow x_j \notin F^+_{exc\_app} \qquad (2)$$

$$- \forall Y \subset T,\ Y \mapsto X \in F^+_{cond\_app} \Rightarrow X \subset T \qquad (3)$$

Conditions *(1)*, *(2)* and *(3)* of this definition respectively match the above rules *(i)*, *(ii)* and *(iii)*. We can, now, reduce the number of conditions by reinforcing the hypotheses. By considering the set of mutual applicability constraints of $IRR(F^+_{mut\_app})$ (minimal cover of $F^+_{mut\_app}$) we can decompose U_{first} into sets of attributes mutually applicable (those sets are denoted X_k and represent groups of coexisting attributes). Then, the selection of substructures among the elements of the power set of U_{first} according to Conditions *(1)*, *(2)* and *(3)* is equivalent to the selection of substructures among the elements of the power set of the X_k sets. Thus Condition *(1)* being satisfied in advance, the selection is made exclusively according to Conditions *(2)* and *(3)*. So, condition *(1)* is replaced by Hypothesis *(j)* in the below-mentioned corollary. Moreover, if we eliminate from these latter elements (elements of $\wp(\{X_1,\ldots,X_k,\ldots\})$) those that cannot coexist because there is at least an exclusive applicability constraint linking two sets of attributes mutually applicable, we can, once more, reduce the number of conditions that must satisfy a substructure. So, Condition *(2)* of the definition is replaced by Hypothesis *(jj)* of the following corollary:

Corollary.

Let:
- C be a class.
- U_{first} be the set of the first level attributes of U: $U_{first} = \{x_1, x_2, \ldots, x_i, \ldots\}$.
- F_{cond_app}, F_{mut_app} and F_{exc_app} be respectively the set of conditioned, mutual and exclusive applicability constraints linking the attributes of U_{first}.
- $F^+_{cond\_app}$, $F^+_{mut\_app}$ and $F^+_{exc\_app}$ be respectively the closure of F_{cond_app}, F_{mut_app} and F_{exc_app}.
- $IRR(F^+_{mut\_app})$ be the minimal cover of $F^+_{mut\_app}$

$$-X_k = \bar{X}_k = \{x_i \in U_{first}, x_i \leftrightarrow x_k \in IRR(F^+_{mut\_app})\} \qquad (j)$$

- $\{T_1, T_2, \ldots, T_m, \ldots\} \subset \wp(\{X_1, X_2, \ldots, X_k, \ldots\})$ such that:

$$\forall X_p \in T_m,\ \forall X_q \in T_m,\ X_p \not\leftrightarrow X_q \notin F^+_{exc\_app} \qquad (jj)$$

We say that T_m is a valid substructure of C if and only if:

$$\forall Y \subset T_m,\ Y \mapsto X \in F^+_{cond\_app} \Rightarrow X \subset T_m$$

Approach for Deducing Substructures.

According to the above rules, it is obvious that the mechanism which calculates all the substructures of a class is based on the analysis of the applicability constraints supplied by the designer. A first naive solution is to deduce all the substructures by selecting among the elements of $\wp(U_{first})$ those verifying the applicability constraints. Another less costly solution is to apply the following mechanism based on the above corollary and detailed in [Lam94b]:
- *Step 1*: determination of the closely linked groups of attributes (sets of attributes mutually applicable to instances of the class).
- *Step 2*: selection, among all the possible unions of the closely linked groups of attributes, of those capable of generating valid substructures (unions that are compatible with the exclusive applicability constraints).
- *Step 3*: selection, among all the selected unions of the closely linked groups of attributes, of those that are self-sufficient to build valid substructures: unions that are compatible with the conditioned applicability constraints.

For example, if the designer supplies the set of applicability constraints between the attributes of the Person class (Figure 2) then the mechanism will provide:

- in *Step 1* the closely linked groups of attributes of Figure 4,

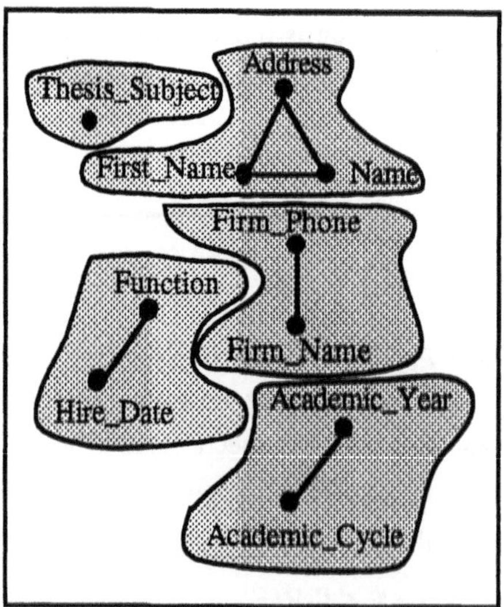

Fig. 4. Groups of coexisting attributes

- then in *Step 2*, the selected unions of closely linked groups of attributes. These unions correspond to the complete subgraphs of Figure 5.

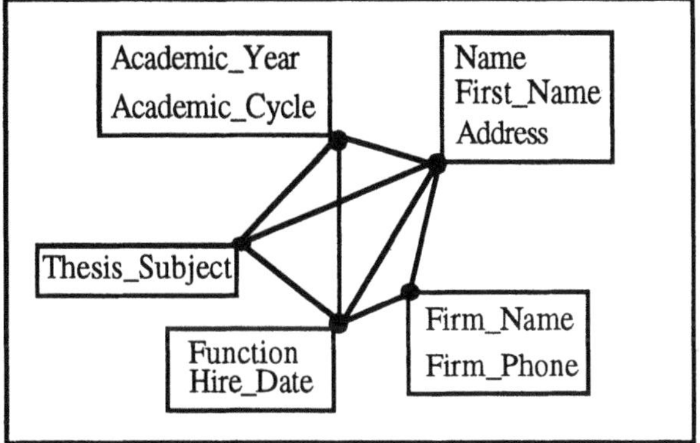

Fig. 5. Possible unions of groups of coexisting attributes

- and then, in *Step 3*, all the valid substructures of Figure 6.

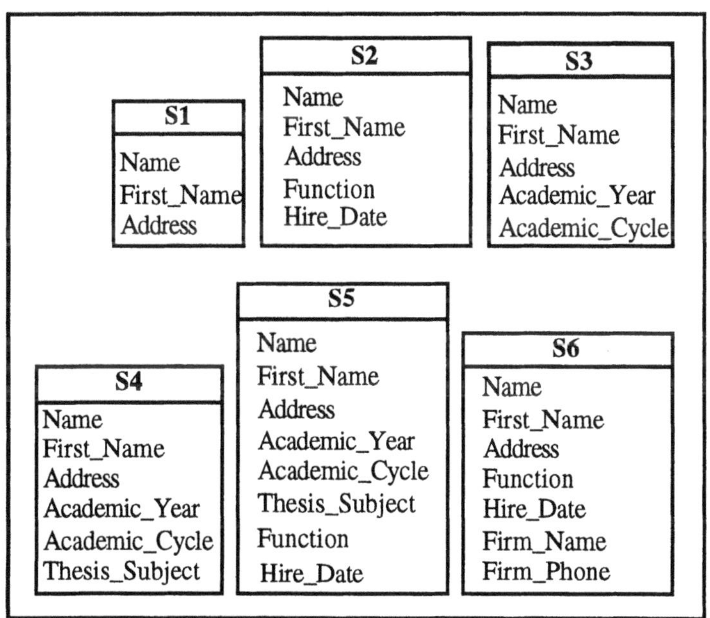

Fig. 6. Valid substructures

The obtained substructures can be organized into an oriented inclusion graph, denoted G(Substructures, Inclusions). G is defined as follows:

Substructures = the set of all the deduced substructures,

$$\text{Inclusions} = \{(S_i, S_j) \in \text{Substructures}^2 \, / \, ((S_j \subset S_i) \wedge (\nexists\, S_k \in \text{Substructures} \, / \, (S_j \subset S_k) \wedge (S_k \subset S_i)))\}$$

This inclusion graph is the starting point of the next phase of the splitting mechanism. For example, the inclusion graph that corresponds to Substructures S1, S2,..., S6 of the class Person is described in Figure 7.

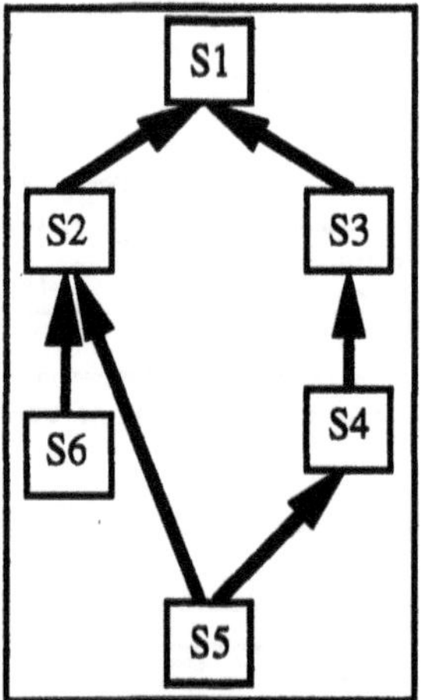

Fig. 7. Inclusion graph

Remark: the inclusion graph has always one sink (S1 in Figure 7) and at least one source (S5 and S6 in Figure 7). It has one sink because we assume that a class has at least one mandatory attribute that gives conceptual meaning to this class (don't forget that we are in the conceptual design stage).

4.2 Determination of the Inheritance Graph

Method Analysis: Linking Methods to Substructures.

As we have used applicability constraints between attributes to deduce substructures, we are going to use the applicability constraints between methods and attributes to decide whether or not a method is to be linked to a substructure. In fact, a necessary condition for Method m to be linked to Substructure S of the initial class is that all the attributes which are necessary to the applicability of m are in S. For example, let us consider Method Display_Students_Cycle_1 and Substructure S3 of Figure 6. The applicability of Display_Students_Cycle_1 is determined by the applicability of the attributes Name, First_Name, Address, Academic_Cycle and Academic_Year. These attributes are in S3. So, the method is able to be linked to S3. This condition can be expressed by the property *(i)* of the following definition.
However, this condition is necessary but not sufficient. To illustrate this, let us refer, once again, to our previous example. Display_Students_Cycle_1 cannot be linked to S4, because its applicability domain and the one of Subject_Thesis are disjoined: Display_Students_Cycle_1 $\not\leftrightarrow$ Subject_Thesis. So, Method m is linked to

Substructure S, if all the attributes that exclude its applicability are not in S. This is expressed in the following definition by the property *(ii)*.

Definition.

Let:
- C be a class,
- S a substructure of C,
- U_{first} the set of the first level attributes of C.
- m a method of C,
- $X_{m,\mapsto} = \{x \in U_{first} / m \mapsto x\}$
- $X_{m,\not\leftrightarrow} = \{x \in U_{first} / m \not\leftrightarrow x\}$.

Method m is linked to Substructure S if and only if these two properties are verified:
- $X_{m,\mapsto} \subseteq S$ *(i)*
- $X_{m,\not\leftrightarrow} \cap S = \varnothing$ *(ii)*

Remark: $X_{m,\mapsto}$ contains the attributes obtained from the conditioned applicability constraints (those inferred are included) and the attributes obtained from the mutual applicability constraints by using the above inference rule:

$$X \leftrightarrow Y \Rightarrow X \mapsto Y \wedge Y \mapsto X.$$

Algorithm for Linking Methods to Substructures.

To determine all the substructures to which Method *m* can be linked, we execute a search in the substructure inclusion graph. The two following properties allow us to reduce the number of comparisons:

(1) $X_{m,\mapsto} \subseteq S_i$, $S_i \in$ Substructures $\Rightarrow (\forall\ S_j \in$ Substructures $, S_j \supset S_i \Rightarrow X_{m,\mapsto} \subseteq S_j)$

(2) $X_{m,\not\leftrightarrow} \cap S_i = \varnothing$, $S_i \in$ Substructures $\Rightarrow$

$$(\forall\ S_j \in \text{Substructures},\ S_j \subset S_i \Rightarrow X_{m,\not\leftrightarrow} \cap S_j = \varnothing)$$

So, the subgraph, the sink of which represents the smallest substructure containing $X_{m,\mapsto}$ (property *(1)*), can be selected in the inclusion graph. To select this subgraph, the search is carried out in depth from the sink to the sources. The selected subgraph will contain all the substructures to which Method *m* can be linked (property *(i)* of the definition). The substructures to which *m* is really linked are obtained by exploring the subgraph from the sources to the sink and by eliminating all sources that don't verify the property *(ii)* of the definition (use of the property *(2)*). We obtain, the following algorithm:

For each Method m **Do**
    Compute $X_{m,\mapsto}$ and $X_{m,\not\leftrightarrow}$;
    $List_m = \varnothing$; /* $List_m$ represents the set of substructures to which m is linked */
    Explore G(Substructures, Inclusions) from the sink to the sources until finding a substructure S including $X_{m,\mapsto}$;
    Studied_Nodes = the set of the substructures of the graph identified by Sink S;
    /* Explore the graph, identified by S, from its sources to S */
    While Studied_Nodes $\neq \varnothing$ **Do**
        let s_i = a substructure of Studied_Nodes;
        If $X_{m,\not\leftrightarrow} \cap S = \varnothing$
        then
                Add to $List_m$ all the descendants of s_i
                Eliminate from Studied_Nodes all the descendants of s_i
        Else eliminate s_i from Studied_Nodes
        End_If;
    End_While;
End_for.

The application of this algorithm to the example (Figure 7) gives the result described in Figure 8.

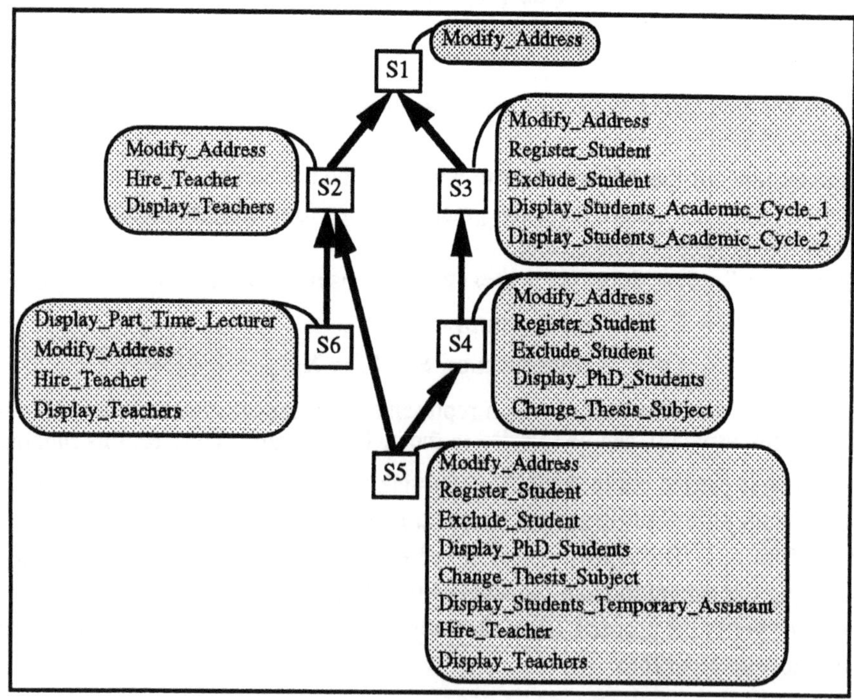

Fig. 8. The linking of methods to substructures

Determination of the Classes and the Inheritance Graph.

This step is the last one in our splitting mechanism. It consists in building the inheritance graph according to the previously defined substructures and according to the set of methods linked to each of them. A class of the inheritance graph is defined by one of the substructures and has a behaviour described by the set of methods which are associated to it. The inheritance graph is not obtained immediately because it may happen that a method could not be linked to all classes of an inheritance branch. It is the case of methods Display_Students_Cycle_1 and Display_Students_Cycle_2 which are linked to S3 but not to S4 and S5 (see Figure 8). The inheritance relationships between some classes cannot, in this case, be defined neatly (without using the concept of masking). To overcome this problem, we define a new class -probably abstract- (in the example C3' of Figure 3) containing only the methods linked to all the classes of an inheritance branch and having as a subclass the class containing the methods which are not linked to all the classes of the inheritance branch (in the example C3 of Figure 3). We obtain, the following algorithm for building the inheritance graph.

Algorithm for building the inheritance graph.

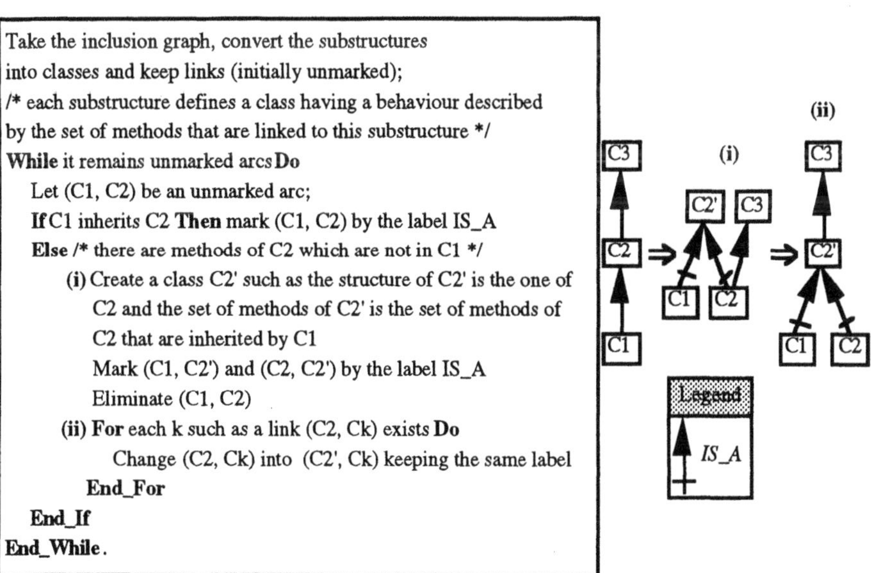

```
Take the inclusion graph, convert the substructures
into classes and keep links (initially unmarked);
/* each substructure defines a class having a behaviour described
by the set of methods that are linked to this substructure */
While it remains unmarked arcs Do
   Let (C1, C2) be an unmarked arc;
   If C1 inherits C2 Then mark (C1, C2) by the label IS_A
   Else /* there are methods of C2 which are not in C1 */
      (i) Create a class C2' such as the structure of C2' is the one of
         C2 and the set of methods of C2' is the set of methods of
         C2 that are inherited by C1
         Mark (C1, C2') and (C2, C2') by the label IS_A
         Eliminate (C1, C2)
      (ii) For each k such as a link (C2, Ck) exists Do
            Change (C2, Ck) into (C2', Ck) keeping the same label
         End_For
   End_If
End_While.
```


The application of this algorithm to Figure 8 gives the inheritance graph of Figure 3. The class C3 can be further reorganized by the designer if there are many methods that are applied to students of academic cycle 1 (or academic cycle 2).

Remark 1: We can merge the above algorithm with the one mentioned in 4.2.1. They have been presented separately for reason of clarity.
Remark 2: If we accept the use of the masking concept in an inheritance graph, the above algorithm is reduced to the initialisation step.
Remark 3: In the general case, at this stage of conceptual design, class methods and instance methods are not distinguished. However, in an object-oreinted implementation and by taking into account the features of the OODBMS used,it may be necessary or convenient to modify the inheritance graph by creating classes to manage (by means of class methods) collections of instances.

5 Conclusion

We have defined a splitting mechanism that derives an inheritance hierarchy from a class. It is based on applicability constraints between characteristics of a class. It is decomposed into three phases. The first phase verifies the consistency of the given set of applicability constraints. The second phase deduces all the substructures included in a class. The third phase builds the classes of the inheritance hierarchy.

The proposed mechanism is a normalization process because it removes from classes all optional attributes that would generate null values in the object implementation stage. Furthermore, this mechanism is a mandatory pre-requisite to any factorization mechanism because those latter don't take optional attributes into account and so can generate "bad" inheritances. It derives specialization inheritances which are the only ones useful to deduce during the conceptual design stage, by opposition to the implementation inheritances. Finally, this mechanism removes all the specified existence constraints. They are expressed through the derived inheritance hierarchy. This is, at the present time, interesting because most of the existant OODBMS don't allow the definition of integrity constraints. So, the designer is obliged to integrate in the class methods some integrity controls. By splitting classes, we avoid the duplication, in methods, of controls related to existence constraints.

The splitting mechanism can be applied at the end of the conceptual design stage of a database with an object-oriented design, preferably with an object-oriented implementation in order to keep all the benefits of the inheritance concept. As mentioned earlier, the maximal decomposition obtained can be reviewed for optimization reasons.

It is also an interesting tool in the perspective of evolving from a traditional design, where data and operations are independent, to an object oriented design where data and operations are encapsulated.

Till now, the implementation of the mechanism is in progress on a Sun station and we intend to integrate it into a case tool [Kar95].
At the present time, we are studying the generalization of the mechanism to a schema including inheritance hierarchies. We are also studying the mean to extract applicability constraints from formal specifications like B or VDM.

References

[And92] Andonnof E., Sallaberry C. and Zurfluh G., *Interactive design of object oriented databases*. 4th International Conference CAISE'92, Manchester, may 1992.

[Atz83] Atzeni P. and Morfuni M., *Functional dependencies and existence constraints in databases relations with null values*. Information System Analysis Institute. Technical report n°R77, december 1983.

[Ber91] Bergstein P. et Lieberherr J., *Incremental Class Dictionary Learning and optimization*. Proceedings de ECOOP'91, Geneve, Suisse, July 91. Lecture Notes in Computer Science 512. Editor Pierre America Springer-verlag.

[Bla94] Blaha M., Premerlani W. et Shen H., *Converting OO Models into RDBMS Schema*. IEEE software Mai 1994. Editor IEEE Computer Society.

[Bou94] Bouzeghoub M., Gardarin G. and Valduriez P., *Du C++ à Merise Objet. Objets: Concepts, Langages, Bases de données, Methodes et interfaces*. Eyrolles, France, 1994.

[Cas93] Castellani X., *Mechanisms of Standardized Reusability of Objects (MCO methodology)*. Proceedings de Working conference on Information system development process, IFIP WG 8.1. Como, Italia, 1-3 september 1993. Editor North-Holland.

[Cod90] Codd E. F., *The relational model for database management. Version 2.* Addison-Wesley Publishing Company, Inc., 1990.

[God93] Godin R. and Mili H., *Building and maintaining analysis-level class hierarchies using Galois Lattices*. OOPSLA'93. ACM SIGPLAN notices, volume 28, number 10. October 1993.

[Gol92] Goldstein R. and Storey V., *Unravelling Is_a Structures*. Information Systems Research Revue 3:2, June 1992.

[Hal91] Halpin T., *A fact-oriented approach to schema transformation*. Proc. MFDBS'91, Springer-Verlag lecture notes in Computer Science, n°495, Rostock, 1991.

[Kar95] Kara-Zaîtri N., Castellani X., *TCO: A Process and aTool to Map Communication Components of Data Flows to Objects*. 33th conference of ACM Southeast Conference. Clemenson, South Caroline. 17 and 18 march 1995.

[Kor95] Kornatzky Y., Shoval P., *Conceptual design of object-oriented database schemas using binary-relationship model*. Data & Knowledge Engineering revue, Volume 14, Number 3, February 1995. North Holland.

[Lal92] Laleau R.,Castellani X. and Jouve M., *Normalized design of the specialization inheritance*. Proceedings Indo-French Workshop on object-oriented systems. Goa, India, November 1992.

[Lam94a] Lammari N., Jouve M., Laleau R. and Castellani X., *Dépendances d'existence: définitions formelles et utilisation pour déterminer des liens d'heritages entre classes.* CEDRIC-CNAM, Paris.Research report, may 1994.

[Lam94b] Lammari N., Jouve M., Laleau R. and Castellani X., *An algorithm for IS_A Hierarchy Derivation.* Proc. OOIS'94 (International Conference on Object-Oriented Information systems), Springer-Verlag editor, London, december 1994.

[Lie91] Lieberherr L., Bergstein P. et Silva-Lepe I., *From objects to classes: algorithms for optimal object-oriented design.* Software Engineering Revue 6:4, july 91.

[Lin92] Ling. T. W, Teo. P. K., *On conflicts in class hierarchies of object-oriented systems.* Department of information systems of the university of Singapore. Technical Report n°TR-C4-92, 1992.

[Mai80] Maier D., *Discarding the Universal Instance Assumption: Preliminary Results.* XP1 Workshop on relational database theory. Suny at Stony Brook, NY, June-July 1980.

[Mai83] Maier D., *The theory of relational databases.* Computer Science Press, Inc., America, 1983.

[Pic90] Pichat E. and Bodin R., *Ingénierie des données.* Masson, Paris, 1990.

[Thi93] Thieme C. et Siebes A., *Schema Integration in Object-Oriented Databases.* Proceedings of CAISE'93.

[Thi94] Thieme C. et Siebes A., *An approach to schema intagration based on transformations and behaviour.* Technical Report n°CS-R9403, january 94.

[Wei91] Wei G. and Teorey T. J., *The Orac model: a unified view of data abstractions.* Proc. of 10th Conference on Entity-relationship Approach, San Mateo, California, USA, october 1991.

[Wir90] Wirfs-Brock R., Wilkerson B. and Wiener L., Designing Object-Oriented Software. Prentice-Hall, Inc. USA 1990.

Author Index

Lecture Notes in Computer Science

For information about Vols. 1–1006

please contact your bookseller or Springer-Verlag

Vol. 1007: A. Bosselaers, B. Preneel (Eds.), Integrity Primitives for Secure Information Systems. VII, 239 pages. 1995.

Vol. 1008: B. Preneel (Ed.), Fast Software Encryption. Proceedings, 1994. VIII, 367 pages. 1995.

Vol. 1009: M. Broy, S. Jähnichen (Eds.), KORSO: Methods, Languages, and Tools for the Construction of Correct Software. X, 449 pages. 1995. Vol.

Vol. 1010: M. Veloso, A. Aamodt (Eds.), Case-Based Reasoning Research and Development. Proceedings, 1995. X, 576 pages. 1995. (Subseries LNAI).

Vol. 1011: T. Furuhashi (Ed.), Advances in Fuzzy Logic, Neural Networks and Genetic Algorithms. Proceedings, 1994. (Subseries LNAI).

Vol. 1012: M. Bartošek, J. Staudek, J. Wiedermann (Eds.), SOFSEM '95: Theory and Practice of Informatics. Proceedings, 1995. XI, 499 pages. 1995.

Vol. 1013: T.W. Ling, A.O. Mendelzon, L. Vieille (Eds.), Deductive and Object-Oriented Databases. Proceedings, 1995. XIV, 557 pages. 1995.

Vol. 1014: A.P. del Pobil, M.A. Serna, Spatial Representation and Motion Planning. XII, 242 pages. 1995.

Vol. 1015: B. Blumenthal, J. Gornostaev, C. Unger (Eds.), Human-Computer Interaction. Proceedings, 1995. VIII, 203 pages. 1995.

VOL. 1016: R. Cipolla, Active Visual Inference of Surface Shape. XII, 194 pages. 1995.

Vol. 1017: M. Nagl (Ed.), Graph-Theoretic Concepts in Computer Science. Proceedings, 1995. XI, 406 pages. 1995.

Vol. 1018: T.D.C. Little, R. Gusella (Eds.), Network and Operating Systems Support for Digital Audio and Video. Proceedings, 1995. XI, 357 pages. 1995.

Vol. 1019: E. Brinksma, W.R. Cleaveland, K.G. Larsen, T. Margaria, B. Steffen (Eds.), Tools and Algorithms for the Construction and Analysis of Systems. Selected Papers, 1995. VII, 291 pages. 1995.

Vol. 1020: I.D. Watson (Ed.), Progress in Case-Based Reasoning. Proceedings, 1995. VIII, 209 pages. 1995. (Subseries LNAI).

Vol. 1021: M.P. Papazoglou (Ed.), OOER '95: Object-Oriented and Entity-Relationship Modeling. Proceedings, 1995. XVII, 451 pages. 1995.

Vol. 1022: P.H. Hartel, R. Plasmeijer (Eds.), Functional Programming Languages in Education. Proceedings, 1995. X, 309 pages. 1995.

Vol. 1023: K. Kanchanasut, J.-J. Lévy (Eds.), Algorithms, Concurrency and Knowlwdge. Proceedings, 1995. X, 410 pages. 1995.

Vol. 1024: R.T. Chin, H.H.S. Ip, A.C. Naiman, T.-C. Pong (Eds.), Image Analysis Applications and Computer Graphics. Proceedings, 1995. XVI, 533 pages. 1995.

Vol. 1025: C. Boyd (Ed.), Cryptography and Coding. Proceedings, 1995. IX, 291 pages. 1995.

Vol. 1026: P.S. Thiagarajan (Ed.), Foundations of Software Technology and Theoretical Computer Science. Proceedings, 1995. XII, 515 pages. 1995.

Vol. 1027: F.J. Brandenburg (Ed.), Graph Drawing. Proceedings, 1995. XII, 526 pages. 1996.

Vol. 1028: N.R. Adam, Y. Yesha (Eds.), Electronic Commerce. X, 155 pages. 1996.

Vol. 1029: E. Dawson, J. Golić (Eds.), Cryptography: Policy and Algorithms. Proceedings, 1995. XI, 327 pages. 1996.

Vol. 1030: F. Pichler, R. Moreno-Díaz, R. Albrecht (Eds.), Computer Aided Systems Theory - EUROCAST '95. Proceedings, 1995. XII, 539 pages. 1996.

Vol.1031: M. Toussaint (Ed.), Ada in Europe. Proceedings, 1995. XI, 455 pages. 1996.

Vol. 1032: P. Godefroid, Partial-Order Methods for the Verification of Concurrent Systems. IV, 143 pages. 1996.

Vol. 1033: C.-H. Huang, P. Sadayappan, U. Banerjee, D. Gelernter, A. Nicolau, D. Padua (Eds.), Languages and Compilers for Parallel Computing. Proceedings, 1995. XIII, 597 pages. 1996.

Vol. 1034: G. Kuper, M. Wallace (Eds.), Constraint Databases and Applications. Proceedings, 1995. VII, 185 pages. 1996.

Vol. 1035: S.Z. Li, D.P. Mital, E.K. Teoh, H. Wang (Eds.), Recent Developments in Computer Vision. Proceedings, 1995. XI, 604 pages. 1996.

Vol. 1036: G. Adorni, M. Zock (Eds.), Trends in Natural Language Generation - An Artificial Intelligence Perspective. Proceedings, 1993. IX, 382 pages. 1996. (Subseries LNAI).

Vol. 1037: M. Wooldridge, J.P. Müller, M. Tambe (Eds.), Intelligent Agents II. Proceedings, 1995. XVI, 437 pages. 1996. (Subseries LNAI).

Vol. 1038: W: Van de Velde, J.W. Perram (Eds.), Agents Breaking Away. Proceedings, 1996. XIV, 232 pages. 1996. (Subseries LNAI).

Vol. 1039: D. Gollmann (Ed.), Fast Software Encryption. Proceedings, 1996. X, 219 pages. 1996.

Vol. 1040: S. Wermter, E. Riloff, G. Scheler (Eds.), Connectionist, Statistical, and Symbolic Approaches to Learning for Natural Language Processing. IX, 468 pages. 1996. (Subseries LNAI).

Vol. 1041: J. Dongarra, K. Madsen, J. Waśniewski (Eds.), Applied Parallel Computing. Proceedings, 1995. XII, 562 pages. 1996.

Vol. 1042: G. Weiß, S. Sen (Eds.), Adaption and Learning in Multi-Agent Systems. Proceedings, 1995. X, 238 pages. 1996. (Subseries LNAI).

Vol. 1043: F. Moller, G. Birtwistle (Eds.), Logics for Concurrency. XI, 266 pages. 1996.

Vol. 1044: B. Plattner (Ed.), Broadband Communications. Proceedings, 1996. XIV, 359 pages. 1996.

Vol. 1045: B. Butscher, E. Moeller, H. Pusch (Eds.), Interactive Distributed Multimedia Systems and Services. Proceedings, 1996. XI, 333 pages. 1996.

Vol. 1046: C. Puech, R. Reischuk (Eds.), STACS 96. Proceedings, 1996. XII, 690 pages. 1996.

Vol. 1047: E. Hajnicz, Time Structures. IX, 244 pages. 1996. (Subseries LNAI).

Vol. 1048: M. Proietti (Ed.), Logic Program Syynthesis and Transformation. Proceedings, 1995. X, 267 pages. 1996.

Vol. 1049: K. Futatsugi, S. Matsuoka (Eds.), Object Technologies for Advanced Software. Proceedings, 1996. X, 309 pages. 1996.

Vol. 1050: R. Dyckhoff, H. Herre, P. Schroeder-Heister (Eds.), Extensions of Logic Programming. Proceedings, 1996. VII, 318 pages. 1996. (Subseries LNAI).

Vol. 1051: M.-C. Gaudel, J. Woodcock (Eds.), FME'96: Industrial Benefit and Advances in Formal Methods. Proceedings, 1996. XII, 704 pages. 1996.

Vol. 1052: D. Hutchison, H. Christiansen, G. Coulson, A. Danthine (Eds.), Teleservices and Multimedia Communications. Proceedings, 1995. XII, 277 pages. 1996.

Vol. 1053: P. Graf, Term Indexing. XVI, 284 pages. 1996. (Subseries LNAI).

Vol. 1054: A. Ferreira, P. Pardalos (Eds.), Solving Combinatorial Optimization Problems in Parallel. VII, 274 pages. 1996.

Vol. 1055: T. Margaria, B. Steffen (Eds.), Tools and Algorithms for the Construction and Analysis of Systems. Proceedings, 1996. XI, 435 pages. 1996.

Vol. 1056: A. Haddadi, Communication and Cooperation in Agent Systems. XIII, 148 pages. 1996. (Subseries LNAI).

Vol. 1057: P. Apers, M. Bouzeghoub, G. Gardarin (Eds.), Advances in Database Technology — EDBT '96. Proceedings, 1996. XII, 636 pages. 1996.

Vol. 1058: H. R. Nielson (Ed.), Programming Languages and Systems – ESOP '96. Proceedings, 1996. X, 405 pages. 1996.

Vol. 1059: H. Kirchner (Ed.), Trees in Algebra and Programming – CAAP '96. Proceedings, 1996. VIII, 331 pages. 1996.

Vol. 1060: T. Gyimóthy (Ed.), Compiler Construction. Proceedings, 1996. X, 355 pages. 1996.

Vol. 1061: P. Ciancarini, C. Hankin (Eds.), Coordination Languages and Models. Proceedings, 1996. XI, 443 pages. 1996.

Vol. 1062: E. Sanchez, M. Tomassini (Eds.), Towards Evolvable Hardware. IX, 265 pages. 1996.

Vol. 1063: J.-M. Alliot, E. Lutton, E. Ronald, M. Schoenauer, D. Snyers (Eds.), Artificial Evolution. Proceedings, 1995. XIII, 396 pages. 1996.

Vol. 1064: B. Buxton, R. Cipolla (Eds.), Computer Vision – ECCV '96. Volume I. Proceedings, 1996. XXI, 725 pages. 1996.

Vol. 1065: B. Buxton, R. Cipolla (Eds.), Computer Vision – ECCV '96. Volume II. Proceedings, 1996. XXI, 723 pages. 1996.

Vol. 1066: R. Alur, T.A. Henzinger, E.D. Sontag (Eds.), Hybrid Systems III. IX, 618 pages. 1996.

Vol. 1067: H. Liddell, A. Colbrook, B. Hertzberger, P. Sloot (Eds.), High-Performance Computing and Networking. Proceedings, 1996. XXV, 1040 pages. 1996.

Vol. 1068: T. Ito, R.H. Halstead, Jr., C. Queinnec (Eds.), Parallel Symbolic Languages and Systems. Proceedings, 1995. X, 363 pages. 1996.

Vol. 1069: J.W. Perram, J.-P. Müller (Eds.), Distributed Software Agents and Applications. Proceedings, 1994. VIII, 219 pages. 1996. (Subseries LNAI).

Vol. 1070: U. Maurer (Ed.), Advances in Cryptology – EUROCRYPT '96. Proceedings, 1996. XII, 417 pages. 1996.

Vol. 1071: P. Miglioli, U. Moscato, D. Mundici, M. Ornaghi (Eds.), Theorem Proving with Analytic Tableaux and Related Methods. Proceedings, 1996. X, 330 pages. 1996. (Subseries LNAI).

Vol. 1072: R. Kasturi, K. Tombre (Eds.), Graphics Recognition. Proceedings, 1995. X, 308 pages. 1996.

Vol. 1073: J. Cuny, H. Ehrig, G. Engels, G. Rozenberg (Eds.), Graph Grammars and Their Application to Computer Science. Proceedings, 1994. X, 565 pages. 1996.

Vol. 1074: G. Dowek, J. Heering, K. Meinke, B. Möller (Eds.), Higher-Order Algebra, Logic, and Term Rewriting. Proceedings, 1995. VII, 287 pages. 1996.

Vol. 1075: D. Hirschberg, G. Myers (Eds.), Combinatorial Pattern Matching. Proceedings, 1996. VIII, 392 pages. 1996.

Vol. 1076: N. Shadbolt, K. O'Hara, G. Schreiber (Eds.), Advances in Knowledge Acquisition. Proceedings, 1996. XII, 371 pages. 1996. (Subseries LNAI).

Vol. 1077: P. Brusilovsky, P. Kommers, N. Streitz (Eds.), Mulimedia, Hypermedia, and Virtual Reality. Proceedings, 1994. IX, 311 pages. 1996.

Vol. 1078: D.A. Lamb (Ed.), Studies of Software Design. Proceedings, 1993. VI, 188 pages. 1996.

Vol. 1079: Z.W. Raś, M. Michalewicz (Eds.), Foundations of Intelligent Systems. Proceedings, 1996. XI, 664 pages. 1996. (Subseries LNAI).

Vol. 1080: P. Constantopoulos, J. Mylopoulos, Y. Vassiliou (Eds.), Advanced Information Systems Engineering. Proceedings, 1996. XI, 582 pages. 1996.

GPSR Compliance
The European Union's (EU) General Product Safety Regulation (GPSR) is a set of rules that requires consumer products to be safe and our obligations to ensure this.

If you have any concerns about our products, you can contact us on

ProductSafety@springernature.com

In case Publisher is established outside the EU, the EU authorized representative is:

Springer Nature Customer Service Center GmbH
Europaplatz 3
69115 Heidelberg, Germany

www.ingramcontent.com/pod-product-compliance
Ingram Content Group UK Ltd.
Pitfield, Milton Keynes, MK11 3LW, UK
UKHW021902190726
13853UKWH00003B/1378

* 9 7 8 3 6 6 2 1 6 2 5 0 7 *